Rick Steves'
ITALY
2002

AVALON
TRAVEL

Other ATP travel guidebooks by Rick Steves
Rick Steves' Best of Europe
Rick Steves' Europe 101: History and Art for the Traveler (with Gene Openshaw)
Rick Steves' Europe Through the Back Door
Rick Steves' Mona Winks: Self-Guided Tours of Europe's Top Museums
   (with Gene Openshaw)
Rick Steves' Postcards from Europe
Rick Steves' France, Belgium & the Netherlands (with Steve Smith)
Rick Steves' Germany, Austria & Switzerland
Rick Steves' Great Britain
Rick Steves' Ireland (with Pat O'Connor)
Rick Steves' Scandinavia
Rick Steves' Spain & Portugal
Rick Steves' Florence (with Gene Openshaw)
Rick Steves' London (with Gene Openshaw)
Rick Steves' Paris (with Steve Smith and Gene Openshaw)
Rick Steves' Rome (with Gene Openshaw)
Rick Steves' Venice (with Gene Openshaw)
Rick Steves' Phrase Books: German, Italian, French, Spanish/Portuguese,
   and French/Italian/German

Avalon Travel Publishing, 5855 Beaudry Street, Emeryville, CA 94608

Printed in the United States of America by R. R. Donnelley
Third printing March 2002

For the latest on Rick's lectures, guidebooks, tours, and public television
series, contact Europe Through the Back Door, Box 2009, Edmonds,
WA 98020, tel. 425/771-8303, fax 425/771-0833, www.ricksteves.com,
or e-mail: rick@ricksteves.com.

ISSN 1084-4422
ISBN 1-56691-354-3

Europe Through the Back Door Editors: Risa Laib, Jacquie Maupin,
   Lauren Mills
Avalon Travel Publishing Editor: Kate Willis
Copy Editor: Donna Leverenz
Research Assistance: Risa Laib, Dave Hoerlein (wrote "More Hill Towns"
   section), Jane Fasce (Santa Margherita Ligure)
Production & Typesetting: Kathleen Sparkes, White Hart Design
Design: Linda Braun
Cover Design: Janine Lehmann
Maps: David C. Hoerlein
Cover Photo: Santa Croce, Florence; copyright © John Elk III

CONTENTS

Top Destinations in Italy

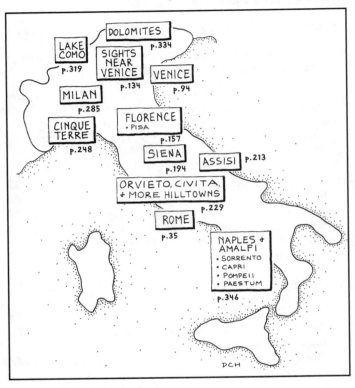

INTRODUCTION

This book breaks Italy into its top big-city, small-town, and rural destinations. It then gives you all the information and opinions necessary to wring the maximum value out of your limited time and money in each of these destinations.

If you plan a month or less in Italy and have a normal appetite for information, this lean and mean little book is all you need. If you're a travel info fiend (like me), you'll find this book sorts through all the superlatives and provides a handy rack upon which to hang your supplemental information.

Italy is my favorite country. Experiencing its culture, people, and natural wonders economically and hassle-free has been my goal for over 25 years of traveling, researching, and tour guiding. With this book, I pass on to you the lessons I've learned, updated (in mid-2001) for 2002.

Rick Steves' Italy is a tour guide in your pocket, offering a comfortable mix of big cities and cozy towns, from brutal but *bello* Rome to *tranquillo*, traffic-free Riviera villages. It covers the predictable biggies and adds a healthy dose of "Back Door" intimacy. Along with marveling at Michelangelo's masterpieces, you'll enjoy a *bruschetta* snack as a village boy rubs fresh garlic on your toast. I've been selective, including only the top sights. For example, after visiting dozens of hill towns, I recommend just the best four (Siena, Assisi, Orvieto, and Civita).

The best is, of course, only my opinion. But after more than two busy decades of travel writing, lecturing, and tour guiding, I've developed a sixth sense for what tickles the traveler's fancy.

This Information Is Accurate and Up-to-Date

This book is updated every year. Most publishers of guidebooks that cover a country from top to bottom can afford an update only every two or three years. Since this book is selective, I'm able to personally update it each summer. Even with an annual update, things change. But if you're traveling with the current edition of this book, I guarantee you're using the most up-to-date information available (for the latest, check www.ricksteves.com/update). This book will help you have an inexpensive, hassle-free trip. Use this year's edition. People who try to save a few bucks by traveling with an old book are not smart. They learn the seriousness of their mistake ... in Italy. Your trip costs about $10 per waking hour. Your time is valuable. This guidebook saves lots of time.

Planning Your Trip

This book is organized by destinations. Each destination is a mini-vacation on its own, filled with exciting sights and comfortable, good-value places to stay. In each chapter, you'll find:

Planning Your Time, a suggested schedule with thoughts on how best to use your limited time.

Orientation, including tourist information, city transportation, and an easy-to-read map designed to make the text clear and your arrival smooth.

Sights with ratings: ▲▲▲—Don't miss; ▲▲—Try hard to see; ▲—Worthwhile if you can make it; no rating—Worth knowing about.

Sleeping and **Eating,** with addresses and phone numbers of my favorite hotels and restaurants.

Transportation Connections to nearby destinations by train, and route tips for drivers.

The **appendix** is a traveler's tool kit, with telephone tips, a climate chart, events calendar, and survival phrases.

Browse through this book, choose your favorite destinations, and link them up. Then have a great trip! You'll travel like a temporary local, getting the absolute most out of every mile, minute, and dollar. You won't waste time on mediocre sights because, unlike other guidebook authors, I cover only the best. Since your major financial pitfalls are lousy, expensive hotels, I've worked hard to assemble the best accommodations values for each stop. And as you travel the route I know and love, I'm happy you'll be meeting some of my favorite Italian people.

Trip Costs

Six components make up your trip cost: airfare, surface transportation, room and board, sightseeing/entertainment, shopping/miscellany, and gelato.

Airfare: Don't try to sort through the mess. Find and use a good travel agent. A basic round-trip USA-to-Milan (or Rome) flight should cost $700 to $1,000 (even cheaper in winter), depending on where you fly from and when. Always consider saving time and money in Europe by flying "open jaw" (into one city and out of another).

Surface Transportation: For a three-week whirlwind trip of all my recommended destinations, allow $300 per person for public transportation (train and buses) or $500 per person (based on 2 people sharing a car) for a three-week car rental, tolls, gas, and insurance. Car rental is cheapest if arranged from the United States. Some train passes are available only outside of Europe. You might save money by getting an Italian railpass or buying tickets as you go (see "Transportation," below).

Room and Board: You can thrive in Italy on $70 a day for room and board (allow $80/day for Rome). This $70/day budget allows $10 for lunch, $20 for dinner, and $40 for lodging (based on 2 people splitting the cost of an $80 double room that includes breakfast). If you've got more money, I've listed great ways to spend it. And students and tightwads can enjoy Italy for as little as $40 a day ($20 for a bed, $20 for meals and snacks). But budget sleeping and eating require the skills covered later in this chapter (and in more depth in my book *Rick Steves' Europe Through the Back Door*).

Sightseeing and Entertainment: In big cities, figure about $5 to $7 per major sight (museums, Colosseum), $2 for minor ones (climbing church towers), and $25 to $30 per person for splurge experiences (such as tours and gondola rides). An overall average of $15 a day works for most. Don't skimp here. After all, this category directly powers most of the experiences all the other expenses are designed to make possible.

Shopping and Miscellany: Figure $1 per postcard, coffee, and soft drink and $2 per gelato. Shopping can vary in cost from nearly nothing to a small fortune. Good budget travelers find that this category has little to do with assembling a trip full of lifelong and wonderful memories.

Exchange Rate

We've priced things throughout this book in euros. Italy, along with 11 other member countries of the European Union, has adopted the euro currency.

---

1 euro (€) = about 90 cents, and €1.10 = about $1.

One euro is broken down into 100 cents. You'll find coins ranging from 1 cent to 2 euros, and bills from 5 euros to 500 euros. To convert prices in euros into dollars, take 10 percent off the price in euros: €25 = about $22, and €140 = about $125. For information on the euro, see the European Central Bank's Web site: www.euro.ecb.int.

Prices, Times, and Discounts

The opening hours and telephone numbers listed in this book are accurate as of mid-2001—but once you pin Italy down, it wiggles. At each major destination, ask the local tourist information office for a current list of the city's sights, hours, and prices. Any guidebook on Italy starts to yellow even before it's printed—especially in this transition year of the euro, when many businesses may adjust their prices at the beginning of the year, depending on the latest exchange rate. Because of that, prices in this book are approximate.

In Italy—and in this book—you'll use the 24-hour clock. It's the same through 12:00 noon, then keep going—13:00, 14:00 . . . . For anything over 12, subtract 12 and add p.m. (14:00 is 2:00 p.m.).

Don't expect discounts on sights in Italy if you're a youth or senior. Discounts are generally available only to people that

are members of the European Union and "reciprocating countries," meaning countries that offer discounts to European youth
and seniors—which America doesn't. Complaining only gets
you the European take on our president.

When to Go

Italy's best travel months are May, June, September, and October.
November through April usually has pleasant weather, with generally none of the sweat and stress of the tourist season (but expect
shorter hours, more lunchtime breaks, and fewer activities available).

Peak season offers the longest hours and the most exciting
slate of activities—but terrible crowds and, at times, suffocating
heat. During peak times, many resort-area hotels maximize business by requiring that guests buy dinner in their restaurants.
August, the local holiday month, isn't as bad as many make it out
to be, but big cities tend to be quiet (with discounted hotel prices),
and beach and mountain resorts are jammed (with higher hotel
prices). If you anticipate crowds, arrive early in the day or call
hotels in advance (call from one hotel to the next; your fluent-
in-Italian receptionist can help you).

Summer temperatures range from the 70s in Milan to the
high 80s and 90s in Rome. Air-conditioning, when available,
doesn't kick in until June 1 and shuts off September 30. Most
mid-range hotels come with air-conditioning—a worthwhile splurge
in the summer. In the winter, it often drops to the 40s in Milan and
the 50s in Rome. Spring and fall can be cold, and many hotels do
not turn on their heat. (See climate chart in the appendix.)

Sightseeing Priorities

Depending on the length of your trip, here are my recommended priorities:

3 days:	Florence, Venice
5 days, add:	Rome
7 days, add:	Cinque Terre
10 days, add:	Civita and Siena
14 days, add:	Sorrento, Naples, Pompeii, Amalfi, Paestum
18 days, add:	Milan, Lake Como, Varenna, Assisi
21 days, add:	Dolomites, Verona, Ravenna

(This includes everything on the "Whirlwind Three-Week
Tour" map on page 7.)

Considering that you're likely to go both broke and crazy driving in Italian cities, and how handy and affordable Italy's trains and
buses are, I'd do most of Italy by public transportation. If you want
to drive, consider doing the big, intense stuff (Rome, Naples area,
Milan, Florence, and Venice) by train or bus and renting a car for
the hill towns of Tuscany and Umbria and for the Dolomites. A car
is a worthless headache on the Riviera and in the Lake Como area.

Red Tape, Business Hours, and Banking

You need a passport but no visa or shots to travel in Italy.

Business Hours: Traditionally, Italy uses the siesta plan. People work from about 08:00 to 13:00 and from 15:30 to 19:00, Monday through Saturday. Many businesses have adopted the government's new recommended 08:00 to 14:00 workday. In tourist areas, shops are open longer.

If you're buying more than $200 worth of souvenirs, ask in the shops about getting the 10 to 19 percent VAT tax back at the airport upon departure.

Banking: You'll want to spend local hard cash. The fastest way to get it is by using plastic: your ATM, credit, or debit card at a cash machine (Bancomat). Bring some traveler's checks only as a backup.

To get a cash advance from a bank machine, you'll need a four-digit PIN (numbers only, no letters, seven-digit PIN won't work) with your bank card. Before you go, verify with your bank that your card will work.

Visa and MasterCard are more commonly accepted than American Express. Bring two cards in case one is demagnetized, eaten by a machine, or rejected by a temperamental cash machine. (If your card is rejected, try again, and request a smaller amount; some cash machines won't let you take out more than about €150—don't take it personally). Just like at home, credit or debit cards work easily at larger hotels, restaurants, and shops, but smaller businesses prefer payment in hard cash.

Regular banks have the best rates for cashing traveler's checks. For a large exchange, it pays to compare rates and fees. Bank of Sicily consistently has good rates. Banking hours are generally 08:30 to 13:30 and 15:30 to 16:30 Monday through Friday, but can vary wildly. Banks are slow; simple transactions can take 15 to 30 minutes. Post offices and train stations usually change money if you can't get to a bank.

Use a money belt. Thieves target tourists. A money belt (call 425/771-8303 for our free newsletter/catalog) provides peace of mind and allows you to carry lots of cash safely.

Don't be petty about changing money. The greatest avoidable money-changing expense is wasting time every few days to return to a bank. Change a week's worth of money, get big bills, stuff them in your money belt, and travel!

Language Barrier

Many Italians in larger towns and the tourist trade speak at least some English. Still, you'll get more smiles and results by using at least the Italian pleasantries. In smaller, nontouristy towns, Italian is the norm. See the "Survival Phrases" near the end of this book (excerpted from *Rick Steves' Italian Phrase Book*). Note that Italian

Italy's Best Three-Week Trip

Day	Plan	Sleep in
1	Arrive in Milan	Milan
2	Milan to Lake Como	Varenna
3	Lake Como	Varenna
4	To Dolomites via Verona (pick up car at Lake Como)	Castelrotto
5	Dolomites	Castelrotto
6	To Venice	Venice
7	Venice	Venice
8	To Florence	Florence
9	Florence	Florence
10	To Cinque Terre	Vernazza
11	Cinque Terre	Vernazza
12	To Siena	Siena
13	Siena	Siena
14	To Orvieto	Orvieto
15	Orvieto	Orvieto
16	To Sorrento via Pompeii	Sorrento
17	Sorrento	Sorrento
18	To Paestum	Sorrento
19	To Rome, drop car	Rome
20	Rome	Rome
21	Rome	Rome
22	Rome, fly home	

This trip is designed to be done by car but works fine by rail with a few modifications. An Italy Rail Card (8 days in 1 month) works well—pay out of pocket for short runs, such as Milan to Varenna, or the hops between villages in the Cinque Terre. While you can fly into Milan or Rome, I'd choose Milan and work my way south, flying out of Rome. Upon landing in Milan, go directly to Lake Como to relax and get over jet lag. Then see Milan for a half day but sleep in cozier Verona. Consider basing in Bolzano in the Dolomites. From Venice, go straight to the Cinque Terre (2 direct trains/day), then do Florence and Siena. A car is efficient in the hill towns of Tuscany and Umbria but a headache elsewhere. Sorrento is a good home base for Naples and the Amalfi Coast. Skip Paestum unless you love Greek ruins. To save Venice for last, start in Milan, seeing everything but Venice on the way south, then sleeping through everything you've already seen by catching the night train from Naples to Venice. This saves you a day and gives you an early arrival in Venice.

Whirlwind Three-Week Tour of Italy

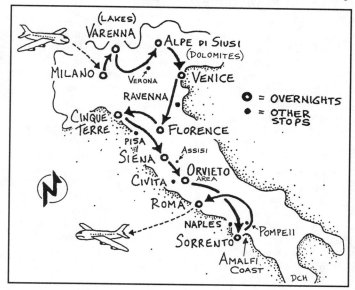

is pronounced much like English, with a few exceptions, such as: *c* followed by *e* or *i* is pronounced *ch* (to ask *"Per centro?"*—"To the center?"—you say pehr CHEN-troh). In Italian, *ch* is pronounced like the hard *c* in Pinocchio (*chiesa*—church—is pronounced kee-AY-zah). Give it your best shot. Italians appreciate your efforts.

Travel Smart

Many people travel through Italy thinking it's a chaotic mess. They feel any attempt at efficient travel is futile. This is dead wrong—and expensive. Italy, which seems as orderly as spilled spaghetti, actually functions quite well. Only those who understand this and travel smart can enjoy Italy on a budget.

Upon arrival in a new town, lay the groundwork for a smooth departure. Write down the schedule for the train or bus you'll take when you depart. Reread this book as you travel, and visit local tourist information offices. Buy a phone card and use it for reservations, reconfirmations, and double-checking hours. Enjoy the friendliness of the local people. Ask questions. Most locals are eager to point you in their idea of the right direction. Keep a notepad in your pocket for organizing your thoughts. Those who expect to travel smart, do.

Sundays have the same pros and cons as they do for travelers in the United States. Sightseeing attractions are generally open

Tips on Sightseeing in Italy

- Churches offer some amazing art (usually free), a cool respite from heat, and a welcome seat. A modest dress code (no bare shoulders or shorts for men, women, and children) is enforced at larger churches such as Venice's St. Mark's and the Vatican's St. Peter's. A coin box near a piece of art often illuminates the art for a coin (and a better photo). Whenever possible, let there be light.

- Reservations are advisable for some of the more famous museums (Florence: Uffizi and Accademia) and mandatory at others (Milan: Da Vinci's *Last Supper*, Padua: Scrovegni Chapel, Rome: Borghese Gallery and Nero's Golden House).

- Hours listed anywhere can vary. On holidays, expect shorter hours or closures. In summer, some sights are open late, allowing easy viewing without crowds. Ask the local TI for a current listing of museum hours. You can confirm sightseeing plans each morning with a quick 10-cent telephone call asking, "Are you open today?" ("*Aperto oggi?*"; ah-PER-toh OH-jee) and "What time do you close?" ("*A che ora chiuso?*"; ah kay OH-rah kee-OO-zoh). I've included telephone numbers for this purpose.

- Art historians and Italians refer to the great Florentine centuries by dropping a thousand years. The *Trecento* (300s), *Quattrocento* (400s), and *Cinquecento* (500s) were the 1300s, 1400s, and 1500s.

- In Italian museums, art is dated with A.D. (for Avanti Cristo, or B.C.) and D.C. (for Dopo Cristo, or A.D.). O.K.?

- Audioguides are becoming increasingly common at museums. These small portable devices give you information in English on what you're seeing. After you dial a number that appears next to a particular work of art, you listen to the spiel (cutting it short if you want). Though the information can be dry, it's usually worthwhile (about €4; extra for 2 earphones—not always available).

- In museums, rooms can begin closing about 30 to 60 minutes before actual closing time. If your heart is set on one piece of art, don't save it for the finale.

- WCs at museums are usually free and clean.

- About half the visitors at Italian museums are English (not Italian) speakers. If a museum lacks audioguides and the only English you encounter explains how to pay, politely ask if there are plans to include English descriptions of the art. Think of it as a service to those who follow.

but have shorter hours, shops and banks are closed, and minor transportation connections are more frustrating (e.g., no bus service to or from Civita). City traffic is light. Rowdy evenings are rare on Sundays. Saturdays are virtually weekdays with earlier closing hours. Hotels in tourist areas are often booked up at Easter, in August, and on Fridays and Saturdays. Religious holidays and train strikes can catch you by surprise anywhere in Italy.

Plan ahead for banking, laundry, post-office chores, and picnics. Mix intense and relaxed periods. Every trip (and every traveler) needs at least a few slack days. Pace yourself. Assume you will return. Drink your water *con gas*.

Tourist Information

During your trip, your first stop in each town should be the tourist office (abbreviated "TI" in this book, and "i," "*turismo*," and "APT" in Italy). While Italian TIs are about half as helpful as those in other countries, their information is twice as important. Prepare. Have a list of questions and a proposed plan to double-check. If you're arriving late, telephone ahead (and try to get a map for your next destination from a TI in the town you're departing from).

Be wary of the travel agencies or special information services that masquerade as TIs but serve fancy hotels and tour companies. They are crooks and liars selling things you don't need.

While the TI is eager to book you a room, use its room-finding service only as a last resort. Across Europe, room-finding services are charging commissions from hotels, taking fees from travelers, and blacklisting establishments that buck their materialistic rules. They are unable to give hard opinions on the relative value of one place over another. The accommodations stakes are too high to go potluck through the TI. You'll do better going direct with the listings in this book.

Italian Tourist Offices in the United States

Before your trip, contact the nearest Italian TI, briefly describe your trip, and request information. You'll get the general packet and, if you ask for specifics (individual city maps, a calendar of festivals, good hikes around Lake Como, info on wine-tasting in Umbria, and so on), an impressive amount of help. If you have a specific problem, they're a good source of sympathy.

Contact the office nearest you...

In **New York:** 630 5th Ave. #1565, New York, NY 10111, brochure hotline tel. 212/245-4822, tel. 212/245-5618, fax 212/586-9249, e-mail: enitny@italiantourism.com.

In **Illinois:** 500 N. Michigan Ave. #2240, Chicago, IL 60611, brochure hotline tel. 312/644-0990, tel. 312/644-0996, fax 312/644-3019, e-mail: enitch@italiantourism.com.

In **California:** 12400 Wilshire Blvd. #550, Los Angeles,

CA 90025, brochure hotline tel. 310/820-0098, tel. 310/820-1898, fax 310/820-6357, e-mail: enitla@earthlink.net.

Web sites: www.italiantourism.com (Italian Tourist Board in the United States), www.museionline.it (museums in Italy, in English), and www.vatican.va (Vatican).

Recommended Guidebooks

Especially if you'll be traveling beyond my recommended destinations, you may want some supplemental information. When you consider the improvements they'll make in your $3,000 vacation, $30 for extra maps and books is money well spent. Especially for several people traveling by car, the weight and expense are negligible. One budget tip can save the price of an extra guidebook.

Lonely Planet's *Italy* is thorough, well-researched, and packed with good maps and hotel recommendations for low- to moderate-budget travelers, but it's not updated annually. Use it only with a one- or two-year-old copyright. The hip *Rough Guide to Italy* (British researchers, more insightful) and the highly opinionated *Let's Go: Italy* (by Harvard students, better hotel listings) are great for students and vagabonds. If you're a low-budget train traveler interested in the youth and night scene (which I have basically ignored), get *Let's Go: Italy*. The Italy section in the bigger *Let's Go: Europe* is sparse.

Cultural and Sightseeing Guides: The colorful Eyewitness series is popular with travelers (editions cover Italy, Tuscany, Rome, Florence, Venice). They are fun for their great, easy-to-grasp graphics and photos, and just right for people who want only factoids. But the Eyewitness written content is relatively skimpy, and the books weigh a ton. I buy them in Italy (no more expensive than in the United States) or simply borrow them for a minute from other travelers at certain sights to make sure I'm aware of that place's highlights. The tall, green Michelin guides to Italy and Rome have minimal information on room and board but do have great maps for drivers and lots of solid encyclopedic coverage of sights, customs, and the culture (sold in English in Italy). The Cadogan guides to various parts of Italy offer an insightful look at the rich and confusing local culture. Those heading for Florence or Rome should read Irving Stone's *The Agony and the Ecstasy* for a great—if romanticized—rundown on Michelangelo, the Medici family, and the turbulent times of the Renaissance.

Rick Steves' Books and Videos

Rick Steves' Europe Through the Back Door 2002 gives you budget travel skills for minimizing jet lag, packing light, planning your itinerary, traveling by car or train, finding budget beds without reservations, changing money, avoiding rip-offs, outsmarting thieves, hurdling the language barrier, staying healthy, taking great photographs, using your bidet, and much more. The book also includes chapters on 35 of my favorite "Back Doors," six of which are in Italy.

Rick Steves' Country Guides are a series of eight guide-books—including this book—covering the Best of Europe; Great Britain; Ireland; Scandinavia; Spain and Portugal; Germany, Austria, and Switzerland; and France, Belgium, and the Netherlands. All are updated annually and come out in December and January.

My **City Guides** cover Paris, London, and Rome (annually updated and available in January), and—new for 2002—Venice and Florence (available in March). These practical guides offer in-depth coverage of the sights, hotels, restaurants, and nightlife in these grand cities along with illustrated tours of their great museums. To make your visit to Italy's secular and religious capital more meaningful, consider getting the Rome city guide.

Rick Steves' Europe 101: History and Art for the Traveler (with Gene Openshaw, 2000) gives you the story of Europe's people, history, and art. Written for smart people who were sleeping in their history and art classes before they knew they were going to Europe, *101* really helps resurrect the rubble.

Rick Steves' Mona Winks: Self-Guided Tours of Europe's Top Museums (with Gene Openshaw, 2001) gives you easy-to-follow, self-guided tours of Europe's top 25 museums and cultural sites. Nearly half of the book is devoted to Italy, with tours of Venice (St. Mark's, Doge's Palace, and Accademia Gallery), Florence (Uffizi Gallery, Bargello, Michelangelo's *David*, and a Renaissance walk through the town center), and Rome (Colosseum, Forum, Pantheon, National Museum of Rome, Borghese Gallery, Vatican Museum, and St. Peter's Basilica). If you want to enjoy the great sights and museums of Italy, *Mona* will be a valued friend.

In Italy, a phrase book is as fun as it is necessary. My *Rick Steves' Italian Phrase Book* will help you meet the people and stretch your budget. It's written by a monoglot who, for more than 25 years, has fumbled through Italy struggling with all the other phrase books. Use this fun and practical communication aid to make accurate hotel reservations over the telephone, ask for a free taste of cantaloupe-flavored gelato at the *gelatería*, have the man in the deli make you a sandwich, and tell your cabbie that if he doesn't slow down, you'll throw up.

My latest television series, *Rick Steves' Europe*, features five new shows on Italy: Venice, Veneto (sights near Venice), Florence, Siena/Assisi, and the Cinque Terre. Of a combined total of 68 episodes (from my new series and the original series, *Travels in Europe with Rick Steves*), 14 of my half-hour shows are on Italy. These air on public television throughout the United States. Episodes are also available in information-packed home videos, as is my two-hour slide-show lecture on Italy (call us at 425/771-8303 for our free newsletter/catalog).

Rick Steves' Postcards from Europe, my autobiographical book, packs more than 25 years of travel anecdotes and insights into the ultimate 3,000-mile European adventure. Through my guidebooks, I share my favorite European discoveries with you. *Postcards* introduces you to my favorite European friends. Half of *Postcards* is set in Italy: Venice, Florence, Rome, and the Cinque Terre.

All of my books are published by Avalon Travel Publishing (www.travelmatters.com).

Maps

The maps in this book, drawn by Dave Hoerlein, are concise and simple. Dave, who is well-traveled in Italy, designed the maps to help you locate recommended places and the tourist offices, where you can pick up more in-depth maps of the city or region (cheap or free).

For an overall map of Europe, consider my Rick Steves' Europe Planning Map—geared to travelers' needs—with sight-seeing destinations listed prominently (for our free newsletter/catalog, contact us at 425/771-8303 or www.ricksteves.com).

Train travelers can do fine with a simple rail map (such as the one that comes with your railpass) and city maps from the TI as they travel. But drivers shouldn't skimp on maps. Excellent maps are available throughout Italy at bookstores, newsstands, and gas stations. Get a good 1:200,000 map to get the most out of your miles; study the key to get the most sightseeing value out of your map.

Tours of Italy

Travel agents will tell you about normal tours of Italy, but they won't tell you about ours. At Europe Through the Back Door, we offer 20-day tours of Italy featuring most of the highlights in this book (departures April–Oct, 24 people on a big roomy bus with 2 great guides) and one-week, off-season getaways to Rome (departures Oct–April, 20 people). For information, call 425/771-8303 or see www.ricksteves.com.

Transportation

By Car or Train?

Each mode of transportation has pros and cons. Public transportation is one of the few bargains in Italy. Trains and buses are inexpensive and good. City-to-city travel is faster, easier, and cheaper by train than by car. Trains give you the convenience and economy of doing long stretches overnight. By train I arrive relaxed and well-rested—not so by car.

Parking, gas (about $4 per gallon), and tolls are expensive in

Italy. But drivers enjoy more control, especially in the countryside. Cars carry your luggage for you, generally from door to door—especially important for heavy packers (such as chronic shoppers and families traveling with children). And groups know that the more people you pack into a car or minibus, the cheaper it gets per person.

Trains

To travel by train cheaply in Italy, simply buy tickets as you go. But Italy's train ticket system confounds even the locals, and, for convenience alone, I'd go with the Italian State Railway's Italy Rail Card (see chart within this chapter).

Whether you're traveling alone or with others, consider Italy's **Kilometric Ticket**. Unlike the Rail Card, the Kilometric Ticket—while a headache, because it doesn't cover fast-train supplements—is especially economical for groups. One to five people can split 3,000 kilometers of travel on it for around $120 second class, $180 first class (buy it in Italy at major train stations or CIT travel agencies; it's also available in the United States but costs much more). The Kilometric Ticket is a little booklet with 20 coupons, each good for a one-way journey for any or all of the listed travelers. Before you board the train, go to a railway clerk at the ticket window (or a CIT travel agent), state where you're going, and the clerk will subtract from your total the number of kilometers your journey takes (kids 4 to 11 "cost" only half as many kilometers as an adult). If any segment of your journey requires a supplement (usually just a few dollars, up to $15 for the fastest trains), pay it at this time, when your ticket is being filled out by the clerk. (If your Ticket is first-class, get a first-class supplement.) You can stop en route; you're allowed an additional six hours to complete trips less than 200 kilometers (or 24–48 hours with unlimited stops for trips longer than 200 kilometers). Don't tear out any of the pages of your Kilometric Ticket. Note that you need to validate your ticket before boarding (see below).

Groups of three to five companions can consider the **Tariffa Mini-Group** to get a 20 percent discount for a single journey (except in July, August, and various holiday seasons). You don't need to have any type of card, but you'll get this deal only if you ask for it at the station.

Before boarding the train, you must **validate** (stamp) your train documents in the machine near the platform. This includes whatever you need to take a particular trip, which can be as simple as a single ticket, or can involve a combination of: the pertinent page of a Kilometric Ticket, a supplement, seat reservation, or a *cuccetta* (overnight berth) reservation. You don't need to stamp Eurailpasses or Italy Rail Cards.

For travel exclusively in Italy, a 17-country **Eurailpass** is a bad value. If you're branching out beyond Italy, the Eurail

Prices listed are for 2001. My free *Rick Steves' Guide to European Railpasses* has the latest on 2002 prices. To get the railpass guide, call us at 425/771-8303 or visit www.ricksteves.com/rail. All Italy passes are also sold in Italy at travel agencies and major train stations.

ITALY RAIL CARD

	1st class	2nd class
8 consec. days	$299	$199
15 consec. days	373	249
21 consec. days	433	289
30 consec. days	522	348
Any 4 days in 1 mo. flexi	239	159
Any 8 days in 1 mo. flexi	334	223
Any 12 days in 1 mo. flexi	429	286

Passes cover supplements EXCEPT for the fast-n-classy Eurostar Italia trains; passes do not cover any reservations. Children 4-11 pay half the adult fare; under 4 free.

ITALIAN KILOMETRIC TICKET

Also known as the "Biglietto Chilometrico," this ticket features coupons for up to 20 trips totaling up to 3,000 kilometers that can be used for up to five people. Sold quick and easy at any major Italian travel agency or train station, the pass costs about $180 for first class or $120 for second class. For example, a group of five could go the 570 km from Venice to Rome on a Kilometric Ticket for $24 each vs. the normal $45 regular ticket price The Kilometric Ticket does not cover supplements charged for the faster intercity trains.

Italy: This schematic map indicates the cost in dollars for a one-way 2nd class trip (first #) and the number of kilometers (second #) between the cities shown.

ITALY RAIL & DRIVE PASS

Any 3 days of rail travel + 2 days of Hertz car rental in 1 month.

Car Category	First Class	2nd class	Extra car day
Economy	$259	$189	$40
Compact	279	209	60
Intermediate	289	215	65
Small Automatic	289	215	65

Rail & Drive prices are approximate per person, two traveling together. Solo travelers pay about 20% more. For more info, call your travel agent or Rail Europe at 800/438-7245.

EURAIL SELECTPASSES

This pass covers travel in three adjacent countries. For details, visit www.ricksteves.com/rail or see *Rick Steves' Guide to European Railpasses*.

	1st cl Selectpass	1st cl Saverpass	2nd cl Youthpass
5 days in 2 months	$328	$280	$230
6 days in 2 months	360	306	252
8 days in 2 months	420	358	294
10 days in 2 months	476	406	334

Saverpass: price is per person for 2 or more adults traveling together at all times.
Youthpasses: Under age 26 only. Kids 4-11 pay half adult fare; under 4: free.

Deciphering Italian Train Schedules

At the station, look for the big yellow posters labeled *Partenze*—Departures (ignore the white posters, which show arrivals). Schedules are listed chronologically, hour by hour, showing the trains leaving the station throughout the day. The first column (*Ora*) lists the time of departure. The next column (*Treno*) shows the type of train. The third column (*Classi Servizi*) lists the services available (first- and second-class cars, dining car, couchettes, etc.) and, more important, whether you need reservations (usually denoted by an *R* in a box). The next column lists the destination of the train (*Principali Fermate Destinazioni*), often showing intermediate stops, followed by the final destination, with arrival times listed throughout in parentheses. Note that *your* final destination may be listed in fine print as an intermediate destination. If you're going from Milan to Florence, scan the schedule and you'll notice that virtually all trains that terminate in Rome stop in Florence en route. Travelers who read the fine print end up with a greater choice of trains. The next column (*Servizi Diretti e Annotazioni*) has pertinent notes about the train, such as "also stops in . . ." (*ferma anche a . . .*), "doesn't stop in . . ." (*non ferma a . . .*), "stops in every station" (*ferma in tutte le stazioni*), and so on. The last column lists the track (*Binario*) the train departs from. Confirm the *binario* with an additional source: a ticket seller, the electronic board listing immediate departures, TV monitors on the platform, or the railway officials who are usually standing by the train unless you really need them. For any odd symbols on the poster, look at the key at the end. Some of the phrasing can be deciphered easily, such as *servizio periodico* (periodical service—doesn't always run). For the trickier ones, ask a local or railway official or simply take a different train.

Selectpass ($476 for 10 days in 2 months—2001 price) allows you to tailor a pass to your trip, provided you're traveling in three adjacent countries directly connected by rail or ferry. For instance, you could choose France-Italy-Greece or Germany-Austria-Italy. For additional countries in the core of Europe, consider a five-country Europass.

Youth and **seniors** can buy €25 cards at the station to get discounts on their train travel (20 percent discount on second-class or first-class tickets, valid 6 months). If you're under 26, ask for a Carta Verde. If you're 60 or over, request a Carta d'Argento.

You'll encounter several **types of trains** in Italy. Along with

Italy's Public Transportation

KEY: — RAIL   ---BUS   ···· SHIP
NOT TO SCALE   ● GOOD OVERNIGHT STOPS

the various milk-run trains, there are the slow IR (Interregional) and *directo* trains, the medium *expresso*, the fast IC (Intercity), and the bullet-train T.A.V. (Treno Alta Velocita). The T.A.V., which requires about a €16 supplement even if you have a railpass, provides two-thirds of the train service from Rome to Milan, Florence, Venice, or Naples. Even with supplements, fast trains are affordable (e.g., a second-class Rome-to-Venice ticket costs about $50 with express supplement). Buying supplements on the train comes with a nasty penalty, and buying them at the station can waste time. Try to buy them at travel agencies (CIT or American Express) in towns. The cost is the same, the lines and language barrier are smaller, and you'll save time.

First-class tickets cost 50 percent more than **second-class**. While second-class cars go as fast as their first-class neighbors, Italy is one country where I would consider the splurge of first class. The easiest way to upgrade a second-class ticket once onboard a crowded train is to nurse a drink in the snack car.

Trains can fill up, even in first class; if a popular train route originates at your departure point (e.g., you're catching the Milan-to-Venice train in Milan), arrive at least 15 minutes before the departure time to snare a seat. If you anticipate a crowd, you can get a firm seat reservation in advance for about €4.

Newsstands sell up-to-date regional and all-Italy **timetables** (€4, ask for the *orario ferroviario*). There is an all-Italy telephone number for train information: tel. 848-888-088 (daily 07:00–21:00, automated, in Italian). On the Web, check www.reiseauskunft.bahn .de/bin/query.exe/en or www.fs-on-line.com.

Italian trains are famous for their thieves. Never leave a bag unattended. There have been cases of bandits gassing an entire car before looting the snoozing gang. I've noticed that police now ride the trains, and things seem more controlled. Still, for an **overnight** trip, I'd feel safe only in a *cuccetta* (a berth in a special sleeping car with an attendant who keeps track of who comes and goes while you sleep—approximately €13 in a 6-bed compartment, €18 in a less cramped 4-bed compartment).

Avoid big-city train station lines whenever you can. For either the same cost or a minimal charge (about €2), you can buy tickets (including Kilometric Tickets) and reserve a *cuccetta* at most travel agencies.

Most stations have **baggage storage** (*deposito* or *bagagli*) where you can safely leave your bag for €3 per 12-hour period (payable when you pick up the bag). Larger stations also have lockers, but they are a bit complicated to figure out (the smiley slot takes bills).

Strikes are common. Strikes generally last a day, and train employees will simply say, "*Sciopero*" (strike). But in actuality, sporadic trains, following no particular schedule, lumber down the tracks during most strikes.

Car Rental

Research car rental before you go. It's cheaper to arrange for car rentals through your travel agent while still in the United States. Rent by the week with unlimited mileage. If you need a car for three or more weeks, it's cheaper to lease (you'll save money on insurance and taxes). Explore your drop-off options (south of Rome can be a problem).

For peace of mind, I spring for the Collision Damage Waiver (CDW) insurance (about $10–15 per day), which gives a zero deductible rather than the standard value-of-the-car "deductible." A few "gold" credit cards cover CDW insurance; quiz your credit-card company on the worst-case scenario. Travel Guard sells CDW insurance for $6 a day (U.S. tel. 800/826-1300, www.travelguard.com).

Theft insurance (separate from CDW insurance) is mandatory when you're renting a car for use in Italy. The insurance usually costs about $10 to $15 a day, payable when you pick up the car.

A rail-and-drive pass (such as a EurailDrive, Europass Drive, Selectpass Drive, or Italy Rail and Drive) can be put to thoughtful use. Certain areas are great by car, such as the Dolomites and the hill towns of Tuscany and Umbria, while most of Italy is best by train.

Driving

Driving in Italy is frightening—a video game for keeps, and you only get one quarter. All you need is a U.S. driver's license and a car. According to everybody but the Italian police, international driver's permits are not necessary. The police fine you if they can't read your license.

Autostradas: Italy's freeway system is as good as our inter-state system, but you'll pay about a dollar for every 10 minutes of use. (I paid €20 for the four-hour drive from Bolzano to Pisa.) While I favor the autostradas because I feel they're safer, cheaper (saving time and gas), and less nerve-racking than smaller roads, savvy local drivers know which toll-free "superstradas" are actually faster and more direct than the autostrada (e.g., Florence to Pisa). For more information, visit www.autostrade.it.

Gas: Most cars take unleaded gas (from green pumps, available everywhere). Autostrada rest stops are self-service stations open daily without a siesta break. Small-town stations are usually cheaper and offer full service but shorter hours. Many 24-hour-a-day stations are entirely automated, with machines that trade gas for paper money.

Metric: A liter is about a quart, four to a gallon; a kilometer is about six-tenths of a mile. Figure kilometers to miles by cutting them in half and adding back 10 percent of the original (120 km: 60 + 12 = 72 miles, 300 km: 150 + 30 = 180 miles).

Parking: White lines generally mean parking is free. Blue lines mean you'll have to pay—usually €0.75 to €1 per hour. If there's no meter, there is probably a roving attendant who will take your money. Study the signs. Many free zones are cleared out (by car owners or tow trucks) one day a week for

Standard European Road Signs

STOP   No Entry For Cars   All Vehicles Prohibited   No Entry   Speed Limit (in km)   Yield   No Passing   Danger   Parking

street cleaning. Often the free zones have a 30- or 60-minute time limit. *Zona disco* has nothing to do with dancing. Italian cars have a time disk (a cardboard clock), which you set at your arrival time and lay on the dashboard so the attendant knows how long you've been parked. This is a fine system that all drivers should take advantage of. (If your rental car doesn't come with a *zona disco*, pick one up at a tobacco shop or just write your arrival time on a piece of paper and place it on the dashboard.) Garages are safe, save time, and help you avoid the stress of parking tickets. Take the parking voucher with you to pay the cashier before you leave.

    Theft: Cars are routinely vandalized and stolen. Try to make your car look locally owned: Hide the "tourist-owned" rental company decals and put a local newspaper in your back window.

Telephones, Mail, and E-mail

Smart travelers use the telephone every day—especially in Italy—to make hotel reservations, call tourist information offices, and phone home. Dialing long distance is easy with an Italian phone card.

    Phone Cards: Italy's phone cards are cards you insert in the phone instead of coins. They're sold in varying denominations at tobacco shops, post offices, and machines near phone booths (many phone booths indicate where the nearest phone-card sales outlet is located). Rip off the perforated corner to "activate" the card before you insert it into the phone.

    The orange SIP public telephones are everywhere and take cards or coins. About a quarter of the phones are broken (which could explain why so many Italians carry cell phones). The rest of the phones work reluctantly. Dial slowly and deliberately, as if the phone doesn't understand numbers very well. Often a recorded message will break in, brusquely informing you that your number does not exist (*non-esistente*), even if you're dialing your own home phone number. Dial again with an increasing show of confidence, in an attempt to convince the phone of your number's existence. If you fail, try a different phone. Repeat as needed.

    Italian phone numbers vary in length; a hotel can have, say, a 10-digit phone number and 11-digit fax number. When spelling out your name on the phone, you'll find *a* (pronounced "ah" in Italian), *e* (pronounced "ay"), and *i* (pronounced "ee") are confusing. Say "*a*, Aosta," "*e*, Empoli," and "*i*, Italia" to clear up that problem. If you plan to access your voice mail from Italy, be advised that you probably can't dial extensions or secret codes once you connect (you're on vacation—relax).

Dialing Direct: Italy has dispensed with area codes. You dial the same number, no matter where you're calling from in Italy. For example, the number of one of my recommended Venice hotels is 041-522-7131. To call it from the Venice train station, dial 041-522-7131. If you call it from Rome, it's the same: 041-522-7131.

When dialing internationally, dial the international access code (00 if you're calling from Europe, 011 from the U.S. or Canada), the country code (of the country you're calling), and the local number. To call the Venice hotel from the United States, dial 011 (the U.S. international access code), 39 (Italy's country code), and then 041-522-7131. To call my office from Italy, I dial 00 (Italy's international access code), 1 (the U.S. country code), 425 (Edmonds' area code), and 771-8303. For **international access codes and country codes**, see the appendix. European time is six/nine hours ahead of the east/west coast of the United States.

Hotel-room phones are reasonable for calls within Italy (the faint beeps stand for €0.10 phone units) but a terrible rip-off for calls to the United States (unless you use a PIN card—see below—or your hotel allows toll-free access to your USA Direct service—see below). If you have phone-card phobia, look for the easy-to-use "talk now, pay later" metered phones in some bars or in the central post office or train station in big cities.

Italy has toll-free numbers that start with 800 (like the U.S.A.'s 800 numbers, though in Italy you don't dial a "1" first). In Italy, you can dial these 800 numbers—called *freephone* or *numero verde* (green number)—free from any phone without using a card or coins.

In 2001, the phone system dropped the initial zero from Italy's cellular phone numbers; if, during your travels, you come across old information that lists cell phone numbers starting with zero, drop the zero and try the number.

PIN Cards: Calling the United States from Italy is now cheapest with the new PIN cards sold at newsstands and hole-in-the-wall long-distance phone shops. Because there are so many brand names, just ask for an international telephone card (specify that you want a card for making calls to America or Canada to avoid getting the PIN cards that are only good within particular regions in Italy). After you buy a card, scratch off and reveal your Personal Identification Number, dial the toll-free number, punch in your PIN, and talk. You'll get about three minutes per dollar. Because you don't insert these cards into a phone, you can use them at most phones, including your hotel room (unless it's an older touch-tone phone).

If the PIN doesn't work on one phone, try another phone. Get a lower denomination in case the card is a dud. On my last trip, I had difficulty using PIN cards to make local calls, so I used Italian phone cards, coins, or hotel room phones for local calls, and saved the PIN card for international calls.

USA Direct Services: While still convenient, these services, such as AT&T, MCI, and Sprint, are no longer a good value. It's much cheaper to call the United States using a PIN card or Italian phone card, but some people prefer to use their easier, pricier calling cards. Each card company has a toll-free number in each European country (for Italy: AT&T–tel. 172-1011, MCI–tel. 172-1022, and Sprint–tel. 172-1877), which puts you in touch with an English-speaking operator. The operator takes your card number and the number you want to call, puts you through, and bills your home phone number for the call. Oddly, you need to use a small-value coin or Italian phone card to dial the toll-free number. Sprint is the priciest, costing $3 for the first minute with a $4.50 connection fee; hanging up when you hear an answering machine is expensive ($7.50). First use a coin or an Italian phone card to call home for five seconds—long enough to say "call me" or to make sure an answering machine is off so you can call back using your USA Direct number to connect with a person. It's outrageously expensive to use USA Direct for calls between European countries; it's much cheaper to call direct using an Italian phone card.

Cell Phones: Affluent travelers like to buy cell phones (about $60 on up) in Europe to use for making local and international calls. The cheaper phones generally work only if you're making calls from the country where you purchased it (e.g., a phone bought in Italy won't work in France). Pricier phones allow you to call from any country, but it'll cost you about $40 to outfit the phone per country with the necessary chip and pre-paid phone time. If you're interested, stop by any European shop that sells cell phones (you'll see an array of phones prominently displayed in the store window). Depending on your trip and budget, ask for a phone that works only in that country or one that can be used throughout Europe. And if you're really on a budget, skip cell phones and use PIN cards instead.

Mail: Mail service is miserable in Italy. Postcards get last priority. If you must have mail stops, consider a few pre-reserved hotels along your route, or use American Express offices. Most American Express offices in Italy will hold mail for one month. This service is free to anyone using an AmEx card or traveler's checks (and available for a small fee to others). Allow 14 days for U.S.-to-Italy mail delivery, but don't count on it. Federal Express makes pricey two-day deliveries. Phoning is so easy that I've completely dispensed with mail stops. If possible, mail nothing precious from Italy.

E-mail: E-mail use among Italian hoteliers is increasing. I've listed e-mail addresses when possible. Little, hole-in-the-wall cybercafés are popular in the bigger cities, giving you inexpensive and easy Internet access.

Sleeping

For hassle-free efficiency, I favor hotels and restaurants handy to your sightseeing activities. Rather than list hotels scattered throughout a city, I describe two or three favorite neighborhoods and recommend the best accommodations values in each, from $20 bunks to plush $200 doubles with all the comforts.

Sleeping in Italy is expensive. Cheap big-city hotels can be depressing. Tourist information services cannot give opinions on quality. A major feature of this book is its extensive listing of good-value rooms. I like places that are clean, small, central, quiet at night, traditional, inexpensive, friendly, with firm beds—and those not listed in other guidebooks. (In Italy, for me, 6 out of 9 attributes means a keeper.)

Hotels

Double rooms listed in this book will range from about $50 (very simple, toilet and shower down the hall) to $200 (maximum plumbing and more), with most clustering around $90 (with private bathrooms). Prices are higher in big cities and heavily touristed cities, and lower off the beaten path. Three or four people economize by requesting larger rooms. Solo travelers find that the cost of a *camera singola* is often only 25 percent less than a *camera doppia*. Most listed hotels have rooms for anywhere from one to five people. If there's room for an extra cot, they'll cram it in for you.

The Italian word for "hotel" is *hotel*, and in smaller, non-touristy towns, *albergo*. A few places have kept the old titles, *locanda* or *pension*, indicating that they offer budget beds.

You normally get close to what you pay for. Prices are fairly standard. Shopping around earns you a better location and more character, but rarely a cheaper price.

However, prices at nearly any hotel can get soft if you do any of the following: arrive direct (without using a pricey middleman like the TI), offer to pay cash, stay at least three nights, or visit off-season. Breakfasts are legally optional (though some hotels insist they're not). Initial prices quoted often include breakfast and a private bathroom. Offer to skip breakfast for a better price.

You'll save $10 to $20 if you ask for a room without a shower and just use the shower down the hall. Generally rooms with a bath or shower also have a toilet and a bidet (which Italians use for quick sponge baths). Tubs usually come with a frustrating "telephone shower" (handheld nozzle). If a shower has no curtain, the entire bathroom showers with you. The cord that dangles

Sleep Code

To pack maximum information into minimum space, I use this code to describe accommodations in this book. When there is a range of prices in one category, the price will fluctuate with the season, size of room, or length of stay. Prices listed are per room, not per person.

   S = Single room or price for one person using a double.

   D = Double or twin room. "Double beds" are often two twins sheeted together and are usually big enough for non-romantic couples.

   T = Three-person room (often a double with a single bed moved in).

   Q = Four-adult room (an extra child's bed is usually cheaper).

   b = Private bathroom with a toilet and shower or tub.

   s = Private shower or tub only. (The toilet is down the hall.)

   CC = Accepts credit cards (Visa and MasterCard, rarely American Express).

   no CC = Does not accept credit cards; pay in local cash.

   SE = Speaks English. This code is used only when it seems predictable that you'll encounter English-speaking staff.

   NSE = Does not speak English. Used only when it's unlikely you'll encounter English-speaking staff.

   According to this code, a couple staying at a "Db-€85, CC, SE" hotel would pay a total of 85 euros (about $78) for a double room with a private bathroom. The hotel accepts Visa or Italian cash. The staff speaks English.

over the tub or shower is not a clothesline. You pull it when you've fallen and can't get up.

Double beds are called *matrimoniale*, even though hotels aren't interested in your marital status. Twins are *due letti singoli*.

Many hotel rooms have a TV and phone. Rooms in fancier hotels usually come with air-conditioning (sometimes you pay an extra per-day charge for this), a tiny safe, and a small stocked fridge called a *frigo* bar (FREE-goh bar).

When you check in, the receptionist will ask for your passport and keep it for a couple of hours. Hotels are required to register each guest with the police. Relax. Americans are notorious for making this chore more difficult than it needs to be.

The hotel breakfast, while convenient, is often a bad value— $8 for a roll, jelly, and usually unlimited *caffè latte*. You can sometimes request cheese or salami (about €2.50 extra). I enjoy taking breakfast at the corner café. It's OK to supplement what you order with a few picnic goodies.

Rooms are safe. Still, zip cameras and keep money out of sight. More pillows and blankets are usually in the closet or available on request. In Italy, towels and linen aren't always replaced every day. Hang your towel up to dry.

While bed-and-breakfasts (*affitta camere*) and youth hostels (*ostello della gioventù*) are not as common in Italy as elsewhere in Europe, I've listed many in this book. Big-city hostels are normally overrun with the *Let's Go* crowd, but small-town hostels can be an enjoyable way to save money and make friends.

Regardless of where you stay, you'll avoid the time-wasting crowd at the reception desk in the morning if you pay the evening before you leave.

Making Reservations

It's possible to travel at any time of year without reservations, but, given the high stakes and the quality of the gems I've found for this book, I'd recommend making reservations. You can call long in advance from home or grab rooms a few days to a week in advance as you travel. (If you have difficulty, ask the fluent recep- tionist at your current hotel to call for you.) If you like more spon- taneity (or if you're traveling off-season), you might make a habit of calling between 09:00 and 10:00 on the day you plan to arrive, when the hotel clerk knows who'll be checking out and just which rooms will be available. I've taken great pains to list telephone numbers with long distance instructions (see "Telephones," above; also see the appendix). Use the telephone and the convenient tele- phone cards. Most hotels listed are accustomed to English-only speakers. A hotel receptionist will trust you and hold a room until 16:00 without a deposit, though some will ask for a credit-card number. Honor (or cancel by phone) your reservations. Long distance is cheap and easy from public phone booths. Don't let these people down—I promised you'd call and cancel if for some reason you won't show up. Don't needlessly confirm rooms through the tourist office; they'll take a commission.

If you know where you want to stay each day (and you don't need or want flexibility), reserve your rooms a month or two in advance from home. To reserve from home, telephone first to confirm availability and then fax or e-mail your formal request. Phone and fax costs are reasonable, e-mail is a steal, and simple English is usually fine. To fax, use the handy form in the appendix (or online at ricksteves.com/reservation). If you don't get an answer to your fax request, consider that a "no." (Many little places get 20 faxes a day after they're full and can't afford to respond.)

A two-night stay in August would be "two nights, 16/8/02 to 18/8/02" (Europeans write the date in this order—day/month/year—and hotel jargon uses your day of departure). You'll often receive a response back requesting one night's deposit. A credit card will usually be accepted. If you use your credit card for the deposit, you can pay with your card or cash when you arrive; if you don't show up, you'll be billed for one night. Always reconfirm your reservations a day in advance by phone.

Agriturismo

Agriturismo (or agricultural tourism) began in the 1960s to encourage farmers to remain on their land, produce food, and offer accommodation to tourists. These rural Italian B&Bs are ideal for couples or families traveling by car.

Some properties are simple and rustic, while others are downright luxurious, offering amenities such as swimming pools. The quality of the rooms varies, but they are usually simple, clean, and comfortable. Most serve tasty home-grown food. And most require a minimum-night stay, usually a week. July and August are especially busy. Off-season shorter stays are possible.

Be aware that agricultural tourism is organized "*alla Italiana*," which means, among other things, a lack of a single governing body. In this book you'll find some *agriturismo* farms you can contact directly—or try this Web site, www.agriturist.it, which lists over 1,700 farms throughout Italy. If you'd prefer to go through an agency, consider Farm Holidays in Tuscany. They book rooms and apartments at 300 farms in Tuscany, Umbria, and elsewhere in Italy (Mon–Fri 09:00–13:00, 15:00–18:00, plus May–Sept Sat 16:00–18:00, closed Sun, Via Manin 20, 58100 Grosseto, tel. 0564-417-418, www.it-farmholidays.it, English spoken, ask for Mr. Andrea Mazzanti). Book several months in advance for high season (May–Sept). Generally, a 25 percent deposit is required (lost if you cancel), and the balance is due one month before arrival.

For more information on *agriturismo*, visit www.initaly.com, www.italyfarmholidays.com, and www.agriturismo.com.

Eating Italian

The Italians are masters of the art of fine living. That means eating...long and well. Lengthy, multi-course lunches and dinners and endless hours sitting in outdoor cafés are the norm. Americans eat on their way to an evening event and complain if the check is slow in coming. For Italians, the meal is an end in itself, and only rude waiters rush you. When you want the bill, mime-scribble on your raised palm or ask for it: "*Il conto?*"

Eating with the Seasons

Italian cooks love to serve you fresh produce and seafood at its tastiest. If you must have porcini mushrooms outside of October and November, they'll be frozen. To get the freshest veggies at a fine restaurant, request *"Il piatto del la stagioni, per favore."* (A plate of what's seasonal, please.)
Here are a few examples of what's fresh when:

April–May:	Calamari, squid, green beans, and zucchini flowers
April, May, Sept, Oct:	Black truffles
May–June:	Mussels, asparagus, zucchini, canteloupe, and strawberries
May–Aug:	Eggplant
Oct–Nov:	Mushrooms and white truffles
Fresh year-round:	Clams, meats, and cheese

Even those of us who liked dorm food will find that the local cafés, cuisine, and wines become a highlight of our Italian adventure. Trust me, this is sightseeing for your palate, and even if the rest of you is sleeping in cheap hotels, your taste buds will relish an occasional first-class splurge. You can eat well without going broke. But be careful; you're just as likely to blow a small fortune on a disappointing meal as you are to dine wonderfully for $20.

Restaurants

When restaurant hunting, choose places filled with locals, not the place with the big neon signs boasting, "We speak English and accept credit cards." Restaurants parked on famous squares generally serve bad food at high prices to tourists. Locals eat better at lower-rent locales. Family-run places operate without hired help and can offer cheaper meals. The word *osteria* (normally a simple, local-style restaurant) makes me salivate.

For unexciting but basic values, look for a *menu turistico* (also called *menu del giorno*—menu of the day), a three- or four-course, set-price meal (price includes service charge, no need to tip). Galloping gourmets order à la carte with the help of a menu translator. (The *Marling Italian Menu Master* is excellent. *Rick Steves' Italian Phrase Book* has enough phrases for intermediate eaters.) Some restaurants have self-serve antipasti buffets, offering a variety of cooked appetizers spread out like a salad bar (pay per plate, not weight; usually costs around €6–8); a plate of antipasti combined with a pasta dish makes a healthy, affordable, interesting meal.

A full meal consists of an appetizer (antipasto, €2.50–5), a first course (*primo piatto*, pasta or soup, €4–7), and a second course (*secondo piatto*, expensive meat and fish dishes, €5–10). Seafood and steak is sometimes sold by weight (if you see "100 g" by the price, you'll pay that price *per* 100 grams—about a quarter pound). Some special dishes come in large quantities meant for two people; the shorthand way of showing this on a menu is "X2" (meaning "times two"). Vegetables (*contorni, verdure*) may come with the *secondo* course or cost extra (€3) as a side dish. Restaurants normally pad the bill with a cover charge (*pane e coperto*, around €1) and a service charge (*servizio*, 15 percent); these charges are listed on the menu. Italian waiters are paid well, and tipping is not expected if the *servizio* charge is included in the bill. At restaurants that don't tack on a service charge, tip 10 to 15 percent.

As you will see, the euros add up in a hurry. Light and budget eaters get by with a *primo piatto* each and a shared antipasto. Italians admit that *secondi* are the least interesting aspect of the local cuisine.

Delis, Cafeterias, Pizza Shops, and Tavola Calda (Hot Table) Bars

Italy offers many cheap alternatives to restaurants. Stop by a *rosticcería* for great cooked deli food; a self-service cafeteria (called "free flow" in Italian) that feeds you without the add-ons; a *tavola calda* bar for an assortment of veggies; or a Pizza Rustica shop for stand-up or take-out pizza.

Pizza is cheap and everywhere. Key pizza vocabulary: *capricciosa* (generally ham, mushrooms, and artichokes), *funghi* (mushrooms), *margherita* (tomato sauce and mozzarella), *marinara* (tomato sauce, oregano, garlic, no cheese), *quattro formaggi* (4 different cheeses), and *quattro stagioni* (different toppings on each of the four quarters for those who can't choose just one menu item). If you ask for *peperoni* on your pizza, you'll get green or red peppers, not sausage. Kids like *margherita* (tomato and cheese) and *diavola* (closest thing in Italy to American "pepperoni"). At Pizza Rustica take-out shops, slices are sold by weight (100 grams, or *un etto*, is a hot, cheap snack; 200 grams, or *due etti*, makes a light meal).

For a fast, cheap, and healthy lunch, find a *tavola calda* bar with a buffet spread of meat and vegetables and ask for a mixed plate of vegetables with a hunk of mozzarella (*piatto misto di verdure con mozzarella*). Don't be limited by what you can see. If you'd like a salad with a slice of cantaloupe and a hunk of cheese, they'll whip that up for you in a snap. Belly up to the bar and, with a pointing finger and key words in the chart in this chapter, you can get a fine mixed plate of vegetables. If something's a mystery, ask for *un assaggio* (a little taste).

Ordering Food at *Tavola Caldas*

plate of mixed veggies	*piatto misto di verdure*	pee-AH-toh MEES-toh dee vehr-DOO-ray
"Heated, please."	*"Scaldare, per favore."*	skahl-DAH-ray, pehr fah-VOH-ray
"A taste, please."	*"Un assaggio, per favore"*	oon ah-SAH-joh, pehr fah-VOH-ray
artichoke	*carciofo*	kar-CHOH-foh
asparagus	*asparagi*	ah-spah-RAH-jee
beans	*fagioli*	fah-JOH-lee
green beans	*fagiolini*	fah-joh-LEE-nee
broccoli	*broccoli*	BROK-oh-lee
canteloupe	*melone*	may-LOH-nay
carrots	*carote*	kah-ROT-ay
ham	*prosciutto*	proh-SHOO-toh
mushrooms	*funghi*	FOONG-ghee
potatoes	*patate*	pah-TAH-tay
rice	*riso*	REE-zoh
spinach	*spinaci*	speen-AH-chee
tomatoes	*pomodori*	poh-moh-DOH-ree
zucchini	*zucchine*	zoo-KEE-nay
breadsticks	*grissini*	gree-SEE-nee

*Excerpted from *Rick Steves' Italian Phrase Book*

Italian Bars/Cafés

Italian "bars" are not taverns, but cafés. These local hangouts serve coffee, mini-pizzas, sandwiches, and cartons of milk from the cooler. Many dish up plates of fried cheese and vegetables from under the glass counter, ready to reheat. This is my budget choice, the Italian equivalent of English pub grub.

For quick meals, bars usually have trays of cheap, ready-made sandwiches (*panini* or *tramezzini*)—some kinds are delightful grilled. To save time for sightseeing and room for dinner, my favorite lunch is a ham and cheese *panini* at a bar (called *tost*, grilled twice to get really hot). To get food "to go," say, "*Da portar via*" (for the road). All bars have a WC (*toilette, bagno*) in the back, and the public is entitled to use it.

Bars serve great drinks—hot, cold, sweet, or alcoholic. Chilled bottled water (*natural* or *frizzante*) is sold cheap to go.

Coffee: If you ask for "*un caffè,*" you'll get espresso. Cappuccino is served to locals before noon and tourists any time of day.

(To an Italian, cappuccino is a breakfast drink and a travesty after anything with tomatoes.) Italians like it only warm. To get it hot, request "*Molto caldo*" (very hot) or "*Più caldo, per favore*" (hotter, please; pron. pew KAHL-doh, pehr fah-VOH-ray).

Experiment with a few of the options...

- *caffè freddo*: sweet and iced espresso
- *cappuccino freddo*: iced cappuccino
- *caffè hag*: espresso decaf (decaf is easily available for any coffee drink)
- *macchiato*: with only a little milk
- *caffè latte*: coffee with lots of hot milk, no foam
- *caffè Americano*: espresso diluted with water
- *caffè corretto*: espresso with a shot of liqueur

Beer: Beer on tap is "*alla spina*." Get it *piccola* (33 cl), *media* (50 cl), or *grande* (a liter).

Wine: To order a glass (*bicchiere*; pron. bee-kee-AY-ree) of red (*rosso*) or white (*bianco*) wine say, "*Un bicchiere di vino rosso/bianco.*" *Corposo* means full-bodied. House wine often comes in a quarter-liter carafe (*un quarto*). Trendy wines with small production (such as Brunello di Montalcino) are good but overpriced. There are better values on wines with greater production and less demand (such as Frescobaldi Montisodi).

Prices: You'll notice a two-tiered price system. Drinking a cup of coffee while standing at the bar is cheaper than drinking it at a table. If you're on a budget, don't sit without first checking out the financial consequences.

If the bar isn't busy, you'll often just order and pay when you leave. Otherwise: 1) decide what you want; 2) find out the price by checking the price list on the wall, the prices posted near the food, or by asking the barman; 3) pay the cashier; and 4) give the receipt to the barman (whose clean fingers handle no dirty euros) and tell him what you want.

Picnics

In Italy, picnicking saves lots of euros and is a great way to sample local specialties. In the process of assembling your meal, you get to deal with the Italians in the market scene. On days you choose to picnic, gather supplies early. You'll probably visit several small stores or market stalls to put together a complete meal, and many close around noon. While it's fun to visit the small specialty shops, a local *alimentari* is your one-stop corner grocery store (most will slice and stuff your sandwich for you if you buy the ingredients there). A *supermercato* gives you more efficiency with less color for less cost.

Juice-lovers can get a liter of O.J. for the price of a Coke or coffee. Look for "100% *succo*" (juice) on the label. Hang onto the half-liter mineral-water bottles (sold everywhere for about €0.50).

Buy juice in cheap liter boxes, drink some and store the extra in your water bottle. (I drink tap water—*acqua del rubinetto*.)

Picnics can be an adventure in high cuisine. Be daring. Try the fresh mozzarella, *presto* pesto, shriveled olives, and any UFOs the locals are excited about. Shopkeepers are happy to sell small quantities of produce. But in a busy market, a merchant may not want to weigh and sell small, three-carrot-type quantities. In this case, estimate generously what you think it should cost, and hold out euros in one hand and the produce in the other. Wear a smile that says, "If you take the money, I'll go." He'll grab the money. A typical picnic for two might be fresh rolls, 100 grams of cheese, 100 grams of meat (100 grams = about a quarter pound, called *un etto* in Italy), two tomatoes, three carrots, two apples, yogurt, and a liter box of juice. Total cost—about $10.

Culture Shock—Accepting Italy as a Package Deal

We travel all the way to Italy to enjoy differences—to become temporary locals. You'll experience frustrations. Certain truths that we find "God-given" or "self-evident," like cold beer, ice in drinks, bottomless cups of coffee, hot showers, body odor smelling bad, and bigger being better, are suddenly not so true. One of the benefits of travel is the eye-opening realization that there are logical, civil, and even better alternatives. A willingness to go local ensures that you'll enjoy a full dose of Italian hospitality.

If there is a negative aspect to the image Italians have of Americans, it is that we are big, loud, aggressive, impolite, rich, and a bit naive. While Italians look bemusedly at some of our Yankee excesses—and worriedly at others—they nearly always afford us individual travelers all the warmth we deserve.

Send Me a Postcard, Drop Me a Line

If you enjoy a successful trip with the help of this book and would like to share your discoveries, please fill out and send the survey at the end of this book to me at Europe Through the Back Door, Box 2009, Edmonds, WA 98020. I personally read and value all feedback. Thanks in advance—it helps a lot.

For our latest travel information on Italy, tap into our Web site at www.ricksteves.com. To check on any updates for this book, visit www.ricksteves.com/update. My e-mail address is rick@ricksteves.com. Anyone is welcome to a free issue of our *Back Door* quarterly newsletter.

Judging from all the positive feedback and happy postcards I receive from travelers who have used this book, it's safe to assume you'll enjoy a great, affordable vacation—with the finesse of an independent, experienced traveler. Thanks, and *buon viaggio!*

BACK DOOR TRAVEL PHILOSOPHY
As Taught in *Rick Steves' Europe Through the Back Door*

Travel is intensified living—maximum thrills per minute and one of the last great sources of legal adventure. Travel is freedom. It's recess, and we need it.

Experiencing the real Europe requires catching it by surprise, going casual... "Through the Back Door."

Affording travel is a matter of priorities. (Make do with the old car.) You can travel—simply, safely, and comfortably—anywhere in Europe for $80 a day plus transportation costs. In many ways, spending more money only builds a thicker wall between you and what you came to see. Europe is a cultural carnival, and, time after time, you'll find that its best acts are free and the best seats are the cheap ones.

A tight budget forces you to travel close to the ground, meeting and communicating with the people, not relying on service with a purchased smile. Never sacrifice sleep, nutrition, safety, or cleanliness in the name of budget. Simply enjoy the local-style alternatives to expensive hotels and restaurants.

Extroverts have more fun. If your trip is low on magic moments, kick yourself and make things happen. If you don't enjoy a place, maybe you don't know enough about it. Seek the truth. Recognize tourist traps. Give a culture the benefit of your open mind. See things as different but not better or worse. Any culture has much to share.

Of course, travel, like the world, is a series of hills and valleys. Be fanatically positive and militantly optimistic. If something's not to your liking, change your liking. Travel is addictive. It can make you a happier American as well as a citizen of the world. Our Earth is home to six billion equally important people. It's humbling to travel and find that people don't envy Americans. They like us, but, with all due respect, they wouldn't trade passports.

Globe-trotting destroys ethnocentricity. It helps you understand and appreciate different cultures. Travel changes people. It broadens perspectives and teaches new ways to measure quality of life. Many travelers toss aside their hometown blinders. Their prized souvenirs are the strands of different cultures they decide to knit into their own character. The world is a cultural yarn shop. And Back Door Travelers are weaving the ultimate tapestry. Come on, join in!

ITALY

- 192,000 square kilometers, or 120,000 square miles (a little larger than Arizona)
- 60 million people (300 people per square kilometer, or 500 people per square mile)
- 1,200 kilometers (800 miles) long, 160 kilometers (100 miles) wide

Bella Italia! It has Europe's richest, craziest culture. If you take it on its own terms, Italy is a cultural keelhauling that actually feels good.

Some people, often with considerable effort, manage to hate it. Italy bubbles with emotion, corruption, stray hairs, inflation, traffic jams, body odor, strikes, rallies, holidays, crowded squalor, and irate ranters shaking their fists at each other one minute and walking arm in arm the next. Have a talk with yourself before you cross the border. Promise yourself to relax and soak in it; it's a glorious mud puddle.

There are two Italys: The north is industrial, aggressive, and "time is money" in its outlook. The south is crowded, poor, relaxed, farm-oriented, and traditional. Families here are very strong and usually live in the same house for many generations. Loyalties are to the family, city, region, soccer team, and country—in that order.

Economically, Italy has had its problems, but somehow things have always worked out. Today, Italy is the Western world's seventh largest industrial power. Its people earn more per capita than the British. Italy is the world's leading wine producer. It is sixth in cheese and wool output. Tourism is big business. Cronyism, which complicates my work, is an integral part of the economy.

Italy, home of the Vatican, is Catholic, but the dominant religion is life—motor scooters, soccer, fashion, girl-watching, boy-watching, good coffee, good wine, and *la dolce far niente* ("the sweetness of doing nothing"). The Italian character shows itself on the streets in the skilled maniac drivers and the classy dressers who star in the ritual evening stroll, or *passeggiata*.

The language is fun. Be melodramatic and talk with your hands. Hear the melody; get into the flow. Italians are outgoing. They want to communicate, and they try harder than any other Europeans. Play with them.

Italy, a land of extremes, is also the most thief-ridden country you'll visit. Tourists suffer virtually no violent crime—but plenty of petty purse-snatchings, pickpocketings, and shortchangings. Wear your money belt! The scruffy-looking women and children loitering around the major museums aren't there for the art.

Take advantage of the cheap, colorful, and dry-but-informative city guidebooks sold on the streets. Use the information telephones you'll find in most historic buildings. Just set the dial on English, pop in your coins, and listen. The narration is often accompanied by a brief slide show.

Some important Italian churches require modest dress: No shorts or bare shoulders on men, women, and sometimes even children. With a little imagination (except at the ultrastrict Vatican's St. Peter's), those caught by surprise can improvise something— a jacket for your knees and maps for your shoulders. I wear a super-lightweight pair of long pants for my hot and muggy big-city Italian sightseeing.

While no longer a cheap country, Italy is still a hit with shoppers. Glassware (Venice), gold, silver, leather, prints (Florence), and high fashion (Rome and Milan) are good souvenirs, but do some price research at home so you'll recognize the good values.

La dolce far niente is a big part of Italy. Zero in on the fine points. Don't dwell on the problems. Accept Italy as Italy. Savor your cappuccino, dangle your feet over a canal (if it smells, breathe through your mouth), and imagine what it was like centuries ago. Ramble through the rabble and rubble of Rome and mentally resurrect those ancient stones. Look into the famous sculpted eyes of Michelangelo's *David* and understand Renaissance man's assertion of himself. Sit silently on a hilltop rooftop. Get chummy with the winds of the past. Write a poem over a glass of local wine in a sun-splashed, wave-dashed Riviera village. If you fall off your moral horse, call it a cultural experience. Italy is for romantics.

ROME
(ROMA)

Rome is magnificent and brutal at the same time. Your ears will ring, if you're careless you'll be run down or pickpocketed, you'll be frustrated by the kind of chaos that only an Italian can understand. You may even come to believe Mussolini was a necessary evil. But Rome is required, and still aglow after the improvements made for Jubilee 2000, it's more exciting and easier than ever.

If your hotel provides a comfortable refuge, if you pace yourself and accept and even partake in the siesta plan, if you're well-organized for sightseeing, and if you protect yourself and your valuables with extra caution and discretion, you'll do fine. You'll see the sights and leave satisfied.

Rome at its peak meant civilization itself. Everything was either civilized (part of the Roman Empire, Latin- or Greek-speaking) or barbarian. Today Rome is Italy's political capital, the capital of Catholicism, and a splendid... "junk pile" is not quite the right term... of Western civilization. As you peel through its fascinating and jumbled layers, you'll find its buildings, cats, laundry, traffic, and 2.6 million people endlessly entertaining. And then, of course, there are its magnificent sights.

Tour St. Peter's, the greatest church on earth, and scale Michelangelo's 100-meter-tall dome, the world's largest. Learn something about eternity by touring the huge Vatican Museum. You'll find the story of creation—bright as the day it was painted—in the newly restored Sistine Chapel. Do the "Caesar Shuffle" through ancient Rome's Forum and Colosseum. Savor Europe's most sumptuous building—the Borghese Gallery—and take an early evening "Dolce Vita Stroll" down the Via del Corso with Rome's beautiful people. Enjoy an after-dark walk from Trastevere to the Spanish Steps, lacing together Rome's Baroque and bubbly night spots.

Rome Area

Planning Your Time

For most travelers, Rome is best done quickly. It's a great city, but it's exhausting. Time is normally short, and Italy is more charming elsewhere. To "do" Rome in a day, consider it as a side trip from Orvieto or Florence and maybe before the night train to Venice. Crazy as that sounds, if all you have is a day, it's a great one.

Rome in a day: Vatican (2 hours in the museum and Sistine Chapel and 1 hour in St. Peter's), taxi over the river to the Pantheon (picnic on its steps), then hike over Capitol Hill, through the Forum, and to the Colosseum. Have dinner on Campo de' Fiori and dessert on Piazza Navona.

Rome in two days: Do the "Caesar Shuffle" from the Colosseum and Forum over Capitol Hill to the Pantheon. After a siesta, join the locals strolling from Piazza del Popolo to the Spanish Steps (see my recommended "Dolce Vita Stroll," below). Have dinner near your hotel.

On the second day, see the Vatican City (St. Peter's, climb the dome, tour the Vatican Museum). Spend the evening walking from Trastevere to Campo de' Fiori—an atmospheric place for dinner—to the Trevi Fountain (see "Night Walk Across Rome," below). With a third day, add the Borghese Gallery (reservations required) and the National Museum of Rome.

Orientation

Sprawling Rome actually feels manageable once you get to know it. It's the old core—within the triangle formed by the train station, Colosseum, and Vatican. Get a handle on Rome by considering it in these layers:

The ancient city had a million people. Tear it down to size by walking through just the core. The best of the classical sights stand in a line from the Colosseum to the Pantheon.

Medieval Rome was little more than a hobo camp of 50,000—thieves, mean dogs, and the pope, whose legitimacy required a Roman address. The medieval city, a colorful tangle of lanes, lies between the Pantheon and the river.

Window-shoppers' Rome twinkles with nightlife and ritzy shopping near Rome's main drag—Via del Corso—in the triangle formed by Piazza del Popolo, Piazza Venezia, and the Spanish Steps.

Vatican City is a compact world of its own with two great, huge sights: St. Peter's Basilica and the Vatican Museum.

Trastevere, the seedy, colorful, wrong-side-of-the-river neighborhood/village, is Rome at its crustiest—and perhaps most "Roman."

Baroque Rome is an overleaf that embellishes great squares throughout the town with fountains and church facades.

Since no one is allowed to build taller than St. Peter's dome, the city has no modern skyline. And the Tiber River is ignored. It's not navigable, and after the last floods (1870) the banks were built up very high and Rome turned its back on its naughty, impassable river.

Tourist Information

While Rome has three main tourist information offices, the dozen or so TI kiosks scattered around the town at major tourist centers are handy and just as helpful. If all you need is a map, forget the TI and pick up one at your hotel.

You'll find TIs at the airport (daily 08:15–19:00, tel. 06-6595-6074) and the train station (daily 08:00–21:00, off-season 09:00–20:00, near track 3, accessible from platforms or lobby, marked "Informazioni Turistiche/Tourist Info," crowded, combined with travel agency, tel. 06-4890-6300).

The central TI office, near Piazza della Repubblica's huge fountain, covers the city and the region. It's a five-minute walk out the front of the train station (Mon–Sat 08:15–19:00, air-con, next to car dealership, Via Parigi 5, seats, table, free Internet access for tourist info: www.romaturismo.com, tel. 06-488-991). It's less crowded, and more helpful than the station TI.

At any TI, ask for a city map, a listing of sights and hours (in the free *Tesori di Roma* booklet), and *L'Evento*, the free bimonthly periodical entertainment guide for evening events and fun.

Rome

All hotels list an inflated rate to cover the hefty commission any TI room-finding service charges. Save money by booking direct.

Smaller TIs (daily 09:00–18:00) include kiosks near the Forum (on Piazza del Tempio della Pace), at Via del Corso (on Largo Goldoni), in Trastevere (on Via Sonnino), on Via Nazionale (at Palazzo delle Esposizioni), at Castel Sant' Angelo, Santa Maria Maggiore, and at San Giovanni in Laterano. For more information, call 06-3600-4399 (daily 09:00–19:00, www.comune.roma.it).

Roma c'è is a cheap little weekly entertainment guide with a helpful English section (at the back) on musical events and the pope's schedule for the week (new edition every Thu, sold at news-stands for €1, www.romace.it, Web site in Italian). Fancy hotels carry a free English monthly, *Un Ospite a Roma* (A Guest in Rome).

Arrival in Rome

By Train: Rome's main train station, Termini, is a minefield of tourist services: a TI (daily 08:00–21:00, off-season 09:00–20:00, near track 3), train info office (daily 07:00–21:45), ATMs, late-hours banks, public showers (downstairs), luggage lockers (near track 24), 24-hour thievery, a pharmacy (daily 07:30–22:00, in the modern mall downstairs), the main city-bus hub (in front of train station), a subway stop, a grocery (oddly named "Drug Store," daily 07:00–24:00, downstairs), and the handy, cheery Chef Express Self-Service Ristorante (daily 11:00–22:30, easy WC at entrance, near east end of station; although there are several Chef Express bars scattered throughout station, the most comfortable is this sit-down Ristorante). The closest Internet point is downstairs near Dunkin Donuts (Thenetgate, daily 06:00–23:30, cheapest to buy a €5.50 60-minute card, can return or use at branches at Trevi Fountain or Vatican). The station has some sleazy sharks with official-looking cards. In general, avoid anybody selling anything at the station if you can.

Most of my hotel listings are easily accessible by foot (those near the train station) or by Metro (those in the Colosseum and Vatican neighborhoods). The train station has its own Metro stop (Termini).

By Bus: Long-distance buses (e.g., from Siena and Assisi) arrive at Rome's small **Tiburtina** station, which is on Metro line B, with easy connections to the main train station (a straight shot 4 stops away) and the entire Metro system.

By Plane: If you arrive at the airport, catch a train (hrly, 30 min, €9) to Rome's train station or take (or share) a taxi to your hotel. For details, see "Transportation Connections," below.

Dealing with (and Avoiding) Problems

Theft Alert: With sweet-talking con artists meeting you at the station, well-dressed pickpockets on buses, and thieving gangs of children at the ancient sites, Rome is a gauntlet of rip-offs. There's no great physical risk, but green tourists will be exploited. Thieves strike when you're distracted. Don't trust kind strangers. Keep nothing important in your pockets. Assume you're being stalked. (Then relax and have fun.) Be most on guard while boarding and leaving buses and subways. Thieves crowd the door, then stop and turn while others crowd and push from behind. The sneakiest thieves are well-dressed businessmen (generally with something in their hands); lately, many are posing as tourists with Tevas, fanny packs, and cameras. Scams abound: Don't give your wallet to self-proclaimed "police" who stop you on the street, warn you about counterfeit (or drug) money, and ask to see your wallet.

If you know what to look out for, the gangs of children picking the pockets and handbags of naive tourists are no threat but an interesting, albeit sad, spectacle. Gangs of city-stained children (sometimes as young as 8–10 years old), too young to be prosecuted but old enough to rip you off, troll through the tourist crowds around the Colosseum, Forum, Piazza Repubblica, and train and Metro stations. Watch them target tourists who are overloaded with bags or distracted with a video camera. The kids look like beggars and hold up newspapers or cardboard signs to confuse their victims. They scram like stray cats if you're onto them. A fast-fingered mother with a baby is often nearby. The terrace above the bus stop near the Colosseum Metro stop is a fine place to watch the action and maybe even pick up a few moves of your own.

Reporting Losses: To report lost or stolen passports and documents or to file an insurance claim, you must file a police report (with Polizia at track 1 or with Carabinieri at track 20, also at Piazza Venezia). To replace a passport, file the police report, then go to your embassy (see below). To report lost traveler's checks, call your bank (Visa tel. 800-874-155, Thomas Cook/MasterCard tel. 800-872-050, American Express tel. 800-872-000; these toll-free 800 numbers are Italian, not American), then file a police report. To report stolen or lost credit cards, call the company (Visa tel. 800-877-232, MasterCard tel. 800-870-866, American Express tel. 800-874-333), then file a police report.

Embassies: United States (Mon–Fri 08:30–13:00, 14:00–17:30, Via Veneto 119, tel. 06-46741) and Canada (Via Zara 30, tel. 06-445-981).

Emergency Numbers: Police tel. 113. Ambulance tel. 118.

Hit and Run: Walk with extreme caution. Scooters don't need to stop at red lights, and even cars exercise what drivers call the "logical option" of not stopping if they see no oncoming traffic. As Vespa scooters become electric, they'll get quieter (hooray) but more dangerous for pedestrians. Follow locals like a shadow when you cross a street (or spend a good part of your visit stranded on curbs).

Staying/Getting Healthy: The siesta is a key to survival in summertime Rome. Lie down and contemplate the extraordinary power of gravity in the eternal city. I drink lots of cold, refreshing water from Rome's many drinking fountains (the Forum has three). There's a pharmacy (marked with a green cross) in every neighborhood, including a handy one in the train station (daily 07:30–22:00, located downstairs, at west end) and a 24-hour pharmacy on Piazza dei Cinquecento 51 (next to train station on Via Cavour, tel. 06-488-0019). Embassies can recommend English-speaking doctors. Consider MEDline, a 24-hour home medical service (tel. 06-808-0995, doctors speak English). Anyone is entitled to free emergency treatment at public hospitals. The hospital closest to the train station is Policlinico Umberto 1 (entrance for emergency treatment on Via Lancisi, translators available, Metro: Policlinico). The American Hospital is a private hospital on the edge of town accustomed to helping Yankees (tel. 06-225-571).

Helpful Hints

Web Sites on Rome: www.romaturismo.com (music, exhibitions, events, kid stuff, in English), www.wantedinrome.com (job openings and real estate, but also festivals and exhibitions, in English), and www.vatican.va (the pope's Web site, in English).

Bookstore: The American Bookstore sells fiction and all the major guidebooks (Via Torino 136, Metro: Repubblica, tel. 06-474-6877).

Train Tickets and Reservations: Get train tickets and rail-pass-related reservations and supplements at travel agencies rather than dealing with the congested train station. Either cost is the same or there's a minimal charge. Your hotel can direct you to the nearest travel agency. Quo Vadis, near the Pantheon, is handy (Via dei Cestari 21, tel. 06-413-1831).

Getting around Rome

Sightsee on foot, by city bus, or by taxi. I've grouped your sight-seeing into walkable neighborhoods.

Public transportation is efficient, cheap, and part of your Roman experience. It starts running around 05:30 and stops around 23:30, sometimes earlier. After midnight, there are a few very crowded night buses, and taxis become more expensive and hard to get. Don't try to hail one—go to a taxi stand.

Buses and subways use the same ticket. You can buy tickets at newsstands, tobacco shops, or at major Metro stations or bus stops, but not on board (€0.80, good for 75 minutes—one Metro ride and unlimited buses); all-day bus/Metro passes cost €3.25 (for more info, visit www.atac.roma.it).

Buses (especially the touristic #64) and the subway are havens for thieves and pickpockets. Assume any commotion is a thief-created distraction.

Metropolitana: Rome's Subway

By Metro: The Roman subway system (Metropolitana) is simple, with two clean, cheap, fast lines. While much of Rome is not served by its skimpy subway, these stops are helpful: Termini (train station, National Museum of Rome at Palazzo Massimo, recommended hotels), Repubblica (Baths of Diocletian/Octagonal Hall, main TI, recommended hotels), Barberini (Cappuccin Crypt, Trevi Fountain), Spagna (Spanish Steps, Villa Borghese, classy shopping area), Flaminio (Piazza del Popolo, start of recommended Dolce Vita Stroll down Via del Corso), Ottaviano (St. Peter's and Vatican City), Cipro-Musei Vaticani (Vatican Museum, recommended hotels), Colosseo (Colosseum, Roman Forum, recommended hotels), and E.U.R. (Mussolini's futuristic suburb).

By Bus: Bus routes are clearly listed at the stops. Punch your ticket in the orange stamping machine as you board (even if you've already stamped it for the Metro)—or you are cheating. Riding without a stamped ticket on the bus, while relatively safe, is stressful. Inspectors fine even innocent-looking tourists €52. If you hop a bus without a ticket, locals who use tickets rather than a monthly pass can sell you a ticket from their wallet bundle. Ideally, buy a bunch of tickets from a tobacco shop so you can hop a bus without first having to search for a tobacco shop that's open. Here are a few buses worth knowing about:

#64: Termini (train station), Piazza della Repubblica (sights), Via Nazionale (recommended hotels), Piazza Venezia (near Forum), Largo Argentina (near Pantheon), St. Peter's Basilica.

Ride it for a city overview and to watch pickpockets in action (can get horribly crowded).

#8: This tram connects Largo Argentina with Trastevere (get off at Piazza Mastai).

Electrico #116: Through the medieval core of Rome from Campo de' Fiori to Piazza Barberini via the Pantheon.

Electrico #117: San Giovanni in Laterano, Colosseo, Via dei Serpenti, Trevi Fountain, Piazza di Spagna, Piazza del Popolo.

"J" buses are bigger, come with a hostess, and provide more convenient access to some places farther out, such as St. Peter's (Cavalleggeri stop) and the catacombs. Purchase tickets (€1) on the bus (info: tel. 800-076-287).

By Taxi: Taxis start at about €2.75 (surcharges of €1 on Sun, €2.75 for night hours of 22:00–07:00, €1 surcharge for luggage, €7.25 extra for airport, tip about 10 percent by rounding up to the nearest euro). Sample fares: Train station to Vatican-€9; train station to Colosseum-€6; Colosseum to Trastevere-€7. Three or four companions with more money than time should taxi almost everywhere. It's tough to wave down a taxi in Rome. Find the nearest taxi stand. (Ask a local or in a shop *"Dov'è* [DOH-vay] *una fermata dei tassi?"* Some are listed on my maps.) Unmarked, unmetered taxis at train stations and the airport are usually a rip-off. Taxis listing their telephone number on the door have fair meters— use them. To save time and energy, have your hotel call a taxi; the meter starts when the call is received. (To call a cab on your own, dial 06-3570, 06-4994, or 06-88177.)

Tours of Rome

Scala Reale—Tom Rankin (an American architect in love with Rome and his Roman wife) runs Scala Reale, a company committed to sorting out the rich layers of Rome for small groups with a longer-than-average attention span. Their excellent walking tours vary in length from two to four hours and start at €16 per person. Try to book in advance, since their groups are limited to six and fill up fast. Their fascinating "Rome Orientation" walks lace together lesser-known sights from antiquity to the present, and give you a sense of how Rome works (tel. 06-474-5673, U.S. tel. 888/467-1986, www.scalareale.org, e-mail: info@scalereale.org).

Through Eternity—This company offers four walking tours, all led by native English speakers with relevant university degrees and an emphasis on storytelling: St. Peter's and Vatican Museum (€31, museum entry not included, 5.5 hrs, daily except Sun); Colosseum and Roman Forum (€18, 2.5 hrs, daily); Rome at Twilight (€18, nightly); and a Wine Sampling Tour (€26, nightly, includes a glass at 4 or 5 wine bars). Call to get the schedule and to book in advance (max of 25 people, tel. 06-700-9336, cellular 347-336-5298, private tours possible, www.througheternity.com).

Walks of Rome—Students working for "Walks of Rome" give tours in fluent American or British English. They offer group tours (that individuals can join) and private tours (at a higher cost). Sample group tours include: Rome Through the Centuries (€34, 3 hrs, Mon, Wed, Fri at 10:00), Vatican City Walk (€52, includes admission to Vatican Museum, 4.5 hrs, Tue, Thu, Sat at 10:00), and the Colosseum (€19, includes admission, 1.5 hrs, offered daily). See their Web site for the latest (www.walksofeurope.com) and book in advance by e-mail (info@walksofeurope.com) or phone (tel. 06-484-853, cellular 347-795-5175). You'll need to give your hotel name and phone number. Your guide will call to let you know the meeting place. Their pub crawl tours meet at 20:00 at the Colosseum Metro stop (year-round) and finish at a disco six pubs later around midnight (€16, no need to reserve). I've never seen 50 young, drunk people having so much fun.

Hop-on Hop-off Bus Tour—The ATAC city bus tour offers your best budget orientation tour of Rome. In 1.75 hours , you'll have 80 sights pointed out to you (by a live guide in English and maybe one other language) and have a chance to get out at nine different stops and catch a later bus. While the guide's spiel is limited to simple identification of the sights, this tour provides an efficient and economical orientation to Rome. The stops are: Piazza Barberini, Via Veneto, Villa Borghese, Piazza Cavour, St. Peter's Square, Corso Vittorio Emanuele (for Piazza Navona), Piazza Venezia, Colosseum, and Via Nazionale (€7.75, bus #110 departs every 30 minutes— at top and bottom of hour—from front of train station, near platform C, buy tickets at info kiosk there—marked "i bus," runs March–Sept 09:00–20:00, Oct–Feb 10:00–18:00, tel. 06-4695-2252).

Archeobus—This handy new hop-on-and-hop-off bus runs hourly from Piazza Venezia way out the Appian Way (buy €7.75 ticket on the bus, good from 09:00–17:00, 16-seat bus with hostess, pick up the guided tour flier in English, tel. 06-4695-4695). They have cheap bike rental at the appropriate Appian Way stop as well.

Sights—From the Colosseum Area to Capitol Hill

Beware of gangs of young thieves, particularly between the Colosseum and the Forum; they're harmless if you know their tricks (see Theft Alert in "Helpful Hints," above).

▲**St. Peter-in-Chains Church (San Pietro in Vincoli)**—Built in the fifth century to house the chains that held St. Peter, this church is most famous for its Michelangelo statue. Check out the much-venerated chains under the high altar, then focus on Moses (free, but pop in a coin to light the statue, Mon–Sat 07:00–12:30, 15:30–19:00, Sun 07:30–12:30, a short walk uphill from the Colosseum, modest dress required).

Museum Tips for Rome

Plan ahead. The marvelous Borghese Gallery and Nero's Golden House both require reservations. For the Borghese Gallery, it's safest to make reservations well in advance of your trip (for specifics, see page 56). You can wait until you're in Rome to reserve a time at Nero's Golden House, though it's easy to book farther ahead (see listing on this page).

Some museums may stay open later in summer (usually on Sat). Get a current listing of museum hours from one of Rome's TIs: ask for the booklet *Tesori di Roma* (Treasures of Rome).

A **special combo ticket**—covering the National Museum of Rome, Colosseum, Palatine Hill, Baths of Caracalla, and a couple of other museums—costs €16 (allows you to see 7 sights for price of 3, purchase at participating sites, valid for 5 days). When you buy this, you can upgrade to a "Coupon Servizi" pass for an extra €5, giving you tours or audioguides at each site (they usually cost €3.60 each). The big plus of this ticket is that you avoid the long lines at the Colosseum (if you purchase it at a participating site other than the Colosseum).

Pope Julius II commissioned Michelangelo to build a massive tomb, with 48 huge statues, crowned by a grand statue of this egomaniacal pope. The pope had planned to have his tomb placed in the center of St. Peter's Basilica. When Julius died, the work had barely been started, and no one had the money or necessary commitment to Julius to finish the project. Michelangelo finished one statue—Moses—and left a few unfinished statues: Leah and Rachel flanking Moses in this church, the "prisoners" now in Florence's Accademia, and the "slaves" now in Paris' Louvre.

This powerful statue of Moses—mature Michelangelo—is worth studying. He worked on it in fits and starts for 30 years. Moses has received the Ten Commandments. As he holds the stone tablets, his eyes show a man determined to stop his tribe from worshiping the golden calf and idols...a man determined to win salvation for the people of Israel. Why the horns? Centuries ago, the Hebrew word for "rays" was mistranslated as "horns."

▲**Nero's Golden House (Domus Aurea)**—The barren remains of Emperor Nero's "Golden House" were reopened to the public in 1999. The original entrance to the house was all the way over at the Arch of Titus in the Forum. This massive house once sprawled across the valley (where the Colosseum now stands)

The Forum Area

1. ARCH OF TITUS
2. BASILICA CONSTANTINE
3. VESTAL VIRGINS HOUSE
4. BASILICA JULIA
5. ARCH OF SEPTIMIUS SEVERUS
6. CURIA
7. BASILICA AEMELIA
8. DRINKING FOUNTAINS (ACQUA!)

and up the hill—the part you tour today. Larger even than Bill Gates' place, it was a pain to vacuum. A colossal, 33-meter-tall bronze statue of Nero towered over everything. The house incorporated an artificial lake (where the Colosseum was later built) and a forest stocked with game. It was decorated with the best multicolored marble and the finest frescoes. No expense was too great for Nero—his mistress soaked daily in the milk of 500 wild asses kept for her bathing pleasure.

Nero (ruled A.D. 54–68) was Rome's most notorious emperor. He killed his own mother, kicked his pregnant wife to death, crucified St. Peter, and—most galling to his subjects—was a bad actor. When Rome burned in A.D. 64, Nero was accused of torching it to clear land for an even bigger house. The Romans rebelled and Nero stabbed himself in the neck, crying, "What an artist dies in me!"

While only hints of the splendid, colorful frescoes survive, the towering vaults and the basic immensity of the place are impressive. As you wander through rooms that are now underground, look up at the holes in the ceiling. Imagine how much of old Rome still hides underground...and why the subway is limited to two lines.

Visits are allowed only with an escort (30 people every 15 minutes) and a reservation (€6.20, Wed–Mon 09:00–19:45, last entry at 18:45, closed Tue, tour lasts 45 min, escort speaks Italian only, audioguides-€1.60 but listen to the intro before entering or you'll be forever behind, 200 meters northeast of Colosseum, through a park gate, up a hill and on the left). To reserve a place, call 06-3996-7700. If you just show up (particularly on a late afternoon on a weekday), you could luck out and get on a tour; if tours aren't booked up, the remaining seats are sold to drop-ins.

▲▲▲**Colosseum**—This 2,000-year-old building is *the* great example of Roman engineering. Using concrete, brick, and their trademark round arches, Romans constructed much larger buildings than the Greeks. But in deference to the higher Greek culture, they finished their no-nonsense megastructure by pasting all three orders of Greek columns (Doric, Ionic, and Corinthian) as exterior decorations. The Flavian Amphitheater's popular name, "Colosseum," comes from the colossal statue of Nero that once stood in front of it.

Romans were into "big." By putting two theaters together, they created a circular amphitheater. They could fill and empty its 50,000 numbered seats as quickly and efficiently as we do our superstadiums. Teams of sailors hoisted canvas awnings over the stadium to give fans shade. This was where ancient Romans, whose taste for violence was the equal of modern America's, enjoyed their Dirty Harry and *Terminator*. Gladiators, criminals, and wild animals fought to the death in every conceivable scenario. The floor of the Colosseum is missing, exposing underground passages. Animals in cages were kept here and then lifted up in elevators; they'd pop out from behind blinds into the arena. The gladiator didn't know where, when, or by what he'd be attacked.

Cost, Hours, Tours: €7, covered by €16 combo-ticket, daily 09:00–19:00, off-season 09:00–15:00 (Metro: Colosseo, tel. 06-3974-9907). To avoid the long lines here, buy your ticket elsewhere. Individual tickets for the Colosseum are sold on Via di San Gregorio (to reach booth, face Forum entrance, with your back to the Colosseum, and go left on street) and at the Palatine Hill booth just inside the Forum. If you buy a €16 combo-ticket (sold at Via di San Gregorio, Palatine Hill, National Museum of Rome, Baths of Caracalla, and more), you can bypass the long line and walk right into the Colosseum. For details, see "Museum Tips for Rome," page 45. Public WCs are behind the Colosseum (face ticket entrance and go right—WC under stairway). The modern-day gladiators outside the Colosseum expect payment if you snap a photo of them; my advice is to negotiate—they have swords.

▲**Arch of Constantine**—The well-preserved arch, which stands between the Colosseum and the Forum, commemorates a military coup and, more importantly, the acceptance of Christianity in the Roman Empire. In A.D. 312, the ambitious Emperor Constantine (who had a vision he could win under the sign of the cross) defeated his rival Maxentius. Constantine became sole emperor and promptly legalized Christianity.

▲▲▲**Roman Forum (Foro Romano)**—This is ancient Rome's birthplace and civic center, and the common ground between Rome's famous seven hills (free admission to Forum, €6.20 for Palatine Hill, both keep the same hours: daily 09:00–19:15 or an hour before dark, off-season 09:00–15:00, Metro: Colosseo, tel. 06-3974-9907).

To help resurrect this confusing pile of rubble, study the before-and-after pictures in the cheap city guidebooks sold on the streets. (Check out the small red *Rome, Past and Present* books with plastic overlays to un-ruin the ruins; they're priced at €11—pay no more than €8.) With the help of the map in this section, follow this basic walk. Enter the Forum near the Arch of Constantine:

1. Start by the small **Arch of Titus** (drinking fountain opposite) overlooking the remains of what was the political, social, and commercial center of the Roman Empire. The Via Sacra—the main street of ancient Rome—cuts through the Forum from here to Capitol Hill and the Arch of Septimius Severus on the opposite side. On the left, a ticket booth welcomes you to the Palatine Hill (described below)—once filled with the palaces of Roman emperors. Study the Arch of Titus—carved with propaganda celebrating the A.D. 70 defeat of the Jews, which began the Diaspora that ended with the creation of Israel in 1947. Notice the gaggle of soldiers carrying the menorah.

2. Ahead of you on the right are the massive ruins of the **Basilica of Constantine.** Follow the path leading there from the Via Sacra. Only the giant barrel vaults remain, looming crumbly and weed-eaten. As you stand in the shadow of the Basilica of Constantine, reconstruct it in your mind. The huge barrel vaults were just side niches. Extend the broken nub of an arch out over the vacant lot and finish your imaginary Roman basilica with rich marble and fountains. People it with plenty of toga-clad Romans. Yeow.

3. Next, hike past the semicircular Temple of Vesta to the **House of the Vestal Virgins.** Here, the VVs kept the eternal flame lit. A set of ponds and a marble chorus line of Vestal Virgins mark the courtyard of the house.

4. The grand **Basilica Julia,** a first-century law court, fills the corner opposite the Curia. Notice how the Romans passed their time; ancient backgammon-type game boards are cut into the pavement.

5. The **Arch of Septimius Severus,** from about A.D. 200, celebrates that emperor's military victories. In front of it, a stone called Lapis Niger covers the legendary tomb of Romulus. To the left of the arch, the stone bulkhead is the Rostra, or speaker's platform. It's named for the ship's prows that used to decorate it as big shots hollered, "Friends, Romans, countrymen...."

6. The plain, intact brick building near the Arch of Septimius Severus was the **Curia,** where the Roman senate sat. (Peek inside.) Roman buildings were basically brick and concrete, usually with a marble veneer, which in this case is long lost.

7. The **Basilica Aemilia** (2nd century B.C.) shows the floor plan of an ancient palace. This pre-Christian "basilica" design was later adopted by medieval churches. From here, a ramp leads up and out (past a WC and a fun headless statue to pose with).

▲**Palatine Hill**—The hill above the Forum contains scanty remains of the Imperial palaces and the Roman Quadrata (Iron Age huts and the legendary house of Romulus—under corrugated tin roof in far corner). We get our word *palace* from this hill, where the emperors chose to live. The Palatine was once so filled with palaces that later emperors had to build out. (Looking up at it from the Forum, you see the substructure that supported these long-gone palaces.) The Palatine museum has sculptures and fresco fragments but is nothing special. From the pleasant garden, you'll get an overview of the Forum. On the far side, look down into an emperor's private stadium and then beyond at the dusty Circus Maximus, once a chariot course. Imagine the cheers, jeers, and furious betting. But considering how ruined the ruins are, the heat, the hill to climb, the €6.20 entry fee, and the relative difficulty in understanding what you're looking at, the Palatine Hill is a disappointment (covered by €16 combo-ticket, same hours as Forum, above; the entrance and ticket office—which also sells Colosseum tickets, enabling smart sightseers to avoid that long line—is near the Arch of Titus at the south end of the Forum).

▲**Mammertine Prison**—The 2,500-year-old, cisternlike prison, which once held Saints Peter and Paul, is worth a look (donation requested, daily 09:00–12:30, 14:30–18:30, at the foot of Capitol Hill, near Forum's Arch of Septimius Severus). When you step into the room, you'll hit a modern floor. Ignore that and look up at the hole in the ceiling, from which prisoners were lowered. Then take the stairs down to the level of the actual prison floor. As you descend, you'll walk past a supposedly miraculous image of Peter's face, created when a guard pushed him into the wall. Downstairs you'll see the column to which Peter was chained. It's said that a miraculous fountain sprang up in this room so Peter could baptize other prisoners. The upside-down cross commemorates Peter's upside-down crucifixion.

Imagine humans, amid fat rats and rotting corpses, awaiting slow deaths. On the walls near the entry are lists of notable prisoners (Christian and non-Christian) and the ways they were executed: *strangolati, decapitato, morto di fame* (died of hunger)....

Sights—Capitol Hill Area

There are several ways to get to the top of Capitol Hill. If you're coming from the north (Piazza Venezia), take the grand stairs located to the right of the big, white Victor Emmanuel Monument (described below). Coming from the Forum, take either the steep staircase or the winding road, which converge at a great Forum overlook and a refreshing water fountain. Block the spout with your fingers; water spurts up for drinking. Romans, who call this *il nasone* (the nose), joke that a cheap Roman boy takes his date out for a drink at *il nasone*.

▲▲**Capitol Hill (Campidoglio)**—This hill was the religious and political center of ancient Rome. It's still the home of the city's government. Michelangelo's Renaissance square is bounded by two fine museums and the mayoral palace. Its centerpiece is a copy of the famous equestrian statue of Marcus Aurelius (the original is behind glass in the museum a few steps away).

Michelangelo intended that people approach the square from the grand stairway off Piazza Venezia. From the top of the stairway, you see the new Renaissance face of Rome with its back to the Forum, facing the new city. Notice how Michelangelo gave the buildings the "giant order"—huge pilasters make the existing two-story buildings feel one-storied and more harmonious with the new square. Notice also how the statues atop these buildings welcome you and then draw you in. The terraces just downhill (past either side of the mayor's palace) offer fine views of the Forum.

▲▲**Capitol Hill Museum**—This museum encompasses two buildings (Palazzo dei Conservatori and Palazzo Nuovo), connected by an underground passage that leads to the vacant Tabularium and a panoramic overlook of the Forum (€8, free on last Sun of month, Tue–Fri and Sun 09:00–19:00, Sat 09:30–23:00, closed Mon, last entry 60 min before closing, tel. 06-3996-7800).

For an orientation to the museum's two buildings, face the equestrian statue on Capitol Hill Square (with your back to the grand stairway). The Palazzo Nuovo is on your left and the Palazzo dei Conservatori is on your right (closer to the river). Ahead is the mayor's palace (Palazzo Senatorio); below it and out of sight are the Tabularium and underground passage.

You can buy your ticket at either building (but if you want to rent a €3.75 audioguide, go to Palazzo dei Conservatori).

The **Palazzo dei Conservatori** is one of the world's oldest museums, at 500 years old. Outside the entrance, notice the marriage announcements and, very likely, wedding-party photo ops. Inside the courtyard, have a look at giant chunks of a statue of Emperor Constantine; when intact, this imposing statue held court in the Basilica of Constantine in the Forum. The museum is worthwhile, with lavish rooms and several great statues. Tops is the original (500 B.C.) Etruscan *Capitoline Wolf* (the little statues of Romulus and Remus were added in the Renaissance). Don't miss the *Boy Extracting a Thorn* or the enchanting *Commodus as Hercules*. The second-floor painting gallery—except for two Caravaggios—is forgettable. The café upstairs has a splendid patio with city views (lovely at sunset).

Connect the two museums with the underground passage that leads to the **Tabularium**. Built in the first century A.D., this once held the archives of ancient Rome. The word *Tabularium* comes from tablet, on which the Romans wrote their laws. You won't see any tablets, but you will see a superb head-on view of the Forum from the windows.

The **Palazzo Nuovo** houses mostly portrait busts of forgotten emperors. But it has three must-see statues: the *Dying Gaul*, the *Capitoline Venus* (both on the first floor up), and the original gilded bronze equestrian statue of Marcus Aurelius (behind glass in museum courtyard). This greatest surviving equestrian statue of antiquity was the original centerpiece of the square. While most such pagan statues were destroyed by Dark Age Christians, Marcus was mistaken for Constantine (the first Christian emperor) and therefore spared.

From Capitol Hill to Piazza Venezia—Leaving Capitol Hill, descend the stairs leading to Piazza Venezia. At the bottom of the stairs, look left several blocks down the street to see a condominium actually built around surviving ancient pillars and arches of Teatro Marcello—perhaps the oldest inhabited building in Europe.

Still at the bottom of the stairs, look up the long stairway to your right (which pilgrims climb on their knees) for a good example of the earliest style of Christian church. While pilgrims find it worth the climb, sightseers can skip it. As you walk toward Piazza Venezia, look down into the ditch on your right and see how modern Rome is built on the forgotten frescoes and mangled mosaics of ancient Rome.

Piazza Venezia—This vast square is the focal point of modern Rome. The Via del Corso, which starts here, is the city's axis, surrounded by Rome's classiest shopping district. In the 1930s, Mussolini whipped up Italy's nationalistic fervor here from a balcony above the square (to your right with back to Victor Emmanuel Monument). Fascist masses filled the square screaming, "Four more years!" or something like that. Fifteen years later, they hung Mussolini from a meat hook in Milan.

Victor Emmanuel Monument—This oversized monument to an Italian king was part of Italy's rush to overcome the new country's strong regionalism and create a national identity after unification in 1870. It's now open to the public, offering a new view of the Eternal City (free, just climb the big stairs, long hours).

Romans think of the monument not as an altar of the fatherland but as "the wedding cake," "the typewriter," or "the dentures."

It wouldn't be so bad if it weren't sitting on a priceless acre of ancient Rome and if they had chosen better marble (this is too in-your-face white and picks up the pollution horribly). Soldiers guard Italy's *Tomb of the Unknown Soldier* as the eternal flame flickers. At this level, stand with your back to the flame and see how Via del Corso bisects Rome.

▲**Trajan's Column, Market, and Forum**—This offers the grandest column and best example of "continuous narration" from antiquity. Over 2,500 figures scroll around the 40-meter-high column, telling of Trajan's victorious Dacian campaign (circa A.D. 103, in present-day Romania), from the assembling of the army at the bottom to the victory sacrifice at the top. The ashes of Trajan and his wife were held in the mausoleum at the base while the sun once glinted off a polished bronze statue of Trajan at the top. Today, St. Peter is on top. Study the propaganda that winds up the column like a scroll, trumpeting Trajan's wonderful military exploits. You can see this close up for free (always open and viewable, just off Piazza Venezia, across the street from the Victor Emmanuel Monument). Viewing balconies once stood on either side, but it seems likely Trajan fans came away only with a feeling that the greatness of their emperor and empire was beyond comprehension (for a rolled-out version of the Column's story, visit the Museum of Roman Civilization at E.U.R., below). This column marked **Trajan's Forum**, built to handle the shopping needs of a wealthy city of over a million. Commercial, political, religious, and social activities all mixed in the Forum.

For a fee, you can go inside **Trajan's Market** (boring) and part of Trajan's Forum; the entrance is uphill from the column on Via IV Novembre. The market was once filled with shops selling goods from all over the Roman Empire (€6.20, summer Tue–Sun 09:00–18:30, winter 09:00–16:30, closed Mon, entrance is uphill from the column on Via IV Novembre, tel. 06-3600-4399).

Pantheon Area

▲▲▲**Pantheon**—For the greatest look at the splendor of Rome, antiquity's best-preserved interior is a must (free, Mon–Sat 08:30–19:30, Sun 09:00–13:00, 14:00–18:00, tel. 06-6830-0230). Because it became a church dedicated to the martyrs just after the fall of Rome, the barbarians left it alone, and the locals didn't use it as a quarry. The portico is called Rome's umbrella—a fun local gathering in a rainstorm. Walk past its one-piece granite columns (biggest in Italy, shipped from Egypt) and through the original bronze doors. Sit inside under the glorious skylight and enjoy classical architecture at its best.

The dome, 47 meters (142 feet) high and wide, was Europe's biggest until the Renaissance. Michelangelo's dome at St. Peter's, while much higher, is one meter smaller. The brilliance of its

Heart of Rome

construction astounded architects through the ages. During the Renaissance, Brunelleschi was given permission to cut into the dome (see the little square hole above and to the right of the entrance) to analyze the material. The concrete dome gets thinner and lighter with height—the highest part is volcanic pumice.

This wonderfully harmonious architecture greatly inspired Raphael and other artists of the Renaissance. Raphael, along with Italy's first two kings, chose to be buried here.

As you walk around the outside of the Pantheon, notice the "rise of Rome"—about five meters (15 feet) since it was built.

▲▲**Churches near the Pantheon**—The **Church of San Luigi dei Francesi** has a magnificent chapel painted by Caravaggio (free, Fri–Wed 07:30–12:30, 15:30–19:00, Thu 07:30–12:30, sightseers should avoid Mass at 07:30 and 19:00, modest dress recommended).

The only Gothic church you'll see in Rome is **Santa Maria sopra Minerva**. On a little square behind the Pantheon to the east, past the Bernini statue of an elephant carrying an Egyptian obelisk, this Dominican church was built *sopra* (over) a pre-Christian temple of Minerva. Before stepping in, notice the high-water marks on the wall (right of door). Inside you'll see that the lower parts of the frescoes were lost to floods. (After the last great flood, in 1870, Rome built the present embankments, finally breaking the spirit of the Tiber River.)

Rome was at its low ebb, almost a ghost town, through much of the Gothic period. Little was built during this time (and much of what was built was redone Baroque). This church is a refreshing exception.

St. Catherine's body lies under the altar (her head is in Siena). In the 1300s, she convinced the pope to return from France to Rome, thus saving Italy from untold chaos.

Left of the altar stands a little-known Michelangelo statue, *Christ Bearing the Cross*. Michelangelo gave Jesus an athlete's or warrior's body (a striking contrast to the more docile Christ of medieval art) but left the face to one of his pupils. Fra Angelico's simple tomb is farther to the left, on the way to the back door. Before leaving, head over to the right (south transept), pop in a coin for light, and enjoy a fine Filippo Lippi fresco showing scenes from the life of St. Thomas Aquinas.

Exit the church via its rear door (behind the Michelangelo statue), walk down Fra Angelico lane (spy any artisans at work), turn left, and walk to the next square. On your right, you'll find the **Chiesa di St. Ignazio** church, a riot of Baroque illusions. Study the fresco over the door and the ceiling in the back of the nave. Then stand on the yellow disk on the floor between the two stars. Look at the central (black) dome. Keeping your eyes on the dome, walk under and past it. Church building project runs out of money? Hire a painter to paint a fake, flat dome. (Both churches open early, take a siesta—Santa Maria sopra Minerva closes at 12:00, St. Ignazio at 12:30—reopen around 15:30, and close at 19:00. Modest dress is recommended.)

A few blocks away, back across Corso Vittorio Emmanuele, is the rich and Baroque **Gesu Church** (daily 06:00–12:30, 16:00–19:15), headquarters of the Jesuits in Rome. The Jesuits powered the Church's Counter-Reformation. With Protestants teaching that all roads to heaven did not pass through Rome, the Baroque churches of the late 1500s were painted with spiritual road maps that said they did.

Walk out the Gesu Church and two blocks down Corso V. Emmanuele to the **Sacred Area** (Largo Argentina), an excavated square facing the boulevard, about four blocks south of the Pantheon. Stroll around this square and look into the excavated pit at some of the oldest ruins in Rome. Julius Caesar was assassinated near here. Today, it's a refuge for cats—some 250 of them are cared for by volunteers. You'll see them (and their refuge) at the far (west) side of the square.

▲**Trevi Fountain**—This bubbly Baroque fountain of Neptune with his entourage is a minor sight to art scholars, but a major nighttime gathering spot for teens on the make and tourists tossing coins (for more information, see "Self-Guided Walks in Rome," below).

East Rome: Near the Train Station

These sights are within a 10-minute walk of the train station. By Metro, use the Termini stop for the National Museum and the Piazza Repubblica stop for the rest.

▲▲▲**National Museum of Rome in Palazzo Massimo**—This museum houses the greatest collection of ancient Roman art anywhere, and includes busts of emperors and a Roman copy of the *Greek Discus Thrower*. The ground floor is a historic yearbook of marble statues from the second century B.C. to the second century A.D., with rare Greek originals.

The first floor is peopled by statues from the first through fourth centuries A.D. The second floor (which requires an appointment, request when you buy ticket) contains frescoes and mosaics that once decorated the walls and floors of Roman villas. Finally, descend into the basement to see fine gold jewelry, dice, an abacus, and vault doors leading into the best coin collection in Europe, with fancy magnifying glasses maneuvering you through cases of coins from ancient Rome to modern times.

Cost and Hours: €6.20, covered by €16 combo-ticket, Tue–Sun 09:00–19:45, closed Mon, open some summer Saturdays until 23:00, last entry 45 min before closing, audioguide-€3.60 (Metro: Termini, tel. 06-481-5576). The museum is about 100 meters from the Termini train station. As you leave the station, it's the sandstone-brick building on your left. Enter at the far end, at Largo di Villa Peretti.

Baths of Diocletian—Around A.D. 300, Emperor Diocletian built the largest baths in Rome. This sprawling meeting place, with baths and schmoozing spaces to accommodate 3,000 bathers at a time, was a big deal in ancient Rome. While much of it is still closed, three sections are open: the Octagonal Hall, the Church of St. Mary of the Angels and Martyrs (both face Piazza della Repubblica), and the Museum of the Bath (across from the train station).

▲▲**Octagonal Hall**—The Aula Ottagona, or Rotunda of Diocletian, was a private gymnasium in the Baths of Diocletian. Built around A.D. 300, these functioned until 537, when the barbarians cut Rome's aqueducts. The floor would have been seven meters lower (look down the window in the center of the room). The graceful iron grid supported the canopy of a 1928 planetarium. Today, the hall's a gallery, showing off fine bronze and marble statues—the kind that would have decorated the baths of imperial Rome. Most are Roman copies of Greek originals...gods, athletes, portrait busts. Two merit a close look:

the *Defeated Boxer* (first century B.C, Greek and textbook Hellenistic) and the *Roman Aristocrat*. The aristocrat's face is older than the body. This bronze statue is typical of the day: Take a body modeled on Alexander the Great and pop on a portrait bust (free, Tue–Sat 09:00–14:00, Sun 09:00–13:00, closed Mon, faces Piazza Repubblica).

▲**Church of St. Mary of the Angels and Martyrs (Santa Maria degli Angeli e dei Martiri)**—From Piazza della Repubblica, step through the Roman wall into what was the great central hall of the baths and is now a church (since the 16th century) designed by Michelangelo. When the church entrance was moved to Piazza Repubblica, the church was reoriented 90 degrees, turning the nave into long transepts and the transepts into a short nave. The 12 red granite columns still stand in their ancient positions. The classical floor was five meters (15 feet) lower. Project the walls down and imagine the soaring shape of the Roman vaults.

Museum of the Bath (Museo Nazionale Romano Terme di Diocleziano)—This museum, located on the grounds of the ancient Baths of Diocletian, has a misleading name. Rather than featuring the baths, it displays ancient Roman inscriptions on tons of tombs, steles, and tablets. Although well-displayed and described in English, the museum is difficult to appreciate quickly, and most travelers will find more history presented on a grander scale in the National Museum of Rome a block away (€4.20, Tue–Sun 09:00–19:45, closed Mon, Viale E. De Nicola 79, entrance faces Termini station, tel. 06-488-0530).

▲**Santa Maria della Vittoria**—This church houses Bernini's statue of a swooning *St. Teresa in Ecstasy* (free, daily 07:00–12:00, 16:00–19:00, on Largo Susanna, about 5 blocks northwest of train station, Metro: Repubblica). Once inside the church, you'll find St. Teresa to the left of the altar.

Teresa has just been stabbed with God's arrow of fire. Now the angel pulls it out and watches her reaction. Teresa swoons, her eyes roll up, her hand goes limp, she parts her lips...and moans. The smiling, Cupidlike angel understands just how she feels. Teresa, a 16th-century Spanish nun, later talked of the "sweetness" of "this intense pain," describing her oneness with God in ecstatic, even erotic, terms.

Bernini, the master of multimedia, pulls out all the stops to make this mystical vision real. Actual sunlight pours through the alabaster windows; bronze sunbeams shine on a marble angel holding a golden arrow. Teresa leans back on a cloud and her robe ripples from within, charged with her spiritual arousal. Bernini has created a little stage setting of heaven. And watching from the "theater boxes" on either side are members of the family that commissioned the work.

North Rome: Villa Borghese and nearby Via Veneto

▲**Villa Borghese**—Rome's scruffy "Central Park" is great for people-watching (plenty of modern-day Romeos and Juliets). Take a row on the lake or visit its fine museums.

▲▲▲**Borghese Gallery**—This private museum, filling a cardinal's mansion in the park, offers one of Europe's most sumptuous art experiences. Because of the gallery's slick mandatory reservation system, you'll enjoy its collection of world-class Baroque sculpture—including Bernini's *David* and his excited statue of Apollo chasing Daphne, as well as paintings by Caravaggio, Raphael, Titian, and Rubens—with manageable crowds.

The essence of the collection is the connection of the Renaissance with the classical world. Notice the second-century Roman reliefs with Michelangelo-designed panels above either end of the portico as you enter. The villa was built in the early 17th century by the great art collector Cardinal Borghese, who wanted to prove that the glories of ancient Rome were matched by the Renaissance.

In the main entry hall, opposite the door, notice the thrilling relief of the horse falling (first century A.D., Greek). Pietro Bernini, father of the famous Bernini, completed the scene by adding the rider.

Each room seems to feature a Baroque masterpiece. The best of all is in Room 3: Bernini's *Apollo chasing Daphne*. It's the perfect Baroque subject—capturing a thrilling, action-filled moment. In the mythological story, Apollo races after Daphne. Just as he's about to reach her, she turns into a tree. As her toes turn to roots and branches spring from her fingers, Apollo is in for one rude surprise. Walk slowly around. It's more air than stone.

Cost and Hours: €7.25, Tue–Sun 09:00–19:00, June–Sept may be open until 23:00 on Sat, closed Mon. No photos are allowed.

Reservations: Reservations are mandatory and easy to get in English over the Internet (www.ticketeria.it) or by phone: call 06-32810 (if you get an Italian recording, press 2 for English; office hours: Mon–Fri 09:00–18:00, Sat 09:00–13:00). Reserve a *minimum* of several days in advance for a weekday visit, at least a week ahead for weekends.

Every two hours, 360 people are allowed to enter the museum. Entry times are 09:00, 11:00, 13:00, 15:00, and 17:00 (plus 19:00 and 21:00 if open late on Sat June–Sept). When you reserve, request a day and time (which you'll be given if available), and you'll get a claim number. While you'll be advised to come 30 minutes before your appointed time, you can arrive a few minutes beforehand, but don't be late, as no-show tickets are sold to stand-bys.

Visits are strictly limited to two hours. Concentrate on the first floor, but leave yourself 30 minutes for the paintings of the Pinacoteca upstairs; highlights are marked by the audioguide icons. The fine bookshop and cafeteria are best visited outside your two-hour entry window.

If you don't have a reservation, just show up (or call first and ask if there are openings; a late afternoon on a weekday is usually your best bet). Reservations are tightest at 11:00 and on weekends. No-shows are released a few minutes after the top of the hour. Generally, out of 360 reservations, a few will fail to show (but more than a few may be waiting to grab them).

Tours: Guided English tours are offered at 09:10 and 11:10 for €4.20; reserve with entry reservation (or consider the excellent audioguide tour for €4.20).

Location: The museum is in the Villa Borghese park. A taxi (tell the cabbie your destination: gah-leh-REE-ah bor-GAY-zay) can get you within 100 meters of the museum. Otherwise, Metro to Spagna and take a 15-minute walk through the park.

Etruscan Museum (Villa Giulia Museo Nazionale Etrusco)—The Etruscan civilization thrived in this part of Italy around 600 B.C., when Rome was an Etruscan town. The Etruscan civilization is fascinating, but the Villa Giulia Museum is extremely low-tech and in a state of disarray. I don't like it, and Etruscan fans will prefer the Vatican Museum's Etruscan section. Still, the Villa Giulia does have the famous "husband and wife sarcophagus" (a dead couple seeming to enjoy an everlasting banquet from atop their tomb; 6th century B.C from Cerveteri), the *Apollo from Veio* statue (of textbook fame), and an impressive room filled with gold sheets of Etruscan printing and temple statuary from the Sanctuary of Pyrgi (€4.20, Tue–Sun 09:00–19:00, plus June–Sept Sat 21:00–23:45, closed Mon, closes earlier off-season, Piazzale di Villa Giulia 9, tel. 06-320-1951).

▲**Cappuccin Crypt**—If you want bones, this is it. The crypt is below the church of Santa Maria della Immaculata Concezione on Via Veneto, just up from Piazza Barberini. The bones of more than 4,000 monks who died between 1528 and 1870 are in the basement, all artistically arranged for the delight—or disgust—of the always-wide-eyed visitor. The soil in the crypt was brought from Jerusalem 400 years ago, and the monastic message on the wall explains that this is more than just a macabre exercise. Pick up a few of Rome's most interesting postcards (donation, Fri–Wed 09:00–12:00, 15:00–18:00, closed Thu, Metro: Barberini). A painting of St. Francis by Caravaggio is upstairs. Just up the street, you'll find the American embassy, Federal Express, and fancy Via Veneto cafés filled with the poor and envious looking for the rich and famous.

Ara Pacis (Altar of Peace)—This will reopen in 2005 once restoration is complete. In 9 B.C, after victories in Gaul and Spain, Emperor Augustus celebrated the beginning of the Pax Romana by building this altar of peace. Peace is almost worshiped here. The north and south walls show a procession with realistic portraits of the imperial family in Greek Hellenistic style. It's a fine combination of Roman grandeur and Greek elegance. Even when the altar is not open, it can sometimes be seen through the windows (a long block west of Via del Corso on Via di Ara Pacis, on east bank of river near Ponte Cavour, nearest Metro: Spagna).

West Rome: Vatican City Area

Vatican City is a tiny independent country (just over 100 acres) that contains two huge sights: the Vatican Museum (with Michelangelo's Sistine Chapel) and St. Peter's Basilica (with Michelangelo's exquisite *Pietà*). A helpful **TI** is just to the left of St. Peter's Basilica (Mon–Sat 08:30–18:30, closed Sun, tel. 06-6988-1662, Vatican switchboard tel. 06-6982, www.vatican.va). The entrances to St. Peter's and the Vatican Museum are a 15-minute walk apart (follow the outside of the Vatican wall, which links the two sights). The nearest Metro stops still involve a 10-minute walk to either sight: for St. Peter's, the closest stop is Ottaviano; for the Vatican Museum, it's Cipro-Musei-Vaticani.

Post Office: The Vatican post, with an office in the Vatican Museum and one on St. Peter's Square, is more reliable than the Italian mail service (comfortable writing rooms, Mon–Sat 08:30–18:30). The stamps are a collectible bonus (Vatican stamps are good throughout Rome; Italian stamps are not good at the Vatican).

Tours: The Vatican TI conducts free 90-minute tours of St. Peter's (depart from TI at 15:00 on Mon, Wed, and Fri, confirm schedule at TI, tel. 06-6988-1662). Tours of the Vatican Gardens offer the only way to see the gardens; book tours at least one day in advance by calling 06-6988-4466 (€9, Mon–Sat 10:00–12:00, tours start at Vatican Museum tour desk and finish on St. Peter's Square). To tour the necropolis of St. Peter's and the saint's tomb, call the Excavations Office at 06-6988-5318 (€8, 2 hrs, office open Mon–Fri 09:00–17:00, tel. 06-6988-5318).

Seeing the Pope: Your best chances for a sighting are on Sundays and Wednesdays. Because he's a travelin' man, the following schedule can vary. The pope gives a blessing at noon on Sunday from his apartment on St. Peter's Square (except Aug–Sept, when he speaks at his summer residence at Castel Gandolfo, 40 km from Rome; train leaves Rome's Termini station at 08:35, returns after his talk). On Wednesday at 10:00, the pope blesses the crowds at St. Peter's from a balcony or canopied platform on the square (except in winter, when he speaks at 11:00 in 7,000-seat Aula Paola VI Auditorium, next to St. Peter's Basilica). To find out the pope's schedule or to book a free spot for the Wednesday blessing (either for a seat on the square or in the auditorium), call 06-6988-3017. Smaller ceremonies celebrated by the pope require reservations. The weekly entertainment guide *Roma c'è* always has

Vatican City Overview

● HOTEL ALIMANDI
● HOTEL SPRING HOUSE
● HOTEL GERBER
● HOSTARIA BASTIONI REST.
● LA RUSTICHELLA REST.
● ENTRANCE TO VATICAN MUSEUM
● TOURIST INFO, POST & WC
● HOTEL SANT' ANNA
● HOTEL BRAMANTE

a "Seeing the Pope" section. If you don't want to see the pope, minimize crowd problems by avoiding these times.

▲▲▲**St. Peter's Basilica**—There is no doubt: This is the richest and most impressive church on earth. To call it vast is like calling God smart. Marks on the floor show where the next-largest churches would fit if they were put inside. The ornamental cherubs would dwarf a large man. Birds roost inside, and thousands of people wander about, heads craned heavenward, hardly noticing each other. Don't miss Michelangelo's

Pietà (behind bullet-proof glass) to the right of the entrance.
Bernini's altar work and seven-story-tall bronze canopy
(*baldacchino*) are brilliant.

For a quick self-guided walk through the basilica, follow
these points (see map on next page):

1. The atrium is larger than most churches. Notice the
historic doors (the Holy Door, on the right, won't be opened
until the next Jubilee Year, in 2025—see point 13 below).

2. The purple, circular porphyry stone marks the site of
Charlemagne's coronation in A.D. 800 (in the first St. Peter's
church that stood on this site). From here, get a sense of the
immensity of the church, which can accommodate 95,000
worshippers standing on its six acres.

3. Michelangelo planned a Greek-cross floor plan rather
than the Latin-cross standard in medieval churches. A Greek cross,
symbolizing the perfection of God, and by association the good-
ness of man, was important to the humanist Michelangelo. But
accommodating large crowds was important to the Church in the
fancy Baroque age, which followed Michelangelo, so the original
nave length was doubled. Stand halfway up the nave and imagine
the stubbier design Michelangelo had in mind.

4. View the magnificent dome from the statue of St. Andrew.
See the vision of heaven above the windows: Jesus, Mary, a ring
of saints, rings of angels, and, on the very top, God the Father.

5. The main altar sits directly over St. Peter's tomb and
under Bernini's 21-meter-tall (70 feet) bronze canopy.

6. The stairs lead down to the crypt to the foundation,
chapels, and tombs of popes. (Do this last since it leads you out
of the church.)

7. The statue of St. Peter, with an irresistibly kissable toe,
is one of the few pieces of art that predate this church. It adorned
the first St. Peter's church.

8. St. Peter's throne and Bernini's starburst dove window
is the site of a daily Mass (Mon–Sat at 17:00, Sun at 17:45).

9. St. Peter was crucified here when this location was simply
"the Vatican Hill." The obelisk now standing in the center of
St. Peter's square marked the center of a Roman racecourse long
before a church stood here.

10. For most, the treasury (in the sacristy) is not worth the
admission.

11. The church is filled with mosaics, not paintings. Notice
the mosaic version of Raphael's *Transfiguration*.

12. Blessed Sacrament Chapel.

13. Michelangelo sculpted his *Pietà* when he was 24 years
old. A pietà is a work showing Mary with the dead body of Christ
taken down from the cross. Michelangelo's mastery of the body is
obvious in this powerfully beautiful masterpiece. Jesus is believably

St. Peter's Basilica

ST. PETER'S SQUARE

1. Holy Door
2. Site of Charlemagne's coronation, 800 AD
3. Extent of the original "Greek Cross" church plan
4. St. Andrew statue (view the dome from here)
5. Main altar directly over Peter's tomb. BERNINI's 70-foot bronze canopy covers the altar
6. Stairs down to the crypt: the foundation of old St. Peter's, chapels and tombs of popes (the entrance moves around)
7. Statue of St. Peter with irresistibly kissable toe
8. BERNINI - Dove window and "St. Peter's Throne"
9. Site of Peter's crucifixion
10. Museum entrance
11. RAPHAEL - "Transfiguration" mosaic
12. Blessed Sacrament Chapel
13. MICHELANGELO - Pieta
14. Elevator to roof and dome-climb (this entrance moves around - sometimes it is even outside)

dead, and Mary, the eternally youthful "handmaiden" of the Lord, still accepts God's will...even if it means giving up her son.

The Holy Door (just to the right of the *Pietà*) was bricked shut at the end of the Jubilee Year 2000 and won't be opened until 2025. Every 25 years, the Church celebrates an especially festive year derived from the Old Testament idea of the Jubilee

Year (originally every 50 years), which encourages new beginnings
and the forgiveness of sins and debts. In the Jubilee Year 2000,
the pope tirelessly—and with significant success—promoted debt
relief for the world's poorest countries.

14. An elevator leads to the roof and the stairway up the
dome (€4.20, allow an hour to go up and down). The dome,
Michelangelo's last work, is (you guessed it) the biggest anywhere.
Taller than a football field is long, it's well worth the sweaty climb
for a great view of Rome, the Vatican grounds, and the inside of
the basilica—particularly heavenly while there is singing. Look
around—Rome has no modern skyline. No building is allowed
to exceed the height of St. Peter's. The elevator takes you to the
rooftop of the nave. From there, a few steps take you to a balcony
at the base of the dome looking down into the church interior.
After that the one-way, 300-step climb (for some people claustro-
phobic) to the cupola begins. The rooftop level (below the dome)
has a gift shop, WC, drinking fountain, and a commanding view.

Dress Code: The church strictly enforces its dress code:
no shorts or bare shoulders (men and women); no miniskirts.
You might be required to check any bags at a free cloakroom
near the entry.

Hours of Church: May–Sept daily 07:00–19:00, Oct–April
daily until 18:00 (ticket booth to treasury closes 1 hour earlier).
All are welcome to join in the hour-long Mass at the front altar
(Mon–Sat at 17:00, Sun at 17:45). The church is particularly
moving at 07:00, while tourism is still sleeping. Volunteers who
want you to understand and appreciate St. Peter's give free 90-
minute tours (3/week, see "Tours," above); these are generally
excellent but non-Christians can find them preachy. Seeing the
Pietà is neat; understanding it is divine.

Cost and Hours of Dome: The view from the dome is
worth the climb (€4.20 elevator plus 300-step climb, May–Sept
daily 08:00–18:00, Oct–April daily 08:30–17:00).

▲▲▲**Vatican Museum**—The six kilometers of displays in this
immense museum—from ancient statues to Christian frescoes
to modern paintings—are topped by the Raphael Rooms and
Michelangelo's glorious Sistine Chapel. (If you have binoculars,
bring them.)

Even without the Sistine, this is one of Europe's top three or
four houses of art. It can be exhausting, so plan your visit carefully,
focusing on a few themes. Allow two hours for a quick visit, three
or four for time to enjoy it. The museum has a nearly impossible-
not-to-follow, one-way system (although, for the rushed visitor,
the museum does clearly mark out 4 color-coded visits of different
lengths—A is shortest, D longest). Tip: The Sistine Chapel has an
exit (optional) that leads directly to St. Peter's Basilica, saving you
the 10-minute walk back to the Vatican Museum exit; if you want

to squirt out at the Sistine, see the Pinacoteca painting gallery first (described below) and don't get an audioguide (which needs to be returned at the entry/exit).

Start, as civilization did, in Egypt and Mesopotamia. Next, the Pio Clementino collection features **Greek and Roman statues**. Decorating its courtyard are some of the best Greek and Roman statues in captivity, including the *Laocoön* group (1st century B.C., Hellenistic) and the *Apollo Belvedere* (a 2nd-century Roman copy of a Greek original). The centerpiece of the next hall is the *Belvedere Torso* (just a 2,000-year-old torso, but one that had a great impact on the art of Michelangelo). Finishing off the classical statuary are two fine fourth-century porphyry sarcophagi; these royal purple tombs hold the remains of Constantine's mother and daughter. Crafted in Egypt at a time when a declining Rome was unable to do such fine work, the details are fun to study.

After long halls of tapestries, old maps, broken penises, and fig leaves, you'll come to what most people are looking for: The Raphael Rooms (or *stanza*) and Michelangelo's Sistine Chapel.

These outstanding works are frescoes. A fresco (meaning "fresh" in Italian) is technically not a painting. The color is mixed into wet plaster, and, when the plaster dries, the painting is actually part of the wall. This is a durable but difficult medium, requiring speed and accuracy, as the work is built slowly, one patch at a time.

After fancy rooms illustrating the "Immaculate Conception of Mary" (a hard-to-sell, 19th-century Vatican doctrine) and the triumph of Constantine (with divine guidance, which led to his conversion to Christianity), you enter the first room completely done by **Raphael** and find the newly restored *School of Athens*. This is remarkable for its blatant pre-Christian classical orientation, wall-papering the apartments of Pope Julius II. Raphael honors the great pre-Christian thinkers—Aristotle, Plato, and company—who are portrayed as the leading artists of Raphael's day. The bearded figure of Plato is Leonardo da Vinci. Diogenes, history's first hippie, sprawls alone in bright blue on the stairs, while Michelangelo broods in the foreground—supposedly added late. Apparently Raphael snuck a peek at the Sistine Chapel and decided that his arch competitor was so good he had to put their personal differences aside and include him in this tribute to the artists of his generation. Today's St. Peter's was under construction as Raphael was working. In the *School of Athens*, he gives us a sneak preview of the unfinished church.

Next (unless you detour through the refreshingly modern Catholic art section) is the brilliantly restored **Sistine Chapel**. The Sistine Chapel, the pope's personal chapel, is where, upon the death of the ruling pope, a new pope is elected. The College of Cardinals meets here and votes four times a day until a two-thirds-plus-one majority is reached and a new pope is elected.

The Sistine is famous for Michelangelo's pictorial culmination of the Renaissance, showing the story of Creation, with a powerful God weaving in and out of each scene through that busy first week. This is an optimistic and positive expression of the High Renaissance and a stirring example of the artistic and theological maturity of the 33-year-old Michelangelo, who spent four years on this work.

Later, after the Reformation wars had begun and after the Catholic army of Spain had sacked the Vatican, the reeling Church began to fight back. As part of its Counter-Reformation, a much older Michelangelo was commissioned to paint the *Last Judgment* (behind the altar). Brilliantly restored, the message is as clear as the day Michelangelo finished it: Christ is returning, some will go to hell and some to heaven, and some will be saved by the power of the rosary.

In the recent and controversial restoration project, no paint was added. Centuries of dust, soot (from candles used for lighting and Mass), and glue (added to make the art shine) were removed, revealing the bright original colors of Michelangelo. Photos are allowed (without a flash) elsewhere in the museum, but as part of the deal with the company who did the restoration, no photos are allowed in the Sistine Chapel.

For a shortcut, a small door at the rear of the Sistine Chapel allows groups and individuals (without an audioguide) to escape directly to St. Peter's Basilica. If you exit here, you're done with the museum. The Pinacoteca is the only important part left. Consider doing it at the start. Otherwise it's a 10-minute, heel-to-toe slalom through tourists from the Sistine Chapel to the entry/exit.

After this long march, you'll find the **Pinacoteca** (the Vatican's small but fine collection of paintings, with Raphael's *Transfiguration*, Leonardo's unfinished *St. Jerome*, and Caravaggio's *Deposition*), a cafeteria (long lines, mediocre food), and the underrated early-Christian art section, before you exit via the souvenir shop.

Cost and Hours: €9.30, March–Oct Mon–Fri 08:45–16:45, Sat 08:45–13:45, Nov–Feb Mon–Sat 08:45–13:45, closed Sun except last Sun of the month when it's free and crowded. The last entry is 75 minutes before closing time. The Sistine Chapel shuts down 30 minutes early. The museum is closed on many holidays (mainly religious ones), including—for 2002: Jan 1 and 6, Feb 11, March 19, Easter and Easter Monday, May 1, 9, and 30, June 29, Aug 14 and 15, Nov 1, Dec 8, 25, and 26. Modest dress (no short shorts or bare shoulders for men or women) is appropriate and often required. Museum tel. 06-6988-4947.

▲**Castel Sant' Angelo**—Built as a tomb for the emperor; used through the Middle Ages as a castle, prison, and place of last refuge for popes under attack; and today, a museum, this giant pile of ancient bricks is packed with history.

Ancient Rome allowed no tombs—not even the emperor's—within its walls. So Hadrian grabbed the most commanding position just outside the walls and across the river and built a towering tomb (circa A.D. 139) well within view of the city. His mausoleum was a huge cylinder (64 meters wide, 21 meters high) topped by a cypress grove and crowned by a huge statue of Hadrian himself riding a chariot. For nearly a hundred years, Roman emperors (from Hadrian to Caracalla in A.D. 217) were buried here.

In the year 590, the Archangel Michael appeared above the mausoleum to Pope Gregory the Great. Sheathing his sword, the angel signaled the end of a plague. The fortress that was Hadrian's mausoleum eventually became a fortified palace, renamed for the "holy angel."

Since Rome was repeatedly plundered by invaders, Castel Sant' Angelo was a handy place of last refuge for threatened popes. The elevated corridor connecting Castel Sant' Angelo with the Vatican was built in 1277. In anticipation of long sieges, rooms were decorated with papal splendor (you'll see paintings by Crivelli, Signorelli, and Mantegna). In the 16th century, during a sack of Rome by troops of Charles V of Spain, the pope lived inside the castle for months with his entourage of hundreds (an unimaginable ordeal, considering the food service at the top-floor bar).

After you walk around the entire base of the castle, take the small staircase down to the original Roman floor. In the atrium, study the model of the castle in Roman times and imagine the niche in the wall filled with a towering "welcome to my tomb" statue of Hadrian. From here, a ramp leads to the right, spiraling 125 meters. While some of the fine brickwork and bits of mosaic survive, the marble veneer is long gone (notice the holes in the wall which held it in place). At the end of the ramp, stairs climb to the room where the ashes of the emperors were kept. These stairs continue to the top, where you'll find the papal apartments. Don't miss the Sala del Tesoro (treasury), where the wealth of the Vatican was locked up in a huge chest. Do miss the 58 rooms of the military museum. The views from the top are great—pick out landmarks as you stroll around—and a restful coffee with a view of St. Peter's is worth the price.

Cost, Hours, Tours: €5, Tue–Sun 09:00–19:00, plus June–Sept Sat 21:00–23:45, closed Mon. You can take an English-language tour with an audioguide (€3.60) or live guide (€4.20, Tue–Fri at 15:00, Sat at 12:15 and 16:30, confirm times, tel. 06-3996-7600, Metro: Lepanto or bus #64, near Vatican City).

Ponte Sant' Angelo—The bridge leading to Castel Sant' Angelo was built by Hadrian for quick and regal access from downtown to his tomb. The three middle arches are actually Roman originals and a fine example of the empire's engineering expertise. The angels were designed by Bernini and finished by his students.

South Rome

Baths of Caracalla (Terme di Caracalla)—Today it's just a shell—a huge shell—with all of its sculptures and most of its mosaics moved to museums. Inaugurated by Emperor Caracalla in A.D. 216, this massive complex could accommodate 1,600 visitors at a time. Today you'll see a huge two-story, roofless brick building surrounded by a garden and bordered by ruined walls. The two large rooms at either end of the building were used for exercise. In between the exercise rooms was a pool flanked by two small mosaic-floored dressing rooms. Niches in the walls once held statues. In its day, this was a remarkable place to hang out. For ancient Romans, the baths were a social experience.

The Baths of Caracalla functioned until Goths severed the aqueducts in the sixth century. In modern times, operas were performed here from 1938 to 1993. For the same reason concerts no longer take place in the Forum—to keep the ruins from becoming more ruined—the performances were discontinued (€4.20, covered by €16 combo-ticket, Mon 09:00–14:00, Tue–Sun 09:00–19:15, ask if audioguides are available, fine €8 guidebook—can read in shaded garden while sitting on a chunk of column; Metro: Circus Maximus, and a 5-minute walk south along Via delle Terme di Caracalla, tel. 06-574-5748). Several of the Baths' statues are now in Rome's Octagonal Hall; the immense *Toro Farnese* (a marble sculpture of a bull surrounded by people) snorts in Naples' Archaeological Museum.

E.U.R.—In the late 1930s, Italy's dictator, Benito Mussolini, planned an international exhibition to show off the wonders of his fascist society. But these wonders brought us World War II, and Il Duce's celebration never happened. The unfinished mega-project was completed in the 1950s and now houses government offices and big, obscure museums.

If Hitler and Mussolini won the war, our world might look like E.U.R. (pronounced "ay-oor"). Hike down E.U.R.'s wide, pedestrian-mean boulevards. Patriotic murals, aren't-you-proud-to-be-an-extreme-right-winger pillars, and stern squares decorate the soulless, planned grid and stark office blocks. Boulevards named for Astronomy, Electronics, Social Security, and Beethoven are more exhausting than inspirational. Today E.U.R. is worth a trip for its Museum of Roman Civilization (described below).

The Metro skirts E.U.R. with three stops (10 min from the Colosseum): Use E.U.R. Magliana for the "Square Colosseum" and E.U.R. Fermi for the Museum of Roman Civilization (both described below). Consider walking 30 minutes from the palace to the museum through the center of E.U.R.

From the Magliana subway stop, stairs lead uphill to the **Palace of the Civilization of Labor (Palazzo del Civilta del Lavoro)**, the essence of fascist architecture. With its giant,

no-questions-asked, patriotic statues and its black-and-white simplicity, this is E.U.R.'s tallest building and landmark. It's understandably nicknamed the "Square Colosseum." Around the corner,
Café Palombini is still decorated in a 1930s style and is now quite
trendy with young Romans (daily 07:00–24:00, good gelato, pastries,
and snacks, Piazzale Adenauer 12, tel. 06-591-1700).

The **Museum of Roman Civilization (Museo della Civilta
Romana)** fills 59 rooms with plaster casts and models illustrating
the greatness of classical Rome. Each room has a theme, from
military tricks to musical instruments. One long hall is filled with
casts of the reliefs of Trajan's Column. The museum's highlight
is the 1:250 scale model of Constantine's Rome—circa A.D. 300
(€4.20, Tue–Sat 09:00–18:45, Sun 09:00–13:00, closed Mon,
Piazza G. Agnelli, from Metro: E.U.R. Fermi, walk 10 min up Via
dell Arte, you'll see its colonnade on the right, tel. 06-592-6041).

Ancient Appian Way (Via Appia Antica)

Since the fourth century B.C., this has been Rome's gateway to
the East. The first section was perfectly straight. It was the largest,
widest, fastest road ever, the wonder of its day, called the "Queen
of Roads." Eventually, this most important of Roman roads
stretched 700 kilometers to the port of Brindisi—where boats
sailed for Greece and Egypt.

Tourist's Appian Way: The road starts about three kilometers south of the Colosseum at the massive San Sebastian
Gate. The Museum of the Walls, located at the gate, offers an
interesting look at Roman defense and a chance to scramble along
a stretch of the ramparts (€2.60, Tue–Sun 09:00–19:00, closed
Mon, tel. 06-7047-5284). A kilometer down the road are the two
most historic and popular catacombs, those of San Callisto and
San Sebastian (described below). Beyond that, the road becomes
pristine and traffic-free, popular for biking and evocative hiking.

To reach the Appian Way, you can hop on the new Archeobus (see "Tours of Rome," above) or take the Metro to the
Colli Albani stop, then catch bus #660 to Via Appia Antica—its
last stop and the start of an interesting stretch of the ancient road
(the café next to the stop sometimes rents bikes). The segment
between the third and 11th milestones is most interesting.

▲▲**Catacombs**—The catacombs are burial places for (mostly)
Christians who died in ancient Roman times. By law, no one
was allowed to be buried within the walls of Rome. While pagan
Romans were into cremation, Christians preferred to be buried.
But land was expensive and most Christians were poor. A few
wealthy landowning Christians allowed their land to be used
as burial places.

The 40 or so known catacombs circle Rome about five kilometers from its center. From the first through the fifth centuries,

Christians dug an estimated 600 kilometers of tomb-lined tunnels, with networks of galleries as many as five layers deep.

In the 800s, when barbarian invaders started ransacking the tombs, Christians moved the relics of saints and martyrs to the safety of churches in the city center. For a thousand years, the catacombs were forgotten. Around 1850, they were excavated and became part of the romantic Grand Tour of Europe.

The underground tunnels, while empty of bones, are rich in early Christian symbolism. The dove symbolized the soul. You'll see it quenching its thirst (worshiping), with an olive branch (at rest), or happily perched (in paradise). Peacocks, known for their "incorruptible flesh," symbolized immortality. The shepherd with a lamb on his shoulders was the "good shepherd," the first portrayal of Christ as a kindly leader of his flock. The fish was used because the first letters of these words—"Jesus Christ, Son of God, Savior"— spelled "fish" in Greek. And the anchor is a cross in disguise. A second-century bishop had written on his tomb: "All who understand these things, pray for me." You'll see pictures of people praying with their hands raised up—the custom at the time.

Catacomb tours are essentially the same. Which one you visit is not important. The **Catacombs of San Callisto**, the official cemetery for the Christians of Rome and burial place of third-century popes, is the most historic. Sixteen bishops (early popes) were buried here. Buy your €4.20 ticket and wait for your language to be called. They move lots of people quickly. If one group seems ridiculously large (over 50 people), wait for the next English tour (Thu–Tue 08:30–12:00, 14:30–17:30, closed Wed and Feb, closes at 17:00 in winter, Via Appia Antica 110, tel. 06-5130-1580).

The **Catacombs of San Sebastian** are 300 meters farther down the road (€4.20, Mon–Sat 08:30–12:00, 14:30–17:30, closed Sun and Nov, closes at 17:00 in winter, Via Appia Antica 136, tel. 06-5130-1580). Dig this: The catacombs have a Web site— www.catacombe.roma.it.

Sights—Near Rome

▲▲**Ostia Antica**—Rome's ancient seaport, less than an hour from downtown Rome, is the next best thing to Pompeii. Ostia had 80,000 people at the time of Christ, later became a ghost town, and is now excavated. Start at the 2,000-year-old theater, buy a map, explore the town, and finish with its fine little museum (note that museum closes at 14:00). To get there, take the Metro's B Line to the Piramide stop (consider popping out to see an ancient Roman pyramid tomb); from the Piramide stop, catch the Lido train to Ostia Antica (2/hr), then follow the signs to (or ask for) "*scavi* Ostia Antica" (€4.20, Tue–Sun 08:30–18:00 in summer, 09:00–16:00 in winter, closed Mon, museum closes for lunch, tel. 06-5635-8099). Just beyond is Rome's filthy beach (*lido*).

Trastevere

① HOTEL SANTA MARIA
② TAVERNA DEL MORO DA TONY
③ TRATTORIA DA LUCIA
④ TRATTORIA DE OLINDO
⑤ OSTERIA PONTE SISTO
⑥ PANIFICIO ARNESE BAKERY
⑦ GELATERIA

Self-Guided Walks in Rome

▲▲▲**Night Walk Across Rome: Trastevere to the Spanish Steps**—Rome can be grueling. But a fine way to enjoy this historian's rite of passage is an evening walk lacing together Rome's floodlit night spots. Enjoying fine urban spaces, observing real-life theater vignettes, sitting so close to a Bernini fountain that traffic noises evaporate, watching water flicker its mirror on the marble, jostling with local teenagers to see all the gelato flavors, enjoying lovers straddling more than the bench, jaywalking past flak-proof vested *polizia*, marveling at the ramshackle elegance that softens this brutal city for those who were born here and can imagine living nowhere else—these are the flavors of Rome best tasted after dark. This walk is about three kilometers (2 miles) long; for a shortcut, start at Campo de' Fiori.

Taxi or ride the bus (from Vatican area, take #23; from Via

From Campo de' Fiori to the Spanish Steps

200 YARDS
200 METERS

TO SPANISH STEPS

PONTE UMBERTO

TIBER

PIAZZA COLONNA

S. LUIGI (CARAVAGGIO)

TREVI

ANCIENT STADIUM ENTRANCE

CORONARI

TRE SCALINI

PIAZZA NAVONA

MUSEUM OF ROME

PANTHEON

S. MARIA SOPRA MINERVA

SAN IGNAZIO

CAMPO DE' FIORI

VITTORIO

LARGO ARGENTINA (CAT HOSPICE)

EMANUELE

GESÙ

PIAZZA VENEZIA

PALAZZO FARNESE

CAMPODOGLIO

TO COLO.

TO TRASTEVERE

FORUM

DCH

Ⓣ - TAXI STAND

Nazionale hotels, take #64, #70, #115, or #640 to Largo Argentina and then transfer to #8) to Trastevere, the colorful neighborhood across (*tras*) the Tiber (*tevere*) River. Consider dinner here (see "Eating," below).

Trastevere offers the best look at medieval-village Rome. The action all marches to the chime of the church bells. Go to Trastevere and wander. Wonder. Be a poet on Rome's Left Bank. This proud neighborhood was long an independent working-class area. It's now becoming trendy, and high rents are driving out the source of so much color. Still, it's a great people scene, especially at night. Start your exploratory stroll at Piazza di Santa Maria in Trastevere. While today's fountain is 17th century, there has been a fountain here since Roman times.

Santa Maria in Trastevere, one of Rome's oldest churches, was made a basilica in the fourth century, when Christianity was legalized (free, daily 07:30–13:00, 15:00–19:00). It was the first church dedicated to the Virgin Mary. The portico (covered area just outside the door) is decorated with fascinating ancient fragments filled with early Christian symbolism. Most of what you see today dates from around the 12th century, but the granite columns come from an ancient Roman temple, and the ancient basilica floor plan (and ambience) survives. The 12th-century mosaics behind the altar are striking, and notable for their portrayal of Mary—the first showing her at the throne with Jesus in heaven. Look below the scenes from the life of Mary to see ahead-of-their-time paintings (by Cavallini, from 1300) that predate the Renaissance by 100 years.

Before leaving Trastevere, wander the back streets. Then, from the church square (Piazza di Santa Maria), take Via del Moro to the river and cross on Ponte Sisto, a pedestrian bridge with a good view of St. Peter's dome. Continue straight ahead for one block. Take the first left, which leads down Via di Capo di Ferro through the scary and narrow darkness to Piazza Farnese, with its imposing Palazzo Farnese. Michelangelo contributed to the facade of this palace, now the French embassy. The fountains on the square feature huge one-piece granite hot tubs from the ancient Roman Baths of Caracalla.

One block from there (opposite the palace) is **Campo de' Fiori** (Field of Flowers), which is my favorite outdoor dining room after dark (see "Eating," below). The statue of Giordano Bruno, a heretic who was burned in 1600 for believing the world was round and not the center of the universe, marks the center of this great and colorful square. Bruno overlooks a busy produce market in the morning and strollers after dark. This neighborhood is still known for its free spirit. When the statue of Bruno was erected in 1889, local riots overcame Vatican protests against honoring a heretic. Bruno faces his executioner, the Vatican Chancellory (the big white building in the corner a bit to his right), while his pedestal reads: "And the flames rose up." The square is lined and surrounded by fun eateries. Bruno also faces La Carbonara restaurant, the only real restaurant on the square. The Forno, next door, is a popular place for hot and tasty take-out *pizza bianco* (plain but spicy pizza bread).

If Bruno did a hop, step, and jump forward and turned right and marched 200 meters, he'd cross the busy Corso Vittorio Emanuele and find **Piazza Navona**. Rome's most interesting night scene features street music, artists, fire-eaters, local Casanovas, ice cream, outdoor cafés (splurge-worthy if you've got time to sit and enjoy the human river of Italy), and fountains by Bernini, the father of Baroque art. The Tartufo "death by chocolate" ice cream (€3, €6.50 at a table) made the Tre Scalini café (left of obelisk) world-famous among connoisseurs of ice cream and chocolate alike. This oblong piazza is molded around the long-gone Stadium of Domitian, an ancient chariot racetrack.

Leave Piazza Navona directly across from Tre Scalini café, go (east) past rose peddlers and palm readers, jog left around the guarded building, and follow the brown sign to the **Pantheon** straight down Via del Salvatore (cheap pizza place on left just before the Pantheon, easy WC at McDonald's). Sit for a while and ponder under the Pantheon's floodlit, moonlit portico.

With your back to the Pantheon, head right, passing Bar Pantheon on your right. The Tazza d'Oro Casa del Caffè, one of Rome's top coffee shops, dates back to the days when this area was licensed to roast coffee beans. Look back at the fine view of the Pantheon from here.

With the coffee shop on your right, walk down Via degli Orfani to Piazza Capranica, with the big, plain, Florentine Renaissance–style Palazzo Capranica. Big shots, like the Capranica family, built stubby towers on their palaces—not for any military use … just to show off. Leave the piazza to the right of the palace, between the palace and the church. Via in Aquiro leads to a sixth-century B.C. Egyptian **obelisk** (taken as a trophy by Augustus after his victory in Egypt over Mark Antony and Cleopatra). Walk into the guarded square past the obelisk and face the huge parliament building. A short detour to the left (past Albergo National) brings you to some of Rome's most famous gelato. **Gelateria Caffè Pasticceria Giolitti** is cheap to go or elegant, pricey, and worth-while for a sit among classy locals (open daily until very late, your choice: cone or *bicchierini*—cup, Via Uffici del Vicario 40). Gelato fans will want to visit the nearby **Gelateria della Palma**, also two blocks away, with better gelato (Via della Maddalena 20). Or head directly from the parliament into the next, even grander, square.

Piazza Colonna features a huge second-century column honoring Marcus Aurelius, the philosopher-emperor. The big, important-looking palace is the prime minister's residence. Cross Via del Corso, Rome's noisy main drag, and jog right (around the Y-shaped shopping gallery from 1928) and head down Via dei Sabini to the roar of the water, light, and people of the Trevi Fountain.

The **Trevi Fountain** is an example of how Rome took full advantage of the abundance of water brought into the city by its great aqueducts. This watery Baroque avalanche was built in 1762 by Nicola Salvi, hired by a pope celebrating his reopening of the ancient aqueduct that powers it. Salvi used the palace behind the fountain as a theatrical backdrop for Neptune's "entrance" into the square. Neptune surfs through his watery kingdom while Triton blows his conch shell.

Romantics toss two coins over their shoulders thinking it will give them a wish and assure their return to Rome. That

may sound silly, but every year I go through this touristic ritual...
and it actually seems to work.

Take some time to people-watch (whisper a few breathy *bello*s
or *bella*s) before leaving. Facing the fountain, go past it on the
right down Via delle Stamperia to Via del Triton. Cross the busy
street and continue to the Spanish Steps (ask, "*Dov'è Piazza di
Spagna?*"; doh-vay pee-aht-zah dee spahn-yah) a few blocks and
thousands of dollars of shopping opportunities away.

The **Piazza di Spagna** (rhymes with "lasagna"), with the
very popular Spanish Steps, got its name 300 years ago, when this
was the site of the Spanish embassy. It's been the hangout of many
Romantics over the years (Keats, Wagner, Openshaw, Goethe,
and others). The Boat Fountain at the foot of the steps, which was
done by Bernini's father, Pietro Bernini, is powered by an aqueduct. The piazza is a thriving night scene. Facing the steps, walk
to your right about a block to tour one of the world's biggest and
most lavish McDonald's. About a block on the other side of the
steps is the Spagna Metro stop, which (usually until 23:30) will
zip you home.

▲**The Dolce Vita Stroll down Via del Corso**—This is the city's
chic and hip "cruise" from Piazza del Popolo (Metro: Flaminio)
down a wonderfully traffic-free section of Via del Corso, and up
Via Condotti to the Spanish Steps each evening around 18:00
(Sat and Sun are best). Strollers, shoppers, and flirts on the prowl
fill this neighborhood of Rome's most fashionable stores (open
after siesta 16:30–19:30). Throughout Italy, early evening is
time to stroll.

Start on **Piazza Popolo**. Historians: This area was once
just inside medieval Rome's main entry. The delightfully car-free
square is marked by an obelisk that was brought to Rome by
Augustus after he conquered Egypt. (It once stood in the Circus
Maximus.) The Baroque Church of **Santa Maria del Popolo**—
with Raphael's Chigi Chapel (pron. kee-gee, third chapel on left)
and two Caravaggio paintings (side paintings in chapel left of
altar)—is next to the gate in the old wall, on the far side of Piazza
del Popolo, to the right as you face the gate (church open Mon–
Sat 07:00–12:00, 16:00–19:00, Sun 08:00–13:30, 16:30–19:30).

From Piazza del Popolo, shop your way down **Via del Corso**.
To rest your feet, join the locals sitting on the steps of various
churches along the street.

At Via Pontefici, historians turn right and walk a block to
see the massive, rotting, round brick **Mausoleum of Augustus**,
topped with overgrown cypress trees. Beyond it, next to the river,
is Augustus' Ara Pacis, or Altar of Peace (which should be reopening in 2005).

From the mausoleum, return to Via del Corso and the 21st
century, continuing straight until **Via Condotti**. Shoppers, take

a left on Via Conditti to join the parade to the **Spanish Steps**. The streets that parallel Via Condotti to the south (Borgogno and Frattini) are just as popular. You can catch a taxi home at the taxi stand a block south of the Spanish Steps (at Piazza Mignonelli, near American Express and McDonald's).

Historians: Ignore Via Condotti. Continue a kilometer down Via del Corso—straight since Roman times—to the Victor Emmanuel Monument. Climb Michelangelo's stairway to his glorious (especially when floodlit) square atop Capitol Hill. From the balconies at either side of the mayor's palace, catch the lovely views of the Forum as the horizon reddens and cats prowl the unclaimed rubble of ancient Rome.

Sleeping in Rome
(€1.10 = about $1, country code: 39)

Sleep Code: **S** = Single, **D** = Double/Twin, **T** = Triple, **Q** = Quad, **b** = bathroom, **s** = shower only, **CC** = Credit Cards accepted, **no CC** = Credit Cards not accepted, **SE** = Speaks English, **NSE** = No English. Breakfast is included in all but the cheapest places.

The absolute cheapest beds (dorms or some cramped doubles) in Rome are €18 in small, backpacker-filled hostels. A nicer hotel (around €130 with a bathroom and air-con) provides an oasis and refuge, making it easier to enjoy this intense and grinding city. If you're going door to door, prices are soft—so bargain. Built into a hotel's official price list is a kickback for a room-finding service or agency; if you're coming direct, they pay no kickback and may lower the price for you. Many hotels have high-season (mid-March–June, Sept–Oct) and low-season prices. If traveling outside of peak times, ask about a discount. Room rates are lowest in sweltering August. Easter, September, and Christmas are most crowded and expensive. On Easter, April 25, and May 1, the entire city gets booked up.

English works in all but the cheapest places. Traffic in Rome roars. My challenge: To find friendly places on quiet streets. With the recent arrival of double-paned windows and air-conditioning, night noise is not the problem it was. Even so, light sleepers should always ask for a *tranquillo* room. Many prices here are promised only to people who show this book and reserve directly, without using a room-finding service. And many places prefer hard cash.

Bed-and-breakfasts are booming in Rome, offering comfy doubles in the old center for around €80. The Beehive hostel is a good contact for booking B&Bs in Rome (www.cross-pollinate .com, see "Sleeping in Hostels and Dorms," below).

Your hotel can point you to the nearest **Laundromat** (usually open daily 08:00–22:00, about €6 to wash and dry a 15-pound load). The Bolle Blu chain comes with Internet access (€4.25/hr, near train station at Via Milazzo 20, Via Palestro 59, and Via Principe Amedeo 116, tel. 06-446-5804).

Most hotels are eager to connect you with a shuttle service to the airport. It's reasonable and easy for leaving, but upon arrival I think it's easiest to simply catch a cab or the shuttle train.

Almost no hotels have parking, but nearly all have a line on spots in a nearby garage (about €21/day).

Sleeping on Via Firenze *(zip code: 00184)*

I generally stay on Via Firenze because it's safe, handy, central, and relatively quiet. It's a 10-minute walk from the central train station and airport shuttle, and two blocks beyond Piazza della Repubblica and the TI. The Defense Ministry is nearby, and you've got heavily armed guards watching over you all night. Virtually all the orange buses that rumble down Via Nazionale (#64, #70, #115, #640) take you to Piazza Venezia (Forum) and Largo Argentina (Pantheon). From Largo Argentina, electric trolley #8 goes to Trastevere (first stop after crossing the river) and #64 (jammed with people and thieves) continues to St. Peter's. Farmacia Piram (Via Nazionale 228, tel. 06-488-4437) is the neighborhood 24-hour pharmacy.

Hotel Oceania is a peaceful slice of air-conditioned heaven. This 16-room, manor house–type hotel is spacious and quiet, with newly renovated and spotless rooms, run by a pleasant father-and-son team (Sb-€105, Db-€135, Tb-€165, Qb-€192, these prices through 2002 with this book only, additional 25 percent off in Aug and winter, phones, CC, Via Firenze 38, 3rd floor, tel. 06-482-4696, fax 06-488-5586, www.hoteloceania.it, e-mail: hoceania@tin.it, son Stefano SE, dad Armando serves world-famous coffee).

Hotel Aberdeen, while more formal and hotelesque, offers the same great value, with mini-bars, phones, and showers in its 36 modern, air-conditioned, and smoke-free rooms. It's warmly run by Annamaria, with support from her cousins Sabrina and Cinzia, and trusty Massimo riding shotgun after dark (Sb-€92, Db-€129, Tb-€154, Qb-€180, prices through 2002 with this book only, €30 less per room in Aug and winter, CC, free Internet access, nearby parking–€21/day, Via Firenze 48, tel. 06-482-3920, fax 06-482-1092, check for deals on Web, www.travel.it/roma/aberdeen, e-mail: hotel.aberdeen@travel.it, SE).

Residence Adler, with its wide halls, breakfast on a garden patio, and eight quiet, elegant, and air-conditioned rooms in a great locale, is another good deal. It's run the old-fashioned way by a charming family (Db-€103, Tb-€145, Qb-€176, prices through 2002 with this book only, CC, additional 5 percent off for cash, elevator, Via Modena 5, 2nd floor, tel. 06-484-466, fax 06-488-0940, gracious Sr. Brando Massini NSE but tries).

Residenza Cellini is a gorgeous new place with six rooms. It offers "ortho/anti-allergy beds" and four-star comforts and service on a small scale (Db-€155, larger Db-€181, €26 discount

Rome's Train Station Neighborhood

1. HOTEL OCEANIA & NARDIZZI
2. HOTEL ABERDEEN
3. RESIDENCE ADLER & RESIDENZA CELLINI
4. HOTEL REX
5. HOTEL BRITANNIA
6. HOTEL SONYA
7. HOTEL PENSIONE ITALIA
8. HOTEL CORTINA & CAFFETTERIA NAZIONALE
9. YWCA CASA STUDENTESSE
10. SUORE SANTA ELISABETTA
11. HOTEL MONTREAL
12. HOTEL FENICIA & MAGIC
13. ALBERGO SILEO
14. HOTEL DUCA D'ALBA
15. HOTEL GRIFO
16. SUORE DI SANT ANNA
17. SNACK BAR GASTRONOMIA
18. PASTICCERIA DAGNINO
19. HOSTARIA ROMANA
20. RISTORANTE GIOVANNI
21. PHARMACY
22. RIST. CINESE INT'L.
23. BEEHIVE HOSTEL & MONTE D.O.C. VINERIA
24. CASA OLMATA HOSTEL
25. PENSIONE PELLIGRINI
26. CLARIN HOTEL
27. TO HOTEL CASA KOLBE
28. HOTEL LANCELOT
29. HOTEL PABA
30. GULLIVER'S HOUSE ROME
31. REST. NERONE

in off-season—Nov–March plus Aug, these prices with this book and payment in cash through 2002, elevator, air-con, Via Modena 5, tel. 06-4782-5204, fax 06-4788-1806, www.residenzacellini.it, e-mail: residenzacellini@tin.it, SE).

Hotel Nardizzi Americana, with 18 simple, pleasant, air-conditioned rooms and a delightful rooftop terrace, is loosely run (Sb-€83, Db-€109, Tb-€129, Qb-€140, prices through 2002 with this book only, discounts for off-season and long stays, CC, additional 10 percent off with cash, elevator, Via Firenze 38, 4th floor, tel. 06-488-0368, fax 06-488-0035, SE).

Hotel Seiler is a quiet, serviceable place with 33 decent rooms (Sb-€83, Db-€119, Tb-€145, Qb-€165, these discounted prices good only with this book, CC, fans, elevator, Via Firenze 48, tel. 06-485-550, fax 06-488-0688, e-mail: acropoli@rdn.it, Silvio and Alessia SE).

Hotel Texas Seven Hills, a stark, institutional throwback to the 1960s, rents 18 dreary rooms (D-€83, Db-€93, often soft prices, CC, single-paned windows, Via Firenze 47, first elevator on the right to 3rd floor, tel. 06-481-4082, fax 06-481-4079, e-mail: reserva@texas7hills.com, NSE). Note: This place may go three stars in 2002.

Sleeping between Via Nazionale and Basilica Santa Maria Maggiore
(zip code: 00184 unless otherwise noted)

Hotel Pensione Italia, in a busy, interesting, and handy locale, is placed safely on a quiet street next to the Ministry of the Interior. Thoughtfully run by Andrea, Lena, and Alberico, it has 31 comfortable, airy, clean, and bright rooms (Sb-€67, Db-€93, Tb-€124, Qb-€145, air-con for €8 extra, prices through 2002 with this book and cash only, all rooms 20 percent off in mid-July–Aug and winter, elevator, Via Venezia 18, just off Via Nazionale, tel. 06-482-8355, fax 06-474-5550, www.hotelitaliaroma.com, e-mail: hitalia@pronet.it, SE). Most rooms have a fan. Their fine singles are all on the quiet courtyard, and the eight annex rooms across the street are a cut above the rest.

Clarin Hotel, a plain and worn slumbermill with 21 rooms, is quiet, safe, and run with a smile (Db-€88, Tb-€109, Qb-€129, prices good with this book and cash, 3 percent extra with CC, Via Palermo 36, tel. 06-4782-5170, fax 06-4788-1393, e-mail: clarinhotel@hotmail.com, Renaldo, Franco, and Marco SE).

Hotel Sonya is a small, family-run, but impersonal place with 20 comfortable, well-equipped rooms, a great location, and decent prices (Db-€119, Tb-€134, Qb-€155, Quint/b-€170, CC, air-con, elevator, facing the Opera at Via Viminale 58, tel. 06-481-9911, fax 06-488-5678, e-mail: hotelsonyaroma @katamail.com, Francesca SE).

Hotel Cortina rents 14 modern, air-conditioned rooms on a busy street. Ask for a quieter room on the courtyard or side street (Db-€129 in 2002 with this book, CC, Via Nazionale 18, tel. 06-481-9794, fax 06-481-9220, www.travel.it /roma/hotelcortina, e-mail: hotelcortina@pronet.it, John Carlo and Angelo SE).

Hotel Montreal, run with care, is a bright, solid, business-class place on a big street a block southeast of Santa Maria Maggiore (Db-usually €103 but €88 July–Aug and €78 in winter, CC, 21 of its 27 rooms have air-con; elevator, good security, 1 block from Metro: Vittorio, 3 blocks west of train station, Via Carlo Alberto 4, 00185 Roma, tel. 06-445-7797, fax 06-446-5522, www.hotelmontrealroma.com).

Splurges: **Hotel Britannia** stands like a marble fruitcake, offering all the comforts in tight quarters. Lushly renovated with over-the-top classical motifs, its 32 air-conditioned rooms are small but comfortable with bright, modern bathrooms (Db-€233 in May–June and Sept–Oct, Db-€152 in Aug, Db-€207 the rest of the year, extra bed-€52, CC, free parking, Via Napoli 64, tel. 06-488-3153, fax 06-488-2343, www.hotelbritannia.it, e-mail: info@hotelbritannia.it).

Hotel Rex is a business-class, Art Deco fortress—a quiet, plain, and stately four-star place with 50 rooms and all the comforts (Sb-€201, Db-€253, Tb-€294, CC, elevator, air-con, Via Torino 149, tel. 06-482-4828, fax 06-488-2743, e-mail: hotel.rex@alfanet.it, SE).

YWCA and Convents: **YWCA Casa Per Studentesse** accepts men and women. It's an institutional place, filled with white-uniformed maids, more-colorful Third World travelers, and 75 single beds (€26 per person in 3- and 4-bed rooms, S-€36, Sb-€46, D-€62, Db-€73, includes breakfast except on Sun, no CC, elevator, Via C. Albo 4, tel. 06-488-0460, fax 06-487-1028). The YWCA faces a great little street market.

Suore di Santa Elisabetta is a heavenly Polish-run convent. While often booked long in advance and a challenge in communication, it's an incredible value (S-€27, Sb-€34, D-€48, Db-€63, Tb-€80, Qb-€98, CC, elevator, fine view roof terrace, a block southwest of Basilica Santa Maria Maggiore at Via dell' Omata 9, tel. 06-488-8271, fax 06-488-4066).

Pensione Per Pelligrini is another nun-run place with 39 big, simple rooms and lots of twin beds. There's a language barrier, but the price is right (S-€34, Sb-€41, D-€67, Db-€78, Tb-€89, breakfast-€4.25, closed Aug, no CC, peaceful garden, elevator, just off Piazza Vittorio Emmanuel II, Istituto Buon Salvatore, Via Leopardi 17, from station take bus #714, #649, or #360 or Metro: Vittorio Emmanuel, tel. 06-446-7147 or 06-446-7225, fax 06-446-1382, Sister Anna Maria SE).

Sleeping Cheap, Northeast of the Train Station
(zip code: 00185)

The cheapest hotels in town are northeast of the station. Some travelers feel this area is weird and spooky after dark, but these hotels feel plenty safe. With your back to the train tracks, turn right and walk two blocks out of the station. The first two hotels are located in the same building.

Hotel Fenicia rents 11 comfortable, well-equipped rooms at a fine price. The bigger rooms upstairs are quieter, but there's no elevator (Sb-€47, Db-€73, Tb-€98, bigger and fancier Db-€83, prices through 2002 with this book only, air-con-€10.50/day, breakfast-€5.25, says she takes CC but doesn't, Via Milazzo 20, tel. & fax 06-490-342, www.fenicia.web-page.net, e-mail: fenicia@tiscalinet.it, Georgio and Anna SE).

Hotel Magic, a clean, marbled, family-run place with 10 rooms, is high enough off the road to escape the traffic noise (Sb-€52, Db-€73, Tb-€103, Qb-€114, air-con-€10.50/day, breakfast-€3.75, prices through 2002 with this book only, cheaper in Aug and winter, CC, thin walls, midnight curfew, Via Milazzo 20, 3rd floor, tel. & fax 06-495-9880, little English spoken).

Albergo Sileo is a shiny-chandeliered, 10-room place with an elegant touch. It has a contract to house train conductors who work the night shift. Most of the simple, pleasant rooms are rented from 19:00 to 09:00 only. If you can handle this, it's a great value. During the day, they store your luggage, and, though you won't have access to a room, you're welcome to hang out in their lobby or bar (D-€39, Db-€47, Tb-€62, Db for 24 hours-€62— a steal, elevator, Via Magenta 39, tel. & fax 06-445-0246, friendly Alessandro and Maria Savioli NSE).

Sleeping near the Colosseum (zip code: 00184)

These places are buried in a very Roman world of exhaust-stained medieval ambience. Take the subway one stop from the train station to Metro: Cavour. The handy *electrico* bus line #117 (San Giovanni in Laterano, Colosseo, Via dei Serpenti, Trevi Fountain, Piazza di Spagna, and Piazza del Popolo) connects you with the sights.

Hotel Paba is a little six-room place, chocolate-box tidy and lovingly cared for by Alberta and Pasquale Castelli. While overlooking busy Via Cavour just two blocks from the Colosseum, it's quiet enough (Db-€124, extra bed-€21, show this book for 5 percent discount, breakfast served in room, CC, air-con, elevator, Via Cavour 266, tel. 06-4782-4902, fax 06-4788-1225, www.hotelpaba.com, e-mail: info@hotelpaba.com).

Hotel Duca d'Alba, a tight and modern pastel-marble-hardwood place, is more professional than homey (Sb-€134, Db-€201, much cheaper July–Aug and winter, extra bed-€21, CC, air-con, safes, phones, TV, elevator, Via Leonina 14, tel.

06-484-471, fax 06-488-4840, check Web site for deals, www
.hotelducadalba.com, SE).

Hotel Grifo has a homey, tangled floor plan with 20
modern rooms and a roof terrace. The double-paned windows
almost keep out the Vespa noise (Db-€119, €109 July–Aug,
CC, elevator, air-con, some rooms have terraces, 2 blocks off
Via Cavour at Via del Boschetto 144, tel. 06-487-1395, fax
06-474-2323, e-mail: alez@dds.nl, SE).

Suore di Sant Anna was built for Ukrainian pilgrims. The
sisters are sweet. It's difficult (little English plus 23:00 curfew),
but once you're in, you've got a comfortable home in a classic
Roman village locale (Sb-€41, Db-€67, Tb-€101, consider
dinner for €15, no CC, off the corner of Via dei Serpenti and
Via Baccina at Piazza Madonna dei Monti 3, tel. 06-485-778,
fax 06-487-1064, e-mail: santasofia@tiscalinet.it).

Behind the Colosseum: **Hotel Lancelot**, a favorite among
United Nations workers, is a big 60-room place with a shady
courtyard, rooftop terrace, bar, and restaurant. It's quiet, safe,
well-run by Faris and Lubna Khan, and popular with returning
guests (Sb-€88–103, Db-€139, Tb-€163, Qb-€178, add €11
for balcony, CC, air-con, no elevator, parking-€11/day, behind
Colosseum near San Clemente Church at Via Capo D'Africa 47,
tel. 06-7045-0615, fax 06-7045-0640, www.venere.com/roma
/lancelot/lancelot.html, e-mail: lancelot@italyhotel.com).

Near the Palatine: The **Hotel Casa Kolbe**, located in a former
monastery, rents out 63 monkish, spartan rooms with no fans or
air-conditioning. With vast public spaces and a peaceful garden, it's
popular with groups. But the location is great: on the river side of
the Palatine ruins, on a quiet side street about a block from a little-
used entrance to the Forum (Sb-€62, Db-€78, Tb-€98, Qb-€109,
breakfast-€5.25, CC, elevator, garden, courtyard, not handy to public transit so taxi from the station, Via S. Teodoro 44, tel. 06-679-
4974 or 06-679-8866, fax 06-6994-1550, Maurizio and Antonio SE).

Sleeping near Campo de' Fiori (zip code: 00186)

You pay a premium to stay in the old center, but all of these
places are romantically set deep in the tangled back streets
near the idyllic Campo de' Fiori and are, for many, worth the
extra money.

Casa di Santa Brigida overlooks the elegant Piazza
Farnese. With soft-spoken sisters gliding down polished hallways, and pearly gates instead of doors, this lavish 23-room
convent makes exhaust-stained Roman tourists feel like they've
died and gone to heaven. If you're unsure of your destiny (and
don't need a double bed), this is worth the splurge (Sb-€78,
Db-€134, 3 percent extra with CC, great €16 dinners, roof
garden, plush library, air-con, physical address: Monserrato 54,

mailing address: Piazza Farnese 96, 00186 Roma, tel. 06-6889-2596, fax 06-6889-1573, www.brigidine.org/case/italy/welcome.html, e-mail: brigida@mclink.it, many of the sisters are from India and speak English). If you get no response to your fax or e-mail within three days, consider that a "no." Groups are very welcome here.

Hotel Smeraldo, while well-run, clean, and air-conditioned, is noisy at night, and its 50 rooms can be somewhat smoky (Sb-€73, D-€73, Db-€103, Tb-€124, CC, Civolo dei Chiodaroli 9, midway between Campo de' Fiori and Largo Argentina, tel. 06-687-5929, fax 06-6880-5495, www.hotelsmeraldoroma.com, e-mail: albergosmeraldoroma@tin.it).

Hotel Arenula, the only hotel in Rome's old Jewish quarter or ghetto, is a fine place in the thick of old Rome with 50 comfy rooms (Sb-€88, Db-€114, Tb-€134; €26 less in July, Aug, and winter; air-con- €10.50/day, CC, just off Via Arenula at Via Santa Maria de' Calderari 47, tel. 06-687-9454, fax 06-689-6188, www.hotelarenula.com, e-mail: hotel.arenula@flashnet.it).

Sleeping near the Pantheon (zip code: 00186)

These four places are buried in the pedestrian-friendly heart of ancient Rome, each within a four-minute walk of the Pantheon. You'll pay more here—but save time and money by being exactly where you want to be for your early and late wandering.

Hotel Due Torri hides out on a tiny, quiet street. It feels professional yet homey, with an accommodating staff, generous public spaces, and 26 comfortable-if-small rooms—four with balconies (Sb-€98, Db-€165, family apartment-€222 for 3 and €248 for 4, CC, air-con, Vicolo del Leonetto 23, a block off Via della Scrofa, tel. 06-6880-6956, fax 06-686-5442, www.hotelduetorriroma.com, e-mail: hotelduetorri@interfree.it).

Piazza Navona: **Hotel Navona**, while pretty ramshackle, is a fine value, offering 35 basic rooms in an ancient building (with a perfect locale) a block off Piazza Navona. Top-floor rooms come with more character (wood beams) and more stairs (D-€98, Db-€109, air-con-€16/day, family rooms, no CC, Via dei Sediari 8, tel. 06-686-4203, fax 06-6880-3802, www.hotelnavona.com, e-mail: info@hotelnavona.com, run by a friendly Australian named Corry, his Italian wife Patricia, and her dad Pino).

Residenza Zanardelli is a sumptuous little place with six classy and quiet rooms. Also owned by Corry, it's two blocks north of Piazza Navona (Db-€134, air-con-€10.50/day, no CC, on busy street but double-paned windows minimize noise, Via G. Zanardelli 7, tiny name next to doorbell, tel. 06-6821-1392 or 06-6880-9760, fax 06-6880-3802).

Hotel Nazionale, a four-star landmark, is a 16th-century palace sharing a well-policed square with the national Parliament.

Hotels and Restaurants in the Heart of Rome

- ❶ CASA DI SANTA BRIGIDA
- ❷ HOTEL SMERALDO
- ❸ TO HOTEL ARENULA
- ❹ HOTEL DUE TORRI
- ❺ HOTEL NAVONA
- ❻ RESIDENZA ZANARDELLI
- ❼ HOTEL NAZIONALE
- ❽ TAVERNA REST., VINERIA REST. & LA CARBONARA REST.
- ❾ OSTARIA DA GIOVANNI AR GALLETTO
- ❿ OSTERIA ENOTECA AL BRIC
- ⓫ FILETTI DE BACCALA & TRATTORIA DER PALLARO
- ⓬ RIST. GROTTE DEL TEATRO DI POMPEO

- ⓭ CUL DE SAC BAR & L'INSALATA RICCA REST.
- ⓮ BREK REST.
- ⓯ IL DELFINO REST.
- ⓰ OSTERIA DA MARIO REST.
- ⓱ REST. MYOSOTIS DI MARSILI
- ⓲ ENOTECA SPIRITI
- ⓳ TO RIST. ALLA RAMPA
- ⓴ RIST. LA TAVERNA DEGLI AMICI
- ㉑ RIST. PIZZERIA SACRO & PROFANO
- ㉒ GIOLITTI GELATERIA
- ㉓ GELATERIA DELLA PALMA

Its 90 rooms are served by lush public spaces, fancy bars, and a uniformed staff. It's a big hotel with a revolving front door, but it's a worthy splurge if you want security, comfort, and the heart of old Rome at your doorstep (Sb-€186, Db-€289, extra person-€62, suite-€439, less in Aug and winter, CC, air-con, elevator, free loaner motorbikes, Piazza Montecitorio 131, tel. 06-695-001, fax 06-678-6677, www.nazionaleroma.it, e-mail: hotel@nazionaleroma .it, SE). See their Web site for weekend and summer discounts of about 25 percent.

Sleeping in Trastevere (zip code: 00153)

Hotel Santa Maria sits like a lazy hacienda in the midst of Trastevere. Surrounded by a medieval skyline, you'll feel as if you're on some romantic stage set. Its 18 small but well-equipped rooms—former cells in a cloister—are all ground floor, circling a gravelly courtyard of orange trees and stay-awhile patio furniture. Because this is the only hotel in Trastevere, you'll pay about 25 percent more—but for poets, it's a deal (Db-€155, Tb-€191, Qb-€217, for this special price it's cash only, prices good with this book through 2002, 3-night min, CC, air-con, a block north of Piazza Maria Trastevere at Vicolo del Piede 2, tel. 06-589-4626, fax 06-589-4815, www.htlsantamaria.com, e-mail: hotelsantamaria @libero.it, Stefano SE).

Sleeping "Three Stars" near the Vatican Museum (zip code: 00192)

To locate hotels, see map on page 60.

Hotel Alimandi is a good value, run by the friendly and entrepreneurial Alimandi brothers: Paolo, Enrico, and Luigi, and the next generation: Marta and Germano. Their 35 rooms are air-conditioned, modern, and marbled in white (Sb-€85, Db-€145, Tb-€168, 5 percent discount with this book and cash, CC, elevator, a grand buffet breakfast is served in their great roof garden, self-service washing machines, Internet access, pool table, grand piano lounge, free parking, down the stairs directly in front of the Vatican Museum, Via Tunisi 8, near Metro: Cipro-Musei Vaticani, reserve by phone, no reply to fax means they are full, tel. 06-3972-6300, toll-free in Italy tel. 800-122-121, fax 06-3972-3943, www.alimandi .org, e-mail: alimandi@tin.it, SE). They offer free airport pickup and drop-off, though you must reserve when you book your room and wait for a scheduled shuttle (every 2 hours, see their Web site). Maria Alimandi rents out three rooms in her apartment, a 20-minute bus ride from the Vatican (Db-€78, see www.alimandi.org).

Hotel Spring House, with a hotelesque feel, offers 51 attractive rooms—some with balconies or terraces (Db-€129, Tb-€155, mention this book, 15 percent discount July–Aug and winter plus additional 5 percent discount for cash payment, weekend deals,

CC, Internet access, air-con, elevator, free loaner bikes, Metro: Cipro-Musei Vaticani, Via Mocenigo 7, 2 blocks from Vatican Museum, tel. 06-3972-0948, fax 06-3972-1047, www.hotelspringhouse.com, Stefano Gabbani SE).

Hotel Gerber is sleek, modern, and air-conditioned, with 27 businesslike rooms set in a quiet residential area (S-€62, Sb-€98, Db-€129, Tb-€150, Qb-€170, 10 percent discount with this book, CC, air-con, Via degli Scipioni 241, a block from Metro: Lepanto, at intersection with Ezio, tel. 06-321-6485, fax 06-321-7048, www.hotelgerber.it, Peter and Simonetta SE).

Hotel Sant' Anna is pricier than the rest, located on a charming-for-Rome pedestrian street that fills up with restaurant tables at dinnertime. Its 20 rooms are overly decorated with classical themes, but the furnishings are comfy (Sb-€145, Db-€181, Db-€145 in July–Aug and winter, CC, air-con, elevator, courtyard, Borgo Pio 133, near intersection with Mascherino, a couple blocks from entrance to St. Peter's, tel. 06-6880-1602, fax 06-6830-8717, www.travel.it/roma/santanna, SE).

Hotel Bramante sits like a grand medieval lodge in the shadow of the fortified escape wall that runs from the Vatican to Castel San Angelo. The public spaces and the 16 rooms are generously sized, with rough wood beams and high ceilings (Sb-€129, Db-€181, Tb-€217, Qb-€253, 8 percent discount with this book, CC, air-con, no elevator, Vicolo delle Palline 24, tel. 06-6880-6426, fax 06-687-9881, www.hotelbramante.com, e-mail: bramante@excalhq.it, Loredana SE).

Sleeping in Hostels and Dorms (zip code: 00184)

For easy communication with young, friendly entrepreneurs, cheap dorm beds, and the very cheapest doubles in town—within a 10-minute hike of the train station—consider the following places:

Casa Olmata is a laid-back backpackers' place midway between the Termini train station and Colosseum (dorm beds €16–18, S-€34, bunk bed D-€36, one queen-size D-€55, no CC, lots of stairs, laundry service, free Internet access, video rentals, games, rooftop terrace with views, communal kitchen, dinners twice weekly, a block southwest of Basilica Santa Maria Maggiore, Via dell' Omata 36, 3rd floor, tel. 06-483-019, fax 06-474-2854, www.casaolmata.com, e-mail: casaolmata30@hotmail.com, Mirella and Marco).

The Beehive is especially good for older vagabonds. This tidy little place has two six-bed dorms (€16 beds) and a guests' kitchen on the main floor. Upstairs are five hotel-type rooms that are a great value (Sb-€39, D-€52, T-€78, Q-€103). It's thoughtfully run by a friendly young American couple, Steve and Linda (CC, dorms closed 13:00–16:00, 2 blocks south of Basilica Santa Maria Maggiore at Via Giovanni Lanza 99, tel. 06-474-0719, www.the-beehive.com). They also run a B&B booking service (fine private rooms in the city's old center, offering comparable quality for €65–95—about half the cost of a hotel, www .cross-pollinate.com).

Gulliver's House Rome is a fun little hostel in a very safe and handy locale, run by Simon and Sara. Its 24 beds in cramped quarters work fine for backpackers (€18 per bunk bed in 8-bed dorm, D-€57, no CC, closed 12:00–16:00, Via Palermo 36, tel. 06-481-7680, www.gullivershouse.com, e-mail: info@gullivershouse.com).

Eating in Rome

Romans spend their evenings eating rather than drinking, and the preferred activity is simply to enjoy a fine, slow meal, buried deep in the old city. Rome's a fun and cheap place to eat, with countless little eateries serving memorable $20 meals.

Although I've listed a number of restaurants, I recommend that you just head for a scenic area and explore. Piazza Navona, the Pantheon area, Campo de' Fiori, and Trastevere are neighborhoods packed with characteristic eateries. Sitting with tourists on a famous square enjoying the scene works fine or, for places more out of the way, consider my recommendations.

For Rome's best gelato, see "Eating near the Pantheon," below.

Eating in Trastevere

Colorful Trastevere is also now pretty touristy. Still, Romans join the tourists to eat on the rustic side of the Tiber River. Start at the central square (Piazza Santa Maria in Trastevere). Then choose: Eat with tourists enjoying the ambience of the famous square, or wander the back streets in search of a mom-and-pop place with barely a menu. Consider these places before making a choice (all are in the tangle of lanes between Ponte Sisto and the Piazza Santa Maria in Trastevere—see map on page 70):

At **Taverna del Moro da Tony**, Tony scrambles—with a great antipasti table—to keep his happy eaters (mostly tourists) well-fed and returning. Until we start telling him to "hold the mayo," his bruschetta will come buried in it (Tue–Sun 12:00–24:00, closed Mon, off Via del Moro at Vicolo del Cinque 36, tel. 06-580-9165).

For good home cooking Roman-style, consider these two fun little places (within a block of each other): **Trattoria da Lucia** (closed Mon, indoor or outdoor seating, Vicolo del Mattonato 2, tel. 06-580-3601) and the homey **Trattoria de Olindo** (closed Sun, Vicolo della Scala 8, tel. 06-581-8835).

Osteria Ponte Sisto, a rough-and-tumble little place, specializes in traditional Roman cuisine. Since it's just outside of the tourist zone, it offers the best value and caters mostly to Romans. It's also easiest to find: As you approach Trastevere, crossing Ponte Sisto (pedestrian bridge), continue across the little square (Piazza Trilussa), and it's on the right (open daily, Via Ponte Sisto 80, tel. 06-588-3411).

Panificio Arnese could be the most respected traditional bakery in town (daily 09:00–21:00, Via del Politeama 27). Pop in and eat something fresh out of the oven. And the fine little *gelateria* (across from the church on Piazza della Scala) dishes up oh-wow pistachio.

Eating on and near Campo de' Fiori

While touristy, Campo de' Fiori offers a classic, romantic square setting. And since it is so close to the collective heart of Rome, it remains popular with locals. For greater atmosphere than food value, circle the square, considering each place. Bars and pizzerias seem to overwhelm the square. The **Taverna** and **Vineria** at numbers 16 and 15 offer good perches from which to people-watch and nurse a glass of wine. The only real restaurant is **La Carbonara**. While not the birthplace of pasta carbonara, it does serve good food (closed Tue, Piazza Campo de Fiori 23, tel. 06-686-4783). Meals on small nearby streets are a better value but lack that Campo de' Fiori magic.

Nearby, on the more elegant and peaceful Piazza Farnese, **Ostaria Da Giovanni Ar Galletto** has a dressier local crowd, great outdoor seating, and moderate prices. Giovanni and his son Angelo serve fine food; but, unfortunately, single diners have been turned away (closed Sun, tucked in corner of Piazza Farnese at #102, tel. 06-686-1714). Of all my listings, Giovanni offers perhaps the best *al fresco* dining experience.

Osteria Enoteca al Bric is a mod Italian/French bistro–type place run by a man who loves to cook and serve good wine. Wine case lids decorate the wall like happy memories. With candlelit elegance and no tourists, it's perfect for the wine snob in the mood for pasta and fine cheese. Choose your bottle (or half bottle) from the huge selection lining the walls as you enter (open from 19:30, closed Mon, CC, 100 meters off Campo dei' Fiori at Via del Pellegrino 51, tel. 06-687-9533).

Filetti de Baccala is a tradition for many Romans. Basically a fish bar with paper tablecloths and cheap prices, it features grease-stained, hurried waiters who serve old-time favorites— fried cod fillets, a strange, bitter *puntarelle* salad, and delightful anchovies with butter—to nostalgic locals (Mon–Sat 17:30–23:00, closed Sun, a block east of Campo de' Fiori tumbling onto a tiny and atmospheric square, Largo dei Librari 88, tel. 06-686-4018).

Trattoria der Pallaro has no menu but plenty of return eaters. Paola Fazi—with a towel wrapped around her head, turban-style—and her family serve up a five-course festival of typically Roman food for €17.50, including wine, coffee, and a wonderful mandarin liqueur. Their slogan: "Here, you'll eat what we want to feed you." Make like Oliver Twist asking for more soup and get seconds on the mandarin liqueur (Tue–Sun 12:00–15:30, 19:30–24:00, closed Mon, indoor/outdoor seating on quiet square, a block south of Corso Vittorio Emmanuele, down Largo del Chiavari to Largo del Pallaro 15, tel. 06-6880-1488).

Ristorante Grotte del Teatro di Pompeo, sitting atop an ancient theater, serves good food at fair prices with a smile (closed Mon, Via del Biscione 73, tel. 06-6880-3686). This is great if you want to dine on a characteristic street busy with people strolling.

Between Campo de Fiori and Piazza Navona: For interesting bar munchies, try **Cul de Sac** on Piazza Pasquino (often crowded, daily 12:00–18:00, 19:00–24:00, a block southwest of Piazza Navona). **L'Insalata Ricca**, next door, is a popular chain that specializes in hearty and healthy salads (daily 12:00–15:45, 18:45–22:00, Piazza Pasquino 72, tel. 06-6830-7881). Another branch is nearby with more spacious outdoor seating (just off Corso Vittorio Emmanuele on Largo del Chiavari).

Eating near the Pantheon

You'll find a mix of cafeterias, groceries, restaurants, wine bars, and gelato shops.

Cafeterias: **Brek**, on Largo Argentina just south of the Pantheon, is an appealing, self-service restaurant with a modern, efficient atmosphere and really cheap prices (daily 12:00–15:30, 18:30–23:00, skip the sandwiches and pizza slices downstairs and go to the cafeteria upstairs, northwest corner of square, Largo Argentina 1, tel. 06-6821-0353).

Il Delfino, also on Largo Argentina, is a tired but handy self-service cafeteria that serves throughout the day (daily 07:00–21:00, not cheap but fast). Across the side street, **Frullati di Frutta** sells refreshing fruity frappés.

Grocery: The *alimentari* on the Pantheon square will make you a sandwich for a temple-porch picnic. Sit at the base of a column in the shade and munch lunch.

Restaurants: **Osteria da Mario**, a great little mom-and-pop joint with a no-stress menu, serves delicious traditional favorites. You'll feel right at home with locals who know a good value. The pop (Mario), who passed away—you'll see his photo on the wall—would be happy with the way his wife and kids are carrying on (Mon–Sat 13:00–15:00, 19:30–23:00, closed Sun, 2 blocks in front of Pantheon and to the left at Piazza delle Coppelle 51, tel. 06-6880-6349).

Ristorante Myosotis di Marsili, a dressy place with black-tie waiters and a coat check, is popular with local politicians and diners classy enough to look into the fish locker and make a knowledgeable choice. It has a traditional yet imaginative menu with a good wine list (Mon–Sat 12:30–15:30, 19:30–23:30, closed Sun, reservations smart, near Osteria da Mario 2 blocks in front of Pantheon at Vicolo Della Vaccarella 3, tel. 06-686-5554).

Wine Bar: **Enoteca Spiriti**, a wine bar two blocks from the Pantheon, is run by Raffaele, son Matteo, and daughter Daria. They serve great wine ("*corposo*" means full-bodied) by the glass and light meals with integrity. Raffaele and I have designed a treat for travelers with this book: "A Taste of Italy for Two" includes two glasses of fine Amarone wine (or the equivalent in value), fresh bread, and a plate decorated with a tasty variety of Italian cheeses and meats for a total of €16. Choose: Cool jazz interior or classic Roman sidewalk exterior (open at 12:30, very busy with local office workers at 13:30, dinner from 19:30, facing Pantheon walk around to the right and take 2 rights to Via S. Eustachio 5).

Gelato: Two of Rome's top ice-cream joints are a minute's walk in front of the Pantheon. The venerable **Giolitti's** (just off Piazza Colonna and Piazza Monte Citorio on Via Uffici del Vicario) is good with cheap take-away prices and elegant Old World seating. But **Gelateria della Palma** is the new king of gelato— fresher, tastier, and with more options, including sugar-free and frozen yogurt varieties (100 flavors, 2 blocks in front of Pantheon at Via della Maddalena 20, tel. 06-6880-6752).

Eating near the Spanish Steps

Ristorante Alla Rampa is a classic old restaurant tucked away just around the corner from the touristy crush of the Spanish Steps. You'll get quality Roman cooking here, with great indoor/outdoor ambience, for a moderate price. They take no reservations, so arrive by 19:30 or be prepared to wait (closed Sun, 100 meters east of Spanish Steps at Piazza Mignanelli 18, tel. 06-678-2621).

Eating near Piazza Venezia

Ristorante La Taverna degli Amici is a dressy yet friendly, candlelit place draped in ivy and tucked away on a sleepy square two blocks toward the Pantheon from the Victor Emmanuel Monument. This is a great and peaceful spot for a break before or after your Capital Hill sightseeing. The waiters are friendly, and the clientele is local and upscale (reserve for dinner to avoid the basement, Tue–Sun 12:30–15:00, 19:30–24:00, closed Mon, Piazza Margana 36, tel. 06-6920-0493).

Eating near the Trevi Fountain

Ristorante Pizzeria Sacro e Profano is a bright and trendy place energetically filling an old church with spicy south Italian (Calabrian) cuisine and great pizzas. Run by friendly and helpful Pasquale and friends, this is just far enough away from the

Trevi mobs (a block off Via del Tritone at Via dei Maroniti 29, tel. 06-6791-836).

Eating between the Colosseum and St. Peter-in-Chains Church

You find good views but poor value in the restaurants directly behind the Colosseum. To get your money's worth, eat a block away from the Colosseum. There are two handy eateries at the top of Terme Di Tito, a block uphill from the Colosseum, near St. Peter-in-Chains Church (of Michelangelo's *Moses* fame).

For a real restaurant meal, try **Ostaria da Nerone**. The Santis family serves traditional Roman cuisine in a homey indoor or outdoor setting (Mon–Sat 12:00–15:00, 19:00–23:00, closed Sun, Via delle Terme di Titi 96, tel. 06-481-7952). Next door at **Caffè dello Studente**, Pina and Mauro serve typical "bar gastronomia" fare (pizza, toasted sandwiches, various drinks). Stand up at the crowded bar, take away, or enjoy the outdoor tables (Mon–Sat 07:30–21:30, closed Sun, tel. 06-488-3240).

Eating near Via Firenze and Via Nazionale Hotels

Snack Bar Gastronomia is a great local hole-in-the-wall for lunch or dinner (daily 07:00–24:00, fresh meat or veggie sandwiches, fresh squeezed juices, and Greek-style yogurt—yummy with fruit—ask the price first, Via Firenze 34). There's a classic old-fashioned *alimentari* (grocery) across the street (7:00–19:30).

Pasticceria Dagnino—popular for its top-quality Sicilian specialties, especially pastries and ice cream—is frequented by people who work at my recommended hotels (daily 07:00–22:00, in Galleria Esedra off Via Torino, tel. 06-481-8660). Their *arancino*—a rice, cheese, and ham ball—is a greasy Sicilian favorite, and their cannoli is sweet. Direct the construction of your meal at the bar, pay for your trayful at the cashier, and climb upstairs, where you'll find the dancing Sicilian girls (free).

Hostaria Romana is a great place for traditional Roman cuisine. For an air-conditioned, classy, local favorite run by a jolly group of men who enjoy their work, eat here (closed Sun, midway between Trevi Fountain and Piazza Barberini, Via del Boccaccio 1, at intersection with Via Rasella, no reservations needed before 20:00, tel. 06-474-5284). Go ahead and visit the antipasto bar in person to assemble your plate. They're happy to serve an *antipasti misto della casa* and pasta dinner. Take a hard look at their *Specialita Romane* list.

Ristorante da Giovanni is a serviceable, hardworking place, feeding locals and tired travelers now for 50 years (tired €12 menu, Mon–Sat 12:00–15:00, 19:00–22:30, closed Sun, CC, just off Via XX Settembre at Via Antonio Salandra 1, tel. 06-485-950).

Cafeteria Nazionale, with woody elegance, offers light

lunches—including salads—at reasonable prices (Mon–Sat 07:00–20:00, closed Sun, CC, Via Nazionale 26-27, at intersection with Via Agostino de Pretis, tel. 06-4899-1716). Their lunch buffet is a delight (€7.50, 12:30–15:00).

Ristorante Cinese Internazionale is your best neighborhood bet for Chinese (daily 12:00–15:00, 18:00–23:00, inexpensive, no pasta, just off Via Nazionale behind Hotel Luxor at Via Agostino de Pretis 98, tel. 06-474-4064).

Restaurant Target is a soulless, modern, but handy place serving decent pizza and pasta near recommended hotels (open daily, indoor and outdoor seating, don't expect great service, Via Torino 33, tel. 06-474-0066).

The **McDonald's** restaurants on Piazza della Repubblica (free piazza seating outside), Piazza Barberini, and Via Firenze offer air-conditioned interiors and salad bars.

Flann O'Brien Irish Pub is an entertaining place for a quick light meal (of pasta or something *other* than pasta, served early or late when other places are closed), fine Irish beer, live sporting events on TV, and perhaps the most Italian crowd of all (daily 07:30–01:00, Via Nazionale 17, at intersection with Via Napoli, tel. 06-488-0418).

Eating near Santa Maria Maggiore

For a classy taste of Tuscany in a woody wine bar filled with local office workers, drop by **Monti D.O.C. Vineria** Wine Bar for lunch (chalkboard shows the daily specials, daily 10:00–24:00, 2 blocks from basilica next to recommended Beehive hostel at Via Giovanni Lanza 93, tel. 06-487-2696).

Eating near the Vatican Museum and St. Peter's

Avoid the restaurant pushers handing out fliers near the Vatican: bad food, expensive menu tricks. Try any of these instead:

Antonio's Hostaria dei Bastioni is tasty and friendly. It's conveniently located midway on your hike from St. Peter's to the Vatican Museum, with noisy streetside seating and a quiet interior (Mon–Sat 12:00–15:00, 19:00–23:30, closed Sun, €5.25–6.25 pastas, €7.75 *secondi*, no cover charge, at corner of Vatican wall, Via Leone IV 29, tel. 06-3972-3034). Antonio is your gracious host.

La Rustichella serves a sprawling antipasti buffet (€7.75 for a meal-sized plate). Arrive when they open at 19:30 to avoid a line and have the pristine buffet to yourself (Tue–Sun 12:30–15:00, 19:30–23:00, closed Mon, near Metro: Cipro-Musei Vaticani stop, opposite church at end of Via Candia, Via Angelo Emo 1, tel. 06-3972-0649). Consider the fun and fruity **Gelateria Millennium** next door.

Viale Giulio Cesare is lined with cheap **Pizza Rustica**

shops and fun eateries, such as **Cipriani Self-Service Rosticcería** (closed Mon, pleasant outdoor seating, near Ottaviano subway stop, Viale Guilio Cesare 195). Restaurants such as **Tre Pupazzi** lining the pedestrian-only Borgo Pio, a block from Piazza San Pietro, are worth a look.

Turn your nose loose in the wonderful **Via Andrea Doria** open-air market, three blocks north of the Vatican Museum (Mon–Sat roughly 07:00–13:30, until 16:30 on Tue and Fri except summer, between Via Tunisi and Via Andrea Doria). If the market is closed, try the nearby **IN's supermarket** (Mon–Sat 08:30–13:30, 16:00–20:00 but closed Thu eve, a half block straight out from Via Tunisi entrance of open-air market, Via Francesco 18).

Transportation Connections—Rome
Termini is the central station (see "Arrival in Rome," on page 39; Metro: Termini). Tiburtina is the bus station (4 Metro stops away from train station; Metro: Tiburtina).

By train from Rome to: Venice (6/day, 5–8 hrs), **Florence** (12/day, 2 hrs, most stop at Orvieto en route), **Pisa** (8/day, 3–4 hrs), **Genova** (7/day, 6 hrs, overnight possible), **Milan** (12/day, 5 hrs, overnight possible), **Naples** (6/day, 2 hrs), **Brindisi** (2/day, 9 hrs), **Amsterdam** (2/day, 20 hrs), **Bern** (5/day, 10 hrs), **Frankfurt** (4/day, 14 hrs), **Munich** (5/day, 12 hrs), **Nice** (2/day, 10 hrs), **Paris** (5/day, 16 hrs), **Vienna** (3/day, 13–15 hrs). All-Italy train info: tel. 848-888-088.

By bus to: Assisi (3/day, 3 hrs), **Siena** (7/day, 3 hrs).

Rome's Airports
Rome's two airports—Fiumicino (a.k.a. Leonardo da Vinci) and the small Ciampino—share the same Web site (www.adr.it).

Fiumicino Airport: Rome's major airport has a TI (Mon–Sat 08:00–19:00, closed Sun, tel. 06-6595-4471), ATMs, banks, luggage storage, shops, and bars.

A slick, direct train connects the airport and Rome's central Termini train station in 30 minutes. Trains run twice hourly in both directions from roughly 07:30 to 22:00. From the airport, trains depart at :07 and :37 past the hour (from airport's arrival gate, follow signs to "Stazione/Railway Station"; buy ticket from a machine or the Biglietteria office; €9, CC). From the Termini train station, trains depart at :21 and :51 past the hour, usually from track 25; look for signs that say "Fiumicino" and confirm with an official or a local on the platform that the train is indeed going to the airport (€9, buy ticket from any *tabacchi* shop in station or at Alitalia desk near entrance to track 25; to reach track 25, walk along track 24 midway through the station, then follow signs that take you inside—to Alitalia desk—and down the escalator). Read your ticket: If it requires validation, stamp it in a yellow machine near the platform before boarding.

Your hotel can arrange a taxi to the airport at any hour for about €40. To get from the airport into town cheaply by taxi, try teaming up with any tourist also just arriving (most are heading for hotels near yours in the center). Splitting a taxi and hopping out once downtown at a taxi stand to take another to your hotel will save you about €15. Avoid unmarked, unmetered taxis.

For airport information, call 06-65951. To inquire about flights, call 06-6595-3640 (Alitalia: tel. 06-65643, British Air: toll-free tel. 848-812-266, Delta: toll-free tel. 800-864-114, KLM/Northwest: tel. 06-6501-1441, Lufthansa: tel. 06-6568-4004, SAS: tel. 06-6501-0771, Swiss Air: tel. 06-847-0555, United: tel. 0266-7481).

Ciampino Airport: Rome's smaller airport (tel. 06-794-941) handles budget and charter flights. To get to downtown Rome from the airport, take the LILA/Cotral bus (2/hr) to the Anagnina Metro stop, where you can connect by Metro to the stop nearest your hotel.

Driving in Rome

Greater Rome is circled by the Grande Raccordo Anulare. This ring road has spokes that lead you into the center. Entering from the north, leave the autostrada at the Settebagni exit. Following the ancient Via Salaria (and the black-and-white "Centro" signs), work your way doggedly into the Roman thick of things. This will take you along the Villa Borghese park and dump you right on Via Veneto (where there's an Avis office). Avoid rush hour and drive defensively: Roman cars stay in their lanes like rocks in an avalanche. Parking in Rome is dangerous. Park near a police station or get advice at your hotel. The Villa Borghese underground garage is handy (€18/day, Metro: Spagna).

Consider this: Your car is a worthless headache in Rome. Avoid a pile of stress and save money by parking at the huge, easy, and relatively safe lot behind the Orvieto station (follow "P" signs from autostrada) and catch the train to Rome (14/day, 75 min).

VENICE
(VENEZIA)

Soak all day in this puddle of elegant decay. Venice is Europe's best-preserved big city. This car-free urban wonderland of a hundred islands—laced together by 400 bridges and 2,000 alleys—survives on the artificial respirator of tourism.

Born in a lagoon 1,500 years ago as a refuge from barbarians, Venice is overloaded with tourists and is slowly sinking (unrelated facts). In the Middle Ages, the Venetians, becoming Europe's clever middlemen for east-west trade, created a great trading empire. By smuggling in the bones of St. Mark (San Marco, A.D. 828), Venice gained religious importance as well. With the discovery of America and new trading routes to the Orient, Venetian power ebbed. But as Venice fell, her appetite for decadence grew. Through the 17th and 18th centuries, Venice partied on the wealth accumulated through earlier centuries as a trading power.

Today Venice is home to about 65,000 people in its old city, down from a peak population of nearly 200,000. While there are about 500,000 in greater Venice (counting the mainland, not counting tourists), the old town has a small-town feel. Locals seem to know everyone. To see small-town Venice away from the touristic flak, escape the Rialto-San Marco tourist zone and savor the town early and late without the hordes of vacationers daytripping in from cruise ships and nearby beach resorts. A 10-minute walk from the madness puts you in an idyllic Venice few tourists see.

Planning Your Time

Venice is worth at least a day on even the speediest tour. Hyper-efficient train travelers take the night train in and/or out. Sleep in the old center to experience Venice at its best: early and late. For a one-day visit, cruise the Grand Canal, do the major sights

Venice

on St. Mark's Square (the square itself, Doge's Palace, and St.
Mark's Basilica), see the Church of the Frari (Chiesa dei Frari)
for art, and wander the back streets on a pub crawl (see "Eating,"
below). Venice's greatest sight is the city itself. Make time to
simply wander. While doable in a day, Venice is worth two.
It's a medieval cookie jar, and nobody's looking.

Orientation

The island city of Venice is shaped like a fish. Its major thoroughfares are canals. The Grand Canal winds through the middle of
the fish, starting at the mouth where all the people and food enter,
passing under the Rialto Bridge, and ending at St. Mark's Square
(San Marco). Park your 21st-century perspective at the mouth
and let Venice swallow you whole.

Venice is a carless kaleidoscope of people, bridges, and odor-
less canals. The city has no real streets, and addresses are hope-
lessly confusing. Each district has about 6,000 address numbers.
Luckily, it's easy to find your way, since many street corners have
a sign pointing you to the nearest major landmark, such as San
Marco, Accademia, Rialto, and Ferrovia (the train station). To
find your way, navigate by landmarks, not streets. Obedient visitors stick to the main thoroughfares as directed by these signs
and miss the charm of backstreet Venice.

Tourist Information

There are TIs at the train station (daily 08:00–20:00, crowded and
surly), at St. Mark's Square (Mon–Sat 09:45–15:15, with your back
to St. Mark's, it's in far corner of square to your left), and near St.
Mark's Square *vaporetto* stop (a *vaporetto* is a motorized bus-boat) on
the lagoon (daily 09:00–18:00, sells *vaporetto* tickets, rents audioguides
for self-guided walking tours). Smaller offices are at Tronchetto,
Piazzale Roma, and the airport. For a quick question, save time by
phoning (tel. 041-529-8711 or 041-522-5150, www.turismovenezia
.it). At any TI, pick up a free city map and the free *Leo* bimonthly
magazine, which comes with an insert, *Leo Bussola*, that lists museum
hours, exhibitions, and musical events (in Italian and English).
Confirm your sightseeing plans. Ask for the fine brochures outlining
three offbeat Venice walks. The free periodical entertainment guide
Un Ospite de Venezia (a monthly listing of events, nightlife, museum
hours, train and *vaporetto* schedules, emergency telephone numbers,
and so on) is available at the TI or fancy hotel reception desks.

Maps: The €3.10 Venice map on sale at postcard racks has
much more detail than the TI's free map, but the new "Illustrated
Venice Map" by Magnetic North is by far the best ever (€6.20,
listing nearly every shop, hotel, and restaurant). Also consider
the little guidebook (sold alongside the postcards), which comes
with a city map and explanations of the major sights.

Arrival in Venice

A three-kilometer-long causeway (with highway and train lines) connects Venice to the mainland. Mestre, Venice's sprawling mainland industrial base, has fewer crowds, cheaper hotels, and plenty of parking lots, but no charm. Don't stop here, unless you're parking your car in a lot. Trains regularly connect Mestre with Venice's Santa Lucia station (6/hr, 5 min). Don't leave your train at Venezia-Mestre—the next stop is Venezia Santa Lucia (end of the line for Venice).

By Train: Venice's Santa Lucia train station plops you right into the old town on the Grand Canal, an easy *vaporetto* ride or fascinating 40-minute walk from St. Mark's Square. Upon arrival, skip the station's crowded TI (the two TIs at St. Mark's Square are better); it's not worth a long wait for a miminal map (buy a good one from a newsstand with no wait). Confirm your departure plan (stop by train info desk or just study the *partenze*—departure—posters on walls). Consider storing unnecessary heavy bags, although lines for baggage check may be very long (baggage check at platform 14, €2.60/12 hrs, €5.20/24 hrs, daily 03:45–00:30; or lockers at platform 1—€1.60–2.60, often either in use or broken). Then walk straight out of the station to the canal. The dock for *vaporetti* #1 and #82 is on your left (for downtown Venice, most recommended hotels, and Grand Canal Tour); the dock for #51 and #52 is on your right (for some recommended hotels). Buy a €3.10 ticket (or €9.25 all-day pass) at the ticket window and hop on a boat for downtown (direction: Rialto or San Marco).

By Car: The freeway ends at Venice. Follow the green lights directing you to a parking lot with space, probably Tronchetto (across the causeway and on the right), which has a huge, multi-story garage (€15.50/day, half price with discount coupon from your hotel, tel. 041-520-7555). From there you'll find travel agencies masquerading as TIs and *vaporetto* docks for the boat connection (#82) to the town center. Don't let taxi boatmen con you out of the cheap (€3.10) *vaporetto* ride. Parking in Mestre is easy and cheap (open-air lots €4.10/day, €5.20/day garage across from Mestre train station).

By Plane: Romantics can jet to St. Mark's Square by Alila-guna speedboat (€9.75, hrly, 70 min, 06:15–24:00 from airport, 04:50–22:50 from St. Mark's Square, generally departing at :50 after each hour). A water taxi zips you directly to your hotel in 30 minutes for €80. Or, buses connect the airport and Piazzale Roma *vaporetto* stop: either the handy blue ATVO shuttle bus (€2.60, 2/hr, 20 min, 05:30–20:40 to airport, 08:30–24:00 from airport, www.atvo.it) or the cheaper orange ACTV bus #5 (€0.75, 1–3/hr, 20–40 min, 04:40–01:00). Airport info: tel. 041-260-611, flight info: tel. 041-260-9260.

Helpful Hints

Venice is expensive for locals as well as tourists. The demand is huge and running a business is costly. Things just cost more here. Perhaps the best way to enjoy Venice is to just succumb to its charms and blow a lot of money. Accept the fact that Venice was a tourist town 400 years ago. It was, is, and always will be crowded. While 80 percent of Venice is actually an untouristy place, 80 percent of the tourists never notice. Hit the back streets.

Get Lost: Venice is the ideal town to explore on foot. Walk and walk to the far reaches of the town. Don't worry about getting lost. Get as lost as possible. Keep reminding yourself, "I'm on an island, and I can't get off." When it comes time to find your way, just follow the directional arrows on building corners or simply ask a local, *"Dov'è San Marco?"* ("Where is St. Mark's?"). People in the tourist business (that's most Venetians) speak some English. If they don't, listen politely, watching where their hands point, say *"Grazie,"* and head off in that direction. If you're lost, pop into a hotel and ask for its business card—it comes with a map and a prominent "you are here."

Rip-Offs, Theft, and Help: While pickpockets work the crowded main streets, docks, and *vaporetti* (wear your money-belt and carry your daybag in front), the dark, late-night streets of Venice are safe. A service called Venezia No Problem tries to help tourists who've been mistreated by any Venetian business (toll-free tel. 800-355-920, for complaints only, not for information).

Water: Venetians pride themselves on having pure, safe, and tasty tap water piped in from the foothills of the Alps; you can actually see the mountains from Venice bell towers on crisp, clear winter days.

Money: ATMs are plentiful and the easiest way to go. Bank rates vary. I like the Banca di Sicilia, a block toward St. Mark's Square from Campo San Bartolomeo. The American Express change desk is just off St. Mark's Square (see "Travel Agencies," below). Non-bank exchange bureaus such as Exacto will cost you $10 more than a bank for a $200 exchange. A 24-hour cash machine near the Rialto *vaporetto* stop exchanges U.S. dollars and other currencies at fair rates.

Travel Agencies: If you need to get train tickets, pay supplements, or make reservations, avoid the time-consuming trip to the crowded station by using a downtown travel agency. Kele & Teo Viaggi e Turismo is good and handy (cash only, Mon–Fri 08:30–18:00, Sat 09:00–12:00, at Ponte dei Bareteri on the Mercerie midway between Rialto and St. Mark's Square, tel. 041-520-8722).

While American Express provides other travel services, it no longer sells train tickets and is of no help with reservations (Mon–Fri 09:00–17:30; change desk: Mon–Sat 08:30–20:00; about

2 blocks off St. Mark's Square at 1471, en route to the Accademia, tel. 041-520-0844).

Post Office: A large post office is off the far end of St. Mark's Square (on the side of square opposite the St. Mark's church, Mon–Sat 08:10–18:00, shorter hours off-season), and a branch is near the Rialto (on St. Mark's side, Mon–Fri 08:10–13:30, Sat 08:10–12:30).

Church Services: The San Zulian Church (the only church in Venice which you can actually walk around) offers a Mass in English at 09:30 on Sunday (May–Sept, 2 blocks toward Rialto off St. Mark's Square). Gregorians would enjoy the sung Gregorian Mass at 11:00 on Sunday at San Giorgio Maggiore church (on island of San Giorgio Maggiore, visible from Doge's Palace, catch *vaporetto* #82 from San Zaccaria dock). Confirm times of Mass at TI.

The "Rolling Venice" Youth Discount Pass: This worthwhile €2.60 pass gives those under 30 discounts on sights and transportation, plus information on cheap eating and sleeping. In summer, they have may have a kiosk in front of the train station (July–Sept daily 08:00–20:00). Their main office, near St. Mark's Square, is open year-round (Mon–Fri 09:00–14:00, from American Express head toward St. Mark's Square, first left, first left again through "Contarina" tunnel, follow white sign to Commune di Venezia and see the sign, Corte Contarina 1529, third floor, tel. 041-274-7651).

Pigeon Poop: If bombed by a pigeon, resist the initial response to wipe it off immediately—it'll just smear into your hair. Wait until it dries and flake it off cleanly.

Laundry: There are two full-service laundrys, both closed on weekends. **Lavanderia Gabriella** is near St. Mark's Square (Mon–Fri 08:00–19:00, 985 Rio Terra Colonne, from San Zulian Church go over Ponta dei Ferali, take first right down Calle dei Armeni, tel. 041-522-1758). **Lavanderia S.S. Apostoli** is near the Rialto on the St. Mark's side (Mon–Fri 08:30–12:00, 15:30–19:00, closed Sat-Sun, just off Campo S.S. Apostoli on Salizada del Pistor, tel. 041-522-6650). At either place, you can get nine pounds of laundry washed and dried for €16—confirm price carefully. Drop it off in the morning; pick it up that afternoon. (Call to be sure they're open.) Don't expect to get your clothes back ironed, folded, or even entirely dry.

Across the canal from the train station, you'll find the modern and much cheaper **Bea Vita** self-serve *lavanderia* (daily 08:00–22:00, from station go over bridge, take first right, first left, first right).

Etiquette: Walk on the right and don't loiter on bridges. Picnicking is technically forbidden (keep a low profile). Dress modestly. Men should keep their shirts on. When visiting St. Mark's or other major churches, men, women, and even children should cover their knees and shoulders (or risk being turned away).

Haircuts: I've been getting my hair cut at Coiffeur Benito for 15 years. Benito has been keeping local men and women trim for 25 years. He's an artist—actually a "hair sculptor"—and a cut here is a fun diversion from the tourist grind (€18, Tue–Sat 08:30–13:30, 15:30–19:30, behind San Zulian Church near St. Mark's Square, Calle S. Zulian Gia del Strazzanol 592A, tel. 041-528-6221).

Getting around Venice

By Vaporetto: The public transit system is a fleet of motorized bus-boats called *vaporetti*. They work like city buses except that they never get a flat, the stops are docks, and if you get off between stops, you may drown. For most, only two lines matter: #1 is the slow boat, taking 45 minutes to make every stop along the entire length of the Grand Canal, and #82 is the fast boat that zips down the Grand Canal in 25 minutes, stopping mainly at Tronchetto (parking lot), Piazzale Roma (bus station), Ferrovia (train station), Rialto Bridge, San Tomá (Church of the Frari), the Accademia Bridge, and San Marco. Buy a €3.10 ticket, ideally before boarding (at the booth at the dock) or from a conductor on board. Families of three or more pay €2.60 per person. A round-trip (*andata e ritorno*) costs €5.20 (good for 2 trips within a day on any line).

A 24-hour pass (€9.25, cheaper for families) pays for itself in three trips. Also consider the 72-hour (€18) and one-week (€31) passes. It's fun to be able to hop on and off spontaneously. Technically, luggage costs the same as dogs—€3.10—but I've never been charged. Riding free? There's a one-in-ten chance a conductor will fine you €20.

Only three bridges cross the Grand Canal, but *traghetti* (little €0.50 ferry gondolas, marked on better maps) shuttle locals and in-the-know tourists across the Grand Canal at several handy locations (see Downtown Venice map). Take advantage of these time-savers. They can also save money. For instance, while most tourists take the €3.10 *vaporetto* to connect St. Mark's with Salute Church, a €0.50 *traghetto* also does the job.

By Taxi: Venetian taxis, like speedboat limos, hang out at most busy points along the Grand Canal. Prices—which average €30–40 (about €75 to the airport)—are a bit soft. Negotiate and settle before stepping in. With lots of luggage or small groups, they can be a worthwhile and time-saving convenience—and extremely scenic to boot.

Walking Tours of Venice

Audioguide Tours—The TI rents audioguides for self-guided walking tours of Venice (2 hours-€5, 24 hrs-€10, just punch the number of what you'd like described—exteriors only, available at TI at lagoon near St. Mark's Square).

American Express Tours—AmEx runs several basic guided

Downtown Venice

- ● 1·82 VAPORETTI STOPS w/ LINE #'s
- ●···● TRAGHETTO ROUTES

400 YARDS
400 METERS

TO GHETTO, TRAIN STN, & TRONCHETTO

CA d'ORO

TO FONDAMENTA NUOVE & BOATS TO MURANO & BURANO

FISH MKT.

HOSP.

CAMPO S. GIO PAOLO

RIALTO

POST

CANAL

CAMPO S.M. FORMOSA

CAMPO S. LUCA

CAMPO MANIN

S. ZAC.

LA FENICE

POST OFFICE
WC
AMEX
LARGA
S. MOISE

CAMP.+

DOGE'S PAL.

SAN MARCO

CAMPO MAURIZIO

- ❶ HOTEL RIVA
- ❷ LOCANDA PIAVE
- ❸ LOCANDA CASA QUERINI
- ❹ HOTEL CAMPIELLO
- ❺ ALBERGO PAGANELLI
- ❻ ALBERGO DONI
- ❼ HOTEL FONTANA
- ❽ ALBERGO CORONA
- ❾ HOTEL ASTORIA
- ❿ LOCANDA GAMBERO
- ⓫ HOTEL BEL SITO
- ⓬ ALLOGGI ALLA SCALA
- ⓭ LOCANDA STURION & HOTEL LOCANDA OVIDIUS
- ⓮ ALBERGO GUERRATO
- ⓯ HOTEL CANADA
- ⓰ HOTEL GIORGIONE
- ⓱ LOCANDA LA CORTE
- ⓲ FORESTERIA DELLA CHIESA VALDESE

tours daily (€16–28, 2–3 hrs, depart from AmEx office, about 2 blocks off St. Mark's Square in direction of Accademia, past TI in arcade, tel. 041-520-0844).

Classic Venice Bars Tour—Debonair local guide Alessandro Schezzini is a connoisseur of Venetian *bacaros*—classic old bars serving traditional *cicchetti* (local munchies). He offers evening tours that involve stopping, eating, and drinking at three of these. The fee (about €26 per person) includes wine, *cicchetti*, and a great insight into this local tradition (4–8 per group, depart at 18:00, tel. & fax 041-534-5367, cellular 33-5530-9024, e-mail: venische@tiscalinet.it).

Venicescapes—Michael Broderick's private theme tours of Venice are demanding intellectually and beyond the attention span of most mortal tourists, but for the curious with stamina, he's enthralling. Michael's challenge: to help visitors gain a more solid understanding of Venice. For a description of all six of his itineraries, see www.venicescapes.org (book well in advance, 6-hour tour: €303 for 2, €28 per person after that, plus admissions and transportation, tel. 041-520-6361, e-mail: info@venicescapes.org).

Local Guides—Alessandro Schezzini gets into offbeat Venice (€90, 2.5 hrs, listed above in "Classic Venice Bars Tour"). Elisabetta Morelli is another good, local, licensed guide (€130, 2 hrs, tel. 041-526-7816, cellular 328-753-5220, e-mail: bettamorelli@inwind.it).

Grand Canal Tour of Venice

For a ▲▲▲ joyride, introduce yourself to Venice by boat. Cruise the entire Canale Grande from Tronchetto (car park) or Ferrovia (train station) all the way to San Marco. You can ride boat #1 (slow and ideal, 45 min) or #82 (too fast, 25 min, be certain you're on a "San Marco via Rialto" boat because some boats don't go farther than Rialto).

If you can't snag a front seat, lurk nearby and take one when it becomes available or find an outside seat in the stern. This ride has the best light and fewest crowds early or late. Twilight is magic. After dark, chandeliers light up the building interiors. While Venice is a barrage on the senses that hardly needs a narration, these notes give the cruise a little meaning and help orient you to this great city. Some city maps (on sale at post-card racks) have a handy Grand Canal map on the back.

Venice, built in a lagoon, sits on pilings driven nearly five meters (15 feet) into the clay (alder wood worked best). About 40 kilometers (25 miles) of **canals** drain the city, dumping like streams into the Grand Canal. Technically, there are three canals: Grand, Giudecca, and Cannaregio. The other 45 "canals" are referred to as *rio* (rivers), but the only natural river is this main street of Venice, about five meters deep. Because of its faster current, sediment never settled here.

Venice is a city of **palaces**. The most lavish were built fronting the Grand Canal. This cruise is the only way to really appreciate the front doors of this unique and historic chorus line of mansions dating from the days when Venice was the world's richest city. Strict laws prohibit any changes in these buildings, so while landowners gnash their teeth, we can enjoy Europe's best-preserved medieval city—slowly rotting. Many of the grand buildings are now vacant. Others harbor chandeliered elegance above mossy, empty ground floors. Ages ago the city was nick-named "Venice the Red" for the uniform, red brick, dust-colored stucco of its buildings. Today you'll see a bit of the original red along with the modern colors.

Start at **Tronchetto** (the bus and parking lot) or the **train station**. The station, one of the few modern buildings in town, was built in 1954. It's been the gateway into Venice since 1860, when the first station was built. "F.S." stands for "Ferrovie dello Stato," the Italian state railway system. The bridge at the station is the first of only three that cross the Canale Grande.

The **ghetto** is shortly after the train station on the left. Look down Cannaregio Canal (opposite the Riva di Biasio stop). The twin pink six-story buildings, known as the "skyscrapers," are a reminder of how densely populated the world's original ghetto was. Set aside as the local Jewish quarter in 1516, the area became extremely crowded. This urban island (behind the San Marcuola stop) developed into one of the most closely knit business and cultural quarters of all the Jewish communities in Italy (Jewish Museum described in "Sights," below).

As you cruise, notice the traffic signs. Venice's main thorough-fare is busy with traffic. You'll see all kinds of **boats:** taxis, police boats, garbage boats, ambulances, and even brown-and-white UPS boats. Venice's sleek, black, graceful **gondolas** are a symbol of the city. While used gondolas cost around $10,000, new ones run up to $30,000 apiece. Today, with over 400 gondoliers joyriding around the churning *vaporetti*, there's a lot of congestion on the Grand Canal. Watch your *vaporetto* driver curse the gondoliers.

Opposite the San Stae stop, look for the faded frescoes. Imagine the grand facades of the Grand Canal in its day.

At the Ca d'Oro stop, notice the lacy Gothic palace. Named the **"House of Gold"**—the frilly edge of the roof was once gilded—it's considered the most elegant Venetian Gothic palace on the canal. Unfortunately, there's little to see inside (€3.10, Mon 08:15–14:00, Tue–Sun 08:15–19:15, free peek through hole in door of courtyard). "Ca" refers to "house." Because only the house of the doge (Venetian ruler) could be called a palace, all other palaces are technically "Ca."

On the right, the outdoor **fish and produce market** bustles with people in the morning, but is quiet the rest of the day. (This is a great scene to wander through—even though new European hygiene standards required a less-colorful remodeling job last year.) Find the *traghetto* gondola ferrying shoppers—standing like Washington crossing the Delaware—back and forth.

Ahead, above the post office, the golden angel of the Campanile (bell tower) faces the wind and marks St. Mark's Square, where this tour will end. The huge **post office**, with *servizio postale* boats moored at its blue posts, is on the left just before the Rialto Bridge.

A major landmark of Venice, the **Rialto Bridge** is lined with shops and tourists. The third bridge on this spot, it was built in 1592. Earlier Rialto Bridges could open to let in big ships. After 1592, much of the Grand Canal was closed to shipping and became a canal of palaces. With a span of 42 meters and foundations stretching 200 meters on either side, the Rialto was an impressive engineering feat in its day. Locals call the summit of this bridge the "icebox of Venice" for its cool breeze. Tourists call it a great place to kiss. *Rialto* means "high river bank." The restaurants with views of the bridge feature high prices and low quality.

Rialto, a separate town in the early days of Venice, has always been the commercial district, while San Marco was the religious and governmental center. Today, a street called the Mercerie connects the two, providing travelers with human traffic jams and a mesmerizing gauntlet of shopping temptations.

Beyond the Rialto on the left, notice the long stretch of important **merchants' palaces**, each with a proud and different facade. Since ships couldn't navigate beyond the Rialto Bridge (to reach the section of the Grand Canal you just came from), the biggest palaces—with the major shipping needs—lie ahead. Many feature the Roman palace design of twin towers flanking a huge set of central windows. These were showrooms designed to let in maximum sunlight.

Take a deep whiff of Venice. What's all this nonsense about stinky canals? All I smell is my shirt. By the way, how's your captain? Smooth dockings? To get to know him, stand up in the bow and block his view.

The rising water level takes its toll. Many canal-level floors are abandoned. Notice how many buildings have a foundation of waterproof white stone (*pietra d'Istria*) upon which the bricks sit high and dry. The posts—historically painted gaily with the equivalent of family coats of arms—don't rot under water. But the wood at the water line does rot. Notice how the rich marble facades are just a veneer covering no-nonsense brick buildings. Look up at the characteristic funnel-shaped chimneys. These forced embers through a loop-the-loop channel until dead—required in the days when stone palaces were surrounded by humble wooden buildings and a live spark could make a merchant's workforce homeless.

After the San Silvestro stop, you'll see (on the right) the

palace of a 13th-century **"captain general of the sea."** The Venetian equivalent of five-star admirals were honored with twin obelisks decorating their palaces.

After the San Tomá stop, look down the side canal (on the right) before the bridge to see the traffic light, the **fire station**, and the fireboats ready to go.

These days, when buildings are being renovated, huge murals with images of the building mask the ugly scaffolding. Corporations hide the scaffolding out of goodwill (and to get their names on the mural).

The wooden Accademia Bridge crosses the Grand Canal and leads to the **Accademia Gallery** (neoclassical facade just after the British consulate on the right), filled with the best Venetian paintings. The bridge was put up in 1932 as a temporary one. Locals liked it, so it stayed.

Cruising under the bridge, you'll get a classic view of the **Salute Church** ahead (daily 09:00–12:00, 15:00–18:00). This Church of Saint Mary of Good Health was built to coax God into delivering the locals from the devastating plague of 1630 (which eventually killed about a third of the city's population). It's claimed that more than a million trees were piled together to build a foundation reaching below the mud to the solid clay.

Much of the surrounding countryside was deforested by Venice. Trees were exported and consumed locally to fuel the furnaces of Venice's booming glass industry, build Europe's biggest merchant marine, and to prop up this city in the mud.

The low white building on the right (between the bridge and the church) is the **Peggy Guggenheim Collection**. She willed to the city a fine collection of modern art.

Next to this notice the early Renaissance building (flat-feeling facade just decorated with Renaissance motifs). The Salviati building (with the fine mosaic) is a glass factory.

Just before the Salute stop (on the right), the house with the big view windows and the red and wild Andy Warhol painting on the living-room wall (often behind white drapes) was inhabited by Mick Jagger. In the 1970s this was famous as Venice's rock-and-roll-star party house.

The building on the right with the golden ball is the **Dogana da Mar**, a 16th-century customs house (not open to the public today). Its two bronze Atlases hold a statue of Fortune riding the ball. While there are few hotels on this side, all the buildings on the left are fancy Grand Canal hotels.

As you prepare to deboat at San Marco, look from left to right out over the lagoon. A wide harborfront walk leads past the town's most elegant hotels to the green area in the distance. This is the public garden, the only park in Venice. Farther out is the

lido, Venice's beach. It's tempting, with its sand and casinos, but its car traffic breaks into the medieval charm of Venice.

The dreamy church that seems to float is the architect Palladio's **San Giorgio Maggiore**. It's just a *vaporetto* ride away (#82 from San Zaccaria dock); if you visit the church, find the Tintoretto paintings (such as the *Last Supper*) and take the elevator up the tower for a terrific view (€2.10 for tower; €5.20 for tower, church, and museum; daily 09:30–12:30, 14:30–18:30, Gregorian Mass at 11:00 on Sun, tel. 041-522-7827). Across the lagoon (to your right) is a residential island called Giudecca.

Get out at the San Marco stop. Directly ahead is Harry's Bar. Hemingway drank here when it was a characteristic no-name *osteria* and the gondoliers' hangout. Today, of course, it's the overpriced hangout of well-dressed Americans who don't mind paying triple for their Bellinis (peach juice with Prosecco wine) to make the scene. St. Mark's Square is just around the corner.

For more *vaporetto* fun, ride a boat around the city and out into the lagoon and back (ask for the *circulare;* pron. cheer-koo-LAH-ray). Plenty of boats leave from San Marco for the beach (*lido*), and speedboats offer tours of nearby islands: Burano is a quiet, picturesque fishing and lace town, Murano specializes in glassblowing, and Torcello has the oldest churches and mosaics but is otherwise dull and desolate. Boat #12 takes you to these remote points slower and cheaper.

Sights—Venice, on St. Mark's Square

▲▲▲**St. Mark's Square (Piazza San Marco)**—Surrounded by splashy and historic buildings, Piazza San Marco is filled with music, lovers, pigeons, and tourists by day and is your private rendezvous with the Middle Ages late at night. Europe's greatest dance floor is the romantic place to be. St. Mark's Square is about the first place in Venice to flood (you might see stacked wooden benches; when the square floods, these are put end to end to make elevated sidewalks).

Venice's best TIs (and WCs) are here; one TI is on the square, the other on the lagoon. To find the TI on the square, stand with your back to the church, and go to the far corner on your left; the office is tucked away in the arcade (daily 09:00–17:00, near this TI is a €0.50 WC open daily 08:00–21:00—it's a few steps beyond St. Mark's Square en route to American Express office and Accademia; see "Albergo Diorno" sign marked on pavement). The other TI is on the lagoon (daily 10:00–18:00, walk out to the water by Doge's Palace, go right; nearby WCs open daily 09:00–19:00).

With your back to the church, survey one of Europe's great urban spaces and the only square in Venice to merit the title "Piazza." Nearly two football fields long, it's surrounded by the offices of the republic. On the right are the "old offices"

(16th-century Renaissance). On the left are the "new offices" (17th-century Baroque). Napoleon, after enclosing the square with the more simple and austere neoclassical wing across the far end, called this "the most beautiful drawing room in Europe."

The clock tower, a Renaissance tower built in 1496, marks the entry to the Mercerie, the main shopping drag, which connects St. Mark's Square with the Rialto. From the piazza, you can see the bronze men (Moors) swing their huge clappers at the top of each hour. In the 17th century one of them knocked an unsuspecting worker off the top and to his death—probably the first-ever killing by a robot. Notice the world's first "digital" clock on the tower facing the square (with dramatic flips every 5 minutes).

For a slow and pricey evening thrill, invest €6.20 (plus €4 if the orchestra plays) in a beer or coffee at one of the elegant cafés with the dueling orchestras. (Caffè Florian is described below in "Nightlife in Venice.") If you're going to sit awhile and savor the scene, it's worth the splurge. If all you have is €1, buy a bag of pigeon seed and become popular in a flurry. To get everything airborne, toss your sweater in the air.

▲▲**St. Mark's Basilica**—Since about A.D. 830, this basilica has housed the saint's bones. The mosaic above the door at the far left of the church shows two guys carrying Mark's coffin into the church. Mark looks pretty grumpy after the long voyage from Egypt.

The church, built in eastern style to underline Venice's connection with Byzantium (thus protecting it from the ambition of Charlemagne and his Holy Roman Empire), is decorated by booty from returning sea captains—a kind of architectural Venetian trophy chest.

To enter the church, modest dress is required even of kids (no shorts or bare shoulders). In peak season, there can be long lines of people waiting to get into the church. People who ignore the dress code hold up the line while they plead fruitlessly with—or put on extra clothes under the watchful eyes of—the dress code police.

The church has 4,000 square meters of Byzantine mosaics, the best and oldest of which are in the atrium (turn right as you enter and stop under the last dome—this may be roped off, but dome is still partially visible). Facing the church, gape up (it's OK, no pigeons), and read clockwise the story of Adam and Eve that rings the bottom of the dome. Now, facing the piazza, look dome-ward for the story of Noah, the ark, and the flood (two by two, the wicked being drowned, Noah sending out the dove, a happy rainbow, and a sacrifice of thanks).

Step inside the church (stairs on right lead to bronze horses) and notice the marble floor richly decorated in mosaics. As in many Venetian buildings, because the best foundation pilings

Floods and a Dying City

Venice floods about 60 times a year—normally in March and November—when the wind blowing up from Egypt and the high barometric pressure on the lower Adriatic Sea are most likely to combine to push water up to this top end of the sea. (There is no real lunar tide in the Mediterranean.) Venetian floods start in St. Mark's Square. The entry of the church is nearly the lowest spot in town. The meters at the base of the outside of the bell tower, or Campanile (near the exit, facing the grand square), show the current sea level (*livello marea*). Find the mark showing the high-water level from the terrible floods of 1966 (waist-level on right). When the water level raises one meter, a warning siren sounds. It repeats if a serious flood is imminent.

In 1965, Venice's population was over 150,000. Since the flood of 1966, the population has been shrinking. Today the population is about 65,000 . . . and geriatric. Sad, yes, but imagine raising a family here: The fragile nature of the city means piles of regulations (no biking, and so on), and costs are high—even though the government is now subsidizing rents to keep people from moving out. You can easily get glass and tourist trinkets, but it's hard to find groceries. And floods and the humidity make house maintenance an expensive pain.

were made around the perimeter, the interior floor rolls. As you shuffle under the central dome, look up for the Ascension (free, Mon–Sat 09:30–17:00, Sun 14:00–17:00, no photos, tel. 041-522-5205). See the schedule board in the atrium, listing free English guided tours (schedules vary but April–Oct there can be up to 4/day). The church is particularly beautiful when lit (unpredictable schedule, maybe middays 11:00–12:00, Sat–Sun 14:00–17:00 plus 18:45 Mass on Sat). During peak times, the line can be very long. Free reservations are available at www.alata.it (just print out your time and present it when you enter—to the left of the general entry).

In the **Galleria and Museum** upstairs, you can see an up-close mosaic exhibition, a fine view of the church interior, a view of the square from the horse balcony, and (inside, in their own room) the newly restored original bronze horses. These well-traveled horses, made during the days of Alexander the Great (4th century B.C.), were taken to Rome by Nero, to Constantinople/Istanbul by Constantine, to Venice by crusaders, to Paris by Napoleon, back "home" to Venice when Napoleon fell, and finally indoors and out of the acidic air (€1.60, daily 09:45–16:00, summer until 17:00, enter from atrium either before or after you tour church).

San Marco's **treasury** (with included and informative audioguide free for the asking) and **altarpiece** (€2.10 each, daily 09:45–17:10, 16:10 in winter) give you the best chance outside of Istanbul or Ravenna to see the glories of Byzantium. Venetian crusaders looted the Christian city of Constantinople and brought home piles of lavish loot (until the advent of TV evangelism, perhaps the lowest point in Christian history). Much of this plunder is stored in the treasury (*tesoro*) of San Marco. As you view these treasures, remember most were made in A.D. 500, while Western Europe was still rutting in the mud. Beneath the high altar lies the body of St. Mark ("Marxus") and the Pala d'Oro, a golden altarpiece made with 80 Byzantine enamels (A.D. 1000–1300). Each shows a religious scene set in gold and precious stones. Both of these sights are interesting and historic, but neither is as much fun as two bags of pigeon seed.

▲▲▲**Doge's Palace (Palazzo Ducale)**—The seat of the Venetian government and home of its ruling duke, or doge, this was the most powerful half-acre in Europe for 400 years (April–Oct daily 09:00–19:00, Nov–March daily 09:00–17:00, last entry 90 min before closing, €5 audioguide, tel. 041-522-4951). The €9.25 combo ticket includes admission to a number of lesser museums: Museo Correr (see below), Palazzo Mocenigo (textiles and costumes, closed Mon), Museo del Vetro di Murano (glass museum on Murano, closed Wed), and Museo del Merletto di Burano (lace museum on Burano, closed Tue). The ticket is valid for three months. If the line is very long here, consider buying the combo ticket at the Correr Museum across the square. With that, you can go directly through the Doge's turnstile.

The fine "Secret Itineraries Tour," which follows the Doge's footsteps through rooms not included in the general admission price, must be booked in advance (€12.50, at 10:00 and 11:30 in English, 1.25 hrs, call 041-522-4951). As they take only 25 people per tour, call two or three days in advance to confirm times and reserve a spot. The cost includes admission only to the Doge's Palace (and allows you to bypass the long line), and while the tour skips the main halls inside, it finishes inside the palace and you're welcome to visit those on your own.

The Doge's palace was built to show off the power and wealth of the republic and remind all visitors that Venice was number one. In typical Venetian Gothic style, the bottom has pointy arches, and the top has an Eastern or Islamic flavor. Its columns sat on pedestals, but in the thousand years since they were erected, the palace has settled into the mud, and the bases have vanished.

Enjoy the newly restored facades from the courtyard. Notice

a grand staircase (with nearly naked Moses and Paul Newman at the top). Even the most powerful visitors climbed this to meet the doge. This was the beginning of an architectural power trip. The doge, the elected-for-life duke or leader of this "dictatorship of the aristocracy," lived with his family on the first floor near the halls of power. From his lavish quarters, you'll follow the one-way tour through the public rooms of the top floor, finishing with the Bridge of Sighs and the prison. The place is wallpapered with masterpieces by Veronese and Tintoretto. Don't worry much about the great art. Enjoy the building.

In room 12, the Senate Room, the 200 senators met, debated, and passed laws. From the center of the ceiling, Tintoretto's *Triumph of Venice* shows the city in all her glory. Lady Venice, in heaven with the Greek gods, stands high above the lesser nations, who swirl respectfully at her feet with gifts.

The Armory—a dazzling display originally assembled to intimidate potential adversaries—shows remnants of the military might the empire employed to keep the east-west trade lines open (and the local economy booming). Squint out the window at the far end for a fine view of Palladio's San Giorgio Maggiore Church and the *lido* (cars, casinos, crowded beaches) in the distance.

The giant Hall of the Grand Council (55 meters/180 feet long, capacity 2,000) is where the entire nobility met to elect the senate and doge. Ringing the room are portraits of 76 doges (in chronological order). One, a doge who opposed the will of the Grand Council, is blacked out. Behind the doge's throne, you can't miss Tintoretto's monsterpiece, *Paradise*. At 520 square meters (1,700 square feet), this is the world's largest oil painting. Christ and Mary are surrounded by a heavenly host of 500 saints. Its message to electors who met here: Make wise decisions and you'll ultimately join that holy crowd.

Walking over the Bridge of Sighs, you'll enter the prisons. In the privacy of his own home, a doge could sentence, torture, and jail his opponents secretly. As you walk back over the bridge, squeeze your arm through the marble lattice window and wave to the gang of tourists gawking at you.

▲▲**Museo Civico Correr**—The city history museum is now included (whether you like it or not) with the admission to the Doge's Palace. In the Napoleon Wing, you'll see fine neoclassical works by Canova. Then peruse armor, banners, and paintings re-creating festive days of the Venetian Republic. The top floor lays out a good overview of Venetian art. And just before the cafeteria is a room filled with traditional games. There are English descriptions and great Piazza San Marco views throughout (€9.25 combo ticket with Doge's Palace and other museums, enter in arcade directly opposite church, daily April–Oct 09:00–19:00, Nov–March 09:00–17:00, last entry 60 min before closing, tel. 041-522-4951).

▲**Campanile di San Marco**—The lofty bell tower was once half as tall—a lighthouse marking the entry of the Grand Canal and part of the original fortress/palace which guarded its entry. Ride the elevator 92 meters (300 feet) to the top of the bell tower for the best view in Venice. This tower crumbled into a pile of bricks in 1902, a thousand years after it was built. For an ear-shattering experience, be on top when the bells ring (€5.20, daily 09:00–21:00 in summer, until 19:00 otherwise). The golden angel at its top always faces into the wind. Beat the crowds and enjoy crisp air at 09:00.

More Sights—Venice

▲▲**Galleria dell' Accademia**—Venice's top art museum, packed with highlights of the Venetian Renaissance, features paintings by Bellini, Veronese, Tiepolo, Giorgione, Testosterone, and Canaletto. It's just over the wooden Accademia Bridge. Expect long lines in the late morning because they allow only 300 visitors in at a time; visit early or late to miss crowds (€6.20, Mon 08:15–14:00, Tue–Sun 08:15–19:15, audioguide-€3.60 or €5.20 with 2 earphones, English info sheets in some rooms, guidebook-€7.75, no photos, tel. 041-522-2247). Hour-long guided tours run daily at 10:00, 11:00, and 12:00 for €5.20 (you can skip to the front of the line if buying a tour).

There's a decent pizzeria at the bridge (Pizzeria Accademia Foscarini; see "Eating," below), a public WC under it, and usually a classic shell game being played on top of it (study the system as partners in the crowd win big money).

▲**Peggy Guggenheim Collection**—This popular collection of far-out art offers one of Europe's best reviews of the art styles of the 20th century. Stroll through Cubism (Picasso, Braque), surrealism (Dalí, Ernst), futurism (Boccione, Carra), American abstract expressionism (Pollock), and a sprinkling of Klee, Calder, and Chagall (€6.20, Wed–Mon 10:00–18:00, Sat until 22:00 April–Oct, closed Tue, audioguide-€5.20, guidebook-€5.20, free baggage check, pricey café, photos allowed only in garden and terrace—a fine and relaxing perch overlooking Grand Canal, near Accademia, tel. 041-240-5411). The place is run (cheaply) by American interns working on art history degrees.

▲▲**Chiesa dei Frari**—My favorite art experience in Venice is seeing art in the setting for which it was designed—at the Chiesa dei Frari. The Franciscan "church of the friars" and the art that decorates it are warmed by the spirit of St. Francis. It features the work of three great Renaissance masters: Donatello, Bellini, and Titian—each showing worshippers the glory of God in human terms.

In Donatello's wood carving of St. John the Baptist (just to the right of the high altar), the prophet of the desert—dressed in animal skins and almost anorexic from his diet of bugs 'n' honey—

announces the coming of the Messiah. Donatello was a Florentine working at the dawn of the Renaissance.

Bellini's *Madonna and the Saints* painting (in the chapel farther to the right) came later, done by a Venetian in a more Venetian style—soft focus without Donatello's harsh realism. While Renaissance humanism demanded Madonnas and saints that were accessible and human, Bellini places them in a physical setting so beautiful it creates its own mood of serene holiness. The genius of Bellini, perhaps the greatest Venetian painter, is obvious in the pristine clarity, believable depth, and reassuring calm of this three-paneled altarpiece. Notice the rich colors of Mary's clothing and how good it is to see a painting *in situ*.

Finally, glowing red and gold like a stained glass window over the high altar, Titian's *Assumption* sets the tone of exuberant beauty found in the otherwise sparse church. Titian the Venetian—a student of Bellini—painted steadily for 60 years…you'll see a lot of his art. As stunned apostles look up past the swirl of arms and legs, the complex composition of this painting draws you right to the radiant face of the once dying, now triumphant Mary as she joins God in heaven.

Be comfortable discreetly freeloading off of passing tours. For many, these three pieces of art make a visit to the Accademia Gallery unnecessary (or they may whet your appetite for more). Before leaving, check out the neoclassical, pyramid-shaped tomb of Canova and (opposite that) the grandiose tomb of Titian. Compare the carved marble Assumption behind his tombstone portrait with the painted original above the high altar (€2.10, Mon–Sat 09:00–18:00, Sun 13:00–18:00, modest dress recommended, tel. 041-522-2637).

▲**Scuola di San Rocco**—Next to the Frari Church, another lavish building bursts with art, including some 50 Tintorettos. The best paintings are upstairs, especially the *Crucifixion* in the smaller room. View the neck-breaking splendor with one of the mirrors (*specchio*) available at the entrance (€5.20, daily 09:00–17:00, or see a concert here and enjoy the art as an evening bonus—see "Nightlife in Venice," below). For *molto* Tiepolo (14 stations of the cross), drop by the nearby Church of San Polo.

▲**Ca' Rezzonico and the Museum of the Venetian 18th Century**—This grand Grand Canal *palazzo* offers the best look in town at the life of Venice's rich and famous in the 1700s. Wandering among furnishings from that most decadent century, you'll see the art of Guardi, Canaletto, Longhi, and Tiepolo (€6.70, Wed–Mon 10:00–18:00, closed Tue, easy *vaporetto* access via Ca' Rezzonico stop, tel. 041-520-4036).

Dalmatian School (Scuola Dalmata dei San Giorgio)—This school (which means "meeting place") is a reminder that Venice was Europe's most cosmopolitan place in its heyday. It was here that the

Dalmatian community (people from the present-day region of Croatia) worshipped in their own way, held neighborhood meetings, and worked to preserve their culture. The chapel on the ground floor happens to have the most exquisite Renaissance interior in Venice, with a cycle painted by Carpaccio ringing the room (€2.60, Tue–Sat 09:30–12:30, 15:30–18:30, Sun 09:30–12:30, closed Mon between St. Mark's and Arsenale, on Calle dei Furlani, 3 blocks southeast of Campo San Lorenzo).

Jewish Ghetto—The word "ghetto" is Venetian for foundry, and was inherited by Venice's Jewish community when it was confined to the site of Venice's former copper foundries in 1516. Notice how an island—dominated by the Campo del Ghetto Nuovo square and connected with the rest of Venice by only three bridges—would be easy to isolate. While little survives from that time or the Jewish community, in its day the square was densely populated—lined with proto-skyscrapers seven to nine stories high. This original ghetto becomes most interesting after touring the Jewish Museum. Entry is by guided tour only, leaving hourly (€2.60, June–Sept Sun–Fri 10:00–19:00, Oct–May Sun–Fri 10:00–17:30, closed Sat; guided tours hourly; look for Campo di Ghetto Nuovo on map; tel. 041-715-359).

Santa Elena—For a pleasant peek into a completely untouristy residential side of Venice, catch the boat from St. Mark's Square to the neighborhood of Santa Elena (at the fish's tail). This 100-year-old suburb lives as if there were no tourism. You'll find a kid-friendly park, a few lazy restaurants, and beautiful sunsets over San Marco.

Gondola Rides

A rip-off for some, this is a traditional must for romantics. Gondoliers charge about €62 for a 50-minute ride during the day; from 20:00 on, figure on €77 to €103 (for *musica*—singer and accordionist, it's an additional €88 during day, €98 after 20:00). You can divide the cost—and the romance—among up to six people. Glide through nighttime Venice with your head on someone else's shoulder. Follow the moon as it sails past otherwise unseen buildings. Silhouettes gaze down from bridges while window glitter spills onto the black water. You're anonymous in the city of masks as the rhythmic thrust of your striped-shirted gondolier turns old crows into songbirds. This is extremely relaxing (and I think worth the extra cost to experience at night). Since you might get a narration plus conversation with your gondolier, talk with several and choose one you like who speaks English well. Women, beware…while gondoliers can be extremely charming, local women say anyone who falls for one of these guys "has hams over her eyes."

For a glimpse at the most picturesque gondola workshop in Venice, visit the Accademia neighborhood. Walk down the Accademia side of the canal called Rio San Trovaso. As you

approach Giudecca Canal, you'll see the beached gondolas on
your right across the canal.

For cheap gondola thrills, stick to the €0.50 one-minute
ferry ride on a Grand Canal *traghetto* or hang out on a bridge
along the gondola route and wave at (or drop leftover pigeon
seed on) romantics.

Festivals

Venice's most famous festival is **Carnevale** (Feb. 2–12 in 2002).
Carnevale, which means "farewell to meat," originated centuries
ago as a wild two-month-long party leading up to the austerity of
Lent. In Carnevale's heyday—the 1600s and 1700s—you could do
pretty much anything with anybody from any social class if you
were wearing a mask. These days it's a tamer 10-day celebration,
culminating in a huge dance lit with fireworks on St. Mark's
Square. Sporting masks and costumes, Venetians from kids to
businessmen join in the fun. Drawing the biggest crowds of the
year, Carnevale has nearly been a victim of its success, driving
away many locals (who skip out on the craziness to go ski in
the Dolomites).

Other typically Venetian festival days that fill the city's hotels
with visitors and its canals with decked-out boats are: **Feast of
the Ascension Day** (May 9, 2002), **Feast and Regatta of the
Redeemer** (parade and fireworks, July 20 and 21, 2002), and
the **Historical Regatta** (old-time boats and pageantry, Sept 1 in
2002). Each November 21 is the **Feast of Our Lady of Good
Health.** On this local "Thanksgiving," a bridge is built over the
Grand Canal so the city can pile into the Salute Church and
remember how it survived the gruesome plague of 1630. On this
day, Venetians eat smoked lamb from Dalmatia (which was the
cargo of the first ship let in when the plague lifted).

Every other year, the city hosts the **Venice Biennale International Art Exhibition** (next scheduled for 2003), a world-class contemporary art exhibition spread over the sprawling Castello Gardens
and the Arsenale. Artists representing 65 nations from around the
world offer the latest in contemporary art forms: video, computer
art, performance art, and digital photography, along with painting
and sculpture (€13, open daily generally March–Nov 10:00–18:00,
Sat until 22:00; for details, see www.labiennale.org).

Venice is always busy with special musical and artistic events.
The free monthly **Un Ospite de Venezia** lists all the latest in
English (free at TI or from fancy hotels).

Shopping

Shoppers like Carnevale masks, lace (a specialty of Burano, see
below, but sold in Venice as well), empty books with handmade
covers, and paintings—especially of Venice. If you're buying a

substantial amount from nearly any shop, bargain. It's accepted and almost expected. Offer less and offer to pay cash; merchants are very conscious of the bite taken by credit-card companies.

Popular **Venetian glass** is available in many forms: vases, tea sets, decanters, glasses, jewelry, lamps, sculptures (such as solid-glass aquariums), and on and on. Shops will ship it home for you; snap a photo of it before it's packed up. For simple, easily-packable souvenirs, consider glass-bead necklaces (sold cheap at vendors' stalls, expensive at shops).

If you're serious about glass, visit the small shops on Murano Island. Murano's glass-blowing demonstrations are fun; you'll usually see a vase and a "leetle 'orse" made from molten glass.

In Venice, glass-blowing demos are given by various companies around St. Mark's Square for tour groups. **Galleria San Marco** offers great demos just off Piazza San Marco every few minutes. They have agreed to let individual travelers flashing this book sneak in with tour groups to see the show (and sales pitch). And, if you buy anything, show this book and they'll take 20 per-cent off the price listed. (The gallery faces the square behind the orchestra nearest the church at #153, go through the arcade facing the square, cross the alley, get in good with the guard, and climb the stairs with the next group, daily 09:30–12:00, 14:00–17:00, manager Adriano Veronese, tel. 041-271-8650).

Salizada San Samuele is a nontouristy street with several artsy shops. Livio de Marchi's wood sculpture shop is delightful even when it's closed. Check out the window displays for his latest creations: socks, folded shirts, teddy bears, "paper" sacks, all carved from wood (Mon–Fri 09:30–12:30, 13:30–18:30, nearest major landmark is Accademia Bridge—on St. Mark's side, Sali-zada San Samuele 3157, *vaporetto* stop: San Samuele, or if approaching by foot, follow signs to Palazzo Grassi, tel. 041-528-5694, www.liviodemarchi.com).

Sights—Venice Lagoon

Several interesting islands hide out in the Venice Lagoon.

Burano, famous for its lace, is a sleepy island with a sleepy community—village Venice without the glitz. Lace fans enjoy Scuola di Merletti (€4.10, Wed–Mon 10:00–17:00, closed Tue, tel. 041-730-034). While the main drag leading from the *vaporetto* stop into town is lined with shops and packed with tourists, simply wander to the far side of the island and the mood shifts. Explore to the right of the leaning tower for a peaceful yet intensely pastel small-town lagoon world.

Torcello, another lagoon island, is dead except for its church, which claims to be the oldest in Venice (€5.20 for church, tower, and museum, Tue–Sun 10:30–17:30, closed Mon, tel. 041-730-761). It's impressive for its mosaics, but not worth a look on a

Venice Lagoon

short visit unless you really have your heart set on Ravenna, but can't make it there.

The island of **Murano**, famous for its glass factories, has the Museo Vetrario, which displays the very best of 700 years of Venetian glassmaking (€4.10, Thu–Tue 10:00–17:00, closed Wed, tel. 041-739-586). You'll be tempted by salesmen offering free speedboat shuttles from Piazza San Marco to the island. If you're interested in glass, it's handy. You must watch the show, but then you're free to buy or escape and see the rest of the island.

The islands are reached easily, cheaply, and slowly by *vaporetto* (depart from San Zaccaria dock nearest the Bridge of Sighs/Doge's Palace, line #12 connects all 3 islands, can also take #41 to Murano, then #12 to the other islands). Four-hour speedboat tours of these three lagoon destinations leave twice a day from the dock near the Doge's Palace (usually at 09:30 and 14:30; 1/day in winter at 14:30, €16, tel. 041-523-8835); the tours are indeed speedy, stopping for roughly 35 minutes at each island.

Nightlife in Venice

Venice is quiet at night, as tour groups are back in the cheaper hotels of Mestre on the mainland, and the masses of daytrippers return to their beach resorts. **Gondolas** can cost nearly double, but are doubly romantic and relaxing under the moon. *Vaporettos* are nearly empty, and it's a great time to cruise the Grand Canal on slow boat #1.

Take your pick of traditional Vivaldi **concerts** in churches throughout town. Vivaldi is as trendy here as Strauss in Vienna and Mozart in Salzburg. In fact, you'll find frilly young Vivaldis all over town hawking concert tickets. The TI has a list of this week's Baroque concerts (tickets from €18, shows start at 21:00 and generally last 90 min). If you see a concert at Scuola di San Rocco, you can enjoy the art (which you're likely to pay €5.20 for during the day) for free during the intermission. The general rule of thumb: musicians in wigs and tights offer better spectacle, musicians in black-and-white suits are better performers. Consider the venue carefully.

On St. Mark's Square, the dueling **café orchestras** entertain. Every night, enthusiastic musicians play the same songs, creating the same irresistible magic. Hang out for free behind the tables (which allows you to easily move on to the next orchestra when the musicians take a break) or spring for a seat and enjoy a fun and gorgeously set concert. If you sit awhile, it can be €10.20 well spent (€6.20 drink plus a one-time €4 fee for entertainment).

Caffè Florian, on St. Mark's Square, is the most famous Venetian café and one of the first places in Europe to serve coffee. It's been the place for a discreet rendezvous in Venice since 1720. Today, it's most famous for its outdoor seating and orchestra, but do walk through its 18th-century richly-decorated rooms, where Casanova, Lord Byron, Charles Dickens, and Woody Allen have all paid too much for a drink (reasonable prices at bar in back, tel. 041-520-5641).

You're not a tourist, you're a living part of a soft Venetian night... an alley cat with money. Streetlamp halos, live music, flood-lit history, and a ceiling of stars make St. Mark's magic at midnight. In the misty light, the moon has a golden hue. Shine with the old lanterns on the gondola piers where the sloppy Grand Canal splashes at the Doge's Palace... reminiscing. Comfort the small statues of the four frightened tetrarchs (ancient Byzantine emperors) where the Doge's Palace hits the basilica. Cuddle history.

Sleeping in Venice
(€1.10 = about $1, country code: 39)
Sleep Code: **S** = Single, **D** = Double/Twin, **T** = Triple, **Q** = Quad, **b** = bathroom, **s** = shower only, **CC** = Credit Cards accepted, **no CC** = Credit Cards not accepted, **SE** = Speaks English, **NSE** = No English. Breakfast is included unless otherwise noted. Air-conditioning, when available, is usually only turned on in summer. See map on page 101 for hotel locations. Virtually all of these hotels are central.

Reserve a room as soon as you know when you'll be in town. Book direct—not through any tourist agency. Most places take a credit card number for a deposit. If everything's full, don't despair.

Call a day or two in advance and fill in a cancellation. If you arrive on an overnight train, your room may not be ready. Drop your bag at the hotel and dive right into Venice.

I've listed prices for peak season: April, May, June, September, and October. Prices can get soft in July, August, and winter. Hotels sometimes give discounts if you stay at least three nights and/or pay cash. If on a budget, ask for a cheaper room or a discount. Always ask. I've listed rooms in two neighborhoods: in the Rialto-San Marco action and in a quiet Dorsoduro area behind the Accademia Gallery. If a hotel has a Web site, check it. Hotel Web sites are particularly valuable for Venice, because they often come with a map that at least gives you the illusion you can easily find the place.

Sleeping between St. Mark's Square and Campo Santa Maria di Formosa (zip code: 30122)

Hotel Riva, with gleaming marble hallways and bright modern rooms, is romantically situated on a canal along the gondola serenade route. You could actually dunk your breakfast rolls in the canal (but don't). Sandro may hold a corner (*angolo*) room if you ask. Confirm prices and reconfirm reservations, as readers have had trouble with both (Sb-€77, 2 D with adjacent showers-€93, Db-€108, Tb-€155, Qb-€232, Ponte dell' Angelo, #5310 Castello, 30122 Venezia, tel. 041-522-7034, fax 041-528-5551, Dante works the night shift). Face St. Mark's cathedral, walk behind it on the left along Calle de la Canonica, take the first left (at blue "Pauly & C" mosaic in street), continue straight, go over the bridge, and angle right to the hotel.

Locanda Piave, with 19 fine rooms above a bright and classy lobby, is fresh, modern, and comfortable (Db-€139, Tb-€181, family suites-€200 for 3, €212 to €232 for 4 or 5 people, prices good through 2002 with this book, CC but 10 percent discount with cash, air-con; *vaporetto* #51 or #82 to San Zaccaria, to the left of Hotel Danieli is Calle de le Rasse, take it, turn left at end, turn right nearly immediately at square—S.S. Filippo e Giacomo—on Calle Rimpeto La Sacrestie, go over bridge, take second left, hotel is two short blocks ahead on Ruga Giuffa #4838/40, Castello, 30122 Venezia, tel. 041-528-5174, fax 041-523-8512, www.elmoro.com/alpiave, e-mail: hotel.alpiave@iol.it, Mirella, Paolo, and Ilaria SE, faithful Molly NSE). They have a couple of apartments for €181 to €227 (for 3–5 people, cash only, includes kitchenette, cheaper in Aug).

Locanda Casa Querini is a plush little six-room place on a quiet square tucked away behind St. Mark's (Db-€165, CC, 5 percent discount with this book, air-con, exactly halfway between San Zaccaria *vaporetto* stop and Campo Santa Maria Formosa at Castello Campo San Giovanni Novo 4388, tel. 041-241-1294, fax 041-241-4231, e-mail: casaquerini@italyhotel.com, Sylvia SE).

Sleeping on or near the Waterfront, East of St. Mark's Square

These places, about one canal down from the Bridge of Sighs, on or just off the Riva degli Schiavoni waterfront promenade, rub drainpipes with Venice's most palatial five-star hotels. The first three—while pricey because of the location—are professional and comfortable. Ride *vaporetto* to San Zaccaria (#51 from train station, #82 from Tronchetto car park).

Hotel Campiello, a lacy and bright little 16-room, air-conditioned place, was once part of a 19th-century convent. It's ideally located 50 meters off the waterfront (Sb-€114, Db-€119–170, CC, 8 percent discount with cash, 30 percent discount mid-Nov–Feb excluding Christmas and Carnevale; behind Hotel Savoia, up Calle del Vin off the waterfront street—Riva degli Schiavoni, San Zaccaria #4647, tel. 041-520-5764, fax 041-520-5798, www.hcampiello.it, e-mail: campiello@hcampiello.it, family-run for 4 generations, sisters Monica and Nicoletta).

Albergo Paganelli is right on the waterfront—on Riva degli Schiavoni—and has a few incredible view rooms (S-€88, Sb-€119, Db-€140–€181, Db with view-€192, request *"con vista"* for view, CC, air-con, prices often soft, at San Zaccaria *vaporetto* stop, Riva degli Schiavoni #4182, Castello, 30122 Venezia, tel. 041-522-4324, fax 041-523-9267, www.hotelpaganelli.com, e-mail: hotelpag@tin.it). With spacious rooms, carved and gilded headboards, chandeliers, and hair dryers, this hotelesque place is a good value. Seven of their 22 rooms are in a less interesting but equally comfortable *dependencia* a block off the canal.

Albergo Doni is a dark, hardwood, clean, and quiet place with 12 dim-but-classy rooms run by a likable smart aleck named Gina (D-€77, Db-€103, T-€103, Tb-€139, ceiling fans, air-con for €10 extra per night, secure telephone reservations with CC but must pay in cash, Riva degli Schiavoni, San Zaccaria N. #4656 Calle del Vin, tel. & fax 041-522-4267, e-mail: albergodoni @libero.it, Niccolo and Gina SE). Leave Riva Degli Schiavoni on Calle del Vin and go 100 meters with a left jog.

Hotel Fontana is a cozy, two-star, family-run place with 14 rooms and lots of stairs on a touristy square two bridges behind St. Mark's Square (Sb-€52–103, Db-€77–155, family rooms, fans, 10 percent discount with cash, CC; *vaporetto* #51 to San Zaccaria, find Calle de le Rasse—to left of Hotel Danieli—take it, turn right at end, continue to first square, Campo San Provolo, Castello 4701, tel. 041-522-0579, fax 041-523-1040, www.hotelfontana.it, e-mail: htlcasa@gpnet.it).

Albergo Corona is a dingy, confusing, Old World place with eight basic rooms, lots of stairs, and no breakfast (D-€57, *vaporetto* #1 to San Zaccaria dock, take Calle de le Rasse—to

the left of Hotel Danieli, turn left at end, take right at square—
Campo S.S. Filippo e Giacomo—on Calle Rimpeto La Sacrestie,
take the first right, then next left on Calle Corona to #4464,
tel. 041-522-9174).

Sleeping North of St. Mark's Square

Hotel Astoria has 24 simple rooms tucked away a few blocks off
St. Mark's Square (D-€103, Db-€124, €10 discount July–Aug if
you pay cash, closed mid-Nov–mid-March, CC, 2 blocks from San
Zulian Church at Calle Fiubera #951; from Rialto *vaporetto* #1
dock, go straight inland on Calle le Bembo, which becomes Calle
dei Fabbri, turn left on Calle Fiubera, tel. 041-522-5381, fax 041-
528-8981, e-mail: info@hotelastoriavenezia.it, Alberto SE).

Locanda Gambero, with 27 rooms, is comfortable and
very central in the San Marco area (Db-€129, Tb-€170, CC;
from Rialto *vaporetto* #1 dock, go straight inland on Calle le
Bembo, which becomes Calle dei Fabbri; or from St. Mark's
Square, go through Sotoportego dei Dai then down Calle dei
Fabbri to #4687, at intersection with Calle del Gambero, tel.
041-522-4384, fax 041-520-0431, e-mail: hotgamb@tin.it).
Gambero runs the pleasant Art Deco–style La Bistrot on the
corner, which serves old-time Venetian cuisine.

Sleeping West/Northwest of St. Mark's Square

Hotel Bel Sito, friendly for a three-star hotel, has Old World
character and a picturesque location—facing a church on a small
square between St. Mark's Square and the Accademia. With solid
wood furniture, its rooms feel elegant (Sb-€123, Db-€186, CC,
air-con, elevator, some rooms with canal or church views, *vaporetto*
#1 to Santa Maria del Giglio stop, take narrow alley to square,
hotel at far end to your right, San Marco 2517, Santa Maria del
Giglio, west of St. Mark's Square, tel. 041-522-3365, fax 041-
520-4083, e-mail: belsito@iol.it).

Alloggi Alla Scala, a seven-room place run by Senora
Andreina della Fiorentina, is homey, central, and tucked away
on a quiet square that features a famous spiral stairway called
Scala Contarini del Bovolo (small Db-€73, big Db-€83, extra
bed-€26, breakfast-€7.75, 5 percent discount for payment in
cash, sometimes overbooks and sends overflow to sister's lesser
place; Campo Manin #4306, San Marco, northwest of St. Mark's
Square, tel. 041-521-0629, fax 041-522-6451, daughter SE). From
Campo Manin follow signs to (on statue's left) "Scala Contarini
del Bovolo" (€2.10, daily 10:00–17:30, views from top).

Sleeping near the Rialto Bridge

The first three hotels are on the west side of the Rialto Bridge
(away from St. Mark's Square) and the last three are on the east side

of the bridge (on St. Mark's side). *Vaporetto* #82 quickly connects the Rialto with both the train station and the Tronchetto parking lot.

On West Side of Rialto Bridge: **Locanda Sturion**, with air-conditioning and all the modern comforts, is pricey because it overlooks the Grand Canal (Db-€129–191, Tb-€181–232, family deals, canal-view rooms cost about €16 extra, CC, piles of stairs, 100 meters from Rialto Bridge opposite *vaporetto* dock, San Polo, Rialto, Calle Sturion #679, 30125 Venezia, tel. 041-523-6243, fax 041-522-8378, www.locandasturion.com, e-mail: info@locandasturion.com, SE). They require a personal check or traveler's check for a deposit.

Hotel Locanda Ovidius, with an elegant Grand Canal view terrace, wood-beam-ceilinged breakfast room, and nine bright, comfortable rooms, is also on the Grand Canal. It has fewer stairs than the Locanda Sturion (Sb-€77–155, Db-€103–201, Db with view-€155–232, CC, air con, Calle del Sturion #677a, tel. 041-523-7970, fax 041-520-4101, www.hotelovidius .com, e-mail: info@hotelovidius.com).

Albergo Guerrato, overlooking a handy and colorful produce market one minute from the Rialto action, is run by friendly, creative, and hardworking Roberto and Piero. Giorgio takes the night shift. Their 800-year-old building is Old World simple, airy, and wonderfully characteristic (D-€77, Db-€103, big top floor Db-€124, T-€98, Tb-€129, Q-€103, Qb-€150, including a €2.10 city map, prices promised through 2002 with this book, cash only; walk over the Rialto away from St. Mark's Square, go straight about 3 blocks, turn right on Calle drio la Scimia— not Scimia, the block before—and you'll see the hotel sign, Calle drio la Scimia #240a, 30125 San Polo, tel. & fax 041-522-7131 or 528-5927, e-mail: hguerrat@tin.it, SE). My tour groups book this place for 50 nights each year. Sorry. If you fax without calling first, no reply within three days means they are booked up. (It's best to call first.) They rent family apartments in the old center (great for groups of 4 to 8) for around €55 per person.

On East Side of Rialto Bridge: **Locanda Novo Venezia**, a charming six-room place run by industrious Claudio and Ivan, is on a great square—Campo dei S.S. Apostoli, just north of the Rialto Bridge (Db-€124 with this book, family deals for up to 6 in a room, CC, air con, Cannaregio #4529, tel. 041-241-1496, fax 041-241-5989, www.locandanovo.com, e-mail: info@locandanova.com).

Hotel Canada has 25 small, pleasant rooms (S-€83, Sb-€119, D-€124, Db-€150, Tb-€181, Qb-€227, CC, air-con-€7.75 extra per night, rooms on canal come with view, noise, and aroma, rooms facing church are quiet and fresh, Castello San Lio #5659, 30122 Venezia, tel. 041-522-9912, fax 041-523-5852, SE). This hotel is ideally located on a small, lively square, just off Campo San Lio between the Rialto and St. Mark's Square.

Hotel Giorgione, a four-star hotel in a 15th-century palace on a quiet lane, is super-professional, with plush public spaces, pool tables, Internet access, a garden terrace, and 70 spacious over-the-top rooms with all the comforts. They have perfect price discrimination down to a science (Sb-€88–145, Db-€129–€248, pricier superior rooms and suites available, extra bed-€52, 20 percent off July–Aug, check Web for discounts, CC, elevator, air con, Piazza S.S. Apostoli #4587, tel. 041-522-5810, fax 041-523-9092, www.hotelgiorgione.com).

Sleeping near S.S. Giovanni e Paoli

Locanda la Corte, a three-star hotel, has 16 attractive, high-ceilinged, wood-beamed rooms—done in pastels—bordering a small, quiet courtyard (Sb-€93, standard Db-€165, superior Db-€181, suites available, CC, air-con; *vaporetto* #52 from train station to Fondamente Nove, exit boat to your left, follow waterfront, turn right after second bridge to get to S.S. Giovanni e Paolo square; facing Rosa Salva bar, take street to left—Calle Bressana, hotel is a short block away at bridge; Castello 6317, tel. 041-241-1300, fax 041-241-5982, www.locanda.lacorte.it, e-mail: info@locanda.lacorte.it).

Sleeping near the Accademia

When you step over the Accademia Bridge, the commotion of touristy Venice is replaced by a sleepy village laced with canals. This quiet area, next to the best painting gallery in town, is a 10-minute walk from St. Mark's Square and the Rialto. The fast *vaporetto* #82 connects the Accademia Bridge with both the train station (in about 15 min) and St. Mark's Square (5 min). The hotels are located near the south end of the Accademia Bridge, except for the last listing (Fondazione Levi), which is at the north end of the bridge (St. Mark's side).

Pensione Accademia fills the 17th-century Villa Maravege. While its 27 comfortable and air-conditioned rooms are nothing extraordinary, you'll feel aristocratic gliding through its grand public spaces and lounging in its breezy garden (Sb-€83–119, standard Db-€129–181, superior Db-€155–227, one big family-of-5 room with grand canal view, family deals, CC; facing Accademia Gallery, take first right, cross first bridge, go right, Dorsoduro #1058, 30123 Venezia, tel. 041-523-7846, fax 041-523-9152, www.pensioneaccademia.it, e-mail: info@pensioneaccademia.it).

Hotel Galleria has 10 compact and velvety rooms, most with views of the Grand Canal (S-€62, D-€88–93, Db-€103, 2 big canal-view Db-€129, includes breakfast in room, CC, fans, some rooms narrow, near Accademia Gallery and next to recommended Foscarini restaurant, Dorsoduro #878a, 30123 Venezia, tel. 041-523-2489, tel. & fax 041-520-4172, www.galleria.it, e-mail: galleria@tin.it, SE).

Accademia Area Hotels and Restaurants

Hotel Agli Alboretti is a cozy, family-run, 25-room place in a quiet neighborhood a block behind the Accademia Gallery. With red carpeting and wood-beamed ceilings, it feels elegant (Sb-€96, 2 small Db-€116, Db-€145, Tb-€170, Qb-€196, CC, air con; 100 meters from the Accademia *vaporetto* stop on Rio Terra a Foscarini at #884 Accademia; facing Accademia Gallery, go left, then forced right, tel. 041-523-0058, fax 041-521-0158, www.aglialboretti.com, e-mail: alborett@gpnet.it, SE).

Hotel American is a small, cushy, three-star hotel on a lazy canal next to the delightful Campo San Vio (a tiny overlooked square facing the Grand Canal). At this Old World hotel with 18 rooms, you'll get better rates Sundays through Thursdays (Sb-€103–155, Db-€155–207, Db with view-€155–232, extra bed-€26–52, CC, air con, 30 meters off Campo San Vio and 200 meters from Accademia Gallery; facing Accademia Gallery, go left, forced right, take second left—following yellow sign to Guggenheim Museum, cross bridge, take immediate right, #628 Accademia, 30123 Venezia, tel. 041-520-4733, fax 041-520-4048, check www.hotelamerican.com for deals, e-mail: reception@hotelamerican.com, Marco SE).

Hotel Belle Arti is a good bet if you want to be in the old center without the commotion and intensity of Venice. With a grand entry and all the American hotel comforts, it's a big, 67-room, modern, three-star place sitting on a former schoolyard (Sb-€114–134, Db-€145–196, Tb-€186–238, the cheaper rates apply to July–Aug and winter, CC, plush public areas, air-con, elevator, 100 meters behind Accademia Gallery; facing Gallery, take left, then forced right, Via Dorsoduro #912, tel. 041-522-6230, fax 041-528-0043, www.hotelbellearti.com, info@hotelbellearti.com).

Domus Cavanis, across the street from—and owned by—Belle Arti, is a big, practical, plain place with a garden, renting 27 quiet and simple rooms (Db-€103, extra beds €21, includes breakfast at Hotel Belle Arti, elevator, TV, phones, Dorsoduro #896, tel. 041-528-7374, fax 041-522-8505, e-mail: info@hotelbellearti.com).

Pensione La Calcina, the home of English writer John Ruskin in 1876, comes with all the three-star comforts in a professional yet intimate package. Its 29 rooms are squeaky clean, with good wood furniture, hardwood floors, and a peaceful canalside setting facing Giudecca (S-€65–77, Sb-€88, Sb with view-€103, Db-€124–139, Db with view-€155–176, prices vary with room size and season, CC, air-con, rooftop terrace, killer sundeck on canal and canalside buffet breakfast terrace, Dorsoduro #780, at south end of Rio di San Vio, tel. 041-520-6466, fax 041-522-7045, e-mail: la.calcina@libero.it). They also rent apartments nearby (max. 2 people, from €130–€233, air-con and amenities). From the Tronchetto car park or station, catch *vaporetto* #51 to Zattere (at *vaporetto* stop, exit right, and walk along canal to hotel).

Next door, **Pensione Seguso** is almost an Addams-Family-on-vacation time warp. Sra. Seguso runs her place as her parents did, with the beds, free-standing closets, lamps, and drapes all feeling like your great-grandmother's. The upside is the commanding canalside setting. The downside is that dinner is required during high season (Db with dinner-€207 for 2 maximum price, slow season Db-€124 without dinner, CC, elevator, tel. 041-522-2340, fax 041-528-6096, e-mail: what's that?).

Locanda San Trovaso is sparkling new, with seven classy, spacious rooms—three with canal views—and a peaceful location on a small canal (Sb-€77–88, Db-€103–124, CC, small roof terrace, Dorsoduro #1351, take *vaporetto* #82 from Tronchetto or #51 from Piazzale Roma or train station, get off at Zattere, exit left, cross bridge, turn right at tiny Calle Trevisan, cross bridge, cross adjacent bridge, take immediate right, then first left, tel. 041-277-1146, fax 041-277-7190, www.locandasantrovaso .com, e-mail: s.trovaso@tin.it, Mark and his son Alessandro SE).

The basic **Hotel Alla Salute** is buried deep in Dorsoduro, ideal for those wanting a quiet Venice with three-star comforts (Db-€134, CC, facing the canal Rio delle Fornace near the Salute church, tel. 041-523-5404, fax 041-522-2271, e-mail: hotel.salute.dacici@iol.com).

Fondazione Levi, a guest house run by a foundation that promotes research on Venetian music, offers 21 quiet, institutional yet comfortable rooms (Sb-€62, Db-€103, Tb-€119, Qb-€134, only twin beds, elevator; 80 meters from base of Accademia Bridge on St. Mark's side; from Accademia *vaporetto* stop, cross Accademia Bridge, take immediate left—crossing the bridge Ponte Giustinian and going down Calle Giustinian directly to the Fondazione, buzz the "Foresteria" door to the right, San Vidal #2893, 30124 Venezia, tel. 041-786-711, fax 041-786-766, www.foresterialevi@libero.it, SE).

Sleeping near the Train Station

Hotel Marin is three minutes from the train station but completely out of the touristic bustle. Just renovated, cozy, and cheery, it seems like a 19-bedroom home the moment you cross the threshold. This is one of the best values in town (S-€57, D-€70, Db-€85, T-€93, Tb-€112, Q-€111, Qb-€122, prices good with this book and if you pay cash, pricier with CC, San Croce #670b, tel. 041-718-022, fax 041-721-485, www.hotelmarin.it). It's family-run by helpful, friendly, English-speaking Bruno, Nadia, and son Samuel (they have city maps). It's immediately across the canal from the train station, behind the green dome (over bridge, right, first left, first right, first right). There's an Internet café and handy laundromat nearby.

Dormitory Accommodations

Foresteria della Chiesa Valdese, warmly run by the local Methodist church, offers cheap dorm beds and doubles, halfway between St. Mark's Square and the Rialto Bridge. This run-down but charming old place has elegant paintings on the ceilings (dorm bed-€18, D-€52, Db-€67, some family apartments-€103 for 5, must check in and out when office is open: 09:00–13:00, 18:00–20:00, from Campo Santa Maria di Formosa, walk past Bar all' Orologio to end of Calle Lunga and cross the bridge, Castello #5170, tel. & fax 041-528-6797, fax 041-241-6328, e-mail: veneziaforesteria@chiesavaldese.org).

Venice's **youth hostel** on Giudecca Island is crowded, cheap, and newly remodeled (€16 beds with sheets and breakfast in 10- to 16-bed rooms, membership required, office open daily 07:00–9:30, 13:30–23:00, catch *vaporetto* #82 from station to Zittele, tel. 041-523-8211). Its budget cafeteria welcomes non-hostelers (nightly 17:00–23:30).

Eating in Venice

While touristy restaurants are the scourge of Venice, and most restauranteurs believe you can't survive in Venice without catering to tourists, there are plenty of places which are still popular with locals and respect the tourists who happen in. First trick: Walk away from triple-language menus. Second trick: Order daily specials.

For a fun change from restaurant fare, consider a pub crawl. You can stop at various atmospheric pubs to make a meal out of appetizers, called *cicchetti* (pron. cheh-KET-tee). For details, see "The Stand-Up Progressive Venetian Pub-Crawl Dinner," below.

To supplement Venice's skimpy hotel breakfasts, drop by any bar and ask for toast (which gets you a grilled ham-and-cheese sandwich).

Eating between Campo Santi Apostoli and Campo S.S. Giovanni e Paolo

Antiche Cantine Ardenghi de Lucia e Michael is a leap of local faith and an excellent splurge. Effervescent Michael and his wife, Lucia, cook proudly Venetian for a handful of people each night by reservation only. You must call first. You pay €41 per person and trust them to wine, dine, and serenade you with Venetian class. The evening can be quiet or raucous, depending on who's eating and how many. While the menu is heavy on crustaceans, Michael promises to serve plenty of veggies and fruit as well. Find #6369. There's no sign, the door's locked, and the place looks closed. But knock, say the password (La Repubblica Serenissima), and you'll be let in. From Campo S.S. Giovanni e Paolo, pass the churchlike hospital (notice the illusions painted on its facade), go over the bridge to the left, and take the first right on Calle della Testa to #6369 (Tue–Sat 20:00–24:00, closed Sun–Mon, tel. 041-523-7691, cellular 389-523-7691).

The following two colorful *osterias* are good for *cicchetti* (munchies), wine-tasting, or a simple, rustic, sit-down meal surrounded by a boisterous local ambience:

Osteria da Alberto is good for *cicchetti* (18:00–19:30) and great for a sit-down meal after 19:30 (closed Sun, CC, midway between Campo Santi Apostoli and Campo S.S. Giovanni e Paolo, next to Ponte de la Panada on Calle Larga Giacinto Gallina, tel. 041-523-8153)

Osteria Al Promessi Sposi does *cicchetti* with gusto and offers a little garden for sit-down meals. This place is proudly Venetian (great cod and polenta) and has a fun ambience (Thu–Tue 09:00–23:00, closed Wed, a block off Campo S.S. Apostoli and a block inland from Strada Nova at Calle dell' Oca, tel. 041-522-8609).

You'll find pubs in the side streets opposite Campo St. Sofia across Strada Nova.

Eating in Dorsoduro, near the Accademia

Restaurant/Pizzeria Accademia Foscarini, next to the Accademia Bridge and Galleria, offers decent €5 to €7 pizzas in a great canalside setting (Wed–Mon 07:00–23:00, closed Tue).

Trattoria Al Cugnai is an unpretentious place run by three gruff sisters serving good food at a good price (Tue–Sun 12:00–15:00, 19:00–22:30, closed Mon, midway between Accademia Gallery and the forgotten and peaceful Campo San Vio, tel. 041-528-9238). Enjoy a quiet sit on Campo San Vio (benches with Grand Canal view) for dessert.

Taverna San Trovaso is an understandably popular restaurant/pizzeria. Arrive early or wait (Tue–Sun 12:00–14:50, 19:00–21:50, closed Mon, CC, air con, 100 meters from Accademia Gallery on San Trovaso canal; facing Accademia take a right, then a forced left at canal). On the same canal, **Enoteca Cantine del Vino Gia Schiavi**—much-loved for its *ciccheti*—is a good place for a glass of wine and appetizers (tel. 041-523-0034). You're welcome to enjoy your wine and finger-food while sitting on the bridge.

Al Gondolieri is considered one of the best restaurants for meat—not fish—in Venice. Its sauces are heavy and prices are high, but carnivores love it (closed Tue, behind Guggenheim Gallery on west end of Rio delle Torreselle, reservations smart, tel. 041-5286396).

Cantinone Storico, also in this neighborhood, is described below under "Romantic Canalside Settings."

Eating near St. Mark's Square

Osteria Da Carla, two blocks west of St. Mark's Square, is a fun and very local hole-in-the-wall where the food is good and the price is right. They have hearty tuna salads and a daily pasta special along with traditional antipasti, polenta, and decent wine

by the glass. While you can eat outside, you don't want table #3
(Mon–Sat 07:00–23:00, closed Sun; from American Express head
toward St. Mark's Square, first left down Frezzeria, first left again
through "Contarina" tunnel, at Sotoportego e Corte Contarina,
tel. 041-523-7855, Carlo SE).

The Stand-Up Progressive Venetian Pub-Crawl Dinner

A tradition unique to Venice in Italy is a *giro di ombre* (pub crawl)—
ideal in a city with no cars. My favorite Venetian dinner is a pub
crawl. I've listed plenty of pubs in walking order for a quick or
extended crawl below. If you've crawled enough, most of these bars
make a fine one-stop, sit-down dinner. *Ombre* means shade, from
the old days when a portable wine bar scooted with the shadow of
the Campanile across St. Mark's Square.

Venice's residential back streets hide plenty of characteristic
bars with countless trays of interesting toothpick-munchie food
(*cicchetti*). This is a great way to mingle and have fun with the
Venetians. Real *cicchetti* pubs are getting rare in these fast-food
days, but locals appreciate the ones that survive.

Try fried mozzarella cheese, gorgonzola, calamari, artichoke
hearts, and anything ugly on a toothpick. Meat and fish (*pesce:*
PAY-shay) munchies can be expensive; veggies (*verdure*) are cheap,
around €3.10 for a meal-sized plate. In many places there's a set
price per munchie (e.g., €1). Ask for a *piatto misto* (mixed plate).
Or try a plate of assorted appetizers for €5 (or more, depending
on how hungry you are); ask for *"Un classico piatto di cicchetti misti
da €5"* (pron. oon KLAH-see-koh pee-AH-toh dee cheh-KET-tee
MEE-stee dah CHEEN-kway ay-OO-roh). Bread sticks (*grissini*)
are free for the asking.

Drink the house wines. A small glass of house red or white wine
(*ombre rosso* or *ombre bianco*) or a small beer (*birrino*) costs about €1.
A liter of house wine costs around €3.60. *Vin bon*, Venetian for fine
wine, may run you from €1.60 to €2.60 per little glass. Remember,
corposo means full-bodied. A good last drink is *fragolino*, the local
sweet wine—*bianco* or *rosso*. It often comes with a little cookie
(*biscotti*) for dipping. Bars don't stay open very late, and the *cicchetti*
selection is best early, so start your evening by 18:00. Most bars are
closed on Sunday. You can stand around the bar or grab a table in
the back—usually for the same price.

Cicchetteria *West of the Rialto Bridge*

Cantina Do Mori is famous with locals (since 1462) and savvy
travelers (since 1982) as a classy place for fine wine and *francobollo*
(a spicy selection of 20 tiny sandwiches called "stamps"). Choose
from the featured wines in the barrel on the bar. Order carefully,
or they'll rip you off. From Rialto Bridge, walk 200 meters down
Ruga degli Orefici away from St. Mark's Square—then ask

Venice's Restaurants

① CANTINA DO MORI
② OSTERIA SORA AL PONTE
③ CANTINA DO SPADE
④ OSTERIA ALLA BOTTE
⑤ ROSTICCERIA SAN BARTOLOMEO
⑥ PASTICCERIA PONTE DELLE PASTE
⑦ OSTERIA AL PORTEGO
⑧ DEVIL'S FOREST PUB & BORA BORA PIZZERIA
⑨ OSTERIA AL DIAVOLO E L'AQUASANTA
⑩ BAR ALL' OROLOGIO
⑪ CIP CIAP PIZZA
⑫ OSTERIA AL MASCARON
⑬ ENOTECA MASCARETA
⑭ GELATERIA
⑮ LA BOUTIQUE GELATERIA
⑯ ANTICHE CANTINE ARDENGHI
⑰ OSTERIA DA ALBERTO
⑱ OSTERIA AL PROMESSI SPOSI
⑲ REST. AL VAGON
⑳ BENITO'S HAIR SALON

(Mon–Sat 17:00–20:30, closed Sun, stand up only, arrive early before *cicchetti* are gone, San Polo 429, tel. 041-522-5401).

A few steps from the Rialto fish market, you'll find Campo delle Becarie and two little places serving traditional munchies. On this square, as you face the restaurant Vini da Pinto, **Ostaria Sora al Ponte** is to your right, just over the bridge (each item €1.30, assemble by pointing, Tue–Sun until 24:00, closed Mon), and **Cantina do Spade** is in the alley directly behind Vini da

Pinto (head around building to your left, take a right through archway; closed Sun).

Eating near the Rialto Bridge and Campo San Bartolomeo (East of the Rialto Bridge)

Osteria "Alla Botte" Cicchetteria is an atmospheric place packed with a young, local, bohemian jazz clientele. It's good for a *cicchetti* snack with wine at the bar (see the posted, enticing selection of wines by the glass) or for a light meal in the small, smoke-free room in the back (2 short blocks off Campo San Bartolomeo in the corner behind the statue—down Calle de la Bissa, notice the "day after" photo showing a debris-covered Venice after the notorious 1989 Pink Floyd open-air concert, closed Mon and Wed, tel. 041-520-9775).

If the statue on the Campo San Bartolomeo walked backward 20 meters, turned left, and went under a passageway, he'd hit **Rosticceria San Bartolomeo.** This cheap—if confusing—self-service restaurant has a likably surly staff (good €4.70 pasta, great fried mozzarella *al* prosciutto for €1.20, delightful fruit salad, and €1 glasses of wine, prices listed on wall behind counter, no cover or service charge, daily 09:30–21:30, tel. 041-522-3569). Take out or grab a table.

From Rosticceria San Bartolomeo, continue over a bridge to Campo San Lio (a good landmark). Here, turn left, passing Hotel Canada and following Calle Carminati straight about 50 meters over another bridge. On the right is the pastry shop (*pasticceria*) and straight ahead is Osteria Al Portego (at #6015), both listed below:

Pasticceria Ponte delle Paste is a feminine and pastel salon *de tè*, popular for its pastries and apéritifs. Italians love a 15-minute break, sipping a "spriz" apéritif with friends after a long day's work before heading home. Ask spritely Monica for a "spriz al bitter" (white wine, amaro, and soda water, €1.30, or choose from the menu on the wall) and munch some of the free goodies on the bar (Wed–Mon after 18:00, closed Tue, Ponte delle Paste).

Osteria Al Portego is a friendly, local-style bar serving great *cicchetti* and good meals (Mon–Fri 09:00–22:00, closed Sat–Sun, tel. 041-522-9038). The *cicchetti* here can make a great meal, or consider sitting down for an actual meal. They have a fine little menu.

The **Devil's Forest Pub**, an air-conditioned bit of England tucked away a block from the crowds, is—strangely—more Venetian these days than the *tipico* places. Locals come here for good English and Irish beer on tap, big salads (€6.70, lunch only), hot bar snacks, and an easygoing ambience (no cover or service charge, fine prices, backgammon and chess boards available-€2.10, meals daily 12:00–15:30, bar snacks all the time, closed Sun in Aug, a block off Campo San Bartolomeo on Calle dei Stagneri, tel. 041-520-0623). Across the street, **Bora Bora Pizzeria** serves pizza and salads from an entertaining menu (daily 12:00–15:00, 19:00–22:30, closed Wed in winter, CC, tel. 041-523-6583).

    Osteria al Diavolo e L'Aquasanta, three blocks west of the Rialto, serves good pasta and makes a handy lunch stop for sightseers (Wed–Mon 12:00–15:00, 19:00–22:00, closed Tue, hiding on a quiet street just off Rua Vecchia S. Giovanni, on Calle della Madonna, tel. 041-277-0307).

Eating on or near Campo Santa Maria di Formosa

Campo Santa Maria di Formosa is just plain atmospheric (as most squares with a Socialist Party office seem to be). For a balmy outdoor sit, you could split a pizza with wine on the square. **Bar all' Orologio** has a good setting and friendly service but mediocre "freezer" pizza (happy to split a pizza for pub crawlers, Mon–Sat 06:00–23:00, closed Sun). For a picnic pizza snack on the square, cross the bridge behind the canalside *gelateria* and grab a slice to go from **Cip Ciap Pizza** (Wed–Mon 09:00–21:00, closed Tue; facing *gelateria*, take bridge to the right; Calle del Mondo Novo). Pub crawlers get a salad course at the fruit-and-vegetable stand next to the water fountain (open until about 19:30, closed Sun).

    From Campo Santa Maria di Formosa, follow the yellow sign to "S.S. Giov e Paolo" down Calle Longa Santa Maria di Formosa and head down the street to **Osteria al Mascaron,** a delightful little restaurant seemingly made to order for pirates gone good (#5225, Gigi's bar, Mon–Sat 12:00–15:00, 19:00–23:00, closed Sun, reservations smart, tel. 041-522-5995). Their *antipasto della casa* (a €13 plate of mixed appetizers) is fun, and the Pasta Scogliera (€26, rock fish spaghetti for 2) makes a grand meal.

    Enoteca Mascareta, a wine bar with much less focus on food, is 30 meters farther down the same street (#5183, Mon–Sat 18:00–01:00, closed Sun, tel. 041-523-0744).

    The *gelateria* on the canal at Campo Santa Maria di Formosa is handy (for more, see "Gelato," below).

Eating on Campo S. Angelo

Ristorante Aqua Pazza (literally "crazy water") provides good pizza in a wonderful setting on a square midway between the Rialto, Accademia, and St. Mark's. The owner is from Naples and he delights locals with Amalfi/Naples cuisine. That means perhaps the best—and most expensive—pizza in Venice (Tue–Sun 12:00–15:00, 19:00–23:30, closed Mon, Campo S. Angelo, tel. 041-277-0688).

Eating in Cannaregio

For great local cuisine far beyond the crowds in a rustic Venetian setting, hike to **Osteria Al Bacco** (closed Mon, Fondamenta

Cappuccine, Cannaregio #3054, halfway between train station
and northernmost tip of Venice, reservations recommended,
tel. 041-717-493).

Eating with a Romantic Canalside Setting

Of course, if you want a canal view, it comes with lower quality
or a higher price. But the memory is sometimes most important.

Restaurant Al Vagon is popular with tourists because
nearly everyone gets a seat right on the canal. The food and
prices are acceptable and the ambience glows (moderate prices,
a 3-minute walk north of Rialto just before Campo S.S. Appos-
toli, overlooking canal called Rio dei Santi Apostoli, tel.
041-523-7558).

Ristorante da Raffaele is *the* place for classy food on a
quiet canal. It's filled with top-end tourists and locals who want
to pay well for the best seafood. The place was a haunt of the
avant-garde a few generations ago. Today it's on a main gondolier
thoroughfare—in fact, many guests arrive or depart by gondola.
Make a reservation if you want a canalside table (you do). While
their multi-lingual menu is designed for the tourists, locals stick
with their daily specials (expensive, exactly halfway between Piazza
San Marco and the Accademia Bridge at Ponte delle Ostreghe,
CC, tel. 041-523-2317). Before leaving, wander around inside
to see the owner's fabulous old weapons collection.

Ristorante Cantinone Storico sits on a peaceful canal
in Dorsoduro between the Accademia Bridge and the Peggy
Guggenheim Collection. It's dressy, specializes in fish, has six
or eight tables on the canal, and is worth the splurge (on the
canal Rio de S. Vio, reservations wise, tel. 041-523-9577).

Dorsoduro Riviera, the long promenade along the south side
of the Dorsoduro (a 5-min walk south of Accademia Bridge), is
lined with canalside restaurants away from the crush of touristic
Venice. Places immediately south of the Accademia Bridge (near
the Zattere *vaporetto* stop) are decent but more touristic. At the
west end (near the S. Basilio *vaporetto* stop), **Trattoria B. Basilio**
and **Pizzeria Riviera** (a local fave for pizza), both come with local
crowds and wet views.

For a Grand Canal view from the Rialto Bridge, consider
Al Buso, at the northeast end of the Rialto Bridge. Of the several
restaurants that hug the canal near the Rialto, this is recommended by locals as offering the best value (daily 09:00–24:00,
Ponte di Rialto #5338, tel. 041-528-9078).

Cheap Meals

A key to cheap eating in Venice is bar snacks, especially stand-
up mini-meals in out-of-the-way bars. Order by pointing.
Panini (sandwiches) are sold fast and cheap at bars everywhere.

Basic reliable ham-and-cheese sandwiches (white bread, crusts trimmed) come toasted—simply ask for "toast." Pizzerias are cheap and easy—try for a sidewalk table at a scenic location. For budget eating, I like small *cicchetti* bars (see "Pub-Crawl Dinner," above); for speed, value, and ambience, you can get a filling plate of local appetizers at nearly any of the bars.

The **produce market** that sprawls for a few blocks just past the Rialto Bridge (best 08:00–13:00, closed Sun) is a great place to assemble a picnic. The adjacent fish market is wonderfully slimy. Side lanes in this area are speckled with fine little hole-in-the-wall munchie bars, bakeries, and cheese shops.

The **Mensa DLF**, the public transportation workers' cafeteria, is cheap and open to the public (daily 11:00–14:30, 18:00–22:00). Leaving the train station, turn right on the Grand Canal, walk about 150 meters along the canal, up eight steps, and through the unmarked door.

Gelato

La Boutique del Gelato is one of the best *gelaterias* in Venice (daily 10:00–20:30, closed Dec–Jan, 2 blocks off Campo Santa Maria di Formosa on corner of Salizada San Lio and Calle Paradiso, next to Hotel Bruno, #5727—just look for the crowd).

For late-night gelato at Rialto, try **Michielangelo**, next to the McDonald's on Campo San Bartolomeo, on the St. Mark's side of the Rialto Bridge (daily 10:00–23:30, closed Wed in winter). At St. Mark's Square, the **Al Todaro** *gelateria* opposite the Doge's Palace is open late (daily 08:00–24:00, closed Mon in winter).

Transportation Connections—Venice

By train to: Verona (hrly, 90 min), **Florence** (6/day, 3 hrs), **Dolomites** (8/day to Bolzano, 4 hrs with 1 transfer; catch bus from Bolzano into mountains), **Milan** (hrly, 3–4 hrs), **Rome** (6/day, 5 hrs, slower overnight), **Naples** (change in Rome, plus 2–3 hrs), **Brindisi** (3/day, 11 hrs), **Cinque Terre** (2 La Spezia trains go directly to Monterosso al Mare daily, 6 hrs, at 09:58 and 14:58), **Bern** (4/day, change in Milan, 8 hrs), **Munich** (5/day, 8 hrs), **Paris** (3/day, 11 hrs), **Vienna** (4/day, 9 hrs). Train and *couchette* reservations (about €18) are easily made at a downtown travel agency. Venice train info: 848-888-088.

SIGHTS NEAR VENICE:
PADUA, VICENZA, VERONA, AND RAVENNA

While Venice is just one of many towns in the Italian region of Veneto, few venture off the lagoon. Four important towns and possible side trips, in addition to the lakes and the Dolomites, make zipping directly from Venice to Milan (3-hr trip, hrly trains) a route strewn with temptation.

Planning Your Time

The towns of Padua, Vicenza, Verona, and Ravenna are all, for various reasons, good stops. Each town gives the visitor a low-key slice of Italy that complements the high-powered urbanity of Venice, Florence, and Rome. But none is an essential part of the best three weeks Italy has to offer. High-speed town-hopping between Venice and Bolzano or Milan—with 3-hour stops at Padua, Vicenza, and Verona—is a good day. Trains run frequently enough to allow flexibility and little wasted time. Of the towns discussed below, only Ravenna (2.5 hours from Padua or Florence) is not on the main Milan–Venice train line.

If you're Padua-bound, note that you need to reserve ahead to see the Scrovegni Chapel (see below). On Monday, most sights in Verona and Vicenza are closed.

PADUA (Padova)

Living under Venetian rule for four centuries seemed only to sharpen Padua's independent spirit. Nicknamed "the brain of Veneto," Padua has a prestigious university (founded 1222) that was home to Galileo, Copernicus, Dante, and Petrarch. The old town, even when packed with modern-day students, is a colonnaded time-tunnel experience. And Padua's museums and churches hold their own in Italy's artistic big league. Note that you need to

Temptations between Venice and Milan

reserve in advance to see the Scrovegni Chapel with its great Giotto paintings (see below).

Arrival in Padua: Enter the station lobby. To get oriented, turn around and face the tracks. Look for the two small offices next to each other, marked in English: Train Information and Tourist Information. To the left of these is an even smaller office, marked Bus Tickets, that sells city bus tickets (€0.80). At the **TI**, pick up a city map and list of sights (Mon–Sat 09:15–19:00, Sun 09:00–12:00, Oct–March Mon–Sat 09:15–5:45, Sun 09:00–12:00, tel. 049-875-2077).

Daytrippers: The station has lockers (€2.10–2.60) and a baggage check office (€3.90, daily 06:00–24:00). If you have reservations for the Scrovegni Chapel, that will dictate the order of your sightseeing. But if you don't plan on seeing the Chapel, here's an efficient plan: Take the bus from the station to the Basilica of St. Anthony, then walk through the old town, sightseeing your way back to the station (buy your €0.80 bus ticket at the Bus Ticket office in the station lobby or at a *tabacchi* stop; catch bus #8, #12, or #18 to Via Luca Belludi, next to Piazza del Santo and the Basilica of St. Anthony). A taxi into town costs about €5. (If you have any train business, such as reservations, note that a CIT office is on the square in front of the station.)

Sights—Padua

▲▲**Basilica of St. Anthony**—Friar Anthony of Padua, "Christ's perfect follower and a tireless preacher of the Gospel," is buried here. For nearly 800 years, his remains and this impressive church (building started immediately after the death of the saint in 1231) have attracted pilgrims to Padua (daily in summer 06:30–19:45, winter 06:30–19:00, modest dress code enforced).

Nod to St. Anthony looking down from the facade, then start your visit at the information desk just inside the cloisters (daily 09:00–12:00, 15:00–18:00, very helpful with an abundance of St. Anthony-related handouts). Wander around the various cloisters. In the far end, a fascinating little museum is filled with votives and folk art recounting miracles attributed to Anthony.

Entering the basilica, you gaze past the crowds and through the incense haze at Donatello's glorious crucifix hanging over the altar, and realize this is one of the most important pilgrimage sites in Christendom.

Along with the crucifix, Donatello's bronze statues— Mary with Padua's six favorite saints—grace the high altar.

On the left, pilgrims file slowly by the chapel containing St Anthony's tomb. This Renaissance masterpiece from 1500 is circled by nine marble reliefs showing scenes and miracles from the life of the saint. The pilgrims believe Anthony is their protector—a confidant and intercessor of the poor. And they believe he works miracles. Votives placed here by the faithful ask for help or give thanks for miracles they believe he's performed. By putting their hand on his tomb while saying a silent prayer, pilgrims show devotion to Anthony and feel the saint's presence.

Next on the pilgrim route is the Chapel of the Reliquaries (behind the altar), where you can see St. Anthony's robe, vocal chords (discovered intact when his remains were examined in 1981), jaw . . . and "uncorrupted tongue" (discovered when the remains were examined in 1263). These relics—considered miraculously preserved— befit the saint who couldn't stop teaching, preaching, and praying.

Outside, on Piazza del Santo, stands Donatello's much-admired equestrian statue of the Venetian mercenary General Gattamelata. Even military commanders—such as this powerful Venetian— wanted to be close to St. Anthony. This statue is famous as the first statue of this size cast out of bronze since ancient Roman times. On the square, you'll find a handy TI and a couple of friendly cafés. A 10-minute stroll up Via del Santo takes you back into the center.

Palazzo della Ragione—This grand 13th-century palazzo once held the medieval law courts. The first floor consists of a huge hall (81 meters long, 27 meters wide) decorated with a series of 15th-century frescoes depicting signs of the zodiac and labors of the month, topped with a keel-shaped roof. Exhibitions are often held here (€3.60, Tue–Sun 09:00–19:00, closed Mon).

▲▲**Market Squares: Piazza Erbe and Piazza Frutta**—The stately Palazzo della Ragione (described above) provides a quintessentially Italian backdrop for Padua's almost exotic-feeling market, filling the surrounding squares—Piazza delle Erbe and Piazza della Frutta—each morning. Make a point to explore this scene. For centuries, locals have come here not only for price and quality but for the variety of produce available. Then, each evening, students gather here, spilling out of colorful bars and cafés—drinks in hand—into the square. This is a classic opportunity to enjoy a real discussion with smart, English-speaking students who see tourists not as pests but as interesting people from far away.

Consider dropping by **Café Pedrocchi**, a sumptuously neoclassical café famous as the place where students plotted an uprising in 1848. Nowadays you get more foam than ferver (at intersection of Oberdan and Febbraio 8, between Piazza delle Erbe and Piazza Cavour, tel. 049-820-5007).

University of Padua—This prestigious university, which requires a reservation to tour, is just across the street from Café Pedrocchi. Founded in 1222, it's one of the first, greatest, and most progressive in Europe. Long a haven for free thinking, it attracted intellectuals from all over Europe. The great astronomer Copernicus made some of his important discoveries here. And Galileo—notorious for disagreeing with the Church's views on science—called his 18 years on the faculty here the best of his life. Students gather in ancient courtyards, surrounded by memories of illustrious alumni—including the first woman ever to receive a university degree (in 1678).

And just upstairs, Europe's first great **anatomy theater,** from the 1500s, is worth a look. While strictly forbidden by the Church, students would pack this theater to watch professors dissect human cadavers. At a moment's notice, the table could be flipped, allowing the corpse to fall into a river below and be replaced with an animal instead (€2.60, reopens in March 2002 after renovation. 1 tour daily except Sun, 45 min, request English, book ahead by calling 049-876-7927, university tel. 049-827-3047).

From Piazza Cavour, it's about a ten-minute walk to the station; en route you'll find the town's artistic wonder, the ...

▲▲**Scrovegni Chapel (Cappella degli Scrovegni)**—Reserve in advance to see this glorious chapel (due to reopen in March 2002 after renovation). It's surrounded by the ruins of a Roman amphitheater, a reminder that Padua was an important Roman town. But the sightseeing thrill here is the chapel wallpapered by Giotto's beautifully preserved cycle of nearly 40 frescoes depicting scenes from the lives of Jesus and Mary. Painted by Giotto and his assistants from 1303 to 1305, and considered by many to be the first piece of modern art, this work makes it clear: Europe was breaking out of the Middle Ages. A sign of the Renaissance to come, Giotto placed real people in real scenes. These frescoes were radical for their 3-D nature, lively colors, light sources, emotion, and humanism.

To protect the paintings from excess humidity, only 25 people are allowed in the chapel at a time for a 15-minute visit. Call 049-820-4551 well in advance, particularly if you want to visit on a weekend (booking office open Mon–Fri 10:00–18:00; if you have difficulty getting through, call 049-820-4500, the neighboring Civic Museum, for help). This is likely the procedure you'll follow: Give your name and choose a day and time. Arrive about 15 minutes early and pay cash for your reserved ticket. If you're late, you'll lose your place. After buying your ticket, go outside and follow the path and signs to the chapel (€6.20, daily 09:00–19:00, people are allowed in every 20 minutes at :00, :20, and :40 past the hour, last admission 18:40, no photos allowed in chapel). Once you're admitted, you'll have to wait in the anteroom for 15 minutes to establish humidity levels before continuing into the chapel. During your enforced wait, you can read the posted information in English, study a guidebook that you purchased beforehand in the gift shop, or play with one of the computers. Summon up Giotto's Scenes by pressing Scene; double-click to enlarge. Two of the most famous are Scene #29—*Il Bacio* (Judas kissing Jesus) and Scene #34—*Il Compianto* (Entombment). Although you have only 15 minutes inside the chapel, it's divine. You're essentially inside a Giotto time capsule, looking back at an artist ahead of his time.

Civic Museum (Musei Civici Eremitani)—This museum, next to the Scrovegni Chapel, displays Roman and Etruscan archaeological finds, buckets of rare coins, and 15th- to 18th-century paintings. The highlight is a crucifix by Giotto (€4.10, Tue–Sun 09:00–19:00, closed Mon, Piazza Eremitani).

Sleeping in Padua
(€1.10 = about $1, country code: 39)
Many travelers make Padua a low-stress, low-price home base from which to tour Venice. I'd rather flip-flop it—sleeping in Venice and side-tripping to Padua, 30 minutes away by train.

In the Center: **Majestic Hotel Toscanelli** is a big, fancy hotel with 32 pleasant rooms, a touch of charm, and a relatively quiet location on a side street (Sb-€96–116, Db-€108–165, superior rooms and suites available at extra cost, includes a wonderful breakfast, CC, Via dell' Arco 2, several blocks south of Piazza delle Erbe, tel. 049-663-244, fax 049-876-0025, e-mail: majestic@toscanelli.com).

Hotel Verdi, much cheaper, has 18 basic rooms and a good attitude (S-€23, D-€36, bus #10 from station to Teatro Verdi, Via Dondi dell' Orologio 7, about four zigzag blocks northwest of Piazza Signori, tel. 049-875-5744).

Down by the Station: For elegant four-star comfort, convenience, and prices, it's **Hotel Grand' Italia**. Housed in a palace, its 57 rooms are comfortable, and the breakfast room is bright and inviting (Db–€124–€186 depending on season and size, includes breakfast, CC, elevator, air-con, Corso del Popolo 81, right outside train station, tel. 049-876-1111, fax 049-875-0850, www.hotelgranditalia.it).

Hotel Monaco, a three-star hotel a few doors away, is plain in comparison, with darkly decorated rooms, but it's a heck of lot cheaper (Db–€93–108, includes breakfast, CC, elevator, air-con, traffic noise, Piazzale Stazione 3, as you leave the station—go right, tel. 049-664-344, fax 049-664-669, www.monacohotel.it).

Hostel: The well-run **Ostello Città di Padova** has four-, six-, and 16-bed rooms (€14 beds with sheets and breakfast, €14.50 in family rooms, bus #3, #8, #12, or #18 from station, Via Aleardi 30, tel. 049-875-2219).

Eating in Padua

These are all centrally located in the historic core. **La Cova Ristorante/Pizzeria**, at Piazza Cavour, offers a pleasing range of pizza and pasta (Wed–Mon 12:00–15:00, 19:00–24:00, closed Tue, Piazza Cavour 20, Via P.F. Calvi, tel. 049-654-312). **Marechiaro Pizzeria/Trattoria** is another good bet, just off Piazza delle Erbe (Tue–Sun 12:00–14:30, 18:30–22:30, closed Mon, Via D. Manin 37, tel. 049-875-8489). **Brek**, tucked into a corner of Piazza Cavour, is an easy self-service *ristorante* (daily 11:30–15:00, 18:30–22:00).

For more of a dining experience, consider **Isola di Caprera** for traditional Veneto cuisine (€21 menu, cheaper à la carte options, Mon–Sat 12:00–15:00, 19:30–23:00, closed Sun, CC, air con, Via Marsilio da Padova 11-15, a half block north of the eastern edge of Piazza della Frutta, tel. 049-876-0244).

VICENZA

To many architects, Vicenza is a pilgrimage site. Entire streets look like the back of a nickel. This is the city of Palladio, the 16th-century Renaissance architect who gave us the Palladian style so influential in Britain (countless country homes). For the casual visitor, a quick stop offers plenty of Palladio (1508–1580)—the last great artist of the Renaissance. Note that Vicenza's major sights are closed on Monday.

Tourist Information: The main TI is at Piazza Matteotti 12 (Mon–Sat 09:00–13:00, 14:30–18:00, Sun 09:00–13:00, tel. 0444-320-854, www.ascom.vi.it/aptvicenza—site has English translations). The train station sometimes has a bleak TI (Aug–Oct only, if at all). Pick up a map, and if staying the night, an entertainment guide. Architect fans will appreciate the free

Vicenza Città del Palladio brochure in English. Guided **tours** are offered Saturday at 10:00 (€13, includes admissions to Olympic Theater and other sights—a super deal, April–Oct, 2 hrs, depart from TI on Piazza Matteotti, booking is required, call 0444-320-854 to reserve and confirm time).

Arrival in Vicenza: From the train station, it's a 5-minute **walk** up wide Viale Roma to the bottom of Corso Palladio. Or it's a short **bus** ride to Piazza Matteotti and the top of Corso Palladio. For a daytrip, consider catching the bus to Piazza Matteotti and doing your sightseeing on the way back to the station. From the station, catch bus #1, #2, #5, or #7 (€0.80, tickets sold at *tabacchi* shop in station and at small white kiosk—marked Vendita Biglietti—across street in the bushes). Validate your ticket in the machine near the back of the bus. Get off at Piazza Matteotti, a skinny, park-like square in front of a white neoclassical building. A **taxi** to Piazza Matteotti costs about €5.20.

At the station, you can store luggage (lockers-€2.60, baggage check-€3.90, daily 06:00–22:00) and rent bicycles (€1/hr, €8/day, daily 08:00–20:00).

Market Days: Vicenza hosts a Tuesday market on Piazza dei Signori and a larger Thursday market that also spills into Piazza Duomo, Piazza del Castello, and Viale Roma (08:00–13:00).

Launderette: The self-service **Lava & Asciuga** is a 10- to 15-minute walk from either the station or central Piazza dei Signori (daily 07:30–22:30, Contra S. Tommaso 46).

Sights—Vicenza

Most of Vicenza's sights are covered by a Biglietto Unico ticket for €6.70, sold only at the Olympic Theater. In addition to the theater, this combo ticket includes the Pinacoteca (paintings, in Palazzo Chiericati on Piazza Matteoti), the Santa Corona Archaeological and Natural History Museum (next to the Church of Santa Corona), and the Basilica Palladiana (in Piazza dei Signori).

▲▲Olympic Theater (Teatro Olimpico)—Palladio's last work is one of his greatest. Begun in 1580 shortly before Palladio died, the theater was actually completed by his pupil Scamozzi. Modeled after the theaters of antiquity, this is a wood-and-stucco festival of classical columns, statues, and an oh-wow stage bursting with perspective tricks. Behind the stage, framed by a triumphal arch, five streets recede at different angles. Many of the statues in niches are modeled after the people who funded the work. In contrast to the stunning stage, the audience's wooden benches are simple and crude. One of the oldest indoor theaters in Europe and considered one of the world's best, it's still used for performances (€6.70 Biglietto Unico ticket, Tue–Sun 09:00–17:00, closed Mon—though hours can vary).

▲Church of Santa Corona (Church of the Holy Crown)— A block away, this church was built in the 13th century to house a thorn from the crown of thorns given to the Bishop of Vicenza by the French King Louis IX (Mon 16:00–18:00, Tue–Sun 08:30–12:00, 15:00–18:00). It has Giovanni Bellini's fine *Baptism of Christ* (c. 1500, put in a coin for light, to the left of the altar). Study the incredible inlaid marble and mother-of-pearl work on the high altar (1670) and the inlaid wood complementing that in the stalls of the choir (1485).

Archaeological and Natural History Museum—Next door to the Church of Santa Corona, this humble museum features Roman antiquities (mosaics, statues, and swords) on its ground floor; prehistoric scraps upstairs; and precious little English information throughout (€6.70 Biglietto Unico, Tue–Sun 9:00–17:00, closed Mon).

Strolling Corso Palladio—From the Olympic Theater or Church of Santa Corona, stroll down Vicenza's main drag, Corso Andrea Palladio, and see why they call Vicenza "Venezia on terra firma." A steady string of Renaissance palaces and Palladian architecture is peopled by Vicenzans (considered by their neighbors to be as uppity as most of their colonnades) and punctuated by upper-class *gelaterias.*

After a few blocks, you'll see the commanding **Basilica Palladiana** dominating (with its 82-meter-tall, 13th-century tower) the Piazza dei Signori, which has been the town center since Roman times. It was young Palladio's proposal to redo Vicenza's dilapidated Gothic palace of justice in the neo-Greek style that established him as Vicenza's favorite architect. (This was not a church, but a meeting place for local big shots.) The rest of Palladio's career was a one-man construction boom. The brick-columned Loggia del Capitaniato, home of the Venetian governor (opposite the basilica) and one of Palladio's last works, gives you an easy chance to compare early Palladio (the basilica) with late Palladio (the loggia). The ground floor of the basilica is filled with shops. Climb up the 15th-century stairs. You'll see the lion's mouth after a few steps; centuries ago, people used to sneak notes into the mouth, complaining anonymously about others. The arcaded upper floor (with a WC in back) contains the entrance to the huge basilica (€6.70 Biglietto Unico, Tue–Sun 09:00–17:00, closed Mon, exhibitions are often held here, Piazza dei Signori). The basilica's ceiling, shaped like an upside-keel, has a nautical feel, augmented by the porthole windows. Set in the wall in front, the winged lion (symbol of St. Mark and Venice) set the course for this little town in the 15th century.

Also in the Piazza dei Signori stand two tall 15th-century columns topped by Jesus and the winged lion. When Venice took over Vicenza in the early 1400s, these columns were added—à la St. Mark's Square—to give the city a Venetian feel. (A rare public WC is behind the basilica; face the belfry and go left through the arch and down the stairs.)

Finish your Corso Palladio stroll at Piazzale Gasperi (where the Pam supermarket is a handy place to grab a picnic for the train ride), dip into the park called Giardino Salvi (for one last Palladio loggia), and then walk five minutes down Viale Roma back to the station. Trains leave about every hour toward Milan/Verona and Venice (less than an hour away).

Villa la Rotonda—Thomas Jefferson's Monticello was inspired by Palladio's Rotonda (a.k.a. Villa Almerico Capra). Started by Palladio in 1566, it was finished by his pupil, Scamozzi. The white, gently domed building, with grand colonded entries, seems to have popped out of the grassy slope. Palladio, who designed a number of country villas, had a knack for using the setting for dramatic effect. This private—but sometimes tourable—residence is on the edge of Vicenza (€2.60 for grounds, mid-March–Oct Tue–Sun 10:00–12:00, 15:00–18:00, closed Mon; €5.20 for interior—open only Wed 10:00–12:00, 15:00–18:00; everything closed Nov–mid-March, Via Rotunda 29, tel. 0444-321-793). To get to the villa from Padua's train station, hop a bus (#8, hrly) or take a taxi (about €5.50). For a quick round-trip any time of day, you can zip out by cab (5 min from train station) to see the building sitting regally atop its hill, and then ride the same cab back.

Sleeping in Vicenza
(€1.10 = about $1, country code: 39)

Hotel Campo Marzio, a four-star, American-style, modern place, faces a park on the main drag a few minutes' walk in front of the station (Db-€155–207 depending on season and size of room—"superior" means bigger, includes breakfast, CC, easy parking, air con, elevator, Viale Roma 27, 36100 Vicenza, tel. 0444-545-700, fax 0444-320-495, www.hotelcampomarzio.com).

Hotel Giardini, with three stars and 17 sleek rooms, has splashy pastel colors and a refreshing feel (Sb-€88, Db-€119, includes breakfast, CC, elevator, air-con, on busy street but has double-paned windows, within a block of Piazza Matteotti/Olympic Theater on Via Giuriolo 10, tel. & fax 0444-326-458, e-mail: hgiardini.vi@iol.it).

Hotel Palladio has a shortage of matching bedspreads, but it's decent for a two-star hotel in the city center (25 rooms, S-€36, Sb-€65, D-€62, Db-€72, Tb-€103, includes breakfast, CC, ask for quieter room, a block off Piazza dei Signori, Via Oratoria dei Servi 25, tel. 0444-321-072, fax 0444-547-328, e-mail: hotelpalladio@libero.it).

Hotel Castello, on Piazza Castello, charges a little too much for its 18 dim, quiet rooms (Sb-€103, Db-€134, includes breakfast, CC, air-con, Contra Piazza del Castello 24, down alley to the right of Ristorante agli Schioppi, 5-minute walk from station, tel. 0444-323-585, fax 0444-323-583, www.hotelcastello.net).

Hostel: **L'Ostello Rimane,** just three years old, has a great location on Piazza Matteotti (84 beds, €13.50 beds in 4–6 bed rooms, €14.50 beds in family room, €16 beds in doubles, non-members pay €2.60 extra, closed 09:30–15:30, Internet access, laundry, best to reserve several weeks in advance by fax, tel. 0444-540-222, fax 0444-547-762).

Eating in Vicenza

The local speciality is marinated cod, called *baccala alla Vicentina*. **Al Pestello** serves typical *cucina Vicentina* a block from the Church of Santa Corona (Santo Stefano 3). Locals like the romantic **Zi Teresa** for good reason (moderately-priced traditional cuisine and pizzas, closed Wed, a couple blocks southwest of Piazza Signori, Contra S. Antonio 11, at intersection with Contra Proti, tel. 0444-321-411). **La Meneghina** is an atmospheric pastry shop (on Contra Cavour, a short street between Piazza dei Signori and Corso Palladio, tel. 0444-323-305). Nearby, on Piazza del Signori, the tiny **Soraru** pastry shop has lots of sidewalk tables within tickling distance of the Palladio statue (next to basilica, at far end of square from the two tall columns). A cheap self-service **Brek Ristorante** is just off Piazza del Castello, in the shadow of the arch where Corso Palladio meets Viale Roma (closed Mon, Corso Palladio 12, tel. 0444-327-829). A few steps from that same arch is the Pam **supermarket**, perfect for picnics (daily 08:30–20:00 but closed Wed afternoon).

VERONA

Romeo and Juliet made Verona a household word. But, alas, a visit here has nothing to do with those two star-crossed lovers. You can pay to visit the house falsely claiming to be Juliet's, with an almost believable balcony (and a courtyard slathered with tour groups), take part in the tradition of rubbing the breast of Juliet's statue to ensure finding a lover (or picking up the sweat of someone who can't), and even make a pilgrimage to what isn't "La Tomba di Giulietta." Despite the fiction, the town has been an important crossroads for 2,000 years and is therefore packed with genuine history. R and J fans will take some solace in the fact that two real feuding families, the Montecchi and the Capellos, were the models for Shakespeare's Montagues and Capulets. And, if R and J had existed and were alive today, they would recognize much of their "hometown."

Verona's main attractions are its wealth of Roman ruins; the remnants of its 13th- and 14th-century political and cultural boom; its 21st-century, quiet, pedestrian-only ambience; and a world-class opera festival each July and August. After Venice's festival of tourism, Veneto's second city (in population and in artistic importance) is a cool and welcome sip of pure Italy, where dumpsters are painted by schoolchildren as class projects. If you like Italy but don't need great sights, this town is a joy.

Ask a Veronese to tell you about Papa del Gnoccho (no-ko). Every year someone from the San Zeno neighborhood is elected Papa del Gnocco. On the Friday before Mardi Gras, he's dressed like a king. But instead of a sceptre, he holds a huge fork piercing a *gnocco* (potato dumpling). Lots of people wear costumes, including little kids who dress as *gnocchi*. The focal point is the Church of San Zeno; the origin is in medieval times. About 500 years ago, at a time when the Veronese were nearly starving, the prince handed out *gnocchi* to everyone. Even now it's customary for the Veronese to eat *gnocchi* on Friday during Lent.

Orientation

The most enjoyable core of Verona is along Via Mazzini between Piazza Bra and Piazza Erbe, Verona's market square since Roman times. Head straight for Piazza Bra—and stroll. For a good day-trip, see the Arena and take the self-guided "Introductory Old Town Walk," outlined below.

Tourist Information: Verona's TI offices are at the station (Mon–Sat 09:00–18:00, closed Sun, shorter hours off-season, tel. 045-800-0861, www.tourism.verona.it) and at Piazza Bra (daily 09:00–19:00 July–Aug, shorter hours off-season, facing the large yellow-white building, TI is across street to your right, tel. 045-806-8680, public WC on Piazza Bra). Pick up the free city map that includes a list of sights, opening hours, and walking tours. Many sights are closed on Monday and are free on the first Sunday of every month. If you're staying the night, ask for the free *Agenda di Verona*, the monthly entertainment guide (it's in Italian, but *concerto di musica classica* is darn close to English).

The **Verona Card**, which covers bus transportation and most of Verona's sights, isn't worth it if you're daytripping (€11.50/3 days, sold at museums). A pricier version of the Verona Card (€19.50) includes Gardaland, an Italian Disneyland that's best reached by car.

Verona's historic **churches**—San Zeno, San Lorenzo, Sant' Anastasia, San Fermo, and the Duomo—charge admission (€2.10 apiece or €4.10 for a combo ticket, sold at the churches, hours roughly Mon–Sat 09:00–18:00, Sun 13:00–18:00, no photos allowed, no touring during Mass, modest dress expected).

Opera: In July and August, Verona's opera festival brings crowds and higher hotel prices (tickets €21–150, box office tel. 045-800-5151, www.arena.it).

Internet Access: Try Internet Train on Via Roma 17a,

a couple of blocks off Piazza Bra toward Castelvecchio (Mon–Fri 11:00–22:00, Sat 11:00–20:00, Sun 14:00–20:00, tel. 045-801-3394) or the tiny Realta Virtuale at platform 1 at the train station (Mon–Sat 07:30–19:00, closed Sun).

Private Guides: For private guides, consider Marina Menegoi (tel. 045-801-2174, e-mail: milanit@libero.it) or the Verona guide association (tel. 045-810-1322, e-mail: veronaguide@katamail.com).

Arrival in Verona

Arriving by train, get off at Verona's Porta Nuova station. The train station is modern, but so cluttered with shops it can be hard to get oriented. In the lobby, with your back to the tracks, lockers are on the far left (€1.60–2.60). To your far right, you'll find the baggage check (€2.60/12 hrs), and, if you search hard, you'll see the TI, tucked inside an office labeled "Centro Accoglienza e Informazioni."

The 15-minute walk from the station (on busy streets) to Piazza Bra is boring; take the **bus**. Directly in front of the station are the buses. You need to buy a ticket before boarding (€0.80, from *tabacchi* shop inside station or at white bus kiosk outside at Platform A). Bus information will likely be posted in English on the window of the bus kiosk (or ask, *Che numero per centro?*, pron. kay NOO-may-roh pehr CHEN-troh). You'll probably have a choice of orange bus #11, #12, or #13, leaving from Platform A. Validate your ticket on the bus by stamping it in the machine in the middle of the bus (good for 60 min). Buses stop on Piazza Bra, the square with the can't-miss-it Roman Arena. The TI is just a few steps beyond the bus stop.

Taxis pick up only at taxi stands (at train station and Piazza Bra) and cost about €5.50 for a ride between the train station and Piazza Bra. All sights of importance are located within an easy walk through the old town, which is defined by a bend in the river. Buses return to the station from the bus stop just outside the city wall (on the right), where Corso Porta Nuova hits Piazza Bra.

Sights—Verona

Arena—This elliptical 140-by-120-meter amphitheater—the third-largest in the Roman world—is well-preserved, dates from the first century A.D., and looks great in its pink marble. Over the centuries, crowds of up to 25,000 spectators have cheered Roman gladiator battles, medieval executions, and modern plays (including the popular opera festival that takes advantage of the famous acoustics every July and August). Climb to the top for a fine city view (€3.10, Tue–Sun 09:00–18:30, closed Mon and at 15:00 during opera season, info boxes near entry, located on Piazza Bra).

House of Juliet—This bogus house is a block off Piazza Erbe (detour right to Via Cappello 23). The tiny, admittedly romantic courtyard is a spectacle in itself, with Japanese posing from the balcony, Nebraskans polishing Juliet's bronze breast, and amorous graffiti everywhere. The info boxes (€0.50 for 2) offer a good history. ("While no documentation has been discovered to prove the truth of the legend, no documentation has disproven it either.") The "museum" is only empty rooms and certainly not worth the €3.10 entry fee (Tue–Sun 09:00–19:00, closed Mon).

▲**Piazza Erbe**—Verona's market square is a photographer's delight, with pastel buildings corralling the stalls, fountains, pigeons, and people that have come together here since Roman times, when this was a forum. Notice the Venetian Lion hovering above the square, reminding locals since 1405 of their conquerors. During medieval times, the stone canopy in the center held the scales where merchants measured the weight of things they bought and sold, such as silk, wool, even wood. The fountain has bubbled here for 2,000 years. Its statue, originally Roman, had lost its head and arms. After a sculptor added a new head and arms—voila— she became Verona's Madonna. She holds a small banner that reads: "I want justice and I bring peace."

▲▲**Evening** *Passeggiata*—For me, the highlight of Verona is the *passeggiata* (stroll)—especially in the evening—from the elegant cafés of Piazza Bra through the old town on Via Mazzini (one of Europe's many "first pedestrian-only streets") to the bustling and colorful market square, Piazza Erbe.

Roman Theater (Teatro Romano)—Dating from the first century A.D., this ancient theater was discovered in the 19th century and restored. To reach the worthwhile museum, high up in the building above the theater, you can take the stairs or the elevator (to find the elevator, start at the stage and walk up the middle set of stairs—continue straight on the path through the bushes). The museum displays Roman artifacts (mosaic floors, busts, clay and bronze votive figures) and a model of the theater; helpful English info sheets are in virtually every room (€2.60, free first Sun of month, Tue–Sun 09:00–17:00, closed Mon, across the river near Ponte Pietra). Every summer, the theater stages Shakespeare plays—only a little more difficult to understand in Italian than in olde English.

Giardini Giusti—If you'd enjoy a Renaissance garden with manicured box hedges and towering cypress trees, you could find this worth the walk and fee (€4.10, daily 09:00–sunset, cross river at Ponte Nuovo, continue 8 blocks up Via Carducci).

Introductory Old Town Walk
This walk will take you from Piazza Erbe to the major sights and end at Piazza Bra. Allow an hour (including tower climb and dawdling but not detours).

Verona

200 YARDS
200 METERS

- ❶ BUS TO STATION
- ❷ BUS FROM STATION
- ❸ HOTEL TORCOLO
- ❹ HOTEL EUROPA
- ❺ LOCANDA CATULLO
- ❻ HOTEL AURORA
- ❼ HOTEL BOLOGNA
- ❽ HOTEL GIULIETTA E ROMEO
- ❾ TO YOUTH HOSTEL
- ❿ OSTERIA AL DUCA
- ⓫ RISTORANTE GREPPIA & BOTTEGA DEL VINO
- ⓬ ORESTE DAL ZOVO CANTINA
- ⓭ PIZZERIA SALVATORE

From the center of Piazza Erbe, head toward the river on Via della Costa. The street is marked by an arch with a whale's rib suspended from it. When you pass through the arch, don't worry. The whale's rib has hung there a thousand years. According to legend, it will fall when someone who's never lied walks under it.

The street soon opens up to a square, **Piazza dei Signori**, which has a white statue of Dante center-stage. The pensive Dante seems to wonder why the tourists choose Juliet over him. Dante—expelled from Florence—was granted exile in Verona by the Scaligeri family. With the whale's rib behind you, you're facing the brick, crenellated, 13th-century Scaligeri residence. Behind Dante is the yellowish 15th-century Venetian Renaissance–style Portico of the Counsel. In front of Dante—and to his right (follow the white "WC" signs) is the 12th-century Romanesque **Palazzo della Ragione**.

Enter the courtyard. The impressive staircase—which goes nowhere—is the only surviving Renaissance staircase in Verona. For a grand city view, you can climb to the top of the 13th-century **Torre dei Lamberti** (€2.10 for stairs, €2.60 elevator, free first Sun of month, Tue–Sun 09:30–18:30, closed Mon). The elevator saves you 245 steps—but you'll need to climb about 45 more to get to the first view platform. It's not worth continuing up the endless spiral stairs to the second view platform.

Exit the courtyard the way you entered and turn right, continuing down the whale-rib street. Within a block you'll find the strange and very **Gothic tombs** of the Scaligeri family, who were to Verona what the Medici family was to Florence. Notice the dogs' heads near the top of the tombs. On the first tomb, the dogs peer over a shield displaying a ladder. The story goes that the Scaligeri family got rich making ladders, but money can't buy culture. When Marco Polo returned from Asia boasting of the wealthy Kublai Khan, the Scaligeris wanted to be associated with this powerful Khan by name. Only they understood "Khan" as "Cane" (dog). One Scaligeri changed his name to Grand Cane (big dog) and another to Cane Signori (lead dog).

Continue straight for one long block and turn left on San Pietro Martire (you'll need to step into the street to check the road sign). After one block, you'll reach Verona's largest church, the brick **Church of Sant' Anastasia**. It was built from the late 13th century through the 15th century, but the builders ran out of steam, for the facade was never finished. You can enter the church for €2.10 (or pay €4.10 for a combo ticket which includes other churches, including the Duomo, which we'll stop at later; ask for English brochure), or just peek in over the screen to get a sense of its size. The highlights of the interior are the grimacing troll holding a basin of holy water on his back (near entrance at base of column) and Pisanello's fragmented fresco of *St. George and the Princess* (above chapel to right of altar). The story of the church is posted in English behind the screen at the entry/exit.

Back to the walking tour. Face the church, then go right and walk along the length of it. Take a left on Via Sottoriva. In a block, you'll reach a small riverfront park that usually has a few modern-day Romeos and Juliets gazing at each other, rather than the view. Get up on the sidewalk right next to the river. You'll see the red-and-white bridge, **Ponte Pietra**. The white stones are from the original Roman bridge that stood here. After the bridge was bombed in World War II, the Veronese fished the marble chunks out of the river to rebuild it.

You'll also see, across the river and built into the hillside, the **Roman Theater** (description in "Sights," above). Way above the theater is the fortress, Castello San Pietro. We'll be heading toward the Roman bridge. That's your chance to break away, cross the bridge, and visit the Roman Theater; or climb the stairs to the left of the theater for a city view; or take the little road Scalone Castello S. Pietro and climb to the top of the hill to the Castello for a tremendous view.

Me? I'm simply passing the bridge on the way to the next church. Leave the riverfront park and take the street to the right, toward the bridge. One block before you reach the bridge (clearly marked by an arch in a tower), turn left on Via Cappelletta. After two long blocks, turn right on Via Duomo (the corner is marked by a little church). Straight ahead you'll see the striped **Duomo**. One of Verona's historic churches, it costs €2.10 to enter (€4.10 combo ticket; borrow the laminated English info sheet). Started in the 12th century, it was built over a period of centuries, showing with its bright interior the tremendous leaps made in architecture. (Okay, so the white paint helps.)

The highlights are Titian's *Assumption* and the ruins of an older church. To find the Titian, stand at the very back of the church, facing the altar; the painting is to your left. Mary calmly rides a cloud—direction up—to the shock and bewilderment of the crowd below.

To find the ruins of an older church, walk up toward the altar to the last wooden door on the left. If the door's not open, ask someone for help. Inside are the 10th-century foundations of the Church of St. Elena, turned intriguingly into a modern-day chapel.

Leave the church, returning down Via Duomo. Continue straight ahead on Via Duomo until you reach the Church of Sant' Anastasia. With your back to this church, walk down Corso S. Anastasia.

In five minutes (at a brisk pace), you'll reach the ghostly white **Porta Borsari**, stretching across the road. This sturdy first-century Roman gate was one of the original entrances to this ancient town.

Continue straight (the name of the street changes to Corso Cavour). In a little park next to the castle is a first-century Roman triumphal arch, **Arco dei Gavi.** After being destroyed by French revolutionary troops in 1796, it was rebuilt at this location in the 1900s.

Castelvecchio, the medieval castle next to the arch, is now a sprawling art museum displaying Christian statuary, some weaponry, and fine 15th- to 17th-century paintings. As you pass outdoors between the buildings of the museum, look for the skinny stairway leading up to the ancient wall overlooking the river. Climb up. It's a dead end but offers a great opportunity to shoot arrows at medieval invaders (€3.10, free first Sun of month, Tue–Sun 09:00–18:30, closed Mon, audioguide-€3.60 or €5.20 for two).

From the castle, you have three options. A grand bridge leads from the castle over the river for a good view. The castle's drawbridge points the way to Via Roma, which takes you to Piazza Bra and a well-deserved rest at a sidewalk café (Brek is good).

Or: A few blocks from the castle is the 12th-century **Basilica of San Zeno Maggiore**. This offers not only a great example of Italian Romanesque but also Mantegna's *San Zeno Triptych* and a set of 48 paneled 11th-century bronze doors that are nicknamed "the poor man's Bible." Pretend you're an illiterate medieval peasant and do some reading.

Sleeping in Verona
(€1.10 = about $1, country code: 39, zip code: 37100)

Usually price ranges are listed. Prices soar in July and August (during opera season) and anytime of year for a trade fair or holiday. The first two are my favorites for their family-run feeling.

Near Piazza Erbe: **Hotel Aurora**, just off Piazza Erbe, has a friendly family management, a terrace overlooking the piazza, and 19 fresh and newly renovated, air-conditioned rooms (S-€62, Sb-€104, Db-€117, Tb-€145, includes good buffet breakfast, lower prices off-season, reserve with traveler's check or personal check for deposit, CC, elevator, church bells ring the hour early, Piazza Erbe, 37121 Verona, tel. 045-594-717, fax 045-801-0860, SE). They also offer two quads (each with 2 rooms, a double bed, 2 twins, and bathroom; €191/night), best for families because the bedrooms aren't private.

Near Piazza Bra: Several fine places are in the quiet streets just off Piazza Bra, within 200 meters of the bus stop and well marked with yellow signs.

Hotel Torcolo provides 19 comfortable, lovingly maintained rooms in a good location near Piazza Bra (Sb-€52–70, Db-€70–99, breakfast-€6.50–10.50 extra, prices vary with season, CC, air-con, fridge in room, elevator, garage-€8–10.25/day, Vicolo Listone 3, tel. 045-800-7512, fax 045-800-4058, well-run by Silvia Pomari, SE).

Hotel Europa offers sleek, modern comfort in the same great neighborhood. Nearly half of its 46 rooms are smoke-free, a rarity in Italy (Db-€129 but €155 July-Aug, includes breakfast, call a day ahead to check for discounts, CC, air-con, elevator,

Via Roma 8, 37121 Verona, tel. 045-594-744, fax 045-800-1852, e-mail: hoteleuropavr@tiscalinet.it, SE).

Hotel Bologna has 30 bright, classy, and well-maintained rooms within a half block of the Roman Arena. It has attractive public areas and an attached restaurant (Sb-€98–124, Db-€119–175, Tb-€150–217, includes breakfast, CC, air-con, Piazzetta Scalette Rubiani 3, tel. 045-800-6830, fax 045-801-0602, e-mail: hotelbologna@tin.it).

Hotel Giulietta e Romeo, just behind the Arena, is on a quiet side street. Its 30 decent rooms are decorated in dark colors, but on the plus side, they have non-smoking rooms (on first floor) and don't take tour groups (Sb-€62–103, Db-€77–160, includes breakfast, CC, air-con, elevator, laundry service, garage-€15.50/day, Vicolo Tre Marchetti 3, tel. 045-800-3554, fax 045-801-0862, www.giuliettaeromeo.com).

Between Piazza Bra and Piazza Erbe: **Locanda Catullo** is a cheaper, quiet, and quirky place deeper in the old town, with 21 good basic rooms up three flights of stairs (S-€39, D-€54, Db-€65, Qb-€124, no breakfast, left off Via Mazzini onto Via Catullo, down an alley between 1D and 3A at Via Valerio Catullo 1, tel. 045-800-2786, fax 045-596-987, e-mail: locandacatullo @tiscalinet.it, SE a little).

Hostel: **Villa Francescatti** is a good hostel (8- to 10-bed rooms, €12 beds with breakfast, €7.25 dinners, launderette, some family rooms, bus #73 from station during the day or #90 at night and Sun, over the river beyond Ponte Nuovo at Salita Fontana del Ferro 15, tel. 045-590-360, fax 045-800-9127). During busy times, hostel members get priority over nonmembers.

Eating in Verona

Near Piazza Erbe: **Osteria al Duca** has an affordable two-course menu (€13) and lots more options. For dessert, try the chocolate salami. Family-run with a lively atmosphere, it's popular—go early (Mon–Sat 12:00–14:15, 18:45–22:00, closed Sun, Via Arche Scaligere 2, half block from Scaligeri Tombs, tel. 045-594-474). Other good choices include **Ristorante Greppia** (Vicolo Samaritana 3, tel. 045-800-4577) and the pricier **Bottega del Vino** (closed Tue, Via Scudo di Francia 3, tel. 045-800-4535); to find these, head from Piazza Erbe up Via Mazzini—they're within a couple of blocks.

For a fun, local wine/grappa bar (no formal food but an abundance of fun and hearty bar snacks), try **Oreste Dal Zovo**, run by Oreste and his wife Beverly from Chicago (no chairs, just a couple of benches; it's on the alley—San Marco in Foro—off Porta Borsari, just a block from Piazza Erbe, tel. 045-803-4369).

On Piazza Bra: For fast food with a great view of Verona's main square, consider the self-service **Brek** (daily 11:30–15:00, 18:30–22:00, indoor/outdoor seating, cheap salad plates, Piazza

Bra 20, tel. 045-800-4561). **Enoteca Cangrande** serves great wine (such as the local *pasito bianco*) and delicious food (closed Sun, Via Dietro Liston 19/D, one block off Piazza Bra and Via Roma, tel. 045-595-022).

Near Ponte Nuovo: **Pizzeria Salvatore**, just across the Ponte Nuovo bridge (and to the left), serves great pizza on funky, modern art tables (Piazza San Tomasso 6, tel. 045-803-0366).

Transportation Connections—Verona

By train to: Florence (5/day, 3 hrs, more with transfer in Bologna; note that all Rome trains stop in Firenze), **Bologna** (nearly hrly, 2 hrs), **Milan** (hrly, 2 hrs), **Rome** (4/day, 4–6 hrs, more with transfer in Bologna), **Bolzano** (hrly, 90 min, note that Brennero-bound trains stop in Bolzano). Hopping between **Verona, Padua, Vicenza,** and **Venice** couldn't be easier: All are 30 minutes apart on the Venice–Milan line (hrly, 3 hrs).

Parking in Verona: Drivers will find lots of free parking at the stadium or cheap long-term parking near the train station. The most central lot is behind the Arena on Piazza Cittadella (guarded, €1/hr). Street parking costs €0.80 for two hours (buy ticket at *tabacchi* shop to put on dashboard). The town center is closed to regular traffic.

RAVENNA

Ravenna is on the tourist map for one reason: Its 1,500-year-old churches, decorated with best-in-the-West Byzantine mosaics. Known in Roman times as Classe, the city was an imperial port for the large naval fleet. Briefly a capital of eastern Rome during its fall, Ravenna was taken by the barbarians. Then, in A.D. 540, the Byzantine emperor Justinian turned Ravenna into the western-most pillar of the Byzantine empire. A pinnacle of civilization in that age, Ravenna was a light in Europe's Dark Ages. Two hundred years later, the Lombards booted out the Byzantines, and Ravenna melted into the backwaters of medieval Italy, staying out of historical sight for a thousand years.

Today the local economy booms with a big chemical industry, the discovery of offshore gas deposits, and the construction of a new ship canal. The bustling town center is Italy's most bicycle-friendly (bike paths are in the middle of pedestrian streets, subtly indicated by white brick paving). Locals go about their business, while busloads of tourists slip quietly in and out of town for the best look at the glories of Byzantium this side of Istanbul.

Ravenna's only a 90-minute detour from the main Venice–Florence train line and worth the effort for those interested in old mosaics. While its sights don't merit an overnight stop, many find that the peaceful charm of this untouristy and classy town makes it a pleasant surprise in their Italian wandering.

Orientation

Central Ravenna is quiet, with a pedestrian-friendly core and more bikes than cars (bike rental at Coop San Vitale on Piazza Farini, on the left just as you exit train station, tel. 0544-37031). On a quick visit to Ravenna, I'd see the basilicas, Mausoleum of Galla Placidia, covered market, and Piazza del Popolo.

Tourist Information: The TI is a 20-minute walk (or a 5-minute pedal) from the train station (Mon–Sat 08:30–18:00, Sun 09:30–12:30, 14:30–17:30, Via Salara 8, tel. 0544-35404, www.turismo.ravenna.it). For directions to the TI, see the section "Orientation Walk," below.

For a private guide, consider Claudia Frassineti (tel. 335-613-2996, www.abacoguide.it).

Combo Tickets: Many top sights can only be seen by purchasing a combo ticket (called *biglietto cumulativo*, €4.70, sold at the sights). It includes admission to the Basilica of San Vitale, Mausoleum of Galla Placiolia, St. Apollinare Nuovo, Spirito Santo, Battistero Neoniano, and Cappella Arcivescoville. There are no individual admissions to these.

A different combo ticket (€5.20) includes admissions to the National Museum and Mausoleum of Teadorico. Pay an extra €1 to include the Sant' Appollinare in Classe. Unlike with the other combo ticket mentioned above, you can buy individual admissions to the sights (National Museum-€4.10, daily Tue–Sun 08:30–19:00, until 18:00 off-season, closed Mon; Mausoleum of Teadorico-€2.10, daily 09:00–19:00, until 17:30 off-season; and Sant' Appollinare in Classe-€2.10, Mon–Sat 08:30–19:30; Sun 13:00–19:00).

Sights—Ravenna

Orientation Walk—A visit to Ravenna can be as short as a three-hour loop from the train station. From the station walk straight down Viale Farini to Piazza del Popolo. This square was built around 1500 during a 60-year period when the city was ruled by Venice. Under the Venetian architecture, the people of Ravenna gather here as they have for centuries. A right on Via IV Novembre takes you a block to the colorful covered market (Mercato Coperto, open Mon–Sat for picnic fixings 08:00–13:00, closed Sun). The TI is a block away (on Via Salaria 8). Ravenna's two most important sights, Basilica di San Vitale and the Mausoleum of Galla Placidia, are two blocks away down Via San Vitale. On the other side of Piazza del Popolo is the Basilica of St. Apollinare Nuovo, also worth a look. From there, you're about a 15-minute walk back to the station.

▲▲▲**Basilica di San Vitale**—Imagine…it's A.D. 540. The city of Rome had been looted, the land was crawling with barbarians, and the infrastructure of Rome's thousand-year Empire was crumbling fast. Into this chaotic world came the emperor of the

Ravenna

❶ HOTEL BISANZIO   **❸ HOTEL RAVENNA**   **❺ RISTORANTE MARCHESINI**
❷ HOTEL GIACIGLIO   **❹ CA DE VEN REST.**   **❻ BIKE RENTAL**

East, Justinian, bringing order and stability, briefly reassembling the empire, and making Ravenna a beacon of civilization. His church of San Vitale—standing as a sanctuary of order in the midst of that chaos—is covered with lavish mosaics—gold and glass chips the size of your fingernail. It's impressive enough to see a 1,400-year-old church. But to see one decorated in brilliant mosaics, still managing to convey the intended feeling that "this peace and stability was brought to you by your emperor and God," is rare indeed.

In a medieval frame of mind, study the scene: High above the altar, God is in heaven—portrayed as Christ sitting on a celestial orb. He oversees his glorious creation—symbolized by the four rivers. And running the show on earth is Justinian (left side)—sporting both a halo and a crown to show he's leader of the church and the state. Here, Justinian brings together the military leaders and the church leaders—all united by the straight line of eyes. The bald bishop of Ravenna—the only person who was actually here—is portrayed most realistically.

Facing the Emperor (from the right side) is his wife, Theodora and her entourage. Decked out in jewels and pearls, the former dancer who became a mistress and then empress carries a chalice to consecrate the new church.

The walls and ceilings sparkle with colorful Bible scenes told with a sixth-century exuberance. This was a transitional time— and many consider the mosiacs of Ravenna both the last ancient Roman and the first medieval European works of art. For instance, you'll see a beardless Christ (as he was depicted by ancient Romans) next to a bearded Christ, his standard medieval portrayal.

The church's octagonal design—clearly eastern—inspired the construction of Hagia Sofia, built ten years later in Constantinople. Charlemagne traveled here in about 800. He was so impressed that when he returned to his capital, Aix le Chapelle (present-day Aachen in Germany), he built what many consider the first great stone building in North Europe—modeled on this church (€3.10, €5.20 for combo ticket, see above, daily 09:00–19:00, until 17:30 off-season).

▲▲**Mausoleum of Galla Placidia**—Just across the courtyard (and included in San Vitale admission) is this tiny, humble-looking mausoleum, with the oldest—and to many, the best—mosaics in Ravenna. The Mausoleum of Galla Placidia (plah-CHEE-deeah) is reputed to be the burial place of the daughter of an emperor who died in 450 after ruling Ravenna for 25 years. The little light that sneaks through the thin alabaster panels brings a glow and a twinkle to the very early Christian symbolism (Jesus the Good Shepherd, Mark's lion, Luke's ox, John's eagle, the golden cross above everything) that fills the little room. Cover the light of the door with your hand to see the standard Roman portrayal of Christ—beardless and as the Good Shepherd. The eastern influence is apparent in the carpet-like decorative patterns (€2.10, daily 09:00–19:00, until 17:30 off-season, reservations necessary March–May when school groups mob the site— call 0544-219-938 to book ahead).

▲▲**Basilica of St. Apollinare Nuovo**—This austere sixth-century church, with a typical early-Christian basilica floor plan, has two huge and wonderfully preserved side panels. One is a procession of haloed virgins, each bringing gifts to the Madonna and the Christ Child. Opposite, Christ is on his throne with four angels, awaiting a solemn procession of 26 martyrs. Ignoring the Baroque altar from a thousand years later, we can clearly see the rectangular Roman hall of Justice or basilica plan—which was adopted by churches and used throughout the Middle Ages (daily 09:30–19:00, until 17:30 off-season).

▲**Church of Sant' Apollinare in Classe**—Featuring great Byzantine art, this church is a favorite among mosaic pilgrims (Mon–Sat 08:30–19:30, Sun 13:00–19:00, tel. 0544-473-643). It's five kilometers out of town. Catch bus #4 from the station or #44 from Piazza Caduti.

Other Sights—The **Basilica San Francesco** is worth a look for its simple interior and flooded, mosaic-covered crypt below the main altar (daily 07:30–12:00, 15:00–19:00). Nearby, the **Tomb of Dante** is the true site of his remains. The Dante memorial—often mistaken for a tomb—in Florence's Santa Croce Church is empty (daily 09:00–19:00, off-season daily 09:00–12:00, 15:00–17:00).

Overrated Sight—The nearby beach town of Rimini is an overcrowded and polluted mess.

Sleeping in Ravenna
(€1.10 = about $1, country code: 39, zip code: 48100)
Hotel Bisanzio is a business-class splurge in the city center (Sb-€98, Db-€124, larger Db-€154, Via Salara 30, tel. 0544-217-111, fax 0544-32539).

Two cheap hotels near the station are **Al Giaciglio** (S-€28, D-€36, Db-€50, Via R. Brancaleone 42, tel. & fax 0544-39403, SE) and **Hotel Ravenna** (S-€40, Sb-€45, D-€50, Db-€60, CC, Via Varoncelli 12, tel. 0544-212-204, fax 0544-212-077, SE).

Hostel: **Ostello Dante** is a 20-minute walk from the station (€13 bed in 4-6 bed rooms, family rooms available, follow signs for Ostello Dante—or catch bus #1 or #70 from the station, Via Nicolodi 12, tel. & fax 0544-421-164, SE).

Eating in Ravenna
The atmospheric **Ristorante-Enoteca Cá de Ven**—or house of wine—fills a 16th-century warehouse with locals enjoying quality wine and traditional cuisine. *Piadina* (pron. peeah-DEE-nah) dominates the menu. An unleavened bread that kids are raised on here, it's served with cheese and proscuitto (Tue–Sun 11:00–14:00, 17:30–22:15, closed Mon, Via C. Ricca 24, 2-min walk from Piazza del Popolo, tel. 0544-30163).

Ristorante Marchesini has a classy, self-serve menu that includes some delicious salads (closed Sun, Via Mazzini 6, 5-min walk from Piazza del Popolo, near Piazza Caduti, tel. 0544-212-309).

Free Flow Bizantino, inside the covered market, is another self-serve (Mon–Fri open lunch only). Or assemble a picnic at the market and enjoy your feast in the shady gardens of the **Rocca Brancaleone** fortress (5-min walk from the station).

Transportation Connections—Ravenna
By train to: Venice (3 hrs with transfer in Ferrara: Ravenna to Ferrara, every 2 hrs, 1 hr; Ferrara to Venice, hrly, 90 min), **Florence** (4 hrs with transfer in Bologna: Ravenna to Bologna, 8/day, 90 min; Bologna to Florence, hrly, 90 min). Train info: tel. 848-888-088.

FLORENCE
(FIRENZE)

Florence, the home of the Renaissance and birthplace of our modern world, is a "supermarket sweep," and the groceries are the best Renaissance art in Europe.

Get your bearings with a Renaissance walk. Florentine art goes beyond paintings and statues—there's food, fashion, and handicrafts. You can lick Italy's best gelato while enjoying some of Europe's best people-watching.

Planning Your Time

If you're in Europe for three weeks, Florence deserves a well-organized day. For a day in Florence, see Michelangelo's *David*, tour the Uffizi Gallery (best Italian paintings anywhere), tour the underrated Bargello (best statues), and do the Renaissance ramble (explained below). Art-lovers will want to chisel out another day of their itinerary for the many other Florentine cultural treasures. Shoppers and ice cream–lovers may need to do the same. Plan your sightseeing carefully. Some sights close Mondays and afternoons. While many spend several hours a day in lines, thoughtful travelers avoid this by making reservations or going late in the day. Places open at night are virtually empty.

Orientation

The Florence we're interested in lies mostly on the north bank of the Arno River. Everything is within a 20-minute walk of the train station, cathedral, or Ponte Vecchio (Old Bridge). The less impressive but more characteristic Oltrarno (south bank) area is just over the bridge. The huge, red-tiled dome of the cathedral (the Duomo) and its tall bell tower (Giotto's Tower) mark the center of historic Florence.

Florence Overview

FORTEZZA BASSO
DAVID
TRAIN STN.
S. LORENZO
RICASOLI
DUOMO
CERRETANI
S.M. NOVELLA
VIA CALZAIUOLI
PONTE VECCHIO
PIAZZA SIG.
S. CROCE
UFFIZI
ARNO
OLTRARNO
DCH
S. SPIRITO
NOT TO SCALE

Tourist Information

There are three TIs in Florence: at the station, near Santa Croce, and on Via Cavour (www.firenze.turismo.toscana.it).

The TI across the square from the train station is most crowded—expect long lines (Mon–Sat 08:30–19:00, Sun 08:30–13:00; off-season Mon-Sat 08:30–17:30, Sun 08:30–13:00; with your back to tracks, it's across square in wall near corner of church; Piazza Stazione, tel. 055-212-245). Note: In the station, avoid the Hotel Reservations "Tourist Information" window (marked Informazioni Turistiche Alberghiere) near the McDonald's; it's not a real TI but a hotel reservation business.

The TI near Santa Croce Church is pleasant, helpful, and uncrowded (Mon–Sat 09:00–19:00, Sun 09:00–14:00, shorter hours off-season, Borgo Santa Croce 29 red, tel. 055-234-0444).

Another winner is the TI three blocks north of the Duomo (Mon–Sat 08:15–19:15, Sun 08:30–13:30, closed winter Sun, Via Cavour 1 red, tel. 055-290-832 or 055-290-833; international bookstore across street, see "Helpful Hints," below).

At any TI, pick up a map, a current museum-hours listing (extremely important since no guidebook—including this one—has ever been able to predict next year's hours), and any information on entertainment. The free, monthly *Florence Concierge Information* magazine lists museums, plus lots of information that I don't: concerts and events, markets, sporting events, church services, shopping ideas, bus and train connections, and an entire similar section on Siena. Get yours at the TI or from any expensive hotel (pick one up as if you're staying there).

Greater Florence

TO BOLOGNA

TO PISA & CINQUE TERRE

A-1

FIRENZE NORD EXIT

A-11

FLORENCE

N

2 MILES
3 KM

FIESOLE

VIA PISTOLESE

VIA BARRACA

RIVER ARNO

VIA BACCIO MONTELUPO

FIRENZE SIGNA EXIT

VIA SENESE

PIAZZALE MICHEL-ANGELO VIEW!

A-1

FIRENZE SUD EXIT

TO ROMA

FIRENZE CERTOSA EXIT

SUPER-STRADA

S-2

TO SIENA

S-222

DCH

Arrival in Florence

By Train: The station soaks up time and generates dazed and sweaty crowds. Try to get your tourist information and train tickets elsewhere. (You can get onward tickets and information at American Express—see "Helpful Hints," below.) With your back to the tracks, to your left are most of my recommended hotels; a 24-hour pharmacy (Farmacia Comunale, near McDonald's); city buses; and the entrance to the underground mall/passage that goes across the square to the church Santa Maria Novella (but because the tunnel, especially the surface point near the church, is frequented by pickpockets, stay above ground).

By Car: From the *autostrada* (north or south), take the Certosa exit (follow signs to *Centro*; at Porta Romana go to the left of the arch and down Via Francesco Petrarca). After driving and trying to park in Florence, you'll understand why Leonardo never invented the car. Cars flatten the charm of Florence. Don't

drive in Florence and don't risk parking illegally (fines up to
€150). The city has plenty of lots. For a short stay, park underground at the train station (€2/hr). The Fortezza da Basso is
clearly marked in the center (€18.50/24 hrs). The least expensive
lots are: Parcheggio Parterre (Firenze Parcheggi, €10.50/24 hrs,
perhaps cheaper with hotel reservation) and Parcheggio Oltrarno
(near Porta Romana—pass through gate and on left, €10.50 per
day). For parking information, call 055-500-1994.

Helpful Hints

Hours of Sights Can Change Suddenly: Because of labor
demands, hours of sights change without warning. Pick up the
latest listing of museum hours at a TI, or you'll miss out on something you came to see. Don't delay; you never know when a place
will unexpectedly close for a holiday, strike, or restoration.

Make Reservations to Avoid Lines: Florence has a great
reservation system for its top five sights—Uffizi, Accademia,
Bargello, Medici Chapel, and the Pitti Palace. You can show up
and wait in line or, make a quick and easy telephone booking.

Two sights come with long lines: the Accademia (*David*)
and the Uffizi (two-hour lines on busy days). These lines are
easily avoided by making a reservation. Frankly, it's stupid not to.

While you can generally make a reservation a day in advance
(upon arrival in Florence), you'll have a wider selection of entry
times by calling a few days ahead. You dial 055-294-883 (Mon–Fri
08:30–18:30, Sat 08:30–12:00), an English-speaking operator walks
you through the process, and two minutes later you say *grazie* with
appointments (15-minute entry window) and six-digit confirmation
numbers for each of the top museums and galleries.

If you don't book ahead, remember that many sights (a breeze
at the minor, less crowded sights) can reserve and sell tickets to
other museums—often for admissions the same day—allowing you
to skip right past the dreary mob scene.

More Tips on Sightseeing: Some museums close at 14:00
and stop selling tickets 30 minutes before that. The biggies (Uffizi
and Accademia) close on Monday. The *Concierge Information* magazine thoughtfully lists which sights are open afternoons, Sundays,
and Mondays (best attractions open Mon: Museo dell' Opera del
Duomo, Giotto's Tower, Brancacci Chapel, Michelangelo's Casa
Buonarroti, Dante's House, Science Museum, Palazzo Vecchio, and
churches). Churches usually close from 12:30 to 15:00 or 16:00.

I like the €2.60 "new map" of Florence that lists the sights
(sold at newsstands). Local guidebooks are cheap and give you a
map and a decent commentary on the sights.

Theft Alert: Florence has particularly hardworking thief
gangs. They specialize in tourists and hang out where you do:
near the train station, the station's underpass (especially where

the tunnel surfaces), and major sights. Also, be on guard at two squares frequented by drug pushers (Santa Maria Novella and Santo Spirito). American tourists—especially older ones—are considered easy targets.

Medical Help: For a doctor who speaks English, call 055-475-411 (reasonable hotel calls, cheaper if you go to the clinic at Via L. Magnifico 59). The TI has a list of English-speaking doctors. A 24-hour pharmacy is at the train station.

Addresses: Street addresses list businesses in red and residences in black or blue (color-coded on the actual street number and indicated by a letter following the number in printed addresses: n = black, r = red). *Pensioni* are usually black but can be either. The red and black numbers each appear in roughly consecutive order on streets but bear no apparent connection with each other. I'm lazy and don't concern myself with the distinction (if one number's wrong, I look for the other) and find my way around fine.

American Express: AmEx offers all the normal services, but is most helpful as an easy place to get your train tickets, reservations, supplements (all the same price as at station), or even just information on train schedules. It's three short blocks north of Palazzo Vecchio on Via Dante Alighieri 22 red (Mon–Fri 09:00–17:30, Sat money exchange only 09:00–12:30, CC, tel. 055-50981).

Long-Distance Telephoning: Small newsstand kiosks sell PIN phone cards giving you cheap international phone calls (6 minutes/$1).

Books: Feltrinelli International, a fine bookstore that sells fiction and guidebooks in English, is a few blocks north of the Duomo and across the street from the TI on Via Cavour (Mon–Sat 09:00–19:30, Via Cavour 20 red). Paperback Exchange also sells fiction and guidebooks (daily 09:00–19:30, shorter hours in Aug, at corner of Via Fiesolana and Via dei Pilastri, 6 blocks east of Duomo, tel. 055-247-8154).

Getting around Florence

I organize my sightseeing geographically and do it all on foot. A €0.75 ticket gives you one hour on the buses, €1.30 gives you three hours, and €3.10 gets you 24 hours (tickets not sold on bus—except after 21:00; buy in *tabacchi* shops or newsstands, validate on bus).

The minimum cost for a taxi ride is €4, or, after 22:00, €5 (rides in the center of town should be charged as tariff #1). A taxi ride from the train station to Ponte Vecchio costs about €8. Taxi fares and supplements are clearly explained in each cab.

Tours of Florence

Walking Tours of Florence—This company offers a variety of tours (up to 4/day Mon–Sat) featuring downtown Florence,

Rick Steves' Italy

Uffizi highlights, or the countryside, presented by informative, entertaining, native English-speaking guides (€24 for 3-hr Original Florence walk, office open Mon–Sat 08:30–18:00, closed for lunch off-season, Piazza Santo Stefano 2 black, a short block north of Ponte Vecchio; go east on tiny Vicolo San Stefano, in Piazza Santo Stefano at #2; booking necessary for Uffizi tour, private tours also available, tel. 055-264-5033 or cellular 0329-613-2730, www .florencewalkingtour.com). The "Original Florence" walk hits the main sights, but gets offbeat to weave a picture of Florentine life in medieval and Renaissance times. You can expect lots of talking, which is great if you like history. Tours start at their office (year-round, regardless of weather, maximum of 22, extra guides available if more show up). For a private tour, consider Rosanne Magers (tel. 055-264-5033, walkingtours@artviva.com).

Scholarly Tours—Simone Gaddini runs Firenze Antica with a group of art historians. They offer top-notch private and "semi-private" tours of Florence and Tuscany, good for thoughtful and well-heeled travelers (semi-private tours start at €50 per person, max 8 per group; private tours start at €198 for half-day tour; reserve in advance, tel. 055-225-535, www.firenzeantica.org, e-mail: info@firenzeantica.org).

A Florentine Renaissance Walk

Even during the Dark Ages, people knew they were in a "middle time." It was especially obvious to the people of Italy—sitting on the rubble of Rome—that there was a brighter age before them. The long-awaited rebirth, or Renaissance, began in Florence for good reason. Wealthy because of its cloth industry, trade, and banking; powered by a fierce city-state pride (locals would pee into the Arno with gusto, knowing rival city-state Pisa was downstream); and fertile with more than its share of artistic genius (imagine guys like Michelangelo and Leonardo attending the same high school)—Florence was a natural home for this cultural explosion.

Take a walk through the core of Renaissance Florence by starting at the Accademia (home of Michelangelo's *David)* and cutting through the heart of the city to Ponte Vecchio on the Arno River. (A 10-page, self-guided tour of this walk is outlined in my museum guidebook, *Rick Steves' Mona Winks;* otherwise, you'll find brief descriptions below.)

At the Accademia, you'll look into the eyes of Renaissance man—humanism at its confident peak. Then walk to the cathedral (Duomo) to see the dome that kicked off the architectural Renaissance. Step inside the baptistery to view a ceiling covered with preachy, flat, 2-D, medieval mosaic art. Then, to learn what happened when art met math, check out the realistic 3-D reliefs on the doors. The painter, Giotto, also designed the bell tower—

Florence

an early example of a Renaissance genius excelling in many areas. Continue toward the river on Florence's great pedestrian mall, Via de' Calzaiuoli (or "Via Calz")—part of the original grid plan given to the city by the ancient Romans. Down a few blocks, compare medieval and Renaissance statues on the exterior of the Orsanmichele Church. Via Calz connects the cathedral with the central square (Piazza della Signoria), the city palace (Palazzo Vecchio), and the Uffizi Gallery, which contains the greatest collection of Italian Renaissance paintings in captivity. Finally, walk through the Uffizi courtyard—a statuary think tank of Renaissance greats—to the Arno River and Ponte Vecchio.

Sights—On Florence's Renaissance Walk

▲▲▲Accademia (Galleria dell' Accademia)—This museum houses Michelangelo's *David* and powerful (unfinished) *Prisoners*. Eavesdrop as tour guides explain these masterpieces. More than any other work of art, when you look into the eyes of *David*, you're looking into the eyes of Renaissance man. This was a radical break with the past. Hello, humanism. Man was now a confident individual, no longer a plaything of the supernatural. And life was now more than just a preparation for what happened after you died.

The Renaissance was the merging of art, science, and humanism. In a humanist vein, *David* is looking at the crude giant of medieval darkness and thinking, "I can take this guy." (David was an apt mascot for a town surrounded by big bully city-states.) Back on a religious track, notice *David*'s large and overdeveloped right hand. This is symbolic of the hand of God that powered David to slay the giant...and enabled Florence to rise above its crude neighboring city-states.

Beyond the magic marble are two floors of interesting pre-Renaissance and Renaissance paintings, including a couple of lighter-than-air Botticellis.

Cost, Hours, Location: €7.75. Open Tue–Sun, 08:15–18:50, maybe summer Sat until 22:00, closed Mon (Via Ricasoli 60, tel. 055-238-8609).

Nearby: Piazza Santissima Annunziata, behind the Accademia, features lovely Renaissance harmony. Brunelleschi's Hospital of the Innocents (Spedale degli Innocenti, not worth going inside), with terra-cotta medallions by Luca della Robbia, was built in the 1420s and is considered the first Renaissance building. The 15th-century Santissima Annunziata church facing the same square is worth a peek.

▲▲Duomo—Florence's Gothic Santa Maria del Fiori cathedral has the third-longest nave in Christendom (free, Mon–Wed and Fri–Sat 10:00–17:00, Thu 10:00–15:30, Sun 13:30–17:00, first Sat of month 10:00–15:30). The church's noisy neo-Gothic facade from the 1870s is covered with pink, green, and white Tuscan marble. Since nearly all of its great art is stored in the Museo dell' Opera del Duomo (behind the church), the best thing about the interior is the shade. The inside of the dome is decorated by one of the largest paintings of the Renaissance, a huge (and newly restored) *Last Judgment* by Vasari and Zuccari.

Think of the confidence of the age: The Duomo was built with a hole awaiting a dome in its roof. This was before the technology to span it with a dome was available. No matter. They knew that someone soon could handle the challenge...and the local architect Brunelleschi did. The cathedral's claim to artistic fame is Brunelleschi's magnificent dome—the first Renaissance dome and the model for domes to follow.

▲**Climbing the Cathedral's Dome**—For a grand view into the cathedral from the base of the dome, a peek at some of the tools used in the dome's construction, a chance to see Brunelleschi's "dome-within-a-dome" construction, a glorious Florence view from the top, and the equivalent of 463 plunges on a Stairmaster, climb the dome (€5.20, Mon–Fri 08:30–19:00, Sat 08:30–17:40, closed Sun, first Sat of month 08:30–15:20, enter from outside church on south or river side, expect a long, dreadfully slow-moving line if you don't arrive by 08:30, tel. 055-230-2885). When planning St. Peter's in Rome, Michelangelo rhymed (not in English), "I can build its sister—bigger, but not more beautiful, than the dome of Florence."

▲**Giotto's Tower**—Climbing Giotto's 82-meter-tall tower (or Campanile) beats climbing the neighboring Duomo's dome because it's 50 fewer steps, faster, not so crowded, and offers the same view plus the dome (€5.20, daily 08:30–19:30).

▲▲**Museo dell' Opera del Duomo**—The underrated cathedral museum, behind the church at #9, is great if you like sculpture. It has masterpieces by Donatello (a gruesome wood carving of Mary Magdalene clothed in her matted hair, and the *cantoria*, a delightful choir loft bursting with happy children) and by Luca della Robbia (another choir loft, lined with the dreamy faces of musicians praising the Lord). Look for a late Michelangelo *Pietà* (Nicodemus, on top, is a self-portrait), Brunelleschi's models for his dome, and the original restored panels of Ghiberti's doors to the baptistery. This is one of the few museums in Florence open on Monday (€5.20, Mon–Sat 09:00–19:30, Sun 09:00–13:40, tel. 055-230-2885). If you find all this church art intriguing, look through the open doorway of the Duomo art studio, which has been making and restoring church art since the days of Brunelleschi (a block toward the river from the Duomo at 23a Via dello Studio).

▲**Baptistery**—Michelangelo said its bronze doors were fit to be the gates of Paradise. Check out the gleaming copies of Ghiberti's bronze doors facing the Duomo. Making a breakthrough in perspective, Ghiberti used mathematical laws to create the illusion of receding distance on a basically flat surface. The earlier, famous competition doors are around to the right (north); Ghiberti, who beat Brunelleschi, got the job of designing these doors.

A local document from 860 A.D. already refers to Florence's oldest building as "ancient." Inside, sit and savor the medieval mosaic ceiling, where it's Judgment Day and Jesus is giving the ultimate thumbs up and thumbs down. Compare that to the "new, improved" art of the Renaissance (€2.60 interior open Mon–Sat 12:00–19:00, Sun 08:30–14:00, bronze doors are on the outside so always "open"; original panels are in the Museo dell' Opera del Duomo).

▲**Orsanmichele**—This 9th-century loggia (a covered courtyard) was a market used for selling grain (stored upstairs). Later, it was closed in to make a church. Notice the grain spouts on the pillars inside. The glorious tabernacle by Orcagna takes you back (1359).

Study the sculpture in the niches outside. You can see man stepping out of the literal and figurative shadow of the church in the great Renaissance sculptor Donatello's *St. George*. Look into George's face; he's a sensitive new-age guy (SNAG). The predella at the base of this statue shows St. George slaying the dragon to protect the wispy, melodramatic maiden. This was groundbreaking Renaissance emotion and perspective (free, daily 09:00–12:00, 16:00–18:00, closed first and last Mon of month, on Via Calzaiuoli; can be closed due to staffing problems, try going through the back door). The iron bars spanning the vaults were the Italian Gothic answer to the French Gothic external buttresses. Across the street is Museo Orsanmichele...

▲**Museo Orsanmichele**—For some peaceful time alone with the original statues that filled the niches of Orsanmichele, climb to the top of the church (entry behind church, across street). Be there at 09:00, 10:00, and 11:00 daily when the door is open and art-lovers in the know climb four flights of stairs to this little-known museum containing statues by Ghiberti, Donatello, and others (info in Italian, but picture guides on wall help you match art with artists). Upstairs is a tower room with city views (free). A block away, you'll find...

▲**Mercato Nuovo**—This market loggia is how Orsanmichele looked before it became a church. Originally a silk and straw market, Mercato Nuovo still functions as a rustic market today (at intersection of Via Calimala and Via Porta Rossa). Prices are soft. Notice the circled X in the center, marking the spot where those who fell into bankruptcy hit after being hoisted up to the top and dropped as punishment. You'll also find Porcellino (a wild boar nicknamed "little pig"), which people rub and give coins to in order to insure their return to Florence. Nearby is a wagon selling tripe (cow innards) sandwiches.

▲**Piazza della Repubblica**—This large square sits on the site of Florence's original Roman Forum. The lone column is the only remaining bit of Roman Florence except for the grid street plan. Look at the map to see the ghost of Rome: A rectangular fort lined up with the compass oblivious to the river with this square marking the intersection of the two main roads (Via Corso and Via Roma). The piazza you see today is really a nationalistic statement from just after the unification of Italy. Florence, the capital of the country (1865–1870) until Rome was liberated, lacked a square worthy of this grand new country. So the neighborhood here was razed to open up a grand modern forum surrounded by grand, circa 1890 buildings.

Medieval writers described Florence as so densely built up that when it rained, pedestrians didn't get wet. Torches were used to light the lanes in midday. The city was prickly with noble family towers (like San Gimignano) and had Romeo and Juliet–type family feuds. But with the rise of the Medicis (c. 1300), no noble family was allowed to have an architectural ego trip taller then their tower, and nearly all were taken down.

▲**Palazzo Vecchio**—This fortified palace, once the home of the Medici family, is a Florentine landmark. But if you're visiting only one palace interior in town, the Pitti Palace is better. The Palazzo Vecchio interior is wallpapered with mediocre magnificence, worthwhile only if you're a real Florentine art and history fan. The museum's most famous statues are Michelangelo's *Genius of Victory*, Donatello's static *Judith and Holerfernes*, and Verrocchio's *Winged Cherub* (a copy tops the fountain in the free courtyard at entrance, original inside).

Scattered throughout the museum are a dozen computer terminals with information in English on the Medici family, Palazzo Vecchio, and the building's architecture and art, including an animation of the relocation of Michelangelo's *David* (€5.70, Sun 09:00–14:00, Mon–Wed and Fri–Sat 09:00–19:00, Thu 09:00–14:00, in summer open until 23:00 on Mon and Fri, WC in second courtyard, tel. 055-276-8465).

Even if you don't go to the museum, do step into the free courtyard (behind the fake *David*) just to feel the essence of the Medici. Until 1873, Michelangelo's *David* stood at the entrance, where the copy is today. While the huge statues in the square are important only as the whipping boys of art critics and rest stops for pigeons, the nearby Loggia dei Lanzi has several important statues. Look for Cellini's bronze statue of Perseus (with the head of Medusa). The plaque on the pavement in front of the fountain marks the spot where the monk Savonarola was burned in MCCCCXCVIII (for more on the monk, see "Museum of San Marco" listing, below).

▲▲▲**Bargello (Museo Nazionale)**—This underrated sculpture museum is behind Palazzo Vecchio in a former prison that looks like a mini-Palazzo Vecchio. It has Donatello's painfully beautiful *David* (the very influential first male nude to be sculpted in a thousand years), works by Michelangelo, and rooms of Medici treasures cruelly explained in Italian only—mention that English descriptions would be wonderful (€4, daily 08:15–13:50 but closed first, third, and fifth Sun and second and fourth Mon of each month, Via del Proconsolo 4, tel. 055-238-8606).

▲▲▲**Uffizi Gallery**—The greatest collection of Italian paintings anywhere is a must, with plenty of works by Giotto, Leonardo, Raphael, Caravaggio, Rubens, Titian, and Michelangelo and a roomful of Botticellis, including his *Birth of Venus*. Because only

780 visitors are allowed inside the building at any one time, during the day there's generally a very long wait. The good news: No Louvre-style mob scenes. The museum is nowhere near as big as it is great: Few tourists spend more than two hours inside. The paintings are displayed on one comfortable floor in chronological order, from the 13th through 17th centuries.

Essential stops are (in this order): Gothic altarpieces (narrative, pre-Realism, no real concern for believable depth) including Giotto's altarpiece, which progressed beyond "totem-pole angels"; Uccello's *Battle of San Romano*, an early study in perspective (with a few obvious flubs); Fra Filippo Lippi's cuddly Madonnas; the Botticelli room, filled with masterpieces, including a pantheon of classical fleshiness and the small *La Calumnia*, showing the glasnost of Renaissance free-thinking being clubbed back into the darker age of Savonarola; two minor works by Leonardo; the octagonal classical sculpture room with an early painting of Bob Hope and a copy of Praxiteles' *Venus de Medici*—considered the epitome of beauty in Elizabethan Europe; a view through the window of Ponte Vecchio—dreamy at sunset; Michelangelo's only surviving easel painting, the round *Holy Family*; Raphael's noble *Madonna of the Goldfinch*; Titian's voluptuous *Venus of Urbino*; and Duomo views from the café terrace at the end (WC near café).

Cost, Hours, Reservations: €9.30, Tue–Sun 08:15 to 18:50, maybe summer Sat until 22:00, closed Mon (last entry 45 min before closing; take elevator or climb 4 long flights of stairs).

Avoid the two-hour peak season midday wait by making a telephone reservation. It's easy, slick, and costs only €1.60 (tel. 055-294-883, explained in "Helpful Hints," above). At the Uffizi, walk briskly past the 200-meter-long line—pondering the IQ of this gang—to the special entrance for those with reservations (labeled in English "Entrance for Reservations Only"), give your number, pay (cash only), and scoot right in. You can reserve in advance for other museums—including the Bargello, Accademia (*David*), Medici Chapel, and Pitti Palace, though the only other one I'd consider reserving would be the Accademia.

If you haven't called ahead, you may be able to book directly at the Uffizi. Ask the clerk (who stands at the entrance for people with reservations) if you can make a reservation in person. He may direct you to the ticket office where you can secure a reservation for later in the day or the next day (depends on luck and availability). Also, Walking Tours of Florence does a guided tour of the museum Tuesday through Saturday (€31 includes admission and reservation, departs from their office at 15:30, 2 hrs, 18 people; see "Tours of Florence," above).

Enjoy the Uffizi square, full of artists and souvenir stalls. The surrounding statues honor the earthshaking: artists, philosophers (Machiavelli), scientists (Galileo), writers (Dante), explorers

(Amerigo Vespucci), and the great patron of so much Renaissance thinking, Lorenzo (the Magnificent) de Medici.

▲**Ponte Vecchio**—Florence's most famous bridge is lined with shops that have traditionally sold gold and silver. A statue of Cellini, the master goldsmith of the Renaissance, stands in the center, ignored by the flood of tacky tourism. Notice the "prince's passageway" above. In less secure times, the city leaders had a fortified passageway connecting the Palace Vecchio and Uffizi with the mighty Pitti Palace, to which they could flee in times of attack. This passageway, called the Vasari Corridor, is open to the persistent by request only (€6.20, Tue–Sat at 09:30, closed Mon, tel. 055-265-4321).

More Sights—Central Florence

▲▲**Santa Croce Church**—This 14th-century Franciscan church, decorated by centuries of precious art, holds the tombs of great Florentines (free, Mon–Sat 09:30–17:30, Sun 15:00–17:30, in winter Mon–Sat 09:30–12:30, 15:00–17:30, Sun 15:00–17:30, modest dress code enforced, tel. 055-244-619). The loud 19th-century Victorian Gothic facade faces a huge square ringed with tempting touristy shops and littered with tired tourists. Escape into the church.

Working counterclockwise from the entrance, you'll find the tomb of Michelangelo (with the allegorical figures of painting, architecture, and sculpture), a memorial to Dante (no body... he was banished by his hometown), the tomb of Machiavelli (the originator of hardball politics), a relief by Donatello of the Annunciation, and the tomb of the composer Rossini. To the right of the altar, step into the sacristy, where you'll find a bit of St. Francis' cowl and old sheets of music with the medieval and mobile C clef (two little blocks on either side of the line determined to be middle C). In the bookshop, notice the photos high on the wall of the devastating flood of 1966. Beyond that is a touristy—but mildly interesting—"leather school." The chapels lining the front of the church are richly frescoed. The Bardi Chapel (far left of altar) is a masterpiece by Giotto featuring scenes from the life of St. Francis. On your way out, you'll pass the tomb of Galileo (allowed in by the church long after his death). The neighboring Pazzi Chapel (by Brunelleschi) is considered one of the finest pieces of Florentine Renaissance architecture.

▲▲**Museum of San Marco**—One block north of the Accademia on Piazza San Marco, this museum houses the greatest collection anywhere of medieval frescoes and paintings by the early Renaissance master Fra Angelico. You'll see why he thought of painting as a form of prayer, and couldn't paint a crucifix without shedding tears. Each of the monks' cells has a Fra Angelico fresco. Don't miss the cell of Savonarola, the charismatic monk who rode in from the Christian right, threw out the Medici, turned Florence into a theocracy, sponsored "bonfires of the vanities" (burning books, paintings, and so on), and was finally burned himself when Florence decided to change channels (€4, daily 08:15–13:50, Sat and Sun until 19:00, but closed the first, third, and fifth Sun and the second and fourth Mon of each month, tel. 055-238-8608). They can sell tickets (often with immediate reservation) to Uffizi and Accademia.

▲**Medici Chapel (Cappella dei Medici)**—This chapel, containing two Medici tombs, is drenched in lavish High Renaissance architecture and sculpture by Michelangelo (€5.70, daily 08:15–17:00 but closed the second and fourth Sun and the first, third, and fifth Mon of each month, tel. 055-238-8602). Behind San Lorenzo on Piazza Madonna is a lively market scene that I find just as interesting. Take a stroll through the huge, double-decker central market one block north.

Science Museum (Museo di Storia della Scienza)—This is a fascinating collection of Renaissance and later clocks, telescopes, maps, and ingenious gadgets. One of the most talked-about bottles in Florence is the one here containing Galileo's finger. Loaner English guidebooklets are available. It's friendly, comfortably cool, never crowded, and just downstream from the Uffizi (€6.20, Mon and Wed–Fri 09:30–17:00, Tue and Sat 09:30–13:00, closed Sun, Piazza dei Giudici 1, tel. 055-239-8876).

▲**Michelangelo's Home, Casa Buonarroti**—Fans enjoy Michelangelo's house, which has some of his early, much-less-monumental statues and sketches (€6.20, Wed–Mon 09:30–14:00, closed Tue, English descriptions, Via Ghibellina 70).

Casa di Dante—Dante's house consists of five rooms in an old building, with little of substance to show but lots of photos relating to the life and work of Dante. Although it's well-described in English, it's interesting only to literary buffs (€2.60, Mon and Wed–Sat 10:00–18:00, Sun 10:00–14:00, closed Tue, across the street and around the corner from Bargello, at Via S. Margherita 1).

Church of Santa Maria Novella—This 13th-century Dominican church is rich in art. Along with crucifixes by Giotto and Brunelleschi, there are fine examples of the early Renaissance mastery of perspective: *The Holy Trinity* by Masaccio; it's opposite the entrance (€2.60, Mon–Thu and Sat 09:30–17:00, Fri and Sun 13:00–17:00).

A palatial **perfumery** is around the corner 100 meters down Via della Scala at #16 (free but shopping encouraged, Mon–Sat 09:30–19:30, closed Sun). Thick with the lingering aroma of centuries of spritzes, it started as the herb garden of the Santa Maria Novella monks. Well-known even today for its top-quality products, it is extremely Florentine. Pick up the history sheet at the desk and wander deep into the shop. From the back room, you can peek at the S. M. Novella cloister, with its dreamy frescoes, and imagine a time before Vespas and tourists.

Museum of Precious Stones (Museo dell' Opificio delle Pietre Dure)—This unusual gem of a museum features mosaics of inlaid marble and semiprecious stones. You'll see remnants of the Medici workshop from 1588, including 500 different semiprecious stones, the tools used to cut and inlay them, and room after room of the sumptuous finished product. The fine loaner booklet describes it all in English (€2, Mon–Sat 08:15–14:00, Thu until 19:00, closed Sun, Via degli Alfani 78, around corner from Accademia). This ticket booth can also sell tickets with reservations (perhaps same-day) to the Uffizi and Accademia.

Sights—Florence, South of the Arno River

▲▲**Pitti Palace**—From the Uffizi follow the elevated passageway (closed to non-Medicis) across the Ponte Vecchio bridge to the gargantuan Pitti Palace, which has five separate museums.

The **Palatine Gallery/Royal Apartments** features palatial room after chandeliered room, their walls sagging with paintings by the great masters. Its Raphael collection is the biggest anywhere (first floor, €7.25, Tue–Sun 08:15–18:50, perhaps summer Sat until 22:00, closed Mon).

The **Modern Art Gallery** features Romanticism, neoclassicism, and Impressionism by 19th- and 20th-century Tuscan painters (second floor, €4, daily 08:15–13:50 but closed second and fourth Sun and first, third, and fifth Mon).

The **Grand Ducal Treasures**, or Museo degli Argenti, is the Medici treasure chest entertaining fans of applied arts with jeweled crucifixes, exotic porcelain, gilded ostrich eggs, and so on (ground floor, €7.75, nearly the same hours as Modern Art Gallery).

Behind the palace, the huge, landscaped **Boboli Gardens** offer a shady refuge from the city heat (€2, daily 09:00–18:30, until 19:30 June–Aug, until 16:30 in winter, but closed first and last Mon of month).

▲**Brancacci Chapel**—For the best look at the early Renaissance master Masaccio, see his restored frescoes here (€3, Mon and Wed–Sat 10:00–17:00, Sun 13:00–17:00, closed Tue, cross Ponte Vecchio and turn right a few blocks to Piazza del Carmine). Since only a few tourists are let in at a time, seeing the chapel often involves a wait. The neighborhoods around here are considered the last surviving bits of old Florence.

▲**Piazzale Michelangelo**—Across the river overlooking the city (look for the huge statue of *David*), this square is worth the 30-minute hike, drive, or bus ride (either #12 or #13 from the train station) for the view of Florence and the stunning dome of the Duomo. After dark it's packed with local schoolkids, feeding their dates slices of watermelon. Just beyond it is the stark and beautiful, crowd-free Romanesque San Miniato Church.

Oltrarno Walk—If you never leave the touristy center, you don't really see Florence. There's more to the city than tourism. Ninety percent of its people live and work—mostly in small shops—where tourists rarely venture. This self-guided tour follows a perfectly straight line (you can't get lost). Cross the Ponte Vecchio and walk west on the road toward Pisa—it changes names, from Borgo San Jacopo and Via di Santo Spirito to Borgo Frediano, until you reach the city wall at Porta San Frediano. Along this route you can check out several of my favorite restaurants (described below). As you walk, consider these points:

After one block, at the fancy **Hotel Lungarno**, belly up to the Arno River viewpoint for a great look at Ponte Vecchio. Recall the story of Kesserling, the Nazi commander-in-chief of Italy who happened to be an art-lover. As the Nazis retreated in 1944, he was commanded to blow up all the bridges. Rather than destroy the venerable Ponte Vecchio, he disabled it by blowing up the surrounding neighborhood. Turn around and cross the street to see the ivy-covered nub of a medieval tower—ruined August 6, 1944.

Along this walk, you'll see plenty of artisans at work and inviting little **shops**. You're welcome to drop in but remember, it's rude not to say "*Buon giorno*" and "*Ciao*." "Can I take a look?" is "*Posso guardare?*" (pron. poh-soh gwahr-dah-ray)

The streets are busy with *motorini* (Vespas and other motor bikes). While these are allowed in the city, non-resident cars are not (unless they are electric). Notice that parked cars have a *residente* permit on their dash. You'll see a police officer (likely a woman) later on the walk, keeping traffic out.

Look for little architectural details. Tiny shrines protect the corners of many blocks. Once upon a time, the iron spikes on the walls impaled huge candles, which provided a little light. Electricity changed all that, but notice there are no electric wires visible. They're under the streets.

This street is lined with apartment flats punctuated by the occasional palazzo. The skyline and architecture are typical of the 13th to 16th centuries. Huge **palazzos** (recognized by their immense doors, lush courtyards, and grand stonework) were for big-shot merchants. Many have small wooden doors designed to look like stones (e.g., 3b on Borgo San Frediano). While originally for one family, these buildings are now subdivided, as evidenced by the huge banks of doorbells at the door.

The **Church of Santa Maria del Carmine**, with its famous Brancacci Chapel and Masaccio frescoes, is a short detour off Borgo San Frediano (described above).

A couple of blocks before Porta San Frediano (and its tower), look left up Piazza dei Nerli. The bold yellow schoolhouse was built during Mussolini's rule—grandly proclaiming the resurrection of the Italian empire.

Porta San Frediano, from about 1300, is part of Florence's medieval wall, which stretches grandly from here to the river. The tower was originally twice as high, built when gravity ruled warfare. During the Renaissance, when gunpowder dominated warfare, the tower—now just an easy target—was topped. In medieval times, a kilometer-wide strip outside the wall was cleared to deny attackers any cover. Notice the original doors— immense and studded with fat iron nails to withstand battering rams. Got a horse? Lash it to a ring.

Tour over. You passed several fun eateries, and the colorful Trattoria Sabatino is just outside the wall (all described in "Eating," below). *Ciao.*

Experiences—Florence

▲▲**Gelato**—Gelato is an edible art form. Italy's best ice cream is in Florence—one souvenir that can't break and won't clutter your luggage. But beware of scams at touristy joints on busy streets that turn a simple request of a cone into a €10 "tourist special."

The **Gelateria Carrozze** is very good (daily 11:00–24:00, closes at 21:00 in winter, on riverfront 30 meters from Ponte Vecchio toward the Uffizi, Via del Pesce 3). **Gelateria dei Neri** is another local favorite worth finding (2 blocks east of Palazzo Vecchio at Via Dei Neri 20 red, daily in summer 12:00–23:00, closed Wed in winter).

Vivoli's is the most famous (Tue–Sun 08:00–01:00, closed Mon, the last 3 weeks in Aug, and winter; opposite the Church of Santa Croce, go down Via Torta a block, turn right on Via Stinche; before ordering, try a free sample of their *riso* flavor— rice). The **Cinema Astro**, across the street from Vivoli's, plays English/American movies in their original language (closed Mon).

If you want an excuse to check out the little village-like neighborhood across the river from Santa Croce, enjoy a gelato at the tiny **no-name gelateria** at Via San Miniato 5 red (just before Porta San Miniato).

Shopping

Florence is a great shopping town. Busy street scenes and markets abound, especially near San Lorenzo, near Santa Croce, on Ponte Vecchio, and at Mercato Nuovo (a covered market square 3 blocks north of Ponte Vecchio, listed above in "Sights"). Leather (often better quality for less than the U.S. price), gold, silver, art prints, and tacky plaster "mini-*Davids*" are most popular. Shops usually have promotional stalls in the market squares. Prices are soft in markets. Many visitors spend entire days shopping.

For ritzy Italian fashions, browse along Via de Tornabuoni, Via della Vigna Nuova, and Via Strozzi. Typical chain depart- ment stores are Coin (Mon–Sat 09:30–20:00, Sun 11:00–20:00, on Via Calzaiuoli, near the Orsanmichele church) and Standa

(Mon–Sat 09:00–19:55, closed Sun, at intersection of Via Panzani and Via del Giglio, near train station).

For shopping ideas, ads, and a list of markets, see the *Florence Concierge Information* magazine described under "Tourist Information," above (free from TI and many hotels).

Side Trips to Fiesole and Siena

For a candid peek at **Fiesole**—a Florentine suburb—ride bus #7 (3/hr, departs from Piazza Adua at the northeast side of the station and also from Piazza San Marco) for about 25 minutes through neighborhood gardens, vineyards, orchards, and large villas to the last stop—Fiesole. This town is a popular excursion from Florence because of its small eateries and its good views of Florence. Catch the sunset from the terrace just below the La Reggia restaurant; from the Fiesole bus stop, face the bell tower and take the very steep Via San Francisco on your left. You'll find the view terrace near the top of the hill.

Connoisseurs of peace and small towns who aren't into art or shopping (and who won't be seeing Siena otherwise) should consider riding the bus to **Siena** (75 min by bus). This can be a daytrip or an evening trip. Siena is magic after dark. Confirm when the last bus returns. For more information, see the Siena chapter.

Sleeping in Florence
(€1.10 = about $1, country code: 39)

Sleep Code: **S** = Single, **D** = Double/Twin, **T** = Triple, **Q** = Quad, **b** = bathroom, **s** = shower only, **CC** = Credit Cards accepted, **no CC** = Credit Cards not accepted, **SE** = Speaks English, **NSE** = No English. Unless otherwise noted, breakfast is included (but usually optional). English is generally spoken.

The accommodations scene varies wildly with the season. Spring and fall are very tight and expensive, while mid-July through August is wide open and discounted. November through February is also generally empty. With good information and a phone call ahead, you can find a stark, clean, and comfortable double with breakfast for about €65, with a private shower for €90 (less at the smaller places, such as the *soggiornos*). You get elegance for €125. Many places listed are old and rickety; I can't imagine Florence any other way. Rooms with air-conditioning cost around €100—worth the extra money in the summer. Virtually all of the places are central, within minutes of the great sights. Few hotels escape Vespa noise at night.

Call direct to the hotel. Do not use the TI, which costs your host and jacks up the price. In slow times, budget travelers call around and find soft prices. Ask if you'll get a discount for paying in cash, for staying for three or more nights (or both), or for using this book. And ask if you can skip breakfast (these

overpriced breakfasts are legally optional, though some hotels
pretend otherwise).

Call ahead. I repeat, call ahead. Places will hold a room
until early afternoon. If they say they're full, mention you're
using this book.

Laundromats: The Wash & Dry Lavarapido chain offers
long hours and efficient self-service Laundromats at several
locations (daily 08:00–22:00, tel. 055-580-480). Close to recommended hotels: Via dei Servi 105 red (near *David*), Via del Sole 29
red and Via della Scala 52 red (between station and river), and
Via dei Serragli 87 red (across the river in Oltrarno neighborhood). East of the station, another handy modern launderette
is just off Via Cavour at Via Guelfa 22 red (daily 08:00–22:00,
12 pounds washed and dried for €6.20).

Sleeping between the Station and Duomo
(zip code: 50123)

Hotel Accademia is an elegant two-star hotel with marble stairs,
parquet floors, attractive public areas, 22 pleasant rooms, and
a floor plan that defies logic (Sb-€83, Db-€124, Tb-€155,
these discounted prices are promised through 2002 only with
this book, CC, air-con, TV, tiny courtyard, Via Faenza 7, tel.
055-293-451, fax 055-219-771, www.accademiahotel.net,
e-mail: info@accademiahotel.net).

Hotel Bellettini rents 33 bright, cool, well-cared-for
rooms with inviting lounges and a touch of class. Its five rooms
in an annex two blocks away are of higher quality with all the
comforts, but you need to come to the main hotel for breakfast (Sb-€83, Db-€108, Tb-€145, Qb-€181, CC, 5 percent
discount with this book only if you claim it upon arrival,
air-con, free Internet access, Via de' Conti 7, tel. 055-213-561,
fax 055-283-551, www.firenze.net/hotelbellettini, e-mail:
hotel.bellettini@dada.it, frisky Gina SE).

Residenza Dei Pucci, a block north of the Duomo, has
12 tastefully decorated rooms—in soothing earth tones—with
aristocratic furniture and tweed carpeting. It's fresh and bright
(Sb-€130, Db-€145, Tb-€165, suite with grand Duomo
view-€207 for 2 people, €233 for 4, claim a 10 percent discount through 2002 with this book, breakfast served in room,
CC, Via dei Pucci 9, tel. 055-281-886, fax 055-264-314, http:
//residenzapucci.interfree.it/, SE).

Palazzo Castiglioni offers 16 grand rooms with all the
conveniences in a peaceful, 19th-century palazzo package.
Most rooms are spacious, several have frescoes, and all make a
fine splurge (Db-€170, Db suite-€232, air con, elevator, Via
del Giglio 8, tel. 055-214-886, fax 055-274-0521, e-mail: torre
.guelfa@flashnet.it, Laura SE).

Hotels in Florence

- **1** HOTEL ACCADEMIA
- **2** HOTEL MORANDI ALLA CROCETTA
- **3** CASA RABATTI
- **4** SOGGIORNO PEZZATI
- **5** HOTEL ENZA
- **6** SOGGIORNO MAGLIANI
- **7** HOTEL LOGGIATO DEI SERVITI
- **8** DUE FONTANE HOTEL
- **9** OBLATE SISTERS OF THE ASSUMPTION
- **10** RESIDENZA DEI PUCCI
- **11** PALAZZO CASTIGLIONI & HOTEL ALDOBRANDINI
- **12** HOTEL BELLETTINI
- **13** HOTEL BASILEA
- **14** PENSIONE CENTRALE
- **15** HOTEL SOLE
- **16** SOGGIORNO BATTISTERO
- **17** HOTEL PENDINI
- **18** PENSIONE MAXIM
- **19** ALBERGO FIRENZE
- **20** HOTEL ELITE
- **21** TORRE GUELFA, HOTEL APOSTOLI & ALESSANDRA HOTELS
- **22** PENSIONE BRETAGNA
- **23** FLORENCE WALKING TOURS

Pensione Centrale, a happy and traditional-feeling place with 18 spacious rooms, is indeed central. Run by aristocratic Marie Therese Blot, spunky Margherita, and Franco, you'll feel right at home (D-€93, Db-€109, CC, quiet, some air-con rooms, often filled with American students, elevator, Via de' Conti 3, tel. 055-215-761, fax 055-215-216, e-mail: info@pensionecentrale.it). They sometimes send people to a nearby, noisier pension; confirm that your reservation is for this place.

Hotel Aldobrandini, a good budget choice, has 15 decent, clean, affordable rooms, with the San Lorenzo market at its doorstep and the entrance to the Medici Chapel a few steps away (Ss-€42, Sb-€52, D-€67, Db-€83, CC, lots of night noise, fans, Piazza Madonna Degli Aldobrandini 8, tel. 055-211-866, fax 055-267-6281, Ignazio and Anna SE).

Sleeping near the Central Market
(zip code: 50129)

Hotel Basilea offers predictable, three-star, air-conditioned comfort in its 38 modern rooms (Db-€109–150 depending on season, CC, elevator, terrace, free e-mail service, Via Guelfa 41, at intersection with Nazionale—a busy street, ask for rooms in the back, tel. 055-214-587, fax 055-268-350, www.florenceitaly .net, e-mail: basilea@dada.it).

Casa Rabatti is the ultimate if you always wanted to be a part of a Florentine family. Its four simple, clean rooms are run with motherly warmth by Marcella and her husband Celestino, who speak minimal English (D-€47, Db-€54, €20 per bed in shared quad or quint, prices good with this book, no breakfast, fans, no sign other than on doorbell, 5 blocks from station, Via San Zanobi 48 black, tel. 055-212-393, e-mail: casarabatti@inwind.it).

Soggiorno Pezzati Daniela is another little place, with six homey rooms (Sb-€44, Db-€60, Tb-€83, cheaper off-season, no breakfast, all rooms have a fridge, air-con extra; marked only by small sign near door, Via San Zanobi 22, tel. 055-291-660, fax 055-287-145, e-mail: 055291660@iol.it, Daniela SE). If you get an Italian recording when you call, hang on—your call is being transferred to a cell phone.

Hotel Enza rents 16 quirky rooms for a decent price (S-€42, Sb-€52, D-€57, Ds-€65, Db-€75, T-€78, Tb-€93, family loft, CC, Via San Zanobi 45 black, tel. 055-490-990, fax 055-473-672, www.hotelenza.it, e-mail: info@hotelenza.it, Katia and Tatyana SE).

Central and humble, with seven rooms, **Soggiorno Magliani** feels and smells like a great-grandmother's place (S-€33, D-€43, cash only but secure reservation with CC, double-paned windows, near Via Guelfa at Via Reparata 1, tel. 055-287-378, e-mail: hotel-magliani@libero.it, run by a friendly family duo, Vincenza and English-speaking daughter Cristina).

Sleeping East of the Duomo

The first two listings are near the Accademia, on Piazza Annunziata (zip code: 50122).

Hotel Loggiato dei Serviti, at the most prestigious address in Florence on the most Renaissance square in town, gives you Renaissance romance with hair dryers. Stone stairways lead you under open-beam ceilings through this 16th-century monastery's elegant public rooms. The 29 cells, with air-conditioning, TVs, mini-bars, and telephones, wouldn't be recognized by their original inhabitants. The hotel staff is both professional and friendly (Sb-€140, Db-€202, family suites from €258, book a month ahead during peak season, discounts in Aug and winter, CC, elevator, Piazza S.S. Annunziata 3, tel. 055-289-592, fax 055-289-595, www.loggiatodeiservitihotel.it, e-mail: info@loggiatodeiservitihotel.it, Simonetta, Francesca, and Andrea SE).

Le Due Fontane Hotel faces the same great square but fills its old building with a smoky, 1970s, business-class ambience. Its 57 air-conditioned rooms are big and comfortable (Sb-€103, Db-€140, Tb-€196, these discounted prices are promised through 2002 but only if you claim them upon reserving, CC, elevator, Piazza S.S. Annunziata 14, tel. 055-210-185, fax 055-294-461, e-mail: leduefontane@dada.it, SE).

At **Hotel Morandi alla Crocetta**, a former convent, you're enveloped in a 16th-century cocoon. Located on a quiet street, with period furnishings, parquet floors, and wood-beamed ceilings, it draws you in (Sb-€93, Db-€150, CC, Via Laura 50, a block off Piazza S.S. Annunziata, tel. 055-234-4747, fax 055-248-0954, www.hotelmorandi.it, e-mail: welcome@hotelmorandi.it).

The **Oblate Sisters of the Assumption** run a 20-room hotel in a Renaissance building with a dreamy garden and a quiet, institutional feel (S-€34, D-€62, Db-€67, elevator, Borgo Pinti 15, 50121 Firenze, tel. 055-248-0582, fax 055-234-6291, NSE).

Sleeping on or near Piazza Repubblica (zip code: 50123)

These are the most central of my accommodations recommendations, though given Florence's walkable core, nearly every hotel can be considered central.

Hotel Pendini, a very well-run three-star hotel with 42 old-time rooms (8 with views of the square), is popular and central, overlooking Piazza Repubblica (Sb-€83–109, Db-€109–150 depending on season, CC, elevator, fine lounge and breakfast room, air-con, Via Strozzi 2, reserve ASAP, tel. 055-211-170, fax 055-281-807, www.florenceitaly.net, e-mail: pendini@dada.it).

Pensione Maxim, right on Via Calz, is a big, institutional-feeling place as close to the sights as possible. Its halls are narrow, but the 29 rooms are comfortable and well-maintained (Sb-€83, Db-€93, Tb-€124, Qb-€155, add €5 per person per day for air-con June–Sept, CC but pay first night in cash, Internet access, elevator, no curfew, Via dei Calzaiuoli 11, tel. 055-217-474, fax 055-283-729, www.firenzealbergo.it/home/hotelmaxim, e-mail: hotmaxim@tin.it, Paolo and Nicola Maioli).

Soggiorno Battistero, next door to the Baptistery, has seven simple, airy rooms, most with urban noise but also great views, overlooking the Baptistery and square. You're in the heart of Florence (S-€52, Db-€93, Tb-€124, breakfast served in room, Internet access, CC, Piazza San Giovanni 1, third floor, tel. 055-295-143, fax 055-268-189, www.soggiornobattistero.it, e-mail: battistero@dada.it, lovingly run by Italian Luca and American wife Kelly).

Albergo Firenze, a big, efficient place, offers good, basic, and spacious rooms in a wonderfully central, reasonably quiet locale two blocks behind the Duomo (Sb-€62, Db-€83, cash only, must prepay first night with a bank draft or traveler's check, elevator, off Via del Corso at Piazza Donati 4, tel. 055-214-203, fax 055-212-370, SE).

Sleeping South of the Train Station near Piazza Santa Maria Novella
(zip code: 50123)

From the station (with your back to the tracks), cross the wide square to reach the church and continue to the Piazza Santa Maria Novella in front of the church (or you can take the underground Galleria S.M. Novella tunnel from the station—with your back to the tracks, it's outside on the left—but beware of thieves in the tunnel, where the tunnel surfaces, and at night). Piazza Santa Maria Novella is a pleasant square by day that becomes a little sleazy after dark.

Hotel Pensione Elite, run warmly by Maurizio and Nadia, is a fine basic value, with eight comfortable rooms and a charm rare in this price range (Ss-€52, Sb-€72, Ds-€67, Db-€83, breakfast-€5, fans, at south end of square with back to church, go right to Via della Scala 12, second floor, tel. & fax 055-215-395, SE).

Hotel Sole, a clean, cozy, family-run place with eight bright, modern rooms, is just off Santa Maria Novella toward the river (Sb-€47, Db-€75, Tb-€103, no breakfast; air-con, elevator, Via del Sole 8, third floor, tel. & fax 055-239-6094, friendly Anna NSE).

Sleeping near Arno River and Ponte Vecchio
(zip code: 50123)

Pensione Bretagna is an Old World, ramshackle place run by helpful Antonio and Maura. Imagine eating breakfast under

...andeliered ceiling overlooking the Arno River
(...   ...-€57, small Db-€93, big Db-€96, Tb-€120,
Qb-   ...3, family deals, prices special with this book through
2002, CC, air-con, just past Ponte San Trinita, Lungarno Corsini
6, tel. 055-289-618, fax 055-289-619, www.bretagna.it, e-mail:
hotel@bretagna.it). They also run Soggiorno Althea, a cheaper
place with nicer rooms, near Piazza San Spirito in the Oltrarno
neighborhood (6 rooms, Db-€67, no breakfast, no reception
desk, call Bretagna to book).

Hotel Torre Guelfa is topped with a fun medieval tower
with a panoramic rooftop terrace, and has a huge living room. Its
16 rooms vary wildly in size (small Db-€129, standard Db-€170,
Db suite-€232). Number 15, with a private terrace—€200—
is worth reserving several months in advance (elevator, air-con, a
couple blocks northwest of Ponte Vecchio, Borgo S.S. Apostoli 8, tel.
055-239-6338, fax 055-239-8577, www.hoteltorreguelfa.com, e-mail:
torre.guelfa@flashnet.it, Giancarlo, Carlo, and Sandro all SE).

Residenza Apostoli, in the same building, is bright, spacious,
and modern, with parquet floors and 12 air-conditioned rooms
(Db-€134, Tb-€155, breakfast in room, CC, 10 percent discount with this book in 2002, elevator, Borgo Santi Apostoli 8,
tel. 055-284-837, fax 055-268-790, e-mail: residenza.apostoli
@infinito.it, run by Mirella and Cinzia).

Hotel Pensione Alessandra is an old 16th-century, peaceful
place with 25 big rooms (S-€72, Sb-€109, D-€109, Db-€140,
T-€140, Tb-€181, Q-€155, Qb-€202, CC but 5 percent discount with cash, air-con, Internet access, Borgo S.S. Apostoli 17,
tel. 055-283-438, fax 055-210-619, www.hotelalessandra.com).

Sleeping in Oltrarno, South of the River
(zip code: 50125)

Across the river in the Oltrarno area, between the Pitti Palace
and Ponte Vecchio, you'll still find small traditional crafts shops,
neighborly piazzas, and family eateries. The following places are
a few minutes' walk from Ponte Vecchio.

Hotel La Scaletta, an elegant, dark, cool place with 13
rooms, a labyrinthine floor plan, lots of Old World lounges, and
a romantic and panoramic roof terrace, is run by Barbara, her
son Manfredo, and daughters Bianca and Diana (S-€52, Sb-€93,
D-€98, Db-€113–124, Tb-€129–145, Qb-€145–155, higher
price is for quieter rooms in back, €5–10 discount if you pay
cash, CC, air-con in 8 rooms and fans in others, elevator, bar
with fine wine at good prices, Via Guicciardini 13b, 150 meters
south of Ponte Vecchio, tel. 055-283-028, fax 055-289-562,
www.lascaletta.com, e-mail: info@lascaletta.it). Secure your
reservation with a personal check or traveler's check. Manfredo
loves to cook. If he's cooking dinner, eat here. He serves a

Florence's Oltrarno Neighborhood

① HOTEL LA SCALETTA
② TO HOTEL SILLA
③ PENSIONE SORELLE BANDINI
④ HOTEL LUNGARNO
⑤ SOGGIORNO PEZZATI ALESSANDRA
⑥ ISTITUTO GOULD
⑦ OSTELLO SANTA MONACA
⑧ TRATTORIA BORDINO

⑨ RISTORANTE BIBO
⑩ BORGO ANTICO REST., OSTERIA SANTO SPIRITO, & RICCHI CAFE
⑪ TRATTORIA CASALINGA
⑫ CAMMILLO TRATTORIA
⑬ OSTERIA DEL CINGHIALE BIANCO
⑭ TRATTORIA ANGIOLINO
⑮ TO TRATTORIA SABATINO

€10 "Taste of Tuscany" deal (plate of quality Tuscan meats and cheeses with bread and 2 glasses of robust Chianti)—ideal for a light lunch on the terrace.

Hotel Silla, a classic three-star hotel with 36 cheery, spacious, pastel, and modern rooms, is a fine value. It faces the river and overlooks a park opposite the Santa Croce Church (Db-€160, Tb-€196, mention this book for a discount, CC, elevator, air-con, Via dei Renai 5, 50125 Florence, tel. 055-234-2888, fax 055-234-1437, www.hotelsilla.it, e-mail: hotelsilla@tin.it, Laura SE).

Pensione Sorelle Bandini is a ramshackle, 500-year-old palace on a perfectly Florentine square, with cavernous rooms, museum-warehouse interiors, a musty youthfulness, cats, a balcony lounge-loggia with a view, and an ambience that, for romantic bohemians, can be a highlight of Florence. Mimmo or Sr. Romeo will hold a room until 16:00 with a phone call (D-€96, Db-€116, T-€133, Tb-€159, includes breakfast—which during low times is optional, saving €9 per person—elevator, Piazza Santo Spirito 9, tel. 055-215-308, fax 055-282-761).

Hotel Lungarno is the place to stay if money is no object. This deluxe, four-star hotel with 70 rooms strains anything stressful or rough out of Italy and gives you only service with a salute, physical elegance everywhere you look, and fine views over the Arno and Ponte Vecchio (Sb-€222, Db-€346, Db facing the river-€424, fancier suites, great riverside public spaces, 100 meters from Ponte Vecchio at Borgo San Jacopo 14, tel. 055-27261, fax 055-268-437, www.lungarnohotels.com, e-mail: bookings@lungarnohotels.com).

Soggiorno Pezzati Alessandra is a warm and friendly place renting five great rooms in the Oltrarno neighborhood (Sb-€44, Db-€60, Tb-€83, Qb-€104, cheaper off-season, no breakfast, all rooms have a fridge, air-con extra, Via Borgo San Frediano 6, tel. 055-290-424, fax 055-218-464, e-mail: alex170169@libero.it, Alessandra). If you get an Italian recording when you call, hang on—your call is being transferred to a cellular phone.

Istituto Gould is a Protestant Church–run place with 33 clean but drab rooms with twin beds and modern facilities (S-€30, Sb-€35, D-€41, Db-€48, Tb-€62, €20 per person in quads, no breakfast, quieter rooms in back, Via dei Serragli 49, tel. 055-212-576, fax 055-280-274, e-mail: gould.reception@dada.it). You must arrive when the office is open (Mon–Fri 09:00–13:00, 15:00–19:00, Sat 09:00–13:00, no check-in Sun).

Ostello Santa Monaca, a cheap hostel, is a few blocks south of Ponte Alla Carraia, one of the bridges over the Arno (€15.50 beds, 4- to 20-bed rooms, breakfast extra, 01:00 curfew, Via Santa Monaca 6, tel. 055-268-338, fax 055-280-185).

Sleeping Away from the Center

Hotel Ungherese is good for drivers. It's northeast of the city center (near Stadio, en route to Fiesole), with easy, free street parking and quick bus access (#11 and #17) into central Florence (Sb-€60, Db-€114, extra bed-€30, these discounted prices available with this book, pay cash for additional 7 percent discount, rooms are 20 percent less off-season, includes breakfast, CC, most rooms air-con, Via G. B. Amici 8, tel. & fax 055-573-474, www.hotelungherese.it, e-mail: hotel.ungherese@dada.it). It has great singles and a backyard garden terrace (ask for a room on the garden). They can recommend good eateries nearby.

Villa Camerata, classy for an IYHF hostel, is on the outskirts of Florence (€14.50 per bed with breakfast, 4- to 12-bed rooms, must have IYHF card, ride bus #17 to Salviatino stop, Via Righi 2, tel. 055-601-451).

Eating in Florence

To save money and time for sights, you can keep lunches fast and simple, eating in one of the countless self-service places and pizzerias or just picnicking (try juice, yogurt, cheese, and a roll for €5). For good sit-down meals, consider the following. Remember, restaurants like to serve what's fresh. If you're into flavor, go for the seasonal best bets—featured in the *Piatti del Giorno* (special of the day) sections of the menus.

Eating in Oltrarno, South of the River

For a change of scene, eat across the river in Oltrarno. Here are a few good places just over Ponte Vecchio.

At Piazza San Felicita: A block south of Ponte Vecchio is the unpretentious and happy Piazza San Felicita, with two good restaurants. The cozy and candlelit **Trattoria Bordino**, just up the street and actually built into the old town wall (c. 1170), serves tasty and beautifully presented Florentine cuisine "with international influence" (moderate prices, Mon–Sat 12:00–14:30, 19:30–22:30, closed Sun, Via Stracciatella 9 red, tel. 055-213-048). Right on the square, the more touristy **Ristorante Bibo** serves *"cucina tipica Fiorentina"* with a pink-tablecloth-and-black-bowties dressiness and leafy candlelit outdoor seating (good €15 3-course meal, CC, reserve for outdoor seating, Wed–Mon 12:00–15:00, 19:00–23:00, closed Tue, Piazza San Felicita 6 red, tel. 055-239-8554).

At Piazza Santo Spirito: This classic Florentine square (lately a hangout for drug pushers, therefore a bit seedy-feeling and plagued by Vespa bag-snatchings) has two popular little restaurants offering good local cuisine every night of the week, indoor and on-the-square seating (reserve for on-the-square), moderate prices, and impersonal service: **Borgo Antico** (Piazza Santo Spirito 6 red, tel. 055-210-437) and **Osteria Santo Spirito** (pricier, more peaceful outdoor seating, Piazza Santo Spirito 16 red, tel. 055-238-2383).

The **Ricchi Caffè**, next to Borgo Antico, has fine *gelato* and shaded outdoor tables. Notice the plainness of the facade of the Brunelleschi church facing the square. Then step inside the café, grab a coffee, and pick your favorite of the many ways it might be finished.

Trattoria Casalinga is an inexpensive standby. Famous for its home-cooking, it's now filled with tourists rather than locals. But it sends them away full, happy, and with euros left for *gelato* (Mon–Sat 12:00–14:30, 19:00–21:45, closed Sun and all of Aug, CC, just off Piazza Santo Spirito, near the church at Via dei Michelozzi 9 red, after 20:00 reserve or wait, tel. 055-218-624).

Restaurants in Florence

① OSTERIA BELLEDONNE

② RIST. LA SPADA

③ TRATTORIA MARIONE

④ TRATTORIA SOSTANZA-TROIA

⑤ TRATTORIA IL CONTADINO

⑥ TRATTORIA DA GIORGIO

⑦ LA GROTTA DI LEO

⑧ MERCATO CENTRALE MARKET

⑨ TRATTORIA LA BURRASCA & OSTERIA LA CONGRAGA

⑩ SELF-SERVICE REST. LEONARDO

⑪ RIST. IL CAVALLINO

⑫ OSTERIA VINI E VECCHI SAPORI

⑬ CANTINETTA DEI VERRAZZANO & RIST. PAOLI

⑭ I FRATELLINI WINE & SANDWICH SHOP

⑮ TRATTORIA ICCHE C'E C'E

⑯ PICNIC SPOT IF IT'S NOT TOO HOT

On Via di Santo Spirito/Borgo San Jacopo: Several good and colorful restaurants line this multi-named street a block off the river in Oltrarno. I'd survey the scene (perhaps following the self-guided Oltrarno walk described above) before making a choice.

At **Cammillo Trattoria,** while Cammillo is slurping spaghetti in heaven, his granddaughter Chiara carries on his tradition, mixing traditional Tuscan with "creative" modern cuisine. With a charcoal grill and a team of white-aproned waiters cranking out wonderful food in a fun, dressy-but-down-to-earth ambience, this place is a hit (full dinners about €36 plus wine, Thu–Tue 12:00–14:30, 19:30–22:30, closed Wed, CC, Borgo San Jacopo 57 red, reservations smart, tel. 055-212-427).

Other inviting places along this street include: **Osteria del Cinghiale Bianco,** popular but cramped (around €30 for dinner plus wine, Borgo San Jacopo 43 red, air-con, closed Tue–Wed, reservations wise, tel. 055-215-706). The more relaxed **Trattoria Angiolino** serves good old-fashioned local cuisine (about €20 for dinner plus wine, closed Mon, Via di Santo Spirito 36 red, tel. 055-239-8976). **Trattoria Sabatino** is spacious and extremely cheap, with family character, red-checkered tablecloths, a simple menu, and the fewest tourists of all. A wonderful place to watch locals munch, it's just outside the Porta San Frediano (medieval gate), a ten-minute walk from Ponte Vecchio (12:00–14:30, 19:20–22:00, Mon–Fri only—because it caters to locals rather than tourists, Via Pisana 2 red, tel. 055-225-955). If you eat here, read my guided walk before hiking out to the gate.

Eating North of the River

Eating near Santa Maria Novella and the Train Station

Osteria Belledonne is a crowded and cheery bohemian hole-in-the-wall serving great food at good prices. I loved the meal but had to correct the bill—read it carefully. They don't take too many reservations. Arrive early or wait (Mon–Fri 12:00–14:30, 19:00–22:30, closed Sat–Sun, Via delle Belledonne 16 red, tel. 055-238-2609).

Ristorante La Spada, nearby, is another local favorite serving typical Tuscan cuisine with less atmosphere and more menu (€11 lunch special, about €20 for dinner plus wine, daily 12:00–14:30, 19:00–22:30, air con, near Via della Spada at Via del Moro 66 red, evening reservations smart, tel. 055-218-757).

Trattoria Marione serves good home-cooked meals to a local crowd in a happy, food-loving ambience (closed Sun, dinners run about €15 plus wine, pretty smoky, Via della Spada 27 red, tel. 055-214-756).

Trattoria Sostanza-Troia, with its shared tables, is a

characteristic and well-established place with a loyal local following. Whirling ceiling fans and walls strewn with old photos create a time-warp ambience. They offer two seatings, requiring reservations: one at 19:30 and one at 21:00 (dinners for about €15 plus wine, lunch 12:00–14:00, great for steaks, closed Sat, Via del Porcellana 25 red, tel. 055-212-691).

Two smoky chowhouses for local workers offer a €9, hearty, family-style, fixed-price menu with a bustling working-class/budget-Yankee-traveler atmosphere (Mon–Sat 12:00–14:30, 18:15–21:30, closed Sun, 2 blocks south of train station): **Trattoria il Contadino** (Via Palazzuolo 69 red, tel. 055-238-2673) and **Trattoria da Giorgio** (across the street at Via Palazzuolo 100 red). Arrive early or wait. The touristy **La Grotta di Leo** (a block away) has a cheap, straightforward menu and edible food and pizza (daily 11:00–01:00, Via della Scala 41 red, tel. 055-219-265). Because these places are a block from the station, they are handy, but the street scene is grotty.

Eating near the Central and San Lorenzo Markets

For mountains of picnic produce or just a cheap sandwich and piles of people-watching, visit the huge Central Market—**Mercato Centrale** (Mon–Sat 07:00–14:00, closed Sun, a block north of the San Lorenzo street market).

Trattoria la Burrasca is a funky family-run place ideal for Tuscan home cooking. It's small (10 tables) and inexpensive (pasta for €4) but Anna and Antonio Genzano have cooked and served here with passion since 1982. If Andy Capp were Italian, he'd eat here for special nights out. Everything but the desserts is homemade. And if you want good wine cheap, order it here (Fri–Wed 12:00–15:00, 19:00–22:00, closed Thu, Via Panicale 6b, at north corner of Central Market, tel. 055-215-827, NSE).

Osteria La Congrega brags it's a Tuscan wine bar designed to help you lose track of time. In a fresh and romantic two-level setting, creative chef/owner Mahyar has designed a fun, easy menu featuring modern Tuscan cuisine with top-notch local meat and produce. He offers fine vegetarian dishes, but only one main meat course per evening. With just 10 uncrowded tables, it requires reservations for dinner (moderate, with €13 dinner plates, CC, daily 12:00–15:00, 19:00–23:00, Via Panicale 43 red, tel. 055-2645027).

Eating near the Accademia and Museum of San Marco

Gran Caffè San Marco, conveniently located on Piazza San Marco, offers reasonably priced pizzas, sandwiches, and desserts (no cover charge, self-service and restaurant, Piazza San Marco 11 red, across square from entrance to Museum of San Marco, tel. 055-215-833).

Eating near the Cathedral (Duomo)

Self-service Restaurant Leonardo is fast, cheap, air-conditioned, and very handy, just a block from the Duomo behind the Baptistery (€3 pastas, €4 main courses, Sun–Fri 11:45–14:45, 18:45–21:45, closed Sat, upstairs at Via Pecori 5, tel. 055-284-446). Luciano ("like Pavarotti") runs the place with enthusiasm.

Eating near Palazzo Vecchio

Piazza Signoria, the square facing the old city hall, is ringed by beautifully situated yet touristic eateries. Any will do for a reasonably priced pizza. Perhaps the best value is **Ristorante il Cavallino** (€10 fixed-price lunch menu, €15.50 fixed-price dinner menu, great outdoor seating in shadow of palace, tel. 055-215-818).

Osteria Vini e Vecchi Sapori is a colorful hole-in-the-wall serving traditional food, including plates of mixed sandwiches (€0.75 each—you choose), half a block north of Palazzo Vecchio (Tue–Sun 10:00–23:00, closed Mon, Via dei Magazzini 3 red, facing the bronze equestrian statue in Piazza della Signoria, go behind its tail into the corner and to your left, Emore NSE).

Cantinetta dei Verrazzano is a long-established bakery/café/wine bar serving delightful sandwich plates in an elegant old-time setting, and hot focaccia sandwiches to go. The *Specialita Verrazzano* is a fine plate of four little *crostini* (like mini-*bruschetta*) featuring different local breads, cheeses, and meats (€7). The *Tagliere di Focacce*, a sampler plate of mini focaccia sandwiches, is also fun. Either of these dishes with a glass of Chianti makes a fine, light meal. Paolo describes things to make eating educational. As office workers pop in for a quick bite, it's traditional to share tables at lunchtime (Mon–Sat 12:30–21:00, closed Sun, just off Via Calzaiuoli on a side street across from Orsanmichele church at Via dei Tavolini 18, tel. 055-268-590).

At **I Fratellini**, a colorful hole-in-a-wall place, the "little brothers" have served peasants rustic sandwiches and cheap glasses of Chianti wine since 1875. Join the local crowd, then sit on a nearby curb or windowsill to munch, placing your glass on the wall rack before you leave (€4 for sandwich and wine, 20 meters in front of Orsanmichele church on Via dei Cimatori).

Ristorante Paoli serves great local cuisine to piles of happy eaters under a richly frescoed Gothic vault. Because of its fame and central location, it's filled mostly with tourists, but for a dressy, traditional splurge meal, this is my choice (Wed–Mon 12:00–14:00, 07:00–22:00, closed Tue, smart to reserve for dinner, €19 tourist menu, à la carte is pricier, CC, midway between the old square and the cathedral at Via de Tavolini 12 red, tel. 055-216-215). Salads are flamboyantly cut and mixed from a trolley right at your table.

Trattoria Icche C'è C'è (dialect for "whatever is, is"; pron. ee-kay chay chay) is a small, family-style place where fun-loving Gino serves good traditional meals (moderate, not too touristy, closed Mon, midway between the Bargello and river at Via Magalotti 11 red, tel. 055-216-589).

Transportation Connections—Florence

By train to: Assisi (3/day, 2 hrs, more frequent with transfers, direction: Foligno), **Orvieto** (6/day, 2 hrs), **Pisa** (2/hr, 1 hr), **La Spezia** (for the Cinque Terre, 2/day direct, 2 hrs, or change in Pisa), **Venice** (7/day, 3 hrs), **Milan** (12/day, 3–5 hrs), **Rome** (hrly, 2.5 hrs), **Naples** (2/day, 4 hrs), **Brindisi** (3/day, 11 hrs with change in Bologna), **Frankfurt** (3/day, 12 hrs), **Paris** (1/day, 12 hrs overnight), **Vienna** (4/day, 9–10 hrs). Train info: tel. 848-888-088.

Buses: The SITA bus station, a block west of the Florence train station, is user-friendly (but remember, bus service drops dramatically on Sunday). Schedules are posted everywhere, with TV monitors indicating imminent departures. You'll find buses to: **San Gimignano** (hrly, 1.75 hrs), **Siena** (hrly, 75-min *corse rapide* fast buses, faster than the train, avoid the 2-hr *diretta* slow buses), and the **airport** (hrly, 15 min). Bus info: tel. 055-214-721 from 09:30 to 12:30; some schedules are in the *Florence Concierge Information* magazine.

Taxi to Siena? For around €100, you can arrange a ride directly from your Florence hotel to your Siena hotel. For a small group or people with more money than time, this can be a good value.

PISA

Pisa was a regional superpower in its medieval heyday (11th, 12th, and 13th centuries), rivaling Florence and Genoa. Its Mediterranean empire, which included Corsica and Sardinia, helped make it a wealthy republic. But the Pisa fleet was beaten (in 1284, by Genoa) and its port silted up, leaving the city high and dry, with only its Field of Miracles and its university keeping it on the map.

Pisa's three important sights (the cathedral, the baptistery, and the bell tower) float regally on the best lawn in Italy. Even as the church was being built, the Piazza del Duomo was nicknamed the Campo dei Miracoli, or Field of Miracles, for the grandness of the undertaking. The style throughout is Pisa's very own "Pisan Romanesque," surrounded by Italy's tackiest ring of souvenir stands. This spectacle is tourism at its most crass. Wear gloves.

The big news for 2002 is that the tower—with its tilt finally stabilized—has recently reopened. To ascend, you'll have to reserve in advance (see "Sights," below).

Planning Your Time

Seeing the tower and the square and wandering through the church are 90 percent of the Pisan thrill. Pisa is a touristy quickie. By car, it's a headache. By train, it's a joy. Train travelers may need to change trains in Pisa anyway. Hop on the bus and see the tower. Sophisticated sightseers stop more for the Pisano carvings in the cathedral and baptistery than for a look at the tipsy tower. There's nothing wrong with Pisa, but I'd stop only to see the Field of Miracles and get out of town. By car, it's a 45-minute detour from the freeway.

Orientation

Tourist Information: One TI is at the train station (summer: Mon–Sat 08:00–19:00, Sun 09:30–15:30; winter: Mon–Sat 09:00–17:00 and possibly closed Sun; to your left as you exit station, tel. 050-42291) and another is near the Leaning Tower (Mon–Fri 09:00–18:00, Sat–Sun 10:30–16:30, outside the medieval wall, hidden behind souvenir stands in a nook of the wall, about 100 meters to the left of the gate before you enter the Field of Miracles, tel. 050-560-464). Another TI is at the airport (tel. 050-503-700).

Internet Access: Pisa Internet Point is next to the station (Mon–Sat 10:00–20:00, closed Sun, exit station to the right, Via Colombo 53, tel. 050-220-0408).

Arrival in Pisa

By Train: To get to the Field of Miracles from the station, you can walk (25–30 min, get free map from TI at station, they'll mark the best route on your map), take a taxi (€8, at taxi stand at station or call 541-600), or catch a bus. The latest information on the bus route to the Field of Miracles is posted in the train information office in Pisa's station lobby (or ask at TI). Even though thousands of travelers come to Pisa every year just to see the tower, Pisa sometimes changes the bus number and route to its most famous sight. Currently, you take bus #3 (3/hr, 10 min, leaves from in front of station, across the street—at the big hotel). Buy a €0.75 ticket from the *tabacchi*/magazine kiosk in the station's main hall or at any *tabacchi* shop (good for 1 hr, round-trip OK, 15-minute ride one-way to tower). Confirm the bus route number or risk taking a long tour of Pisa's suburbs. The correct bus will let you off at Piazza Manin, in front of the gate to the Field of Miracles. To return to the station, catch the bus from across the street where you got off (confirm the stop with a local or at either TI).

You can store your bag at Pisa's train station in lockers (which take coins or bills in a complicated process) or usually faster at the *deposito bagaglio* counter (€2.60, tucked into a bleak corner 12 meters to the left of the lockers). With your back to the tracks, the lockers and baggage counter are to the far right.

By Car: To get to the Leaning Tower, follow signs to the Duomo or Campo dei Miracoli, located on the north edge of town. Drivers (coming from the Pisa Nord autostrada exit) don't have to mess with the city center (although you will have to endure some terrible traffic). There's no option better than the €1-per-hour pay lot just outside the town wall a block from the tower.

By Plane: From Pisa's airport, take bus #3 into town (€0.75, 3/hr, 5 min) or a taxi (€6).

Prices

Pisa has a scheme to get you into its neglected secondary sights: the baptistery, cathedral museum (Museo dell' Opera del Duomo), Camposanto cemetery, and fresco museum (Museo delle Sinopie). For any one monument, you'll pay €4.75; for two monuments the cost is €6.20; for four monuments it's €8.30; and for the works (including the cathedral) you'll pay €9.80. In comparison, the cathedral alone is a bargain (€1.60). You can buy any of these tickets at the usually crowded ticket office (behind tower and cathedral entrance), or more easily at the Camposanto cemetery, Museo dell' Opera del Duomo, or Museo delle Sinopie (near Baptistery, almost suffocated by souvenir stands); note that you can buy a ticket just for, say, the cathedral at any of these points.

Sights—Pisa

▲▲**Leaning Tower**—Started in the 12th-century, this most famous example of Pisan Romanesque architecture was leaning even before its completion. Notice how the architect for lack of a better solution, kinked up the top section. The 294 tilted steps to the top were closed for years as engineers worked to keep the bell tower from toppling. The formerly clean and tidy area around the tower was turned into a construction zone as engineers used steam pipes to dry out the subsoil and huge weights to stabilize (but not straighten out) the tower.

The tower finally reopened in December 2001. You'll need a reservation to ascend with an escorted group of 30 (€15, daily 09:00–17:40, probably until 19:40 in summer, to reserve call 050-560-547 or visit www.duomo.pisa.it).

The following Web site contains scads of Tower photos, plus information on its history and the attempts to halt the lean: http://torre.duomo.pisa.it.

▲▲**Cathedral**—The huge Pisan Romanesque church (known as the Duomo), with its carved pulpit by Giovanni Pisano, is artistically more important than its more famous bell tower (€1.60, hours from spring through fall: Mon–Sat 10:00–19:40, Sun 13:00–19:40; winter: Mon–Sat 10:00–12:45, Sun 15:00–16:45). Shorts are OK as long as they're not short shorts. Big backpacks are not allowed, nor is storage provided (but ticket-taker might let you leave bag at entrance).

Pisa

PIAZZA OF MIRACLES
- ❶ BAPTISTERY
- ❷ CAMPOSANTO
- ❸ DUOMO
- ❹ TOWER
- ❺ MUSEO DEL DUOMO

TO AUTOSTRADA

VIALE CASCINE

TO LUCCA

VIA CONTESSA MATILDE

OLD CITY WALLS

PIAZZA MANIN

VIA GABBA

VIA BONANNO

VIA PISANO

TACKY SOUVENIR STANDS

VIA ROMA

VIA SANTA MARIA

VIA MILLE

PIAZZA CAVALIERI

S. STEFANO

VIA UDINI

PIAZZA CAVALOTTI

PIAZZA DANTE

MARKET

VIA BORGO STRETTO

PONTE DI MEZZO

PONTE SOLFERINO

RIVER ARNO

SANTA MARIA DELLA SPINA

VIA FRAN. CRISPI

VIA MANZ.

CORSO ITALIA

N

VIA BATTISTI

PIAZZA VITTORIO EMANUELE

VIA BONAINI

BUS STOP

ⓘ

❻

TRAIN STATION

¼ MILE

400 METERS

DCH

- ❻ HOTEL MILANO
- ❼ HOTEL VILLA KINZICA
- ❽ LA BUCA REST.
- ❾ TAXI STAND

Baptistery—The baptistery, the biggest in Italy, is interesting
for its great acoustics (open daily, summer: 08:00–17:40; spring/
fall: 09:00–17:40; winter: 09:00–16:40; located in front of cathedral). If you ask nicely and leave a tip, the ticket-taker uses the
place's echo power to sing haunting harmonies with himself.
The pulpit, by Nicolo Pisano (1260), inspired Renaissance art to
follow, but the same artist's pulpit and carvings in Siena were just
as impressive to me—in a more enjoyable atmosphere. Notice
that even the baptistery leans about five feet.

Other Sights at the Field of Miracles—For Pisan art, see the
Museo dell' Opera del Duomo, featuring treasures of the cathedral: From sculptures (12th–14th century), paintings, and silverware
to ancient Egyptian, Etruscan, and Roman artifacts (open daily,
summer: 08:00–19:20; spring/fall: 09:00–17:20; winter: 09:00–16:20;
housed behind tower, Piazza Arcivescovado 18). Skip the **Camposanto** cemetery bordering the cathedral square, even if its "Holy
Land dirt" does turn a body into a skeleton in a day (open daily,
summer: 08:00–19:40; spring/fall: 09:00–17:40; winter: 09:00–
16:40). The **Museo delle Sinopie**, housed in a 13th-century hospital, features the sketchy frescoes that were preparatory work for
the frescoes in the cemetery (same hours as baptistery, hidden
behind souvenir stands, across street from baptistery entrance).
The much-advertised **Panoramic Walk on the Wall**, which
includes just a small section of the medieval wall (entrance near
baptistery, at Porta Leone), isn't worth your time or €2.20.

More Sights—The **Museo Nazionale di San Matteo**, in a
former convent, displays 12th to 15th century sculptures,
illuminated manuscripts, and paintings by Martini, Ghirlandaio,
Masaccio, and others (€4.20, Tue–Sat 09:00–19:00, Sun 09:00–
14:00, closed Mon, on the river near Piazza Mazzini at Lungarno
Mediceo, tel. 050-541-865).

Walking between the station and Field of Miracles shows
you a student-filled, classy, Old World town with an Arno-scape
much like its rival upstream. A **fruit market** is pinched and
squeezed into Piazza Vettovaglie (Mon–Sat 07:00–18:00, near
river, between station and tower). The **flea market** attracts
itchy shoppers Wednesday and Saturday mornings on Via del
Brennero (just outside of wall, about 6 blocks east of tower).

Sleeping and Eating in Pisa
(€1.10 = about $1, country code: 39)
Consider **Hotel Milano**, near the station, offering 10 spacious
rooms with faded—but clean—bedspreads (D-€47, Db-€65,
breakfast extra, CC, air-con, Via Mascagni 14, tel. 050-23162,
fax 050-44237, e-mail: hotelmilano@csinfo.it). For a splurge, try
Hotel Villa Kinzica, with 34 modern rooms within a block of
the Field of Miracles—ask for a room with a view of the tower

(Db-€95, CC, elevator, most rooms air-con, attached restaurant, Piazza Arcivescovado 2, tel. 050-560-419, fax 050-551-204).

Eating: For a quick lunch or dinner, the pizzeria/trattoria **La Buca**—just a block from the tower—has a good reputation among locals (Sat–Thu 12:00–15:30, 19:00–23:00, closed Fri, CC, at Via Santa Maria and Via G. Tassi, tel. 050-560-660).

Transportation Connections—Pisa

By train to: Florence (hrly, 1 hour), **La Spezia** (hrly, 1 hr, most trains heading to Torino and Ventimiglia stop in La Spezia; small trains run from La Spezia to Cinque Terre), **Siena** (change at Empoli: Pisa-Empoli, hrly, 30 min; Empoli-Siena, hrly, 1 hr). Even the fastest trains stop in Pisa, and you might be changing trains here whether you plan to stop or not. Train info: tel. 848-888-088.

Route Tips for Drivers

To Florence and Siena: The drive from Pisa to Florence is that rare case where the non-autostrada highway (free, more direct, and at least as fast) is a better deal than the autostrada. When departing for Florence, San Gimignano, or Siena, follow the blue "*superstrada*" signs (green signs are for the autostrada) for the SS road (along the city wall east from the tower—away from the sea) for Florence (and later Siena).

To the Cinque Terre: From Pisa, catch the Genova-bound autostrada. The white stuff you'll see in the mountains as you approach La Spezia isn't snow—it's Carrara marble, Michelangelo's choice for his great art. From Pisa to La Spezia takes about an hour.

SIENA

Break out of the Venice-Florence-Rome syndrome and savor Italy's hill towns. Experience the texture of Tuscany, the slumber of Umbria, and the lazy towns of Lazio.

For starters, here's one of my favorites. Tuscany's Siena seems to be every Italy connoisseur's pet town. In my office, whenever Siena is mentioned, someone moans, "Siena? I luuuv Siena!" Nearby San Gimignano (see end of chapter) is the quintessential hill town, with Italy's best surviving medieval skyline.

Seven hundred years ago, Siena was a major military power in a class with Florence, Venice, and Genoa. With a population of 60,000, it was even bigger than Paris. In 1348, a disastrous plague weakened Siena. Then, in the 1550s, her bitter rival, Florence, really "salted" her, forever making Siena a nonthreatening backwater. Siena's loss became our sightseeing gain, as its political and economic irrelevance pickled it purely Gothic. Today Siena's population is still 60,000, compared to Florence's 420,000.

Siena's thriving historic center, with red-brick lanes cascading every which way, offers Italy's best Gothic city experience. Most people do Siena, just 50 kilometers south of Florence, as a daytrip, but it's best experienced at twilight. While Florence has the blockbuster museums, Siena has an easy-to-enjoy soul: Courtyards sport flower-decked wells, alleys dead-end at rooftop views, and the sky is a rich blue dome. Right off the bat, Siena becomes an old friend.

Pleasing those who dream of a Fiat-free Italy, pedestrians rule in the old center of Siena. Sit at a café on the red-bricked main square. Take time to savor the first European city to eliminate automobile traffic from its main square (1966) and then, just to be silly, wonder what would happen if they did it in your city.

Hill Towns

Planning Your Time

On a quick trip, consider spending three nights in Siena (with a whole-day side trip into Florence and a day to relax and enjoy Siena). Whatever you do, enjoy a sleepy medieval evening in Siena. After an evening in Siena, its major sights can be seen in half a day. San Gimignano is an overrun, pint-sized Siena. Don't rush Siena for San Gimignano (with less than 24 hours for Siena, skip San Gimignano). Note that San Gimingnano, with good bus connections, also makes an easy daytrip from Florence.

Orientation

Siena lounges atop a hill, stretching its three legs out from Il Campo. This main square, the historic meeting point of Siena's neighborhoods, is for pedestrians only. And most of those pedestrians are students from the local university. Everything I mention is within a 15-minute walk of the square. Navigate by landmarks,

Hill Towns: Public Transportation

TO GENOVA   TO MILAN   TO VENICE

CINQUE TERRE →   FERRARA
LA SPEZIA   FLORENCE   BOLOGNA
LUCCA   RAVENNA
PISA →   EMP.   TEREN-TOLA   RIMINI
SAN GIM.   POGG.   CORTONA   PESARO
ELBA   SIENA →   PERUGIA   FALCONARA
CHIUSI   ASSISI   FOSSATO
ORVIETO   TODI
CIVITA DI BAGNOREGIO →   FOLIGNO   ANCONA
VITERBO   SPOLETO
ORTE   DCH
ROMA   PESCARA
ANZIO   NAPLES

NOT TO SCALE

KEY: — RAIL --- BUS .... SHIP
○ GOOD OVERNIGHT STOPS

following the excellent system of street-corner signs. The typical visitor sticks to the San Domenico-Il Campo axis.

Siena is one big sight. Its essential individual sights come in two little clusters: the square (city hall, museum, tower) and the cathedral (baptistery, cathedral museum with its surprise viewpoint). Check these sights off and you're free to wander.

Tourist Information: Pick up a free town map from the main TI at #56 on Il Campo; look for the yellow "Change" sign— bad rates, good information (mid-March–mid-Nov Mon–Sat 08:30–19:30, mid-Nov–mid-March Mon–Sat 08:30–14:00, 15:00– 19:00, tel. 0577-280-551, www.siena.turismo.toscana.it). The little TI at San Domenico is for hotel promotion only and sells a Siena map for €0.60.

Museum Passes: Siena offers a variety of passes. If you're staying for two days or more, consider getting the €16 combo ticket (called Siena Itinerari d'Arte) that covers eight sights, including Museo Civico, Santa Maria della Scala, Museo dell' Opera, Baptistery, Piccolomini Library (in the cathedral), and more (valid for 7 days, sold at participating sites). This pass covers a wider range of sights than the other passes that cost and cover less (e.g., just religious sights or just city museums). In general, if you see two-thirds of the sights covered by a pass, you'll save money.

Helpful Hints

Local Guide: Roberto Bechi, a hardworking Sienese guide, specializes in off-the-beaten-path tours of Siena and the surrounding countryside. Married to an American (Patti) and having run restaurants in Siena and the U.S., Roberto communicates well with Americans. His passions are Sienese culture, Tuscan history, and local cuisine. Book well in advance for full-day tours (ranging in cost from $60–90 per person). Half days ($30–50 per person) cannot be pre-booked during high season but may be available at the last minute (tel. & fax 0577-704-789, www.toursbyroberto.com, e-mail: tourrob@tin.it; for U.S. contact, fax Greg Evans at 540/434-4532).

Internet Access: In this university town, there are lots of places to get plugged in. **Internet Point** is just off Piazza Matteotti, on Via Paradiso (across street from McDonald's), and **Internet Train** is near Il Campo, at Via di Città 121 (tel. 0577-226-366).

Markets: On Wednesday morning, the weekly market—consisting mainly of clothes—sprawls near Piazza Gramsci along Viale Cesare Maccabi and the adjacent Viale XXV Aprile. The produce market is held a block from Il Campo, behind the city hall (Mon–Sat mornings).

Arrival in Siena

By Train: The small train station has a bar, bus office, luggage storage (€2), and lockers (€2.25–2.75, at far end of station, to your left with back to tracks). If you're daytripping, note that luggage can be stored only until 18:30 (that goes for lockers, too).

The station is located on the outskirts of town. To get to the city center, take a taxi or a city bus. The **taxi stand** is to your far right as you exit the station; allow about €8 to your hotel (for taxis at station, call 0577-44504, for taxis at Piazza Matteotti in the center, call 0577-49222). For the **city bus**, buy a €0.75 ticket from the Bus Ticket Office in the station lobby (daily 06:15–19:30, ask for city map—it's free and just a bus route map, but helps get you started). You can also buy a bus ticket from the blue machine in the lobby (touch screen for English and select "urban" for type of ticket). Then cross the parking lot and the street to reach the sheltered bus stop. Catch any orange city bus to get into town (punch ticket in machine on bus to validate it). You'll end up at one of three stops—Piazza Gramsci/Lizza, Piazza Sale, or Stufa Secca—all within several blocks of each other (buses run about every 7 min, fewer on Sun; if you get off at Stufa Secca's tiny square, you're soon faced with two uphill roads—take the one to the right for one block to reach the main drag, Banchi di Sopra).

To get to Siena's train station from the center of Siena, catch the city bus at Piazza del Sale or Stufa Secca; note that bus stops are rarely marked with a "bus stop" sign, but instead with a posted schedule and sometimes with yellow lines painted on the pavement, showing a bus-sized rectangle and the word "bus." Confirm with the driver that the bus is going to the *stazione* (stat-zee-OH-nay). Remember to purchase your ticket in advance from a *tabacchi* shop.

By Bus: Some buses arrive in Siena at the train station (see "Arrival By Train," above), others at Piazza Gramsci (a few blocks from city center), and some stop at both. The main bus companies are Sena and Tran. You can store baggage underneath Piazza Gramsci in Sotopassaggio la Lizza (€2.75, daily 07:00–19:30, no overnight).

By Car: Drivers coming from the autostrada take the Porta San Marco exit and follow the "Centro," then "Stadio," signs (stadium, soccer ball). The soccer-ball signs take you to the stadium lot (Parcheggio Stadio, €1.50/hr, €12.50/day) at the huge, bare-brick San Domenico Church. The Fortezza lot nearby charges the same. Or park in the lot underneath the railway station. You can drive into the pedestrian zone (a pretty bold thing to do) only to drop bags at your hotel. You can park free in the lot below the Albergo Lea, in white-striped spots behind Hotel Villa Liberty, and behind the Fortezza. (The signs showing a street cleaner and a day of the week indicate which day the street is cleaned; that's a €105 tow-fee incentive to learn the days of the week in Italian.)

Sights—Siena's Main Square

▲▲▲**Il Campo**—Siena's great central piazza is urban harmony at its best. Like a people-friendly stage set, its gently tilted floor fans out from the tower and city hall backdrop. It's the perfect invitation to loiter. Think of it as a trip to the beach without sand or water. Il Campo was located at the historic junction of Siena's various competing districts, or *contrada*, on the old marketplace. The brick surface is divided into nine sections, representing the council of nine merchants and city bigwigs who ruled medieval Siena. At the square's high point, look for the Fountain of Joy, the two naked guys about to be tossed in, and the pigeons politely waiting their turn to gingerly tightrope down slippery spouts to slurp a drink (you can see parts of the original fountain, of which this is a copy, in an interesting exhibit at Siena's Santa Maria della Scala museum, listed below). At the square's low point is the city hall and tower. The chapel located at the base of the tower was built in 1348 as thanks to God for ending the Black Plague (after it killed more than a third of the population). The market area behind the city hall, a wide-open expanse since the Middle Ages, originated as a farming area within the city walls to feed the city in times of siege. Now the morning produce market is held here Monday through Saturday. (The closest public WCs to Il Campo are each about a block away: at Via Beccheria—a few steps off Via de Città—and on Casato di Sotto; €0.60.)

To say Siena and Florence have always been competitive is an understatement. In medieval times, a statue of Venus stood on

Siena

1. PICCOLO HOTEL ETRURIA
2. ALBERGO TRE DONZELLE
3. ALBERGO LA PERLA
4. TO HOTEL DUOMO
5. HOTEL CANNON D'ORO
6. LOCANDA GARIBALDI
7. ALBERGO BERNINI
8. ALMA DOMUS
9. HOTEL CHIUSARELLI
10. TO ALBERGO LEA & HOTEL LIBERTY
11. JOLLY HOTEL SIENA
12. PIZZERIA SPADAFORTE
13. RISTORANTE GALLO NERO
14. OSTERIA IL TAMBURINO
15. OSTERIA DA DIVO
16. IL VERROCHIO
17. CIAO CAFETERIA
18. PALIO MOVIE
19. TO PENSIONE PAL. RAVIZZA
20. HOTEL SANTA CATARINA & PALAZZO VALLI
21. SOTTOPASSAGGIO LA LIZZA
22. LAUNDROMATS

Il Campo (where the Fountain of Joy is today). After the plague hit Siena, the monks blamed this pagan statue. The people cut it to pieces and buried it along the walls of Florence.

▲**Museo Civico**—The Palazzo Publico (City Hall), at the base of the tower, has a fine and manageable museum housing a good sample of Sienese art. In the following order, you'll see: the Sala Risorgimento, with dramatic scenes of Victor Emmanuel's unification of Italy (surrounded by statues that don't seem to care); the chapel, with impressive inlaid wood chairs in the choir; and the Sala del Mappamondo, with Simone Martini's *Maesta* (Enthroned Virgin) facing the faded *Guidoriccio da Fogliano* (a mercenary providing a more concrete form of protection). Next is the Sala della Pace—where the city's fat cats met. Looking down on the oligarchy during their meetings were two interesting frescoes showing the effects of good and bad government. Notice the whistle-while-you-work happiness of the utopian community ruled by the utopian government (in the better-preserved fresco) and the fate of a community ruled by politicians with more typical values (in a terrible state of repair). The message: Without justice, there can be no prosperity. The rural view out the window is essentially the view from the top of the big stairs—enjoy it from here (€6.25, combo ticket with tower-€9.50, daily March–Oct 10:00–19:00, July–Sept 10:00–23:00, Nov–Jan 10:00–16:00, last entry 45 min before closing, audioguide-€3.75 for 1 person, €5.25 for 2, tel. 0577-292-111).

▲**City Tower (Torre del Mangia)**—Siena gathers around its city hall, not its church. It was a proud republic; its "declaration of independence" is the tallest secular medieval tower in Italy. The 100-meter-tall Torre del Mangia was named after a hedonistic watchman who consumed his earnings like a glutton consumes food (his chewed-up statue is in the courtyard, to the left as you enter). Its 300 steps get pretty skinny at the top, but the reward is one of Italy's best views (€5.25, combo ticket with Museo Civico-€9.50, daily 10:00–19:00, mid-July–mid-Sept until 23:00, closed in rain, sometimes long lines, limit of 30 towerists at a time, avoid midday crowd).

▲**Pinacoteca (National Picture Gallery)**—Siena was a power in Gothic art. But the average tourist, wrapped up in a love affair with the Renaissance, hardly notices. This museum takes you on a walk through Siena's art, chronologically from the 12th through the 15th centuries. For the casual sightseer, the Sienese art in the city hall and cathedral museums is adequate. But art fans enjoy this opportunity to trace the evolution of Siena's delicate and elegant art (€4.25, Sun–Mon 08:30–13:15, Tue–Sat 08:15–19:15, plus possibly 20:30–23:30 on Sat in summer, tel. 0577-281-161). From Il Campo, walk out Via di Città to Piazza di Postierla and go left on San Pietro.

Sights—Siena's Cathedral Area

▲▲▲**Duomo**—Siena's cathedral is as Baroque as Gothic gets. The striped facade is piled with statues and ornamentation, and the interior is decorated from top to bottom. The heads of 172 popes peer down from the ceiling, over the fine inlaid art on the floor. This is one busy interior.

To orient yourself in this *panforte* of Italian churches, stand under the dome and think of the church floor as a big clock. You're the middle, and the altar is high noon; you'll find the *Slaughter of the Innocents* roped off on the floor at 10:00, Pisano's pulpit between two pillars at 11:00, Bernini's chapel at 3:00, two Michelangelo statues (next to doorway leading to a shop, snacks, and WC) at 07:00, the library at 08:00, and a Donatello statue at 09:00. Take some time with the floor mosaics in the front. Nicola Pisano's wonderful pulpit is crowded with delicate Gothic storytelling from 1268. To understand why Bernini is considered the greatest Baroque sculptor, step into his sumptuous *Cappella della Madonna del Voto*. This last work in the cathedral, from 1659, is enough to make a Lutheran light a candle. Move up to the altar and look back at the two Bernini statues: Mary Magdalene in a state of spiritual ecstasy, and St. Jerome playing the crucifix like a violinist lost in beautiful music.

The Piccolomini altar is most interesting for its two Michelangelo statues (the lower big ones). Paul, on the left, may be a self-portrait. Peter, on the right, resembles Michelangelo's more famous statue of Moses. Originally contracted to do 15 statues, Michelangelo left the project early (1504) to do his great *David* in Florence.

The Piccolomini Library—worth the €1.50 entry—is brilliantly frescoed with scenes glorifying the works of a pope from 500 years ago. It contains intricately decorated, illuminated music scores and a statue (a Roman copy of a Greek original) of the Three Graces (library open Sun 14:30–19:30, Tue–Sat same as church hours, below). Donatello's bronze statue of St. John the Baptist, in his famous rags, is in a chapel to the right of the library.

Hours: The church is open mid-March–Oct daily 09:00–19:30, but Sun 10:15–13:30 is reserved for worship only, Nov–mid-March Mon–Sat 10:00–13:00, 14:30–17:00, Sun 14:30–17:30 (modest dress required). In September, when much of the elaborate mosaic floor is uncovered, you'll pay a fee to enter the church (€2.75 for Pavimento Cattedrale).

Audioguides: There's a daunting number of audioguides. An audioguide for just the church costs €2.75; to add the library, it's €3.75; and to add the Cathedral Museum (Museo dell' Opera de Panorama), pay €5.25. For the church and museum only, it's €4.25. Two headphones are available at a price break.

▲▲**Santa Maria della Scala**—This renovated old hospital-turned-museum (opposite the Duomo entrance) was used as a hospital as recently as the 1980s. Now it displays a lavishly frescoed hall, a worthwhile exhibit on Quercia's *Fountain of Joy* (downstairs), and a so-so archaeological museum (subterranean, in labyrinthine tunnels). The entire museum is a maze, with various exhibitions and paintings plugged in to fill the gaps.

The frescoes in the **Pellegrinaio Hall** show medieval Siena's innovative health care and social welfare system in action (c. 1442, wonderfully described in English). The hospital was functioning as early as the 11th century, nursing the sick and caring for abandoned children (see frescoes). The good work paid off, as bequests and donations poured in, creating the wealth that's evident in the chapels elsewhere on this floor. The Old Sacristy was built to house precious relics, including a Holy Nail thought to be from Jesus' cross.

Downstairs, the engaging exhibit on Jacopo della Quercia's early 15th-century *Fountain of Joy* doesn't need much English description—fortunately—because there isn't much. In the 19th century, the *Fountain of Joy* in Il Campo was deteriorating. It was dismantled and plaster casts were made of the originals. Then replicas were made, restoring the pieces as if brand-new. The *Fountain of Joy* that stands in Il Campo today is a replica. In this exhibit, you'll see the plaster casts of the original, eroded panels paired with their restored twins. Statues originally stood on the edges of the fountain (see the statues and drawings). In general, the pieces at the beginning and end of the exhibit are original. If there's a piece in a dim room near the exit of the exhibit, it's likely an original chunk awaiting cleaning.

The **Archaeological Museum**, way downstairs, consists mainly of pottery fragments in cases lining tunnels after tunnels. It's like being lost in a wine cellar without the wine. Unless there's an exhibition, it's not worth the trip.

Cost and Hours: €5.25, daily 10:00–18:00, Fri–Sat in summer until 23:00, off-season 11:00–16:30. The chapel just inside the door to your left is free (English description inside chapel entrance).

▲**Baptistery**—Siena is so hilly that there wasn't enough flat ground on which to build a big church. What to do? Build a big church and prop up the overhanging edge with the baptistery. This dark and quietly tucked-away cave of art is worth a look (and €2) for its cool tranquility and the bronze panels and angels—by Ghiberti, Donatello, and others—adorning the pedestal of the baptismal font (daily mid-March–Sept 09:00–19:30, Oct 09:00–18:00, Nov–mid-March 10:00–13:00, 14:30–17:00).

▲▲**Cathedral Museum (Museo dell' Opera e Panorama)**— Siena's most enjoyable museum, on the Campo side of the church (look for the yellow signs), was built to house the cathedral's art. The ground floor is filled with the cathedral's original Gothic sculpture by Giovanni Pisano (who spent 10 years in the late 1200s carving and orchestrating the decoration of the cathedral) and a fine Donatello *Madonna and Child*. Upstairs to the left awaits a private audience with Duccio's *Maesta* (Enthroned Virgin). Pull up a chair and study one of the great pieces of medieval art. The flip side of the *Maesta* (displayed on the opposite wall), with 26 panels—the medieval equivalent of pages—shows scenes from the Passion of Christ. Climb onto the "Panorama dal Facciatone." From the first landing, take the skinnier second spiral for Siena's surprise view. Look back over the Duomo and consider this: When rival republic Florence began its grand cathedral, proud Siena decided to build the biggest church in all Christendom. The existing cathedral would be used as a transept. You're atop what would have been the entry. The wall below you, connecting the Duomo with the museum of the cathedral, was as far as Siena got before a plague killed the city's ability to finish the project. Were it completed, you'd be looking straight down the nave—white stones mark where columns would have stood (€5.25, worthwhile €2.75, 40-minute audioguide, daily mid-March–Sept 09:00–19:30, Oct 09:00–18:00, Nov–mid-March 09:00–13:30, tel. 0577-283-048).

Sights—Siena's San Domenico Area

Church of San Domenico—This huge brick church is worth a quick look. The bland interior fits the austere philosophy of the Dominicans. Walk up the steps in the rear for a look at various paintings from the life of Saint Catherine, patron saint of Siena. Halfway up the church on the right, you'll see a metal bust of Saint Catherine and her finger in a case. And in the adjacent chapel (to the left), you'll see her actual head (free, daily May–Oct 07:00–13:00, 15:00–19:00, Nov–April 09:00–13:00, 15:00–18:00; WC for €0.60 at far end of parking lot—facing church entrance, it's to your right).

Sanctuary of Saint Catherine—Step into Catherine's cool and peaceful home. Siena remembers its favorite hometown girl, a simple, unschooled, but almost mystically devout girl who, in the mid-1300s, helped convince the pope to return from France to Rome. Pilgrims have come here since 1464. Since then, architects and artists have greatly embellished what was probably a humble home (her family worked as wool dyers). Enter through the court-yard and walk to the far end. The chapel on your right was built over the spot where Saint Catherine received the stigmata while praying. The chapel on your left used to be the kitchen. Go down the stairs to the left of the chapel/kitchen to reach the saint's room. The saint's bare cell is behind see-through doors. Much of the art throughout the sanctuary depicts scenes from the saint's life (free, daily 09:00–12:30, 14:30–18:00, winter 09:00–12:30, 15:30–18:00, Via Tiratoio). It's a few downhill blocks toward the center from San Domenico (follow signs to the Santuario di Santa Caterina).

Nightlife—Join the evening *passeggiata* (peak strolling time is

19:00) along Via Banchi di Sopra with gelato in hand. **Nannini's** at Piazza Salimbeni has fine gelato (daily 11:00–24:00).

The **Enoteca Italiana** is a good wine bar in a cellar in the Fortezza/Fortress (Mon 12:00–20:00, Tue–Sat 12:00–24:00, closed Sun, sample glasses in 3 different price ranges: €1.50, €2.75, €5.25, bottles and snacks available, CC, cross bridge and enter fortress, go left down ramp, tel. 0577-288-497).

Shopping—Shops line Via Banchi di Sopra, the *passeggiata* route. For a department store, try Upim on Piazza Matteotti (Mon–Sat 09:30–19:50, closed Sun). The large, colorful scarves/flags, each depicting the symbol of one of Siena's 17 different neighborhoods (such as the wolf, the turtle, and snail, etc.), are easy-to-pack souvenirs, fun for decorating your home (€7.25 apiece for large size, sold at souvenir stands).

Siena's Palio

In the Palio, the feisty spirit of Siena's 17 *contrada* (neighborhoods) lives on. These neighborhoods celebrate, worship, and compete together. Each even has its own historical museum. *Contrada* pride is evident any time of year in the colorful neighborhood banners and parades. (If you hear distant drumming, run to it for some medieval action.) But *contrada* pride is most visible twice a year—on July 2 and August 16—when they have their world-famous Palio di Siena. Ten of the 17 neighborhoods compete (chosen by lot), hurling themselves with medieval abandon into several days of trial races and traditional revelry. On the big day, jockeys and horses go into their *contrada*'s church to be blessed ("Go and win," says the priest). It's considered a sign of luck if a horse makes droppings in the church.

On the evening of the big day, Il Campo is stuffed to the brim with locals and tourists, as the horses charge wildly around the square in this literally no-holds-barred race. A horse can win even if its rider has fallen off. Of course, the winning neighborhood is the scene of grand celebrations afterward. The grand prize: Simply proving your *contrada* is numero uno. All over town, sketches and posters depict the Palio. This is not some folkloristic event. It's a real medieval moment. If you're packed onto the square with 15,000 people who each really want to win, you won't see much, but you'll feel it. While the actual Palio packs the city, you could side trip in from Florence to see horse-race trials each of the three days before the big day (usually at 09:00 and around 19:30).

▲**Palio al Cinema**—This 20-minute film, *Siena, the Palio, and its History*, helps recreate the craziness of the Palio. See it at the Cinema Moderno in Piazza Tolomei, two blocks from Il Campo (€5.25, with this book pay €4.25, or €7.75 for 2; Mon–Sat 09:30–17:30, English showings generally hourly at :30 past the hour, schedule posted on door, closed Sun, air-con, tel. 0577-289-201).

Call or drop by to confirm when the next English showing is scheduled—there are usually seven a day. At the ticket desk, you can buy the same show on video (discounted from €13 to €10.50 with this book, video must be labeled "NTSC American System" or it'll be a doorstop at your home).

Sleeping in Siena
(€1.10 = about $1, country code: 39, zip code: 53100)

Sleep Code: **S** = Single, **D** = Double/Twin, **T** = Triple, **Q** = Quad, **b** = bathroom, **s** = shower only, **CC** = Credit Cards accepted, **no CC** = Credit Cards not accepted, **SE** = Speaks English, **NSE** = No English. Breakfast is generally not included. Have breakfast on Il Campo or in a nearby bar.

Finding a room is tough during Easter or the Palio in early July and mid-August. Call ahead any time of year, as Siena's few budget places are listed in all the budget guidebooks. While daytripping tour groups turn the town into a Gothic amusement park in midsummer, Siena is basically yours in the evenings and off-season. Nearly all listed hotels lie between Il Campo and the Church of San Domenico. About a third of the listings don't take credit cards, no matter how earnestly you ask. Cash machines are plentiful on the main streets.

Siena has two modern, self-service **Laundromats:** Lavarapido Wash and Dry (daily 08:00–22:00, Via di Pantaneto 38, near Logge del Papa) and Onda Blu (daily 08:00–22:00, Via del Casato di Sotto 17, 50 meters from Il Campo).

Sleeping near Il Campo

Each of these first listings is forgettable but inexpensive, and just a horse wreck away from one of Italy's most wonderful civic spaces.

Piccolo Hotel Etruria, a good bet for a hotel with 19 decent rooms but not much soul, is just off the square (S-€39, Sb-€44, Db-€73, Tb-€91, Qb-€114, breakfast-€4.75, CC, with your back to the tower, leave Il Campo to the right at 2:00, Via Donzelle 1-3, tel. 0577-288-088, fax 0577-288-461, e-mail: hetruria@tin.it, Fattorini family).

Albergo Tre Donzelle has 27 plain, institutional rooms, next door to Piccolo Hotel Etruria, which make sense only if you think of Il Campo as your terrace (S-€34, D-€47, Db-€60, CC, Via Donzelle 5, tel. 0577-280-358, fax 0577-223-933, Signora Iannini SE).

Hotel Cannon d'Oro, a few blocks up Via Banchi di Sopra, is spacious and group-friendly (30 rooms, Sb-€62, Db-€76.50, Tb-€101, Qb-€119, these discounted prices promised through 2002 with this book, family deals, breakfast-€5, CC, Via Montanini 28, tel. 0577-44321, fax 0577-280-868, e-mail: cannondoro@libero.it, Maurizio and Debora SE).

Locanda Garibaldi is a modest, very Sienese restaurant

and *albergo*. Gentle Marcello wears two hats, as he runs a fine, busy restaurant downstairs and seven pleasant rooms up a funky, artsy staircase (Db-€67, Tb-€78, family deals, no CC, takes reservations only a few days in advance, half a block downhill off the square at Via Giovanni Dupre 18, tel. 0577-284-204, NSE).

Albergo La Perla is a funky, jumbled, 13-room place. Its narrow maze of hallways, stark rooms, old bedspreads, miniscule bathrooms, and laissez-faire environment works for backpackers (Sb-€41, Db-€57, Tb-€78, no CC, a block off the square on Piazza Independenza at Via della Terme 25, tel. 0577-47144). Attilio and his American wife, Deborah, take reservations only a day or two ahead. Ideally, call the morning you'll arrive.

Splurges: **Hotel Duomo** is a classy place with 23 spacious rooms (Sb-€103, Db-€129, Tb-€170, Qb-€186, includes breakfast, CC, air-con, picnic-friendly roof terrace, free parking, follow Via di Città, which becomes Via Stalloreggi, to Via Stalloreggi 38, 10-min walk to Il Campo, tel. 0577-289-088, fax 0577-43043, www.hotelduomo.it, e-mail: hduomo@comune.siena.it, Stefania SE). If you arrive by train, take a taxi (€8); if you drive, go to Porta San Marco and follow the signs to the hotel, drop off your bags, and then park in nearby "Il Campo" lot.

Pensione Palazzo Ravizza has an aristocratic feel and a peaceful garden. Elegant and friendly, it's a 10-minute walk from Il Campo (Db-€196–212, suites available, includes breakfast and dinner, cheaper mid-Nov–Feb, CC, elevator, back rooms face open country, good restaurant, parking, Via Pian dei Mantellini 34, tel. 0577-280-462, fax 0577-221-597, www.palazzoravizza.it).

Sleeping near San Domenico Church

These hotels are listed in order of closeness to Il Campo—a maximum 10-minute walk. The first two enjoy views of the old town and cathedral (which sits floodlit before me as I type) and are the best values in town.

Albergo Bernini makes you part of a Sienese family in a modest, clean home with nine fine rooms. Friendly Nadia and Mauro welcome you to their spectacular view terrace for breakfast and picnic lunches and dinners (the resident bird on the terrace is named Romeo). Outside of breakfast and checkout time, Mauro, an accomplished accordionist, might play a song for you if you ask (Sb-€67, D-€62, Db-€78, breakfast-€6.25, less in winter, no CC, midnight curfew, on the main San Domenico-Il Campo drag at Via Sapienza 15, tel. & fax 0577-289-047, www.albergobernini.com, e-mail: hbernin@tin.it, their son, Alessandro, SE).

Alma Domus is ideal—unless nuns make you nervous, you need a double bed, or you plan on staying out past the 23:30 curfew (no mercy given). This quasi-hotel (not a convent) is run with firm but angelic smiles by sisters who offer clean and quiet rooms for a steal and save the best views for foreigners. Bright lamps, quaint balconies, fine views, grand public rooms, top security, and a friendly atmosphere make this a great value. The check-out time is strictly 10:00, but they will store your luggage in their secure courtyard (Db-€57, Tb-€70, Qb-€88, breakfast-€5.75—not always available, no CC, ask for a view room—*con vista*, elevator, from San Domenico walk downhill with the church on your right toward the view, turn left down Via Camporegio, make a U-turn at the little chapel down the brick steps to Via Camporegio 37, tel. 0577-44177 and 0577-44487, fax 0577-47601, NSE).

Hotel Chiusarelli, a proper hotel in a beautiful building with a handy location, comes with lots of traffic noise at night—ask for a quieter room in the back (50 rooms, S-€55, Sb-€70, Db-€101, Tb-€134, includes big buffet breakfast, CC, suites available, air-con, pleasant garden terrace, across from San Domenico at Viale Curtatone 15, tel. 0577-280-562, fax 0577-271-177, www.essentia.org/chiusarelli, e-mail: chiusare@tin.it, SE).

Jolly Hotel Siena, for people who want a four-star hotel, has 126 rooms that are modern but not plush. Across the street from Piazza Gramsci, it's convenient if you're arriving by bus and if you've got lots of luggage—and money (Sb-€124–160, Db-€170–233, includes breakfast, CC, nonsmoking floor, Piazza La Lizza, tel. 0577-288-448, fax 0577-41272, e-mail: siena@jollyhotels.it).

Hotel Villa Liberty has 18 big, bright, comfortable rooms (S-€78, Db-€124, includes breakfast, CC, only one room with twin beds, elevator, bar, air-con, TVs, courtyard, etc., facing fortress at Viale V. Veneto 11, tel. 0577-44966, fax 0577-44770, www.villaliberty.it, SE).

Albergo Lea is a sleepable place in a residential neighborhood a few blocks away from the center (past San Domenico) with 11 rooms and easy parking (S-€52, Db-€85, Tb-€105, cheaper in winter, includes breakfast, CC, rooftop terrace, Viale XXIV Maggio 10, tel. & fax 0577-283-207, SE).

Sleeping Farther from the Center
The first three listings are near Porta Romana.

Hotel Santa Caterina is a three-star, 18th-century place best for drivers who need air-conditioning. It is professionally run, with a real attention to quality, it has 22 comfortable rooms with a delightful garden (Sb-€98, small Db-€98, Db-€133, Tb-€179, mention this book to get these prices, includes breakfast, CC; garden side is quieter but street side—with multipaned windows—isn't bad, fridge in room, parking-€12/day—request when you reserve, 100 meters outside Porta Romana at Via E.S. Piccolomini 7, tel. 0577-221-105, fax 0577-271-087, www.sienanet.it/hsc, e-mail: hsc@sienanet.it, SE). A city bus runs frequently (Mon–Sat 4/hr, Sun 2/hr) to the town center. A taxi to/from the station runs around €8.

Palazzo di Valli, with 11 spacious rooms and a garden, is 800 meters beyond Porta Romana (the Roman gate) and feels like it's in the country. Catch the city bus into town (Db-€140, Tb-€170, includes breakfast, CC, parking, Via E.S. Piccolomini, bus to center Mon–Sat 4/hr, Sun 2/hr; tel. 0577-226-102, fax 0577-222-255, Camarda family). From the autostrada, exit at Siena Sud in the direction of Porta Romana.

Casa Laura has five clean, well-maintained rooms, some with brick-and-beam ceilings (Db-€83 with breakfast, €73 without; cheaper off-season, CC, Via Roma 3, 10-min walk from Il Campo, tel. 0577-226-061, fax 0577-225-240, e-mail: labenci@tin.it).

Frances' Lodge is a small farmhouse B&B 1.5 kilometers out of Siena. English-speaking Franca and Franco rent four modern rooms in a rustic yet elegant old place with a swimming pool, peaceful garden, eight acres of olive trees and vineyards, and great Siena views (Db-€135–165, easy parking, near shuttle bus into town, Strada di Valdipugna 2, tel. & fax 0577-281-061, www.franceslodge.it).

Hostel: Siena's **Guidoriccio Youth Hostel** has 120 cheap beds, but, given the hassle of the bus ride and the charm of downtown Siena at night, I'd skip it (office open 15:00–01:00, €13 beds in doubles, triples, and dorms with sheets and breakfast, CC, bus #10 from train station or bus #15 from Piazza Gramsci, Via Fiorentina 89 in Stellino neighborhood, tel. 0577-52212, SE).

Eating in Siena

Sienese restaurants are reasonable by Florentine and Venetian standards. Even with higher prices, lousy service, and lower-quality food, consider eating on Il Campo—a classic European experience. **Pizzeria Spadaforte**, at the edge of Il Campo, has a decent setting, mediocre pizza, and tables steeper than its prices (daily 12:00–16:00, 19:30–22:30, CC, to far right of city tower as you face it, tel. 0577-281-123).

For authentic Sienese dining at a fair price, eat at **Locanda Garibaldi**, down Via Giovanni Dupre at #18, within a block of Il Campo (€14.50 *menu*, Sun–Fri opens at 12:00 for lunch and 19:00 for dinner, arrive early to get a table, closed Sat). Marcello does a nice, little *piatto misto dolce* for €2.75, featuring several local desserts with sweet wine.

Ristorante Gallo Nero is a friendly "grotto" for authentic Tuscan cuisine. This "black rooster" serves a mean *ribollita* (hearty Tuscan bean soup) and offers a €21 "medieval menu," as well as several Tuscan *menus*, starting at €14.50 (daily

12:00–15:30, 19:00–24:00, CC, 3 blocks down Via del Porrione from Il Campo at #65, tel. 0577-284-356).

Il Verrochio, a block away, is tucked between a church and loggia, and serves a decent €11.50 *menu* in a cozy, wood-beamed setting (daily 12:00–14:30, 19:00–22:00, closed Wed in winter, CC, Logge del Papa 1, tel. 0577-284-062).

Antica Osteria Da Divo is the place for a fine €40 meal. The kitchen is creative, the food is fresh and top-notch, and the ambience is candlelit. You'll get a basket of exotic fresh breads. The "black pearls"—with a truffle sauce—are sumptuous. The lamb goes baaa in your mouth. And the chef is understandably proud of his desserts (daily 12:00–14:30, 19:00–22:00, CC, Via Franciosa 29, facing baptistery door, take the far right and walk one long curving block, reserve for summer eves, tel. 0577-284-381).

Osteria la Chiacchera, while touristy, is an atmospheric, tasty, and affordable hole-in-the-brick-wall (daily 12:00–15:30, 19:00–24:00, CC, 2 rooms, below Pension Bernini at Costa di San Antonio 4, reservations wise, skip the *trippa*—tripe, tel. 0577-280-631).

Osteria Nonna Gina wins praise from locals for its good quality and prices (Tue–Sun 12:30–14:30, 19:30–20:30, closed Mon, CC, Piano dei Mantellini 2, 10-min walk from Il Campo, near Hotel Duomo, tel. 0577-287-247).

Trattoria La Tellina has patient waiters and great food, including homemade tiramisu. Arrive early to get a seat (Via dell Terme 52, between St. Catherine's House and Piazza Tolomei—where Palio film is shown, tel. 0577-283-133).

Le Campane, two blocks off Il Campo, is classy and a little pricey (daily 12:15–14:30, 19:15–22:00, closed Mon in winter, CC, indoor/outdoor seating, a few steps off Via di Città at Via delle Campane 6, tel. 0577-284-035).

Osteria il Tamburino is friendly, small, and intimate and serves up tasty meals (Mon–Sat 12:00–14:30, 19:00–20:30, closed Sun, CC, follow Via di Città off Il Campo, becomes Stalloreggi, Via Stalloreggi 11, tel. 0577-280-306).

Snack with a view from a small balcony overlooking Il Campo. Survey these three places from Il Campo to see which has a free table. On Via di Città, you'll find **Gelateria Artigiana**, which has perhaps Siena's best ice cream, and **Barbero d'Oro**, which serves cappuccino and *panforte* (€1.75/100 grams; balcony with 2 tables, closed Sun). **Bar Paninoteca** is on Vicolo di S. Paolo, on the stairs leading down to Il Campo (sandwiches, has a row of chairs on balcony, closed Mon).

At the bottom of Il Campo, a **Ciao** cafeteria offers easy self-service meals, no ambience, and no views. The crowded **Spizzico**, a pizza counter in the front half of Ciao, serves huge, inexpensive quarter-pizzas; and on sunny days, people

take the pizza, trays and all, out on Il Campo for a picnic
(daily 12:00–15:00, 19:00–21:00, nonsmoking section—
non fumatori—in back, CC only in cafeteria, to left of city
tower as you face it).

Cheap Meals and Picnics: Budget eaters look for *pizza al
taglio* shops, scattered throughout Siena, selling pizza by the slice.
Picnickers enjoy the market held mornings (except Sun) behind
Il Campo, on Piazza del Mercato. Of the grocery shops scattered
throughout town, the biggest is called simply **Alimentari**; it's
one block off Piazza Matteotti, toward Il Campo. Their pesto is
the besto (Mon–Sat 08:00–19:30, Via Pianigiani).

Sienese Sweets: All over town, Prodotti Tipici shops sell
Sienese specialties. Siena's claim to caloric fame is its *panforte*, a
rich, chewy concoction of nuts, honey, and candied fruits that
impresses even fruitcake-haters (although locals prefer a white
macaroon-and-almond cookie called *ricciarelli*).

Transportation Connections—Siena

By bus to: Florence (2/hr, 1.25–2 hrs, by Tran bus), **Rome**
(7/day, 3 hrs, by Sena bus, arrives at Rome's Tiburtina station),
Assisi (2/day, 2 hrs, by Sena bus; the morning bus goes direct
to Assisi, the afternoon bus might terminate at Santa Maria
Angeli, from here catch a local bus to Assisi, 2/hr, 20 min), **San
Gimignano** (6/day, 1.25 hrs, by Tran bus, more frequent with
transfer in Poggibonsi). Schedules get sparse on Sunday.

Buses depart Siena from Piazza Gramsci, the train station,
or both; confirm when you purchase your ticket. You can get
tickets for Tran buses or Sena buses at the train station (Tran
bus office: Mon–Sat 05:50–19:30; for Sena, buy tickets at *tabacchi*
shop unless they've opened a separate office in the station), or
easier and more central, under Piazza Gramsci at Sottopassaggio
La Lizza (Tran bus office: daily 05:50–19:30, tel. 0577-204-246,
toll-free 800-373-760; Sena bus office: Mon–Sat 07:45–19:45,
Sun 15:30–19:30, tel. 0577-283-203).

Sottopassaggio La Lizza, under Piazza Gramsci, has a cash
machine (neither bus office accepts credit cards), luggage storage
(€2.75/day, €1.50/half day, daily 07:00–19:30, no overnight
storage), posted bus schedules, TV monitors (listing imminent
departures), an elevator, and expensive WCs (€0.55). If you
decide to depart Siena after the bus offices close, you can buy
the ticket directly from the driver.

On schedules, the fastest buses are marked *corse rapide*.
Note that if a schedule lists your departure point as Via Tozzi
or La Lizza, you catch the bus at Piazza Gramsci (Via Tozzi
is the street that runs alongside Piazza Gramsci and La Lizza
is the name of the bus station).

By train to: Florence (9/day, 1.75 hrs, last one at 21:00).

NEAR SIENA: SAN GIMIGNANO

The epitome of a Tuscan hill town, with 14 medieval towers still standing (out of an original 72!), San Gimignano is a perfectly preserved tourist trap, so easy to visit and visually pleasing that it's a good stop. In the 13th century, back in the days of Romeo and Juliet, towns were run by feuding noble families. They'd periodically battle things out from the protective bases of their respective family towers. Pointy skylines were the norm in medieval Tuscany. But in San Gimignano, fabric was big business, and many of its towers were built simply to hang dyed fabric out to dry.

While the basic three-star sight here is the town of San Gimignano itself, there are a few worthwhile stops. From the town gate, shop straight up the traffic-free town's cobbled main drag to Piazza del Cisterna (with its 13th-century well). The town sights cluster around the adjoining Piazza del Duomo. Thursday is market day (08:00–13:00), but, for local merchants, every day is a sales frenzy.

Tourist Information: The TI is in the old center on Piazza Duomo (March–Oct daily 09:00–13:00, 15:00–19:00, Nov–Feb 09:00–13:00, 14:00–18:00, changes money, tel. 0577-940-008, www.sangimignano.com, e-mail: prolocsg@tin.it). To see virtually all of the city's sights, consider a €10.50 combo ticket (covers Collegiata, Torre Grossa, Museo Civico, archaeological museum, and more).

Sights—San Gimignano

Collegiata—This Romanesque church, with round windows and wide steps, is filled with fine Renaissance frescoes (€3.25, Mon–Fri 09:30–19:30, Sat 09:30–17:00, Sun 13:00–17:00).

Torre Grossa—The city's tallest tower can be scaled (€4.25, 60 meters tall, March–Oct daily 09:30–19:20; Nov–Feb Sat–Thu 10:30–16:20, closed Fri), but the free *rocca* (castle), a short hike behind the church, offers a better view and a great picnic perch, especially at sunset.

Museo Civico—This museum, on Piazza Popolo, has a classy little painting collection with a 1422 altarpiece by Taddeo di Bartolo, honoring Saint Gimignano. You can see the saint with the town in his hands surrounded by events from his life (€3.75, €6.25 combo ticket with Torre Grossa, same hours as Torre Grossa).

Sleeping and Eating in San Gimignano
(€1.10 = about $1, country code: 39, zip code: 53037)

Carla Rossi offers rooms—most with views—throughout the town (Db-from €52, no CC, Via di Cellole 81, tel. & fax 0577-955-041, cellular 36-8352-3206, www.appartamentirossicarla.com). For a listing of private rooms, stop by or call **Associazione Strutture Extralberghiere** (Db-€52, no breakfast, no CC, Piazza della Cisterna, tel. 0577-943-190). **Osteria del Carcere** has good food and prices (Via del Castello 13, just off Piazza della Cisterna, tel. 0577-941-905). Shops guarded by wild boar statues sell boar by the gram; carnivores buy some boar (*cinghiale*—cheen-GAH-lay), cheese, bread, and wine and enjoy a picnic in the garden by the castle.

Transportation Connections—San Gimignano

To: Siena (5 buses/day, 1.25 hrs, or can change in Poggibonsi to catch train to Siena), **Florence** (hrly buses, 75 min, change in Poggibonsi; or catch the frequent 20-min shuttle bus to Poggibonsi and train to Florence), **Volterra** (6 buses/day, 2 hrs, change in Poggibonsi and Colle di Val d'Elsa). In San Gimignano, bus tickets are sold at the bar just inside the town gate. The town has no baggage-check service.

Drivers: You can't drive within the walled town of San Gimignano, but a parking lot awaits just a few steps outside.

ASSISI

Assisi is famous for its hometown boy, St. Francis, who made very good.

Around the year 1200, a simple friar from Assisi challenged the decadence of church government and society in general with a powerful message of non-materialism, simplicity, and a "slow down and smell God's roses" lifestyle. Like Jesus, Francis taught by example. A huge monastic order grew out of his teachings, which were gradually embraced (some would say co-opted) by the church. Clare, St. Francis' partner in poverty, founded the Order of the Poor Clares. Catholicism's purest example of simplicity is now glorified in beautiful churches. In 1939, Italy made Francis and Clare its patron saints.

Francis' message of love and sensitivity to the environment has a broad and timeless appeal. But any pilgrimage site will be commercialized, and the legacy of St. Francis is Assisi's basic industry. In summer, this Umbrian town bursts with flash-in-the-pan Francis fans and Franciscan knickknacks. Those able to see past the tacky friar mementos can actually have a "travel on purpose" experience.

Planning Your Time

Assisi is worth a day and a night. The town has half a day of sightseeing and another half a day of wonder. The essential sight is the Basilica of St. Francis. For a good visit, take the Assisi Welcome Walk (below), ending at the basilica. Schedule time to linger on the main square. Hikers enjoy sunset at the castle.

Most visitors are daytrippers. While the town's a zoo by day, it's a delight at night. Assisi after dark is closer to a place Francis could call home.

Orientation

Crowned by a ruined castle at the top, Assisi spills downhill to its famous Basilica of St. Francis. The town is beautifully preserved and rich in history. The 1997 earthquake did more damage to the tourist industry than to the local buildings. Fortunately tourists are returning—whether art-lovers or pilgrims or both—drawn by Assisi's powerful sights.

Tourist Information: The TI is in the center of town on Piazza del Comune (Mon–Sat 08:00–14:00, 15:30–18:30, Sun 09:00–13:00, tel. 075-812-534; visit www.umbria2000.it for info on Umbria).

Also on (or just off) Piazza Commune, you'll find the Roman temple of Minerva, a Romanesque tower, banks, a finely frescoed pharmacy, and an underground Roman Forum. A combo ticket (*biglietto cumulativo*) for €5.25 covers three sights—Rocca Maggiore, Pinacoteca (paintings), and Roman Forum; you'd need to see all three sights to save money (sold at participating sites). Your hotel may give you an Assisi Card, which offers discounts at some restaurants and on parking. Market day is Saturday on the Piazza Matteotti.

Arrival in Assisi

By Train and Bus: Buses connect Assisi's train station with the old town of Assisi on the hilltop (€0.60, 2/hr, about 15–20 min), stopping at Piazza Unita d'Italia (near Basilica of St. Francis), then Largo Properzio (near Basilica of St. Clare), and finally Piazza Matteotti (top of old town). Going to the old town, buses usually leave from the station at :16 and :46 past the hour. Going to the station from the old town, buses usually run from Piazza Matteotti at :10 and :40 past the hour, and from Piazza Unita d'Italia at :17 and :47 past the hour. At Piazza Unita d'Italia, there are two bus stops (*fermata bus*): one sign reads *per f.s. S.M. Angeli* (take this bus to get to the train station), and the other reads *per P. Matteotti* (this bus goes to the top of the old town).

By Taxi: Taxis from the station to the old town run about €10. There are legitimate extra charges for luggage and night service, but beware: Many taxis rip off tourists by using tariff #2; the meter should be set on tariff #1 (€2.50 drop). You can check bags at the train station (€2.50, daily 07:00–19:30) but not in the old town. When departing the old town of Assisi, you'll find taxi stands at Piazza Unita d'Italia and the Basilica of St. Clare (or have your hotel call for you, tel. 075-812-600).

By Car: Drivers just coming in for the day should follow the signs to Piazza Matteotti's wonderful underground parking garage at the top of the town (which comes with bits of ancient Rome in the walls, €1.20/hr, or €11.50/day with Assisi Card—offered by many hotels; open 07:00–21:00, until 23:00 in summer).

Helpful Hints

Travel Agency: You can get bus and train tickets at Agenzia Viaggi Stoppini, between Piazza del Comune and the Basilica of St. Clare (Mon–Fri 09:00–12:30, 15:30–19:00, Sat 09:00–12:30, closed Sun, Corso Mazzini 31, tel. 075-812-597). Note that they don't sell tickets to Siena; you buy these on the bus (see "Transportation Connections," below).

Internet Access: Internet World has several computers and a nonsmoking room (Thu–Tue 11:00–13:00, 14:00–22:00, Wed 16:00–22:00, Via San Gabriele 25, a long block off Piazza Comune, tel. 075-812-327).

Guide: Anne Robichaud, an American who has lived here since 1975, gives pricey though informative tours of the town and the countryside. Make it clear what you want (half day–from €66 per person, full day–from €99, tel. 075-802-334, fax 075-813-698, www.annesitaly.com). Thanks to Anne for her help with the following self-guided walk.

Assisi Welcome Walk

There's much more to Assisi than St. Francis and what all the blitz tour groups see.

This walk, rated ▲▲, covers the town from Piazza Matteotti at the top, down to the Basilica of St. Francis at the bottom. To get to Piazza Matteotti, ride the bus from the train station (or from Piazza Unità d'Italia) to the last stop, or drive there (underground parking with Roman ruins).

The Roman Arena: Start 50 meters beyond Piazza Matteotti (at intersection at far end of parking lot, away from the city center—see map). A lane, named Via Anfiteatro Romano, leads to a cozy circular neighborhood built around a Roman arena. Assisi was an important Roman town. Circle the arena counterclockwise (the chain stretched across the road is to keep cars out, not you). Imagine how colorful the town laundry must have been in the last generation, when the women of Assisi gathered here to do their wash. Adjacent to the laundry is a small rectangular pool filled with water; above it are the coats of arms of the town's leading families. A few steps farther, hike up the stairs to the top of the hill for an aerial view of the oval arena. The Roman stones have long been absorbed into the medieval architecture. It was Roman tradition to locate the arena outside of town...which this was. Continue on. The lane leads down to a city gate.

Umbrian view: Leave Assisi at the Porta Perlici for a commanding view. Umbria, called the "green heart of Italy," is the country's geographical center and only landlocked state. Enjoy the greens: silver green on the valley floor (olives), emerald green 10 meters below you (grape vines), and deep green on the hillsides (evergreen oak trees). Also notice Rocca Maggiore (big castle),

Assisi

① HOTEL ASCESI
② HOTEL BELVEDERE
③ CAMERE ANNALISA
④ HOTEL IDEALE
⑤ ALBERGO DUOMO
⑥ HOTEL FORTEZZA
⑦ SRA. GAMBACORTA'S STORE
⑧ LA PALLOTTA ROOMS
⑨ LA PALLOTTA REST.
⑩ HOTEL SOLE & PRIORI
⑪ HOTEL UMBRA

NOT TO SCALE...
PIAZZA COMUNE TO:
• BASILICA = 10 MIN. WALK DOWNHILL
• ROCCA MAGGIORE = 10 MIN. WALK UPHILL
• ROCCA MINORE = 15 MIN. WALK UPHILL

ROCCA MINORE
5 KM TO HERMITAGE
PORTA PERLICI
START WALK
ROCCA MAGGIORE
EREMO CARC.
PORTA CAPP.
PIAZZA MATTEOTI
ROCCA
TEMPLE OF MINERVA
COLLE
S. RUFINO
PORTA NUOVA AND LARGO PROP.
ALESSI
PORTA S. GIACOMO
VIA S. CROCE
S. PABLO
PORTO
PIAZZA COMUNE
ARETINO
METASTASIO
SEM.
AGNESE
BASILICA S. CHIARA
BASILICA OF ST FRANCIS
VIA S. FRANCESCO
CRISTOFANI
FONTEBELLA
S. APOLL.
VIA BORGO S.P.
WALLS
CITY
P
PIAZZA UNITA D'ITALIA
TO PERUGIA & FLORENCE
3 KILOMETERS TO TRAIN STATION & S.M. ANGELI
DCH

a fortress providing townsfolk a refuge in times of attack, and, behind you, atop the hill, Rocca Minore (little castle). Now walk back to Piazza Matteotti. Go to the opposite end of this piazza, to the corner with the blobby stone tower. As you walk down the lane next to this tower, you'll see the big dome of the Church of San Rufino. Walk to the courtyard of the church; the big bell tower is on your left.

Church of San Rufino: While Francis is Italy's patron saint, Rufino is Assisi's—the town's first bishop (he was martyred and buried here in the third century). The church is 12th-century Romanesque with a neoclassical interior. Enter the church (daily 07:00–12:00, 14:00–19:00). To your right (in the back corner of the church) is the baptismal font where Francis and Clare were baptized. Traditionally, the children of Assisi are still baptized here.

The striking glass panels in the church floor reveal ancient foundations dating from Roman times, discovered only recently. You're walking on history. After the 1997 earthquake, the church was checked from ceiling to floor by structural inspectors. When they looked under the paving stones, they discovered bodies (it used to be a common practice to bury people in church, until

Napoleon decreed otherwise) and underneath the graves, Roman foundations and some animal bones (suggesting the possibility of animal sacrifice). There might have been a Roman temple here. It's plausible, because churches were often built on the sites of ruined Roman temples. Standing at the back of the church (facing the altar), look left at the Roman cistern (enclosed with a black iron fence). This was once the town's water source when under attack.

Underneath the church, alongside the Roman ruins, are the foundations of an earlier Church of San Rufino, now the crypt. When it's open in summer, you can go below to see the saint's sarcophagus.

Medieval Architecture: When you leave the church, take a sharp left (on Via Dono Doni—say it fast three times), following the sign to Santa Chiara. Take the first right, down the stairway. At the bottom, notice the pink limestone pavement. The medieval town survives. The arches built over doorways indicate that the buildings date from the 12th through the 14th century. The vaults that turn lanes into tunnels are reminders of medieval urban expansion (mostly 15th century). While the population grew, people wanted to live protected within the walls, so Assisi became more dense. Medieval Assisi had five times the population density of today's Assisi. Notice the floating gardens. Assisi has a flowering balcony competition each June. When you arrive at a street, turn left, going slightly uphill for a block, then jog right, following the "S. Chiara" sign down to the Basilica of St. Clare.

When you reach the basilica, turn left and walk to the arch sprouting out of the back of the church. Across the street from the arch is a remarkable manger scene, created by Silvano Gionbolina. Jesus and mom are in the foreground of a village that is going about its business, as an angel with gently fluttering wings perches on the manger. People chat and stroll, the sheep graze in motion, and a worker scoops water from a well. On the manger is written, *Io sono la via, la verita, e la vita*, translated "I am the way, the truth, and the light." No one in the town seems to be listening except his mom.

Basilica of St. Clare (Santa Chiara): For a description, see "More Sights—Assisi," below.)

Another Umbrian View: Belly up to the viewpoint in front of the basilica. On the left is the convent of St. Clare; below you, the olive grove of the Poor Clares since the 13th century; and, in the distance, a grand Umbrian view. Assisi overlooks the richest and biggest valley in otherwise hilly and mountainous Umbria. The municipality of Assisi has 29,000, but only 1,000 live in the old town. The lower town grew up with the coming of the railway in the 19th century. In the haze, the blue-domed church is St. Mary of the Angels (Santa Maria degli Angeli, see description below), the cradle of the Franciscan order, marking the place

St. Francis lived and worked. This church, a popular pilgrimage sight today, is the first Los Angeles. Think about California. The Franciscans named L.A. (after this church), San Francisco, and even Santa Clara.

Arches and Artisans: From Via Santa Chiara, you can see two arches over the street. The arch at the back of the church dates from 1265. (Beyond it—out of view, the Porta Nuova, from 1316, marks the final expansion of Assisi.) Toward the city center (on Via Santa Chiara, the high road), an arch indicates the site of the Roman wall.

Forty meters before this arch, pop into the souvenir shop at #1b. The plaque over the door explains that the old printing press (a national monument now, just inside the door) was used to make fake documents for Jews escaping the Nazis in 1943 and 1944. The shop is run by a couple of artisans: The man makes frames out of medieval Assisi timbers; the woman makes the traditional Assisi, or Franciscan, cross-stitch.

Just past the gate and on your left is the La Pasteria natural products shop at Corso Mazzini 18b (across from entrance of Hotel Sole). Cooks love to peruse Umbrian wines, herbs, pâtés, and truffles, and sample an aromatic "fruit infusion." Ahead at Corso Mazzini 14d, the small shop (Poiesis) sells olive-wood carvings. Drop in. It's said that St. Francis made the first nativity scene to help teach the Christmas message. That's why you'll see so many of these in Assisi. Even today, nearby villages are enthusiastic about their "living" manger scenes. The Lisa Assisi shop (at Corso Mazzini 25b, across the street and to your right) has a delightful bargain basement with surviving bits of a 2000-year-old mortarless Roman wall. Ahead of you, the columns of the Temple of Minerva mark the Piazza del Comune (described below). Sit at the fountain on the square for a few minutes of people-watching—don't you love Italy? Within 200 meters of this square, on either side, were the medieval walls. Imagine a commotion of 5,000 people confined within these walls. No wonder St. Francis needed an escape for some peace and quiet. I'll meet you over at the temple on the square.

Roman Temple/Christian Church: Assisi has always been a spiritual center. The Romans went to great lengths to make this Temple of Minerva a centerpiece of their city. Notice the columns cutting into the stairway. It was a tight fit here on the hilltop. The stairs probably went down triple the distance you see today. The church of Santa Maria sopra (over) Minerva was added in the ninth century. The bell tower is 13th century. Pop inside the temple/church (Mon–Sat 07:15–19:00, from 08:30 on Sun, closes at 17:00 in winter). Today's interior is 17th-century Baroque. Flanking the altar are the original Roman temple floor stones. You can even see the drains for the bloody sacrifices that took place here. Behind the statues of Peter and Paul, the original Roman embankment peeks through.

A few doors back toward the fountain, step into the 16th-century vaults from the old fish market. Notice the Italian flair for design. Even a smelly fish market was finely decorated. The art style is "grotesque"—literally a painting in a grotto. This was painted in the early 1500s, a few years after Columbus brought turkeys back from the New World. The turkeys painted here may just be that bird's European debut. (Public WCs are a few steps off Piazza del Comune; near the fountain, go through Via dell' Arco dei Priori, then down the street on the left.)

Church of San Stefano: From the main square, hike past the temple up the high road, Via San Paolo. After 200 meters, a sign directs you down a lane to San Stefano, which used to be outside the town walls in the days of St. Francis. Legend is that its bells miraculously rang on October 3, 1226, the day St. Francis died. Surrounded by cypress, fig, and walnut trees, it's a delightful bit of offbeat Assisi. Step inside. This is the typical rural Italian Romanesque church—no architect, just built by simple stone-masons who put together the most basic design. The lane zigzags down to Via San Francesco. Turn right and walk under the arch toward the Basilica of St. Francis.

Via San Francesco: This was the main drag leading from the town to the basilica holding the body of St. Francis. Francis was a big deal even in his own day. He died in 1226 and was made a saint in 1228—the same year the basilica's foundations were laid—and his body was moved in by 1230. Assisi was a big-time pilgrimage center, and this street was a booming place. Notice the fine medieval balcony just below the arch. A few meters farther down (on the left), cool yourself at the fountain. The hospice next door was built in 1237 to house pilgrims. Notice the three surviving faces of its fresco: Jesus, Francis, and Clare.

Basilica of St. Francis

A ▲▲▲ sight, the Basilica de San Francesco is one of the artistic and religious highlights of Europe. In 1226, St. Francis was buried (with the outcasts he had stood by) outside of his town on the "Hill of the Damned." Now called the "Hill of Paradise," it's frescoed from top to bottom by the leading artists of the day: Cimabue, Giotto, Simone Martini, and Pietro Lorenzetti. A 13th-century historian wrote, "No more exquisite monument to the Lord has been built."

From a distance you see the huge arcades "supporting" the basilica. These were 15th-century quarters for the monks. The arcades lining the square leading to the church housed medieval pilgrims.

There are three parts to the church: the upper basilica, the lower basilica, and the saint's tomb (below the lower basilica). In the 1997 earthquake, the lower basilica (with nine-foot-thick walls) was undamaged. The upper basilica (with three-foot-thick walls and bigger windows) was damaged. After restoration was completed, the entire church was reopened to visitors in late '99 (free, daily 06:30–19:00, relic chapel in lower basilica closes at 18:30, tel. 075-819-0084, e-mail: assisisanfrancesco@krenet.it; a WC is a half block away—from basilica's courtyard, look up the road at the squat brick building; walk alongside the right of it to find the WC). Note that modest dress is required in the basilica—no sleeveless tops or shorts for men or women.

The Basilica of St. Francis, a theological work of genius, can be difficult for the 21st-century tourist/pilgrim to appreciate. Since the basilica is the reason most visit Assisi, and the message of St. Francis has even the least devout blessing the town Vespas, I've designed a *Mona Winks*–type tour with the stress on the place's theology rather than art history. It's adapted from the excellent *The Basilica of Saint Francis—A Spiritual Pilgrimage*, by Goulet, McInally, and Wood (€2 in bookshop).

Start at the lower entrance in the courtyard. The information center (Mon–Sat 09:00–12:00, 14:00–17:00, Sun 14:00–17:00, tel. 075-819-0084) is opposite the entry to the lower basilica. At the doorway of the lower basilica, look up and see St. Francis (in a small gold triangle), who greets you with a Latin inscription (arching over the doorway). Sounding a bit like John Wayne, he says the equivalent of "Slow down and be joyful, pilgrim. You've reached the Hill of Paradise, and this church will knock your spiritual socks off." Start with the tomb (turn left into the nave, midway down the nave to your right follow signs and go downstairs to the tomb). Grab a pew (for more light to read by, sit in back).

The message: Francis' message caused a stir. He traded a life of power and riches for one of obedience, poverty, and chastity. The Franciscan existence (Brother Sun, Sister Moon, and so on) is a space where God, man, and the natural world frolic harmoniously. Franciscan friars, known as the "Jugglers of God," were a joyful part of the community. In an Italy torn by fighting between towns and families, Francis promoted peace and the restoration of order. (He set an example by reconstructing a crumbled chapel.) While the Church was waging bloody Crusades, Francis pushed ecumenism and understanding. Even today the leaders of the world's great religions meet here for summits.

This rich building seems to contradict the teachings of the poor monk it honors, but it was built as an act of religious and civic pride to remember the hometown saint. It was also designed, and still functions, as a pilgrimage center and a splendid classroom.

The tomb: In medieval times, pilgrims came to Assisi because St. Francis was buried here. Holy relics were the "ruby slippers" of medieval Europe. They gave you power—got your prayers answered and helped you win wars—and ultimately helped you get back to your eternal Kansas. Assisi made no bones about promoting the saint's relics, but hid his tomb for obvious reasons of security. Not until 1818 was the tomb opened to the public. The saint's remains are above the altar in the stone box with the iron ties. His four closest friends are buried in the corners of the room. Opposite the altar, up four steps in between the entrance and exit, notice the small gold box behind the metal grill; this contains the remains of Francis' rich Roman patron, Jacopa dei Settesoli. Climb back to the lower nave.

The lower basilica is appropriately Franciscan, subdued and Romanesque. The nave was frescoed with parallel scenes from the lives of Christ and Francis—connected by a ceiling of stars. Unfortunately, after the church was built and decorated, the popularity of the Franciscans meant side chapels needed to be built. Huge arches were cut out of some scenes, but others survive. In the fresco directly above the entry to the tomb, Christ is being taken down from the cross (just the bottom half of his body can be seen, to the left), and it looks like the story is over. Defeat. But in the opposite fresco (above the tomb's exit), we see Francis preaching to the birds, reminding the faithful that the message of the Gospel survives.

These stories directed the attention of the medieval pilgrim to the altar, where, through the sacraments, he met God. The church was thought of as a community of believers sailing toward God. The prayers coming out of the nave (*navis*, or ship) fill the triangular sections of the ceiling—called *vele*, or sails—with spiritual wind. With a priest for a navigator and the altar for a helm, faith propels the ship.

Stand behind the altar (toes to the bottom step) and look up. The three scenes in front of you are, to the right, "Obedience" (Francis wearing a yoke); to the left, "Chastity" (in a tower of purity held up by two angels); and straight ahead, "Poverty." Here Jesus blesses the marriage as Francis slips a ring on Lady Poverty. In the foreground two "self-sufficient" merchants (the new rich of a thriving North Italy) are throwing sticks and stones at the bride. But Poverty, in her patched wedding dress, is fertile and strong, and even those brambles blossom into a rosebush crown.

Putting your heels to the altar and bending back like a drum major, look up at Francis, who traded a life of earthly simplicity for glory in heaven. Now, turn to the right and march...

In the corner, steps lead down into the relic chapel. Circle the room clockwise. You'll see the silver chalice and plate Francis used for the bread and wine of the Eucharist (in small dark windowed case set into wall, marked *Calice con Patena*). Francis believed that his personal possessions should be simple, but the items used for worship should be made of the finest materials. In the corner display case is a small section of the hair cloth worn by Francis as penitence. In the next corner are the tunic and slippers Francis wore during his last days. Next, find a prayer (in a fancy silver stand) that St. Francis wrote for Brother Leo, signed with his taw cross. Next is a papal document (1223) legitimizing the Franciscan order and assuring his followers that they were not risking a (deadly) heresy charge. Finally, see the tunic lovingly patched and stitched by followers of the five-foot, four-inch-tall St. Francis.

Return up the stairs to the lower basilica. You're in the transept. This church brought together the greatest Sienese (Martini and Lorenzetti) and Florentine (Cimabue and Giotto) artists of the day. Look around at the painted scenes. In 1300, this was radical art—believable homespun scenes, landscapes, trees, real people. Study the crucifix (by Giotto) with the eight sparrowlike angels. For the first time, holy people are expressing emotion: One angel turns her head sadly at the sight of Jesus, and another scratches her hands down her cheeks, drawing blood. Mary, previously in control, has fainted in despair. The Franciscans, with their goal of bringing God to the people, found a natural partner in Europe's first modern painter, Giotto.

To see the Renaissance leap, look at the painting to the right. This is by Cimabue—it's Gothic, without the 3-D architecture, natural backdrop, and slice-of-life reality of the Giotto work. Cimabue's St. Francis is considered by some to be the earliest existing portrait of the saint. To the left, at eye level, enjoy the Martini saints and their exquisite halos.

Francis' friend, "Sister Death," was really not all that terrible. In fact, Francis would like to introduce you to her now (above and to the right of the door leading into the relic chapel). Go ahead, block the light and meet her. I'll wait for you upstairs, in the courtyard, next to the fine bookstore. By the way, monks in robes are not my idea of easy-to-approach people, but the Franciscans are still God's jugglers (and most of them speak English).

From the courtyard, climb the stairs to the **upper basilica**. Built later than the lower, the upper basilica is brighter, Gothic (the first Gothic church in Italy, 1228), and nearly wallpapered by Giotto. This gallery of frescoes by Giotto and his assistants shows 28 scenes from the life of St. Francis.

Look for these scenes:

• **A common man spreads his cape before Francis** (immediately to right of altar, as you're facing altar) out of honor and recognition to a man who will do great things. Symbolized by the rose window, God looks over the 20-year-old Francis, a dandy imprisoned in his selfishness. A medieval pilgrim fluent in symbolism would understand this because the Temple of Minerva (which you saw today on Assisi's Piazza del Comune) was a prison at that time. The rose window, which never existed, is symbolic of God's eye.

• **Francis offers his cape to a needy stranger** (next panel). Prior to this act of kindness, Francis had been captured in battle, held as a prisoner of war, and then released.

• **Francis is visited by the Lord in a dream** (next panel) and told to leave the army and go home.

• **Francis relinquishes his possessions** (two panels down), giving his dad his clothes, his credit cards, and even his time-share condo on Capri. Naked Francis is covered by the bishop, symbolizing his transition from a man of the world to a man of the church.

• **The pope has a vision** (next panel) of a simple man propping up his teetering church. This led to the papal acceptance of the Franciscan reforms.

• **Christ appears to Francis** being carried by a seraph— a six-winged angel (other side of church, fourth panel from the door). For the strength of his faith, Francis is given the marks of his master, the "battle scars of love"...the stigmata. Throughout his life, Francis was interested in chivalry; now he's joined the spiritual knighthood.

• **Francis preaches to the birds** (to the right of the exit). Francis was more than a nature-lover. The birds, of different species, represent the diverse flock of humanity and nature, all created and loved by God and worthy of each other's love.

Before you leave, look at the ceiling above the altar and front entrance to see large tan patches; these careful repairs were made after the basilica was damaged in the 1997 earthquake. It's a blessing that so many of the frescoes remain.

Near the outside of the upper basilica are the Latin pax (peace) and the Franciscan taw cross in the grass. Taw, the last letter in the Hebrew alphabet, is symbolic of faithfulness to the end. Francis signed his name with this simple character. Taw and pax. (For more pax, take the high lane back to town, up to the castle, or into the countryside.)

More Sights—Assisi

▲**Basilica of Saint Clare (Basilica di Santa Chiara)**—Dedicated to the founder of the order of the Poor Clares, this Umbrian Gothic church is simple, in keeping with the Poor Clares' dedication to a life of contemplation. The church was built in 1265, and the huge buttresses were added in the next century. The interior's fine frescoes were whitewashed in Baroque times. The Chapel of the Crucifix of San Damiano, on the right (actually an earlier church incorporated into this one), has the crucifix that supposedly spoke to St. Francis, leading to his conversion in 1206. Stairs lead from the nave down to the tomb of Saint Clare. Her tomb is at the far end. The walls depict scenes from Clare's life and death (1193–1253); the saint's robes are in a large case between the stairs. The attached cloistered community of the Poor Clares has flourished for 700 years (church open 09:00–12:00, 14:00–19:00).

Unless you've already seen it on the "Assisi Welcome Walk" (above), make sure you dip into the wondrous mechanical, water-powered manger scene of Silvano Gionbolina (Via Sermei 2b, opposite arch at back end of church).

Roman Forum (Foro Romano)—For a look at Assisi's Roman roots, tour the Roman Forum, which is actually under the Piazza del Comune. The floor plan is sparse, the odd bits and pieces obscure, but it's well-explained in English (a 10-page booklet is loaned to you when you enter), and you can actually walk on an ancient Roman road. For an orientation, look at the poster for sale at the entry to get an idea of the original setting of Forum and Temple (€2, or included in €5.25 combo ticket, daily 10:00–13:00, 15:00–19:00, closes at 17:00 in winter; from Piazza Comune, go one-half block down Via San Francesco, it's on your right).

Pinacoteca—This small museum attractively displays its 13th- to 17th-century art (mainly frescoes), with general information in English in nearly every room. There's a Giotto Madonna (damaged) and a rare secular fresco (to right of Giotto), but it's mainly a peaceful walk through a pastel world, best for art-lovers (€2.75, included in €5.25 combo ticket, daily 10:00–13:00, 15:00–18:00, Via San Francesco 10, on main drag between Piazza del Comune and Basilica of St. Francis, tel. 075-812-033).

▲**Rocca Maggiore**—The "big castle" offers a good look at a 14th-century fortification and a fine view of Assisi and the Umbrian countryside (€2.75, included in €5.25 combo-ticket, daily 10:00–sunset, opens at 09:00 July–Aug). If you're counting euros, the view is just as good from outside the castle, and the interior is pretty bare. For a picnic with the same birdsong and views that inspired St. Francis, leave all the tourists and hike to the Rocca Minore (small castle) above Piazza Matteotti.

Santa Maria degli Angeli

This flat, modern part of Assisi has one major sight: The basilica that marks the spot where Francis lived, worked, and died.

▲▲**St. Mary of the Angels (Basilica di Santa Maria degli Angeli)**—This huge basilica, towering above the buildings below Assisi, was built around the tiny but historic Porziuncola Chapel (now directly under the dome). When the pope gave Francis his blessing, he was given this *porziuncola*, or "small portion"—a little land with a fixer-upper chapel—on which Francis and his followers established their order. As you enter, notice the sketch on the door showing the original little chapel with the monks' huts around it and Assisi before it had its huge basilica. Francis lived here after he founded the Franciscan Order in 1208, and this was where he consecrated St. Clare as the Bride of Christ. A chapel called Cappella del Transito marks the place where Francis died (behind and to the right of the Porziuncola Chapel). Follow signs to the Roseta (Rose Garden). Francis, fighting off a temptation that he never named, threw himself onto roses. As the story goes, the thorns immediately dropped off the roses. Ever since, thornless roses have grown here. Look through the window at the rose garden (to the right of the statue of Francis petting a sheep). The Rose Chapel (Cappella delle Rose) is built over the place where Francis lived. The bookshop has some books in English and the free *museo* has a few monastic cells interesting to pilgrims (museum open Mon–Sat 09:30–12:00, 15:30–18:30, Sun 15:30–18:30).

Hours: The basilica is open May–Oct 07:00–18:30, Nov–April 07:00–12:00, 14:00–sunset. There's a little TI with unpredictable hours (to your right as you face the church, tel. 075-80511). A WC is 40 meters to the right of the TI, behind the hedge.

Transportation Connections: To get to Basilica di Santa Maria degli Angeli from Assisi's train station, it's quicker to walk (exit station left, take first left at McDonald's, 5-minute walk) than to take the orange city bus' circuitous route (though with lots of luggage, you might prefer the bus). When you're leaving the basilica, you can catch the bus directly to the station and on to the old town of Assisi (as you leave church, stop is to your right, next to basilica). The orange city buses run twice hourly (buses to the old town depart the basilica at :10 and :40 after the hour; tickets cost €0.60 if you buy at *tabacchi* or newsstand, €1.10 if you buy from driver; 15–20 minute ride up to old town).

It's efficient to visit this basilica either on your way to the old town of Assisi or when you leave. You can easily walk to the basilica from the station (baggage check available, €2.75, access through shop). If you're heading to Siena next, visit the basilica right before you leave, because that's where you'll catch the bus to Siena (as you leave basilica, stop is to your right, across the street, buy ticket on bus); see "Transportation Connections—Assisi," below.

Sleeping in Assisi
(€1.10 = about $1, country code: 39, zip code: 06081)
Sleep Code: **S** = Single, **D** = Double/Twin, **T** = Triple, **Q** = Quad, **b** = bathroom, **s** = shower only, **CC** = Credit Cards accepted, **no CC** = Credit Cards not accepted, **SE** = Speaks English, **NSE** = No English.

The town accommodates large numbers of pilgrims on religious holidays. Finding a room any other time should be easy. See map on page 216 for hotel locations.

Splurges

Hotel Umbra, the best splurge in the center, feels like a quiet villa in the middle of town (25 rooms, Sb-€67, Db-€88–103 depending upon season and size of room, Tb-€109, includes breakfast, CC, air-con, peaceful garden and view terrace, most rooms have views, good restaurant, 100 meters below Piazza di Comune at Via degli Archi 6, tel. 075-812-240, fax 075-813-653, www.charmerelax.com/en73.html, family Laudenzi).

Hotel Dei Priori is a three-star, palace-type place in the old center with big, quiet rooms that have all the comforts (Db-€103–116, superior Db-€140–150, includes breakfast, CC, elevator, air-con, Corso Mazzini 15, tel. 075-812-237, fax 075-816-804, www.assisihotel.net, e-mail: hpriori@edisons.it).

Hotels

Hotel Belvedere, which offers 16 comfortable rooms and good views, is run by friendly Enrico and his American wife, Mary (Db-€73, breakfast-€5.25, elevator, 2 blocks past Basilica of St. Clare at Via Borgo Aretino 13, tel. 075-812-460, fax 075-816-812, e-mail: assisihotelbelvedere@hotmail.com, SE). Their attached restaurant is good.

Hotel Ideale is on the top edge of town overlooking the valley, and has 12 bright, modern rooms, view balconies, peaceful garden, free parking, and a warm welcome (Sb-€47, Db-€78, includes big-for-Italy breakfast, CC, most rooms with views, Piazza Matteotti 1, tel. 075-813-570, fax 075-813-020, e-mail: hotelideale@libero.it, sisters Lara and Ilaria SE).

Hotel Sole is well-located, with 35 spacious, comfortable rooms in a 15th-century building (Sb-€41, Db-€62, Tb-€81, breakfast-€6.25, CC, half its rooms are in a newer annex across the street, some rooms have views and balconies, elevator in annex, Corso Mazzini 35, 100 meters before Basilica of St. Clare, tel. 075-812-373, fax 075-813-706, e-mail: sole@tecnonet.it, NSE).

Hotel Ascesi has an inviting little lobby, nine pleasant rooms, and a tiny terrace, located within a block of the Basilica of St. Francis (Sb-€34, Db-€52, breakfast-€3.75, CC, air-con, Via Frate Elia 5, walk up from Piazza Unita d'Italia, take a left at Piazzetta Ruggero Bonghi, see sign on right, tel. & fax 075-812-420, e-mail: hotelideale@libero.it). Both of these hotels—at the top and bottom of town—are close to bus stops (and parking lots), handy if you're packing lots of luggage.

Hotel La Fortezza is a simple, modern, and quiet place with seven rooms (Db-€49, Tb-€67, Qb-€78, CC, a short block above Piazza del Comune at Vicolo della Fortezza 19b, tel. 075-812-993, fax 075-819-8035, www.lafortezzahotel.com, SE).

Albergo Il Duomo is tidy and *tranquillo*, with nine rooms on a stair-step lane one block up from San Rufino (S-€26, Sb-€28,

D-€35, Db-€41, breakfast-€4.25, CC, Vicolo S. Lorenzo 2; from
Church of San Rufino follow sign, then turn left on stair-stepped
alley; tel. 075-812-742, fax 075-812-762, e-mail: ilduomo@retein.it,
Carlo SE).

Other Accommodations

Camere Annalisa Martini is a cheery home swimming in vines
and roses in the town's medieval core. Annalisa speaks English
and enthusiastically accommodates her guests with a picnic garden, a washing machine (small load-€2.75), a refrigerator, and
six homey rooms (S-€20, Sb-€23, D-€31, Db-€36, Tb-€47,
Qb-€57, 3 rooms share 2 bathrooms, no breakfast, no CC,
1 block from Piazza del Comune, go downhill toward basilica,
turn left on Via S. Gregorio to #6, tel. & fax 075-813-536).

La Pallotta, a recommended restaurant (see "Eating," below),
offers seven clean, bright rooms (note that rooms and restaurant
are in different locations). Rooms #12 and #18 have views (Db-
€47, CC, view terrace, Via San Rufino 4, go up short flight of
stairs outside building to reach entrance, a block off Piazza del
Comune, tel. & fax 075-812-307, www.pallottaassisi.it).

Signora Gambacorta rents several decent rooms and has a
roof terrace on a quiet lane (Via Sermei 9) just above St. Chiara.
There is no sign or reception desk, so you'll need to check in at her
shop a half block east of Piazza Comune at San Gabriele 17—look
for the sign "Bottega di Gambacorta" (S-€20 Db-€40, Tb-€60,
2-night stays preferred, no breakfast; store is open Mon–Wed and
Fri–Sat 08:00–13:00, 16:30–19:30, Thu 08:00–13:00, closed Sun—
if you can't arrive when store is open, call when you arrive, tel.
075-812-454, fax 075-813-186, www.ilbongustaio.com/inglese
/eerooms.htm, e-mail: geo@umbrars.com, NSE). She also has
two apartments for stays of at least four nights (3 rooms-€90/day,
5 rooms-€140/day, kitchen, no breakfast).

Hostel: Francis probably would have bunked with the peasants
in Assisi's **Ostello della Pace** (€13 beds in 4- to 8-bed rooms, Qb-
€15 apiece, includes breakfast, dinner-€7.75, no CC, laundry, get
off at Assisi's Piazza Unita d'Italia stop on the station–town bus, then
a 10-min walk to Via di Valecchie 177, tel. & fax 075-816-767, SE).

Eating in Assisi

For a fine Assisian perch and good regional cooking, relax on a
terrace overlooking Piazza del Comune at **Taverna dei Consoli**
(€13 4-course *menu*, also à la carte, Thu–Tue 12:00–14:30, 19:00–
21:30, closed Wed, CC, tel. 075-812-516, friendly owner Moreno
SE and recommends the *bruschetta*, *stringozzi*—noodles, *agnello*—
lamb, and *cinghiale*—boar).

La Pallotta, a local favorite run by a friendly, hardworking
family, offers excellent regional specialties, such as *piccione* (pigeon),

coniglio (rabbit), and more typical food (€13.50 *menu*, Wed–Mon 12:00–14:30, 19:15–22:00, closed Tue, CC, also rents rooms—see listing above, a few steps off Piazza del Comune, through gate across from temple/church, Vicolo della Volta Pinta, tel. 075-812-649).

Osteria Piazzetta Dell Erba is a fun, little, family-run place a block above Piazza del Comune, serving good, basic Umbrian specialties next to the Gambacorta grocery (Tue–Sun 12:00–14:00, 19:00–21:45, closed Mon, CC, Via San Gabriele, tel. 075-815-352).

Pizzeria/Tavola Calda Dal Carro is popular, affordable, and friendly (good pizzas and €11.50 *menu*, closed Wed, Vicolo di Nepis 2, leave Piazza del Comune on Via San Gabriele, then take first right—down a stepped lane, tel. 075-815-249).

Ristorante San Francesco is the place to splurge for dinner (Thu–Tue 12:00–14:30, 19:30–22:00, closed Wed, CC, facing Basilica of St. Francis at Via San Francesco 52, tel. 075-812-329).

Transportation Connections—Assisi

By train to: Rome (5/day, 1.75–2.5 hrs), **Florence** (5/day, 2–2.75 hrs, more with transfers at Terontola and Cortona), **Orvieto** (7/day, 2 hrs, transfer in Terontola), **Siena** (6/day, 3.25 hrs, transfers in Chiusi and Terontola; bus is more efficient). Train station: 075-804-0272, train info: tel. 848-888-088.

By bus to: Siena (1/day, 2 hrs, €8.25, departs Basilica di Santa Maria degli Angeli near Assisi train station—as you face basilica, stop is to your left across the street), **Rome** (3/day, 3 hrs, departs Assisi's Piazza Unita d'Italia, arrives at Rome's Tiburtina station). Unless you like getting up really early, don't take the bus to Florence (1/day, departs Assisi's Piazza Unita d'Italia at 06:45, 2.75 hrs); the train is better.

ORVIETO, CIVITA, AND MORE HILL TOWNS

Orvieto, one of the most famous hill towns, is an ideal springboard for a trip (by car or bus) to the tiny hill town of Civita di Bagnoregio. Stranded alone on its pinnacle in a vast canyon, Civita's lovable. If you have more time and a car, you'll find sun-soaked regions of Tuscany, Umbria, and Le Marche spiked with hill towns.

Planning Your Time

These two towns are worth a day and an overnight—ideally, an afternoon, night, and morning. Most people start with Orvieto, which is an easy train stop on the Florence-Rome line, then continue to Civita by bus.

Orvieto has a good half day of sightseeing. Spend the night in Orvieto if you want a variety of restaurants, or in Civita if you want peace. Civita is also worth a half day; a chunk of that time is spent hiking to and from the town from Bagnoregio (connected by bus with Orvieto, daily except Sun).

ORVIETO

Umbria's grand hill town, while no secret, is worth a quick look. Just off the freeway, with three popular claims to fame (cathedral, Classico wine, and ceramics), it's loaded with tourists by day and quiet by night. Drinking a shot of wine in a ceramic cup as you gaze up at the cathedral lets you experience Orvieto all at once.

The town sits majestically on a big chunk of tufa rock. Streets are lined with exhaust-stained buildings made from the volcanic stuff.

Piazza Cahen is a key transportation hub at the entry to the hilltop town. As you exit the funicular, the town center is straight ahead.

Tourist Information: The TI is at Piazza Duomo 24 on

Orvieto and Civita Area

the cathedral square (Mon–Fri 08:15–14:00, 16:00–19:00, Sat
10:00–13:00, 16:00–19:00, Sun 10:00–12:00, 16:00–18:00, tel.
0763-341-772). Pick up the free city map and ask about train
and bus schedules. The TI sells a €1.50 admission ticket for the
Chapel of St. Brizio (within the cathedral). For a longer visit,
consider buying the €10.50 "Carta Unica" which covers entry
to the chapel, Archaeological Museum (Museo Claudio Faina e
Museo Civico), Underground Orvieto Tours, and Torre del Moro
(tower), plus your public transportation (bus and funicular) for
one day (or 5 hrs of parking at *parcheggio* Campo della Fiera).

Market Days: Drop by Piazza del Popolo with your cloth
shopping bag on Tuesday and Saturday mornings.

Arrival in Orvieto

By Train: If you're daytripping, you can check your bag at the
station (€2.75, access from platform, knock if door closed).

A handy funicular/bus shuttle will take you quickly from the
train station and parking lot to the top of the town. Buy your ticket at
the entrance to the *funiculare*; look for the "biglietteria" sign (4–6/hr,
€0.85, ticket includes the minibus from Piazza Cahen to Piazza
Duomo—where you'll find everything that matters; or pay €0.65

for funicular only—best choice if you're staying at Hotel Corso; funicular runs Mon–Sat 07:20–20:30, Sun 08:00–20:30).

As you exit the funicular at the top, to your left is a ruined fortress with a garden, WC, and a commanding view, and to your right—St. Patrick's Well (described below), Etruscan ruins, and another sweeping view. Just in front of you is an orange bus waiting to shuttle you to the town center. It'll drop you off at the TI (last stop, in front of cathedral).

If you forgot to check at the station for the train schedule to your next destination (and now the station is far, far below), Orvieto is ready for you. You can peruse the loose-leaf timetable at the TI or the train schedule posted at the top of the *funiculare*.

By Car: Drivers park at the base of the hill at the huge, free lot behind the Orvieto train station (follow the "P" and "funiculare" signs) or at the pay lot to the right of Orvieto's cathedral (€0.75, for first hour, €0.60/hr thereafter).

Sights—Orvieto's Piazza Duomo

▲▲**Duomo**—The cathedral has Italy's most striking facade (from 1330), thanks to architect Lorenzo Maitani and many others. Grab a gelato (to the left of the church) and study this fascinating, gleaming mass of mosaics and sculpture.

At the base of the cathedral, the broad marble pillars carved with Biblical scenes tell the story of the world from left to right. The pillar on the far left shows the Creation (see the snake and Eve), next is the Tree of Jesse, next the New Testament (look for Mary in a manger, etc.), and on the far right—the Last Judgment (with hell, of course, at the bottom). Each pillar is topped by a bronze symbol of one of the evangelists: angel (Matthew), lion (Mark), eagle (John), and bull (Luke). The bronze doors are modern, by Emilio Greco. (A museum devoted to Greco's work is to the right of the church; it's labeled simply "Museo.") In the mosaic below the rose window, Mary is transported to heaven. In the uppermost mosaic, Mary is crowned.

Why such an impressive church in a little tufa town? Because of a blood-stained cloth. In the 1260s, a Bohemian priest—who doubted that the bread used in communion was really the body of Christ—came to Rome on a pilgrimage. On his return journey, he worshiped in Bolsena, near Orvieto. During Mass, the bread bled, staining a linen cloth. The cloth was brought to the pope, who was visiting Orvieto at the time. Such a miraculous relic required a magnificent church. You can see the actual cloth from the Miracle of Bolsena displayed in the chapel to the left of the altar.

Hours: The cathedral is open April to September daily 07:30–12:45, 14:30–19:15, closing at 18:15 March and Oct, and at 17:15 Nov–Feb. Admission is free, but there is a charge for the Chapel of St. Brizio.

Orvieto

- ❶ HOTEL CORSO
- ❷ HOTEL DUOMO
- ❸ HOTEL POSTA
- ❹ ISTITUTO S.S. DOMENICANE
- ❺ TO HOTEL PICCHIO
- ❻ HOTEL VIRGILIO
- ❼ GRAND HOTEL ITALIA
- ❽ MUSEO EMELIO GRECO
- ❾ TORRE DEL MORO
- ❿ BUY BUS TICKETS TO CIVITA

Cost and Hours of Chapel: Buy the €1.50 ticket at the TI or the shop across the square; it's included in Carta Unica. The chapel is usually free 07:30–10:00—drop by to check; Mon–Sat 10:00–12:45, 14:30–19:15, Sun 14:30–17:45, it closes an hour earlier in winter; only 25 people are allowed in the chapel at a time.

Chapel of St. Brizio: This chapel, to the right of the altar, features Luca Signorelli's brilliantly lit frescoes of the Apocalypse

(1449–1451). Step into the chapel and you're surrounded by vivid scenes, including the *Preaching of the Antichrist* (to your left as you enter—the figure standing on far left is a self-portrait of Signorelli, next to Fra Angelico, who worked on the ceiling); the *Calling of the Elect to Heaven* (left of altar—hear that celestial band); the *Damned in Hell* (right of altar—the scariest mosh pit ever); and the *Resurrection of the Bodies* (to your right as you enter; people dreamily climb out of the earth as skeletons chatter in the corner, wondering where to snare some skin). On the same wall is a gripping *Pietà*. Fra Angelico started the ceiling and Signorelli finished it, turning the entire room into Orvieto's artistic must-see sight.

After leaving the cathedral, if you want a break at a viewpoint park, exit left and pass the small parking lot. The nearest WCs are in the opposite direction (exit cathedral to the right), down the stairs from the left transept.

Archaeological Museum (Museo Claudio Faina e Museo Civico)—Across from the entrance to the cathedral is a fine Etruscan art museum (two upper floors) combined with a miniscule city history museum on the ground floor, featuring a sarcophagus and temple bits. The Faina art—consisting largely of Etruscan vases, plates, and coins, with some jewelry and bronze dishes—was collected by Mauro Faina and his nephew starting in the late 19th century. They bought some of the art, and dug up the rest in haphazardly conducted excavations. Many of the vases came from the Etruscan necropolis (Crocifisso del Tufo) just outside Orvieto. The English placards in most rooms offer some information, especially on the Faina family (€4.25, included in Carta Unica, April–Sept Tue–Sun 09:30–18:00, Oct–March 10:00–17:00, closed Mon, audioguide, WC after ticket desk and on top floor, tel. 0763-341-216). Look out the windows at the Duomo's glittering facade.

▲**Museo Emilo Greco**—This museum displays the work of Emilio Greco (1913–1995), the Sicilian artist who designed the doors of Orvieto's cathedral. His sketches and bronze statues show his absorption with gently twisting and turning nudes. In the back left corner of the museum, look for the sketchy outlines of women—simply beautiful. The artful installation in a palazzo, with walkways and even a spiral staircase up to the ceiling, allow you to view his work from different directions (€2.75, €4.25 includes St. Patrick's Well, April–Sept daily 10:30–13:00, 14:00–18:30, closes 1 hour earlier Oct–March, no English but not essential, next to Duomo, marked "Museo," tel. 0763-344-605).

Underground Orvieto Tours (Parco delle Grotte)—Guides weave a good archaeological history into an hour-long look at about 100 meters of caves (€5.25, included in Carta Unica, tours daily at 11:00, 12:15—English, 16:00, and 17:15—English, tel. 0763-344-891 or the TI). Orvieto is honeycombed with Etruscan and medieval caves. You'll see only the remains of an old olive press, two impressive 40-meter-deep Etruscan well shafts, and the remains of a primitive cement quarry; but, if you want underground Orvieto, this is the place to get it.

More Sights—Orvieto

Torre del Moro—For yet another viewpoint, this distinctive square tower comes with 250 steps and an elevator. The elevator goes only partway up, leaving you with a mere 173 steps to scurry up (€2.75, included in Carta Unica, April–Oct daily 10:00–19:00, July–Aug until 20:00, Nov–Dec 10:30–13:00, 14:30–17:00, terrace on top, at intersection of Corso Cavour and Via Duomo).

St. Patrick's Well (Pozzo di S. Patrizio)—Engineers are impressed by this deep well (53 meters deep and 13 meters wide), designed in the 16th century with a double-helix pattern. The two spiral stairways allow an efficient one-way traffic flow, intriguing now, but critical then. Imagine donkeys and people, balancing jugs of water, trying to go up and down the same stairway. At the bottom is a bridge that people could walk on to scoop up water.

The well was built because a pope got nervous. After Rome was sacked in 1527 by renegade troops of the Holy Roman Empire, the pope fled to Orvieto. He feared that even this little town (with no water source on top) would be besieged. He commissioned a well, which was started in 1527 and finished 10 years later. It was a huge project. Even today, when a local is faced with a difficult task, people say, "It's like digging St. Patrick's Well." The unusual name came from the well's supposed resemblance to the Irish saint's cave. It's not worth climbing up and down a total of 495 steps; a quick look is painless but pricey (€3.25, €4.25 includes Museo Emilio Greco; bring a sweater if you descend to the chilly depths; the well is to your right as you exit *funiculare*).

View Walks—For short, pleasant walks, climb the medieval wall (at western end of town, between Piazza S. Gionvenale and Via Garibaldi) or stroll the promenade park on the northern edge of town, along Viale Carducci, which becomes Gonfaloniera).

Sights Near Orvieto

Wine-Tasting—Orvieto Classico wine is justly famous. For a short tour of a local winery with Etruscan cellars, visit Tenuta Le Velette, where English-speaking Corrado and Cecilia Bottai will welcome you—if you've called ahead to set up an appointment (€8 for tour and tasting, Mon–Fri 08:30–12:00, 14:00–17:00, Sat 08:30–12:00, closed Sun, tel. 0763-29144, fax 076-329-114). From their sign (5 minutes past Orvieto at top of switchbacks just before Canale, on Bagnoregio road), cruise down a long tree-lined drive, then park at the striped gate (must call ahead; no drop-ins).

Sleeping in Orvieto
(€1.10 = about $1, country code: 39, zip code: 05018)
All of these are in the old town except the last one, which is in a more modern neighborhood near the station.

Hotel Corso is small, clean, and friendly, with 18 comfy, modern rooms, some with balconies and views (Sb-€57, Db-€78, 10 percent discount with this book, buffet breakfast-€6.50, CC, elevator, air-con at no extra charge, garage on the main street up from funicular toward Duomo at Via Cavour 339, tel. & fax 0763-342-020, www.argoweb.it/hotel _corso, e-mail: hotelcorso@libero.it).

Hotel Virgilio is a decent hotel with bright and modern— if overpriced—rooms shoehorned into an old building, ideally located on the main square facing the cathedral (Sb-€62, Db-€85, breakfast-€7.75, send personal or traveler's check for first night's deposit, CC, elevator, noisy church bells every 15 min, Piazza Duomo 5, tel. 0763-341-882, fax 0763-343-797, SE). They also have a cheaper *dependencia*—a double and quad in a one-star hotel a few doors away (Db-€57, Qb-€103, e-mail: hotel.virgilio@orvienet.it).

Hotel Duomo, centrally located, is super-duper modern, with splashy art and 17 sleek rooms named after artists who worked on the Duomo (Db-€93, Db suite-€114, includes breakfast, CC, elevator, air-con, double-paned windows keep out noise, a block from Duomo, behind *gelateria* at Via di Maurizio 7, tel. 0763-341-887, fax 0763-394-973).

Hotel Posta is a five-minute walk from the cathedral into the medieval core. It's a big, old, formerly elegant but well-cared-for-in-its-decline building with a breezy garden, a grand old lobby, and 20 spacious, clean, plain rooms with vintage rickety furniture and good mattresses (S-€31, Sb-€36, D-€39, Db-€49–54, breakfast-€5.25, no CC, some air-con, Via Luca Signorelli 18, tel. & fax 0763-341-909).

The sisters of the **Istituto SS Domenicane** rent 15 spotless twin rooms in their heavenly convent with a peaceful terrace (Sb-€36, Db-€52, 2-night min, breakfast-€5.25, no CC, elevator, parking, just off Piazza del Populo at Via del Populo 1, tel. & fax 0763-342-910, www.argoweb.it/istituto _sansalvatore/istituto.uk.html).

Hotel Picchio is a concrete-and-marble place, more comfortable but with less character than others in the area. It's in the lower, plain part of town, 300 meters from the train station (Sb-€34, Db-€46, Tb-€57, ask for the Rick Steves discount; some rooms with air-con, fridge, and phone; Via G. Salvatori 17, 05019 Orvieto Scalo, tel. & fax 0763-301-144, family-run by Marco and Picchio). A trail leads from here up to the old town.

Eating in Orvieto

Near the Duomo, consider **Pergola**—its affordable menu is popular with locals (Thu–Tue 12:30–14:30, 17:30–19:45, closed Wed, Via dei Magoni 9). **La Palomba** is also a good bet (Thu–Tue 12:30–14:15, 19:30–22:00, closed Wed, Via Cipriano Manenta, just off Piazza della Republica). For a bit of a splurge, try **Antico Bucchero** for its classy candlelit ambience and fine food (Thu–Tue 12:30–15:00, 19:00–24:00, closed Wed, CC, indoor/outdoor seating, Via de Cartori, a half block south of Corso Cavour, between Torre del Moro and Piazza della Repubblica). **Osteria San Patrizio**, near the funicular, is good (closed Sun eve and Mon, Corso Cavour 312, tel. 0763-341-245).

For dessert, try the *gelateria* **Pasqualetti** (daily 12:30–01:00, until 20:00 Nov–March, Piazza Duomo 14, next to left transept of church; another branch is at Corso Cavour 56).

Transportation Connections—Orvieto

By train to: Rome (14/day, 75 min, consider leaving your car at the large car park behind the Orvieto station), **Florence** (8/day, 2.25 hrs), **Siena** (8/day, 2–3 hrs, change in Chiusi; all Florence-bound trains stop in Chiusi). The train station's Buffet della Stazione is surprisingly good for a quick focaccia sandwich or pizza picnic for the train ride.

By bus to Bagnoregio (near Civita): It's a 70-minute, €1.50 bus ride. Departures in 2001 from Orvieto's Piazza Cahen on the blue Cotral bus, daily except Sunday: 05:30, 06:50, 09:50, 10:10, 13:00, 14:25, 17:20. During the school year (roughly Sept–June), buses also run at 06:35, 13:35, and 16:40. Buy your ticket at the *tabacchi* stop on Corso Cavour (also confirm the schedule) a block up from *funiculare*. To find the bus stop, face the *funiculare*; the stop is at the far left end of Piazza Cahen where the blue buses are parked (no schedule posted; confirm departure and return times with driver; schedule *is* posted at bus stop in Bagnoregio). Each bus stops at Orvieto's train station five minutes later.

CIVITA DI BAGNOREGIO

Perched on a pinnacle in a grand canyon, the traffic-free village of Civita is Italy's ultimate hill town. Curl your toes around its Etruscan roots.

Civita is terminally ill. Only 15 residents remain as, bit by bit, the town is being purchased by rich big-city Italians who come here to escape. Apart from its permanent (and aging) residents and those who have weekend homes here, there is a group of Americans—introduced to the town through a small University of Washington architecture program—who have bought into the rare magic of Civita. When the program is in session, 15 students live with residents and study Italian culture and architecture.

Civita is connected to the world and the town of Bagno-regio by a long pedestrian bridge—and a new Web site (www .civitadibagnoregio.it). While Bagnoregio lacks the pinnacle-town romance of Civita, it is a pure and lively bit of small-town Italy. It's actually a healthy, vibrant community (unlike Civita, the suburb it calls "the dead city"). Get a haircut, sip a coffee on the square, walk down to the old laundry (ask, *"Dov'è la lavanderia vecchia?"*). A Grand Spesa supermarket is 300 meters from the bus stop (Mon–Sat 08:30–13:00, 17:00-20:00, closed Sun; take main drag from town gate—away from Civita, angle right at pyramid monument). A lively market fills the bus parking lot each Monday.

From Bagnoregio, yellow signs direct you along its long, skinny spine to its older neighbor, Civita. Enjoy the view as you walk up the bridge to Civita. Be prepared for the little old ladies of Civita, who can be aggressive at getting money out of visitors—tourists are their only source of support. Off-season Civita, Bag-noregio, and Al Boschetto (see "Sleeping," below) are all deadly quiet—and cold. I'd side-trip in quickly from Orvieto or skip the area altogether.

Arrival in Bagnoregio, near Civita

If you're arriving by bus from Orvieto, you'll get off at the bus stop in Bagnoregio. Look at the posted bus schedule and write down the return times to Orvieto. (Drivers, see "Transportation Connections," below.)

Baggage Check: While there's no official baggage-check service in Bagnoregio, I've arranged with Laurenti Mauro, who runs the Bar/Enoteca/Caffè Gianfu, to let you leave your bags there (€1/bag, Fri–Wed 07:00–24:00 with a 13:00–13:30 lunch break, closed Thu; to get to café from Orvieto bus stop where you got off, continue in same direction the Orvieto bus headed and round the corner).

From Bagnoregio to Civita

From Bagnoregio, you can walk or take a little orange shuttle bus to the base of the bridge to Civita. From here, you have to walk the rest of the way. It's a 10-minute hike up a pedestrian bridge that gets steeper near the end. There's no bus—only you and your profound regret that you didn't get in better shape before your trip.

You can take the little shuttle **bus** from Bagnoregio to the base of the bridge (€1, 10-min ride, first bus at 07:39, last at 18:20, 1–2/hr except during 13:00–15:30 siesta, catch bus at stop across from gas station). If you'll want to return to Bagnoregio by bus, check the schedule posted near the bridge (at edge of car park, where bus let you off) before you head up to Civita.

To **walk** from Bagnoregio to the base of Civita's bridge (about 20 min, fairly level), take the road going uphill (overlooking the big parking lot), then take the first right and an immediate left onto the main drag, Via Roma. Follow this straight out to the *belvedere* for a superb viewpoint. From the viewpoint, backtrack a few steps, and take the stairs down to the road leading to the bridge.

Civita Orientation Walk

Civita was once connected to Bagnoregio. The saddle between the separate towns eroded away. Photographs around town show the old donkey path, the original bridge. It was bombed in World War II and replaced in 1965 with the new **bridge** you're climbing today. The town's hearty old folks hang on the bridge's hand railing when fierce winter weather rolls through.

Entering the town, you'll pass through a cut in the rock (made by Etruscans 2,500 years ago) and under a 12th-century Romanesque **arch**. This was the main Etruscan road leading to the Tiber Valley and Rome.

Inside the town gate, on your left is the old **laundry** (in front of the WC). On your right, a fancy wooden door and windows (above the door) lead to thin air. This was the facade of a Renaissance palace—one of five that once graced Civita. It fell into the valley riding a chunk of the ever-eroding rock pinnacle. Today the door leads to a remaining chunk of the palace—complete with Civita's first hot tub—owned by the "Marchesa," a countess who married into Italy's biggest industrialist family.

Peek into the museum next door if it's open (Wed and Sat–Sun 10:00–13:00, marked "Benvenuti a Civita") and check out the **viewpoint** a few steps away. Nearby is the long-gone home of Civita's one famous son, Saint Bonaventure, known as the "second founder of the Franciscans."

Now wander to the **town square** in front of the church, where you'll find Civita's only public phone, bar, and restaurant—and a wild donkey race on the first Sunday of June and the second Sunday of September. The church marks the spot where an Etruscan temple, and then a Roman temple, once stood. The pillars that stand like giants' bar stools are ancient—Roman or Etruscan.

Go into the **church**. You'll see frescoes and statues from "the school of Giotto" and "the school of Donatello," a portrait of the patron saint of your teeth (notice the scary-looking pincers), and an altar dedicated to Marlon Brando (or St. Ildebrando).

The basic grid street plan of the ancient town survives. Just around the corner from the church, on the main street, is Rossana and Antonio's cool and friendly **wine cellar** (their sign reads: *bruschette con prodotti locali*). Pull up a stump and let them or their children, Arianna and Antonella, serve you *panini* (sandwiches), *bruschetta* (garlic toast with optional tomato topping), wine, and a local cake called *ciambella*. Climb down into the cellar and note the traditional wine-making gear and the provisions for rolling huge kegs up the stairs. Tap on the kegs in the cool bottom level to see which are full.

The rock below Civita is honeycombed with ancient cellars (for keeping wine at the same temperature all year) and cisterns (for collecting rainwater, since there was no well in town). Many of these date from Etruscan times.

Explore farther down the street but, remember, nothing is abandoned. Everything is still privately owned. After passing an ancient Roman tombstone on your left, you'll come to Vittoria's **Antico Mulino**, an atmospheric collection of old olive presses. The huge press in the entry is about 1,500 years old and was in use as recently as the 1960s (donation requested, give about €1). Vittoria's sons, Sandro and Felice, running the local equivalent of a lemonade stand, toast delicious *bruschetta* on weekends and holidays (roughly 11:00–19:00). Choose your topping (chopped tomato is super) and get a glass of wine for a fun, affordable snack.

Farther down the way and to your left, Maria (for a donation of about €1) will show you through her **garden** with a grand view (Maria's Giardino) and share historical misinformation (she says Civita and Lubriano were once connected). Maria's husband,

Peppone, used to carry goods on a donkey back and forth on the path between the old town and Bagnoregio.

At the end of town, the main drag winds downhill past small **Etruscan caves** to your right. The first two were used as stables until last year. The third cave is an unusual chapel, cut deep into the rock, with a barred door—this is the **Chapel of the Incarcerated** (Cappella del Carcere). In Etruscan times, the chapel may have originally been a tomb, and in medieval times it was used as a jail. When Civita's few residents have a religious procession, they come here, in honor of the Madonna of the Incarcerated.

After the chapel, the paving-stone path peters out into a dirt trail leading down and around to the right to a **tunnel**. Dating from the Etruscan era, the tunnel may have served as a shortcut to the river below. It was widened in the 1930s so farmers could get between their scattered fields more easily, and now the residents use it as a shortcut in fall to collect chestnuts from the trees that cover the hillside. Backtrack to the town square.

Evenings on the town square are a bite of Italy. The same people sit on the same church steps under the same moon, night after night, year after year. I love my cool, late evenings in Civita. If you visit in the cool of the morning, have cappuccino and rolls at the small café on the town square.

Whenever you visit, stop halfway up the donkey path and listen to the sounds of rural Italy. Reach out and touch one of the monopoly houses. If you know how to turn the volume up on the crickets, do so.

Sleeping in Civita and Bagnoregio
(€1.10 = about $1, country code: 39, zip code: 01022)
When you leave the tourist crush, life as a traveler in Italy becomes easy, and prices tumble. Finding a room is easy in small-town Italy.

Franco Sala, who runs Civita's only restaurant, **Antico Forno**, rents three comfortable rooms overlooking Civita's main square. Call a minimum of one day in advance. English-speaking Franco might meet you at the base of the bridge to beam up your luggage (Db-€67, D-€57, €13 more for optional half-pension, CC, Piazza Del Duomo Vecchio, 01022 Civita di Bagnoregio, tel. 0761-760-016, cellular 34-7611-5426, e-mail: fsala@pelagus.it).

For information about a fully furnished and equipped two-bedroom **Civita apartment** with a terrace and cliffside garden that's rentable May through October ($800/week, one-week minimum Sat to Sat, personal checks OK), call Carol Watts in Kansas (tel. 785/539-0815, evenings or weekends, http://homepage.mac.com/cmwatts/civita.html).

Hotel Fidanza, in Bagnoregio near the bus stop, is tired but decent and the only hotel in town. Of its 25 rooms, #206 and #207 have views of Civita (Sb-€52, Db-€62, breakfast-€5.50, no CC, attached restaurant, Via Fidanza 25, Bagnoregio/Viterbo, tel. & fax 0761-793-444).

Just outside Bagnoregio is **Al Boschetto.** The Catarcia family speaks no English, so have an English-speaking Italian call for you (Sb-€34, D-€44, Db-€49, breakfast-€3, CC, Strada Monterado, Bagnoregio/Viterbo, tel. 0761-792-369). Most of the 25 rooms, while very basic, have private showers. The Catarcia family (Angelino, his wife Perina, sons Gianfranco and Domenico, daughter-in-law Giuseppina, and the grandchildren) offers a candid look at rural Italian life. Meals are uneven in quality, and the men are often tipsy (which can pose a problem for women). If the men invite you down deep into the gooey, fragrant bowels of the cantina, be warned: The theme song is *"Trinka Trinka Trinka,"* and there are no rules unless the female participants set them. The Orvieto bus drops you at the town gate (no bus on Sun). The hotel is a 15-minute walk out of town past the old arch (follow "Viterbo" signs); turn left at the pyramid monument and right at the first fork (follow "Montefiascone" sign). Civita is a pleasant 45-minute walk (back through Bagnoregio) from Al Boschetto.

Casa San Martino, in the village of Lisciano Niccone (near Cortona and Perugia), is a 250-year-old farmhouse run as a B&B by American Italophile, Lois Martin. Using this comfortable hilltop countryside as a home base, those with a car can tour Assisi, Orvieto, and Civita. While Lois reserves the summer (June–Aug) for one-week stays, she'll take guests staying a minimum of three nights for the rest of the year (Db-€154, 10 percent discount for my readers—mention this book when you reserve, includes breakfast, views, pool, washer/dryer, house rental available, Casa San Martino 19, Lisciano Niccone, tel. 075-844-288, fax 075-844-422). Lois' neighbors, Ernestine and Gisbert Schwanke, run the charming **La Villetta di San Martino B&B** (Db-€110 includes hearty country breakfast, minimum 2-night stay, kitchen, sitting room, fireplace, San Martino 36, tel. & fax 075-844-309, e-mail: erni@netemedia.net, SE).

For drivers only: Outside the village of Baschi is the outstanding **Agriturismo Le Casette**, with rooms in several restored stone farmhouses clustered around a grassy lawn and a swimming pool with a fabulous view of the green Umbrian landscape (Db-€70, includes breakfast; for a room, breakfast, and a home-cooked dinner, pay €60 per person per day; minimum 1-week stays preferred July–Aug, no CC, tel. 0744-950-190, fax 0744-950-500, www.pomurlovecchio-lecasette.it, e-mail: pomurlovecchio @tiscalinet.it, run by charming Minghelli family, Daniela speaks "a leetle" English). The same family also owns **Pomurlo Vecchio**, a 12th-century tower house with three rooms a few kilometers away (same prices and phone numbers).

Eating in and near Civita

In Civita, try **Trattoria Antico Forno**, which serves up pasta at affordable prices (daily for lunch at 12:00 and sporadically for dinner at 19:00, on the main square, also rents rooms—see above, tel. 0761-760-016). From October through March, Franco shifts his restaurant from outdoors (on the square) inside to an atmospheric dining room in his Antico Forno B&B, a few steps away and also on the square. At **Da Peppone**, the small café/bar on the square, you can get a simple sandwich and treats (daily 09:30–12:30, 14:30–19:00, closed in winter Mon or Tue).

Hostaria del Ponte offers light, creative cuisine at the parking lot at the base of the bridge to Civita (Tue–Sat 12:30–16:00, 19:30–24:00, Sun 12:30–16:00, closed Mon, great view terrace, tel. 0761-793-565).

In Bagnoregio, check out **Ristorante Nello il Fumatore** (Sat–Thu 12:00–15:00, 19:00–22:00, closed Fri, on Piazza Fidanza). At **Al Boschetto,** you'll get country cooking, such as bunny (just outside Bagnoregio; see "Sleeping," above).

Transportation Connections—Bagnoregio

To Orvieto: Public buses (7/day, 70 min) connect Bagnoregio to the rest of the world via Orvieto. Departures in 2001 from Bagnoregio, daily except Sunday: 06:20, 09:10, 12:40, 13:55, 15:45, 17:40, 18:20. During the school year (roughly Sept–June), there are additional departures at 07:20 and 07:50 (for info on Orvieto, see "Connections—Orvieto," above).

Driving from Orvieto to Bagnoregio: Orvieto overlooks the autostrada (and has its own exit). The shortest way to Civita from the freeway exit is to turn left (below Orvieto) and follow the signs to Lubriano and Bagnoregio.

The more winding and scenic route takes 20 minutes longer: From the freeway, pass under hill-capping Orvieto (on your right, signs to Lago di Bolsena, on Viale I Maggio); take the first left (direction: Bagnoregio), winding up past great Orvieto views through Canale, and through farms and fields of giant shredded wheat to Bagnoregio.

Either way, just before Bagnoregio, follow the signs left to Lubriano and pull into the first little square by the church on your right for a breathtaking view of Civita. Then return to the Bagnoregio road. Drive through Bagnoregio (following yellow "Civita" signs) and park at the base of the steep pedestrian bridge leading up to the traffic-free, 2,500-year-old, canyon-swamped pinnacle town of Civita di Bagnoregio.

MORE HILL TOWNS

If you haven't gotten your fill of hill towns, here are more to check out. There are three main regions in central Italy, listed here in order of touristic popularity and accessibility: Tuscany, Umbria, and Le Marche.

Tuscany is our image of village Italy, with its manicured hills, rustic farms, and towns clinging to nearly every hill. Yet many who visit Tuscany, famous as the cradle of the Renaissance, never get out of the crowds of Florence. You'll find good train and bus connections throughout most of the region, but a car is fun.

Landlocked **Umbria**, the "Green Heart of Italy," is known for Assisi, famous worldwide as the hometown of St. Francis. Yet a short distance away from Assisi's touristic bustle, you'll find plenty of pleasant towns with more of the peace that Francis was seeking.

Le Marche is much less discovered. Its landscape is more wild and less manicured. The town of Urbino is the region's highlight. To unlock Le Marche's charms, a car is essential.

TUSCANY

▲▲**Cortona**—Cortona clings by its fingernails to the top of a mountain, dangling above views of the Tuscan and Umbrian landscape below. Frances Mayes' books, such as *Under the Tuscan Sun*, have placed this town in the touristic limelight, just as Peter Mayle's books popularized (and populated) the Luberon region in France. But even before Mayes ever published a book, Cortona was considered one of the classic Tuscan hill towns.

Unlike many hill towns, Cortona is worth visiting for its art alone. The Museo Diocesano has a small but interesting collection, including powerful works by native son Signorelli and two wonderful luminous Fra Angelicos. The Museo dell'Accademia Etrusca, housed in a former palace, has an eclectic collection of paintings, Etruscan artifacts and jewelry, and Egyptian mummies.

Cortona lies above the Terontola station (8 km away) on the Florence–Perugia line. Frequent buses connect the station with Piazza Garibaldi and the sights. The **TI** is at Via Nazionale 42 (tel. 0575-630-352). There are lots of cafés for lunch, or assemble a picnic and dine *al fresco*. Cortona's San Marco hostel, housed in a remodeled 13th-century palace, is one of Italy's best (Via Maffei 57, tel. 0575-601-392).

▲**Chiusi**—This small hill town (rated ▲▲ for Etruscan fans), which was once one of the most important Etruscan cities, is now a key train junction on the Florence–Rome line. The region's trains (to Siena, Orvieto, and Assisi) go through or change at this hub.

Highlights include the Archaeological Museum (Mon–Sat 09:00–14:00, Sun 09:00–13:00, tel. 0578-20177) and the Etruscan tombs located just outside of town near Lago di Chiusi. One of the tombs is multi-chambered with several sarcophagi, while another, the Tomba della Scimmia (Tomb of the Monkey) has some well-preserved frescoes. Visiting the tombs requires a guide, arranged through the TI or the Archaeological Museum.

Troglodyte alert! The Cathedral Museum on the main square has an underground labyrinth of Etruscan tunnels (dark, so bring a flashlight!). The tour, for which you'll need a guide, ends in a large Roman cistern from which you can climb the church bell tower for an expansive view of the countryside.

The **TI** on the main square (daily in summer 08:30–12:30, 15:30–18:30, otherwise mornings only, tel. 0578-227-667). Trains connect Chiusi with Rome, Florence, Siena, and more. Buses link the station (3 km away) with the town center.

▲▲**Montepulciano**—Long and skinny, Montepulciano stretches out lazily across a ridge. Due to its time under Medici rule, Montepulciano has an interesting mix of Renaissance buildings. You can begin your look at this Tuscan gem at Piazza San Agnese and walk uphill from here, but it's easier to take the shuttle bus from Piazza San Agnese up to Piazza Grande and walk downhill.

At Piazza Grande, the Palazzo Comunale, a mini-version of Florence's Palazzo Vecchio, looms across from Palazzo Contucci. Here you'll find an *enoteca* (wine bar) where you can sample the famous Vino Nobile di Montepulciano. From Piazza Grande, take Viale Sangallo downhill. The road snakes its way past shops, palaces, and *enotecas* through the old Porta al Prato gate to Piazza San Agnese. Just outside the city walls is the Church of San Biagio, a Renaissance masterpiece by Sangallo.

Buses take you from Montepuliciano's train station on the Florence–Rome line to the parking lot below Piazza San Agnese at the bottom of town. From here, it's a 25-minute walk up to Piazza Grande (or a quick bus ride). Buses connect Montepulciano with Siena as well.

▲**Montalcino**—Famous for its Brunello di Montalcino red wines, this hill town (rated ▲▲▲ for wine-lovers), once part of Siena's empire, is worth a visit for its *enoteca*, housed inside the 14th-century fortezza at the edge of town (tel. 0577-849-211, www.enotecalafortezza.it). After sampling a glass of the local *vino*, wander down into the heart of town at Piazza Garibaldi. The TI is on this square (tel. 0577-849-331). Besides the fortezza and the Brunello, Montalcino's main sight is the Museo Civico on Via Ricasoli, where you'll find art from the late Gothic/early Renaissance period. An atmospheric café is Antica Fiaschetteria on Piazza del Popolo. Non-wine lovers may find Montalcino a bit too focused on *vino*, but one sip of Brunello makes even wine skeptics believe that Bacchus was onto something. Note that the Rosso di Montalcino wine is also good at half the price. Sweet-tooths will enjoy munching Ossi di Morta ("bones of the dead"), a crunchy cookie with almonds.

Buses connect Montalcino with Siena.

▲**Pienza**—In the 1400s, local pope Pius II of the Piccolomini family decided to remodel his hometown in the current Renaissance style.

Propelled by papal clout, the town of Corsignano was transformed into a jewel of Renaissance architecture and renamed Pienza. The focal point is the Piazza Pio II, with the Duomo and Palazzo Piccolomini. The TI is in Palazzo Pubblico (tel. 0578-749-071).

Buses connect Pienza with Siena and Montepulciano.

▲▲**Crete Senese Drive**—Sometimes it seems that all of Tuscany is one big scenic route, but my favorite drive is this one between Montepulciano and Montalcino on the S-146 road. This area is known as the Crete Senese ("Crests of Siena"), a series of undulating hills that provides postcard views at every turn. You'll see an endless parade of classic Tuscan scenes, with rolling hills topped with medieval towns, olive groves, rustic stone farmhouses, rows of vineyards, and a skyline punctuated with cypress trees.

San Galgano Monastery—Southern Tuscany has several evocative monasteries, and many feel that San Galgano is the best. Way off the beaten track, this sight is for drivers. San Galgano was a 12th-century saint who renounced his past as a knight by miraculously burying his sword up to its hilt into a stone. After his death, a large monastery complex grew up. Today, all you'll see is the roofless, ruined abbey and, on a nearby hill, the Chapel of San Galgano with its fascinating dome and sword in the stone. The adjacent gift shop sells a little bit of everything from wine to postcards to herbs. Other more accessible Tuscan monasteries worth visiting include San Antimo (10 km south of Montalcino) and Monte Oliveto Maggiore (25 km south of Siena).

One bus a day from Siena stops at San Galgano. Buses link Montalcino with San Antimo, and Siena with Monte Oliveto Maggiore.

▲**U.S. Cemetery**—Whatever one's feelings about war, the sight of endless rows of white marble crosses and Stars of David never fail to be moving. This particular cemetery is the final resting place of more than 4,000 Americans who died in the liberation of Italy during World War II. Their memory lives on in two Italian cemeteries, one in Nettuno near Rome and this one just south of Tavernuzze, 12 kilometers south of Florence. Climb the hill past the perfectly manicured grassy lawn, lined with grave markers, to the memorial, where maps and history of the Italian campaign detail the Allied advance (daily mid-April–Sept 08:00–18:00, Oct–mid-April 08:00–17:00, WC, just off Via Cassia road that parallels the superstrada between Florence and Siena, 3 km south of Florence Certosa exit on A-1 autostrada). Buses from Florence stop just outside the cemetery.

UMBRIA

▲**Gubbio**—This handsome town climbs Monte Ingino in northeast Umbria. Tuesday is market day, when Piazza 40 Martiri (named for 40 locals shot by the Nazis) bustles. Nearby, the ruins of the Roman amphiteater are perfect for a picnic. Head up Via della Repubblica to reach the main square with the imposing Palazzo dei Consoli. Farther up, Via San Gerolamo leads to the funky lift that will carry you up the hill in two-person "baskets" for a stunning view from the top, where the basilica of St. Ubaldo is worth a look.

Buses run to Perugia, Rome, and Florence. The TI is at Piazza Odersi (tel. 075-922-0693).

▲**Deruta**—Pottery-lovers the world over start to salivate when the name Deruta is mentioned. Colorful Deruta pottery, considered to be Italy's best, features designs popular since Renaissance times. The high-quality local clay attracted artisans centuries ago, and today artists still practice their craft. Deruta is actually two towns: the upper hill town and the lower strip. The upper town, full of small shops run by local artisans, is worth a wander; prices and quality are higher up here. Ceramic fans drop by the Museo Regionale della Ceramica (closed Tue), in the upper town, next to the TI on the main square. Below, a commercial strip parallel to the super-strada is lined with larger commercial outlets and factories. Many offer demonstrations of their time-honored craft. Prices are about one-third cheaper than in the United States, and most will ship your purchases home with a guarantee of safe delivery.

Buses connect Deruta with Perugia.

▲**Bevagna**—This sleeper of a town south of Assisi has Roman ruins, interesting churches, and more. Locals offer their guiding services for free (usually Italian-speaking only) and are excited to show visitors their town. Get a map at the **TI** on Piazza Silvestri (tel. 0742-361-667) and wander. Highlights are the Roman mosaics, remains of the arena that now houses a paper-making shop, the Romanesque church of San Silvestro, and a gem of a 19th-century theater. Bevagna has all the elements of a hill town except one—a hill. A couple hours is plenty to see the main sights.

Buses connect Bevagna with Foligno.

Montefalco—Famous for its Sagrantino wine and its site (Montefalco means Falcon's Mountain), this village is dubbed the "Balcony of Umbria" for its expansive views. Intact medieval walls surround the town. The Museo Civico San Francesco displays frescoes by Gozzoli (Fra Angelico's pupil) of the Life of St. Francis. There is no TI, but the people at the museum can answer questions.

A few buses a day run to Bevagna.

▲**Spello**—Umbrian hill town aficionados always include Spello on their list. Just 10 kilometers south of Assisi, this town is much less touristy than its neighbor to the north. Spello will give your legs a workout. Via Consolare goes up up to the top of town. Views from the terrace of the restaurant Il Trombone will have you singing a tune. The **TI** is on Piazza Matteotti 3 (tel. 0742-301-009).

Spello is on the Perugia-Assisi-Foligno train line. Buses run to Assisi.

LE MARCHE

▲▲**Urbino**—Urbino is famous for being the hometown of the artist Raphael and architect Bramante, yet the town owes much of its fame to the Duke of Montefeltro. This mercenary general turned Urbino into an important Renaissance center, attracting artists such as Piero della Francesca, Uccello, and Raphael's papa, Giovanni Santi.

The Ducal Palace, with more than 300 rooms, is the main course of a visit to Urbino. Highlights include great paintings such as Raphael's *La Muta*, the remarkable *intarsio* (inlaid wood) walls of the duke's study, the vast cellars, and the Renaissance courtyard (€4.20, Sun–Mon 09:00–14:00, Tue–Sat 09:00–19:00). Note that during busy periods you need to reserve a ticket for the palace in person. For details, call the **TI** (Piazza Duca Federico 35, across from palace, tel. 0722-2613, e-mail: iat@comune.urbino.ps.it) or the booking office in the palace (tel. 0722-32-90-57).

Stop by the Oratory of St. John to see its remarkable frescoed interior. Nearby the Church of San Giuseppe has a dreamy stucco ceiling, with angels peering down through whipped-cream clouds at the huge nativity diorama below. In the adjacent church, a Baroque trompe d'oeil ceiling is worth a look. Fans visit the Casa di Raffaello, but the artist's famous works are in Florence and Rome. For a fabulous view, climb up to the Giardini Pubblici park, where a grassy hillside provides a panorama of Urbino and the hills of Le Marche.

A couple good restaurants are Taverna degli Artisti (great pizzas, Via Bramante) and Il Coppiere (Via Santa Margherita), where your entire meal, including the post-dinner grappa, can involve truffles, if you like. The *enoteca* on Via Raphael is worth a stop, but the action in town is at the bustling Piazza della Repubblica, with an endless parade of students and locals.

Urbino is well off the beaten tourist path. Frequent buses connect Pesaro (on the Ravenna–Pescara train line) with Urbino, terminating at the Borgo Mercatale parking lot below the town, where an elevator lifts you up to the base of the slender towers of Ducal Palace (or walk 5 minutes steeply up Via Mazzini to Piazza della Repubblica).

THE CINQUE TERRE

The Cinque Terre (CHINK-wuh TAY-ruh), a remote chunk of the Italian Riviera, is the traffic-free, lowbrow, underappreciated alternative to the French Riviera. There's not a museum in sight. Just sun, sea, sand (well, pebbles), wine, and pure unadulterated Italy. Enjoy the villages, swimming, hiking, and evening romance of one of God's great gifts to tourism. For a home base, choose among five villages, each of which fills a ravine with a lazy hive of human activity—calloused locals, sunburned travelers, and no Vespas. While the place is now well-discovered (www.cinqueterre .it), I've never seen happier, more relaxed tourists. Vernazza is my favorite home base.

The area was first described in medieval times as "the five castles." Tiny communities grew up in the protective shadows of the castles ready to run inside at the first hint of a Turkish "Saracen" pirate raid. Many locals were kidnapped and ransomed or sold into slavery somewhere far to the east. As the threat of pirates faded, the villages grew, with economies based on fish and grapes. Until the advent of tourism in this generation, the towns were remote. Even today, traditions survive, and each of the five villages comes with a distinct dialect and proud heritage. The region has just become a national park, and its natural and cultural wonders will be carefully preserved.

Now that the Cinque Terre is a national park, you need to pay a park entrance fee. You have two options: buying a Hiking Pass or a Cinque Terre Card. The Hiking Pass costs €2.60 (kids under 4 free; comes with map) and is valid for one day. The pricier Cinque Terre Card covers the park entrance fee and your transportation on the local trains (from Levanto to La Spezia, including all Cinque Terre towns) plus the shuttle buses that run twice an hour within each Cinque Terre town (€5.20/1 day, €10.50/3 days, €15.50/week, kids 4-12 pay half-price, under 4 free; includes map, brochure, and train schedule). Passes, valid until midnight of the day they expire, are sold at participating train stations and hotels, and some trailheads. Validate your Cinque Terre Card at a station (punch into machine).

Over the next decade, Italy has quiet plans for the Cinque Terre. For the sake of tranquility, a new train line will be built inland for the noisy fast trains, leaving the Cinque Terre tracks for just the pokey milk-run trains.

Sadly, a few ugly, noisy Americans are giving tourism a bad name here. Even hip young locals are put off by loud, drunken tourists. They say (and I agree) that the Cinque Terre is a special place. It deserves a special dignity. Party in Viareggio or Porto-fino but be mellow in the Cinque Terre. Talk softly. Help keep it clean. In spite of the tourist crowds, it's still a real community, and we are guests.

Planning Your Time

The ideal minimum stay is two nights and a completely uninterrupted day. The Cinque Terre is served by the milk-run train
from Genoa and La Spezia. Speed demons arrive in the morning,
check their bags in La Spezia, take the five-hour hike through all
five towns, laze away the afternoon on the beach or rock of their
choice, and zoom away on the overnight train to somewhere back
in the real world. But be warned: The Cinque Terre has a strange
way of messing up your momentum.

The towns are each just a few minutes apart by hourly train
or boat. There's no checklist of sights or experiences; just a hike,
the towns themselves, and your fondest vacation desires. Study
this chapter in advance and piece together your best day, mixing
hiking, swimming, trains, and a boat ride. For the best light and
coolest temperatures, start your hike early.

Market days are Tuesday in Vernazza, Wednesday in Levanto,
Thursday in Monterosso, and Friday in La Spezia (08:00–13:00).

Getting around the Cinque Terre

By Train: At La Spezia, the gateway to the Cinque Terre, you'll
transfer to the milk-run Cinque Terre train. There might be a
TI at the station. If not, skip the 20-minute hike to La Spezia's
main TI at Via Mazzini near the waterfront (daily in summer
09:00–13:00, 15:00–18:00; winter Mon–Sat 09:00–13:00, 14:00–
17:00, Sun 09:00–13:00; tel. 0187-718-997).

At the station, buy your €1.20 ticket or Cinque Terre Card,
and take the half-hour train ride into the Cinque Terre town of
your choice. Once in the Cinque Terre, you'll get around the
villages more cheaply by train but more scenically by boat.

Cinque Terre Train Schedule: Since the train is the Cinque
Terre lifeline, many shops and restaurants post the current schedule. Try to get a photocopied schedule—it'll come in handy
(included with Cinque Terre Card).

Trains leave La Spezia for the Cinque Terre villages (last
year's schedule) at 07:17, 08:10, 10:00, 11:23, 12:40, 13:20, 14:16,
15:00, 16:27, 17:19, 18:16, 19:16, 21:09, and 23:05.

Trains leave Monterosso al Mare for La Spezia (departing
Vernazza about 10 minutes later, last year's schedule) at 06:30,
7:04, 08:07, 09:04, 10:16, 11:00, 12:13, 13:05, 13:41, 14:08, 15:12,
16:15, 17:23, 18:24, 19:14, 20:07, 22:13, and 23:31.

Do not rely on these train times. Check the current posted
schedule and then count on half the trains being 15 minutes or
so late (unless you're late, in which case they are right on time).

To orient yourself, remember that directions are "*per* [to]
Genoa" or "*per* La Spezia," and any train that stops at any of the
villages other than Monterosso will stop at all five. (Note that many
trains leaving La Spezia skip them all or stop only in Monterosso.)

The five towns are just minutes apart by train. Know your stop. After leaving the town before your destination, go to the door to slip out before mobs pack in. Since the stations are small and the trains are long, you might get off the train deep in a tunnel, and you might need to flip open the handle of the door yourself.

The train stations should be staffed at all five Cinque Terre towns. Stations sell train tickets; the combination pass, which covers the park fee, train, and bus travel on the Cinque Terre (€5.20/1 day, €10.50/3 days, and €15.50/week); and maybe the park–entrance-only pass (€2.60).

The Cinque Terre Card, which includes the national park entry fee, is convenient, but if you're on a tight budget, you can save a bit of money by buying a one-day Hiking Pass (€2.60) and paying separately for your train travel.

It's cheap to buy individual train tickets to travel between the towns. Since a one-town hop costs the same as a five-town hop (€0.90) and every ticket is good for six hours with stopovers, save money and explore the region in one direction on one ticket. Stamp the ticket at the station machine before you board.

If you have a Eurailpass, don't spend one of your valuable flexi-days on the cheap Cinque Terre.

By Boat: From Easter to late October (through Nov if weather is good), a daily boat service connects Monterosso, Vernazza, Manarola, Riomaggiore, and Portovenere. This provides a scenic way to get from town to town and survey what you just hiked. It's also the only efficient way to visit the nearby resort of Portovenere (the alternative is a tedious train/bus connection via La Spezia). In peaceful weather, the boats are more reliable than the trains. Boats go about hourly, from 10:00 until 18:00 (about €3 per single hop or €11.50 for an all-day pass to the Cinque Terre towns, buy tickets at little stands at each town's harbor, tel. 0187-777-727). A more frequent boat service connects Monterosso and Vernazza (tel. 0187-817-452). Schedules are posted at docks, harbor bars, and hotels.

By Foot: A scenic trail runs along the coast, connecting each of the five Cinque Terre towns (see "Hiking," below). Sometimes severe rains can wash out trails, especially in winter. Ask around if the trails are open.

Tour of the Cinque Terre

For a guided tour, consider spending a day with a hard-working and likable American student, Sean Risotti, who liked the Cinque Terre so much he moved in (€40, almost daily April–Oct, departing Monterosso at 10:00 or Vernazza at 10:45, book at cinqueterretrek @hotmail.com or at the Fishnet Internet Lounge in Monterosso). The day—which is a great way to meet other travelers—includes a hike from Vernazza to Manarola, lots of information, special glimpses of the area, and a dinner that evening.

Events on the Cinque Terre

May 11	Monterosso: Lemon Festival
June 2	Monterosso: Corpus Domini (procession on carpet of flowers)
June 24	Riomaggiore and Monterosso: Festival in honor of St. John the Baptist
June 29	Corniglia: Festival of St. Peter and St. Paul
July 20	Vernazza: Festival for patron saint, St. Margaret
Aug 10	Manarola: Festival for patron saint, St. Lawrence
Aug 15	All towns: Ascension of Mary
Sept 8	Monterosso: Maria Nascente, or "Rising Mary" (fair with handicrafts)

VERNAZZA

With the closest thing to a natural harbor—overseen by a ruined castle and an old church—and only the occasional noisy slurping up of the train by the mountain to remind you of the modern world, Vernazza is my Cinque Terre home.

The action is at the harbor, where you'll find a kids' beach, plenty of sunning rocks, outdoor restaurants, a bar hanging on the edge of the castle (great for evening drinks), and a tailgate-party street market every Tuesday morning. In the summer, the beach becomes a soccer field, where teams fielded by local bars and restaurants provide late-night entertainment. In the dark, locals fish off the promontory, using glowing bobs that shine in the waves.

The town's 500 residents, proud of their Vernazzan heritage, brag that "Vernazza is locally owned. Portofino has sold out." Fearing the change it would bring, keep-Vernazza-small proponents stopped the construction of a major road into the town and region. Families are tight and go back centuries; several generations stay together. Leisure time is devoted to the *passeggiata*—strolling lazily together up and down the main street. Sit on a bench and study the passersby. Then explore the characteristic alleys, called *carugi*. In October, the cantinas are draped with drying grapes. In the winter, the population shrinks, as many people move to more comfortable big-city apartments.

A steep five-minute hike in either direction from Vernazza gives you a classic village photo op (for the best light, head toward Corniglia in the morning, toward Monterosso in the evening). Franco's Bar, with a panoramic terrace, is at the tower on the trail toward Corniglia.

Vernazza

NARROW ROAD!
(TO AUTOSTRADA)

BANK · POST · BAR
SORRISO'S ANNEX

TO CEMETERY

PENSION SORRISO

LA TORRE REST.

TRAIL TO CORNIGLIA

Tunnel

TRAIN STN.

Tunnel

TO/PER MONTEROSSO + GENOVA

TO / PER LA SPEZIA + PISA

BLUE MARLIN BAR + LAUNDRY

BAKERY

PIZZA

"MAIN STRADA" (A.K.A. VIA ROMA)

TRAIL TO MONTEROSSO

ALBERGO BARBARA

FARMACIA

BARS, RESTAURANTS, GROC. STORES + TEL

GROC

TRAT. + PIVA

CHURCH

PIAZZA MARCONI

GELATI

FRANZI ROOMS

SUNNING + SWIMMING

KIDS BEACH

TRAT. GIANNI

HARBOR

CASTLE

TO MONTEROSSO

BREAKWATER

SHOWERS

BAR/REST.

CASTELLO RESTAURANT (GREAT VIEW!)

L I G U R I A N S E A

DOCK

SUNNING + SWIMMING

STATI UNITI

✳ NOTE: MAP NOT TO SCALE— TRAIN STN. TO BREAKWATER IS A 5 MINUTE WALK. (BUT DON'T RUSH IT!)

☲ = STEPPED ALLEYS

DCH

Vernazza has ATMs and two banks (center and top of town). A shuttle bus runs twice an hour up and down the main street, (free with Cinque Terre Card, otherwise €1). The slick new Internet Point, run by Alberto and Isabella, is in the village center (fast connections, daily 09:30–23:30, tel. 0187-812-949). The Blue Marlin bar (run by Franco and Massimo, open daily in Aug, otherwise closed Thu) also offers Internet access plus a self-service laundry (€4.70 wash, €4.70 dry, super easy machines with automatic detergent and English instructions, buy tokens at Blue Marlin bar any day except Thu, laundry open daily 08:00–22:00— earlier if the bar is open and every day in Aug, Via Roma 49, 30 meters below train station).

You can buy train tickets, Hiking Passes, and Cinque Terre

Cards at the Vernazza train station. You can also store luggage
(€0.50 hr) if the station is staffed (open daily in summer 08:00–19:30,
in winter 08:00–18:00, tel. 0187-812-533, a little English spoken).
Accommodations are listed near the end of this chapter.

Sights—Vernazza

▲▲**Vernazza Top-Down Orientation Walk**—Walk uphill
until you hit the parking lot—with a bank, a post office, and a
barrier that keeps all but service vehicles out. The tidy new square
is called Fontana Vecchia, after a long-gone fountain. Older locals
remember the river filled with townswomen doing their washing.
Begin your saunter downhill to the harbor.

Just before the "Pension Sorriso" sign, you'll see the ambulance barn (big brown wood doors) on your right. A group of
volunteers is always on call for a dash to the hospital, 30 minutes
away in La Spezia. Opposite that is a big empty lot next to
Pension Sorriso. Like many landowners, Sr. Sorriso had plans
to expand, but the government said no. The old character of
these towns is carefully protected.

Across from Pension Sorriso is the honorary clubhouse for
the ANPI (members of the local WWII resistance). Only five
ANPI old-timers survive. Cynics consider them less than heroes.
After 1943, Hitler called up Italian boys over 15. Rather than
die on the front for Hitler, they escaped to the hills. Only to
remain free did they become "resistance fighters."

A few steps farther along you'll see a monument (marble
plaque in wall to your left) to those killed in World War II. Not
a family was spared. Study this: Soldiers *"morti in combattimento"*
fought for Mussolini, some were deported to *Germania*, and
"partisans" were killed later fighting against Mussolini.

The tiny monorail *trenino* (as you're facing plaque, look up
on the wall on your right) is parked quietly here except in September
and October, when it's busy helping locals bring down the grapes.
The path to Corniglia leaves from here (it runs above plaque, starting at your left). Behind you is a tiny square playground, decorated
with three millstones, which no longer grind local olives into oil.
From here, Vernazza's tiny river goes underground.

In the tunnel under the railway tracks, you'll see a door
marked "Croce Verde Vernazza" (Green Cross). Posted on the
other side of the tunnel is the "P.A. Croce Verde Vernazza" (in
a small green display case), the list of volunteers ready for ambulance duty each day of the month.

The train tracks are above you. The second set of tracks
(nearer the harbor) was recently renovated to lessen the disruptive
noise; locals say it made no difference.

Follow the road downhill. Until the 1950s, Vernazza's river
ran open through the center of town from here to the *gelateria*.

Wandering through this main business center, you'll pass many locals doing their *vasca* (laps) past the entrepreneurial Blue Marlin bar (about the only nightspot in town) and the tiny Chapel of Santa Marta (the small stone building with iron grillwork over the window, across from Il Baretto), where Mass is celebrated only on special Sundays. Next you'll see a grocery, *gelateria*, bakery, pharmacy, another grocery, and another *gelateria*.

On the left, in front of the second *gelateria*, an arch leads to what was a beach where the river used to flow out of town. Continue on down to the harbor square and breakwater. Vernazza, with the only natural harbor of the Cinque Terre, was established as the sole place boats could pick up the fine local wine. (The town is named for a kind of wine.) Peek into the tiny street behind the Vulnetia restaurant with the commotion of arches. Vernazza's most characteristic side streets, called *carugi*, lead up from here. The trail (above the church toward Monterosso) leads to the classic view of Vernazza (best photos just before sunset).

▲▲▲**The Burned-Out Sightseer's Visual Tour of Vernazza—** Sit at the end of the harbor breakwater (perhaps with a glass of local white wine or something more interesting from Bar Capitano— borrow the glass, they don't mind), face the town, and see . . .

The harbor: In a moderate storm you'd be soaked, as waves routinely crash over the *molo* (breakwater, built in 1972). The train line (to your left), constructed 130 years ago to tie a newly united Italy together, linked Turin and Genoa with Rome. A second line (hidden in a tunnel at this point) was built in the 1960s. The yellow building alongside the tracks was Vernazza's first train station. You can see the four bricked-up alcoves where people once waited for trains. Vernazza's fishing fleet is down to three small fishing boats (with the net spools); the town's restaurants buy up everything they catch. Vernazzans are more likely to own a boat than a car. In the '70s, tiny Vernazza had one of the top water polo teams in Italy, and the harbor was their "pool." Later, when a real pool was required, Vernazza dropped out of the league.

The castle: On the far right, the castle, which is now a grassy park with great views, still guards the town (€1, daily 10:00–18:30, from harbor, take stairs by Trattoria Gianni and follow signs to Castello restaurant, tower is a few steps beyond, see the photo and painting gallery rooms). It's called *Belforte*, or "loud screams," for the warnings it made back in pirating days. The highest umbrellas mark the recommended Castello restaurant (see "Eating," below). The square, squat tower on the water is great for a glass of wine (follow the rope to the Belforte Bar, open Wed–Mon 08:00–24:00, closed Tue; inside the submarine-strength door, a photo of a major storm shows the entire tower under a wave).

The town: Vernazza has two halves. "*Sciuiu,*" on the left (literally "flowery"), is the sunny side, and "*luvegu,*" on the right (literally "dank"), is the shady side. The houses below the castle were connected by an interior arcade—ideal for fleeing attacks. The pastel colors are regulated by a commissioner of good taste in the community government. The square before you is locally famous for some of the region's finest restaurants. The big red central house, the 12th-century site where Genoan warships were built, used to be a kind of guardhouse.

Above the town: The small, round tower above the guardhouse, another part of the city fortifications, reminds us of Vernazza's importance in the Middle Ages, when it was a key ally of Genoa (whose archenemies were the other maritime republics of Pisa, Amalfi, and Venice). Franco's Bar, just behind the tower, welcomes hikers finishing, starting, or simply contemplating the Corniglia–Vernazza hike, with great town views. Vineyards fill the mountainside beyond the town. Notice the many terraces. Someone calculated that the vineyard terraces of the Cinque Terre have the same amount of stonework as the Great Wall of China. Wine production is down nowadays, as the younger residents choose less physical work. But locals still work their plots and proudly serve their family wines. A single steel train line winds up the gully behind the tower. This is for the vintner's *trenino*, the tiny service train.

The church, school, and city hall: Vernazza's Ligurian Gothic church, built with black stones quarried from Punta Mesco (the distant point behind you), dates from 1318. The gray-and-red house above and to the left of the spire is the local elementary school (which about 25 children attend). High school is in the "big city," La Spezia. The red building to the right of (and below) the schoolhouse is the former monastery and present city hall. Vernazza and Corniglia function as one community. Through most of the 1990s, the local government was communist. In 1999, they elected a coalition of many parties working to rise above ideologies and simply make Vernazza a better place. Finally, on the top of the hill, with the best view of all, is the town cemetery, where most locals plan to end up.

Cinque Terre Hiking and Swimming

▲▲▲**Hiking**—All five towns are connected by good trails. Experience the area's best by hiking from one end to the other. The entire 11-kilometer (7-mile) hike can be done in about four hours, but allow five for dawdling. While you can detour to dramatic hilltop sanctuaries (one trail leads from Vernazza's cemetery uphill), I'd keep it simple by following the easy red-and-white-marked low trails between the villages. Good hiking maps (about €5, sold everywhere, not necessary for this described walk) cover the expanded version of this hike, from Portovenere through all five Cinque Terre towns to Levanto, and more serious hikes in the high country. Get local advice to make sure trails are open, particularly in spring.

Since I still get the names of the Cinque Terre towns mixed up, I think of the towns by number: Riomaggiore (town #1), Manarola (#2), Corniglia (#3), Vernazza (#4), and resorty Monterosso (#5).

Riomaggiore–Manarola (20 min): Facing the front of the train station in Riomaggiore (town #1), go up the stairs to the right, following signs for the Via dell' Amore. The film-gobbling promenade—wide enough for baby strollers—leads down the coast to Manarola. While there's no beach here, stairs lead down to sunbathing rocks.

Manarola–Corniglia (45 min): The walk from Manarola (#2) to Corniglia (#3) is a little longer and a little more rugged than that from #1 to #2.

Ask locally about the more difficult six-mile inland hike to Volastra. This tiny village, perched between Manarola and Corniglia, hosts the Five-Terre wine co-op; stop by the Cantina Sociale. If you take this high road between Manarola and Corniglia, allow two hours; in return, you'll get sweeping views and a closer look at the vineyards.

Corniglia–Vernazza (90 min): The hike from Corniglia (#3) to Vernazza (#4)—the wildest and greenest of the coast— is most rewarding. From the Corniglia station and beach, zigzag up to the town (taking the steeper corkscrew stairs, the longer road, or the shuttlebus). Ten minutes past Corniglia toward Vernazza, you'll see the well-hung Guvano beach far below (see below). The trail leads past a bar and picnic tables, through lots of fragrant and flowery vegetation, and scenically into Vernazza.

Vernazza–Monterosso (90 min): The trail from Vernazza (#4) to Monterosso (#5) is a scenic up-and-down-a-lot trek. Trails are rough (and some readers report "very dangerous") but easy to follow. Camping at the picnic tables midway is frowned upon. The views just out of Vernazza are spectacular.

▲**Swimming**—Wear your walking shoes and pack your swim gear. Several of the beaches have showers (no shampoo, please) that may work better than your hotel's. Underwater sightseeing is full of fish—goggles are sold in local shops. Sea urchins can be a problem if you walk on the rocks; consider using fins or Aquasocks.

Here's a beach review:

Riomaggiore: The beach is rocky, but clean and peaceful. It's a two-minute walk from the harbor: face the harbor, then take the path to your left. At the La Conchiglia bar, go down the stairs to the right of the bar. Follow the path to the beach.

Manarola: Manarola has no sand, but the best deepwater swimming of all. The first "beach," with a shower, ladder, and wonderful rocks (with daredevil high-divers), is my favorite.

The second has tougher access and no shower, but feels more remote and pristine (follow paved path around point).

Corniglia: This hilltop town has a rocky man-made beach below its station. It's clean and uncrowded, and the beach bar has showers, drinks, and snacks.

The nude Guvano (GOO-vah-noh) beach (between Corniglia and Vernazza) made headlines in Italy in the 1970s, as clothed locals in a makeshift armada of dinghies and fishing boats retook their town beach. But big-city nudists still work on all-around tans in this remote setting. From the Corniglia train station, follow the road north, go over the tracks, then zigzag below the tracks, following signs to the tunnel in the cliff (walk past the *proprieta privata* sign). When you buzz the intercom, the hydraulic *Get Smart*-type door is opened from the other end. After a 15-minute hike through a cool, moist, and dimly lit unused old train tunnel, you'll emerge at the Guvano beach—and be charged €5 (€4 with this guidebook). The beach has drinking water, but no WC. A steep (free) trail leads from the beach up to the Corniglia-Vernazza trail. The crowd is Italian counterculture: pierced nipples, tattooed punks, hippie drummers in dreads, and nude exhibitionist men. The ratio of men to women is about three to two. About half the people on the pebbly beach keep their swimsuits on.

Vernazza: The village has a children's sandy cove, sunning rocks, and showers by the breakwater. There's a ladder on the breakwater for deepwater access. The tiny *acque pendente* (waterfall) cove which locals call their *laguna blu*, between Vernazza and Monterosso, is accessible only by small hired boat.

Monterosso: The town's beaches, immediately in front of the train station, are easily the Cinque Terre's best and most crowded. It's a sandy resort with everything rentable...lounge chairs, umbrellas, paddleboats, and usually even beach access. Beaches are free only where you see no umbrellas.

Cinque Terre Towns
(Note: Readers of this book fill Vernazza. For this reason, you might prefer to stay in one of these towns with fewer Americans. See "Sleeping," below, for accommodations for each town.)

▲▲**Riomaggiore (town #1)**—The most substantial non-resort town of the group, Riomaggiore is a disappointment from the train station. But walk through the tunnel next to the train tracks (or ride the elevator through the hillside to the top of town), and you land in a fascinating tangle of pastel homes leaning on each other as if someone stole their crutches. There's homemade gelato at the Bar Central on main street, and, if Ivo is there, you'll feel right at home. When Ivo closes, the gang goes down to the harborside with a guitar.

Riomaggiore's **TI** is inside the train station (Mon–Fri 10:30–12:00, 14:30–17:30, Sat–Sun 10:30–12:00, 15:00–17:30,

Riomaggiore and Manarola

tel. 0187-920-633). The bus shuttles locals and tourists up and down
Riomaggiore's steep main street (free with Cinque Terre Card,
2/hr, just flag it down); a larger blue bus helps out in the morning.

Here's an easy loop trip through Riomaggiore that maximizes
views and minimizes walking uphill (this is easiest if you arrive by
train; if you arrive by boat, take the tunnel alongside the tracks to
the station and start from there). From the train station, take the
elevator up to the top of town (€1, included with Cinque Terre
Card, entrance at railway tunnel). At the top, go right, following
the walkway—with spectacular sea views—around the cliff. Ignore
the steps marked *Marina Seacost* (harbor). Instead, continue along
the path; it's a five-minute, fairly level walk to the church. Continue past the church and then take a right down the stairs to Via
Columbo, Riomaggiore's main street. Stroll down Via Columbo.
Just past the WC, you'll see flower boxes on the street, sometimes
blocking it; these slide back electrically to let the little bus get
past. On your way down the hill, you'll pass colorful, small shops,
including a bakery and a couple of groceries. When Via Columbo
dead-ends, on your left you'll find the stairs down to the harbor,
boat dock, and a 200-meter trail to the beach (*spiaggia*). To your
right is the tunnel, running alongside the tracks, that takes you
directly to the station. Either take a train or hop a boat (from
the harbor) to your next destination.

For hikes from Riomaggiore, consider the cliff-hanging
trail that leads from the beach to a hilltop botanical garden
(free entrance with Cinque Terre Card) and old WWII bunkers.
Another climbs scenically to the Madonna di Montenero sanctuary
high above the town. Riomaggiore also has a diving center (scuba,
snorkeling, boats, Via San Giacomo, tel. 0187-920-011).

▲**Manarola (town #2)**—Like town #1, #2 is attached to its
station by a 200-meter-long tunnel. Manarola is tiny and picturesque, a tumble of buildings bunny-hopping down its ravine

Corniglia and Monterosso

to the fun-loving harbor. Notice how the I-beam crane launches the boats. Facing the harbor, look at the hillside to your right, dotted with a bar in the middle. It's Punta Bonfiglio, an entertaining park/game area/bar with the best view playground on the coast. The gate farther up the hillside is the entrance to the cemetery. From here you can get poster-perfect views of Manarola (2-minute walk from the harbor on path to Corniglia).

Within Manarola, the small bus shuttles people between main street and the parking lot (free with Cinque Terre Card, 2/hr, just flag it down). In the middle of town, across from the railway tunnel, you'll see Bar Aristide, which sometimes shows outdoor movies on weekends in August by hanging a screen over part of the tunnel entrance (closed Mon, Via Discovolo 138, tel. 0187-920-000). At the top of the town, you'll find great views, the church, and a cluster of accommodations, including a super hostel (see "Sleeping," below).

The simple, wooden, religious scenes that you'll likely see on the hillside are the work of local resident Mario Andreoli. Before his father died, Mario promised him he'd replace the old cross on the family's vineyard. Mario's been adding figures ever since. After recovering from a rare illness, he redoubled his efforts. The scenes, which do change (a sheep here, an apostle there), are sometimes left up year-round. On religious holidays, everything's lit up: the Nativity, the Last Supper, the Crucifixion, the Resurrection, and more.

▲▲**Corniglia (town #3)**—From the station, a footpath zigzags up nearly 400 stairs to the only town of the five not on water. Take the bus (free with Cinque Terre Card, 2/hr). Originally settled by a Roman farmer who named it for his mother, Cornelia (how Corniglia is pronounced), the town and its ancient residents produced a wine so famous that vases found at Pompeii touted its virtues. Today, wine is still its lifeblood. Follow the pungent smell of ripe grapes into an alley cellar and get a local to let you dip a straw into a keg. Remote and less visited, Corniglia has fewer tourists, cooler temperatures, a windy belvedere (on its promontory), a few restaurants, and plenty of private rooms for rent. Past the train station (toward Manarola) you'll find Corniglia's beach. The nude Guvano beach is in the opposite direction (toward Vernazza).

▲▲▲**Vernazza (town #4)**—See beginning of chapter.

▲▲**Monterosso al Mare (town #5)**—This is a resort with cars, hotels, rentable beach umbrellas, and crowds. The town is split into the old and new, connected by a tunnel. The train station is in the new town, along with the TI (daily Mon–Sat 09:30–12:30, 15:30–17:30, closed Sun and Nov–Easter, exit station and go left a few doors, tel. 0187-817-506), several recommended accommodations, and a statue—*Il Gigante*. This 14-meter-tall statue, which once held a trident, looks as if it were hewn from the rocky cliff, but it's made of reinforced concrete, and dates from the beginning of the 20th century.

Monterosso's old town contains Old World charm, small crooked streets, and plenty of Internet access. Kate's Fishnet Internet Lounge is a welcoming, well-run, and good center for local information (daily until 24:00, Via Roma 17, can book rooms, tel. 0187-817-373, www.fishnet.it). Or try The Net (Via Vittorio Emanuele 55, also books rooms, guides, tel. 0187-817-288, www.cinqueterrenet.com). From the old town harbor, boats run nearly hourly to Vernazza and points beyond. From the breakwater (and the new town), look for all the towns of the Cinque Terre.

The small shuttle buses that run along the waterfront connect the old and newtowns with outlying areas (free with Cinque Terre Card, 2/hr).

You can easily stroll the short tunnel between the new and old towns, but hikers prefer the trail. It's like a mini-Cinque Terre trail, combining scenery and greenery. Heading from the train station to the old town, take the path to the right of the tunnel entrance. The path leads to views of a German WWII bunker below on the rocks (worth seeing, but not worth climbing down to).

Continuing on the path gets you into the old town. Or, at the point where you see the bunker, take the path up to the top of the hill (where you'll see a statue of St. Francis), and up farther still through the woods to reach a gate (marked *Convento e Chiesa Cappuccini*) leading to a church with a Van Dyck painting of the Crucifixion (accommodations next to church, see "Sleeping," below). You're a world away from the resort town below.

A trail to the right of the church leads up to the cemetery; appreciate its flowers, photos, and your beating heart. Backtrack to the St. Francis statue, and take the trail down into the old town. (Reversing this, if you're going from the old town to the new, take the trail to the right of the tunnel entrance; go right on Zii di Frati to see the church, or continue straight to get to the new town). Allow a total of 30 minutes if you include the church and cemetery.

Cinque Terre Cuisine 101

A few menu tips: *Accuighe* (pron. ah-CHOO-gay) are anchovies, a local specialty—always served the day they're caught. If you've always hated anchovies (the harsh, cured-in-salt American kind), try them fresh here. *Tegame alla Vernazza* is the most typical main course in Vernazza: anchovies, potatoes, tomatoes, white wine, oil, and herbs. *Pansotti* is ravioli with ricotta and spinach, often served with a hazelnut sauce...delightful and filling. While antipasto is cheese and salami in Tuscany, here you'll get *antipasti di mare*, a big plate of mixed fruits of the sea and a fine way to start a meal. For many, splitting this and a pasta dish is plenty. Try the fun local dessert: "grandmother's cake," with a glass of *sciacchetrà* for dunking (see "Wine," below).

▲▲**Pesto**—This is the birthplace of pesto. Basil, which loves the temperate Ligurian climate, is mixed with cheese (half *Parmigiano* cow cheese and half pecorino sheep cheese), garlic, olive oil, and pine nuts, and then poured over pasta. Try it on spaghetti, *trenette*, or *trofie* (made of flour with a bit of potato, designed specifically for pesto). Many also like pesto lasagna. If you become addicted, small jars of pesto are sold in the local grocery stores.

▲▲**Wine**—The *vino delle Cinque Terre*, respected throughout Italy, flows cheap and easy throughout the region. It is white—great with the local seafood. D.O.C. is the mark of top quality. Red wine is better elsewhere. For a sweet dessert wine, the local *sciacchetrà* wine is worth the splurge (€2.60 per glass, often served with a cookie). While 10 kilos of grapes yield seven liters of local wine, *sciacchetrà* is made from near-raisins, and 10 kilos of grapes make only 1.5 liters of *sciacchetrà*. The word means "push and pull"...push in lots of grapes, pull out the best wine. If your room is up a lot of steps, be warned: *Sciacchetrà* is 18 percent alcohol, while regular wine is only 11 percent. In the cool, calm evening, sit on the Vernazza breakwater with a glass of wine and watch the phosphorescence in the waves.

Sleeping and Eating on the Cinque Terre
(€1.10 = about $1, country code: 39)

Sleep Code: **S** = Single, **D** = Double/Twin, **T** = Triple, **Q** = Quad, **b** = bathroom, **s** = shower only, **CC** = Credit Cards accepted, **no CC** = Credit Cards not accepted, **SE** = Speaks English, **NSE** = No English. Breakfast is included only in real hotels.

If you're trying to avoid my readers, stay away from Vernazza. Monterosso is a good choice for the younger crowd (more night-life) and rich, sun-worshiping softies (who prefer firm reservations for hotels with private bathrooms). Wine-lovers and mountain goats like Corniglia. Sophisticated Italians and Germans choose Manarola. Travelers who show up without reservations enjoy Riomaggiore for its easy room-booking services.

While the Cinque Terre is too rugged for the mobs that ravage the Spanish and French coasts, it's popular with Italians, Germans, and Americans in the know. Hotels charge the most and are packed on Easter, in August, and on summer Fridays and Saturdays. August weekends are worst. But €60 doubles abound throughout the year. Outside of August weekends, you can land a comfortable €60 double in a private home on any day by just arriving in town (ideally by noon) and asking around at bars and restaurants or simply approaching locals on the street. This seems scary, but it's true.

For the best value, visit three private rooms and snare the best. Going direct cuts out a middleman and softens prices. Plan on paying cash. Private rooms are generally bigger and more comfortable than those offered by the pensions.

If you want the security of a reservation, make it long in advance for a hotel (small places generally don't take reservations made weeks ahead). If you don't get a reply to your faxed request for a room, assume the place is fully booked.

Sleeping in Vernazza
(zip code: 19018)

Vernazza, the essence of the Cinque Terre, is my favorite. There are three pensions and piles of private rooms for rent. Anywhere you stay here will require some climbing. Night noises can be a problem if you're near the station. Address letters to 19018 Vernazza, Cinque Terre, La Spezia. Better yet, call, fax, or e-mail. A new parking lot and a hard-working shuttle service make driving to Vernazza a reasonable option for drivers with nerves of steel. The little shuttle bus runs twice an hour (generally with helpful, English-speaking Beppi behind the wheel).

Usually, when a price range is listed, the lower price is charged during winter (roughly Nov–March) and the higher price the rest of the year.

Pensions

Albergo Barbara, on the harbor square, is run by kindly Giuseppe and his Swiss wife, Patricia. Their nine clean, modern rooms share three public showers and WCs (S-€36–€47 depending on season, D without view-€43, D with small view-€45, D with big view-€55, bunky family Q-€67, 2-night stay preferred, loads of stairs, fans, closed Dec–Jan, Piazza Marconi 30, call to reserve instead of fax, tel. & fax 0187-812-398, cellular 338-7933261, SE). The two big doubles on the main floor come with grand harbor views and are the best value (top-floor doubles have small windows and small views). The office is on the top floor of the big, red, vacant-looking building facing the harbor.

Trattoria Gianni rents 23 small rooms just under the castle. The funky ones are artfully decorated à la shipwreck and are up lots of tight, winding, spiral stairs, and most have tiny balconies and grand views. The new, comfy rooms lack views but have modern bathrooms and a super scenic, cliff-hanger private garden. Marisa (who doles out smiles like a rich gambler on a losing streak) requires a two-night minimum and check-in before 16:00 (S-€34, D-€47, sinks and bathrooms down the hall; Db-€65, Tb-€78, CC but 10 percent discount for cash, Piazza Marconi 5, closed Jan–Feb, tel. & fax 0187-812-228, tel. 0187-821-003). Pick up your keys at Trattoria Gianni's restaurant/reception on the harbor square and hike up dozens of stairs to #41 (funky, *con vista mare*) or #47 (new, *nuovo*) at the top. As a matter of principle, no English is spoken here. (Note: My tour company books this place 50 nights of the season.) Telephone three days in advance and leave your first name and time of arrival.

Pension Sorriso offers 20 good rooms without views or an exuberant welcome. Prices include breakfast and an obligatory dinner (D-€103, Db-€113, 50 meters up from station, reception in bar, closed Nov–Feb, tel. 0187-812-224, fax 0187-821-198, some English spoken). While train sounds rumble through the front rooms of the main building, the annex up the street is quieter.

Private Rooms (Affitta Camere)

These are the best values in Vernazza. The town is honey-combed year-round with pleasant, rentable private rooms and apartments with kitchens (cheap for families). They are usually reluctant to reserve rooms far in advance. It's easiest to call a day or two ahead or simply show up in the morning and look around. The rooms cost about €45 to €60 for a double, depending on the view and plumbing. Some have killer views, and cost the same as a small dark place on a back lane over the train tracks. Little or no English is spoken at these places. Any main-street business has a line on rooms for rent.

Franca Maria rents two sharp, comfortable rooms overlooking the harbor square (Db-€47–72, Qb-€83–103 depending on season, the 2 side-by-side doubles can turn into a quad, Piazza Marconi 30, tel. 0187-812-002, fax 0187-812-956, son's e-mail: metalgearsolid@inwind.it). It's just a few steps up from the harbor—a rarity in vertical Vernazza.

Martina Callo rents three fine, lofty rooms overlooking the square, up piles of steps near the church tower (Db-€47–57, Qb-€93–103; room #1-Qb with harbor view, room #2-Qb is huge family room with no view, room #3-Db with grand view terrace;

heating in winter; ring bell at Piazza Marconi 26, tel. & fax 0187-812-365, e-mail: roomartina@supereva.it).

Affitta Camere da Anna-Maria offers three pleasant rooms up spiral staircases (D-€60, Db-€65 with view or terrace—the terrace room is best, Via Carattino 64, turn left at pharmacy, climb Via Carattino to #64, tel. 0187-821-082).

Tonino Basso rents four super rooms—clean and modern—near the post office, in the only building in Vernazza that has an elevator. Rooms come with a private bath but no views (Sb-€47, Db-€62, Tb-€78, CC, tel. 0187-821-264, fax 0187-821-260, e-mail: toninobasso@libero.it, cellular 335-269-436; when you arrive, call cellular number from train station—phones at bottom of stairs—and Tonino will meet you; or the Gambero Rosso restaurant at harbor can find him—but then you'll have to backtrack to get to his rooms).

Mike and Franca Castiglione, who speak New Yorkish, rent a small, basic room that has a private ramshackle garden with a sea view (€57, Via Carratino 16, turn left at pharmacy, climb Via Carattino to #16, tel. 0187-812-374).

Giuseppina's Villa, a cozy apartment with a low-ceilinged loft, has one window, no view, and a kitchen. The woman at the grocery store nearest the harbor (with *Salumi e Formaggi* on the awning) can check if it's available (Db-€42, Qb-€83, Via S. Giovanni Battista 7, only a short climb from harbor, tel. 0187-812-026). She also has a double room up the street (Db-€47, no view, but has a garden).

Nicolina rents four decent rooms: a large one with a view, two overlooking Vernazza's main drag, and one without any view. Inquire at Pizzeria Vulnetia on the harbor square or reserve in advance by phone (Db-€62, Qb with terrace and view-€127, Piazza Marconi 29, tel. & fax 0187-821-193, Frederica).

Armanda rents a one-room apartment without a view near the Castello (€62, Piazza Marconi 15, tel. 0187-812-218, cellular 347-306-4760).

Giuliano Basso rents three fine rooms that share a view balcony (Db-€62, CC, open year-round, above train station, direction: Corniglia, take a right before Sorriso's, then take left fork, 5-min walk to harbor, cellular 333-341-4792, www.cdh.it/giuliano).

Eating in Vernazza

If you enjoy Italian cuisine, Vernazza's restaurants are worth the splurge. All take pride in their cooking and have similar prices. Wander around at about 20:00 and compare the ambience.

The **Castello**, run by gracious and English-speaking Monica, her husband Massimo, kind Mario, and the rest of her family, serves great food with great views, just under the castle (Thu–Tue 12:00–15:00 for lunch, 15:00–19:00 for drinks and snacks,

19:00–22:00 for dinner, closed Wed and Nov–April, tel.
0187-812-296).

Four fine places fill the harborfront with happy eaters:
Gambero Rosso, considered Vernazza's best restaurant, feels
classy and costs only a few euros more than the others (Tue–
Sun 12:00–15:00, 19:00–22:00, closed Mon and Nov–March,
CC, Piazza Marconi 7, tel. 0187-812-265). **Trattoria del Capitano** might serve the best food for the money (Thu–Tue 12:00–
15:00, 19:00–22:30, closed Wed except in Aug, closed Dec–Jan,
CC, Paolo speaks English, tel. 0187-812-201). **Trattoria Gianni**
is also good, especially for seafood (daily 12:30–15:00, 18:30–
22:00 in July–Aug, otherwise closed Wed). **Pizzeria Vulnetia**
serves the best harborside pizza (Tue–Sun 12:00–16:00, 18:30–
23:00, closed Mon, Piazza Marconi 29).

Trattoria da Sandro, on the main drag, mixes Genovese
and Ligurian cuisine with friendly service, and can be a peaceful
alternative to the harborside scene (Wed–Mon 12:00–15:00,
19:00–22:00, closed Tue, CC, just below train station, Via
Roma 60, tel. 0187-812-223, Gabriella SE). The more offbeat
and intimate **Trattoria da Piva** may come with late-night guitar
strumming (Tue–Sun 12:00–15:30, 19:00–01:00, closed Mon,
Via Carattino 6, around corner from pharmacy).

For basic grub, a grand view, and perfect peace, hike to
Franco's **Ristorante "La Torre"** for a dinner at sunset (Wed–
Mon 20:00–21:30, closed Tue, on trail toward Corniglia,
tel. 0187-821-082).

The main street is creatively determining tourists' needs
and filling them. The **Blue Marlin** bar offers a good selection
of sandwiches, salads, and *bruschetta*. Try the **Forno** bakery
for good focaccia and veggie tarts, and the several bars for sandwiches and pizza by the slice. Grocery stores make inexpensive
sandwiches to order (Mon–Sat 07:30–13:00, 17:00–19:30, Sun
07:30–13:00). The town's two *gelaterias* are good. **La Cantina
del Molo**, the new wine shop, will uncork the bottle you buy
and supply cups to go (daily 11:00–20:00, until 22:00 in summer,
owner makes 5 of the wines, tasting possible). Most harborside
bars will let you take your glass on a breakwater stroll.

Breakfast: Locals take breakfast about as seriously as floss-
ing. A cappuccino and a pastry or a piece of focaccia does it.
The two harborfront bars offer the most ambience (you can
walk out with the cup, grab a view picnic bench, and return
the cup when you're done). The bakery opens early, offering
freshly-made focaccia. The Blue Marlin serves a special €6.20
breakfast: ham and cheese focaccia, an assortment of fresh local
pastries, juice, and cappuccino (Fri–Wed 06:45–24:00, closed
Thu; open daily in Aug; just below station, tel. 0187-821-149,
www.bluemarlin5terre.com).

Sleeping in Riomaggiore
(zip code: 19017)

Riomaggiore has organized its private room scene better than its neighbors. Several agencies within a few meters of each other on the main drag (with regular office hours, English-speaking staff, and e-mail addresses) manage a corral of local rooms for rent. Expect lots of stairs. The town's shuttle bus service makes getting in and out of town from the parking lot easier.

Room-Finding Services

Edi's Rooms rents five fine rooms and 12 apartments—half have views (Db-€52–78, Qb-€83–124 depending on view, season, and number of people, CC, office open 08:00–20:00 in summer, otherwise 09:00–13:00, 15:00–19:00, Via Colombo 111, tel. & fax 0187-920-325, tel. 0187-760-842, e-mail: edi-vesigna@iol.it).

Mar Mar Rooms, run by Mario Franceschetti, has pleasant rooms and a mini-hostel (€21 dorm beds, Db-€47–62, bunky family deals, can request kitchen and balcony, CC, Internet access and small self-service laundry in office, 30 meters above train tracks on the main drag next to Lampara restaurant, Via Malborghetto 8, tel. & fax 0187-920-932, e-mail: marmar @5terre.com). Mar Mar also rents kayaks (double kayaks €8/hr, cheaper by the half day).

Luciano and Roberto Fazioli have five apartments, nine rooms, and a basic 11-bed mini-hostel (€15.50–21 for dorm bed, D-€31–41, Db-€47–62, apartments-€21–52 per person, prices increase with view and in summer, Via Colombo 94, tel. 0187-920-904 or 0187-920-822, e-mail: robertofazioli@libero.it).

At **Bar Central**, friendly Ivo and Alberto can help you find a room (daily 07:00–01:00, closed Mon in winter only, Via Colombo 144, tel. 0187-920-208, e-mail: barcentr@tin.it). Ivo lived in San Francisco, fills his bar with only the best San Franciscan rock, and speaks great English. His Bar Central, a good stop for breakfast, cheeseburgers, Internet access, and live music (sometimes in summer), is a shaded place to relax with other travelers. It's got the only lively late-night action in town. And there's prize-winning gelato next door.

Accommodations

In the center: **Michielini Anna** rents four clean, attractive apartments with kitchens and no views (€26 per person mid-April–Sept, otherwise €21 per person, CC to reserve but please pay cash, cheaper for longer stays, 2 nights preferred June–Sept, across from Bar Central at Colombo 143, door opens hard, tel. 0187-920-950 for friendly Daniela who speaks good English, tel. & fax 0187-920-411 for solo-Italiano-speaking mother, e-mail: anna .michielini@tin.it, another e-mail: michielinis@yahoo.it).

At the top of town: **Albergo Caribana** has six new rooms, with views and shared terraces. At the edge of town, it's a five-minute walk to the center. The easy parking makes this especially appealing to drivers (Db-€62–83, depending on season, includes breakfast, Via Sanctuario 114, tel. 0187-920-773, tel. & fax 0187-920-932, e-mail: marmar@5terre.com).

For a real hotel, consider **Villa Argentina**. It's on the top ridge of town, with 15 crisply clean, modern rooms, fine balconies (for 9 rooms), and sea views. While this is a good choice for drivers, the little bus which shuttles people (and their luggage) between the top and bottom of town makes this hotel a possibility for train travelers (Db-€114, includes breakfast, no CC, Via de Gasperi 37, go through tunnel from station, wait for bus or walk 15 minutes uphill, then take a left at the parking booth, tel. 0187-920-213, fax 0187-920-213, e-mail: villaargentina@libero.it).

Eating in Riomaggiore

Ristorante La Lampara serves a *frutti di mare* pizza, *trenete al pesto*, and the aromatic *spaghetti al cartoccio*—spaghetti with mixed seafood cooked in foil (€13 tourist menu, Wed–Mon 12:00–15:30, 18:00–24:00, Closed Tue, CC, on Via Colombo just above tracks, tel. 0187-920-120). Groceries and delis (such as Da Simone) on Via Columbo sell food to go, including pizza slices (picnic at the harbor). While the late-night fun is at Ivo's Bar Central, take a walk down to the harborside **Dau Cila** bar (closed Tue) for jazz, nets, and mellow *limoncino*—a drink of lemon juice, sugar, and pure alcohol (a.k.a. *limoncello* elsewhere in Italy).

Sleeping in Manarola
(zip code: 19010)

Manarola has plenty of private rooms. Ask in bars and restaurants. Otherwise, you'll find a modern three-star place halfway up the main drag, a cluster of great values around the church at the peaceful top of town a five-minute hike above the train tracks, and a salty place on the harbor. The town's handy shuttle bus service makes getting to and from your car easier.

Up the hill, the utterly normal **Albergo ca' d'Andrean** is quiet, comfortable, modern, and very hotelesque, with 10 big, sunny rooms and a cool garden oasis complete with lemon trees (Sb-€52, Db-€67, breakfast-€5, closed Nov, Via A. Discovolo 101, tel. 0187-920-040, fax 0187-920-452, www.cadandrean.it, e-mail: cadandrean@libero.it, Simone SE).

Affitta Camere de Baranin rents eight airy, refreshing rooms (Db-€55, Db with view and breakfast-€85, Internet access, CC to reserve but please pay cash, climb stairway against wall beyond church square—with your back to the church, stairway is at 07:00, follow sign to Trattoria dal Billy, Via Rollandi 29, tel. & fax 0187-920-595, www.baranin.com, Sara and Silvia SE).

La Torretta has four compact apartments with kitchens, five doubles, and one quad, all attractively designed by the young English-speaking architect/manager Gabriele Baldini (student Db-€26–36, Db-€52–72, Db apartment-€57–77, Qb-€83–124, prices vary with season, reserve with CC, views, big garden, with your back to church, it's at 10:00—look left across the square toward the sea, Piazza della Chiesa, Vico Volto 14, tel. & fax 0187-920-327, check Web for deals involving their Tuscan mountain villa, www.cinqueterre.net/torretta, e-mail: torretta@cdh.it).

Casa Capellini rents four fine rooms; one has a view balcony, another a 360-degree terrace (D-€42, €36 for 2 or more nights; Db-€47, €42 for 2 or more nights; the *alta camera* on the top, with a kitchen, private terrace, and knockout view-€57, €52 for 2 or more nights; 2 doors down the hill from the church, with your back to the church, it's at 2:00, Via Ettore Cozzani 12, tel. 0187-920-823 or 0187-736-765, e-mail: casa.capellini@tin.it, NSE).

Ostello 5-Terre, Manarola's modern and well-run hostel, stands like a Monopoly hotel behind the church square. It's smart to reserve at least two weeks in advance in high season (one week in off-season). You book with your credit card number; if you cancel with less than three days' notice, you'll be charged (May–Sept: beds-€15.50, Qb-€62, off-season: beds-€13, Qb-€52, closed early Jan–mid-Feb, CC, 48 beds in 4- to 6-bed rooms, not co-ed except for families, office closed 13:00–17:00, rooms closed 10:00–17:00, curfew–01:00, off-season: office and rooms closed until 16:00 and curfew at 24:00, open to anyone of any age, laundry, safes, phone cards, Internet access, book exchange, elevator, breakfast and dinner, great roof terrace with showers and sunsets, Via B. Riccobaldi 21, tel. 0187-920-215, fax 0187-920-218, www.cinqueterre.net/ostello/, e-mail: ostello@cdh.it). They rent bikes, kayaks, and snorkeling gear.

Marina Piccola has 10 bright, modern rooms on the water, so they figure a warm welcome is unnecessary (Db-€72 for 1-day stays, otherwise half-pension required at €67 per person, CC, Via Discovolo 192, tel. 0187-920-103, fax 0187-920-966, www .marinapiccola.com).

Sleeping in Corniglia
(zip code: 19010)
Perched high above the sea on a hilltop, Corniglia has plenty of private rooms (generally Db-€52). To get to the town from the station, catch the small shuttle bus or take a 15-minute uphill hike. If you hike, choose between a long road or lots of stairs. At the top of the stairs, turn left to reach the town (if you've taken the

road, just stay on the road). The main drag is Via Fieschi, stretching to the tip of the promontory and its viewpoint park.

For this first listing, take the road (rather than the stairs) up from the station. **Domenico Spora** has eight apartments scattered throughout town, all with views and private bath (Db-€65, Qb-€110, Via Villa 19, tel. 0187-812-293, NSE). Her place is about three-fourths of the way up the hill from the station.

For the following listings, if you've taken the stairs up from the station, turn left at the top of the stairs. These are listed in the order you'll encounter them as you walk up Via Fieschi. At the main square, you'll see **La Lanterna** bar, which rents 10 sleepable rooms in town, some with a view (Db-€52, also has 6 new rooms in Comeneco a 30-min walk away—better for drivers, tel. 0187-812-291).

Continue up Via Fieschi. Detour left—up the stairs—on Via Solferino (then go right, left, and left) to find #34 for **Pelligrini** (3 comfortable rooms including 1 with balcony, terrace for all, tel. 0187-812-184 or 0187-821-176). Return to Via Fieschi.

Next on the main drag comes **Villa Sandra**, which consists of five good doubles (D-€47—2 have terraces, Db-€52) and an apartment (Db-€57; Via Fieschi 212, tel. & fax 0187-812-384). Next...

Louisa Cristiana rents a great apartment with three doubles and a big comfy living room/kitchen with a view terrace on the tiny soccer court at the top of the town (Db-€52, grand apartment for 2 people-€103, for 4 people-€114, for 6 people-€130, cheaper in winter, Via Fieschi 215, call English-speaking daughter Cristiana at 0187-812-236—she works at Bar Matteo on Via Fieschi, below main square; also tel. & fax 0187-812-345; daughter rents small apartment for €57). Finally, near the town promontory, you'll see the door for **Signora Silvana** (Via Fieschi 220, tel. 0187-513-830) and next door, **La Rocca** (Via Fieschi 222, tel. 0187-812-178); both offer rooms at this scenic cliff-hanging edge of town.

Villa Cecio is more of a hotel (Db-€60, views, on the main road 200 meters toward Vernazza, tel. 0187-812-043).

Sleeping in Monterosso
(zip code: 19016)

Monterosso al Mare, the most beach-resorty of the five Cinque Terre towns, offers maximum comfort and ease. There are plenty of hotels and rentable beach umbrellas, shops, and cars. The TI (Pro Loco) can give you a list of €30-per-person doubles (pricier for a single) in a private home (Mon–Sat 10:00–12:00, 15:30–17:30, Sun 10:00–12:00; exiting station, TI is to your left; tel. 0187-817-506).

Monterosso is 30 minutes off the freeway (exit: Carrodano). Parking is easy in the huge beachfront guarded lot (€6.20/day).

A self-serve **laundry** is in the old town (daily 09:00–12:30, 15:00–20:00, Via Mazzini 4, just off Via Roma).

Recommended hotels are listed for the old town and the new town (connected by a tunnel), with a convent-run place in between. My favorite is the Hotel Villa Steno in the old town. To get to the old town from the station, exit left, walk along the waterfront, and go through the tunnel.

Sleeping in the Old Town: These are listed in the order you'll encounter them, whether you're emerging from the tunnel or getting off the boat.

Albergo Pasquale is next to the tunnel entrance, train tracks, and boat dock. Run by the same family who owns Hotel Villa Steno (see listing below), this is a decent place with more comfort than character. It's just a few steps from the beach. The air-conditioning (used with closed windows) minimizes the train noise (Sb-€80, Db-€120, Tb-€140, Qb-€160, includes breakfast, CC, €10 discount per room per night if you pay cash and show this book, readers get a free glass of the local sweet wine—*sciacchetrà*—at check-in, Via Fegina 4, tel. 0187-817-550 or 0187-817-477, fax 0187-817-056, e-mail: pasquale@pasini.com, Felicita and Marco SE).

The next two places, next door to each other on a quiet street, both require half-pension during peak season: the fancy **Albergo degli Amici** (36 modern rooms, Db-€77–90, breakfast extra, Db with half-pension-€129—required July-Aug, CC, no views from rooms, peaceful above-it-all view garden with "sun beds"—lawn chairs with movable sun shades, Via Buranco 36, tel. 0187-817-544, fax 0187-817-424, www.cinqueterre.it/hotel _amici/) and the less fancy **Albergo Marina** (23 decent rooms, Db with required half-pension April–Aug-€103–124, CC, elevator, air con, garden with lemon trees, next door at Via Buranco 40, tel. & fax 0187-817-242 or 0187-817-613, www .cinqueterre.it/hotel_marina/). To get to the Amici and Marina from the old town harbor, go to the left of the arcaded building with the bell tower and turn left after a block; for the next listing go to the right of the arcaded building up Via Roma.

Ristorante al Carugio rents 10, no-view rooms in an apartment flat at the no-character top end of town (Db-€70, CC, office at Via S. Pietro 15—just off Via Roma, rooms at Via Roma 100, tel. & fax 0187-817-453).

Hotel La Colonnina, a comfy, modern place on a sleepy side street, takes reservations in advance only for three-night stays. For a shorter stay, just call a day or two ahead to see if they have space (Db-€88, no breakfast, elevator, garden, rooftop terrace, Via Zuecca 6, tel. 0187-817-439). By the tracks, look for the play-ground and the square with a statue of Garibaldi; Via Zuecca is directly behind him (the hotel is one block up, to the right).

Farther on is the best place in town: The lovingly managed **Hotel Villa Steno**, featuring great view balconies, private gardens off some rooms, TVs, telephones, air-conditioning, and the friendly help of English-speaking Matteo. Of his 16 rooms, 12 have view balconies (Sb-€80, Db-€120, Tb-€140, Qb-€160, includes hearty buffet breakfast, CC, €10 discount per room per night if you pay cash and show this book, Internet access, self-service laundry—guests only, 10-min hike from the station to the top of the old town at Via Roma 109, tel. 0187-817-028 or 0187-818-336, fax 0187-817-354, www.pasini.com, e-mail: steno@pasini.com). Readers get a free glass of the local sweet wine, *sciacchetrà*, when they check in—ask. The Steno has a tiny parking lot (free, but call to reserve a spot).

Sleeping Between the Old and New Towns: The religious **Convento dei Cappuccini** rents 14 spartan rooms, named after monks, on the hill above the tunnel that connects the old and new parts of town. Their terrace, overlooking the garden and a long stretch of coastline, has a tremendous panoramic view. On foot it's a steep hike, or you can take a taxi (€8) to the cemetery 200 meters away—go around or walk through cemetery to reach the convent (S-€34, Sb-€39, D-€72, Db-€78, all twins, includes breakfast, dinner extra and optional, attached church and cloister, reserve ahead, must send a deposit of 30 percent—personal check OK, 19016 Monterosso, tel. 0187-817-531, e-mail: monterosso .convento@libero.it, truly NSE). If you're hiking from the station, exit left, go through the tunnel, then take a hairpin left. Zigzag up the side of the hill until you reach the gate, the church (Chiesa Cappuccin), and *convento* (15-min walk from station).

Sleeping in the New Town: Turn left out of the station to **Pension Agavi,** which has eight bright, airy rooms (Sb-€47, Db-€83, refrigerators, Fegina 30, tel. 0187-817-171, fax 0187-818-264, cellular 336-258-467, spunky Hillary SE).

Turn right leaving the station for the rest of the listings.

The central, waterfront **Hotel Baia** has appealing, high-ceilinged rooms, but the staff is rude (Db-€129, includes breakfast, CC, slow elevator, balconies, request view—same price, Via Fegina 88, tel. 0187-817-512, fax 0187-818-322).

Consider the newly remodeled **Hotel Punta Mesco** (Db-€100, no views, exit right from station, take first right, Via Molinelli 35, tel. 0187-817-495, www.cinqueterre.it/belvedere).

Villa Mario, good for backpackers, has five basic rooms with a view terrace and a squawky bird learning to talk (Db-€62–72, exit right from station, take second right, walk 5 min uphill, Via Padre Semeria 28, tel. & fax 0187-818-030).

Villa Adriana, run by brusque Austrian nuns, has 55 decent, clean rooms divided between a 19th-century villa and an adjacent, modern annex. With a strict 23:00 curfew, a lofty setting (up off the street with a tropical garden as its front yard), and a religious, institutional atmosphere, it's peaceful (Sb-€65, Db-€120, includes breakfast; half-pension required June–Aug: Sb-€69, Db-€130; CC, double and twins available, some views, attached chapel, parking, exit right from station, walk along waterfront, turn right at Via IV Novembre, 300 meters off beach, Via IV Novembre 23, reception at back of building, tel. 0187-818-109, fax 0187-818-128, SE).

Eating in Monterosso
Ristorante Belvedere is a good bet for good value in the old town (Wed–Mon 12:00–14:30, 19:00–22:00, closed Tue, CC, right on the harbor, across from Albergo Pasquale, tel. 0187-817-033). Lots of shops and bakeries sell pizza and focaccia for an easy picnic at the beach. **Il Frantoia** makes tasty pizza to go (Wed–Fri 09:00–14:00, 16:00–20:00, closed Thu, Via Gioberti 1, just off Via Roma in old town).

Transportation Connections—Cinque Terre
The five towns of the Cinque Terre are on a milk-run train line described earlier in this chapter. Hourly trains connect each town with the others, La Spezia, and Genoa. While a few of the milk-run trains go to more distant points (Milan or Pisa), it's faster to change in La Spezia or Monterosso to a bigger train. Train info: Monterosso tel. 0187-817-458 or 848-888-088.

From La Spezia by train to: Rome (10/day, 4 hrs), **Pisa** (hrly, 1 hr, direction: Livorno, Rome, Salerno, Naples, etc.), **Florence** (hrly, 2.5 hrs, change at Pisa), **Milan** (hrly; 3 hrs, 3 direct; or 4 hrs with change in Genoa), **Venice** (2 direct 6-hr trains/day).

From Monterosso by train to: Venice (2/day, 6 hrs), **Milan** (3/day, 3 hrs), **Genova** (9/day, 1.25 hrs), **Turin** (5/day, 3.25 hrs), **Pisa** (3/day, 1.5 hrs), **Sestri Levante** (hrly, 15 min, most trains to Genova stop here), **La Spezia** (nearly hrly, 20 min), **Levanto** (nearly hrly, 6 min).

Driving in the Cinque Terre
Milan to the Cinque Terre (210 km/130 miles): Drivers speed south by autostrada from Milan, skirt Genoa, and drive along some of Italy's most scenic and impressive freeways toward the port of La Spezia. The road via Parma is faster but less scenic.

It is possible to snake your car down the treacherous little road into the Cinque Terre and park in the new parking lot above Vernazza, then take the shuttle bus into town. Monterosso has a big, guarded beachfront parking lot that fills only on August weekends (€6.20/day). Riomaggiore and Manarola both offer parking and a shuttle bus to get you into town. To drive

Our Liguria

to Monterosso or Vernazza, exit the autostrada at Uscita Carrodano west of La Spezia. To drive to Riomaggiore, leave the freeway at La Spezia.

   You can park your car near the train stations in La Spezia or
Levanto (the first town past Monterosso). Confirm that parking
is OK and leave nothing inside to steal. In La Spezia, a nearby
garage can store your car for about €13 per day.

TOWNS NEAR THE CINQUE TERRE

La Spezia, a gateway to the Cinque Terre, is simply a place to
stay if you can't find a room in the Cinque Terre (20–30 min
away by train). Carrara is a quickie for marble-lovers who are
driving between Pisa and La Spezia. The picturesque village of
Portovenere, near La Spezia, has scenic boat connections with
Cinque Terre towns. Levanto has a long beach and a scenic trail
to Monterosso (2.5-hour hike, or easier, 6 min by train). Sestri
Levante, on a narrow peninsula flanked by two beaches, is for sun
seekers (15 min by train from Cinque Terre). Santa Margherita
(75 min by train from the Cinque Terre) is more of a real town,
with actual sights, beaches, and easy connections with Portofino
(by trail, bus, or boat).

LA SPEZIA

When all else fails, you can stay in a noisy, bigger town such as La Spezia. While a quick train ride into the fanciful Five-Terre, La Spezia feels like work-a-day Italy.

The TI is a 20-minute walk from the station, near the waterfront (Mon–Sat 09:00–13:00, 14:30–17:30, Sun 09:00–13:00, Mazzini 45, tel. 0187-718-997 or 0187-770-900). Let's hope they have a branch at the station in 2002. If not, skip it.

Sights are slim. On Friday morning, a huge open-air market sprawls along Via Garibaldi (about 6 blocks from station). The **Museo Amedeo Lia** displays Italian paintings from the 13th to 18th centuries (€6.20, Tue–Sun 10:00–18:00, closed Mon, no photos allowed, 10-min walk from station at Via Prione 234, tel. 0187-731-100, www.castagna.it/mal).

Sleeping in La Spezia
(€1.10 = about $1, country code: 39)

The first three hotels are within a block of the train station; the fourth is a five-minute walk from the station. The last two are for drivers only. Only the first has air-conditioning.

The grand, old, but newly restored **Hotel Firenze e Continentale** has 68 rooms with all the classy comforts (Db-€103, maybe €93 in slow time, includes buffet breakfast, CC, air-con, some nonsmoking rooms, elevator, parking-€15.50/day, Via Paleocapa 7, tel. 0187-713-200, fax 0187-714-930, www.hotelfirenzecontinentale.it, SE). **Hotel Venezia**, across the street, has a plain lobby, but its 19 rooms are modern (Db-€88, CC, elevator, Via Paleocapa 10, tel. & fax 0187-733-465, NSE). **Albergo Parma**, tight, bright, and bleachy clean, is located just below the station, down the stairs (D-€44, Db-€57, CC, Via Fiume 143, tel. 0187-743-010, fax 0187-743-240, some English spoken). **Hotel Astoria**, with 56 decent rooms, has a combination lobby and breakfast room as large as a school cafeteria. It's a fine backup if the hotels nearer the station are full (Db-€73–103, includes breakfast, elevator, Via Roma 139, take street left of Albergo Parma—Via Milano, go 3 blocks and turn left on Via Roma, tel. 0187-714-655, fax 0187-714-425, e-mail: hotelastoria @worldonline.it).

Il Gelsomino, for drivers only, is a small B&B in the hills above La Spezia (3 rooms, D-€62, Db-€75, Tb-€85, views, Via dei Viseggi 9, tel. & fax 0187-704-201, run by Carla Massi).

Santa Maria del Mare Monastery, a last resort for drivers, rents 100 comfortable rooms high above La Spezia in a scenic but institutional setting (Db-€78, Castellazzo Stra, tel. 0187-700-365 or 0187-711-332, e-mail: mare@tamnet.it).

CARRARA

Perhaps the world's most famous marble quarries are just east of
La Spezia in Carrara. Michelangelo himself traveled to these valleys
to pick out the marble, which he'd work into his masterpieces. The
towns of the region are dominated by marble. The quarries higher
up are vast digs that dwarf their hard-working trucks and machinery.
The Carrara museum allows visitors to trace the story of marble-
cutting here from pre-Roman times until today. For a guided visit,
Sara Paolini is excellent (€78 per group for a half-day tour, tel.
0585-632-617, e-mail: casara00@hotmail.com). She is accustomed
to meeting and joining drivers at the Carrara freeway exit.

PORTOVENERE

While the gritty port of La Spezia offers little in the way of redeem-
ing touristic value, the nearby resort of Portovenere is enchanting.
This Cinque Terre-esque village clings to a rocky promontory
jutting into the sea, protecting the harbor from the crashing waves.
On the harbor, next to colorful bobbing boats, a row of restaurants—
perfect for al fresco dining—feature local specialities such as *trenette*
pasta with pesto and spaghetti *frutti di mare*.

Local boats take you on excursions to nearby islands or over
to Lerici, the town across the bay. Lord Byron swam to Lerici
(not recommended). Hardy hikers enjoy the 2-hour (or more)
hike to Riomaggiore, the nearest Cinque Terre town.

Portovenere is an easy daytrip from the Cinque Terre by
boat (Easter to late Oct, nearly hourly 10:00–18:00). Or take
the bus from La Spezia (25 min). In peak season, buses shuttle
drivers from the parking lot just outside Portovenere to the
harborside square.

Sleeping: If you forgot your yacht, try **Albergo Il Genio**,
in the castle-like building where the main street hits the piazza
(Db-from €62, tel. 0187-790-611). If your *vita* is feeling *dolce*,
consider **Grand Hotel Portovenere** (prices soar from €100 for a
viewless double off-season to €300 for a view suite in summer, tel.
0187-792-610, fax 0187-790-661, e-mail: ghp@rphotels.com).

LEVANTO

Graced with a long, sandy beach, Levanto is packed in summer.
The rest of the year, it's just a small, sleepy town, with less colorful charm and fewer tourists than the Cinque Terre towns. Levanto has a new section (gridded-street plan) and a twisty old town
(bisected by a modern street), plus a few pedestrian streets, a
castle (not open), and a scenic, no-wimps-allowed hike to Monterosso (1.5 hrs).

For an energetic daytrip, hike from Monterosso to Levanto,
play in the surf (or collapse on the beach), take a look at the town,
and catch the boat or the train back home.

From the Levanto train station to the TI, it's a 10-minute walk (head down the stairs in front of the station, cross the bridge, then follow "i" and *centro* signs). At the TI, pick up a map (summer Mon–Sat 09:00–13:00, 14:00–18:00, Sun 09:00–13:00; in winter Sun 09:30–12:30 and closes at 17:00 Mon–Sat, Piazza Cavour, tel. 0187-808-125). The train schedule is posted outside the TI's door.

The beach is just two blocks away from the TI. During the summer, half the beach is free (*libero*), the other half is broken up into private sections that require an admission fee. Off-season, roughly October through May, when the sea is free, you can stroll the entire beach. Facing the harbor, the boat dock is to your far left and the diving center is at your far right (you can rent boats in summer at either place).

The old town, several blocks from the TI and beach, clusters around Piazza del Popolo. Until 10 years ago, the town market (*mercato*) was held at the 13th-century loggia in the square. Explore the back streets. To get to the trailhead to Monterosso: From Piazza del Popolo, head uphill to the striped church, Chiesa di S. Andrea (with your back to the loggia, go straight ahead—across the square and up Via Don Emanuele Toso to the church). From the church courtyard, follow the sign to the *castello* (castle), go around the castle, and turn left. You'll see the sign for Punta Mesco, the rugged tip of the peninsula. From here you can hike up (1.5 hrs to Monterosso), or—if you have second thoughts—hike down, taking the stairs to the beach. You'll end up near the dock, where you can catch the boat for the Cinque Terre towns.

For picnic supplies, try Levanto's modern, covered *mercato* (Mon–Sat 09:00–13:00, fish and produce market, between train station and TI; the street it's on—only a decade old—hasn't yet been officially named). On Wednesday morning, an open-air market fills the street in front of the *mercato*. For an inexpensive meal a block from the beach, consider Antico Caffè Roma (closed Tue, Piazza Staglieno 10, near playground, tel. 0187-808-514).

To get to the Cinque Terre, take the train (nearly hrly, 6 min to Monterosso) or the boat (2/day, stops at every Cinque Terre town except Corniglia, Easter–Oct).

Sleeping in Levanto
(€1.10 = about $1, country code: 39, zip code: 19015)
In the popular beach town, a number of hotels require you to take half-pension (lunch or dinner) in summer. The first and last listings don't.

Ristorante La Loggia has eight pleasant rooms perched above the old loggia on Piazza del Popolo (Db-€47–62, includes breakfast, air-con, request balcony, quieter rooms in back, apartment available, attached restaurant, closed Feb, Piazza del Popolo 7, tel. & fax 0187-808-107).

Albergo Primavera has 17 comfortable rooms—10 with terraces but no views—just a half a block from the beach (Db-€88, Db with half-pension required June–Aug-€124, buffet breakfast, closed Nov–Jan, CC, Via Cairoli 5, a block from TI, tel. 0187-808-023, fax 0187-801-588, e-mail: www.primavera.com, friendly staff speaks a little English).

Hotel Europa, also a block from the TI, is a good bet, with 22 decent, well-maintained rooms (Db-€83, Db with half-pension required April–Aug-€103, CC, roof terrace, elevator, Via Dante Alighieri 41, tel. 0187-808-126, fax 0187-808-594, e-mail: albeurop@tin.it).

For a major splurge (which includes dinner), consider **Hotel Stella Maris**, an 18th-century palazzo with original furnishings: chandeliers, frescoed ceilings, and massive beds and armoires. The rooms on the busy street are bigger and grander than the two quieter rooms in the back (Db with required half-pension-€196, cheaper rooms in modern annex also require half-pension: Db-€145, CC, closed Nov, Via Marconi 4, a few steps from Piazza Cavour and TI, tel. 0187-808-258, fax 0187-807-351, www.hotelstellamaris.it).

Hostel: The **Ostello Ospitalia del Mare** offers 60 beds, bright rooms, Internet access, and a terrace in a well-built building in the old town (beds-€15.50–€24 in 4-, 6-, and 8-bed rooms with private bath, includes breakfast and sheets, CC, anyone welcome, not co-ed except for families, no curfew, no reservations accepted in high season—call same day or just show up, office closed 13:30–15:30, Via San Nicolo 1, tel. 0187-802-562, fax 0187-803-696, www.ospitaliadelmare.it).

SESTRI LEVANTE

This peninsular town is squeezed as skinny as a hot dog between its two beaches. The pedestrian-friendly Corso Columbo, which runs down the middle of the peninsula, is lined with shops selling pizza to go, pastries, and beach paraphernalia. The rocky, forested bluff at the end of the peninsula is inaccessible to the public (it's the huge backyard of the fancy Hotel Castelli). Market day is Saturday at Piazza Aldo Moro (08:00–13:00).

The best, quick visit from the station (luggage storage-€2.60) starts with a five-minute walk to the TI to get a map (May–Sept daily 09:30–12:30, 15:30–18:30, Oct–April Mon–Sat 09:30–12:30, 14:30–17:30, closed Sun; go straight out of station on Via Roma, turn left at fountain in park, TI at next square—Piazza S. Antonio 10, tel. 0185-457-011). Roads fan out from Piazza S. Antonio like spokes. From the TI, you're one "spoke" away from Corso Columbo (to the left of the Bermuda Bar). Stroll this street until nearly the end (about 5 min). Just before you get to the large white church at the end, turn off for either beach (the free public beach, Baia del Silencio, is on your left). Or head uphill behind the church to the Hotel Castelli for a drink at their view café (so-so view, reasonably priced drinks, café is at end of parking lot to your right). On the way up the hill you'll pass the evocative arches of a ruined chapel, bombed during WWII, and left as a memorial.

Most people are here for the sun. The beaches are named after the bays (*baias*) they border. The bigger beach, Baia delle Favole, is divided up most of the year (May–Sept) into sections that you pay to enter. The fees, which can soar up to €24 in August, generally include chairs, umbrellas, and fewer crowds. There are several small free sections: at the ends and in the middle (look for *libere* signs). The town's other beach, Baia del Silencio, is narrow, virtually all free, and packed, providing a good chance to see Italian families at play. There isn't much more to do than unroll a beach towel and join in.

You're in good company. Hans Christian Andersen enjoyed his visit here in the mid-1800s, writing, "What a fabulous evening I spent in Sestri Levante!" One of the bays—Baia delle Favole—is named in his honor (*favole* means fairy tale). The last week of May is a street festival, culminating in a ceremony for locals who write the best fairy tales (4 prizes for 4 age groups, from pre-kindergarten to adult). The "Oscar" awards are little mermaids. The small mermaid curled on the edge of the fountain (behind the TI) is another nod to the beloved Danish storyteller.

Even Hans found Sestri Levante easy to reach by train, just 15 minutes away from Monterosso (hrly connections with Monterosso, nearly hrly with other Cinque Terre towns).

Sleeping and Eating in Sestri Levante
(€1.10 = about $1, country code: 39, zip code: 16039)
Hotel Due Mari has three stars, 29 fine rooms, and a rooftop terrace with a super view of both beaches. Ideally, reserve well in advance (Db-€101–114 depending on view, Db with half-pension required in July–Aug-€145, CC, some air-con, elevator, garden, take Corso Columbo to the end, hotel is behind church, free parking first day—then €8/day, Vico del Coro 18, tel. 0185-42695, fax 0185-42698, e-mail: hotelduemari@inwind.it, SE).

Hotel Helvetia, overlooking Baia del Silencio, is another good three-star bet, with 24 bright rooms, a large view terrace, and a peaceful atmosphere (Db-€114–155 depending on view/balcony, includes breakfast, CC, air-con, elevator, parking-€10 /day, from Corso Columbo turn left on Palestro and angle left at square, Via Cappuccini 43, tel. 0185-41175, fax 0185-457216, www.rainbownet.it/helvetia, SE).

Hotel Elisabetta, less central and cheaper, has comfortable rooms on a busy street at the end of Baia delle Favole, a block from the beach (Db-€75–85 depending on season, half-pension available but not required, CC, ask for quieter room in back, Via Novara 7, walk straight out of station, then turn right at park, 12-minute walk, tel. 0185-41128, fax 0185-487-206, NSE).

Hotel dei Fiori has 15 basic rooms across Piazza S. Antonio from the TI office (Db-€52–65, includes breakfast, CC, double-paned windows, request a *tranquillo* room in back, Via Nazionale 12, tel. & fax 0185-41147, NSE).

Eating: At **L'Osteria Mattana**, where everyone shares long tables, you can mix with locals while enjoying the local cuisine (Tue–Sun 19:30–22:30, also Fri–Sun 12:30–14:30, closed Mon, Via XXV Aprile 26, take Corso Columbo from TI, turns into XXV Aprile, restaurant on right, tel. 0185-457-633). **Polpo Mario** is classier but affordable, with a good people-watching location on the main drag (Tue–Sun 12:00–14:30, 19:30–22:00, closed Mon, Via XXV Aprile 163, tel. 0185-480-203).

SANTA MARGHERITA LIGURE

If you need the movie star's Riviera, park your yacht at Portofino. Or you can settle down in the nearby and more personable Santa Margherita Ligure (15 min by bus from Portofino and 75 min by train from the Cinque Terre). While Portofino's velour allure is tarnished by snobby residents and a nonstop traffic jam in peak season, Santa Margherita tumbles easily downhill from its train station. The town has a fun resort character with a breezy promenade.

On a quick daytrip, walk the beach promenade, see the small old town, and catch the bus (or boat) to Portofino to see what all the fuss is about. With more time, Santa Margherita makes a fine overnight stop.

Tourist Information: Pick up a map at the TI (daily 09:00–12:30, 15:00–18:00, in winter Mon–Sat 09:00–12:30, 14:30–17:30, closed Sun, Via XXV Aprile 2b, tel. 0185-287-485, www.apttigullio.liguria.it).

Arrival by Train: To get to the city center from the station, take the stairs marked *Mare* (Sea) down to the harbor. The harbor-front promenade is as wide as the skimpy beach. (The real beaches, which are pebbly, are a 10-minute walk farther on, past the port).

To get to the pedestrian-friendly old town and the TI, take a right at Piazza Veneto (with the roundabout, flags, and park) onto Largo Antonio Giusti. To reach the TI, angle left on Via XXV Aprile. For the old town (a block off Piazza Veneto), head toward the TI, but turn left on Via Torino, which opens almost immediately onto Piazza Caprera, a square with a church and fruit vendors (Mon–Sat morn) in the midst of pedestrian streets.

Daytrippers: If the train station still doesn't store luggage, check it at Hotel Terminus, next to the station (€5/day).

Internet Access: Internet Point gives readers with this book an additional 30 minutes for free (€5.20/30 min, daily 09:00–21:00, Via Guinchetto 39, off Piazza Mazzini, tel. 0185-293-092, run by owners of recommended Hotel Fasce).

Sights—Santa Margherita Ligure

Villa Durazzo—If you need a sight more than a beach or hike, wander through this 17th-century villa. It's the distinctive (garish?) green-shuttered, rust-colored building atop the hill, a couple of blocks inland from Piazza Martiri della Liberta. The building has changed aristocratic hands several times, and, in the early 20th century, even served as a grand hotel. It was sold to the city in 1973. The interior has some period furniture, several grand pianos, chandeliers, and paintings strewn with cupids on the walls and ceilings. Even with the furniture, it's a bit stark. You can tour it on your own with an English info sheet, or, if you call ahead—even on the same day—you might snare a tour in English (€5.15, or €6.20 with tour, summer Tue–Sun 09:30–18:30, winter Tue–Sun 09:30–12:30, 14:30–16:30, closed Mon, WC in adjacent building, tel. 0185-205-449).

The **garden** surrounding the villa is laced with dirt trails and stone-mosaic paths. The greenery, unkempt and evocative at the base of the hill, is tamed on top, with manicured hedges, statuary, and a wide mosaic terrace offering a view of the sea and marina. Bring a picnic and find a bench (free, daily 09:00–19:00 in summer, until 17:00 in winter).

Castle—The small castle overlooking the harbor, just off Piazza Martiri della Liberta, might be open in 2002. If it isn't, walk uphill just past the castle to the church, for the view from its terrace.

Markets—Around 16:00 on weekdays, fishing boats dock at the fish market to unload their catch, which is then sold to waiting customers. The market—Mercato del Pesce—is the rust-colored building with arches and columns on Via Marconi, on the harbor, just past the castle. The **open-air market**, a commotion of clothes and produce, is held every Friday morning on Salita S. Giacomo (between the castle and harbor).

Side-trip to Portofino

Santa Margherita, with its aristocratic architecture, hints of old money; whereas Portofino, with its sleek shops, reeks of the new. Fortunately, a few pizzerias, bars, and grocery shops are mixed in with Portofino's jewelry shops, art galleries, and clothing boutiques, making the town bearable. The *piccolo* harbor, classic Italian architecture, and wooded peninsula can even turn Portofino into an appealing package, if you look past the glitzy wrapping.

Portofino's **TI** is downhill from the bus stop, on your right (daily in summer 09:30–13:30, 14:00–19:00, in winter Tue–Sun

09:30–12:30, 14:00–17:00, closed Mon, Via Roma 35, tel. 0185-269-024). Pick up a free town map and a rudimentary hiking map. Trails are signed well enough.

For hikers, the best thing about Portofino is leaving it. Options include the well-trodden path that leads out to the lighthouse at the point (20 min, nonstop views; medieval castle en route costs €1.60, daily 10:00–17:00); the pedestrian promenade to Paraggi (20 min, parallels main road, ends at ritzy beach where it's easy to catch the bus back to Santa Margherita); the trail to Santa Margherita (1.5 hrs); and the trail to San Fruttuoso Abbey (2.5 hrs, steep at beginning and end).

The 11th-century **San Fruttuoso Abbey,** accessible only by foot or boat (from Portofino or Santa Margherita) isn't the main attraction. The intriguing draw is a statue of Christ of the Abyss (Cristo degli Abissi), 18 meters underwater. Boats run from the abbey to the Christ, where you can look down to see him, his arms outstretched, reaching upward.

Getting to Portofino from Santa Margherita: Portofino is an easy daytrip by bus, boat, or foot. Catch **bus #82** from Santa Margherita's train station or at bus stops along the harbor (€0.90, 2–3/hr, 15 min, buy tickets at bar at station, at bus kiosk at Piazza Veneto—open daily 07:10–19:40, or at any shop that displays a *Biglietti Bus* sign). The **boat** makes the trip with more class and without the traffic jams (€3.50 one-way, €6 round-trip, hrly in summer, 2/day in spring and fall, 2/day only on Sun in winter, dock is off Piazza Martiri della Libertà, a 2-min walk from Piazza Veneto, tel. 0185-284-670, www.traghettiportofino.it); the boats run between Rapallo and the San Fruttuoso Abbey, stopping in between at Santa Margherita Ligure and Portofino. Hikers call the 1.5-hour **Santa Margherita–Portofino hike** one of the best on the Riviera (5 km, start at Via Maragliano, several blocks past the castle).

Sleeping in Santa Margherita Ligure
(€1.10 = about $1, country code: 39, zip code: 16038)
Hotel Fasce is a hardworking place with 18 bright rooms and a happy clientele (Sb-€77, Db-€88, Tb-€116, Qb-€134, includes breakfast, CC, free round-trip train tickets to Cinque Terre for 3-night stays, parking-€16/day, free bikes, English newspapers, roof garden, laundry service-€16, a 10-min walk from the station at Via Bozzo 3, taxi from station costs about €10, tel. 0185-286-435, fax 0185-283-580, www.hotelfasce.it, run enthusiastically by Jane Fasce—an Englishwoman—and her husband Aristide).

Hotel Fiorina, with 55 airy rooms decorated in a light-and-dark color scheme, is on a busy square with quieter rooms in the back. It's family-run with pride and care (Db-€85 with breakfast, Db-€70 without breakfast, half-pension possible, CC, fans in every room, sun terrace—no view, Piazza Mazzini 26, 2 blocks inland from pedestrian Piazza Caprera, tel. 0185-287-517, fax 0185-281-855, www.paginegialle.it/hfiorina, e-mail: fiorinasml@libero.it, SE).

At the **Hotel Nuova Riviera**, a stately old villa, the Sabini family offers 12 nonsmoking rooms (Db-€88, Tb-€114, Qb-€145, discount of €5 per day if you pay cash, includes breakfast, CC, mother Angela cooks dinner—optional, fans in every room, some balconies, Internet access, free parking—first come, first serve, peaceful garden, 10-minute walk from the station; walking or driving, follow signs to hospital, on Piazza Mazzini see hotel signs, Via Belvedere 10, tel. & fax 0185-287-403, www.nuovariviera.com, e-mail: info@nuovariviera.com, daughter Cristina and son Gian Carlo SE). Their annex is cheaper (3 nights preferred, D-€62, T-€88, Q-€104, 4 rooms share 2 bathrooms, includes breakfast, cash only). Note that if you cancel your reservations, you'll be billed for one night.

These three hotels, close to the train station, all come with train noise: **Hotel Terminus**, with 24 rooms right at the station, works hard to keep its customers satisfied (Db-€83, includes huge breakfast, CC, terrace, good meals, some view rooms, ask for room away from tracks, tel. 0185-286-121, fax 0185-282-546, Angelo SE). **Nuovo Hotel Garden** is tucked away down a side street. From its 32 comfortable rooms to its restaurant, the quality is high (Db-€57–114 depending on season, CC, terrace, bar, double-paned windows on train side, Via Zara 13, a block from train station—instead of taking the stairs down to harbor, face stairs and go right, tel. 0185-285-398, fax 0185-290-439, www.nuovohotelgarden.com, SE). Next door, **Hotel Conte Verde** rents 33 rooms of varying quality and prices. Ask if a room with a big terrace is available (Sb-€36–67, D-€44–70, Db-€65–103, price depends on season and size, includes breakfast, CC, garden, big public areas, parking-€11/day, Via Zara 1, tel. 0185-287-139, fax 0185-284-211, www.tigullio.net/ftpcv/index.html, e-mail: cverde@zeus.omninet.it, SE).

Eating in Santa Margherita Ligure

Ristorante Il Faro, which serves good seafood and more, is atmospheric, with rows of wine bottles lining its wainscoted walls (€23 and €28 menus, à la carte options, lunch from 12:20, dinner from 19:20, closed Tue, 2 blocks inland from port, Via Maragliano 24a, tel. 0185-286-867).

Ristorante Il Nostromo, cheaper and more central, offers a €16 menu (closed Tue, Via dell' Arco 6, a block off Piazza Veneto, take Via Gramsi and turn inland on Via dell' Arco, tel. 0185-281-390). **Papiluc's Bar**, a rare Internet café that's actually a café, is on the same street, a few doors down (Fri–Wed 06:30–02:00, closed Thu, Via dell' Arco 20, tel. 0185-282-580).

Ristorante Giardino, near Hotel Fasce, serves pasta and

pizza to happy customers (Tue–Sun 12:00–14:30, 19:00–22:00, closed Mon, CC, Piazza S. Bernardo 6, tel. 0185-289-047). **Dal Baffo,** nearby, is another good pizzeria (Wed–Mon 12:00–15:00, 19:00–24:00, closed Tue, Corso Matteotti 56, tel. 0185-288-987).

The Doro Centry **supermarket** is just off Piazza Mazzini (Mon–Sat 08:00–13:00, 15:00–19:30, Sun 08:30–12:30, Dogali 34, across from Hotel Fiorina).

Transportation Connections— Santa Margherita Ligure

By train to: Sestri Levante (hrly, 20 min), **Monterosso** (hrly, 1 hr), **La Spezia** (hrly, 1.5 hrs), **Pisa** (3/day, 2.25 hrs, more with transfer in La Spezia), **Genoa** (hrly, 45 min), **Milan** (4/day, 2 hrs, more with transfer in Genoa), **Ventimiglia** (2/day, 3.5 hrs, to French border), **Venice** (2/day, 5.25 hrs). For **Florence**, you'll transfer in La Spezia or Pisa or both (allow 3.5–4 hrs).

MILAN
(MILANO)

For every church in Rome, there's a bank in Milan. Italy's second city and the capital of Lombardy, Milan is a hardworking, fashion-conscious, time-is-money city of 1.5 million. Milan is a melting pot of people and history. Its industriousness may come from the Teutonic blood of its original inhabitants, the Lombards, or from the region's Austrian heritage. Milan is Italy's industrial, banking, TV, publishing, and convention capital. The economic success of modern Italy can be blamed on this city of publicists and pasta power lunches.

As if to make up for its shaggy parks, blocky fascist architecture, and recently bombed-out feeling (World War II), its people are works of art. Milan is an international fashion capital with a refined taste. Window displays are gorgeous, cigarettes are chic, and even the cheese comes gift wrapped.

Three hundred years before Christ, the Romans called this place Mediolanum, or "the central place." By the fourth century A.D., it was the capital of the Western half of the Roman Empire. It was from here that Emperor Constantine issued the Edict of Milan, legalizing Christianity. After some barbarian darkness, medieval Milan rose to regional prominence under the Visconti and Sforza families. By the time of the Renaissance, it was called "the New Athens" and was enough of a cultural center for Leonardo to call home. Then came 400 years of foreign domination (Spain, Austria, France, more Austria). Milan was a center of the 1848 revolution against Austria and helped lead Italy to unification in 1870.

Mussolini left a heavy fascist touch on the city's architecture (such as the central train station). His excesses also led to the WWII bombing of Milan. But Milan rose again. The 1959 Pirelli Tower (the skinny skyscraper in front of the station) was a trendsetter in its day. Today Milan is people-friendly, with a great transit system and inviting pedestrian zones.

Many tourists come to Italy for the past. But Milan is today's Italy, and no Italian trip is complete without seeing it. While it's not big on the tourist circuit, Milan has plenty to see.

And seeing Milan is not difficult. My coverage focuses on the old center. Nearly all the sights and hotels covered are within a 10-minute walk of the cathedral (Duomo), which is one straight eight-minute shot on the Metro from the train station. Milan, no more expensive than other Italian cities, is well-organized and completely manageable.

For a pleasant daytrip from Milan, consider Stresa on Lake Maggiore. This resort town has easy boat connections to lovely islands brimming with lush, exuberant gardens. Stresa, about an hour from Milan by train, is covered at the end of this chapter.

Planning Your Time

OK, it's a big city, so you probably won't linger. But with two nights and a full day, you can gain an appreciation for the town and see the major sights. (Note that about half of Milan's sights close on Monday.) With 36 hours, I'd sleep in Milan and focus on the center. Tour the Duomo, hit what art you like (Brera Gallery, Michelangelo's last *Pietà*, Leonardo's *Last Supper*—which requires a reservation), browse through the elegant shopping area and the Galleria, and try to see an opera. Technology buffs like the Science and Technology Museum, while medieval art buffs dig the city's early Christian churches. People-watchers and pigeon feeders could spend their entire visit never leaving sight of the Duomo.

Since Milan is a cold Italian plunge, and most flights to the United States leave Milan early in the morning, you may want to start your Italian trip softly by going directly from Milan to Lake Como (1-hour train ride to Varenna), Lake Maggiore (about an hour by train to Stresa—see end of chapter), or the Cinque Terre (4 hours to Vernazza). Then spend a night or two in Milan at the end of your trip before flying home.

Three-hour tour: If you're just changing trains in Milan (as sooner or later you will), consider this blitz tour: Check your bag at the station, pick up a city map at the station TI, ride the subway to the Duomo (in front of the train station, follow yellow line 3 direction "per San Donato" 4 stops to "Duomo"), peruse the square, explore the cathedral's rooftop and interior, have a scenic coffee in the Galleria, spin on the Taurus, see a museum or two (most are within a 10-minute walk of the main square), and return by subway to the station (yellow line 3, direction "Zara"). Art fans might make time for the Duomo's museum, Leonardo (if you have reservations, Metro: Cadorna), or the Michelangelo (no reservations necessary, Metro: Cairoli).

Orientation

Tourist Information: Milan has two TIs. One is in the central
train station (Mon–Sat 09:00–19:00, Sun 09:00–12:30, 13:30–18:00,
tel. 02-7252-4360). At track level (with your back to the tracks),
look for the sign "APT Tourist Information" near the blinking
orange-and-white *T*. The TI is tucked away down a corridor next
to a Telecom telephone center (Internet access with phone card).

The other TI is on Piazza Duomo (Mon–Fri 08:30–20:00,
Sat 09:00–13:00, 14:00–19:00, Sun 09:00–13:00, 14:00–17:00,
closes 1 hour earlier Oct–April, tel. 02-7252-4301). As you face
the church, it's to your right in a skinny three-story building.

At either TI, confirm your sightseeing plans and pick up
the free map and the classy *Museums in Milan* booklet (with latest
museum hours). For events, concerts, films in English, expatriate
groups, and cultural insights, ask for the free *Hello Milano* monthly
newspaper (www.hellomilano.it) or the less-helpful *Milano Mese*
(events are listed in Italian by category rather than date). The
80-page *Where, When, How* booklet—useful, but overkill for
most short visits—details several self-guided walking tours and
provides a listing of sights, shopping ideas, bookstores, restaurants, nightlife, sports events, and much more (€1.60).

The TI sells a Welcome Card packet for €7.75, which
includes a 24-hour transit pass (value: €2.60, good on Metro,
trams, and buses), a coupon booklet good for discounts on their
city bus tour (about €5 off) and several museums, a CD of opera
music, and an unnecessary vinyl pouch. This is a decent value
if you want the CD.

While I've listed enough sights to keep you hectic for two
days, there's much more to see in Milan. Its many thousand-year-
old churches make it clear that Milan was an important beacon
in the Dark Ages. The TI, the *Where, When, How* booklet, and
other local guidebooks can point you in the right direction if you
have more time.

Arrival in Milan

By Train: The huge, sternly decorated, Fascist-built (in 1931)
train station is a city and a sight in itself. You'll get off the train
and enter the lobby at track level; another floor is downstairs.

Orient from the track-level lobby with your back to the
tracks. On your right: train information (daily 07:00–21:00, validate railpasses here at refund windows #7 or 8, tel. 848-888-088
for info in Italian), baggage check (€2.60/12 hrs), and a 24-hour
pharmacy *(farmacia,* look for green neon cross). On your left are
cash machines (near track 14) and the TI (see above, look for
blinking orange *T*). Out the side exit on the left (down the escalator under the "Gran Bar" sign), you'll find airport shuttle buses
(to Malpensa and Linate, run by STAM) lined up. Across the

curb from those buses is the handy Passaggi Travel Agency (can help you with your air and rail needs with far fewer lines than inside the station—a real time-saver).

From the track level, go downstairs straight ahead to find train-ticket windows, Hertz/Avis/Europcar offices, and a great and huge supermarket/cafeteria that's hidden away (daily 07:30–24:00, after you descend stairs from track-level lobby, go right to the far end and enter Pellini bar, snake your way through the cafeteria to the SuperCentrale market, also called Supermercato Sigma). Just outside the front of the station is the taxi stand (figure on €8 to Duomo) and escalators, which take you down into the Metro system.

Warning: Locals call the change offices in the train station *ladri auttorizzati* (authorized thieves). Ignore them and their 10 percent commission. Use a cash machine (from track 14, enter the lobby—you'll find a Bancomat cash machine to your left and another across the hall) or exit the station straight ahead and cross the square to Banca Commerciale Italiana (Mon–Fri 08:30–13:30, 15:00–16:30).

For most quick visits, the giant city is one simple axis from the train station to the Duomo. To get downtown, go straight into the Metro (look for red *M*) and buy a €1 ticket (from the underground ticket office at the Metro stop—with all prices in English over the window, or from a machine—push green button). Follow signs for line 3 (yellow), direction "S. Donato," and in eight minutes you'll be facing the cathedral. To return to the station, take the yellow line 3, direction "Zara." After one trip on the Metro, you'll dream up other excuses to use it.

By Car: Driving is bad enough in Milan to make the €20/day fee for a downtown garage a blessing. If you're driving, do Milan (and Lake Como) before or after you rent. If you have a car, use the well-marked suburban *parcheggi* (parking lots), which offer affordable and safe parking at city-edge subway stations.

By Plane: Frequent shuttle trains and buses run between Milan's airports and the central train station. For details, see "Transportation Connections," below.

Helpful Hints

Theft Alert: Be on guard. Milan's thieves target tourists. At the station and around the Duomo, thieves roam dressed as beggars, sometimes in gangs of three too-young-to-arrest children. Watch out for ragged people carrying newspaper and cardboard. If you're ripped off, ask the police to fill out a report; it's necessary if you plan to file a claim with your insurance company (Polizia, Piazza San Sepolcro, behind Pinacoteca Ambrosiana, near Duomo, tel. 02-806-051). For lost or stolen credit cards or traveler's checks, contact Visa in Italy at 800-877-232; MasterCard at 800-68086;

or American Express at 800-864-046 (for credit cards) or 800-72000 (for traveler's checks).

U.S. Consulate: Monday–Friday 08:30–5:30, Via Principe Amedeo 2, tel. 02-290-351.

Scheduling: Monday is a terrible sightseeing day, since most museums are closed. August is rudely hot and muggy. Locals who can, vacate, leaving the city pretty quiet. Those visiting in August find many shops and restaurants closed, nightlife sleepy, and hotels empty and discounted. I've indicated which recommended hotels offer air-conditioning—worth the money for a summer visit.

Buying Train Tickets: You can buy train tickets and reserve *couchettes* for the station price without the station lines alongside the station or near the Duomo. At the station, head out the side (under the "Gran Bar" sign to the airport shuttle buses) and find the Passaggi Travel Agency. Near the Duomo, go to CIT (Mon–Fri 09:00–19:00, Sat 09:00–13:00, 14:00–18:00, closed Sun, must place order at least 30 min before closing, CC, in center of Galleria Vittorio Emanuele, tel. 02-8637-0228). American Express is also near the Duomo (Mon–Fri 09:00–12:30, 14:30–17:00, pay cash or use AmEx credit card, up Via Verdi from La Scala, Via Brera 3, tel. 02-7200-3694).

Bookstores: The handiest major bookstore is Libreria Feltrinelli, under the Galleria Vittorio Emanuele. The books in English—fiction and guidebooks—are at opposite ends of the store (daily 09:00–23:00, Aug 10:00–23:00, CC, store is huge but entrances are subtle: Either enter at Ricordi Mediastore next to McDonald's in center of Galleria and go downstairs, or enter through Autogrill restaurant on Piazza Duomo, also sells maps, tel. 02-8699-6903). The American Bookstore is at Via Camperio 16 (near Sforza Castle, tel. 02-878-920).

Internet Access: Major phone offices (e.g., at central train station and in the Galleria) have phone card–operated computers online which work well. The Leonardo da Vinci Science Museum has a wonderful room filled with computers for free Internet access (see "Sights," below).

Street Market: Milan's most popular flea market is Fiera di Senigallia, which spills down Viale D'Annunzio every Saturday from 08:30 to 17:00 (Metro: San Agostino, walk down Viale Papiniano—where market starts—to D'Annunzio, where it gets bigger); be wary of pickpockets at any street market.

Getting around Milan

Use Milan's great subway system. The clean, spacious, fast, and easy three-line Metro zips you anywhere you may want to go. Transit **tickets** are good for one subway ride followed by 75 minutes of bus or tram travel (€1 at newsstands, at machines in the station: Push green "rete urbana di Milano" button; note

Milan's Metro

that some machines sell only the €1 ticket—just feed in the money). Other options include: a *carnet* (€7.25 for 10 rides; you get 5 tickets that can be used twice—flip over to use a second time; these can be shared), the **24-hour pass** (€2.60, worthwhile if you take 4 rides; can usually cover a journey the following morning since it's a 24-hour rather than a 1-day pass), and a **48-hour pass** (€4.65). Transit info: toll-free tel. 800-016-857 (underground ATM Point office at Duomo stop, open Mon–Sat 08:00–19:45, www.atm.mi.it).

I've keyed sightseeing to the subway system. While most sights are within a few blocks of each other, Milan is an exhausting city for walking. You'll rarely wait more than five minutes for a subway train, and the well-marked trams can be useful (especially to the *Last Supper*, #24 from Cordusio).

Small groups go cheap and fast by **taxi** (metered, drop charge €3.10 and €0.70 per km, often easier to walk to a taxi stand than flag a cab down).

Tours of Milan

Bus Tours—Consider the three-hour **Autostradale** city bus tour with a live guide, which includes visits to the La Scala museum, Sforza Castle, and, best of all, Leonardo's *Last Supper* (€39, discounted to €33.50 with TI's Welcome Card, includes entry fees—a good value, CC, departs Tue–Sun at 09:30 year-round from Piazza Duomo at Via Marconi, a second daily departure at 15:00 offered April–Oct except Aug, book at TI on Piazza Duomo, tel. 02-7252-4301). The **Ciao Milano** vintage tram, which does a circle-eight trip around the city with a taped spiel, isn't worth €15.50 for the transportation, because Milan's sights cluster in the center (3/day, multilingual tour, you can hop on and off but what's the point, departs Piazza Duomo at roughly 11:00, 13:00, and 15:00, tel. 02-805-5323).

Walking Tour—The TI offers a walking tour at 10:00 Mondays only (the day the city bus tour doesn't run), covering the Duomo, Galleria Vittorio Emanuele, and the La Scala Museum (€13, 3 hrs, in English, runs year-round, book at TI, tel. 02-7252-4301).

Private Guide—Lorenza Scorti, a hardworking young woman who speaks English well, knows her local history and how to teach it. She can be booked well in advance (necessary in May and Sept) or with short notice (€100 for a 3-hour tour, evenings OK, €200 for a full day, price the same for individuals or groups, tel. 02-4801-7042, e-mail: lorenza.scorti@libero.it).

Sights—Milan's Cathedral and Museum

▲▲**Duomo**—The cathedral, the city's centerpiece, is the fourth-largest church in Europe—after the Vatican's, London's, and Sevilla's. (Get the most out of your visit by starting with the adjacent museum, located just outside the church, directly across from the south transept, and described below.)

Back when Europe was fragmented into countless tiny king-doms and dukedoms, the dukes of Milan wanted to impress their counterparts in Germany and France. Their goal was to earn Milan recognition and respect from both the Vatican and the kings and princes of northern Europe by building a massive, richly ornamented cathedral. Even after Renaissance domes were in vogue elsewhere in Italy, Milan's cathedral stayed on Gothic target. The dukes—thinking northerners would relate better to Gothic—loaded it with pointed arches and spires. For good measure, the cathedral was built not of stone but of marble—pink marble of Candoglia, from top to bottom—rafted from a quarry 70 kilometers away to a canal port at the cathedral.

Interior: At 160 meters long and 93 meters wide, with fifty-two 30-meter-tall sequoia pillars inside and more than 2,000 statues, the place seats 12,000 worshippers. If you do two laps, you've done your daily walk. Built from 1386 to 1810, this construc-tion project originated the Italian phrase meaning "never-ending": "like building a cathedral." It started Gothic (best seen in the apse behind the altar) and was finished under Napoleon. While this is a good example of the flamboyant, or "flamelike," overripe final stage

Milan

of Gothic, architectural harmony is not its forte (church free, €3 for 1-hr audioguide, daily 07:00–19:00, enforced dress code: No shorts or bare shoulders for anyone of any age, Metro: Duomo). For most, the treasury (*tesoro*) under the altar (10:00–12:00, 14:30–18:00) isn't worth the time or the fee (but if you're going to the Museo del Duomo, a combo ticket purchased here saves you €3.60). The west front (wonderful late in the day, with the sun low in the sky) was finished in the early 1800s under Napoleon.

Standing inside (at the back rear) notice two tiny lights: The little red one above the altar marks where a nail from the cross of Jesus is kept. This relic was brought to Milan by St. Helen (Emperor Constantine's mother) in the fourth century ,when Milan was the capital of the Western Roman Empire. It's on display for three days a year (in September). Now look high to the right and find a tiny pinhole of white light. This shines a 10-inch sunbeam onto the bronze line running across the floor here at noon (13:00 in summer) indicating where we are on the zodiac.

Wander deeper into the church up the right aisle. Notice the windows. Those on the right are 15th century (mosaics of colored glass connected by lead, more brilliant and expensive—afforded by wealthy families seeking the Church's favor). Those on the left are from the time of Napoleon (painted glass—dimmer, cheaper). Belly up to the bar facing the high altar. While the church is Gothic, the altar was made Baroque—the style of the Vatican in the 1570s (a Roman Catholic statement to counter the Protestant churches of the north which were mostly Gothic). Look up at the arches. Structurally, they are round (providing the necessary strength to hold up the massive roof), but visually, they're Gothic—filled in with decorative fittings to look pointed and fit the general style of the building. Now look to the rear up at the ceiling and see the fancy carving—nope, that's painted. It looks expensive, but, being painted, it was more affordable than carved stone.

Paleo-Christian Baptistery: In the rear of the church (buy tickets at the kiosk), climb down into the church which stood here long before the present one. Milan was an important center of the early Christian church. In Roman times, Mediolanum's street level was three meters (10 feet) below today's level. You'll see the scant remains of an eight-sided baptistery (where saints Augustine and Ambrogio were baptized) and a little church. Back then, since you couldn't enter the church until you were baptized—which didn't happen until the age of 18—churches had a little "holy zone" just outside for the unbaptized. This included a baptistery.

Cathedral Rooftop: This is the most memorable part of a Duomo visit. You'll wander through a fancy forest of spires with great views of the city, the square, and—on clear days—even the Swiss Alps. And, 100 meters above everything, overlooking everything: "La Madonnina." This four-meter-tall (13 feet) gilt Virgin Mary is a symbol of the city. In fact, locals refer to their town as "the city of la Madonnina." (Climb the stairs for €3; or ride the elevator for €4.65, €6.20 combo ticket—sold only at the elevator—includes elevator and Museo del Duomo; daily mid-Feb–mid-Nov 09:00–17:45, mid-Nov–mid-Feb 09:00–16:15, enter outside from the north transept; clue: in Europe old churches face roughly east.)

▲▲**Museo del Duomo**—To really understand Milan's cathedral, visit the cathedral museum first. While admission is €5, they encourage attendance by selling deeply discounted combo tickets at the church (treasury and museum for €4; elevator to rooftop and museum for €6.20—purchasable only at elevator). The museum is open daily (09:30–12:30, 15:00–18:00, located in Ducal Palace next to south side of Duomo, Piazza Duomo 14, Metro: Duomo, tel. 02-860-358). Here's a tour:

Room 1: After you buy your ticket, look up. Greeting you, as he did pilgrims 500 years ago, is God the Father, made of wood, wrapped in copper, and gilded. In 1425, this covered the keystone connecting the tallest arches directly above the high altar of the Duomo.

Room 2: Meet St. George. Among the oldest cathedral statues, it once stood on the highest spire and shows nearly 600 years of pollution and aging. Some think this is the face of Duke Visconti—the man who started the cathedral. The museum is filled with originals like this. On the right, finger a raw piece of *marmo di Candoglia*—the material of the church, spires, and statues. The duke's family gave the entire Candoglia quarry to the church for all the marble it would ever need.

Room 3: This room (which used to be the stable for the Duke's horses) shows how Gothic was an international style. Gothic craftsmen, engineers, and artists roamed across Europe to work on huge projects such as Milan's cathedral. The statues in this room show the national differences: Peter (near the door, showing off his big keys) is Italian. His expressive face is made even more expressive by his copper-button pupils. The smaller statues (which were models for the big ones) behind glass are German (showing inner strength) and French (most graceful). Pope Martino V, overlooking the room from his perch at the end (to the left as you enter), celebrated the first Mass in the cathedral in 1418 (look at "Papa Martino V" closely—we'll see a 20th-century rendition later in the tour). Study the 15th-century stained-glass windows close up. The grotesque gargoyles (originals), protruding over the door you entered, served two purposes: to scare away evil spirits and to spew rainwater away from the building. Leaving the room, you'll walk under a stylized sun—symbol of both Jesus and the Visconti family.

Room 5: A lit panel shows how the church was built in stages from 1386 to 1774. Building resumed whenever the community had the money.

Room 6: The brick backdrop reminds us what the church would have looked like if not for the dandy with the rolled-up contract in his hand. That's Galeazzo Sforza, making it official— the church now owns the marble quarry (and it makes money on it to this day). A photo of the contract is opposite.

Room 7: The crucifix (again, copper-sheet gilded with real gold nailed onto wood) is 900 years old. It hung in the church that stood here previously, as well as in today's cathedral. The two-sided miniature altar painting has been carried through the city on festival days since the 16th century.

Room 8: These statues, from around 1500, are originals. Copies now fill their niches in the church. St. Paul the Hermit (in front of the blue curtain) got close to God by living in the desert. While wearing only a simple robe, he's filled with inner richness. The intent is for pilgrims to stare into his eyes and feel at peace. (But I couldn't stop thinking of the Cowardly Lion.)

Room 9 (discreet WC behind wooden door): Five hundred years ago, this sumptuous Flanders-style tapestry hung from the high altar. Note the exquisite detail, down to the tears on Mary's cheeks. In the hall is more fancy fabric—this one has silk, silver, and gold embroidery. The tapestries were gifts from big shots hoping to gain favor with the Church.

Room 10: The sketchy red cartoons were designs for huge paintings (see photographs nearly opposite) that still hang between the columns (October through Christmas). Notice the inlaid 16th-century marble floor. The black (from Lake Como) and red (from Verona) marble is harder. Go ahead, wear down the white a little more.

Room 12: Enter room 12 and turn around to see the artwork lining the wall. The terra-cotta was clay—worked in a creative frenzy and then baked. Study the quick design below the careful marble originals (flanking the doorway you entered). You will notice what 300 years of acidic pigeon droppings do to marble.

The statues all around this room (c. 1600) were sculpted 100 years later than the statues in room 8, and therefore are more expressive.

Find the painting of Saint Carlo Borromeo in the black robe, to your right. The 16th-century saint carries a cross showing the holy nail (the church's top relic) as he leads the plague out of Milan. In the background, see the 13th-century original church's facade with today's church—before spires—behind it.

Start circling the room clockwise. Crespi's monochrome painting of the *Creation of Eve* (*Creazione di Eva*) came first (1628). From that the terra-cotta model was made (1629), and this served as the model for the marble statue that still stands above the center door on the church's west portal (1643). Three other sets line the wall.

Opposite *Eve*, see the swirling *Dance of Angels* and its terra-cotta model. This is the original, which decorated the ceiling over the door.

Room 20: If the vestments are still on loan from the Treasury, you'll find them here, off room 12. Showing off rich red robes with lavish gold brocade, it's like a priestly fashion show from the 16th through 20th centuries.

Room 13: Standing like a Picasso is the original (1772) iron frame for the statue of the Virgin Mary that still crowns the Cathedral's tallest spire. In 1967, a steel replacement was made for the 33 pieces of gilded copper bolted to the frame. The carved wood face of Mary (in the corner) is the original mold for Mary's cathedral-crowning copper face.

Room 15: At the modern doors with the thin orange-white marble windows, turn right into a tunnel-like hall. Along the left wall, you'll see a painting of the earlier church, competition designs proposing possible facades for the cathedral, and a photo of the actual west portal. Along the right, the evolution of the church and the Ducal Palace (which you're in now).

Room 16: This huge wooden model of the cathedral was the actual model—necessary in that pre-computer age—used in the 16th century by the architects and engineers to build the church. The more recent facade wasn't used. Climb around the back to see the spire-filled rooftop, which you'll explore later if you like.

Room 17: Look around this room. The art seems a mixture of old and new, but it's all from the 20th century. Notice the vibrant Pope Martin V popping out of the wall (bronze panel to the left as you enter; artist Lucio Fontana). To see the gigantic leap that art has made over the centuries, compare this with the static statue of the same pope in room 3. On the opposite wall, see Fontana's *Ascension of Mary* (*Mary Assunta*). She's making a jump shot into heaven. Her veil looks like flowing hair, like the wings of an angel. Without regret, she soars above the grief of the world.

The last rooms are technical, showing the recent restoration work and the stabilization and reinforcement of the main pylons. To exit, retrace your steps.

Sights—Milan

Compared to Rome and Florence, Milan's art is mediocre, but the city does have unique and noteworthy sights. To maximize your time, use the Metro and note which places stay open through the siesta. I've listed sights in a logical geographical order.

▲**Piazza Duomo**—Milan's main square is a classic European scene and a popular local gathering point. Professionals scurry, label-conscious kids loiter, young thieves peruse. For that creepy-crawly, pigeons-all-over-you experience, buy a bag of seed.

Standing in the square, you're surrounded by history. The statue is of Victor Emanuel II, first king of Italy. He's looking at the grand Galleria named for him. Stand midway between the statue and the Galleria, which was a gift from the people to their king. The words above the entrance read: To Victor Emanuel II from the people of Milan.

Behind the statue (opposite the cathedral) is the center of medieval Milan—Piazza Mercanti. The medieval city hall (look for its red brick arches), dating from 1220, marked the center of town back when the entire city stood within its immense fortified walls. The merchant's square is a strangely peaceful place today, with a fine smattering of old-time Milano architecture.

Opposite the Galleria are two fascist towers (one houses the TI). Mussolini made grandiose speeches from these balconies. You can still see relief panels illustrating the power of the fascist state. Between these towers and the cathedral (set back a bit) is the palace of Maria Theresa from the late 1700s—when Milan was ruled by the Austrian Hapsburgs.

The Duomo Center is a modern mall with a mega-music store, a one-hour photo service, a decent Spizzico pizzeria, and the handy Ciao cafeteria. For a fine view of the Duomo and the piazza, climb the steps (unless strewn with litter and derelicts) to the balcony above the TI. Behind the Duomo is a vibrant, pedestrian shopping zone along Vittorio Emanuele II.

▲▲**Galleria Vittorio Emanuele**—Milan is symbolized by its great four-story, glass-domed arcade on the cathedral square. Here you can turn an expensive cup of coffee into a good value with Europe's best people-watching (or enjoy the same view for peanuts from the strategically placed McDonald's). Bar Zucca (at the entry), with an interior typical of the 1920s, is the birthplace of Campari. (If you try one, you'll pay €3.50 standing or €8 seated.)

Wander around the gallery. Its art is a reminder that the gallery was a gift from the people to the king to celebrate the establishment of Italy as an independent country. Stand under the central dome and enjoy the patriotic mosaics symbolizing the four major continents. The mosaic floor is also patriotic. The white cross in the center is a symbol of the king. The she-wolf with Romulus and Remus (on the south side facing Rome) honors the city, which since 1870 has been the national capital. On the west side (facing Torino, the provisional capital of Italy from 1861–1865), you'll find that city's symbol: a torino (little bull). For good luck, locals step on his irresistible little testicles. Two local girls explained to me that it works better if you spin. Find the poor little bull and just observe for a few minutes . . . it's a cute scene. With so much spinning, the mosaic is replaced every two years.

Also under the Galleria dome is the CIT travel agency (sells train tickets and *couchettes*; see "Helpful Hints," above) and a cluster of SIP public phone booths (Internet access).

Piazza delle Scala—This smart little traffic-free square, out the back between the Galleria and the Opera House, is dominated by a statue of Leonardo da Vinci. The statue (from 1870) is a reminder that Leonardo spent many years in Milan working for the Sforza family (Milan's answer to the Medici). Under the great Renaissance genius stand four of his greatest "Leonardeschi." (He apprenticed a sizable group of followers.) The reliefs show his various contributions—painter, architect, and engineer. Leonardo, wearing his hydroengineer hat, designed Milan's canal system complete with locks. (Until the 1920s, Milan was one of Italy's major ports, with canals connecting it to the Po River and Lake Maggiore.)

▲▲**La Scala Opera House and Museum**—From the Galleria, you'll see a statue of Leonardo. He's looking at a plain but famous neoclassical building, possibly the world's most prestigious opera house, Milan's Teatrale alla Scala. La Scala opened in 1778 with an opera by Antonio Salieri (of *Amadeus* fame). Milan's famous Opera House and its adjacent museum are closed while the venerable hall is renovated, and will reopen in September 2004.

Until then, opera buffs can see the museum's extensive collection elsewhere (probably at the Institute of San Carlo next to Santa Maria della Grazie, which houses Leonardo's *Last Supper*). The collection features things that mean absolutely nothing to the MTV crowd: Verdi's top hat, Rossini's eyeglasses, Toscanini's baton, Fettuccini's pesto, and original scores, busts, portraits, and death masks of great composers and musicians (check with the TI for hours and location).

Opera: While La Scala is being renovated, the show will go on (likely at the Theater Arcimbaldi, far from the center). Schedules vary, but the opera season is December to July, and ballet and classical concerts are held from September to November. No performances are held in August (from Sept–July, box office open daily 12:00–18:00, CC, tel. 02-7200-3744—live, tel. 02-860-775—automated booking, or book online at La Scala's fine Web site: www.teatroallascala.org, show time usually 20:00). Tickets generally go on sale two months before a performance. The expensive seats sell out quickly. At noon on the day of the show, any remaining seats (usually in the affordable, sky-high gallery) are sold at a 50 percent discount at the box office and on the Internet (Web sales cease 1 hour before show time). Due to safety regulations, standing-room spots are no longer available.

▲**Via Speronari**—A block off Piazza Duomo, this is one of Milan's oldest streets and the most charming street in the old center. Via Speronari—named for the spurs once made and sold here—is worth a wander. Streets around here recall their medieval crafts: Speronari—spurs, Spadari—swords, Armorari—armor. The weaponry made on these streets was high fashion among Europe's warrior class . . . like having an Armani dagger. While right in the city center, the neighborhood feels vital. That's because it's also a residential street. Banks of doorbells indicate that families live above the shops. Start at the recommended Hotel Speronari, formerly a dorm for monks from the church across the street. The classy Vino Vino wine shop next door welcomes tasters (€2/glass—today's specials are posted at the door, Tue–Sat 09:00–19:30, closed Sun–Mon). The sign next door— "L'Ortolan Pusae Vecc de Milan"—brags in the old Milanese language that this is the oldest fruit and veggie store in the city. The Princip bakery next door is understandably popular. Its brioches are rarely more than a few minutes old. In the back, a busy *tavola calda* serves locals a quick, fresh, and tasty hot meal (around €4 per plate, 12:00–14:00 only, pay at cashier first).

Where Via Speronari hits Via Torino, go 20 meters to the left to find the **Church of Santa Maria presso San Satiro** hiding behind its Baroque facade (daily 07:30–11:30, 15:30–18:00). It was the scene of a temper tantrum in 1242, when a losing gambler vented his anger by hitting the baby Jesus in the

Madonna-and-Child altarpiece. Blood "miraculously" spurted out, and the beautiful little church has been on the pilgrimage trail ever since. While I've never seen any blood, I'd swear I've seen a 3-D background behind the basically flat altar (a trompe l'oeil illusion by Bramante). This church—squeezed between the earlier church of San Satiro and a street—had no room for a real apse, so, with the help of math, the Renaissance architect Bramante made what looks like an apse. In the north transept, you'll find that original ninth-century church of San Satiro (brother of St. Ambrogio, patron saint of Milan). This tiny church—with surviving bits of Byzantine fresco—predated the rest (note the name means Church of St. Mary at St. Satiro). From this chapel, look back at the main altar to see Bramante's 3-D work collapsed. On the opposite side (near entry)—with dimensions mirroring this old chapel—an eight-sided baptistery by Bramante from the 1480s shows the mathematically-based values of the Renaissance. If you have a prayer in need of an extra boost, pop a coin into the box and "light" an electric candle.

▲▲**World-Class Window-Shopping**—The "Quadrilateral," the elegant, high-fashion shopping area around Via Montenapoleone, is worth a wander (except in Aug, when most shops close). In this land where fur is still fun, the people-watching is as entertaining as the window-shopping. Notice also the exclusive penthouse apartments with roof gardens high above the scene. Via Montenapoleone and the pedestrianized Via Spiga are the best streets. From La Scala, walk up Via Manzoni to the Metro stop at Montenapoleone, browse down Montenapoleone to Piazza San Babila, then (for less expensive shopping thrills) walk down the pedestrians-only Corso Vittorio Emanuele II to the Duomo. Rinascente is a Nordstrom-type department store with reasonable prices and a good selection of toys (Mon–Sat 09:00–22:00, Sun 10:00–21:00, faces north side of Duomo on Piazza Duomo).

▲**Brera Art Gallery**—Milan's top collection of paintings (Italian, 14th–20th centuries) is world class, but it can't top Rome's or Florence's. Established in 1809 to house Napoleon's looted art, it fills the first floor above an art college. On the ground level, wander past the nude *Napoleon* (by Canova) in the courtyard and straight through the art school to a great, cheap cappuccino machine (with all the lingo).

Back in the courtyard, climb the stairway following signs to "Pinacoteca" (€5, €6.20 if there's an exhibition, Tue–Sun 08:30–19:15, maybe June–Sept Sat until 23:00, closed Mon, last entry 45 min before closing, shorter hours Nov–April, Via Brera 28, Metro: Lanza, tel. 02-722-631).

The gallery's highlights include works by Gentile da Fabriano (room IV), the Bellini brothers and Mantegna (his textbook example of feet-first foreshortening, *The Dead Christ*, room VI), Crivelli (for someone new, in room XXI), Raphael (*Wedding of the Madonna*, room XXIV), and Michelangelo Merisi (a.k.a. Caravaggio, *Supper at Emmaus*, room XXIX). Since there are no English descriptions, consider the €3.60 audioguide.

▲**Risorgimento Museum**—With a quick 30-minute swing through this quiet, one-floor, and thoughtfully described-in-English museum, you'll learn the interesting story of Italy's rocky road to unity: from Napoleon (1796) to the victory in Rome (1870). It's just around the block from the Brera Gallery at Via Borgonuovo 23 (free, Tue–Sun 09:00–13:00, 14:00–18:00, closed Mon, Metro: Montenapoleone).

Poldi Pezzoli Museum—This classy house of art features top Italian paintings of the 15th through the 18th centuries, old weaponry, and lots of interesting decorative arts, such as a roomful of old sundials and compasses (€5, or €7.25 combo ticket with Bagatti Valsecchi Museum, Tue–Sun 10:00–18:00, closed Mon, not a word of English, Via Manzoni 12, Metro: Montenapoleone, tel. 02-796-334).

Bagatti Valsecchi Museum—This unique 19th-century collection of Italian Renaissance furnishings was assembled by two aristocratic brothers who spent a wad turning their home into a Renaissance mansion (€5, half price on Wed, Tue–Sun 13:00–17:45, closed Mon, good English descriptions, Via Santo Spirito 10, Metro: Montenapoleone).

▲**Sforza Castle (Castello Sforzesco)**—The castle of Milan tells the story of the city in brick. Built in the late 1300s as a military fortress, it guarded the gate to the city wall (see the diagram on the flip side of the entry sign) and defended the city from enemies "within and without." It was beefed up by the Sforza Duke in 1450 in anticipation of a Venetian attack. Later, it was the Renaissance palace of the Sforza family and even housed their in-house genius, Leonardo. During the centuries of foreign rule (16th to 19th), it was a barracks for occupying soldiers. Today, it houses several museums. This immense, much-bombed-and-rebuilt brick fortress—exhausting at first sight—can only be described as heavy. But its courtyard has a great lawn for picnics and siestas, and its free museum is filled with interesting medieval armor, furniture, early Lombard art, an Egyptian collection, and, most important, Michelangelo's unfinished *Rondanini Pietà*. Michelangelo died while still working on this piece, which hints at the elongation of the Mannerist style that would follow. This is a rare opportunity to enjoy a Michelangelo with no crowds (free, Tue–Sun 09:00–17:30, closed Mon, study posted diagram at castle entrance to find the museum—marked #12 on diagram, on the right at the beginning of second courtyard, photos OK without flash, English info fliers throughout, Metro: Cairoli,

tel. 02-8846-3701). A big park—with a couple of cheap eateries—
sprawls behind the fortress.

▲**Leonardo da Vinci's** *Last Supper* **(***Cenacolo***)**—You must have
a reservation to see this Renaissance masterpiece in the refectory
of the church of Santa Maria delle Grazie. Because of Leonardo's
experimental use of oil rather than the normal fresco technique,
deterioration began within six years of its completion. The church
was bombed in World War II, but—miraculously, it seems—the
wall holding the *Last Supper* remained standing. The 21-year
restoration project (completed in 1999) peeled 500 years of touch-
ups away, leaving a faint but vibrant scene. In a big, vacant, whitewashed room, you'll see faded pastels and not a crisp edge. The
feet under the table look like negatives. But the composition is
dreamy—Leonardo captures the psychological drama as the Lord
says, "One of you will betray me," and the apostles huddle in
stressed-out groups of three, wondering, "Lord, is it I?" Some
are scandalized. Others want more information. Simon (on the far
right) gestures as if to ask a question that has no answer. It's a very
agitated atmosphere, and only Judas (fourth from left and the only
one with his face in shadow)—clutching his 30 pieces of silver and
looking pretty guilty—is not shocked.

The circle means life and harmony to Leonardo. Deep into
a study of how life emanates in circles—like ripples on a pool hit by
a pebble—Leonardo positions the 13 characters in a semicircle. Jesus
is in the center, from whence the spiritual force of God emanates.

The building is an architectural extension of the building.
The disciples form an apse, with Jesus the altar—in keeping with the
Eucharist. Jesus anticipates his sacrifice—his face sad, all-knowing,
and accepting. His feet even foreshadowed his crucifixion. Had the
door, which was cut out in 1652, not been added, you'd see how
Leonardo placed Jesus' feet atop each other, ready for the nail.

The room was a refectory or dining room for the Dominican
friars. Traditionally, they'd gather here to eat with a last supper
scene on one wall facing a crucifixion scene on the opposite wall.
The perspective is mathematically correct. In fact, restorers found
a tiny nail hole in Jesus' right ear, which anchored the strings
Leonardo used to establish these lines. The table is cheated out to
show the meal. Notice the exquisite lighting. The walls are lined
with tapestries (as they would have been) and the one on the right is
brighter—to fit the actual lighting in the refectory (with windows
on the left). With the extremely natural effect of the light and the
drama of the faces, Leonardo created an effective masterpiece.

Reservations are mandatory. To minimize the humidity problem—even though the damage has already been done—25 tourists
are allowed in every 15 minutes for just 15 minutes. Prior to your
appointment time, you wait in several rooms, while doors close
behind you and open up slowly in front of you. The information

posted on Leonardo is mainly in Italian. For a reservation, call 028-942-1146 (or from the U.S., call 011-39-028-942-1146) a minimum of three days in advance for a weekday visit and at least a week ahead for a weekend visit. It's a simple two-minute process, and you'll hang up with an appointed entry time and a number. Long-range planners can book up to three or four months in advance (€6.20 plus €1 reservation fee, cash only). Hours of booking office: Mon–Fri 09:00–18:00, Sat 09:00–14:00, closed Sun.

Hours of *Last Supper*: Tue–Sun 08:15–18:45 (last visit), July–Sept also open Sat until 21:45 (last visit), always closed Mon. You'll be asked to show up 30 minutes before your scheduled time (15 min should be enough, but if you're a minute late, you get no supper). Consider the €2.60 15-minute audioguide (€4.15 with 2 headphones). You might want to listen to it in the waiting room while studying the reproduction of the actual *Last Supper* on that wall until you're let in.

To get to Santa Maria delle Grazie, you can either take the Metro to Cadorna (plus a 5-minute walk), or, even better, hop on tram #24 from Via Mazzini (catch it in front of Rolex store at intersection of Via Dogana and Via Mazzini, just off Piazza Duomo) which drops you off in front of the church. The Museum of Science is two blocks away, and the temporary La Scala Opera museum will likely be across the street in 2002.

People who show up without a reservation can sometimes get in (even if "Sold Out" sign is posted). You'll be told that entry is by reservation only—but if fewer than 25 people show up for a particular time slot, you can get lucky. Still, for guaranteed entry, it's best to call ahead. Note that the city bus tour (see "Tours of Milan," above) includes entry to *Last Supper*.

▲**National Leonardo da Vinci Science and Technology Museum (Museo Nazionale della Scienza e Tecnica)**—The spirit of Leonardo lives here. Most tourists visit for the hall of Leonardo designs illustrated in wooden models, but Leonardo's mind is just as easy to appreciate by paging through a coffee-table edition of his notebooks in any bookstore. The rest of this immense collection of industrial cleverness is fascinating, with trains, radios, old musical instruments, computers, batteries, telephones, chunks of the first transatlantic cable, and on and on. Some of the best exhibits (such as the Marconi radios) branch off the Leonardo hall (€6.20, Tue–Fri 09:30–16:50, Sat–Sun 09:30–18:30, closed Mon, Via San Vittore 21, bus #50 from Duomo, or Metro: San Ambrogio, tel. 02-485-551). Complain politely about the lack of English descriptions. There's a great Internet access room off the Leonardo hall (free).

Pinacoteca Ambrosiana—Newly reopened after seven years of work, this museum forgot that non-Italians may visit. The only English words are in the price list at the turnstile—ask if there are any plans to add English descriptions to the art. While a prestigious collection, there are few recognizable names for most tourists except for the impressive drawing Raphael used as a design for his *School of Athens* in the Vatican (€7.25, small English guidebook for €6.20 covers museum's highlights, Tue–Sun 10:00–17:30, last ticket sold at 16:30, closed Mon, a couple of blocks from Piazza Duomo at Piazza Pio XI, tel. 02-864-105).

Nightlife—For evening action, check out the arty, student-oriented Brera area in the old center and Milan's formerly bohemian, now gentrified "Little Venice," the Navigli neighborhood. Specifics change so quickly that it's best to rely on the entertainment information in periodicals from the TI.

Soccer—The Milanese claim their soccer team is the best in Europe. For a dose of Europe's soccer mania (which many believe provides a necessary testosterone vent to keep Europe out of a third big war), catch a match in Milan. Games are held in the 85,000-seat Meazza stadium most Sunday afternoons, September through June (tickets €10–40, sold at several downtown outlets, tel. 02-4870-7123, Metro: Lotto—no kidding, or tram #24 from Duomo directly to stadium—last stop).

Sleeping in Milan
(€1.10 = about $1, country code: 39)

Sleep Code: **S** = Single, **D** = Double/Twin, **T** = Triple, **Q** = Quad, **b** = bathroom, **s** = shower only, **CC** = Credit Cards accepted, **no CC** = Credit Cards not accepted, **SE** = Speaks English, **NSE** = No English.

I have tried to minimize traffic noise problems in my listings. All are within a few minutes' walk of Milan's subway system. With Milan's fine Metro, you can get anywhere in town in a flash. Anytime in April, September, October, and November, the city can be completely jammed by conventions, and hotel prices increase by €5 to €10. Summer is usually wide open, though many hotels close in August for vacation. Hotels cater more to business travelers than to tourists. Everyone speaks at least some English.

Sleeping near the Duomo

The Duomo area is thick with people-watching, reasonable eateries, and the major sightseeing attractions. From the central train station to the Duomo, it's just four stops on a direct Metro line (yellow line 3, direction "S. Donato") to Metro: Duomo. There is no self-service laundry in the center.

Hotel Speronari is perfectly located, safe, and fairly quiet, with 32 bright, clean rooms on a great pedestrian street full of delis and food shops. Enjoy a free cappuccino upon arrival. Note that this is a one-star hotel. If you want an elevator, air-conditioning, and more comfort, please choose any of the pricier hotels listed below (S-€44, Ss-€52, D-€68, Db-€88, T-€88, Tb-€119, Qb-€135, these discounted prices promised through 2002 with this book—mention it when you reserve, CC but €3 off per person per night if you pay cash, lots of stairs, no breakfast, ceiling fans, 200 meters off Piazza Duomo, Via Speronari 4, 20123 Milano, tel. 02-8646-1125, fax 02-7200-3178, e-mail: hotelsperonari@inwind.it, run by the friendly Isoni family: father Paolo and John Paolo, Maurizio, Carla, and Fara). For breakfast, I like the Chicco D'Oro Bar across the intersection (from 07:00, closed Sun), or grab a fresh brioche at the Princip bakery next door to have with your coffee in the Speronari lobby. If you're flying out of Malpensa airport, they can get you there via car much cheaper than a taxi—which charges €80 (2 people-€47, 3 people-€57, 4 people-€68, request 1 day in advance).

Hotel Grand Duca di York is a real hotel with 33 pleasant rooms and lavish public spaces, oddly stuck in the middle of banks and big-city starkness three blocks southwest of Piazza Duomo (Sb-€98, Db-€145, Tb-€170, includes breakfast, CC, air-con, elevator, closed Aug, near Metro stops: Piazza Cordusio or Duomo, Via Moneta 1, 20123 Milano, tel. 02-874-863, fax 02-869-0344, SE).

Hotel Gritti, facing a peaceful square just off Via Torino, is a bright, classy, professionally run three-star hotel that comes with 48 comfortable rooms and a big, sleepy dog, Boris. Run by a jolly trio of English-speaking gentlemen (Mario, Bruno, and Evandro), Hotel Gritti feels like home in a hurry (Sb-€93, Db-€132, Tb-€183, includes big breakfast, same price all seasons, open year-round, family deals, CC but 10 percent off with cash, elevator, air-con, some smoky rooms, 2 blocks southwest of Piazza Duomo, Piazza S. Maria Beltrade 4, 20123 Milano, tel. 02-801-056, fax 02-8901-0999, www.hotelgritti.com, e-mail: hotel.gritti@iol.it).

Hotel Santa Marta is a shiny little hotel on a small street with 15 fresh, tranquil, and spacious rooms (Db-€129 most of year but €165 during conventions and as low as €98, includes breakfast, CC, air-con, elevator, closed Aug, Via Santa Marta 4, 20123 Milano, tel. 02-804-567, fax 02-8645-2661, e-mail: htls.marta@tiscalinet.it).

Hotel Nuovo, with 36 fine, smallish rooms and a lukewarm reception, is central on a noisy square east of the Duomo near a pedestrian street (S-€34, D-€52, Db-€83–98, Tb-€108–129, CC, no breakfast, some air-con, request third floor for less noise, no public space, Piazza Beccaria 6, tel. 02-8646-4444, fax 02-7200-1752).

Splurge: The **Hotel Spadari** is for art-lovers. Designed by the Milanese artist Art Deco, the 39 rooms have billowing drapes, big paintings, and designer doors. It's in the midst of the three Peck eateries (see below), two blocks from the Duomo (standard

Milan's Center

1. ELEVATOR TO ROOF
2. STAIRS TO ROOF
3. CIT TRAVEL AGENCY, TEL. CENTER, McD's & TAURUS
4. PINACOTECA AMBROSIANA
5. HOTEL SPERONARI
6. LONDON HOTEL
7. HOTEL GIULIO CESARE
8. HOTEL GRAND DUCA DI YORK
9. HOTEL SANTA MARTA
10. HOTEL GRITTI
11. ANTICA LOCANDA MERCANTI
12. HOTEL STAR
13. HOTEL NUOVO
14. LA RINASCENTE BISTROT AND BRUNCH
15. ODEON GELATERIA
16. PECK GROCERY & HOTEL SPADARI
17. PECK ROSTICCERIA
18. PIZZERIA DOLLARO
19. CIAO RISTORANTE (2 LOCATIONS)
20. PIZZERIA CALAFURIA UNIONE
21. REST. FAMILIARE CIMBRACCOLA
22. TRATTORIA MILANESE

M - METRO STN.

200 YARDS
200 METERS

DCH

Db-€217–269, no need for pricier suites, includes breakfast, CC, Via Spadari 11, tel. 02-7200-2371, fax 02-861-184, www .spadarihotel.com, e-mail: spadari@tin.it).

Sleeping between La Scala and Sforza Castle

London Hotel, a 30-room hotel with all the comforts, is warmly run by the friendly Gambino family (S-€78, Sb-€88, D-€109, Db-€134, T-€129, Tb-€171, breakfast-€7.75, cheaper in July and closed Aug, CC but 10 percent off with cash except during special events, elevator, TVs, phones, air-con, near Metro: Cairoli at Via Rovello 3, on relatively quiet side street, 20121 Milano, tel. 02-7202-0166, fax 02-805-7037, www.traveleurope.it /hotellondon.htm, e-mail: hotel.london@traveleurope.it, Tanya and Licia SE).

Hotel Giulio Cesare, across the street from London Hotel, is bigger, basic, and impersonal but quiet and comfortable (Sb-€88, Db-€140, 10 percent discount with this book, CC, air-con, Via Rovello 10, 20121 Milano, tel. 02-7200-3915, fax 02-7200-2179, www.hotelgiuliocesare.com).

Antica Locanda dei Mercanti feels like a library in heaven, well-located and seriously quiet (no TVs, lots of books). It lacks public spaces and a breakfast area but comes with fresh flowers in each of its 10 rooms (standard Db-€129, master Db-€155, Db with air-con and terrace-€207, optional €7.75 breakfast served in room, CC, fans, elevator, no young children, no sign—only a name on doorbell at their address—Via San Tomaso 6, second floor, Metro: Cordusio, tel. 02-805-4080, fax 02-805-4090, www.locanda.it, e-mail: locanda@locanda.it).

Hotel Star is a comfortable, modern 30-room place with fancy, modern plumbing and, more important, helpful staff (Sb-€108, Db-€155, includes big breakfast, CC, closed Aug, air-con, fridge, Via dei Bossi 5, tel. 02-801-501, fax 02-861-787, www.starhotel.it, e-mail: information@starhotel.it).

Sleeping near the Train Station

If you like to drop your bag near the station, this is a handy, if dreary, area. The neighborhood between the train station and Corso Buenos Aires, in spite of its shady characters in the park and its 55-year-old prostitutes after dark, is reasonably safe. Many soulless business hotels have desperately discounted prices for those who drop in during slow times. Just walk down Via Scarlatti (leave the station's upper hall—with your back to the tracks—to the left). Decent options include **"The Best" Hotel** (19 rooms, Sb-€75, Db-€110, includes breakfast, CC, Via B. Marcello 83, 5-minute walk from station, tel. 02-2940-4757, e-mail: thebesthotel@tiscalinet.it), **Hotel Valley** (small, dark, inexpensive, Via Soperga 19, tel. 02-669-2777), **Hotel Virgilio** (inexpensive business hotel, Via P.L. da Palestrina 30, tel. 02-669-1337), and **Hotel Andreola Central** (4-star business hotel with occasional door-breaker prices, Via Scarlatti 24, tel. 02-670-9141).

Eating in Milan

This is a fast-food city, but fast food in a fashion capital isn't a burger and fries. The bars, delis, *rosticcerie*, and self-service cafeterias cater to people with plenty of taste and more money than time. You'll find delightful eateries all over town (but many close in Aug for vacation).

I found the price between basic and classy restaurants was negligible (e.g., pastas €7–10, *secondi* €8–12, cover €1–2), so it is worth springing for the places giving the best experience. To eat mediocre food on a famous street with great people-watching, choose an eatery on the pedestrians-only Via Mercanti or Via Dante. To eat with students in trendy little trattorias, explore the Brera neighborhood. To eat well near the Duomo, consider the recommended places below. Many restaurants close for much of August.

Locals like to precede a lunch or dinner with an aperitif (Campari made its debut in Milan). Bars fill their counters with inviting baskets of munchies, which are served free with these drinks. A cheap drink (if you're either likable or discreet) can become a light meal.

Breakfast is a bad value in hotels and fun in bars. It's OK to quasi-picnic. Bring in a banana (or whatever) and order a toasted ham-and-cheese *panino* (*calda* = hot/toasted) or croissant with your cappuccino.

Eating Classy near the Duomo

Trattoria Milanese, a classy family-run place, is a €30 splurge. It has an enthusiastic and local clientele (the restaurant didn't even bother to get a phone until 1988). Expect a Milanese ambience and quality traditional cuisine (Wed–Mon 12:30–15:00, 19:30–23:00, closed Tue and mid-July–Aug, CC, air-con, Via Santa Marta 11, 5-minute walk from Duomo near Pinacoteca Ambrosiana, tel. 02-8645-1991).

Ristorante Bruno serves Tuscan cuisine with dressy waiters, hearty food, inexpensive desserts, and the best antipasto buffet I've seen (a plate full of Tuscan specialties for €7). You can eat inside or on the sidewalk under Fascist columns (Sun–Fri 12:00–15:00, 19:00–22:45, closed Sat, moderate prices, CC, air-con, Via M. Gonzaga 6, reservations wise, tel. 02-804-364).

Ristorante Al Mercante is *the* place to dine elegantly inside or outside under historic arches in a peaceful square a block from the cathedral. You'll pay extra for the location, but the food is very good (moderately expensive, €16 *secondi*, 12:00–14:30,

19:00–22:30, closed Sun, CC, near Piazza Cordusio at Piazza Mercanti 17, tel. 02-805-2198).

Pizzeria Ristorante al 50 da Geggio is a bustling little favorite packed with locals eating Tuscan food under fans (Wed–Mon 12:00–14:30, 19:00–23:00, closed Tue and Aug, moderate prices, good daily specials, Via Torino 50, tel. 02-8645-2244).

The big department store **La Rinascente,** alongside the Duomo, has three rooftop eateries, each with a terrace overlooking the ornate top of the cathedral (terrace dining only May–Sept): **Bistrot** is a dressy restaurant serving modern Mediterranean cuisine (5-course Tasting Menu-€62, CC, closed Sun, tel. 02-877120). The **Brunch** is a cafeteria with a much simpler and less expensive menu (Mon–Sat 12:00–22:00, closed Sun). Anyone can pop up to the **bar** for a look over at the cathedral. While you can go through the department store, a side entrance (on the Galleria Emanuele side) has a direct elevator.

Eating Simple near the Duomo

Ristorante Pizzeria Calafuria Unione serves tasty €6 pizzas in a nonsmoking room (Mon–Sat 11:00–15:00, 19:00–01:00, closed Sun and Aug, CC, near where Via Falcone hits Via dell' Unione at Via dell' Unione 8, tel. 02-866-103). **Ristorante/Pizzeria Al Dollaro** is a mod, happy place with well-fed locals (Mon–Sat 12:00–15:00, 19:00–23:00, closed Sun and Aug, air-con, smoke-free section, 4 blocks south of Duomo at Via Paolo da Cannobio 11, tel. 02-869-2432).

Latteria Cucina Vegetariana is a very local little hole-in-the-wall serving a good vegetarian Italian lunch. This busy joint is actually a tiny grocery store overrun with dining tables, where local workers enjoy soup, salads, and pasta dishes (€5–8 meals, Mon–Sat 11:30–16:30, closed Sun, just off Via Torino at Via dell' Unione 6, tel. 02-874401, Giorgio Notari).

Pastarito Pizzarito is a pasta-and-pizza chain with a wonderful formula. In a bright atmosphere under literally walls of pasta, you can choose from 10 fresh pastas and lots of sauces to create a huge dish (€4.50–9.50); splitting is welcome. Pizzas go €5 to €8 (daily 12:00–24:00, CC, air-con, 4 blocks from Duomo, a block behind Opera House at Via Verdi 6, tel. 02-862-210).

Primafila, tucked alongside Galleria Vittorio Emanuele, is busy pleasing tourists and locals alike with a varied selection of pizza, pasta, and grilled food, plus a good antipasti buffet (Thu–Tue 11:00–15:00, 19:00–01:00, closed Wed, indoor seating extends into street, CC, facing Galleria, it's on first street to the right, past Burger King, Via Ugo Foscolo 1, tel. 02-862-020).

Ciao, a self-service cafeteria, offers a low-stress, affordable meal on Piazza Duomo (daily 11:30–15:00, 18:30–23:00, next to TI, on second floor, view tables from top "terrace" floor, easy public WC). Fast-food cheapskates enjoy the best people-watching in Milan inside the Galleria at **McDonald's** (salad/pasta plate and tall orange juice for €5).

Floodlit Mary gazes down from the top of the Duomo on the **Odeon Gelateria** for good reason (next to McDonald's on Piazza Duomo, facing the Duomo, open nightly until 01:00).

Picnics near the Duomo

For a fun adventure, assemble an elegant dinner **picnic** by hitting the colorful deli, cheese, and produce shops on Via Speronari. The Princip bakery is mobbed with locals vying for focaccia, olive breadsticks, and luscious pastry. At the small bar in the back, you get free, fresh munchies with your drink (Mon–Sat 07:00–20:00, on Via Spernari, off Via Torino, a block southwest of Piazza Duomo).

Peck is an aristocratic deli with a fancy coffee/pastry shop upstairs, a gourmet grocery on the main level, and an *enoteca* wine cellar in the basement (Mon 15:00–19:30, Tue–Sat 08:45–19:30, closed Sun, Via Spadari 9). The nearby Peck *rosticceria* serves fancy food to go for a superb picnic dinner in your hotel. It's delectable, beautiful, sold by weight (order by the *etto*—100-gram unit— about a quarter pound) and not cheap (try the risotto, Tue–Fri 08:45–14:30, 16:00–19:30, Sat 08:00–13:15, 15:45–19:30, Sun 08:00–13:00, closed Mon, nearby at Via C. Cantu, off Via Orefici).

Supermarket: Standa Superfresco is within a few blocks of the Duomo (Mon–Sat 08:30–20:00, small deli on ground level, big supermarket in basement, on Via Torino, at intersection with San Maurilio).

Eating near Sforza Castle

Le Briciole Pizzeria draws a local crowd for its good prices, pizza, and varied meat dishes; it's packed by 21:00, go earlier (Tue–Fri and Sun 12:15–14:30, 19:15–23:30, Sat 19:15–13:30, closed Mon, Via Camperio 17, a block in front of castle, on small street at end of Via Dante, tel. 02-877-185).

Garbagnati is a tasty self-service cafeteria on Via Dante 13, a couple of blocks in front of the castle (Mon–Sat 12:00–15:00 only, snacks otherwise, closed Sun; a smaller Garbagnati, with sweets and no seats, is near Peck deli at Via Hugo 3; tel. 02-875-301).

Another **Ciao** Autogrill cafeteria is on Via Dante, just off Piazza Cordusio, with outdoor seating on the pedestrian-only street.

At **Ristorante Familiare della Cimbraccola,** the atmosphere is more memorable than the food. Stefanini Arnaldo, with his imaginary mother in the kitchen (she's 92 and now retired back in Tuscany) and using the same pots and pans since 1974, throws his entire menu at his guests—a series of uninspired appetizers, pastas, and entrées; endless wine, water, coffee, and *grappa* (fire water); and three desserts—all for €15. The food is Tuscan and plain.

After six or eight courses, you'll get a big plate of meats. (This is your cue to say "Oh, my gosh!) The walls are plastered with model ships, pipes, dusty paper money, and pins for each hungry client on a U.S. map (Mon–Sat 19:00–22:30, closed Sun and Aug, an olive toss off Via Dante, midway between Duomo and Fortress at Via S. Tomaso 8, tel. 02-869-2250).

Eating near the Brera Art Gallery
The Brera neighborhood surrounding the Church of St. Carmine is laced with narrow, inviting pedestrian streets. Find your own *ristorante* or consider **Al Pozzo**, which offers Tuscan cuisine (Tue–Fri and Sun 11:00–15:00, 19:00–24:00, Sat 19:00–24:00, closed Mon, Via S. Carpoforo 7, tel. 02-877-775). For a splurge, locals like **Trattoria dell' Orso** (pasta-€10, meat-€15, lunch from 12:30, dinner from 17:30, closed Sat–Sun lunch, CC, Via Ciovasso 5, tel. 02-8646-3400).

Eating Cheap near Montenapoleone
For inexpensive, healthy food near the classy shopping street, **Brek** is best. This self-service cafeteria chain is a step above Ciao in quality. One Brek is near one end of Montenapoleone (2 Via dell' Annunciata, 2 blocks from Montenapoleone, tel. 02-653-619), and another is near the other end, a half block off Piazza San Babila (daily 11:30–15:00, 18:30–22:30, Piazza Giordano 1; on Piazza Babila, with back to "egg monument" and facing fountain, Brek is through arch in building on right, tel. 02-7602-3379). One of the ubiquitous **Ciao** Autogrill cafeterias is also on Piazza San Babila (self-service, at the end of pedestrian zone).

Eating Near the Train Station
Again, it's **Brek**, for better food than you'll find at the station (with back to tracks, exit station to left, it's within a block, Via Lepetit 20, tel. 02-670-5149).

Transportation Connections—Milan
By train to: Venice (departures :05 after each hour, 3 hrs), **Florence** (hrly, 3 hrs, also check schedule for trains going to Rome and Naples—these stop in Florence), **Genoa** (hrly, 2 hrs), **Rome** (hrly, 4.5 hrs), **Brindisi** (4/day, 10–12 hrs), **Cinque Terre** (hrly, 3–4 hrs to La Spezia, some direct trains to Monterosso, sometimes changing in Genoa; trains from La Spezia to the villages go nearly hourly), **Varenna** on Lake Como (the small line to Lecco/Sondrio/Tirano leaves every 2 hours for the 1-hour trip to Varenna—maybe 08:15, 09:15, 12:15, 14:16, 16:15, 18:00, 19:10, 20:15), **Stresa** (hrly, 50 min to 1.25 hrs, faster trains require reservations; trains going to Domodossola and some international destinations stop at Stresa), **Como** (around :25 after each hour,

30 min, ferries go from Como to Varenna until 19:00). Train
info (automated in Italian): tel. 848-888-088.

International destinations: Amsterdam (4/day, 14 hrs),
Barcelona (2 changes, 17 hrs—before paying extra for Pablo Casals
express, consider flying), **Bern** (7/day, 3 hrs), **Frankfurt** (5/day,
9 hrs), **London** (2/day, 18 hrs), **Munich** (5/day, 8 hrs), **Nice** (5/day,
7–10 hrs), **Paris** (4/day, 7 hrs), **Vienna** (4/day, 14 hrs).

Milan's Airports

To get flight information for either airport or the current phone
number of your airline, call 02-74851 or 02-7485-2200.

Malpensa: Most international flights land at the manageable Malpensa airport, 45 kilometers northwest of Milan.
Customs guards fan you through, and even the sniffing dog
seems friendly. You'll most likely land at Terminal 1 (international flights) rather than Terminal 2 (charter flights); buses
connect the two. Both have cash machines (at Terminal 1,
near exit 4 at Banca Nazionale del Lavoro), banks, and change
offices. Terminal 1 has a pharmacy, eateries, and a TI (daily
08:00–20:00; when you exit the baggage-carousel area, go right;
tel. 02-5858-0080 or 02-5858-0230). At the *tabacchi* shop, buy
a phone card and confirm your hotel reservation.

You have three easy ways to get to downtown Milan: by train,
shuttle bus, or taxi.

The Malpensa Express **train** zips between Malpensa airport and Milan's Cadorna station (which is both a Metro stop
and a small train station), closer to the Duomo than the central
train station (€9.50, discounted to €6 for Alitalia passengers,
40 min, 2/hr, departing airport at :15 and :45 past the hour,
departing Cadorna at :20 and :50 past the hour, runs from
06:00 to 24:00, no railpasses, tel. 02-27763 or 02-20-222, www
.malpensaexpress.com). At the airport, follow signs (*Treni* and
Malpensa Express) down the stairs; you'll go through a glass
tunnel to the ticket office. After buying your ticket, take the
ramp down to the tracks. If you're leaving Milan to go to the
airport, take the Metro to the Cadorna stop, surface, and buy
a ticket at the Malpensa Express office in the station. Purchase
your ticket before you board, or you'll pay €2.60 extra to buy
it on the train.

Two companies run **buses** between Malpensa airport and
Milan's central train station. The buses are virtually identical
in everything except price, using the same departure points: in
front of the airport and from Piazza Luigi di Savoia at the east
side of the train station. Buy your ticket from the driver for
the 50-minute trip. Each company's buses depart every 20 to
30 minutes, but because the schedules are generally staggered,
you'll find buses running every 10 to 15 minutes. The cheaper

Malpensa Shuttle bus costs €4.20 (runs from station 04:30–22:30, runs from airport 06:40-00:15, at airport you can buy ticket on bus or at Airport 2000 office between exits 5 and 6, catch bus at exit 5, tel. 02-5858-3185, www.malpensa-shuttle.com). The Malpensa Bus Express costs €5 (runs from station 05:10–22:30, from airport 06:30-23:50, catch bus at exit 6, buy ticket from driver).

Taxis into Milan cost up to €80 (insist on meter, avoid hustlers in airport halls).

Linate: Most European flights fly into Linate, eight kilometers east of Milan. The airport has a bank (just past customs, decent rates) and a TI (daily 08:30–20:00, tel. 02-7020-0443). Linate is linked by STAM buses with the central train station (Piazza Luigi di Savoia on east side of Milan's central station; buy €2.60 tickets from driver, 2/hr, runs from station 05:40–21:35, from airport 06:05–23:35, in general buses leave at :05 and :35 after the hour in either direction, tel. 02-717-106 or 02-711-6982); from the station, take the Metro or a taxi to your hotel. Taxis from Linate to the Duomo cost €18.

Between Malpensa and Linate: The Malpensa Shuttle company runs a bus between the airports every 90 minutes (€7.75, from 06:00–20:00, 75 min).

NEAR MILAN: STRESA, BORROMEO ISLANDS, AND LAKE MAGGIORE

Lake Maggiore is ringed by mountains, snow-capped in spring and fall, and lined with resort towns such as Stresa. This town is special mainly because of its boat dock—launching you to the islands of Lake Maggiore.

The three islands are named for the Borromeo family who—from the 16th to the 19th centuries—lovingly turned them into magical retreats with elaborate villas and fragrant gardens. Isola Bella has the palace and terraced garden; Isola Madre has a villa and sprawling garden; and Isola Pescatori is simply small, peaceful, and residential. The Borromeos, who made their money from banking and trading, enjoyed the arts—from paintings (hung in lavish abundance throughout the palace and villa) to plays (performed in an open-air theater on Isola Bella) and marionette shows (you'll see the puppets that performed here).

Tourists flock to the lakes in May and June (when flowers are in luscious bloom) and in September. Concerts held in scenic settings draw music-lovers, particularly the Musical Weeks in August (concert schedules in English at www.stresa.net/settimanemusicali). For fewer crowds, visit in April, in July and August (when Italians prefer the Mediterranean beaches), and October. In winter, the snow-covered mountains attract skiers.

Stresa and Borromeo Islands

Planning Your Time

This region is best visited on a sunny day, when the mountains are clear, the lake is calm, and the heat of the sun brings out the scent of the blossoms.

The two top islands for sightseeing are Isola Bella and Isola Madre. Isola Pescatori has no sights but is a peaceful place for lunch.

Daytrip from Milan: Catch an early train from Milan (there are two 50-minute fast trains, leaving at 08:10 and 09:10, each requiring a reservation). In Stresa, walk 10 minutes downhill to the boat dock, and catch a boat to Isola Madre first (try

to see it before it closes for lunch). Continue on to the Villa
Taranto gardens on the mainland, or backtrack to Isola Pescatori
for a lazy lunch. Save Isola Bella for the afternoon, because tour
groups mob it in the morning.

From Isola Bella, you have two choices: Catch the boat to
the Stresa dock, see the town, and walk back to the train station.

Or, if you'd like to ride the mountain cable car, take the boat
from Isola Bella to Carciano (5 min) to reach the lift. From either
dock, it's about a 10-minute walk to the train station.

Overnight: Small and touristy Stresa could make a fine first
or last stop in Italy, because its connections to Milan's airport
don't involve a transfer in big Milano (see "Transportation
Connections," below).

Orientation

Stresa clings to its shore, stretched thin from one end (main boat
dock and a little downtown that's like an open-air shopping mall)
to the other (the Lido, with the Carciano boat dock and a mountain cable car). The docks are a 15-minute walk apart. In between
is a string of stately expensive lakeside hotels. (Hemingway set
part of his novel *A Farewell to Arms* in the Grand Hotel des Iles
Borromées, where the luxurious "Hemingway Suite" goes for
€2,750 a night.) A narrow promenade runs along most of the
waterfront, offering expansive views of the lake, islands, and
mountains. Market day is on Friday morning at Piazza Capucci,
several blocks inland from the main square, Pizza Matteotti.

Tourist Information: The TI, located between the station
and downtown, gives out free maps and boat schedules without
enthusiasm (daily 10:00–12:30, 15:00–18:30, Via Canonica 3,
tel. 0323-30150, www.stresa.net).

Arrival in Stresa: At the train station, ask for a free city map
at the newsstand (marked *Libri Giornali Riviste*). To get to the
downtown, exit right from the station and take your first left (on
Viale Duchessa di Genova). This takes you straight down to the
lake (the boat dock is about four blocks to your right; ask for a boat
schedule at the ticket window). To get to the TI, follow above
directions, heading down Viale Duchessa di Genova, and take a
right on Via Martini. After two blocks, you'll reach the square
with the TI. A taxi to the TI or boat dock costs about €6.50.

Getting Around Lake Maggiore

Boats link the islands and towns on opposite shores, running about
twice hourly (allow roughly 10 minutes between stops). Short hops
cost €2.30. It's simplest to get a day pass. For the three islands, it's
€5.75. For the islands and Pallanza (a town on the opposite shore),
it's €7.75. For €9.50, add Villa Taranto (gardens).

If you're planning to tour Isola Bella and Isola Madre, you'll save money if, when you buy your boat pass, you ask to include the admission fee (*entrada*) to the sights. The total package for the boat rides and admissions is €21.50—a good deal since the admissions alone total over €16. The ticket office might not display a sign advising you of this opportunity—you need to ask.

Boats run daily from March through October. (Although the boats sail in almost any weather and the rides are short, choppy water can make for a queasy ride.) The map in this chapter shows the route: Stresa, Isola Bella, Isola Pescatori, Baveno (lakeside town), Isola Madre, Pallanza, and Villa Taranto. This route is part of a longer one. To follow the boat schedule (free, available at boat docks, TI, and maybe your hotel), look at the Arona–Locarno timetable for trips from Stresa to the islands, and the Locarno-Arona timetable for the return trip to Stresa. A short five-minute boat ride connects the Carciano dock (and cable-car lift) and Isola Bella. If you're doing the lift and the islands, transfer at Isola Bella.

Go right to the dock to buy your ticket. The little booths promoting private taxi boats outside the docks will overcharge you. At the main Stresa dock, go to the ticket window inside the building in front of the dock; at Carciano, go to the booth directly next to the dock, not the booth near the stream (boat info: tel. 800-551-801).

Sights—Stresa, Islands, and Gardens

▲▲▲**Isola Bella**—The palace dominating the island was named by Charles Borromeo for his wife, Isabella. The island itself is touristy, with a gauntlet of souvenir stands and a corral of restaurants. A few back streets provide evidence that people actually live here.

The sight consists of the impressive palace, a chilly lower floor built to look like a series of grottos, and a formal, terraced garden nearly covering the island.

The **palace** has Murano glass chandeliers, Gobelin-covered chairs, intricate tapestries, plenty of paintings, and even some historic importance. The Conference of Stresa was held in the palace's Music Room in 1935, when Mussolini met with British and French diplomats in an attempt to scare Germany out of starting World War II; this "Stresa Front" soon fizzled when Mussolini attacked Ethiopia and joined forces with Hitler. In Napoleon's Room in August of 1797, the emperor himself and his wife spent two nights—without a private bath, hair-dryer, or cable TV. Fresh from conquering Venice, Napoleon hadn't called ahead for reservations for his party of 62. Count Borromeo wrote later: "We may thank God that the stay was a short one." The puppetry room is fun, with dragons, donkeys, King Kong, servants, and the uppity upper-class, each with its own personality.

The 18th-century **grotto** downstairs, decorated from ceiling to floor with shell motifs and black-and-white stones, still serves its original function of providing a cool refuge from Italy's heat.

The terraced Baroque **gardens**, which give the island the look of a stepped pyramid from the water, are topped with a nautically-themed wall and a rearing unicorn—the symbol of the Borromeo family (€8.50, April–mid-Oct daily 09:00–12:00, 13:30–17:30, English descriptions in palace, WC at entrance to garden, tel. 0323-30556). Picnicking is not allowed in the garden, but you can picnic at the point of the island (free and open to the public); take the mosaic sidewalk to the left of the palace entrance.

▲**Isola Pescatori**—This sleepy island, the smallest and most residential of the three, has a couple of good seafood restaurants, picnic benches, views, and blissfully nothing to do—under arbors of wisteria.

▲▲▲**Isola Madre**—This island consists almost solely of this sight: An interesting, furnished villa and a lovely garden with some exotic birds and plants.

The 16th-century **villa**, which has enough furniture and art to give it warmth, is notable for its 19th-century puppet theater and many marionettes—angels, soldiers, villains, Asian visitors, and more—made out of wood, fabric, and porcelain. The smaller Hell Theater has suitably spooky skeleton puppets and devilish dragons. You'll also see canopied beds, clothes, and jewelry, along with Countess Borromeo's 19th-century doll collection (not a Barbie in the bunch).

The **gardens**, which bloom from April through October, are especially beautiful in May, when the azaleas and rhododendrons perform. The slow-moving, sleepy birds call this island home; careful not to step on their plumage.

A one-way route of the sight is clearly signed for you, taking you through the gardens first and then the villa, ending at the chapel and WC. The route is flip-flopped before the lunch break and before closing, allowing you to see the villa first (before it closes 13:00-14:00, and at 17:00), then the gardens, which stay open until 18:00. It's pointless to arrive on the island between 12:30 and 13:30 when the entry is closed. If you're inside during that time, it's no problem—though the villa is closed for part of that time (€7.75, daily 09:00–12:30, 13:30–17:30, no photos in villa, WC next to chapel outside villa, tel. 0323-31261).

Visit this island only if you intend to tour the sight, because there's nothing else here except go to the La Piratera Ristorante Bar (daily 08:00–17:30, €18 tourist menu, sit-down meals and simple sandwiches to go, picnic at rocky beach a minute's walk from restaurant).

▲**Villa Taranto Botanical Gardens**—Garden-lovers will enjoy this large landscaped park, located on the mainland a 10-minute boat ride from Isola Madre. The gardens are a Scotsman's labor

of love. Starting in the 1930s, Neil MacEacharn created this
garden of delights—bringing in thousands of plants from all over
the world—and here he stays, in the small mausoleum. The park's
highlight is the terraced garden with a series of cascading pools.

Villa Taranto is directly across the street from the boat dock
(€6.20, April–Oct 08:30–19:30, ticket office closes at 18:30, parking, on outskirts of Pallanza, tel. 0323-404-555). A simple bar is by
the dock and a ristorante/bar (and WC) is at the park entrance.

Mountain Cable Car—From Stresa's Lido, a cable car takes you
up—in two stages and a 20-minute ride—to the top of Mottarone
(1,385 meters). From here, you get great views, and, by taking a
short hike, a bird's-eye view of the small, neighboring Lake Orta.
The biggest snowcapped mountain you see is Monte Rosa, Italy's
second-highest mountain.

Cable-car options include a round-trip (€10.50); a one-way
up (€6.20) and a hike or bike ride down; or consider the midway
Alpina stop, where a 10-minute walk leads to the Alpine Gardens
(free and open daily April–mid-Oct Tue–Sun 09:00–18:00, closed
Mon, about 1 km from cable car). From the Alpine Gardens (a
great picnic spot), you get an incredible view of the islands floating
in the lake below, but the gardens on the islands and at Taranto
blow this humble collection of alpine plants out of the water. If
you're hiking down, bring a good map and allow 3.5 hours from
the top of Mottarone, or 1.5 hours from Alpine Gardens.

You can rent a bike at the base of the cable-car lift (full-
suspension mountain bike-€23.50/day, €18/half day, regular
bikes about €5 less, helmets, tel. 0323-30399) and bring it on
the cable car with you (€6.20 extra).

The cable cars run every 20 minutes, unless it's windy, lunch
time (roughly 12:10–13:50), or November. Try this well before
or right after the lunch break; otherwise you'll be either rushed
or bored at the top (WCs at base and top, tel. 0323-30399).

Sidetrips from Stresa

▲**Scenic Boat and Rail Trip to Locarno and Centovalli**—
An enjoyable all-day excursion from Stresa involves three seg-
ments. Take the boat to the end of Lake Maggiore past loads of
small lakeside hamlets to Locarno, in the Italian-speaking Swiss
canton of Ticino (bring your passport). Spend an hour or so
exploring this lakeside town. Then catch the "Centovalli" train
for a 90-minute ride that links together remote mountain villages,
as you return to Italy and the town of Domodossola. From here,
frequent trains run to Stresa.

▲**Lake Orta**—Just on the other side of Mount Mottarone is
the small lake of Orta. The main town, Orta San Giulia, has a
beautiful lakeside piazza ringed by picturesque buildings. The
piazza faces the lake and a view of Isola San Giulia. Taxi boats

(€2.60 round-trip) make the five-minute trip throughout the day. The island is worth a look for the church of San Giulio and the circular "path of silence" that takes about 10 minutes. In peak season, Orta is anything but silent, but off-season or early or late in the day, this place is full of peace and magic.

The train ride from Stresa to Orta-Miasino (a short walk from the lakeside piazza) takes just under two hours and requires a change in Domodossola.

Sleeping in Stresa
(€1.10 = about $1, country code: 39)

Because Stresa town is just a resort, I'd daytrip from Milan, but here are good options if you'd like to stay.

Hotel Moderno offers 56 soothing pastel rooms on a pedestrian street a block from the main square (Db-€93–119, ask for quiet room on courtyard, closed mid-Oct–mid-March, CC, elevator, Via Cavour 33, in Piazza Matteotti with your back to the lake, go right—up small street, tel. 0323-933-773, fax 0323-933-775, e-mail: hotmoder@tin.it).

Hotel Milan Speranza is a four-star hotel, with 176 predictably comfortable rooms in two separate buildings, both across from the boat dock (Db-€98–176, CC, air-con, elevator, tel. 0323-31178, fax 0323-32729, e-mail: hotmispe@tin.it).

Albergo Luina is a cheap sleep without a tour group in sight. The seven rooms, above a restaurant, are basic and clean (S/Sb-€31–34, D/Db-€47–62, no CC, 10 percent discount with this book, Via Garibaldi, 2 blocks off Piazza Matteotti, with back to lake, go left up small street, tel. 0323-30285).

Transportation Connections—Stresa

By train to: Milan (hrly, 50 min fast train, 1.25-hr slow train), **Venice** (1/day, 4 hrs), **Domodossola**—French border (hrly, 35 min).

To Malpensa Airport: Take the train toward Milan (hrly), get off at Gallarate (about 40 min from Stresa), where frequent, cheap (€2.60) shuttle buses run to the airport. Airport buses may start running between Stresa and Malpensa in 2002. Taxis to the airport cost €60 and take about an hour (your hotel can arrange the trip for you).

LAKE COMO
(LAGO DI COMO)

Commune with nature where Italy is welded to the Alps, in the lovely Italian Lakes District. The million-euro question is: Which lake? For the best mix of accessibility, scenery, and offbeatness, Lake Como is my choice. And the sleepy midlake town of Varenna is the handiest base of operations. Here you'll get a complete dose of Italian-lakes wonder and aristocratic-old-days romance. Bustling Milan, just an hour away, doesn't even exist. Now it's your turn to be *chiuso per ferie* (closed for vacation).

Lake Como, lined with elegant, 19th-century villas, crowned by snowcapped mountains, and busy with ferries, hydrofoils, and little passenger ships, is a good place to take a break from the intensity and obligatory turnstile culture of central Italy. It seems half the travelers you'll meet have tossed their itineraries into the lake and are actually relaxing.

Today the hazy, lazy lake's only serious industry is tourism. Thousands of lakeside residents travel daily to nearby Lugano, in Switzerland, to find work. The lake's isolation and flat economy have left it pretty much the way the 19th-century Romantic poets described it.

Planning Your Time

If relaxation's not on your agenda, Lake Como shouldn't be either. Even though there are no essential activities, plan for at least two nights so you'll have an uninterrupted day to see how slow you can get your pulse.

Lake Como is Milan's quick getaway, and the charming little village of Varenna is the gateway. With its handy connections to Milan and midlake destinations, Varenna is my favorite home base.

The Italian Lakes

Arrival in Varenna

I zip directly by train from Milan to Varenna, set up, and limit
my activities to midlake (Varenna and Bellagio). From Milan's
central station, catch a train heading for Sondrio or Tirano (often
confused with Torino—wrong city). Be certain your train stops
in Varenna; look at the fine print on the *Partenze* (departures)
schedule posted at Milan's train station to make sure Varenna is
listed. Trains leave about hourly (at :15 past the hour). Sit on
the left for maximum lake-view beauty. Get off at Varenna-Esino.
(Note that the name Varenna-Esino appears only at the station.
Train schedules list simply Varenna. Same place.)

You can also get to Varenna from Milan via the town of
Como. Trains take you from Milan to Como (50-minute rides
usually leave at :25 past each hour), where you can catch a boat
for the two-hour ride (about hourly, last departure at 19:00,
€5.20) up the lake to Varenna.

Getting around Lake Como

By Boat: Lago di Como is well-served by boats and hydrofoils.
The lake service is divided into three parts: south-north from
Como to Colico; midlake between Varenna, Bellagio, Menaggio,
and Cadenabbia (Villa Carlotta); and the southeastern arm to Lecco.
Unless you're going through Como, you'll probably limit your cruising to the midlake service (boat info: tel. 031-579-211 or toll free
800-551-801). Boats go about hourly between Varenna, Menaggio,
and Bellagio (€2.50 per hop, 15 min, daily 07:00–21:00).

Lake Como

Passengers pay the same for car or passenger ferries, but 50 percent more for the enclosed, stuffy, speedy-but-less-scenic hydrofoil. The free schedule (available at TIs, hotels, and boat docks) lists times and prices. Stopovers aren't allowed, and there's no break for round-trips, so buy a ticket for each ride. The one-day, €6.75 midlake pass saves you money if you make three rides.

Boat schedule literacy tips: *Feriale* = workdays, Monday–Saturday. *Festivo* = Sunday and holidays. *Partenze da* = departing from. *Autotraghetto* = car ferry. *Aliscafo* = hydrofoil. *Battello* = passenger-only ferry.

By Car: With the parking problems, constant traffic jams, and expensive car ferries, this is no place to drive if you don't need to. While you can easily drive around the lake, the road is narrow, congested, and lined by privacy-seeking walls, hedges, and tall fences. It costs €7.50 to take your car onto a ferry. And parking is rarely easy where you need it, especially in Bellagio. Park in

Varenna and cruise. White lines (near Varenna's ferry dock and south of the monastery) indicate free parking; blue lines mean metered parking (€1/hr, 2 hrs max, 08:00–19:00, overnight plus 2 hrs is OK); and yellow lines mean residents only.

Varenna

This town of 800 people offers the best of all lake worlds. Easily accessible by train, on the less-driven side of the lake, Varenna has a romantic promenade, a tiny harbor, narrow lanes, and its own villa. It's the right place to savor a lakeside cappuccino or *aperitivo*. There's wonderfully little to do here, and it's very quiet at night. The *passerella* (lakeside walk, unlit but safe after dark) is adorned with caryatid lovers pressing silently against each other in the shadows.

Tourist Information: Varenna's TI is on the main square to the right of the church (Pro Varenna, Tue–Sat 10:00–12:30, 15:30–18:30, Sun 10:00–12:30, closed Mon, Nov–April only Sat–Sun 10:00–12:30, tel. 0341-830-367, www.varennaitaly.com).

A bank, cash machine, and small post office (Mon–Fri 08:00–13:30, Sat 08:00–11:30) are also on the main square. For accommodations, see "Sleeping and Eating on Lake Como," below.

Hello Varenna Walk

Since you came here to relax, this short walk gives you just the town basics.

Bridge near train station: This main road bridge, just below the train station, spans the tiny Esino River. The river divides two communities, Perledo (which sprawls up the hill—notice the church spire high above) and the old fishing town of Varenna (huddled around its harbor). While the towns were joined in fascist times, today they are separate and not without animosity. Perledo used to have a fine beach (where the river hits the lake) until recent storms washed it away. Varenna wanted to collaborate, remaking and sharing an inviting public beach here. Perledo refused. The train station is called Varenna-Esino for a third community higher in the hills. Now, follow the river down to the lakeside promenade by the ferry dock.

Varenna ferry landing: Since the coming of the train, Varenna has been *the* convenient access point from "mid-lake" (the communities of Bellagio, Menaggio, and Varenna) to Milan. From this viewpoint, you can almost see how Lake Como is shaped like a man. The head is the north end (to the right, up by the Swiss Alps). Varenna is the left hip. Menaggio, across the lake, is the right hip. And Bellagio (hiding behind the wooded hill) is where the legs come together—you can see the point (Punta Spartivento—"where the wind is divided"). In a more colorful description, a local poem says "Lake Como is a man

Varenna

(TRAIN STN. TO CHURCH IS A 10 MIN. WALK)

---- PASSERELLA (LAKESIDE WALK)
IIIII STEPPED STREETS

TRAIN STATION

TRAIN TUNNEL

TRAIL TO CASTLE VEZIO

TRAIN TUNNEL

TO MILANO

TRAVEL AGENCY

❹

TO TIRANO

❸

TRAIL TO ❿ + FIUMELATTE

MAIN ROAD

BANK

❶

CHURCH

MAIN RD. TO LECCO

❼

WC

PASSENGER BOAT DOCK + TICKETS

❶❶

❷

❻

PIAZZA SAN GIORGIO

BANK

❾

GARDENS

GROC

CAR FERRY DOCK

❶❷

HARBOR

POST

❶❸

❺

LAKE

TO MENAGGIO

TO BELLAGIO + COMO

COMO

❽

DCH

❶ ALBERGO OLIVEDO
❷ ALBERGO MILANO
❸ HOTEL MONTE CODENO
❹ ALBERGO BERETTA
❺ VILLA ELENA ROOMS
❻ ALBERGO DEL SOLE
❼ VILLA CIPRESSI

❽ HOTEL DU LAC
❾ HOTEL VICTORIA
❿ TO HOTEL EREMO GAUDIO
❶❶ RISTORANTE IL CAVATAPPI
❶❷ VECCHIA VARENNA REST.
❶❸ NILUS BAR & LA FRULLERIA / IL GELATO

with Colico the head, Lecco and Como the feet, and Bellagio the testicles, (in the local dialect, Bellagio and testicles rhyme). Ask a local to say it for you. The ridges high above the right hip are the border of Switzerland. The region's long-time poverty shapes the local character (much like the Great Depression shaped a generation of Americans' outlooks). Many still remember that this side of the lake was the poorest, because those on the other (Menaggio) side controlled the lucrative cigarette smuggling business over the Swiss border. Today the entire region is thriving (with tourism and a booming—if mysterious—iron and steel industry . . . convenient to secret Swiss bank accounts). Walk past the Hotel Olivedo (Olivedo means the place where olive trees grow—

Varenna is the only such place on this side of the lake) and past
the ferry dock to the *passerella*, Varenna's elevated shoreline walk.

Passerella: A generation ago, a local eccentric (who won big
time on an Italian TV game show) and a determined town carpenter
successfully promoted the idea to build Varenna's elegant lakeside
walk, which connects the ferry dock with the old town center. Strolling this, you'll come to the tiny two-dinghy concrete breakwater
of a local villa. Lake Como is lined with elegant 19th-century villas.
Their front doors faced the lake to welcome boats. At this point,
the modern passerella cuts between this villa's watergate and its
private harbor. Around the next corner and over the hump look
up at another typical old villa—with a veil of serious wisteria and
a prime lakeview terrace. Many of these villas are owned by the
region's "impoverished nobility"—bred and raised not to work
and, therefore, unable now to cover the upkeep of their sprawling
houses. From here, also enjoy a good Varenna town view. These
buildings are stringently protected. You can't even change the
color of your paint.

Varenna harborfront: Walk past the community harbor
and under the old-time arcades to the fisherman's pastel homes,
which face the harbor. Notice there are no streets in town...
just characteristic stepped lanes called *contrada*. Varenna was
originally a fishing community. Even today, old-timers enjoy
Lago di Como's counterpart to lutefisk—air-dried and salted lake
"sardines." Called *missoltino*, these sardines are served with this
region's polenta (different from Venice's because buckwheat is
mixed in with the corn). At the south end of the harbor (across
from the gelato shop), belly up to the bannister for another fine
pastel town view. Another local ditty goes "if you love Lake Como
you know Bellagio is the pearl...but Varenna is the diamond."
Continue straight, leaving the harbor. A lane leads around past
Hotel du Lac (its a fine lakeside terrace welcomes nonresidents
for a drink) to the tiny and pebbly town beach (the only place
for a swim). From here climb uphill to the town square.

Piazza San Giorgio: Four churches face Varenna's town
square. The main church dates from the 14th century. Romantic
Varenna is an understandably popular spot for a wedding—rice
litters the church's front yard. Stepping inside, you'll find a few
humble but centuries-old bits of carving and frescoes. The black
marble floor was quarried right in town. Outside, past the WWI
monument, is the TI. From here you can hike up to the castle,
head south to the gardens, or follow the road north back to the
train station.

Sights—Varenna

Castle—A steep trail leads to Varenna's ruined hilltop castle,
Castello di Vezio. Start at the stairs to the left of Hotel Monte

Codeno and figure on 30 minutes one-way (€2.20, daily 10:00–
18:00 in summer, sometimes open late into the evening, closed
when rainy, spring and fall open only Sat–Sun 10:00–18:00, closed
Oct–April, tel. 335-465-186). The castle is pretty barren, apart from
a couple of medieval contraceptive devices, but comes with a sleepy
café at its entrance and a peaceful, traffic-free, one-chapel town.

Gardens—Two manicured lakeside gardens—Villa Cipressi and
the adjacent monastery—are tourable for a €2.75 combo ticket
available at Villa Cipressi or the monastery (€1.75 for one garden
only, March–Oct daily 09:00–18:00).

Fiumelatte—This town, a kilometer south of Varenna, was named
for its milky river. It's the shortest river in Italy at 277 meters (800
feet) and runs—like most of the local tourist industry—only April
through September. The *"La Sorgente del Fiumelatte"* brochure,
available at Varenna's TI, lays out a walk from Varenna to the
Fiumelatte to the castle and back. It's a 30-minute hike to the
source (*sorgente*) of the milky river (at Varenna's monastery, take
high road, drop into peaceful and evocative cemetery, and climb
steps to the wooded trail leading to peaceful and refreshing cave
where the river sprouts). For a longer lakeside hike, ask about the
Sentiera di Viadante (hike one-way up the lake and return by train).

Tours—For bus and boat tours, consider Varenna's travel agency,
I Viaggi del Tivano, next to Albergo Beretta below the train
station. They book planes, trains, and automobiles and can offer
half-day and day-long tours of the region and into Switzerland
(Mon–Fri 08:30–12:00, 15:00–19:00, Sat 09:00–12:00, cash only,
Via per Esino 3, tel. 0341-814-009, e-mail: sberet@tin.it, helpful
Silvia and Luana SE). They may offer town walks in 2002.

More Sights—Lake Como

▲▲**Bellagio**—The self-proclaimed "Pearl of the Lake" is a classy
combination of tidiness and Old World elegance. If you don't
mind that "tramp in a palace" feeling, it's a fine place to surround
yourself with the more adventurous of the posh travelers and
shop for ties and umbrellas. The heavy curtains between the
arcades keep the visitors and their poodles from sweating. Thriving yet still cute, Bellagio is a much more substantial town than
Varenna, which has almost no shops.

Steep-stepped lanes rise from the harborfront. While Johnny
Walker and jewelry sell best at lake level, the locals shop up the hill.
Piazza Chiesa, near the top of town, has a worth-a-look church.
The TI is right downtown (daily 09:00–12:00, 15:00–18:00, off-
season closed Sun and Tue, tel. 031-950-204, e-mail: prombell
@tin.it). If you need a destination, you can tour the Villa Serbelloni
Park—overlooking the town—with a guide (€5.20, 2 tours daily
at 11:00 and 16:00, April–Oct, 90 min, ask at TI).

For something offbeat, clink glasses with Tony the Wine

Bellagio

King. He runs a fun little cantina festooned in cobwebs and mold near the car-ferry dock (March–Oct daily 11:00–13:30, 15:00–19:30, Salita Genazzini 3, behind camera shop, tel. 031-950-935). Tony, who speaks a little English, greets you with a smile, an empty glass, and 20 open bottles of wine and liqueurs to taste. The tasting's free. After 58 years in his cantina, Tony looks darn good. Local wine tips: The best full-bodied (*corposo*) local reds are Sassella, Grumello, and Inferno. Amaretto di Saronno is a sweet local speciality. And the local grappa del Contadino will curl your passport.

The administrative capital of the midlake region, Bellagio is located where the two southern legs of the lake split off. For an easy break in a park with a great view, wander right on out to the crotch. Meander past the rich and famous Hotel Villa Serbelloni, and walk five minutes to Punta Spartivento, literally "the point that divides the wind." You'll find a Renoir atmosphere complete with an inviting bar/restaurant, a tiny harbor, and a chance to sit on a park bench and gaze north past Menaggio, Varenna, and the end of the lake to the Swiss Alps.

For another stroll, head south from the car-ferry dock down the tree-shaded promenade. Ten minutes later, you'll hit Bellagio's beach. The Lido di Bellagio has a chilly pool, lounge chairs, and a diving board into the lake (€3.75).

For more active entertainment, consider a downhill mountain-bike run. Cavalcalario Club shuttles you uphill, then lets you go (€29–34 includes bike rental, several itineraries, reservations necessary, tel. & fax 031-964-814, www.bellagio-mountains.it).

Bellagio has two docks a few minutes' walk apart: The northern dock is for the passenger-only ferry (*battello*) and the hydrofoil (*aliscafo*); the southern dock is for the car ferry, which also takes foot passengers (*autotraghetto*). To make sure you're waiting at the right dock for the boat you want to take, check the boat schedule carefully (posted near dock, free brochure from kiosk at dock). Its timetable is divided into three different schedules: *battello* (passengers only), *aliscafo* (passengers in a hurry), and *autotraghetto* (passengers and cars). Confirm your intentions at the kiosk near either dock.

▲**Menaggio**—Menaggio has more urban bulk than its neighbors. Since the lake is too dirty for swimming, consider its fine public pool. This is the starting point for a few hikes. Only 25 years ago, these trails were used by cigarette smugglers, sneaking at night from Switzerland back into Italy with tax-free cigarettes. The hostel (see "Sleeping," below) has information about mountain biking and catching the bus to trailheads on nearby Mount Grona.

Villa Carlotta—This is the best of Lake Como's famed villas (€6.50, April–Sept daily 09:00–18:00, Oct daily 09:00–12:00, 14:00–16:30, closed Nov–March, tel. 034-440-405). I see the lakes as a break from Italy's art, but, if you're in need of a place that charges admission, Villa Carlotta offers an elegant neoclassical interior, a famous Canova statue, and a garden (its highlight, best in spring). If you plan to tour one villa on the lake, this is the best. Nearby Tremezzo and Cadenabbia are pleasant lakeside resorts an easy walk away. Boats serve all three places.

Isola Comacina—This remote little island (just south of Bellagio) offers peace, ancient church foundations, goats, sheep, and a lovely view of Lago di Como. It takes 30 minutes to walk around the island, but longer to savor it. Bring a picnic or try the snack bar at the dock. Look for trips to Isola Comacina on the Colico-Como schedule (listed in Lago di Como boat timetable brochure, free at ticket booths at ferry docks). The *isola* is accessible from Varenna (1 hr), Menaggio (45 min), or Bellagio (30 min). Check return times carefully (Como-Colico direction) and don't miss your boat. Usually only one trip a day each way works out for a visit.

Como—On the southwest tip of the lake, Como has a good, traffic-free old town, an interesting Gothic/Renaissance cathedral, and a pleasant lakefront with a promenade (TI tel. 031-330-0111).

It's an easy walk from the boat dock to the train station (from Milan in 30 min, usually leaving at :25 past each hour). Boats leave Como about hourly for midlake (ferries-€6.20, 2 hrs; hydrofoils-€9, 1 hr; departures from 07:00 to 19:00, tel. 031-579-211).

Sleeping and Eating on Lake Como
(€1.10 = about $1, country code: 39)
Sleep Code: **S** = Single, **D** = Double/Twin, **T** = Triple, **Q** = Quad, **b** = bathroom, **s** = shower only, **CC** = Credit Cards accepted, **no CC** = Credit Cards not accepted, **SE** = Speaks English, **NSE** = No English.

The area is tight in August, snug in July, and wide open most of the rest of the year. Many places close in winter. All places listed are family-run and have lakeview rooms, and some English is spoken. If you're expecting friendliness, especially during peak season, you'll likely be disappointed. Enjoy the view. View rooms are given (sometimes for no extra cost) to those who telephone for reservations and request a *"camera con vista."* Prices get soft off-season (Nov–May). Varenna's TI, on the main square, can find private rooms (tel. 0341-830-367).

Sleeping in Varenna *(zip code: 23829)*
Albergo Olivedo, facing the ferry dock, is a tidy, elegant, old hotel with old-time furniture and squeaky hardwood floors. Many rooms have glorious little lakeview balconies. It's a fine place to hang out and watch the children, boats, and sun come and go (prices vary with season and views: S-€32–58, D-€55–70, Db-€72–93, includes breakfast, no CC, some lumpy mattresses, closed mid-Nov–mid-Dec, tel. & fax 0341-830-115, www.olivedo.it, e-mail: olivedo@tin.it, hardworking Laura SE). In May, June, July, and September, half-pension (dinner) is required—and rarely regretted—with the best rooms (€23 per person for dinner).

Albergo Milano, located right in the old town, is great with eight comfy, well-plumbed rooms (Sb-€95, Db-€110, includes breakfast, light lunches available, optional three-course dinner-€20 per person, CC, Via XX Settembre 29, tel. & fax 0341-830-298, U.S. fax 781/634-0094, www.varenna.net, e-mail: hotelmilano@varenna.net, Bettina SE). Lakeside rooms 1 and 2 are small and have royal balconies (best in sunny weather). Lakeside rooms 5 and 6 are bigger but have small balconies. This place whispers *luna di miele* (honeymoon).

Hotel Monte Codeno, with 11 functional rooms and no views, is on the main road between the train station and lake (2 Sb-€67.50, Db-€88, includes breakfast buffet, extra bed-€16, 10 percent discount for 3 nights, CC, attached restaurant serves fresh fish and a curious €20 "Rick Steves" menu—see below, Via della Croce 2, tel. 0341-830-123, fax 0341-815-227, e-mail:

ferrcas@tin.it, Marina Castelli SE). They rent a few apartments nearby (as low as €83 for 2 people, up to €186 for 6 people).

Albergo Beretta, on the main road a block below the station, has 10 decent rooms, several with balconies (D-€47, Db-€60, Qb-€78, up to €18 extra for balcony, breakfast-€5.20, CC, coffee shop on ground floor, Via per Esino 1, tel. & fax 0341-830-132, e-mail: hotelberetta@iol.it, Tosca NSE, daughter Julia and Laura SE).

Villa Elena, a grandmotherly, low-energy place on the main square, offers the best budget beds in town. English-speaking Signora Vitali rents her four rooms at the same price—room #1 has a bathroom and view terrace; the others don't even have sinks (Db-€42 with fine breakfast, €37 without, no CC, it's the vine-covered facade on Piazza San Giorgio near Via San Giovanni, tel. 0341-830-575). **Albergo del Sole**, a restaurant on the same square, may rent eight rooms in 2002 (Piazza San Giorgio 17, tel. 0341-815-218, NSE).

Villa Cipressi, in a huge, quiet garden, is a sprawling, centuries-old mansion with 32 plain, modern rooms and a garden people pay to see (Sb-€73–83, Db-€91, Db with view but no balcony-€104, Tb-€145, Qb-€176, includes breakfast, CC, garden access, elevator, Internet access, Via IV Novembre 18, tel. 0341-830-113, fax 0341-830-401, e-mail: villacipressi @libero.it, Elena SE).

Hotel du Lac, stylish, sleek, and the only place in town with air-conditioning, overlooks the water (17 rooms, Db with view and balcony-€170, less without, suite Db-€206, includes breakfast, CC, parking-€10, Via del Prestino 4, tel. 0341-830-238, fax 0341-831-081, e-mail: albergodulac@tin.it, Ileana SE).

Hotel Victoria, on the main square, is a typical big hotel with a fine lakeview garden and a pool but no air-conditioning (43 rooms, Db-€140, add €31 for view, includes breakfast, CC, Piazza San Giorgio 5, tel. 0341-815-111, fax 0341-830-722, e-mail: hotelroyalvictoria@promo.it, SE).

Eremo Gaudio, standing isolated halfway up the hill with a commanding lakeview high above Varenna, is unique. Built in the 1940s as an orphanage by the Pirelli family (of tire fame), it was then given to the church to be a hermitage. Since 2000, the church has run it as a hotel. Perfect for monks with champagne taste, it's peaceful, with awe-inspiring view balconies and breakfast terrace. They rent 12 bright and comfortable rooms in the main building and 11 simpler, less expensive rooms below in a quarter that still feels like a priest's dorm. From Varenna's main square, walk south about 200 meters. Across from Villa Monastero, veer left up the high road where you'll find the lower of two private elevator-like lifts which slide you up the mountainside to your perch (open March–Oct only, Sb-€67, Db-€83,

Db with balcony-€93, Tb-€125, Qb-€150, lower rooms:
Sb-€47, Db-€62, no CC, free shuttle service from station,
Via Roma 11, tel. 0341-815-301, fax 0341-815-314, www
.eremogaudio.it, e-mail: eremogaudio@yahoo.it).

Eating in Varenna
On the waterfront: **Albergo Olivedo's** restaurant serves fine food
with no-nonsense service across from the ferry dock. Sit either
curbside under an awning with a lake view, or in a classy
old dining hall. While Laura and her staff serve simple pasta
lunches, evening meals are a set three-course affair with wine
(€33, €23 for hotel guests, daily 12:15–14:00, 19:30–21:15,
CC, tel. 0341-830-115).

Vecchia Varenna, on the harbor, is respected, pricey, and
the most romantic place in town. The menu features old-time
traditional cuisine and lake specialties (€25–40 meals, Tue–Sun
12:30–14:00, 20:00–22:00, also closed Tue in winter, dressy
indoors or on harborside deck, CC, reservations smart, tel.
0341-830-793).

The **Nilus Bar**, with a stainless steel diner interior and the
best harborfront seating in town, is *the* place for a light meal.
The young waitstaff serves dinner crêpes, pizzas, salads, hot
sandwiches, and cocktails with a smile (daily 12:00–23:00, Dec–
Feb only Sat–Sun, Fulvia and Giovanni SE). For cold, sweet,
and fruity treats, check out the harborfront **La Frulleria/Il
Gelato** (next to Nilus Bar).

Eating off the water, on or near Piazza San Giorgio:
Ristorante del Sole, facing the town square, serves edible meals
and Naples-style pizzas (€5–8). Making few concessions to the
tourist crowds, this restaurant caters to locals, providing a fun
ambience and a garden in back (daily 12:00–14:30, 19:00–22:00,
closed Wed in winter, Piazza San Giorgio 17, tel. 0341-815-218).

Victoria Grill, also on the square, is more modern, with a
cheery, neon-and-red-checkered-tablecloth atmosphere. They
serve good, well-priced meals and pizza (daily 12:00–14:00,
19:00–22:00, closed Mon in winter, CC, under fancy Hotel
Victoria). Hotel Victoria also has a tired upscale restaurant welcoming non-guests with a set menu and lakeview terrace seating.

Ristorante Il Cavatappi, a five-table place on a quiet lane
30 meters off the town square, is the new place in town. Helpful
owner-chef Mario serves old-time specialties (such as *missoltino*—
the air-dried lake fish locals like more than tourists) as an antipasto. He's serious about his wine. Plan on spending €25 plus
wine (daily 11:30–15:30, 18:30–24:00, closed off-season Wed,
CC, reservations smart, tel. 0341-815-349).

Ristorante Monte Codeno, on the main road without a
hint of lake ambience, serves a special "Rick Steves" menu

designed to give visitors a sampler of lake cuisine. For €20 you
get eight different fishy appetizers, including *missoltino* and *carpione*,
a *secondi* with polenta and risotto, a bit of the local taleggio cheese,
and wine—all explained in a souvenir info sheet (CC, Via della
Croce 2, tel. 0341-830-123).

Picnics: The two little grocery stores, on and just off the main
square, have all you need for a classy balcony or breakwater picnic
dinner (daily 07:30–12:30, 15:30–19:30).

Sleeping in Bellagio (zip code: 22021)

The first five are on the waterfront. The last two places are inland.

Hotel Suisse, next to the fancy places, has 10 simple rooms,
hardwood floors, dim lights, fine bathrooms, unpredictable
beds, and some great views and balconies (Db-€70 with this
book in 2002, breakfast-€8, 10 percent discount in hotel restaurant with this book, CC, Piazza Mazzini 8, tel. 031-950-335,
fax 031-951-755, e-mail: hsuisse@tiscalinet.it, Guido SE).

Hotel du Lac, a good splurge, comes with 48 rooms, a roof
garden, and old-time elegance with no loss of comfort (Sb-€88,
Db-€171, plusher superior Db-€192, includes breakfast, view
rooms cost the same as viewless rooms, CC, parking-€8, air-con,
TVs, mini-bars, closed Nov–March, Piazza Mazzini 32, tel.
031-950-320, fax 031-951-624, www.bellagiohoteldulac.com,
e-mail: dulac@tin.it, Leoni family SE).

Hotel Florence, a few doors away and 150 years old, is
family-run and similar, with hardwood, pastels, and a rich touch
of Old World elegance (30 rooms, Sb-€103–120, Db-€135–170
depending on view and balcony, Db suite-€195–250, includes
breakfast, CC, closed Nov–March, elevator, hand-held showers
only, tel. 031-950-342, fax 031-951-722, www.bellagio.co.nz,
e-mail: hotflore@tin.it, Ketzlar family SE). Enjoy live jazz in
the Florence Bar on Sunday nights.

Hotel Metropole, a tired but grand old place, dominates
Bellagio's waterfront with 42 spacious and reasonably comfortable
rooms and plush public spaces (Db-€109, Db with view balcony-
€114, CC, elevator, fridge, tel. 031-950-409, fax 031-951-534).

Grand Hotel Villa Serbelloni, a famous 19th-century
palace, comes with history, doormen, two pools (inside and out),
a garden, an elite clientele, and sky-high prices. While the grounds
and public spaces are fancy, the rooms don't quite merit the high
price (83 rooms, standard Db-€342, deluxe Db-€454, executive
double-€585, pricier rooms have views, CC, air-con and all the
comforts, tel. 031-950-216, fax 031-951-529,
www.villaserbelloni.com).

Hotel Giardinetto, at the top of town near the TI, 100
steps above the waterfront, offers 14 squeaky-clean and quiet
rooms. The rooms are stark, but the breezy, peaceful garden

is a joy (S-€29, D-€42 Db-€52, Tb-€70, breakfast-€6.20,
no CC but personal checks and traveler's checks OK, Via Roncati
12, tel. 031-950-168, Eugene and Laura Ticozzi SE).

Albergo Europa, run with low energy, is in a concrete annex
behind a restaurant, away from the waterfront with no charm
but reasonable comfort (10 rooms, Db-€93, CC, balconies lack
views but are quiet, parking, Via Roma 21, tel. & fax 031-950-471,
e-mail: albeuropa@tiscalinet.it, family Marchesi).

Eating in Bellagio

Ristorante Bilicus, a busy and jolly place serving regional and lake
cuisine with passion, is up a steep lane from the waterfront. You
can eat indoors or on a gravelly shaded terrace. While a little pricey,
the restaurant is famous for value and quality cooking (daily 12:00–
14:30, 19:00–21:30, CC, Salita Serbelloni, tel. 031-950-480).

Trattoria S. Giacomo, across the street, is less expensive
and respected for its home cooking and traditional cuisine such
as *riso e filetto di pesce* (Wed–Mon 12:00–14:30, 19:00–21:30,
closed Tue, CC, Salita Serbelloni 45, tel. 031-950-329).

The **Hotel Metropole Ristorante**'s terrace offers the
best waterfront dining, though a mediocre food value.

Try **La Grotta** for pizza and pasta (daily 12:00–14:30, 19:00–
24:00, closed Mon Oct–June, Salita Cernaia 14, tel. 031-951-152).

Punto Spartivento, the dramatic park just north of town, has
a **La Punta Ristorante** (tel. 031-951-888) and a great setting for
a picnic. Pick up picnic supplies at **Gastronomica Mini Market**
(at Via Centrale and Via Monastero, uphill from Hotel Florence).
You'll find picnic benches at the park, along the waterfront in
town, and lining the promenade south of town.

Sleeping in or near Menaggio

La Primula Youth Hostel is a rare hostel. Now family-run in
its second generation by Alberto and Marta, it caters to a quiet,
savor-the-lakes crowd. Located 300 meters south of the Menaggio
dock, it has a view terrace; games galore; a members' kitchen; a
washing machine; bike, canoe, and kayak rentals (€10.50/day,
€18.50 for non-hostelers); plus easy parking. (Closed 10:00–17:00
and Nov–mid-March, €11.50 per night in a 4- to 6-bed room
with sheets and breakfast, €12 per bed with private plumbing,
hearty dinners for €9, reserve dinner by 18:00, no CC.) Show
this book for a free half-hour Internet connection (Ostello La
Primula, Via IV Novembre 86, 22017 Menaggio, tel. 0344-
32356, fax 034-131-677, www.menaggiohostel.com, e-mail:
menaggiohostel@mclink.it). The have plenty of ideas for hikes
and bike rides in the area.

La Marianna B&B is run by a husband-and-wife team,
Ty and Paola (whose daughter now runs the youth hostel).

They rent eight rooms and run a fine restaurant in Cadenabbia, two kilometers south of Menaggio (Db with view-€62, attached restaurant with lakeside terrace, CC, tel. 0344-43095, e-mail: inn@la-marianna.com). The hourly Como-Menaggio bus C-10 stops at its doorstep.

Buses run between Milan's Malpensa airport and Menaggio (2/day year-round, 2 hrs, €13 one-way). Last year's departures: Direct from Menaggio to Malpensa at 06:30; Malpensa to Menaggio at 12:00.

Other Hostels on Lago di Como: The Villa Olmo hostel is at the south end of the lake in Como (tel. 031-573-800), and another hostel is in the north at Domaso (tel. 0344-97449).

Transportation Connections—Varenna

From any destination covered in this book, you'll get to Lake Como via Milan. The quickest Milan connection to any point midlake (Bellagio, Menaggio, or Varenna) is via the train to Varenna. If leaving Varenna by train, note that the Varenna station doesn't sell tickets. Purchase a ticket either at the Albergo Beretta bar or the helpful and friendly travel agency, I Viaggi del Tivano, next door. Stamp your ticket in the machine at the station before boarding.

Milan to Varenna: Catch a train at Milano Centrale (last year's schedule: 08:15, 09:15, 12:15, 14:15, 16:15, 18:00, 19:10, 20:15, and 21:10, 60 min, €4.20). In Milan, the large overhead train schedules list Sondrio and Tirano rather than Varenna, a small stop en route (look at the fine print in the departure schedule posted at the station to make sure Varenna is listed). Some cars on long trains don't even get a platform. Ask for help so you don't miss the stop. You may have to open the door yourself.

Varenna to Milan: Trains leave Varenna for Milano Centrale at 06:18, 07:24, 08:23, 10:19, 12:23, 14:23, 16:22, 18:22, 20:20, and 22:30. (Confirm these times.) Varenna makes a comfy last stop before catching the shuttle from Milan's station to the airport.

Varenna to St. Moritz in Switzerland: From Varenna, you have fantastic access to the Bernina Express and scenic train to St. Moritz. First take the train to Tirano and then transfer to St. Moritz (3/day, allow 6 hrs with transfer).

THE DOLOMITES

Italy's dramatic limestone rooftop, the Dolomites, offers some of the best mountain thrills in Europe. Bolzano is the gateway to the Dolomites, and Castelrotto is a good home base for your exploration of Alpe di Siusi, Europe's largest alpine meadow.

The sunny Dolomites are well-developed, and the region's famous valleys and towns suffer from *après-ski* fever. The cost for the comfort of reliably good weather is a drained-reservoir feeling. Lovers of the Alps may miss the lushness that comes with the unpredictable weather farther north. But the bold limestone pillars, flecked with snow over green meadows under a blue sky, offer a worthwhile mountain experience.

A hard-fought history has left the region bicultural, with an emphasis on the German. Locals speak German first, and some wish they were still part of Austria. In the Middle Ages, as part of the Holy Roman Empire, the region faced north. Later it was firmly in the Austrian Hapsburg realm. By losing World War I, Austria's South Tirol became Italy's Alto Adige. Mussolini did what he could to Italianize the region, including giving each town an Italian name. But even in the last decade, local secessionist groups have agitated violently for more autonomy.

The government has wooed locals with economic breaks that make it one of Italy's richest areas (as local prices attest), and today all signs and literature in the province of Alto Adige/Süd Tirol are in both languages. Many include a third language, Ladin, the ancient Latin-type language still spoken in a few traditional areas. (I have listed both the Italian and German, so the confusion caused by this guidebook will match that caused by your travels.)

In spite of all the glamorous ski resorts and busy construction cranes, the local color survives in a warm, blue-aproned,

Dolomites

ruddy-faced, long-white-bearded way. There's yogurt and yodeling for breakfast. Culturally as much as geographically, the area is reminiscent of Austria. The Austrian Tirol is named for a village that is now part of Italy.

Planning Your Time

Train travelers should side-trip in from Bolzano (90 min north of Verona). To get a feel for the alpine culture, spend a night in Castelrotto. With two nights in Castelrotto, you can actually get out and hike. Tenderfeet ride the bus, catch a chairlift, and stroll. For mountain thrills, do a six-hour hike. And for a thrill that won't soon fade away, spend a night in a mountain hut. This means two nights in Castelrotto straddling a night in a hut.

Car hikers with a day can drive the three-hour loop from Bolzano or Castelrotto (Val Gardena-Sella Pass-Val di

Fassa) and ride one of the lifts to the top for a ridge walk. Connecting Bolzano and Venice by the Great Dolomite Road takes two hours longer than the autostrada but is far more scenic (see below).

Hiking season is mid-June through mid-October. The region is packed, booming, and blooming from mid-July through mid-September. Spring is dead, with no lifts running, huts closed, and the most exciting trails still under snow. Ski season (Dec–Easter) is busiest of all.

Helpful Hints
Study Ahead: The South Tirol's Web site is www.hallo.com.

Sleeping: Most towns offer hotels, which charge about €34 to €36 per person, and private homes, which offer beds for as low as €16 but are often a long walk from the town centers. Beds nearly always come with a hearty breakfast. Those traveling in peak season or staying for only one night pay more. Local TIs can always find budget travelers a bed in a private home (*Zimmer*). Drivers on a tight budget should pick remote *Zimmer*s. Most mountain huts offer reasonable doubles, cheap dorm (*lager*) beds, and inexpensive meals. Call any hut to secure a spot before hiking there (most huts open mid-June–Sept only).

Eating: In local restaurants, there is no cover charge, and tipping is not expected. A *Jausenstation* is a place that serves cheap, hearty, and traditional mountain-style food to hikers.

BOLZANO (BOZEN)
Willkommen to the Italian Tirol! If it weren't so sunny, you could be in Innsbruck. This enjoyable old town of 100,000 is the most convenient gateway to the Dolomites, especially if you're relying on public transportation. It's just the place to take a Tirolean stroll.

Bolzano is easy. Everything mentioned in Bolzano is a 10-minute walk from Piazza Walther. Leaving the train station, veer left up the tree-lined Viale Stazione (Bahnhofsallee) and walk past the bus station (on your left) two blocks to Piazza Walther, where you'll find the helpful TI on your right (Mon–Fri 09:00–18:30, Sat 09:00–12:30, closed Sun, tel. 0471-413-808). Pick up the city map (includes a walking tour). The excellent Dolomites information center is a block past the big church down Via Posta (Mon–Fri 09:00–12:00, 15:00–17:00, Parrocchia 11, tel. 0471-413-809). For Internet access, try Happy Time at Piazza Erbe.

The medieval heart of town is just beyond Piazza Walther. Follow your favorite Italian and head down the arcaded Via dei Portici to Piazza Erbe, with its ancient and still-thriving open-air produce market (wash your produce in the handy drinking fountain in the middle of the market).

Sights—Bolzano

▲▲**South Tirol Museum of Archaeology (Museo Archeo-logico dell'Alto Adige)**—This excellent museum features the original Ice Man. "Oetzi the Ice Man" is a 5,000-year-old body found frozen with his gear in a glacier by some German tourists a few years ago. With the help of informative displays and a great audioguide, you'll learn about life in this prehistoric period way before ATM machines. You'll see a convincing reconstruction of Oetzi, and yes, you actually get to see the man himself lying peacefully inside a specially built freezer (€6.70, €4.70 if you're 65 or over, audioguide-€1.60, Tue–Sun 10:00–18:00, Thu until 20:00, last entry 60 min before closing, closed Mon, Via Museo 43, near the river, tel. 0471-982-098, www.iceman.it).

Domenican Church (Chiesa dei Domenicani)—If you're an art-lover who won't make it to Padua to see Giotto's Scrovegni Chapel, drop by this 13th-century church to see its Chapel of St. John/San Giovanni (chapel near altar to the right), frescoed by the Giotto School. It lacks the high quality and that divine "Smurf" blue of the Scrovegni Chapel, but gives you a sense of Giotto's vision (free, Mon–Sat 09:30–17:30, peaceful cloisters to the right of the church, Piazza Domenicani).

Cable Car to Oberbozen—Of the three different cable cars that can whisk you out of Bolzano, the most popular is the Ritten lift to the touristy town of Oberbozen. More interesting than the town are the nearby "earth pyramids," a 20-minute walk from the lift. The pyramids are Bryce-like pinnacles rising out of the ridge (Rittner Sielbahn cable car runs hrly, €5.20; from Bolzano train station, walk about 5 blocks down Via Renon to reach the lift). A little train runs along the ridge, connecting Oberbozen nearly hourly with other villages.

Many are tempted to wimp out on the Dolomites and see them from a distance by hiking from Oberbozen to the Pemmern chairlift, riding to Schwarzseespitze, and walking 45 more minutes to the Rittner Horn. You'll be atop a 2,200-meter (7,000-foot) peak with distant but often hazy Dolomite views. It's not worth the trouble. (But if you're determined to do it and it's outside of summer, call the nearby Collabo TI at 0471-356-100 to make sure trails are clear of snow.)

Markets—In additon to the produce market on Piazza Erbe (Mon–Sat, closed Sun), a Saturday market is held on Piazza Vittoria (morning only).

Sleeping in Bolzano
(€1.10 = about $1, country code: 39, zip code: 39100)
Sleep Code: **S** = Single, **D** = Double/Twin, **T** = Triple, **Q** = Quad, **b** = bathroom, **s** = shower only, **CC** = Credit Card, **no CC** = Credit Cards not accepted, **SE** = Speaks English, **NSE** = No English.

All of the listed hotels are in the city center, listed here from the most expensive to the least.

Splurge: **Hotel Grief** is right on Piazza Walther. When you walk into any of their 33 rooms, designed by artists, you feel like you're in a modern art installation. It's not cozy, but it is striking. In rainy weather, the shiny silver umbrellas by the door are for guests to use (3 types of rooms: comfort/superior/deluxe—priciest, Sb-€124–170, Db-€170–232, includes buffet breakfast, CC, most rooms nonsmoking, air-con, laundry, parking-€16/day, Piazza Walther, entrance on Via della Rena, tel. 0471-318-000, fax 0471-318-148, www.greif.it, SE).

Moderately-priced: **Hotel Figl**, warmly run by Helga Mayr, has 23 comfortable rooms and an attached café on a pedestrian square a block from Piazza Walther (Sb-€72, Db-€93, junior suite-€98, apartment available, breakfast extra, CC, air-con, elevator, Kornplatz 9, tel. & fax 0471-978-412, www.figl.net, SE).

Cheaper Options: **Gasthof Weisses Kreuz**, with 10 basic rooms, is a great value, but it's usually booked up (S-€28, D-€49, Db-€57, Tb-€72, includes breakfast, 1 block off Piazza Walther in old town at Kornplatz 3, tel. 0471-977-552, fax 0471-972-273, e-mail: weisseskreuzbz@yahoo.it, NSE).

The modern, clean, church-run **Kolpinghaus Bozen** has plenty of rooms with twin beds and all the comforts. It makes one feel thankful (Sb-€46, Db-€72, Tb-€108, includes breakfast, CC, confusing elevator, 4 blocks from Piazza Walther, near Piazza Domenicani at Spitalgasse 3, tel. 0471-308-400, fax 0471-973-917, www.kolping.it/bz, e-mail: kolping@tin.it, SE). The lineup in front of the building at lunchtime is workers waiting for the institutional cafeteria to open up (€8 meals, open to the public, Mon–Fri 11:45–13:45, 18:30–19:30).

Eating in Bolzano

All listings are in the downtown core.

Weisses Rosl offers affordable Italian, German, and veggie options in a pub-like setting (closed Sat eve and all Sun, Via Bottai, 2 blocks north of Piazza Municipio, tel. 0471-973-267).

The next three places cluster at the southern edge of Piazza Erbe. **Hopfen and Co.** offers delicious meals (Mon–Sat 09:30–01:00, closed Sun, Piazza Erbe 17, tel. 0471-300-788). **Vogele**, a half block south, serves German/Italian cuisine and has a rare non-smoking floor upstairs, bigger than it initially looks (closed Sat eve and all day Sun, Via Goethe 3, tel. 0471-973-938). **Enoteca Bacaro**, a wine bar a half block east, is an intriguing spot for a glass of wine and bar snacks amid locals (closed Sun, located on alley off Via Argentieri 17, tel. 0471-971-421).

Hostaria Argentieri, pricier than the rest, serves Italian and

German cuisine plus seafood in a classy setting (closed Sun, Via Argentieri 14, tel. 0471-981-718).

On Sundays, when virtually all restaurants are closed, try **Gasthaus Batzenhausl** (closed Thu, Andreas Hofer Strasse 30, tel. 0471-976-183) or the cheaper **Restaurant Blaues Schiff** (Lauben 57, tel. 0471-979-089).

Picnic: Assemble the ingredients at the **Piazza Erbe** market; dine in a superb setting in Piazza Walther or in the park along the Talvera River. A **DeSpar** supermarket is on Via della Rena near Piazza Walther (Mon–Fri 08:00–19:00, Sat 08:00–18:00, closed Sun; from Piazza Walther, facing the TI, take the street to the left for two blocks).

Transportation Connections—Bolzano
By train to: Milan (2/day, 3.5 hrs), **Verona** (hrly, 90 min), **Trento** (hrly, 40 min), **Venice** and **Florence** (via Verona, 3–4 hrs), **Innsbruck** (hrly, 2.5 hrs). Train info: tel. 848-888-088.

By bus to: Castelrotto (2/hr, 40 min, leaves Bolzano at :10 and :40 virtually every hour).

CASTELROTTO (KASTELRUTH)
Castelrotto (population 6,000, altitude 1,060 meters), the ideal home base for exploring the Alpe di Siusi, has more village character than any other town I know of in the region. Friday morning is the farmers' market (June–Oct), and a crafts market fills the town square most Thursday mornings. It's touristy but not a full-blown resort—it's full of real people. Pop into the church to hear the choir practice or be on the town square weekdays at 14:45 when the moms gather their kinder-gartners, chat, and then head home or stop by the playground on Plattenstrasse. On Fridays, the bells peal at 15:00, commemo-rating Christ's sacrifice. On Sundays, townspeople and farmers attend church and linger to visit. Against a backdrop of moun-tains, Castelrotto conveys the powerful message that simple pleasures are enough. The folk-singing group Kastelruther Spatzen has an avid following in town, produces "more CDs than Michael Jackson" (a local told me proudly), and holds a concert here every October.

The TI is on the main square (Mon–Sat 08:30–12:30, 13:30–18:00, Sun 09:00–12:00, tel. 0471-706-333). The bus park has a little building with an ATM, WC, and phones; take the stairs to the right of this building to get to the main square. Another cash machine is across the street from the TI (look for "Meine Bank" sign and go inside).

For a scenic viewpoint, take a short walk uphill from the TI (facing TI, take road under arch to the right, then follow signs to Kalvarienberg/Calvario; you'll pass the stations of the cross).

Sleeping in Castelrotto
(€1.10 = about $1, country code: 39, zip code: 39040)
Albergo Torre (in German, **Gasthof Zum Turm**) is comfortable, clean, and traditional, with great beds and modern bathrooms (prices vary with season and amenities, Db-€50–110, Tb-€64–150, includes breakfast, €3 extra for 1-night stays, CC, closed April and Nov, elevator, behind TI at Kofelgasse 8, tel. 0471-706-349, fax 0471-707-268, www.zumturm.com, e-mail: info@zumturm.com, Gabi and Günther SE). If you're driving, go right through the traffic-free town center (very likely with a police escort). Under the bell tower, enter the white arch to the right of the TI and park (free for guests) in the lot opposite the front door.

Gasthof zum Wolf (in Italian, **Al Lupo**) is pure Tirolean with all the comforts (Sb-€37-52, Db-€68-101, prices vary with season and view, includes breakfast, CNN in rooms, a block below main square at Wolkensteinstrasse 5, tel. 0471-706-332, fax 0471-707-030, www.hotelwolf.it, e-mail: info@hotelwolf.it, Arno SE).

Hotel Cavallino D'Oro (in German, **Goldenes Rossl**), on the main square, has plenty of Tirolean character and is run by friendly and helpful Stefan. Every room is different, and locals frequent the bar. If you love antiques by candlelight (or have only credit cards), this 600-year-old hotel is the best in town (Sb-€53–70, Db-€83–98 depending on season, discount for 3-night stay, CC, no elevator, Krausplatz 1, tel. 0471-706-337, fax 0471-707-172, www.cavallino.it, e-mail: cavallino@cavallino.it, SE). Stefan converted his 500-year-old wine cellar into a spa and sauna, complete with heated tile seats and tropical plants.

Haus Harderer, below Pensione Castelrotto, rents three rooms (Ss-€25, Ds-€50, includes breakfast, no CC, minimum 2 nights in summer) and a fine apartment for longer stays (€93/day, sleeps 4–6, no breakfast, no CC, Plattenstrasse 20, tel. 0471-706-702, run by Inge—SE, plus Oswald, Heinz—SE, Ida, and Mimme the cat). As you enter the driveway, the Harderer house is the one to the right.

Tirler Hof, the storybook Jaider family farm, has 35 cows, one friendly *hund*, four Old World–comfy guest rooms, and a great mountain view (D-€41, includes breakfast, practical only for drivers, it's the first farm outside of town on the right on road to St. Michael, Paniderstrasse 44, tel. 0471-706-017, e-mail: jaider.klaus@rolmail.net, NSE). The ground-floor double has a private bath. The top-floor rooms share a bathroom and a great balcony. Take a stroll before breakfast.

Eating in Castelrotto
The hotels' restaurants are good. Consider **Cavallino D'Oro** (on one side of hotel is the *ristorante*, on the other side is the bar— each side gets the same menu; Wed–Mon 12:00–14:00, 18:00–02:00,

closed Tue) or the less expensive **Albergo Torre** (Thu–Tue 12:00–13:30, 18:00–20:30, closed Wed, April, and Nov). The **Hexankellar**, or the "Witch Cellar," dishes up affordable German and Italian cooking (Mon–Sat 17:00–22:00, closed Sun, a block from TI on Plattenstrasse; facing TI, go left through arch).

For strudel, locals like the simple **Stella** (Tue–Sun 07:30–19:00, closed Mon, on Plattenstrasse; facing TI, go left through arch) and **Café Doris** (closed Tue, on main road at Wolkenstein 29, tel. 0471-706-340); both have terraces. Even better, for strudel *mit* view, take the little Marinzen cable car up the mountain to the **Marinzenhutte** café (tel. 0471-707-158, has animal park for kids). The lift runs from the end of May through October (€4.10 one-way, €6.20 return, base of lift is 2 blocks from bus park; facing A&O Supermarket, go left). You can hike down from Marinzen or return on the lift.

Castelrotto has two groceries: **Silbernagl Kaufhaus** (Mon–Sat 08:00–12:00, 15:00–19:00, closed Sun, on Wolkenstein) and the smaller **A&O Supermarket** (Mon–Sat 08:00–12:00, 15:00–18:30, closed Sun, 2 blocks away, also on main drag).

Transportation Connections—Castelrotto
Catch buses to get into the heart of the Alpe di Siusi. Buy tickets on the bus.

By bus to: Saltria (4–15/day, toll-free info tel. 800-846-047 or tel. 0471-706-633); **Val di Fassa, Vigo di Fassa,** and **Canazei** (late June–mid Sept only, 4/day, 2 hrs); and **Val Gardena, Ortisei/St. Ulrich,** and **St. Cristina** (summer only, 4/day, 1 hr). Buses leave Castelrotto at :00 and :30 for **Bolzano** (40 min).

Summer Shuttle Buses: From June through mid-October, Buxi shuttle buses go about twice hourly from Castelrotto through Alpe di Siusi to Saltria (8:00–17:00, discounted return tickets). Off-season, SAD buses take over, running four a day in both directions between Castelrotto and Saltria. Guests at some Castelrotto hotels ride free on Buxi buses—ask.

ALPE DI SIUSI (SEISER ALM)
Europe's largest high alpine meadow, Alpe di Siusi, separates two of the most famous Dolomite ski-resort valleys. Measuring five kilometers by 12 kilometers and soaring from 1,800 to 2,000 meters high, Alpe di Suisi is dotted by farm huts and wildflowers (mid-June–July), surrounded by dramatic (if distant) Dolomite peaks and cliffs, and much appreciated by hordes of walkers.

The Sasso Lungo (Langkofel) mountains at the head of the meadow provide a storybook Dolomite backdrop, while the spooky Schlern peak stands boldly staring into the haze of the peninsula. The Schlern, looking like a devilish *Winged Victory*, gave ancient peoples enough willies to spawn legends

Alpe di Siusi

NOTE: This 3-D view looks southeast & is not to scale. Elevations in meters

KEY:
● = TOWN
— = ROAD
•--• = LIFT
······· = TRAIL
▲ = MTN. HUT (HUTTE/RIFUGIO)

★ = PENSION SEELAUS

DCH

of supernatural forces. The Schlern witch, today's tourist bro-chure mascot, was the cause of many a broom-riding medieval townswoman's fiery death.

The Alpe di Siusi is my recommended one-stop look at the Dolomites because of Castelrotto's charm as a home base, its easy accessibility to those with and without cars, its variety of walks and hikes, and its quintessentially Dolomite mountain views.

A natural preserve, Alpe di Siusi is closed to cars past Compatsch. The Buxi park bus shuttles hikers to and from key points along the tiny road all the way to Saltria at the foot of the postcard-dramatic Sasso peaks (Sasso Lungo, 3,180 meters). Meadow walks, for flower-lovers and strollers, are pretty—or maybe pretty boring. Chairlifts are springboards for more dramatic and demanding hikes.

Trails are well-marked, and the brightly painted numbers are keyed into local maps. The Kompass Bolzano map #54 covers everything in this chapter (scale 1:50,000, €4.10). The Wander-karte map of Alpe di Siusi (produced by Tabacco) offers more detail and focuses on just Alpe di Siusi (scale 1:25,000, €2.60).

Compatsch, a kilometer in and as far as you're allowed to drive, is the tourist village (1,870 meters) and has a TI (Mon–Sat 09:00–17:00, Sun 09:00–12:00, free WCs behind TI, tel. 0471-727-904). There's also a grocery store (open mid-June–mid-Oct), mountain bike rentals (€5.20/1 hr, €13/4 hrs), an ATM, parking (€3.10/day), hotels, restaurants, shops, and so on. Trocker rents horses and provides guides (€13/1 hr, €23/2 hrs, €32/3 hrs, April–Oct, 100 meters before Compatsch TI, tel. 0471-727-807, NSE).

Sleeping near the Park Entrance: Pension Seelaus, a 10-minute walk downhill from Compatsch, is a cozy, friendly, family-run place with a Germanic feel and down comforters (Sb-€52–69, Db-€103–138, prices vary with season and type of room, includes buffet breakfast and hearty dinner, no CC, Via Compatsch 8, tel. 0471-727-954, fax 0471-727-835, www.hotelseelaus.it, e-mail: info@hotelseelaus.it, Roberto SE).

Hikes in the Alpe di Siusi

Easy meadow walks abound, giving tenderfeet classic Dolomite views from baby-stroller trails. Experienced hikers should consider the tougher and more exciting treks. Before attempting a hike, call or stop by the local TI to confirm your understanding of the time and skills required. Many lifts operate mid-June through mid-October and during the winter ski season. The Panorama and Puflatsch lifts (both near Compatsch) run further into the off-season.

Three Easy Walks from Compatsch: Take a lift to Puflatsch for the two-hour loop north to Arnikahütte (has café) and back (elevation gain about 200 meters).

Or: Ride the lift to Panorama, then hike 90 minutes to Molignonhütte (2,050 meters) and back down to Compatsch; or continue 2.5 hours (fairly level) to Zallingerhütte (2,050 meters) and another 90 minutes to Saltria and the Buxi bus stop.

Or: Bus to Saltria and hike the 2.5-hour loop to Zallingerhütte (2,050 meters, 200-meter altitude gain).

Summit Hike of Schlern (Sciliar): For a challenging 19-kilometer (12-mile), six-hour hike with a possible overnight in a traditional mountain refuge, consider hiking to the summit of Schlern and spending a night in Rifugio Bolzano (Schlernhaus). Start at the Spitzbühl lift (1,725 meters, free parking lot, first bus stop in park). The Spitzbühl chairlift drops you at Spitzbühl (1,935 meters). Trail #5 takes you through a high meadow, down to the Saltner Schwaige dairy farm (1,830 meters), across a stream, and steeply up the Schlern mountain. You'll meet trail #1 and walk across the rocky tabletop plateau of Schlern to the mountain hotel, Rifugio Bolzano/Schlernhaus, three hours into your hike (2,450 meters, D-€35, dorm beds-€10, tel. 0471-612-024, call for reservation). From this dramatic setting, you get a great view of the Rosengarten range. Hike 20 more minutes up the nearby peak (Mount Pez, 2,560 meters) for a 360-degree alpine panorama. From the Schlernhaus, you can hike back the way you came or walk farther along the Schlern (12 km, 2 hrs, past the Rifugio Alpe di Tires, tel. 0471-727-958, 2,440 meters) and descend back into Alpe di Siusi and the road where the Buxi bus will return you to your starting point or hotel.

Loop around Sasso Lungo: Another dramatic but easy hike is the eight-hour walk around Sasso Lungo (Langkofel). You can ride the bus to Saltria (end of the line), take the chairlift to Williamshütte, walk past the Zallingerhütte (overnight possible, tel. 0471-727-947), and circle the Sasso group.

More Sights in the Dolomites

▲▲**Great Dolomite Road**—This is the definitive Dolomite drive: Belluno/Cortina/Pordoi Pass/Sella Pass/Val di Fassa/Bolzano. Connecting Venice with Bolzano this way (the Belluno-Venice autostrada is slick) takes two hours longer than the Bolzano-Verona-Venice autostrada. No public transit does this trip. In spring and early summer, passes labeled "closed" are often bare, dry, and, as far as local drivers are concerned, wide open.

▲▲**Abbreviated Dolomite Loop Drive**—See the biggies in half the kilometers (allow 3 hours, Bolzano/Castelrotto/Val Gardena/Sella Pass/Val di Fassa/Bolzano). Val Gardena (Grodner Tal) is famous for its skiing and hiking resorts, traditional Ladin culture, and wood-carvers (the wood-carver ANRI is from the Val Gardena town of St. Cristina). It's a bit overrated, but even if its culture has been suffocated by the big bucks of hedonistic European fun-seekers, it remains a good jumping-off point for trips into the mountains. Within an hour, you'll reach Sella Pass (2,240 meters). After a series of tight hairpin turns a mile or so over the pass, you'll see some benches and cars. Pull over and watch the rock climbers. Val di Fassa is Alberto Tomba country. The town of Canazei, at the head of the valley and the end of the bus line, has the most ambience and altitude (1,415 meters). From there, a lift takes you to Col dei Rossi Belvedere, where you can hike the Bindelweg trail past Rifugio Belvedere along an easy but breathtaking ridge to Rifugio Viel del Pan. This three-hour round-trip hike has views of the highest mountain in the Dolomites—the Marmolada—and the Dolo-mighty Sella range.

▲▲**Reifenstein Castle**—For one of Europe's most intimate looks at medieval castle life, let the friendly lady of Reifenstein (Frau Blanc) show you around her wonderfully preserved castle. She leads tours on the hour, in Italian and German, squeezing in whatever English she can (€3.10, open Easter–Oct, tours on Mon at 14:00 and 15:00, Tue–Thu and Sat–Sun at 09:30, 10:30, 14:00, and 15:00, closed Fri, picnic spot at drawbridge, tel. 0472-765-879).

To drive to the castle, exit the autostrada at Vipiteno (Sterzing) and follow signs toward Bolzano. The castle is just west of the freeway; park at the base of the castle's rock. Of the two castles here, Reifenstein is the one to the west. While this is easy by car, it's probably not worth the trouble by train (from Bolzano, 6/day, 70 min).

▲**Glurns**—Drivers connecting the Dolomites and Lake Como by the high road via Meran and Bormio should spend the night in the amazing little town of Glurns (45 minutes west of touristy Meran between Schluderns and Taufers). Glurns still lives within its square wall on the Adige River, with a church bell tower that has a thing about ringing and real farms, rather than boutiques, filling the town courtyards. There are several small hotels in the town, but I'd stay in a private home (Family Hofer, 6 rooms, Db-€41–46 with breakfast, less for 3 nights, no CC, 100 meters from town square, near church, just outside wall on river, tel. 0473-831-597).

NAPLES AND THE AMALFI COAST

If you like Italy as far south as Rome, go farther south. It gets better. If Italy is getting on your nerves, think twice about going farther. Italy intensifies as you plunge deeper. Naples is Italy in the extreme—its best (birthplace of pizza and Sophia Loren) and its worst (home of the Camorra, Naples' "family" of organized crime).

Serene Sorrento, without a hint of big-city Naples and just an hour to the south, makes a great home base. It's the gateway to the much-loved Amalfi Coast. From the jet-setting island of Capri to the stunning scenery of the Amalfi Coast, from ancient Pompeii to even more ancient Paestum, this is Italy's coast with the most.

Planning Your Time

On a quick trip, give the area three days. With Sorrento as your sunny springboard, spend a day in Naples, a day exploring the Amalfi Coast, and a day split between Pompeii and the town of Sorrento. While Paestum, the crater of Vesuvius, Herculaneum, and the island of Capri are decent options, they are worthwhile only if you give the area more time.

For a blitz tour, you could have breakfast on the early Rome-Naples express train (about 07:00–09:00), do Naples and Pompeii in a day, and be back in Rome in time for Letterman. That's exhausting but more memorable than a fourth day in Rome. Remember that in the afternoon, Naples' street life slows and many sights close as the temperature soars. The city comes back to life in the early evening.

For a small-town vacation from your vacation, spend a few more days on the Amalfi Coast, sleeping in Positano, Atrani, or Marina del Cantone.

For most, driving south of Rome is not only stressful, it's impractical. Take advantage of the wonderful public transportation:

the slick two-hour Rome–Naples express trains (or direct 5-hour express connections with Florence); the handy Circumvesuviana commuter train (lacing together Naples, Pompeii, and Sorrento); and the regular bus service between Sorrento and the Amalfi Coast (where parking and car access are severely limited).

NAPLES (NAPOLI)

Italy's third-largest city (with 1.2 million people, 2 million in greater Naples) has almost no open spaces or parks, which makes its position as Europe's most densely populated city plenty evident. Watching the police try to enforce traffic sanity is almost comical in Italy's grittiest, most polluted, and most crime-ridden city.

But Naples surprises the observant traveler with its good humor, decency, and impressive knack for living, eating, and raising children in the streets. Overcome your fear of being run down or ripped off long enough to talk with people—enjoy a few smiles and jokes with the man running the neighborhood tripe shop or the woman taking her day-care class on a walk through the traffic. (Ask a local about the New Year's Eve tradition of tossing chipped dinner plates off of balconies into the streets.)

Twenty-five hundred years ago, Neapolis ("new city") was a thriving Greek commercial center. It remains southern Italy's leading city, offering a fascinating collection of museums, churches, and eclectic architecture. The pulse of Italy throbs in Naples. This tangled mess—the closest thing to "reality travel" you'll find in Western Europe—still somehow manages to breathe, laugh, and sing—with a captivating Italian accent.

Planning Your Time

For a quick visit, start with the archaeology museum, do the Slice-of-Neapolitan-Life Walk (see "Sights," below), and celebrate your survival with pizza. Of course, Naples is huge. But even with limited time, if you stick to the described route and grab a cab when you're lost or tired, it's fun. Treat yourself well in Naples; the city is cheap by Italian standards.

Orientation

Tourist Information: The TI is in the central train station (Mon–Sat 09:00–20:00, Sun 09:00–13:00; with your back to the tracks, TI is in the lobby to your left; then, within the lobby, TI is to your right, tel. 081-268-779). Pick up a map, and, even though the odds are against you, ask for the *Qui Napoli* booklet—when they say they're "finished," ask for an old one.

Arrival in Naples: There are several Naples stations. You want Naples Centrale (facing Piazza Garibaldi), which has a TI, baggage check, and the Circumvesuviana stop for commuter trains to Sorrento and Pompeii. As Centrale is a dead-end station,

From Naples to Paestum

through trains often stop at Piazza Garibaldi (actually a subway station just downstairs from Centrale), Campi Flegrei, or Napoli Mergellina across town. The stations of Campi Flegrei and Mergellina (which also has a TI) are connected to Centrale by a direct subway route; a railpass or train ticket to Napoli Centrale covers the ride (subway trains depart about every 10 min, less often on Sun). While on the train to Naples, ask the conductor which Naples stations your train stops at. Get off at Mergellina or Campi Flegrei only if your train does not stop at Centrale or Garibaldi.

Helpful Hints

Traffic: In Naples, red lights are discretionary, and pedestrians need to be wary, particularly of the Vespa motorcycles.

Theft Alert: Lately Naples, under a new activist mayor, has been occupied by an army of police and feels much safer. Still, err on the side of caution. Don't venture into neighborhoods that make you uncomfortable. Walk with confidence, as if you know where you're going and what you're doing. Assume able-bodied beggars are thieves. Tighten your money belt and keep it completely hidden. Stick to busy streets and beware of gangs of hoodlums. A third of the city is unemployed, and past local governments set an example the Mafia would be proud of. Assume con artists are cleverer than you. Any jostle or commotion is probably a thief team smokescreen.

Naples Transportation

Any bags are probably safest checked at the central train station (€2.60, *deposito bagagli* near track #24).

Perhaps your biggest risk of theft is catching or riding the Circumvesuviana commuter train. Remember, if you're connecting from a major train, you'll be stepping from a relatively secure compartment into a crowded Naples subway filled with thieves hunting disoriented American tourists with luggage. While I ride the Circumvesuviana comfortably and safely, each year I hear of many who get ripped off on this ride. You won't be mugged— just conned or pickpocketed. Con artists may say you need to "transfer" by taxi to catch the Circumvesuviana; you don't. There are no porters at the Centrale station or in the basement where the Circumvesuviana station is located; anyone offering to help you with your bags is likely a thief. Wear your money belt, hang on to your bag, and don't display any valuables. For €80, you can ride a **taxi** from Naples 50 kilometers (30 miles) directly to your Sorrento hotel; agree on a fixed price without the meter and pay upon arrival. As another option, consider the Naples–Sorrento **boat**; it's faster, safer, and more scenic than the Circumvesuviana. Naples' port (Beverello) is near the Castel Nuovo at the low end of the described walk and a quick taxi ride from the museum. (For details, see "Sorrento," below.)

Getting around Naples

Naples' subway, the Servizio Metropolitano, runs from the Centrale station through the center of town (direction: Pozzouli), stopping at Piazza Cavour (Archaeological Museum), Piazza Dante, and Monte-santo (top of Spanish Quarter and Spaccanapoli). Tickets, which cost €0.75, are good for 90 minutes. All-day tickets cost €2.35. If you can afford a taxi, don't mess with the buses. A short taxi ride costs €3 to €5 (insist on the meter; supplement charged on Sun).

Getting to the Museum: From the Centrale train station, follow signs to *Metropolitano* (downstairs, buy tickets from window on right, ask which track—"*Binario?*" to Piazza Cavour—it's usually track 4, "*quattro*," go through a *solo metropolitano* turnstile and ride the subway one stop). As you leave the Metro, take the exit to the right. Walk through the park. At the end of cluttered Piazza Cavour, you'll see several pink buildings ahead. The museum is the pink building on the right side of the street.

Sights—Naples

▲▲▲**Museo Archeologico**—For lovers of antiquity, this museum alone makes Naples a worthwhile stop. It offers the only possible peek into the artistic jewelry boxes of Pompeii and Herculaneum. The actual sights are impressive but barren; the best art and all the artifacts ended up here.

Hours, Cost, and Information: €6.20, Wed–Mon 09:00–20:00, summer Sat until 23:00, closed Tue. Tours in English are offered weekdays at 11:30 and 15:30 (except on Tue when museum is closed) and on Sat and Sun at 10:00, 11:00, 12:00, and 15:30 (€3, 1.5 hrs, depart from entry, confirm tour times by calling 081-440-166). Audioguides cost €3.75 (at bookshop, rentable for 3 hrs). Photos are allowed without a flash. The shop sells a worthwhile green guidebook, titled *National Archeological Museum of Naples* (€7.75).

Orientation: At the desk next to the ticket booth, you can sign up for a free 20-minute tour of the Secret Room (containing erotic art from Pompeii and Herculaneum). You'll be given a tour time; meet at the Secret Room (*Gabinetto Segreto*) on the mezzanine near the *Battle of Alexander* mosaic. These short tours, generally offered at the top and bottom of every hour, are usually given in Italian, but English tours are possible—ask.

After passing through the turnstile, orient yourself this way: Face the grand staircase. For the Farnese Collection of marble statues, turn right just before the staircase (and walk way back). The Pompeii mosaics and the Secret Room are on the small mezzanine level (up the grand staircase and on your left). The huge first floor (top of the grand staircase) contains bronze statues from Herculaneum, frescoes from Pompeii, and vases from Paestum. Stairs behind the grand staircase lead to the basement WCs.

Statues, Frescoes, and Artifacts (top floor): Climb the stairs to the top floor. Before you enter the great hall, look right to locate the entrance to the bronze statues of Herculaneum. This large collection—including a dozen bronze statues, plus busts and marble statues—came from Villa Papiri (Papyrus) in Herculaneum. Look into the lifelike blue eyes of the two intense *atleta* (athletes); they are bent on doing their best.

Step inside the great hall. With your back to the entrance,

Naples

PIAZZA CAVOUR

MUSEO ARCHEO-LOGICO

VIA FORIA

CENTRALE STATION F.S.

NOVARA

❷ ❶

VIA CARBONARA

SAN SEVERO

LARGO DONNA

Duomo

PIAZZA GARIBALDI

MONTE SANTO METRO + FUNICULAR

PESSINA

S. BIAGIO FORCELLA

PIAZZA GARIBALDI

EMAN.

VIA TARSIA

S. BROCE

VIA B. CROCE

Gesù Nuovo

UMBERTO

FISH MKT. PORTA (NOLANA)

CORSO GARI.

❸

CIRCUM-VESUVIANA STAZIONE

VOMERO

CORSO VIT.

VIA P. SCURA

PIAZZA DANTE

TOLEDO

MORG.

S. CHIARA

CORSO

N. MARINA

SPANISH QUARTER

PIAZZA CARITA

VIA ROMA

VIA DIAZ

A. DEPRETIS

VIA COLOMBO

N. MARINA

PORT

Opera

GALLERIA UMBERTO I

CASTEL NUOVO

STAZIONE MARITIMA

PIAZZA PLEBI-SCITO

VIA

MOLO BEV.

CAR FERRIES TO SICILY & SARDINIA

CHAIA

S. FRAN. E PAOLO

VITTORIO TUNNEL

PALAZZO REALE

TO SORRENTO, CAPRI, ISCHIA & PROCIDA

TO MERGELLINA & CAMPO FLEGREI

SAURO

N

VIA PARTENOPE

800 YARDS

800 METERS

CASTEL DELL' OVO →

DCH

❶ HOTEL GINEVRA   ❸ GRAND HOTEL TERMINUS
❷ HOTEL EDEN

the rooms on your left feature the Pompeii frescoes, paintings, artifacts, and an interesting model of the town of Pompeii (called *plastico di Pompeii*; near the glass objects). The rooms on your right feature ancient Greek art: a model of Paestum and ancient vases discovered on-site. (Paestum, a temple complex south of Naples, was part of a once-thriving region known as Greater Greece; for more info, see "Paestum," below.) If you contrast all of this ancient art with the darkness of medieval Europe, it becomes clear that classical art greatly inspired and enlightened the Renaissance greats.

Mosaics (mezzanine): On the mezzanine floor below (directly under the bronze statues from Herculaneum), you'll find a small, exquisite collection of Pompeian mosaics and the sexy Secret Room. Most of these mosaics were taken from the House of the Faun, which you'll see at Pompeii. Don't miss the house's delightful centerpiece: a bronze statue (a half-meter high) of the *Dancing Faun*. A highlight of the mosaics is the grand *Battle of Alexander* (a first-century B.C. copy of a fourth-century B.C. Greek original). It decorated a floor in the House of the Faun.

The **Secret Room**, to the left of the *Battle of Alexander* mosaic, contains a small assortment of frescoes, pottery, and statues that once decorated bedrooms, brothels, and even shops at Pompeii and Herculaneum (enter only with a guide, see "Orientation," above). If you didn't bother with making an appointment, you can still peek through the iron gate.

When this earthy art was unearthed in the mid-18th century, people were upset to find their view of the Romans as wise administrators and lawmakers upended. Actually, the meaning of an erect penis was more complex back then than today—dealing with abundance and good luck, as well as good sex.

Farnese Collection (ground floor): This floor has enough Egyptian, Greek, Roman, and Etruscan art to put any museum on the map. Its highlight is the Farnese Collection, a giant hall of huge, bright, and wonderfully restored statues excavated from Rome's Baths of Caracalla. The Toro Farnese—a tangled group with a woman being tied to a bull—is the largest intact statue from antiquity. Actually a third-century copy of a Hellenistic original, it was carved out of one piece of marble and restored by Michelangelo and others.

Once upon an ancient Greek time, King Lykos was bewitched by Dirce and abandoned his pregnant wife (standing regally in the background). The single mom gave birth to twin boys (shown here) who grew up to kill their deadbeat dad and tie Dirce to the horns of a bull to be bashed against a mountain.

You can almost hear the bull snorting. Read the worthwhile descriptions on the walls. At the far end of the hall (opposite the Toro, behind Hercules), a small room contains the sumptuous Farnese Cup, a large ancient cameo made of agates (well-described).

▲▲▲**The Slice-of-Neapolitan-Life Walk**—Walk from the museum through the heart of town and back to the station (allow at least 2 hours plus lunch and sightseeing stops). Sights are listed in the order you'll see them on this walk.

Naples, a living medieval city, is its own best sight. Couples artfully make love on Vespas surrounded by more fights and smiles per cobble here than anywhere else in Italy. Rather than seeing Naples as a list of sights, see the one great museum and then capture its essence by taking this walk through the core of the

Naples Walk

¼ MILE

400 METERS

MUSEO ARCHEOLOGICO

ONE STOP ON SUBWAY TO PIAZZA GARIBALDI & CENTRAL STATION

PIAZZA CAVOUR FORIA

CAVOUR METRO STOP

VIA FORIA

Start

GALLERIA PRINCIPE

DUOMO

VIA DUOMO

VIA PESSINA

PIAZZA BELLINI

SAN SEVERO

VICARIA

COLLETTA

PIAZZA DANTE

VIA PORT'ALBA

SAN DOM.

CROCE

PIZZA

GESU NUOVO

MADDALONI

SPACCA-NAPOLI

CORSO UMBERTO I

TO PIAZZA GARIBALDI (10 MIN. WALK)

VIA TOLEDO

SANTA CHIARA

PIAZZA CARITA

VIA MORGANTINI

N

SPANISH QUARTER

VIA DIAZ

GALLERIA UMBERTO I

BAY

PIAZZA MUNICIPO

STAZIONE MARITTIMA

SAN CARLO

CASTEL NUOVO

OF

ROYAL PALACE

BEVERELLO PORT (BOATS TO SORRENTO) & CAPRI

S. FRAN. DI PAOLA

PIAZZA PLEBISCITO

DCH

NAPLES

city. Should you become overwhelmed or lost, step into a store and ask for help: "*Dov'è la stazione centrale?*" (DOH-vay lah staht-zee-OH-nay chen-TRAH-lay?) or point to the next sight in this book.

Via Toledo and the Spanish Quarter (city walk, first half): Leaving the Archaeological Museum at the top of Piazza Cavour (Metro: Piazza Cavour), cross the street and walk through

the ornate *galleria* (the grand, arched gallery) on your way to
Via Pessina. The first part of this walk is a straight 1.5-kilometer
ramble down this boulevard to Galleria Umberto I near the
Royal Palace.

Busy Via Pessina leads downhill to Piazza Dante—marked
by a statue of Dante. Originally, a statue of a Spanish Bourbon
king stood here. The grand red-and-gray building is typical of
the Bourbon buildings from that period. In 1861, with the unification of Italy, the king—symbolic of Italy's colonial subjugation—
was replaced by Dante—considered the father of the Italian
language and a strong symbol of Italian nationalism.

Poor old Dante looks out over the urban chaos with a hope-
less gesture. Unknowingly, he points the way to the Alba Gate
(part of Naple's old wall and the entrance to a small street often
lined with streetside book vendors). Via Pessina, the long, straight
road we're walking, originated as a military road built by Spain
around 1600. It skirted the old town wall to connect the Spanish
military headquarters (now the museum) with the royal palace
(down by the bay).

A new subway station has recently been built here on Piazza
Dante. Construction was slowed by the city's rich underground
history: four meters down—Roman ruins, seven meters down—
Greek ruins.

Continue walking downhill, remembering that here in Naples
red lights are considered "decorations." The people here are sur-
vivors; a long history of corrupt and greedy colonial overlords has
taught Neapolitans to deal with authority creatively. Many credit
this aspect of Naples' past for the advent of organized crime here.

Via Pessina becomes Via Toledo, Naples' principal shopping
street. In 1860, from the white marble balcony (on the neoclassical
building) overlooking Piazza Sette Settembre, the famous revolutionary Garibaldi declared Italy united and Victor Emanuel its first
king. A year later, the dream of Italian unity was actually realized.

Continue straight on Via Toledo (even though the arterial
jogs left). About five blocks below Piazza Dante, at Via Maddaloni,
you cross the long, straight street called **Spaccanapoli** (literally,
"split Naples"). Look left. Look right. Since ancient times, this
thin street (which changes names several times) has bisected the
city. (We'll be coming back to this point later. If you want to
abbreviate this walk, turn left here and skip down to the Spaccanapoli section.)

Via Toledo runs through Piazza Carita (also known by its
new name, Piazza Salvo D'Acquisto), with fascist architecture
(from 1938, sternly straight and obedient lines) overlooking the
square. Wander down Via Toledo a few blocks, past more fascist
architecture—the two banks on the left. Try robbing the second
one (Banco di Napoli, Via Toledo 178).

Up the hill to your right is the **Spanish Quarter**, Naples at its rawest, poorest, and most historic. Thrill-seekers (or someone in need of a prostitute) can take a stroll up one of these streets and loop back to Via Toledo.

The only thing predictable about this Neapolitan tide pool is the ancient grid plan of its streets (which survives from Greek times), the friendliness of its shopkeepers, and the boldness of its mopeds. Concerned locals will tug on their lower eyelids, warning you to be wary. Pop into a grocery shop and ask the man to make you his best ham and mozzarella sandwich. Trust him on the price—it should be around €3.

Continue down Via Toledo to Piazza Plebiscito. From here, you'll see the Church of San Francesco di Paola with its Pantheon-inspired dome and broad, arcing colonnades. Opposite is the **Royal Palace**, which has housed Spanish, French, and even Italian royalty. The lavish interior is open for tours (€4, Thu–Tue 09:00–20:00, Sat until 23:00, closed Wed, shorter hours off-season; a TI is inside the Royal Palace). Next door, peek inside the neoclassical Teatro San Carlo, Italy's second-most-respected opera house (after Milan's La Scala). The huge castle on the harborfront just beyond the palace houses government bureaucrats and is closed to tourists.

Under the Victorian iron and glass of the 100-year-old **Galleria Umberto I**, enjoy a coffee break or sample a unique Neapolitan pastry called *sfogliatella* (crispy scallop shell–shaped pastry filled with sweet ricotta cheese). Go through the tall yellow arch at the end of Via Toledo or across from the opera house. Gawk up.

Spaccanapoli back to the station (city walk, second half): To continue your walk, double back up Via Toledo past Piazza Carita to Via Maddaloni. (Consider going via the back streets.) You're back at the straight-as-a-Greek-arrow Spaccanapoli. Formerly the main thoroughfare of the Greek city of Neapolis, it starts up the hill near the Montesanto funicular.

The rest of this walk is basically a straight line down a series of streets locals nicknamed Spaccanapoli. Turn right off Via Toledo and walk down Via Maddaloni to two bulky old churches on Piazza Gesu Nuovo. The square is marked by a towering monument to the Counter-Reformation (Baroque, early 18th century). With its Spanish heritage, Jesuits were powerful in Naples. But locals never attacked Protestants with the full fury of the Spanish Inquisition.

Check out the austere, fortresslike church of **Gesu Nuovo.** The unique pyramid grill facade was from a fortress (1470), which predated the church (1600s). Step inside for a brilliant Baroque interior. The second chapel on the right features a much-kissed statue of Giuseppe Moscati, a Christian doctor famous for helping the poor. Moscati was made a saint in 1987. Continue on to the third chapel and enter the Sale Moscati for a huge room filled with Ex Voto—tiny red-and-silver plaques of thanksgiving for miracles attributed to Saint Moscati. Each has a relief symbolic of the ailment cured. Naples' practice of "Ex Voto," while incorporated into its Catholic rituals, goes back to its pagan Greek roots. A glass case displays possessions and photos of the great doctor. As you leave, notice the big bomb casing hanging in the corner. It fell through the church's dome in 1943 but never exploded... yet another miracle.

Across the street, the simpler Gothic church of **Santa Chiara** dates from a period of French Angevin rule (14th century). Notice the stark Gothic/Baroque contrast between this church and the Gesu Nuovo. The faded Trinity (from the school of Giotto, left of entry) is an example of the fine frescoes that once covered the walls (most removed during Baroque times). The altar is adorned with the finely carved Gothic tomb of an Angevin king (free, Mon–Sat 08:30–13:00, 15:30–18:30, Sun 08:30–13:00).

Continue straight down traffic-free Via B. Croce. Since this is a university district, you'll see lots of students and bookstores. This neighborhood is also extremely superstitious. You may see incense-burning women with carts of good-luck charms for sale. At Via Santa Chiara, a detour left leads to shops of antique musical instruments.

The next square is Piazza S. Domenico Maggiore—marked by an ornate 17th-century plague monument. The venerable **Scaturchio Pasticceria** is another good place to try Naples' *sfogliatella* pastry (€1 to go, costs double at a table in the square).

From this square, detour left (along the right side of the castlelike church, then follow yellow signs and take first right) to **Cappella Sansevero** (€4, Mon and Wed–Sat 10:00–18:20, Sun 10:00–13:30, closed Tue, Via de Sanctis 19). No photos are allowed in the chapel (postcards available in gift shop).

This small chapel is a Baroque explosion mourning the body of Christ, who lies on a soft pillow under an incredibly realistic veil. It's also the personal chapel of Raimondo de Sangro, an eccentric Freemason. The monuments to his relatives have a second purpose: To share the Freemason philosophy of freedom through enlightenment. For example, the statue of *Despair* struggling with a marble rope net (carved out of a single piece of marble) shows how knowledge—in the guise of an angel— frees the human mind.

Study the incredible *Veiled Christ* in the center. It's all carved out of marble and is like no other statue I've seen (by Giuseppe "howdeedoodat" Sammartino, 1753). The Christian message (Jesus died for our salvation) is accompanied by a Freemason message. (The veil represents how the body and ego are an obstacle to real spiritual freedom.) As you walk from Christ's feet to his head, notice how the expression of

Jesus' face goes from suffering to peace. When you stand directly behind Him, the veil over the face and knees disappears.

Raimondo de Sangro, an inventor, created the deep green pigment used on the ceiling fresco. De Sangro is even credited with a crude 18th-century version of Gore-Tex.

To the right of *Despair* and the net, an inlaid Escher-esque maze on the floor leads to de Sangro's tomb. The maze is another Freemason reminder of the importance of how the quest for knowledge gets you out of the maze of life. Your Sansevero finale is downstairs: two mysterious...skeletons. Perhaps another of the mad inventor's fancies: Injecting a corpse with a fluid to fossilize the veins so they'll survive the body's decomposition.

Return to Via B. Croce, turn left, and continue your Spaccanapoli cultural scavenger hunt. At the intersection of Via Nilo, find the statue of *The Body of Naples*, with the abundant cornucopia symbolizing the abundance of Naples. (I asked a Neapolitan man to describe the local women, who are famous for their beauty. He replied simply, "Abundant.") This intersection is considered the center of old Naples.

At Via San Gregorio Armeno, a left leads you into a very colorful district (kitschy Baroque church on left with a Vesuvius lava shrine in its portico, lots of shops selling tiny components of fantastic manger scenes).

As Via B. Croce becomes Via S. Biagio dei Librai, notice the gold and silver shops. Some say stolen jewelry ends up here, is melted down immediately, and appears in a saleable form as soon as it cools. The wonderful Sr. Grassi runs the Ospedale delle Bambole (doll hospital) at #81.

Cross busy Via Duomo. The street and side-street scenes along Via Vicaria intensify. Paint a picture with these thoughts: Naples has the most intact street plan of any ancient Roman city. Imagine this city then (retain these images as you visit Pompeii), with street-side shopfronts that close up after dark to form private homes. Today it's just one more page in a 2,000-year-old story of a city: all kinds of meetings, beatings, and cheatings; kisses, near misses, and little-boy pisses.

You name it, it occurs right on the streets today, as it has since ancient times. People ooze from crusty corners. Black-and-white death announcements add to the clutter on the walls. Widows sell cigarettes from buckets. For a peek behind the scenes in the shade of wet laundry, venture down a few side streets. Buy two carrots as a gift for the woman on the fifth floor if she'll lower her bucket to pick them up. The neighborhood action seems best around 18:00.

At the tiny fenced-in triangular park, veer right onto Via Forcella. Turning right on busy Via Pietro Colletta, walk 50 meters and step into the North Pole. Reward yourself for surviving this safari with a stop at the **Polo Nord Gelateria** (Via Pietro Colletta 41, sample their *bacio* or "kiss" flavor before ordering). Via Pietro Colletta leads past Napoli's two most competitive **pizzerias** (see "Eating," below) to Corso Umberto.

Turn left on the grand-boulevardian Corso Umberto. From here to the station, it's a 10-minute walk (if you're tired, hop on a bus; they all go to the station). To finish the walk, continue on Corso Umberto—past a gauntlet of purse/CD/sunglasses salesmen and shady characters hawking stolen camcorders—to the vast, ugly Piazza Garibaldi. On the far side is the Centrale station. **Markets**—Naples' **fish market** is fun for photos, with sawed-off swordfish, wriggly eels in pans, and mussels taking a shower. It's at Piazza Nolana, a few blocks southwest of the train station (at the piazza, follow your nose and go through the old gate; market spills down small street, Vico Sopramuro). A bigger **general market** starts at the far corner of Piazza Capuana (several blocks northwest of the train station), filling the street Via Sant' Antonio Abate with a mix of clothes, olives, bags of gnocchi, hanging hams, shoes, produce, umbrellas, and shoppers on foot or on Vespas. These colorful markets are both open daily from early in the morning until about 16:00 Monday to Saturday, 13:00 on Sunday.

Sleeping in Naples
(€1.10 = $1, country code: 39)
Sleep Code: **S** = Single, **D** = Double/Twin, **T** = Triple, **Q** = Quad, **b** = bathroom, **s** = shower only, **CC** = Credit Cards accepted, **no CC** = Credit Cards not accepted, **SE** = Speaks English, **NSE** = No English.

With Sorrento just an hour away, I can't imagine why you'd sleep in Naples. But, if needed, here are several places, all within 200 meters of the station. The area can feel unnerving, especially after dark.

Hotel Ginevra is quiet, bright, and cheery, and has 16 rooms with comfortable beds, floral wallpaper, and a €6-per-load washing machine. It's run by a friendly family: Bruno and son Lello speak English, Anna speaks Italian (S-€25, Sb-€40, D-€40, Db-€50, T-€55, Tb-€70, Q-€65, Qb-€80, breakfast in room-€4, CC, turn right out of the station onto Corso Novara and walk two blocks, turn right on Via Genova to #116, second floor, tel. & fax 081-283-210, www.mds.it/ginevra, e-mail: hginevra@tin.it).

Grand Hotel Terminus, a four-star place across the street from the station (left side), feels perfectly safe, with 168 rooms and all the comforts (Db-€165 or so, includes breakfast, CC, air-con, elevator, nonsmoking rooms on second floor, gym, roof garden, bar, restaurants, Piazza Garibaldi 91, tel. 081-779-3111, fax 081-206-689, www.starhotels.it, SE).

Hotel Eden, a big old establishment run with panache by

English-speaking Nicola and his brother Vincenzo, rents 45 dreary rooms. Front rooms get traffic noise; request a room in the back (Sb-€29, Db-€44, Tb-€60, Qb-€73, prices good through 2002 with this book and cash, no CC, no breakfast, elevator, turn right out of the station and walk one to Corso Novara 9, tel. 081-285-344, fax 081-285-690). Reserve by phone and reconfirm the day before you arrive.

Eating in Naples

Drop by one of the two most traditional pizzerias. Naples, baking just the right combination of fresh dough, mozzarella, and tomatoes in traditional wood-burning ovens, is the birthplace of pizza. **Antica Pizzeria da Michele**, a few blocks from the train station, is for purists (Mon–Sat 11:00–23:00, closed Sun, cheap, filled with locals, 50 meters off Corso Umberto on Via Cesare Sersale, look for the vertical red "Antica Pizzeria" sign, tel. 081-553-9204). It serves two kinds: *margherita* (tomato sauce and mozzarella) or *marinara* (tomato sauce, oregano, and garlic, no cheese). A pizza with beer costs €5. Some locals prefer **Pizzeria Trianon** across the street. Da Michele's archrival offers more choices, higher prices, air-conditioning, and a cozier atmosphere (daily 10:00–15:30, 18:30–23:00, Via Pietro Colletta 42, tel. 081-553-9426).

Transportation Connections—Naples

By boat to: Sorrento (7/day, 40 min, €6.75), **Capri** (6 hydrofoils/day, 45 min, €10.50).

By train to: Rome (hrly, 2–3 hrs), **Florence** (6/day, 5 hrs), **Brindisi** (2/day, 7 hrs, overnight possible; from Brindisi, ferries sail to Greece), **Milan** (7/day, 7–9 hrs, overnight possible, more with a change in Rome), **Venice** (4/day, 8–10 hrs), **Nice** (4/day, 13 hrs), **Paris** (3/day, 18 hrs). Naples train information: tel. 848-888-088.

The Circumvesuviana: This handy commuter train laces together Naples, Herculaneum, Pompeii, and Sorrento. At Naples' Central Station, signs direct you downstairs. In the long corridor in the basement, the ticket windows—marked "Circumvesuviana"—are on your left. Schedules are posted on the wall. When you buy your ticket, ask which track your train will depart from (*"Che binario?"*—kay bee-NAH-ree-oh). Don't go through the turnstiles opposite the ticket windows. Instead, continue down the corridor and jog right when it does, down another long corridor that has turnstiles at the end (insert your ticket). The platforms are just beyond. (The Circumvesuviana also has its own terminal one stop or a 10-minute walk beyond the Central Station, but there's no reason to use it.) Two trains per hour marked "Sorrento" take you to Herculaneum (Ercolano) in 15 minutes, Pompeii in 40 minutes, and Sorrento, the end of the line, in 70 minutes (€2.50 one-way, not covered by railpasses, not all of the trains go as far

Circumvesuviana Stops
Between Naples and Sorrento

I list these so you can look at the scenery rather than your watch.

Napoli	V. Viuli
Piazza Garibaldi	Trecase
Gianturco	Torre Annunziata
S. Giovanni	Pompei Scavi
Barra	(Pompeii site)
S. Maria d. Pozzo	Moregine
S. Giorgio	Ponte Persica
Cavalli di Bronzo	Pioppaino
Bellavista	V. Nocera
V. Liberta	C. Mare Stabia
Ercolano Scavi	C. Mare Terme
(Herculaneum site)	Pozzano
Ercolano	Scraio
Miglio D'Oro	Vico Equense
Torre del Greco	Seiano
V.S. Antonio	Meta
V. del Monte	Piano di Sorrento
V. Monaci	S. Agnello
Villa della Ginestra	Sorrento
Leopardi	

as Sorrento—look at the schedule carefully or confirm with a local before boarding to make sure the train is going where you want to). Express trains marked DD (12/day) get you to Sorrento 30 minutes quicker. When returning to Naples' Centrale station on the Circumvesuviana, get off at the second-to-the-last station, the Collegamento FS or Garibaldi stop (Centrale station is just up the escalator). **Note:** Many readers report being ripped off on this train (see theft alert in "Helpful Hints," above).

SORRENTO

Wedged on a ledge under the mountains and over the Mediterranean, spritzed by lemon and olive groves, Sorrento is an attractive resort of 20,000 residents and—in the summer—as many tourists. It's as well-located for regional sightseeing as it is a fine place to stay and stroll. The Sorrentines have gone out of their way to create a completely safe and relaxed place for tourists to come and spend money. (None of its 40 banks has ever been robbed.) Everyone seems to speak fluent English and work for the Chamber of Commerce. This gateway to the Amalfi Coast has an unspoiled old quarter, a lively main shopping street, and a spectacular cliffside setting. Skip the port and its poor excuse for a beach unless you're taking a ferry. Locals are proud of the many world-class romantics who've vacationed here. In 1921, the famed tenor Enrico Caruso chose Sorrento as his place to die.

Orientation

Sorrento is long and narrow. The main drag, Corso Italia (50 meters in front of the Circumvesuviana train station), runs parallel to the sea from the station through the town center and out to the cape, where it's renamed Via Capo. Everything mentioned (except the hotels on Via Capo) is within a 10-minute walk of the station. Sorrento hibernates in January and February when many places close down.

Tourist Information: The TI, located inside the Foreigner's Club, hands out a free *Sorrentum* magazine with a great city map and schedules of boats, buses, and events (Mon–Sat 08:45–19:15, closed Sun, shorter hours off-season, tel. 081-807-4033). To reach the TI (*Soggiorno e Turismo*) from the station, go left on Corso Italia and walk five minutes to Piazza Tasso; turn right at the end of the square, then head down Via L. de Maio through Piazza Sant Antonino to the Foreigners' Club mansion at #35. You'll pass fake "tourist offices" (travel agencies selling bus and boat tours). If you arrive after the TI closes, look for key TI handouts in the lobby of the Foreigners' Club (open until midnight).

The Foreigners' Club provides reasonably priced snacks and drinks, relaxation, views, and a handy place for visitors to meet locals (behind TI, public WC). It's lively with concerts or dancing every summer evening (starting at 21:00, tel. 081-877-3263; see "Late-Night Sorrento," and "Eating," below). Drop in for an orientation view of the harbor and a commanding view of the Bay of Naples.

Getting around Sorrento

Orange city buses all stop in the main square (Tasso). They run to the Meta beach (bus A), the port (Marina Piccola, buses B and C), the fishing village (Marina Grande, bus D), and to the hotels on Via Capo (€1 tickets within the center, sold at *tabacchi* shops, purchase before boarding and stamp upon entering). Sorrento Rent-a-Car also rents mopeds and Vespas (€29/3 hrs, daily 08:00–13:00, 16:00–21:00, Corso Italia 210, tel. 081-878-1386). In summer, forget renting a car unless you enjoy traffic jams. Taxis are expensive, charging at least €10 for the short ride from the station to hotels.

Sights—Sorrento

▲**Strolling**—Take time to explore the surprisingly pleasant old city between Corso Italia and the sea. Views from the public park next to Imperial Hotel Tramontano are worth the detour. Duck into the Church of England. The evening *passeggiata* (along Corso Italia and Via San Cesareo) peaks around 22:00. Check out the old-boys' club playing cards, oblivious to the tourism, under their portico (with great 3-D frescoes) at Via San Cesareo and Via Tasso.

Lemon Grove Garden (L'Agruminato)—This small park consists of an inviting lemon and orange grove lined with paths. It's dotted with benches and a little stand often offering free tastes of *limoncello*, a local specialty made of lemons, sugar, and pure alcohol (May–Aug 10:00–20:00, Sept–April 10:00–16:00). Enter the garden on Corso Italia (across from Panetteria da Franco—Corso Italia 165, see door flanked by tiles, marked "L'Agruminato, il giardino della città") or at Via Rota (next to Hotel La Meridiana Sorrento).

Tennis—The Sorrento Sport Snack Bar has fine courts open to the public (€9.30/hr, €11.35/hr after dark for two, including use of rackets and balls, call for reservation, across from recommended Ambasciatori Hotel at Via Califano 5, tel. 081-807-1616).

Late-Night Sorrento—This town is filled with Brit-friendly pubs. These two are most popular and within a few blocks of each other: The **Merry Monk Irish Pub** offers good draft beer, darts, live dance music nightly, hamburgers and fries, free transfer back to your hotel if necessary, and noisy Internet access. And you haven't heard "Mustang Sally" until you've heard it in Italian (at the west end of town at Via Capo 4, tel. 081-877-2409).

The English Inn is another place designed to make English guests feel right at home. Its rough-feeling pub serves baked beans on toast, fish and chips, and draft beer with fun music and a more refined-feeling garden out back (Corso Italia 53, tel. 081-807-4357). The **Foreigners' Club** has live music nightly at 21:00 and is just right for old-timers feeling frisky (in the center, see "Tourist Information," above).

Swimming near Sorrento—If you need immediate tanning, you can rent a chair on the pier by the port. There are no great beaches near Sorrento. The best sandy, family-friendly beach is three kilometers east at Meta (easy Orange bus connection from Sorrento—take bus A from Piazza Tasso). Tarzan might take Jane to the wild and stony beach at **Punta del Capo**, a 15-minute bus ride west of town (2/hr from Piazza Tasso to American Bar, then walk 10 minutes past the ruined Roman Villa di Pollio). Beyond that, **Marina di Poulo** is a tiny fishing town popular in the summer for its sandy beach, surfside restaurants, and beachfront disco.

Sleeping in Sorrento
(€1.10 = about $1, country code: 39, zip code: 80067)
Sorrento offers the whole range of rooms. Hotels often charge the same for a room whether it has a view, balcony, or neither. At hotels that offer sea views, ask for a room "*con balcone, con vista sul mare*"—with a balcony, with a sea view. "*Tranquillo*" is taken

Sorrento

N

TO POMPEII & NAPLES

VIA ROTA

NIZZA

VIA CALIFANO

TENNIS

MUSEUM

VIA CARPASSO

ARANCI

TRAIN STATION

VIA CORREALE

PIAZZA LAURO

PIAZZA TASSO

MARINA PICCOLA

TO CAPRI & NAPLES

VIA DEGLI ITALIA

CATHEDRAL

GULF OF NAPLES

VIA CORSO

MARINA GRANDE

VIA CAPO

TO PUNTA DEL CAPO

300 YARDS
300 METERS

❶ HOTEL LORELEY &
   HOTEL AMBASCIATORI
❷ HOTEL LA MERIDIANA &
   PENSIONE MARA
❸ HOTEL NICE
❹ HOTEL MIGNON MEUBLE
❺ HOTEL DEL CORSO
❻ OSTELLO LE SIRENE DI SORRENTO
❼ PENSION LA TONNERELLA &
   HOTEL DESIREE

❽ HOTEL MINERVA
❾ LA MINERVETTA PENSION
❿ PENSION ELIOS
⓫ RIST. IL BUCO
⓬ L'ANTICA TRATTORIA &
   DAVIDE GELATO
⓭ RIST. ZI 'NTONIO
⓮ PIZZERIA GIARDINIELLO
⓯ SANT ANTONINO REST.

⓰ OSTERIA GATTO NERO
⓱ STANDA SUPERMARKET
⓲ FOREIGNERS' CLUB
⓳ MERRY MONK IRISH PUB
⓴ LAUNDRY
㉑ BUS STOP FOR ORANGE (CITY) BUSES
㉒ BUS STOP FOR BLUE (SITA) BUSES
㉓ LEMON GROVE GARDEN
㉔ OLD BOY'S PORTICO CLUB

as a request for a room off the street. Every place includes breakfast unless otherwise noted. Hotels listed are either near the
station and city center or along the way to Punta del Capo, a
20-minute walk (or short bus ride) from the station. While many
hotels close for the winter, you should have no trouble finding
a room any time outside of August, when the place is jammed
and many hotel prices go way up. Spring for a hotel with air-
conditioning if you wilt in the heat. Note: The spindly, more
exotic, and more tranquil Amalfi Coast town of Positano (below)
is also a good place to spend the night.

Laundromat: A handy coin-op laundry is at Corso Italia 30;
turn right down the alley for the side entrance (1 load-€7.75,
2 loads-€13).

Sleeping East of the Center

A block in front of the station, turn right onto Corso Italia,
then left down Via Capasso, which winds right and becomes Via
Califano. At the Loreley and Ambasciatori, the "private beach" is
actually a sun deck built out over the water.

Hotel Loreley—a rambling, spacious, colorful, old Sorren-
tine villa—feels a bit like a sanitorium. It's ideal for those wishing
to sit on the bluff and stare at the sea. Of its 27 rooms, 19 are
quiet and have seaview balconies. The noisy, streetside rooms lack
views but are air-conditioned. A €2.60 elevator takes you to the
hotel's beach (Db-€83; from July–mid-Sept half-pension at €62
per person is required but the dinner's good; CC, unpredictable
management cannot guarantee view rooms but promises these
prices through 2002 with this book, some free parking, Via Califano 2, tel. 081-807-3187, fax 081-532-9001).

Grand Hotel Ambasciatori, next door, is a sumptuous
four-star hotel with a cliffside setting, sprawling garden, and
pool. This is Humphrey Bogartland with plush public spaces,
a stay-awhile relaxing ambience, and an elevator to its beach
(Db-€238, occasionally less, CC, air-con, some balconies, parking, Via Califano 18, tel. 081-878-2025, fax 081-807-1021,
www.manniellohotels.it).

Hotel La Meridiana Sorrento, a fine three-star place with
everything but character, offers 45 air-conditioned modern rooms
and business-class public spaces (Db-€108, Tb-€145, half-pension
at €85 per person required, Aug–Sept 15, plus €10 for air-con,
prices soft when slow, CC, big rooftop terrace with grand views,
next door to public lemon grove garden, Via Rota 1, tel. 081-807-
3535, fax 081-807-3484, www.wel.it/hlameridiana).

Pensione Mara is a dirty ashtray kind of place, with 13 simple rooms in a dull building with a good location (S-€26, D-€47,
Db-€54, T-€70, Tb-€75, cheap quads and family room, prices
promised through 2002, no breakfast, no CC; from Via Capasso,

turn right at Hotel La Meridiana to Via Rota 5, tel. & fax 081-878-3665, Adelle speaks a little English).

Sleeping in the Town Center

Hotel Nice rents basic rooms 100 meters in front of the station on the noisy main drag. Ask for a room off the street (Sb-€47, Db-€67, Tb-€88, Qb-€103, prices increase about €5 July–Aug, CC, air-con, Corso Italia 257, tel. 081-878-1650, fax 081-878-3086, e-mail: albergo.nice@katamail.com).

    Hotel Mignon Meuble, with 23 big, clean, and pleasant rooms, is Old-World simple on a quiet street off Corso Italia. A 10-minute walk from the station, this is the best hotel value in the town center (Db-€72, Tb-€93, CC, some balconies, no views, air-con, owned by Hotel Loreley, Via Sersale 9; from station, turn left on Via del Corso, tel. & fax 081-807-3824, smart aleck Palmina SE).

    Hotel Del Corso, a funky Old-World, three-star hotel, is clean, family-run, and comfortable, with 20 spacious rooms (Db-€99, Tb-€140, CC, air con, cheap Internet access, roof-top sun terrace, Corso Italia 134, in town center near Piazza Tasso, tel. & fax 081-807-3157, tel. 081-807-1016, www.hoteldelcorso.com, helpful Luca SE).

    Ostello le Sirene di Sorrento, a tiny hostel four blocks from the train station, offers the cheapest beds in town (50 beds in triples and quads—€18 with bath, €16 without, Db-€57, no CC, Internet access, Via degli Aranci 160, tel. & fax 081-877-1371, www.hostel.it, e-mail: info@hostel.it, SE).

Sleeping with a View on Via Capo

These hotels are outside of town, near the cape (straight out Corso Italia, which turns into Via Capo; from the city center, it's a 15-minute walk, a €13 taxi ride, or a cheap bus ride). The bus situation is goofy because there are two competing companies. To get from the train station to Via Capo, you can catch a blue SITA bus (any except those heading for Positano/Amalfi) or an orange Circumvesuviana bus. Tickets for both are sold at the station newsstand and tobacco shops but not on the bus. Orange is more frequent (3/hr). If you're in Sorrento to stay put and luxuriate, these accommodations are ideal (although I'd rather luxuriate on the Amalfi Coast).

    Pension La Tonnarella is a well-worn Sorrentine villa with several terraces, stylish tiles, sea views, a dreamy chandeliered dining room, and uninterested owners (15 of its 21 rooms come with a view, Db-around €134 with view, less without view, obligatory €83 per person half-pension with dinner in Aug, CC, air-con, free Internet access, many rooms with great view balconies, small beach with free elevator access,

Via Capo 31, tel. 081-878-1153, fax 081-878-2169, www
.latonnarella.com, e-mail: latonnarella@syrene.it).

Hotel Désirée, run by friendly Corinna, is a simpler
affair with humbler views but no traffic noise, all the comforts,
a fine roof terrace, and no half-pension requirements (maximum
prices: Sb-€52, small Db-€67, Db-€83, Tb-€98, Qb-€114,
price promised through 2002 with this book, no CC, laundry-
€7.75, shares La Tonnarella's driveway and beach, Via Capo 31,
tel. & fax 081-878-1563). Corinna is hugely helpful with tips
on exploring the peninsula.

Hotel Minerva is like a sun worshipper's temple. Catch
the elevator at Via Capo 32. Getting off at the fifth floor, you'll
step into a spectacular terrace with outrageous Mediterranean
views and a small, cliff-hanging swimming pool complementing
48 large, tiled *limoncello* rooms. Looking for the room numbers,
you'll wonder if you're on *Candid Camera* (Db-€125, Tb-€140,
Qb-€155, plus €26 in Sept, these discounted prices promised
with this book through 2002 *only* if claimed at time of reservation—
fail to do this and you pay €30 more, no summer half-pension
requirement, CC, air-con, Via Capo 30, tel. 081-878-1011, fax 081-
878-1949, www.acampora.it, e-mail: minerva@acampora.it, SE).

La Minervetta Pension rents 12 fine rooms built into the
cliff below its restaurant and far below the noisy street. Each
room comes with perfect quiet and an awesome Mediterranean
view (Db-€98, half-pension—at €67 per person—is required in
Aug, extra bed–€23, bunky family rooms, price good through
2002 with this book, no CC, parking, Via Capo 25, tel. 081-
877-3033, fax 081-807-3069, Salvatore SE).

The humble **Pension Elios**, run by Luigi, Maria, and
daughter Gianna, offers 14 simple but spacious rooms, most with
balconies and views, and a panoramic sun terrace (Db-€47–52,
Tb-€62, family rooms, cheaper off-season, free parking, Via
Capo 33, tel. 081-878-1812).

Eating in Sorrento

Dining Downtown—Splurges
In a town proud to have no McDonald's, consider eating well for a
few extra bucks. Each of these places is a worthwhile splurge in the
old center.

Ristorante Il Buco, once the cellar of an old monastery,
is now a small, dressy restaurant serving delightfully presented,
top-quality food with good wine. The owner, Peppe, designs
his menu around whatever's fresh and travels in the winter to
assemble a wine list sure to offer connoisseurs something new
and memorable (Thu–Tue 12:00–14:30, 19:00–24:00, closed
Wed, dinners run about €36 plus wine, CC, just off Piazza

Sant Antonino at Il Rampe Marina Piccola 5, reservations smart, tel. 081-878-2354).

L'Antica Trattoria serves hearty portions of more traditional cuisine (minimum order of €42 per person) in a *romantico* candlelit ambience, full of contagiously fun waiters and enthusiastic eaters. Its wine list is more predictable, featuring well-known domestic wines. Walk around before you select a place to sit (daily 12:00–15:00, 19:00–23:30, closed Mon off-season, air-con, nonsmoking sections, reservations smart for eves, CC, Via P.R. Giulani 33, tel. 081-807-1082; Tony will take good care of you).

Eating Well and Cheaply Downtown

Ristorante Pizzeria Zi 'Ntonio, just as fancy as L'Antica Trattoria but about half the price, is popular for its local cuisine and its specialty: homemade pasta. Italians like its woody, hanging-hams, and happy-tiled ambience. Its fine self-serve antipasti and seafood buffet makes a great quick lunch or light dinner (Wed–Mon 12:00–16:00, 18:30–01:30, closed Tue, CC, air-con, Via Luigi de Maio 11, tel. 081-878-1623).

Pizzeria Giardiniello is a family show offering good food, good prices, friendly smiles, and a peaceful, tropical garden setting (daily 12:00–24:00, Via Accademia 7, tel. 081-878-4616). Like an old sailor checking the lines, Franco makes sure you're well-fed.

Sant Antonino's offers friendly service, red-checkered table-cloths, an outdoor patio, decent prices, and edible food (closed Mon off-season, CC, just off Piazza Sant Antonino on Santa Maria delle Grazie 6, tel. 081-877-1200). Nearby, the smaller and livelier **Pizzeria Da Gigino** is better (first road to the right of Sant Antonino as you face it, daily 12:00–15:00, 18:30–24:00, closed Tue off-season, CC, tel. 081-878-1927).

Osteria Gatto Nero is a fresh and modern place catering more to trendy young locals out for good traditional cooking, especially pasta and seafood. Chagall would eat here (Tue–Sun 19:00–24:00, closed Mon, CC, eat indoors or out back in the garden, a few minutes walk east of the old center at Via Correale 19, tel. 081-877-3686, Gaetano).

If you fancy a picnic dinner on your balcony, on the hotel terrace, or in the public garden, you'll find many markets and take-out pizzerias in the old town. The **Standa supermarket** at Corso Italia 223 has it all (Mon–Wed and Fri–Sat 08:30–13:00, 16:30–20:30, Thu 08:30–13:00 only, closed Sun, CC).

Gelato: A few doors downhill from L'Antica Trattoria, **Davide Gelato** has many repeat customers—so many flavors, so little time. Walk the most enticing chorus line in Italy before ordering (daily and nightly, Via P.R. Giuliani 39, off Corso Italia).

Cliffside Dinners with Sea Views

For a decent dinner on either side of town near recommended hotels or right in the center, these three places come with great view terraces.

La Minervetta, a 10-minute walk west of town across the street from the recommended Hotel Minerva, is ideal for tired tourists in need of a low-stress, reasonably priced, quality meal and a soothing view (closed Nov–March, Via Capo 25, tel. 081-807-3069). **Hotel Loreley's** restaurant serves reasonably priced, so-so meals with a spectacular sea view (if it's busy, non-guests may be turned away, 10-min walk east of town center, Via Califano 2, listed in "Sleeping," above).

The **Foreigners' Club Restaurant** is a place where the English Patient could recuperate. It has the best sea views in town (under breezy palms), live music nightly at 21:00, and passable meals (March–Nov daily 09:30–24:00, closed in winter, Via L. De Maio 35, tel. 081-877-3263).

Transportation Connections—Sorrento

It's impressively fast to zip by boat from point to point during the summer, when there are many more departures. In fact, many locals get around quicker by fast boat than by car or train.

By boat to: Naples (7/day, 40 min, €6.70), **Positano** (2/day in summer, weekends only in late spring and early fall, 75 min, €6.20), **Capri** (at least hrly, 40 min, €6.20; quicker and pricier by hydrofoil and jet boat: 20 min, €7.75). For an untouristy alternative to Capri, consider the nearby island of **Ischia**, where part of *The Talented Mr. Ripley* was filmed (easy boat connections from Sorrento as well as Naples—pick up schedules at local TI).

To get from Sorrento's Piazza Tasso to the port, walk or take the orange shuttle bus B or C (3/hr). Tickets are sold only at the port. Several lines compete, using boats and hydrofoils. Buy one-way tickets only (there's no round-trip discount) for schedule flexibility, so you can take any company's boat back. Prices are the same among the companies. Check times for the last return crossing upon arrival. The first boats leaving Sorrento can be jammed (either arrive early to buy your ticket or leave closer to 10:00).

To the Amalfi Coast: See "Amalfi Coast," below.

To Pompeii, Herculaneum, and Naples by Circumvesu-viana train: This handy commuter train runs about every 40 minutes between Naples and Sorrento. From Sorrento, it's 30 minutes to Pompeii, 45 minutes to Herculaneum, and 70 minutes to Naples (€2.50 one-way). See "Transportation Connections—Naples," above, for more information on the Circumvesuviana and theft precautions. Note: The risk of theft is limited mostly to suburban Naples. Sorrento to Herculaneum is much safer.

Sorrento Peninsula

Marina del Cantone, a tiny fishing village near Nerano, on a Sorrento Peninsula dead end, is the place to establish a sleepy, fun-in-the-sun residency (5 buses/day from Sorrento to Marina del Cantone, 60 min, or a 30-min, €40 taxi ride). There are some good hikes from here: Punto Penna is about a four-hour loop with great views. A more strenuous hike leads along the coast, past the stunning Gulf of Salerno to Torca, where buses go to Sant Agata (and from there, back to Sorrento). Along the trail, you might detour down to the cliff-hugging fishing village of— get this—Crapolla. Bring water and a good map.

Sleeping in Marina del Cantone: For a peaceful place to call home, sleep literally on the beach at the friendly **Pensione La Certosa**. This family-run place offers 16 basic, air-conditioned rooms (6 with sea view), a great beachfront restaurant, boat excursions, and can direct you to a number of peaceful little beaches (Db-€83 June–Aug, otherwise Db-€62, half-pension required in Aug for €62/person, family rooms, CC, 80068 Massa Lubrense, tel. 081-808-1209, fax 081-808-1245, www.hotelcertosa.com, run by Alfonso, SE).

THE AMALFI COAST

The bus trip from Sorrento to Salerno along the Amalfi Coast is a ▲▲▲ sight and one of the world's great bus rides. It will leave your mouth open and your film exposed. You'll gain respect for the Italian engineers who built the road—and even more respect for the bus drivers who drive it. As you hyperventilate, notice that the Mediterranean, a sheer 500-foot drop below, really twinkles.

Cantilevered garages, hotels, and villas cling to the vertical terrain, and beautiful sandy coves tease from far below and out of reach. If you know where to look, you'll see the villa of Sophia Loren. Gasp from the right side of the bus as you go out and from the left on the way back. Those on the wrong side really miss out. Traffic is so heavy that private tour buses are only allowed to go east—summer traffic is infuriating. Even with a car, you may be glad you took the bus or hired a taxi. Some enjoy doing the coast by motorbike (rented in Sorrento).

Amalfi Coast towns are pretty but generally touristy, congested, overpriced, and a long hike above tiny beaches. The real thrill is the scenic drive. Catch a blue SITA bus from the Sorrento train station (see "Transportation Connections—Amalfi Coast," below).

If you're thinking of taking a round-trip bus ride from Sorrento along the Amalfi Coast to Salerno and back, consider these two options instead: Get off at a prettier town (such as Cetera) near Salerno and return from there by bus rather than go into the big, plain town of Salerno. Or take the bus to Salerno, then catch the ferry back to Amalfi or Positano, and from either town,

Amalfi Coast

hop a ferry to Sorrento; Salerno's ferry dock is conveniently located at the bus stop (see "Transportation Connections—Salerno," at the end of this chapter).

This is perhaps the simplest option: Take the bus to Positano and boat from there back to Sorrento (or vice versa).

Transportation Connections—Amalfi Coast

From Sorrento to the Amalfi Coast by bus: The big tourist activity from Sorrento is riding the bus along the Amalfi Coast. Blue SITA buses depart from Sorrento's train station nearly hourly (in peak season, 20/day) and stop at all Amalfi Coast towns (Positano in 45 min, €1.20; Amalfi in another 45 min, €2.25), ending up in Salerno at the far end of the coast in just under three hours (one easy transfer in Amalfi). Buses start running as early as 06:30 and run as late as 20:00. Buy tickets at the tobacco shop nearest any bus stop before boarding. (There's a *tabacchi*/newsstand at street level at the Sorrento station.) Line up under the "Riservato SITA" sign (where a schedule is posted on the wall) in front of the station (10 steps down). Leaving Sorrento, grab a seat on the right for the best views. Returning, it's fun to sit directly behind the driver for a box seat over the hairpin twisting action.

Crowds on the Amalfi bus: Buses are routinely unable to handle the demand during summer months. Occasionally an extra bus is added to handle the overflow but, generally, if you don't get on, you're well-positioned to catch the next bus (bring a book). In the morning, arrive early (count the line: buses pull in empty and seat 49). The congestion can be so bad in the summer that return buses don't even stop in Positano (they were filled in Amalfi), and those trying to get back to Sorrento have no option but extortionist taxis (or, if stranded in Positano, check boat schedules).

If crowds are horrendous, consider gathering a small group and sharing a taxi from Sorrento (4 by car one-way to Positano for around €50, or 6 by minibus taxi for €63, 50 percent more to Amalfi; while taxis must use meter within city, a fixed rate is OK otherwise—negotiate; ask about a round-trip).

Amalfi Coast tours by taxi: Given the hairy driving, impossible parking, congested buses, and potential fun, you might consider splurging to hire your own car and driver for the Amalfi day. Fun-loving **Carmine Monetti** (a jolly, singing, in-love-with-life, grand-fatherly type who speaks "inventive English") and his son Raffaele (much better English, fewer smiles, more information) have long taken excellent care of my readers' transportation needs from Sorrento. Sample trips and rates: "Amalfi Coast Day" (Positano-Amalfi-lunch in Ravello), 7 hours, €145; "Amalfi Coast and Paestum," 10 hours, €233; "Pompeii and Vesuvius," 7 hours, €145; transfer to Naples airport or train station, 1 hour, €73; tailored family research in Campania (Carmine only) €32/hour; cash only; up to four passengers in their air-conditioned taxi, Raffaele's cellular 33-5602-9158, Carmine's cellular 33-8946-2860, "office" run by Raffaele's Finnish (and English-speaking) wife, Susanna: tel. & fax 081-878-4795, e-mail: monettitaxi17@libero.it. Their reservation system is simple, easy-going, and reliable. Be careful: Many cabbies are claiming to be the Monettis. The Monettis drive taxi #17. Couples wanting to cut their cost in half can tell Susanna they're open to sharing, allowing her to try to fill a cab. If in any kind of a jam, call Raffaele's cellular phone for information.

POSITANO

Specializing in scenery and sand, Positano hangs halfway between Sorrento and Amalfi on the most spectacular stretch of the coast. The village, a three-star sight from a distance, is a pleasant gathering of cafés and expensive women's clothing stores, with a good but pebbly beach. Squished into a ravine, the center of town has no main square, unless you count the beach. There's little to do here but eat, window-shop, and enjoy the beach and views (hence the town's popularity). Consider seeing Positano as a daytrip from Sorrento: take the bus out and the afternoon ferry home. If you stay the night, save the day for the beach and the cooler morning and evening for hiking up and down this hilly town. The town has a local flavor at night, when the grown-ups stroll and the kids play soccer on the church porch.

Tourist Information: The TI is a half block from the beach, in a small building at the bottom of the church steps (daily 08:30–13:50, 16:00–19:30; shorter hours off-season and closed Sun; tel. 089-875-067).

Arrival in Positano: The town has only two scheduled bus stops: Chiesa (at Bar Internazionale, nearer Sorrento) and Sponda (nearer Amalfi Town). To minimize your descent, take the Sponda stop (the second Positano stop if you're coming from Sorrento). It's a 15-minute stroll/shop/munch from here to the beach (and TI).

If you're catching the bus back to Sorrento, remember it may leave from Sponda five minutes before the printed departure. There's no place for the bus to wait, so in case the driver is early, you should be, too. If the walk up is too tough, take the little orange bus (marked Interno Positano) which does a loop from the center of Positano (at Via Columbo and Via del Mulini, across from Bar Mulino Verde) up to the main highway and the SITA bus stops (€0.75, 2/hr, buy tickets for the orange bus on board; buy tickets for SITA from Bar Mulino Verde or Positour Agency—both are on Via Columbo). Drivers must go with the one-way flow entering the town only at the Chiesa bus stop (closest to Sorrento) and exiting at Sponda.

Sights—Positano

Beach—Positano's wide beach, colorful with beach umbrellas, is mostly public (free) but also has a private section (April–Oct, €9.50/person, includes use of sun beds and umbrellas). At the harbor, the nearest WC is behind the waterfront Bucca di Bacco bar.

Boat Trips—At the right side of the beach (as you face the sea), you'll see a series of booths selling boat tickets. Boats to Fornillo make three-minute, €0.75 journeys to Fornillo Beach—a quieter beach nearby (or an easy 10-minute walk, take trail near ticket booths).

You could catch a boat to Amalfi (9/day, 30 min), Capri (7/day, 30 min), Sorrento (4/day in afternoon, 25 min), or Naples (1/day, 50 min on hydrofoil); fewer boats run off-season. Consider renting a rowboat or taking various boat tours of a nearby cave (La Grotta dello Smeraldo—Emerald Cave), fishing village (Nerano), and small islands.

Sleeping in Positano
(€1.10 = about $1, country code: 39, zip code: 84017)
These hotels (but not the hostel) are all on Via Colombo, which leads from the Sponda SITA bus stop down into the village. You'll encounter them in the order listed as you walk downhill. Neither laundry in town offers self-service or guarantees same-day service (Lavanderia Elisa, at Via Columbo 175, is near recommended hotels).

Hotel Marincanto, newly restored into a four-star hotel in 2002, may be worth the expected high price (private stairs to beach, large sun deck, Via Colombo 36, tel. 089-875-130, fax 089-875-595, www.marincanto.it, SE).

Albergo California has great views, spacious rooms (12 of 17 with sea views), and a grand terrace draped with vines

Positano

200 YARDS
200 METERS

—— ROADS FOR CARS
—‑— PEDESTRIAN STREETS

N-163

TO SORRENTO

VIA MARCONI N-163

VIALE CRISTOFORO

VIA MARCONI

VIA COLOMBO N-163

CHIESA ←BUS STOP

VIA MULINI

SPONDA BUS STOP

VIALE PASITEA

VIA T. GENOINO

CHURCH

TO AMALFI

VIA FORNILLO

VIA POSITANESI

SPIAGGIA GRANDE

FORNILLO BEACH

MEDITERRANEAN SEA

TO CAPRI, SORRENTO & NAPLES

TO AMALFI & SALERNO

❶ HOTEL MARINCANTO
❷ ALBERGO CALIFORNIA
❸ RESIDENCE LA TAVOLOZZA
❹ HOTEL SAVOIA
❺ HOTEL BOUGAINVILLE
❻ BRIKETTE HOSTEL
❼ LA TRE SORRELLE REST.
❽ DA VINCENZO REST.

(Db-€120–130 depending on season and amenities, viewless Db-€93, includes breakfast, CC; view rooms are air-con, free parking, can arrange tours, Via Colombo 141, tel. 089-875-382, fax 089-812-154, www.hpe.it/california/, e-mail: albergo .california@hpe.it, Maria SE).

Residence La Tavolozza is an attractive eight-room hotel, warmly run by Celeste (cheh-LES-tay). Flawlessly restored, each room comes with a view, a balcony, fine tile, and silence (Db-€72 in 2002 with this book, breakfast extra, also has small apartment and royal family apartment with six beds, no CC, Via Colombo 10, tel. & fax 089-875-040, e-mail: celestedileve@tiscalinet.it).

Hotel Savoia rents 39 three-star, air-conditioned rooms (prices vary with season: Db-€98–129, deluxe Db-€119–150, CC, some sea views, elevator, Via Colombo 73, tel. 089-875-003, fax 089-811-844, www.starnet.it/savoia, e-mail: savoia@starnet.it, SE).

Hotel Bougainville is spotless, with eager-to-please owners and 14 basic rooms (Db-€78–88 with view balcony, Db without view-€62–72, includes breakfast only with this book, CC, some traffic noise and fumes, Via Colombo 25, tel. 089-875-047, fax 089-811-150, www.bougainville.it, Carlo, Luisa, and son Christian SE).

Brikette Hostel offers your best cheap, dorm-bed option in this otherwise ritzy town. It's bright and clean with the normal hostel rules: locked up from 10:00 to 16:00, curfew at midnight, must check out by 09:00, no luggage storage or lockers (late March–Nov only, dorm bed-€20, D-€42–47, Db-€52–57, breakfast-€2.50, no CC; Via G. Marconi 358, leave bus at Chiesa/Bar Internazionale stop and backtrack uphill 150 meters, tel. 089-875-857, www .brikette.com, e-mail: info@brikette.com).

Eating in Positano

The pizzerias on the beach, while overpriced, are pleasant and convenient. At the waterfront, I like **La Tre Sorrelle** (daily 12:00–16:00, 19:00–24:00, CC) but the neighboring places also leave people fat and happy. A 10-minute hike uphill rewards you with the very Italian **Da Vincenzo.** This is a jolly festival of food with tasty surprises, compliments of Gjosue and Marcella Porpora (Tue 19:00–24:00, Wed–Mon 13:00–15:00, 19:00–24:00, Viale Pasitea 172, tel. 089-875-128). The family-run **Da Costantino**, so high on the hill that the restaurant sends a van to pick you up and take you home, offers reasonably priced, simple, filling meals (closed Wed, Via Montepertuso 127, ask your hotel to call for the van, tel. 089-875-738).

If a picnic dinner on your balcony or the beach sounds good, Emilia at **Enogastromia Delikatessen** can supply the ingredients (daily in summer 07:00–14:00, 16:00–22:00, in winter and on Sun closes at 20:00, just below the car park at Via del Mulini 5). **Vini e Panini**, another small grocery, is a block from the beach and TI (Mon–Sat 08:00–14:00, 16:30–21:30, Sun 08:00–14:00, just off church steps).

AMALFI AND ATRANI

Amalfi Town was once a powerful maritime republic. Today, the waterfront of this most famous of the Amalfi Coast villages is dominated by a bus station, a parking lot, and two gas stations. But step into the town, and you find its once rich and formidable medieval shell filled with trendy shops and capped by an impressive cathedral. The main street through the village—hard for pedestrians to avoid—is packed with cars and bully mopeds.

Amalfi's **cathedral** is the only sight marginally worth visiting. Climb the imposing stairway. Its 1,000-year-old bronze door was given to Amalfi by a wealthy local merchant, who had it made in Constantinople. When leaving the church, head right to tour the "Cloister of Paradise," the Basilica of the

Crucifix (the original 9th-century church, now a museum filled with the art treasures of the cathedral), and the Crypt of St. Andrew. Andrew was the apostle who left his nets to become the original "fisher of men"; his remains were brought here in 1206 during the Crusades—an indication of the wealth and importance of Amalfi then (€2, daily in summer 09:00–21:00, winter 10:00–17:00, pick up the English flier).

Atrani, just a 15-minute stroll away, is a world apart. Amazingly, it has none of the trendy resort feel of Amalfi, relatively few tourists, a delightful town square, and a free, sandy beach. For a classic Amalfi hike, walk from Atrani to Ravello (a venerable cliff-hanging resort town) and then to Amalfi.

Sleeping in Amalfi Town or Atrani

If you're marooned in Amalfi, stay at the 40-room **Hotel Amalfi** (Db-€62–114, roof-terrace restaurant, July–Aug obligatory half-pension is €78 per person, CC, no sea views, on a garden, 50 meters from cathedral, Via dei Pastai 3, 84011 Amalfi, tel. 089-872-440, fax 089-872-250, www.starnet.it/hamalfi, e-mail: hamalfi@starnet.it). **Hotel La Conchiglia** is also good (11 rooms, Db-€88, no CC, Piazzale dei Protontini, tel. 089-871-856).

In Atrani: **A'Scalinatella** is an informal hostel—with a honeycomb of cramped two- to five-bed dorms, private rooms, family apartments, and a washer (€5/load). It's ideal for a small-town Amalfi hideaway, without the glitz and hill-climbing of Positano. The English-speaking owners, Filippo and Gabriele, are friendly and helpful (€13–21 per bed in D or T, D-€36–47, Db-€47–62, no CC; from the main square, hike up the ravine and look for signs, 84010 Atrani, tel. 089-871-492, e-mail: scalinatella@amalficoast.it).

CAPRI

Made famous as the vacation hideaway of Roman emperors Augustus and Tiberius, these days Capri is a world-class tourist trap packed with gawky visitors in search of the rich and famous and finding only their prices. The six-by-three-kilometer "Island of Dreams" is a zoo in July and August—tacky low-grade group tourism at its worst. Other times of year, it provides a relaxing and scenic break from the cultural gauntlet of Italy. While Capri has some Roman ruins and an interesting 14th-century Carthusian monastery, its chief attraction is its famous Blue Grotto, and its best activity is a scenic hike.

Tourist Information: The TI at the ferry dock offers a room-finding service (April–Oct Mon–Sat 08:30–20:30, Sun 09:00–15:00; Nov–March Mon–Sat 09:00–13:00, 15:30–18:45, closed Sun, tel. 081-837-0634). The Caremar baggage storage service is in front of the dock (€1.60/day per bag). As you exit the pier, the ticket

windows (for your return trip) are to your right, and the funicular
is across the street to your left. Bar Augusto, next to the funicular,
has Internet access.

Getting around Capri: The buses and funicular are covered
by the same ticket options: €1.25 one-way on the bus or funicular,
€2.10 for 60 minutes of unlimited use, or €7 for an all-day pass.
You can hire a convertible taxi for about €42 an hour—negotiate.
From the ferry dock at Marina Grande, the funicular lifts you
150 meters (500 feet) to the town of Capri (5 min, 4/hr). From
Capri, cliff-hanging buses run to Anacapri (7 min, 4/hr).

Sights—Capri

Capri Town—This is a cute but touristy shopping town. The
TI is in a closet on the main square (to the left as you exit funicular, same hours as ferry dock TI—listed above, tel. 081-837-0686,
WC down stairs behind TI). For a view restaurant with good
seafood, try **Da Gemma** (daily, Via Madre Serafina 6, from town
square go up stairs near church and follow the sign, tel. 081-837-
0461). Overall, Capri Town is most useful as a place to catch the
bus to Anacapri (from funicular exit, walk straight on shop-lined
street; the bus station is about 100 meters ahead on your right).
Anacapri—This is the island's second town (TI tel. 081-837-1524).
Oddly, there are no ocean views from the town, but there are
hikes worth taking and one sight worth seeing. **St. Michael's
Church** has a remarkable tile floor showing paradise on earth
(€2, daily 09:30–18:00, until 17:00 off-season). Ristorante
Materita on Piazza Diaz is good.

Sleeping in Anacapri: Villa Eva, a 10-minute walk from
town on the Blue Grotto road, is a friendly, family-run place
with 20 rooms, a lush setting, and a swimming pool. They'll
pick guests up at the port for free (Db-€78–98 depending on
season, Via la Fabbrica 8, tel. 081-837-1549, fax 081-837-2040,
www.caprionline.com/villaeva). The cheap **Alla Bussola di
Hermes** is ideal for students and backpackers (dorm bed-€21,
D-€62, laundry services, Internet access, can pick you up from
port, in center of Anacapri, Via Traversa la Vigna 14, tel. 081-
838-2010, e-mail: bus.hermes@libero.it, run by lovely Rita).
Hike down Monte Solaro—From Anacapri, ride the €5.20 chairlift
to the 570-meter (1,900-foot) summit of Monte Solaro for a commanding view of the Bay of Naples and a pleasant downhill hike
through lush vegetation and ever-changing views, past the 14th-
century Chapel of Santa Maria Cetrella, and back into Anacapri.
Blue Grotto—To most, a visit to Capri's Blue Grotto is an overrated and overpriced "must." The boat from Marina Grande costs
€5.20. Once you reach the Grotto, you pay €4 for a rowboat to
take you in, then €4.20 to cover the admission (total €13.40). You
can lop off €5.20 if you catch the bus to Anacapri and hike briskly

for one hour to the Grotto (instead of taking the boat from Marina Grande to the Grotto). Hikers can dive in for free. And so can anyone after 17:00, when the boats stop running. Touristy as this is, the Grotto, with its eerily

beautiful blue sunlight reflecting through the water, is impressive (daily 09:00 until an hour before sunset, boats don't run in stormy weather).

Villa Jovis—Emperor Tiberius' now-ruined villa is a scenic 45-minute hike from Capri Town. Supposedly, Tiberius ruled Rome from here for a decade in about A.D. 30 (€2, daily 09:00 until an hour before sunset).

Transportation Connections—Capri

By boat to: Sorrento (nearly hrly, €6.20 for 40-min ride, €7.75 for 20-min jet-boat ride), **Naples** (6 hydrofoils/day, 45 min, €10.50).

POMPEII, HERCULANEUM, AND VESUVIUS

▲▲▲**Pompeii**—Stopped in its tracks by the eruption of Mount Vesuvius in A.D. 79, Pompeii offers the best look anywhere at what life in Rome must have been like 2,000 years ago. An entire city of well-preserved ruins is yours to explore. Once a thriving commercial port of 20,000, Pompeii grew from Greek and Etruscan roots to become an important Roman city. Then, it was buried under nine meters (30 feet) of hot mud and volcanic ash. For archaeologists, this was a shake-and-bake windfall, teaching them almost all they know about daily Roman life. Pompeii was rediscovered in the 1600s; excavations began in 1748.

Cost, Hours, Information: €8.25, €13.50 combo ticket includes Herculaneum and three lesser sites—valid three days, April–Oct daily 08:30–19:30, Nov–March daily 08:30–17:00. The ticket office closes 1.5 hours before closing time. A good map is included with admission (for more information, check www.pompeiisites.org). A free baggage check is near the ticket window.

Stop by the bookshop. A guidebook on Pompeii makes this site more meaningful. (Books are also on sale in Sorrento.) The small Pompeii and Herculaneum "past and present" book has a helpful text and allows you to recreate the ruins with plastic overlays—with the "present" actually being 1964 (available for €9.50 in bookstore unless they're "finished"; if you buy from a street vendor, pay no more than €9.50). Audioguides may be

Pompeii

- ❶ FORUM
- ❷ TERME DEL FORO & CAFE
- ❸ HOUSE OF FAUN
- ❹ HOUSE OF VETTI
- ❺ BAKERY & MILL
- ❻ TABERNA HEDONES
- ❼ BROTHEL (LUPANARE)
- ❽ TEMPLE OF ISIS
- ❾ THEATER
- ❿ TO AMPHITHEATER

available—ask. Live guides cluster near the ticket booth. If you gather 10 people, the price is reasonable when split (around €10 apiece, total cost about €100, 2 hrs). For a local guide, consider Gaetano Manfredi (tel. 081-863-9816, cellular 33-033-7567).

Background: Pompeii was a booming Roman trading city. Most streets would have been lined with stalls and jammed with customers from sunup to sundown. Chariots vied with shoppers for street space, and many streets were off-limits to chariots during shopping hours (you'll still see street signs with pictures of men carrying vases—this meant pedestrians only).

Fountains overflowed into the streets, flushing the gutters into the sea (thereby cleaning the streets). The stones you see at intersections allowed pedestrians to cross the constantly gushing streets. A single stone designated a one-way street (just enough room for one chariot, stone straddled by its two oxen), and two stones meant a two-way chariot street. There were no posh neighborhoods. Rich and poor mixed it up, as elegant homes existed side by side with simple homes throughout Pompeii. While nearby Herculaneum would have been a classier place to live (traffic-free streets, more elegant homes, far better drainage), Pompeii was the place for action and shopping. It served its estimated 20,000 residents with more than 40 bakeries, 30 brothels, and 130 bars, restaurants, and hotels. Rome controlled the entire Mediterranean 2,000 years ago—making it a kind of free-trade zone—and Pompeii was a central and booming port town. With most buildings covered by brilliant, white ground-marble stucco, Pompeii in A.D. 79 was an impressive town. Remember, Pompeii's best art is in the Naples Archaeological Museum, described above.

Tour of Pompeii: Allow at least three hours to tour the site. Consider the following route, starting at the Porta Marina (town gate) after the ticket booth. Before Vesuvius blew, the sea came nearly to this gate. As you approach the Porta Marina, notice the two openings—big for chariots, small for pedestrians.

From the Porta Marina, Via Marina leads strait to Pompeii's main square, the Forum.

The **Forum** (*Foro*), Pompeii's commercial, religious, and political center, stands at the intersection of the city's two main streets. While the most ruined part of Pompeii, it's grand nonetheless—with temples, lots of pedestals which once sported statues (now in the museum in Naples), and the basilica (Pompeii's largest building, the ancient equivalent of law courts and stock market—on the right as you enter). The Curia (home of the government) stands at the end of the Forum. It's built of brick and mortar—a Roman invention. While brick now, it was once faced with marble. Note that while Pompeii was destroyed by the eruption of A.D. 79, it was also devastated by an earthquake in A.D. 62. It's safe to assume any brick you see dates from between A.D. 62 and A.D. 79—restoration work done by Pompeians after the quake.

Walk (away from the Curia) along the fenced, roofed area that runs alongside the Forum. Behind the iron fence are piles of pottery and, at the end, some eerie casts of volcano victims. With the unification of Italy in the 1860s, national spirit fueled efforts to excavate Pompeii. During this period, archaeologists made these molds (detecting hollows under foot—left by decomposed bodies—as they dug, they'd pour liquid plaster into them, let dry, and dig up).

Such a busy square needed a public toilet. Just past the warehouse, turn left into an ancient public WC. Notice the ditch which led to the sewer (marked by an arch in the corner). The stone supports once held wooden benches with the appropriate holes. Even back then, this area had pay toilets.

Continue on, leaving the Forum through the gate at the end. Take an immediate right, then a left. You're on Via del Foro, passing a convenient 21st-century cafeteria (decent value, gelato, books, WCs upstairs; a fancier restaurant in a more elegant ancient gymnasium setting is adjacent).

Head down Via del Foro and enter the impressive baths, **Terme del Foro** (on the left, past the cafeteria). You'll enter through the gymnasium. After working out, clients would find four rooms: a waiting room, warm bath (*tepidarium*), hot bath (*caldarium*), and cold-plunge bath (*frigidarium*).

The *tepidarium* is ringed by mini-statues or *telamones* (male caryatids, figures used as supporting pillars), which divided clients' lockers. They'd undress and warm up here, perhaps stretching out on one of the benches near the bronze heater for a massage. Notice the ceiling: half crushed by the eruption and half surviving with its fine blue-and-white stucco work.

Next, in the *caldarium*, you'd get hot. Notice the engineering. The double floor was heated from below—so nice with bare feet (look into the grate to see the brick support towers). The double walls with brown terra-cotta tiles held the heat. Romans soaked in the big tub, which was filled with hot water. To keep condensation from dripping annoyingly from the ceiling, the fluting (ribbing) was added to carry the drips down the walls.

Next came the cold plunge in the *frigidarium*—a circular marble basin with the spout spewing frigid water, opposite the entry.

Exit the baths. Notice the oxcart wheel grooves and stepping stones in the street. During ancient rainstorms, streets would turn into filthy rivers. Do as the ancient Romans did. Keep your feet dry by using the stepping stones to cross the street. Directly in front of you is an ancient fast-food stand (notice the holes in the counters for pots). To your left, a few doors down, is the **House of the Tragic Poet** (*Casa de Poeta Tragico*), with its famous "Beware of Dog" (*Cave Canum*) mosaic in the entryway. On either side, grooves in the doorway indicate a shop with sliding doors.

Face the House of the Tragic Poet, then walk to your right two blocks to the House of the Faun (*Casa del Fauno, Danzante*). Notice the holes drilled into the curbs—to hitch your animal or perhaps to support an awning from your storefront.

Pompeii's largest home (with 40 rooms), the **House of the Faun,** provided Naples' Archaeological Museum with many of its top treasures, including the original dancing faun (you'll see a copy here) and the famous mosaic of the "Battle of Alexander." Wander past the welcome mosaic (*HAVE* or "hail to you") and through its courtyards. The back courtyard leads to the exit.

It's lined by pillars rebuilt after the A.D. 62 earthquake. Take a close look at the brick, mortar, and fake marble stucco veneer.

Back on the street, turn right and look for the exposed 2,000-year-old lead pipes in the wire cage (ahead and down on the ground to your right). The lead was imported from Roman Britannia. A huge water tank—fed by an aqueduct—stood at the high end of town. Three independent pipe systems supplied water to the city from here: one each for baths, private homes, and public water fountains. In the case of a water shortage, supply could be limited. Democratic priorities prevailed: first the baths were cut, then the private homes. The last water to be cut was that which fed the public fountains (where the people got their water for drinking and cooking).

Take your first left on Vicolo dei Vetti. Enter Pompeii's best-preserved home, the House of the Vetti (*Casa dei Vetti*).

The **House of the Vetti**, which has retained its mosaics and frescoes, was the bachelor pad of two wealthy merchant brothers. In the entryway, see if you can spot the erection. This is not pornography. There's a meaning here: The penis and the sack of money balance each other on the goldsmith scale above a fine bowl of fruit. The meaning: Only with a balance of fertility and money can you have abundance.

Step into the atrium with its open sky to collect light and rain water. The pool, while decorative, was a functional water-supply tank. It's flanked by large money boxes anchored to the floor. They were certainly successful merchants, and possibly moneylenders, too.

Exit on the right, passing the tight servant quarters, and go into the kitchen, with its bronze cooking pots (and a touchable lead pipe on the back wall). The passage dead-ends in the little Venus Room with its erotic frescoes behind glass.

Return to the atrium and pass into the big colonnaded garden. It was planted according to the plan indicated by traces of roots excavated in the volcanic ash. This courtyard is ringed by richly frescoed entertainment rooms. Circle counterclockwise. The dining room is finely decorated in "Pompeian red" (from iron rust) and black. Study the detail. Notice the lead humidity seal between the wall and the floor designed to keep the wet-sensitive frescoes dry. (Had Leonardo taken this clever step, his *Last Supper* in Milan might be in better shape today.) Continuing around, notice the square white stones inlaid in the floor. Imagine them reflecting like cat eyes as the brothers and their friends wandered around by oil lamp late at night. Frescoes in the Yellow Room (near the exit) show off the ancient mastery of perspective, which was not matched elsewhere in Europe for nearly 1,500 years.

Leaving the House of the Vetti, go left past the pipes again. Then turn right, following Vicolo dei Vetti to Via della

Fortuna, where you'll see a public fountain. Intersections like this were busy neighborhood centers, where the rent was highest and people gathered.

Turn left on Via della Fortuna and take a quick right on Vicolo Storto, which leads down a curving street to the **bakery and mill** *(forno e mulini)*. The ovens look like a modern-day pizza oven. And the stubby stone towers are flour grinders: After grain was poured into the top, donkeys pushed wooden bars that turned the stones, and eventually powdered grain dropped out the bottom as flour—flavored with tiny bits of rock.

Take the first left after the bakery onto Via degli Augustali, and check out the mosaics on the left at the Taberna Hedones. This must be the tavern of hedonism—see the cute welcome mosaic reading *HAVE* ("hail to you"), with the bear licking his wounds.

Next turn right, over the street dam, and follow the signs to the **brothel** *(lupanare)*, at #18. Prostitutes were nicknamed *lupas* (she-wolves). Wander into the brothel, a simple place with stone beds and pillows. The ancient graffiti includes stroke tallies and exotic names of the girls, indicating they came from all corners of the Mediterranean. The faded frescoes above the cells may have served as a kind of menu for services offered. Note the idealized portrayal of women (white, considered beautiful) and man (dark, considered horny). Outside at #17 is a laundry—likely to boil the sheets (thought to guard against venereal disease).

Leaving the brothel, go down the hill to Pompeii's main drag, Via Abbondanza. The Forum (and exit) is to the right. (The huge amphitheater—which you can skip—is 10 minutes to your left.) Go straight down Via dei Teatri, then left before the columns, downhill to the **Temple of Isis** (on the right). This Egyptian temple served Pompeii's Egyptian community. The little shrine with the plastic roof housed holy water from the Nile. Pompeii must have had a synagogue, but it has yet to be excavated.

Immediately upon leaving, follow the lane at #17 to our last stop, the **Theater**. Originally a Greek theater (Greeks built theirs with the help of a hillside), this marks the spot of the birthplace of the Greek port here in 470 B.C. During Roman times, it sat 5,000 in three price ranges: the five marble terraces up close (filled with romantic wooden seats for two), the main section, and the cheap nosebleed section (surviving only on the right). The square stones above the cheap seats used to support a canvas rooftop. Notice the high-profile boxes, flanking the stage, for guests of honor. From this perch, you can see the gladiator barracks—the colonnaded courtyard beyond the theater. They lived in tiny rooms, trained in the courtyard, and fought in the nearby amphitheater.

There's much more to see; 75 percent of Pompeii's 164 acres has been excavated. But this tour's over. *Ciao!*

Getting to Pompeii: Pompeii is halfway between Naples

and Sorrento, about 30 minutes from either by direct Circumvesuviana train (runs at least hrly). Get off at the "Pompei Scavi,
Villa dei Misteri" stop. Note: You want "Pompei Scavi" on the
Naples–Sorrento train line. A different line, which does *not* go to
Sorrento, has a Pompeii stop that leaves you far from the excava-
tion site entrance. Check your bag at the train station (at the bar)
for €0.75, or, better yet, near the Pompeii ticket desk for free.
From the train station, turn right and walk down the road about
a block to the entrance (first left turn). The TI is farther down
the street, but not a necessary stop for your visit.

▲▲**Herculaneum (Ercolano)**—Smaller, less ruined, and less
crowded than its famous big sister, Herculaneum offers a closer
peek into ancient Roman life but with none of the grandeur of
Pompeii. (There's barely a colonnade.) It's extremely low-tech, so
you'll find no information or books at the site (guidebooks are on
sale in nearby gift shops). Caked and baked by the same A.D. 79
eruption, Herculaneum is a small community of intact buildings
with plenty of surviving detail (€8.25, €13.50 combo ticket
includes Pompeii and 3 lesser sites—valid 3 days, daily March–
Sept 08:30–19:30, Oct–Feb 08:30–17:00, ticket office closes 90
min earlier, free baggage check, 15 min from Naples and 45 min
from Sorrento on the same Circumvesuviana train that goes to
Pompeii, leave station and turn right, following yellow signs,
8 blocks straight downhill from Ercolano station to end of road,
tel. 081-739-0963).

▲**Vesuvius**—The 1,200-meter (4,000-foot) summit of Vesuvius,
mainland Europe's only active volcano (sleeping restlessly since
1944), is accessible year-round by car, taxi (€36 round-trip), or
by the blue Transporti Vesuviani bus (often 5/day but irregular,
roughly hrly departures 09:00–14:00 from Herculaneum station;
60 min up with stop at bar, 40 min down). The bus trip, with
a two-hour wait on the mountain, costs about €8 (including
the €1.50 admission to the site). From the bus and car park, it's
a steep, often cold and windy 30-minute hike to the top for a
sweeping view of the Bay of Naples. Up here, it's desolate and
lunar-like. The rocks are hot. Walk the entire crater lip for the
most interesting views; the far end overlooks Pompeii. Be still
and alone to hear the wind and tumbling rocks in the crater.
Any steam? Closed when erupting.

PAESTUM

Paestum is one of the best collections of Greek temples anywhere—and certainly the most accessible to Western Europe.
Serenely situated, it's surrounded by fields and wildflowers and
has only a modest commercial strip.

This town was founded as Poseidonia by Greeks in the sixth
century B.C. and became a key stop on an important trade route.

In the fifth century B.C., the Lucans, a barbarous inland tribe, conquered Poseidonia, changed its name to Paistom, and tried to adopt the cultured ways of the Greeks. The Romans, who took over in the third century B.C., gave Paestum the name it bears today. The final conquerors of Paestum, malaria-carrying mosquitoes, kept the site wonderfully deserted for nearly a thousand years. Rediscovered in the 18th century, Paestum today offers the only well-preserved Greek ruins north of Sicily (TI: daily in summer 08:00–19:00, off-season daily 09:00–16:30, hours may vary, tel. 082-881-1016, e-mail: aastp@oneonline.it).

Arrival at Paestum: Buses from Salerno (see "Transportation Connections," below) stop near a corner of the ruins (at a little bar/café). Arriving by train, exit the station and walk through the old city gate; the ruins are an eight-minute walk straight ahead. Stop by the TI (next to museum) to pick up a free map of the site. If you ask politely, you can store luggage at the TI, site, or museum.

Cost, Hours, Information: €4 for the museum, €4 for the site, €6.20 for a combo ticket. Both the museum and site open daily at 09:00 (except the first and third Mon of month, when museum is closed, though the site is open). Year-round, the museum closes at 19:00 (last ticket sold at 18:30). The site closes one hour before sunset (as late as 19:30 June–Aug, as early as 15:45 in Dec, last ticket sold an hour before closing). Several mediocre guidebooks are offered at the museum's bookshop, including a past-and-present guide. The book with the jumbled title, *Archaeologic Site Temples Museum Paestum*, is the most informative (€7.75). The site and museum have separate entrances. The museum, just outside the ruins, is in a cluster with the TI and a small paleo-Christian basilica.

Planning Your Time: Allow two hours, including the museum. Depending on your interest and the heat of the day, start with either the museum or the site.

Museum: This offers you the rare opportunity to see artifacts—dating from prehistoric to Greek to Roman times— at the site where they were discovered. These beautifully crafted works help bring Paestum to life.

The large ground floor (the most impressive part) contains Greek artifacts. Upstairs, you'll find the prehistory exhibits (in a walkway hugging the walls of the building, with displays of pottery, blades, and arrowheads, and nothing in English) as well as the Roman Room (near the elevator; contains statues, busts, and inscriptions dating from the time of the Roman occupation). No matter where you start, you'll feel like you've come in on the middle of something, but about half of the work is described in English, and the art speaks for itself.

On the ground floor, the large carvings overhead—wrapping

Paestum

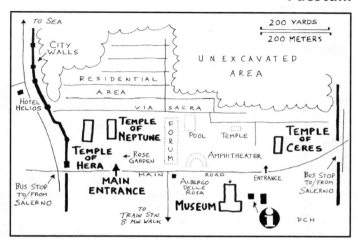

around the first room you see as you enter the museum—once adorned a sanctuary of the goddess Hera (wife of Zeus) outside the city. Some of the carvings show scenes from the life of Hercules. In the various ground-floor rooms, you'll see startlingly well-preserved Greek vases, crumbling armor, and paintings. The highlight of the museum is a rare example of Greek painting, known as the Diver's Tomb (480 B.C.). These slabs—showing a diver and four scenes of banqueting—originally were the sides of a tomb. The simple painting of a diver arcing down into a pool was the top of the tomb (painting faced inward). Though the deceased might have been a diver, it's thought the art more likely represents our dive from life to death. It's rare to see a real Greek statue (most are Roman copies), even rarer to see a Greek painting. The many other painted slabs in the museum date from a later time under Lucan rule. The barbarous people who conquered the Greeks tried to appropriate their art and style, but lacked the Greeks' distinct, light touch. Regardless, the Lucan paintings, as well as the crisply drawn pictures on dozens of Greek vases, are instructive and enjoyable—consider them ancient snapshots.

Site: The key ruins are the impossible-to-miss Temples of Neptune, Hera, and Ceres, but the scattered village ruins are also interesting. Lonely Ceres, in an evocative setting, is about a 10-minute walk from Neptune and Hera, which stand together. The entry to the site may return to its original place in front of Neptune (once the scaffolding is off) or it may be still be in front of Ceres.

The misnamed Temple of Neptune is a textbook example of the Doric style. Constructed in 450 B.C. and actually dedicated to Hera, the Temple of Neptune is simply overwhelming. Better preserved than the Parthenon in Athens, this huge structure is a tribute to Greek engineering and aesthetics. Contemplate the word "renaissance"—the rebirth of this grand Greek style of architecture. Notice how the columns angle out and the base bows up (scan the short ends of the temple). This was a trick ancient architects used to create the illusion of a perfectly straight building. All important Greek buildings were built using this technique. Now imagine it richly and colorfully decorated with marble and statues.

Adjacent to the Temple of Neptune is the almost-delicate Temple of Hera, dedicated to the Greek goddess of marriage in 550 B.C.

Sleeping near Paestum: Paestum at night, with views of the floodlit ruins, is magic. **Hotel delle Rose**, which has 12 small, fine rooms and a respectable restaurant, is near the site entry, on the street bordering the ruins (Db-€52, includes breakfast, no CC, Via Magna Grecia 193, tel. 082-881-1070, NSE, www .hoteldellerose.com). The **Seliano Estate for Agritourism** offers spacious, spotless rooms on a farm, complete with horses, buffalo, a pool, and great cooking (Db-€62 with breakfast, €67 in July– Aug, no CC, run by an English-speaking baroness, serves a fine dinner, near beach, 1.5 kilometers from ruins, tel. 082-872-4544, fax 082-872-3634).

Hotel Helios is a three-star hotel with one-star rooms. After you're wowed by a classy lobby with stained glass and mar- ble, as well as by the inviting swimming pool, the basic rooms are a disappointment (Db-€78, includes breakfast, Via Principe di Piedmonte 1, tel. 082-881-1451, fax 082-872-1047). Ask to visit the owner's mozzarella farm, located nearby.

Transportation Connections— Salerno and Paestum

Salerno, the big city just north of Paestum, is the nearest transpor- tation hub. From Naples or Sorrento, you'll change buses or trains in Salerno to get to Paestum. Salerno's TI has bus, ferry, and train schedules (Mon–Sat 09:00–14:00, 15:00–20:00, closed Sun, shorter hours off-season, on Piazza Veneto, just outside train station, tel. 089-231-432, toll-free 800-213-289, www.crmpa.it/ept/).

Salerno to Paestum by bus: Four companies (CSTP, SCAT, Giuliano, and Lettieri) offer a Salerno-Paestum bus service, all conveniently leaving from the same stop at Piazza Concordia on the waterfront (2–3/hr, 70 min, schedules extremely sparse on Sun). Buy the €2.85 ticket on the bus, except on CSTP buses (CSTP prefers you buy a ticket at their office, next to TI at Piazza Veneto/train station, but driver will grumpily sell you a ticket on bus if necessary). No clear schedule is posted at the

Salerno Connections

Salerno stop. Simply ask a local or a bus rep at the stop for the next bus to Paestum; otherwise, get a schedule at the TI (more impartial, since they don't represent a particular company and their schedule shows all companies and times). Note that orange city buses use the same stop; ignore these.

When leaving Paestum, catch a northbound bus from either of the intersections that flank the ruins (see map on page 385). Flag down any bus, ask "Salerno?", and buy the ticket onboard (except for CSTP buses—try to buy ticket at bar closest to stop).

Salerno to Paestum by train: The train from Salerno to Paestum (3–4/day, 40 min, direction: Paola or Sapri) runs far less frequently than the buses, though it's a quicker ride because it's immune from traffic jams; check schedules at Salerno's TI or train station (luggage storage-€2.60/12 hrs). The Paestum train station is an eight-minute walk from the ruins (from station, go through old city wall, ruins are straight ahead). If you plan to leave Paestum by train, buy your train ticket at the bar/café near the TI (the station is unstaffed, train schedules at TI). Leaving Paestum, trains bound for Salerno (direction: Battipaglia) usually continue to Naples.

Naples to Salerno by train: Hourly, 1.5 hour trip (some trains stop at Pompeii).

Sorrento to Salerno by bus: The scenic three-hour Amalfi Coast drive (blue SITA bus, 12/day, 3 hrs, easy transfer in Amalfi) drops you in Salerno, on the waterfront at Piazza Concordia, at the same place where the buses to Paestum depart. Salerno's train station and TI are two blocks inland.

If you plan to take a bus from Salerno to Sorrento (or points in between), buy your bus ticket at Salerno's Bar Ciofi (CHOH-fee), across the square from Piazza Concordia (see map on page 387). Ticket vendors change periodically; if Bar Ciofi no longer sells tickets, ask anyone or a clerk at a *tabacchi* shop, "Who sells bus tickets to ____?" by saying *"Chi vendi i biglietti dell'autobus per ___?* (kee VEHN-dee ee beel-YET-tee del-OW-toh-boos pehr ___).

Salerno by ferry to Amalfi towns: If you take the bus to Salerno, consider returning by boat. Catch the ferry from Salerno's Piazza Concordia (where the SITA bus drops you off) to **Amalfi** (12/day, 35 min, €2), **Positano** (11/day, 70 min, €3.65), or **Capri** (2 hrs, €10.35) (tickets and info at TravelMar, Piazza Concordia, tel. 089-873-190 or 089-872-950).

Sorrento to Salerno by train: Ride the Circumvesuviana to Naples Centrale station (hrly, 70 min) and catch the Salerno train (hrly, 1 hr). Or ask about connecting in Pompeii.

Drivers: While the Amalfi Coast is a thrill to drive off-season, summer traffic is miserable. From Sorrento, Paestum is 100 kilometers (60 miles) and three hours via the coast and a much smoother two hours by autostrada. To reach Paestum from Sorrento via the autostrada, drive toward Naples, catch the autostrada (direction: Salerno), skirt Salerno (direction: Reggio), exit at Eboli, and drive straight through the modern town of Paestum. You'll hit the ruins just about the time you start to worry you missed the turnoff. Along the way, you'll see many signs for *"mozzarella di bufala,"* the cheese made from the milk of water buffalo that graze here. Try it here—it can't be any fresher.

APPENDIX

Let's Talk Telephones

This is a primer on telephoning in Europe. For specifics on Italy, see "Telephones" in the Introduction.

Making Calls within a European Country: What you dial depends on the phone system of the country you're in. About half of all European countries have phone systems that use area codes; the other half uses a direct-dial system without area codes. If you're calling within a country that uses a direct-dial system (Italy, Belgium, Denmark, France, Norway, Portugal, Spain, and Switzerland), you dial the same number whether you're calling across the street or across the country.

In countries that use area codes (such as Austria, Britain, the Czech Republic, Finland, Germany, Ireland, the Netherlands, and Sweden), you dial the local number when calling within a city, and you add the area code if calling long-distance within the country. Example: The phone number of a hotel in Munich is 089/264-349. To call it in Munich, dial 264-349; to call it from Frankfurt, dial 089-264-349.

Making International Calls: You always start with the international access code (011 if you're calling from America or Canada, or 00 from virtually anywhere in Europe), then dial the country code of the country you're calling (see list of country codes, below).

What you dial next depends on the particular phone system of the country you're calling. If the country uses area codes, you drop the initial zero of the area code, then dial the rest of the area code and the local number. Example: To call the Munich hotel (mentioned above) from Spain, dial 00, 49 (Germany's country code), then 89-264-349.

Countries that use direct-dial systems (no area codes) differ in how they're accessed internationally by phone. For instance, if you're making an international call to Italy, Denmark, Norway, Spain, and Portugal, you simply dial the international access code, country code, and the phone number in full. But if you're calling Belgium, France, or Switzerland, you drop the initial zero of the phone number. Example: The phone number of a Paris hotel is 01 47 05 49 15. To call it from Rome, dial 00, 33 (France's country code), then 1 47 05 49 15 (the phone number without the initial zero).

Calling America or Canada from Europe: Dial the international access code (00 for virtually all of Europe), then dial 1, the area code, and local phone number. Example: Our number here at Europe Through the Back Door (in Edmonds, WA) is 425/771-8303. To call us from Europe, dial 00-1-425-771-8303.

International Access Codes
When dialing direct, first dial the international access code. For the U.S. and Canada, it's 011. Virtually all European countries use "00" as their international access code; the only exceptions are Finland (990) and Lithuania (810).

Country Codes
After you've dialed the international access code, dial the code of the country you're calling.

Austria—43	Greece—30
Belgium—32	Ireland—353
Britain—44	Italy—39
Canada—1	Morocco—212
Czech Rep.—420	Netherlands—31
Denmark—45	Norway—47
Estonia—372	Portugal—351
Finland—358	Spain—34
France—33	Sweden—46
Germany—49	Switzerland—41
Gibraltar—350	United States—1

Useful Italian Phone Numbers
Emergency (English-speaking police help): 113 or 112
Ambulance: 118
Road Service: 116
Directory Assistance (for €0.50, an Italian-speaking robot gives the number twice, very clearly): 12
Telephone help (in English; free directory assistance): 170 or 176

U.S. Embassies
In Rome: American Embassy at Via Veneto 119, tel. 06-46741; Canadian Embassy at Via Zara 30, tel. 06-445-981.
In Milan: U.S. Consulate at Via Principe Amedeo 2, tel. 02-290-351.

Public Holidays and Festivals
Italy (including most major sights) closes down on these national holidays: January 1, January 6 (Epiphany), Easter Sunday and Monday (March 31, April 1), April 25 (Liberation Day), May 1 (Labor Day), May 9 (Ascension Day), August 15 (Assumption of Mary), November 1 (All Saints' Day), December 8 (Immaculate Conception of Mary), and December 25 and 26.

Each town has a local festival honoring its patron saint. For more information on Italian festivals, check out www.whatsonwhen.com, www.italiantourism.com, www.hostetler.net, and www.carnivalofvenice.com.

Here's a partial list of events:

Feb 2–12	Carnevale (Mardi Gras), Venice
March 24–April 1	Holy Week and Good Friday (processions), All Italy
March 31	Scoppio del Carro (fireworks) on Easter, Florence
May 9	Annual Cricket Festival (music, food, crickets sold in cages), Florence
June 2	Battle of the Bridge (medieval festival), Pisa
First Week in June	Regatta of the Great Maritime Republics (rowing competition, parade), Pisa
June 11–24	St. John the Baptist Festival (parades, dances), Florence
June 21–Aug 31	Outdoor Opera in Roman Arena, Verona
June 24	Calcio Fiorentino (costumed soccer game, fireworks), Florence
July 2	Il Palio (horse race), Siena
July 20–21	Feast of the Redeemer (parade, fireworks), Venice
July 20–26	Festa de'Noantri (neighborhood fair), Rome
August 16	Il Palio (horse race), Siena
Sept 1	Historical Regatta (boat parade, pageantry), Venice
Sept 19	Festival of San Genarro (religious festival), Naples
Nov 21	Feast of Our Lady of Good Health (religious festival), Venice
Dec 1–24	Christmas Market, Rome, Piazza Navona

Numbers and Stumblers

- Europeans write a few of their numbers differently than we do: 1 = 1 , 4 = 4 , 7= 7. Learn the difference or miss your train.
- Europeans write dates as day/month/year (Christmas is 25/12/02).
- Commas are decimal points, and decimals are commas. A dollar and a half is 1,50. There are 5.280 feet in a mile.
- When pointing, use your whole hand, palm downward.
- When counting with fingers, start with your thumb. If you hold up your first finger to request one item, you'll probably get two.
- What we Americans call the second floor of a building is the first floor in Europe.
- Europeans keep the left "lane" open for passing on escalators and moving sidewalks. Keep to the right.

Metric Conversion (approximate)

1 inch = 25 millimeters	32 degrees F = 0 degrees C
1 foot = 0.3 meter	82 degrees F = about 28 degrees C
1 yard = 0.9 meter	1 ounce = 28 grams
1 mile = 1.6 kilometers	1 kilogram = 2.2 pounds
1 centimeter = 0.4 inch	1 quart = 0.95 liter
1 meter = 39.4 inches	1 square yard = 0.8 square meter
1 kilometer = 0.62 mile	1 acre = 0.4 hectare

Climate Chart

First line, average daily low; second line, average daily high; third line, days of no rain.

	J	F	M	A	M	J	J	A	S	O	N	D
Rome												
	40°	42°	45°	50°	56°	63°	67°	67°	62°	55°	49°	44°
	52°	55°	59°	66°	74°	82°	87°	86°	79°	71°	61°	55°
	13	19	23	24	26	26	30	29	25	23	19	21
Milan												
	32°	35°	43°	49°	57°	63°	67°	66°	61°	52°	43°	35°
	40°	46°	56°	65°	74°	80°	84°	82°	75°	63°	51°	43°
	25	21	24	22	23	21	25	24	25	23	20	24

Italian Survival Phrases

Hello (good day).	**Buon giorno.**	bwohn **jor**-noh
Do you speak English?	**Parla inglese?**	**par**-lah een-**glay**-zay
Yes. / No.	**Si. / No.**	see / noh
I'm sorry.	**Mi dispiace.**	mee dee-spee**ah**-chay
Please.	**Per favore.**	pehr fah-**voh**-ray
Thank you.	**Grazie.**	**graht**-seeay
Goodbye!	**Arrivederci!**	ah-ree-vay-**dehr**-chee
Where is...?	**Dov'è...?**	doh-**veh**
...a hotel	**...un hotel**	oon oh-**tehl**
...a youth hostel	**...un ostello della gioventù**	oon oh-**stehl**-loh **day**-lah joh-vehn-**too**
...a restaurant	**...un ristorante**	oon ree-stoh-**rahn**-tay
...a supermarket	**...un supermercado**	oon soo-pehr-mehr-**kah**-doh
...the train station	**...la stazione**	lah staht-seeoh-nay
...tourist information	**...informazioni per turisti**	een-for-maht-see**oh**-nee pehr too-**ree**-stee
...the toilet	**...la toilette**	lah twah-**leht**-tay
men	**uomini, signori**	**woh**-mee-nee, seen-**yoh**-ree
women	**donne, signore**	**don**-nay, seen-**yoh**-ray
How much is it?	**Quanto costa?**	**kwahn**-toh **kos**-tah
Cheap(er).	**(Più) economico.**	(pew) ay-koh-**noh**-mee-koh
Is it included?	**È incluso?**	eh een-**kloo**-zoh
I would like...	**Vorrei....**	vor-**rehee**
...a ticket.	**...un biglietto.**	oon beel-**yay**-toh
...a room.	**...una camera.**	**oo**-nah **kah**-may-rah
...the bill.	**...il conto.**	eel **kohn**-toh
one	**uno**	**oo**-noh
two	**due**	**doo**-ay
three	**tre**	tray
four	**quattro**	**kwah**-troh
five	**cinque**	**cheeng**-kway
six	**sei**	**seh**ee
seven	**sette**	**seht**-tay
eight	**otto**	**ot**-toh
nine	**nove**	**nov**-ay
ten	**dieci**	**deeay**-chee
hundred	**cento**	**chehn**-toh
thousand	**mille**	**mee**-lay
At what time?	**A che ora?**	ah kay **oh**-rah
now / soon / later	**adesso / presto / tardi**	ah-**dehs**-soh / **prehs**-toh / **tar**-dee
today / tomorrow	**oggi / domani**	**oh**-jee / doh-**mah**-nee

For 192 more pages of survival phrases for your next trip to Italy, check out *Rick Steves' Italian Phrase Book and Dictionary*.

Faxing Your Hotel Reservation

Use this handy form for your fax (or find it online at
www.ricksteves.com/reservation). Photocopy and fax away.

One-Page Fax

To: _____ @ _____
            hotel   *fax*

From: _____ @ _____
            name   *fax*

Today's date: ____ /_____ /____
                day   *month*   *year*

Dear Hotel _____,

Please make this reservation for me:

Name: _____

Total # of people: _____   # of rooms: _____   # of nights: _____

Arriving: ____ /_____ /____ My time of arrival (24-hr clock): _____
            day   *month*   *year* (I will telephone if I will be late)

Departing: ____ /_____ /____
            day   *month*   *year*

Room(s): Single___ Double___ Twin___ Triple___ Quad___

With: Toilet___ Shower___ Bath___ Sink only___

Special needs: View___ Quiet___ Cheap___ Ground Floor___

Credit card: Visa___ MasterCard___ American Express___

Card #: _____

Expiration date:_____

Name on card: _____

You may charge me for the first night as a deposit. Please fax, e-mail, or
mail me confirmation of my reservation, along with the type of room
reserved, the price, and whether the price includes breakfast. Please also
inform me of your cancellation policy. Thank you.

_____
Signature

_____
Name

_____
Address

_____
City   **State**   **Zip Code**   **Country**

_____
E-mail Address

Road Scholar Feedback for Italy 2002

We're all in the same travelers' school of hard knocks. Your feedback helps us improve this guidebook for future travelers. Please fill this out (or use the on-line version at www.ricksteves.com/feedback), attach more info or any tips/favorite discoveries if you like, and send it to us. As thanks for your help, we'll send you our quarterly travel newsletter free for one year. Thanks! Rick

Of the recommended accommodations/restaurants used, which was:

Best _____

     Why? _____

Worst _____

     Why? _____

Of the sights/experiences/destinations recommended by this book, which was:

Most overrated _____

     Why? _____

Most underrated _____

     Why? _____

Best ways to improve this book:

_____

_____

I'd like a free newsletter subscription:

_____ Yes   _____ No   _____ Already on list

_____
Name

_____
Address

_____
City, State, Zip

_____
E-mail Address

Please send to: ETBD, Box 2009, Edmonds, WA 98020

INDEX

Free, fresh travel tips, all year long.

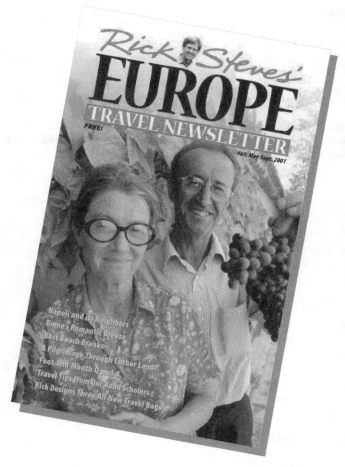

Call (425) 771-8303 to get Rick's free
64-page newsletter, or visit
www.ricksteves.com for even more.

FREE-SPIRITED TOURS FROM

Rick Steves

Great Guides

Big Buses

Small Groups

No Grumps

**Best of Europe ■ Village Europe ■ Eastern Europe ■ Turkey ■ Italy ■ Britain
Spain/Portugal ■ Ireland ■ Heart of France ■ South of France ■ Village France
Scandinavia ■ Germany/Austria/Switzerland ■ London ■ Paris ■ Rome**

Looking for a one, two, or three-week tour that's run in the Rick Steves style? Check out Rick Steves' educational, experiential tours of Europe.

Rick's tours include much more in the "sticker price" than mainstream tours. Here's what you'll get with a Europe or regional Rick Steves tour...

■ **Group size:** Your tour group will be no larger than 26.

■ **Guides:** You'll have two guides traveling and dining with you on your fully guided Rick Steves tour.

■ **Bus:** You'll travel in a full-size 48-to-52-seat bus, with plenty of empty seats for you to spread out and read, snooze, enjoy the passing scenery, get away from your spouse, or whatever.

■ **Sightseeing:** Your tour price includes all group sightseeing. There are no hidden extra charges.

■ **Hotels:** You'll stay in Rick's favorite small, characteristic, locally-run hotels in the center of each city, within walking distance of the sights you came to see.

■ **Price and insurance:** Your tour price is guaranteed for 2002. Single travelers do *not* pay an extra supplement (we have them room with other singles). ETBD includes prorated tour cancellation/interruption protection coverage at no extra cost.

■ **Tips and kickbacks:** All guide and driver tips are included in your tour price. Because your driver and guides are paid salaries by ETBD, they can focus on giving you the best European travel experience possible.

Interested? Call (425) 771-8303 or visit www.ricksteves.com for a free copy of Rick Steves' 2002 Tours booklet!

Rick Steves' Europe Through the Back Door
130 Fourth Avenue North, PO Box 2009, Edmonds, WA 98020 USA
Phone: (425) 771-8303 ■ Fax: (425) 771-0833 ■ www.ricksteves.com

FREE TRAVEL GOODIES FROM

Rick Steves

EUROPEAN TRAVEL NEWSLETTER

My *Europe Through the Back Door* travel company will help you travel better *because* you're on a budget—not in spite of it. To see how, ask for my 64-page *travel newsletter* packed full of savvy travel tips, readers' discoveries, and your best bets for railpasses, guidebooks, videos, travel accessories and free-spirited tours.

2002 GUIDE TO EUROPEAN RAILPASSES

With hundreds of railpasses to choose from in 2002, finding the right pass for your trip has never been more confusing. To cut through the complexity, ask for my 64-page *2002 Guide to European Railpasses.* Once you've narrowed down your choices, we give you unbeatable prices, including important extras with every Eurailpass, **free:** my 90-minute *Travel Skills Special* video or DVD; your choice of one of my 16 country guidebooks and phrasebooks; and answers to your "top five" travel questions.

RICK STEVES' 2002 TOURS

We offer 18 different one, two, and three-week tours (180 departures in 2002) for those who want to experience Europe in Rick Steves' Back Door style, but without the transportation and hotel hassles. If a tour with a small group, modest family-run hotels, lots of exercise, great guides, and no tips or hidden charges sounds like your idea of fun, ask for my 48-page 2002 Tours booklet.

YEAR-ROUND GUIDEBOOK UPDATES

Even though the information in my guidebooks is the freshest around, things do change in Europe between book printings. I've set aside a special section at my website (www.ricksteves.com/update) listing *up-to-the-minute changes* for every Rick Steves guidebook.

*Call, fax, or visit **www.ricksteves.com** to get your...*

- ☑ **FREE EUROPEAN TRAVEL NEWSLETTER**
- ☑ **FREE 2002 GUIDE TO EUROPEAN RAILPASSES**
- ☑ **FREE RICK STEVES' 2002 TOURS BOOKLET**

Rick Steves' Europe Through the Back Door

130 Fourth Avenue North, PO Box 2009, Edmonds, WA 98020 USA
Phone: (425) 771-8303 ■ Fax: (425) 771-0833 ■ www.ricksteves.com

Rick Steves' Phrase Books

Unlike other phrase books and dictionaries on the market, my well-tested phrases and key words cover every situation a traveler is likely to encounter. With these books you'll laugh with your cabby, disarm street thieves with insults, and charm new European friends.

Each book in the series is 4" x 6", with maps.

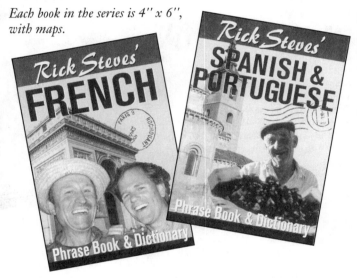

RICK STEVES' FRENCH PHRASE BOOK & DICTIONARY
U.S. $6.95/Canada $10.95

RICK STEVES' GERMAN PHRASE BOOK & DICTIONARY
U.S. $6.95/Canada $10.95

RICK STEVES' ITALIAN PHRASE BOOK & DICTIONARY
U.S. $6.95/Canada $10.95

RICK STEVES' SPANISH & PORTUGUESE PHRASE BOOK & DICTIONARY
U.S. $8.95/Canada $13.95

RICK STEVES' FRENCH, ITALIAN & GERMAN PHRASE BOOK & DICTIONARY
U.S. $8.95/Canada $13.95

**AVALON
TRAVEL**
publishing

How far will our travel guides take you? As far as you want.

Discover a rhumba-fueled nightspot in Old Havana, explore prehistoric tombs in Ireland, hike beneath California's centuries-old redwoods, or embark on a classic road trip along Route 66. Our guidebooks deliver solidly researched, trip-tested information—minus any generic froth—to help globetrotters or weekend warriors create an adventure uniquely their own.

And we're not just about the printed page. Public television viewers are tuning in to Rick Steves' new travel series, *Rick Steves' Europe*. On the Web, readers can cruise the virtual black top with *Road Trip USA* author Jamie Jensen and learn travel industry secrets from Edward Hasbrouck of The *Practical Nomad*.

In print. On TV. On the Internet.

We supply the information. The rest is up to you.

Avalon Travel Publishing

Something for everyone

www.travelmatters.com

Avalon Travel Publishing guides are available at
your favorite book or travel store.

FOGHORN OUTDOORS guides are for campers, hikers, boaters, anglers, bikers, and golfers of all levels of daring and skill. Each guide focuses on a specific U.S. region and contains site descriptions and ratings, driving directions, facilities and fees information, and easy-to-read maps that leave only the task of deciding where to go.

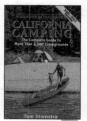

"Foghorn Outdoors has established an ecological conservation standard unmatched by any other publisher." **~Sierra Club**

WWW.FOGHORN.COM

TRAVEL SMART guidebooks are accessible, route-based driving guides focusing on regions throughout the United States and Canada. Special interest tours provide the most practical routes for family fun, outdoor activities, or regional history for a trip of anywhere from two to 22 days. Travel Smarts take the guesswork out of planning a trip by recommending only the most interesting places to eat, stay, and visit.

"One of the few travel series that rates sightseeing attractions. That's a handy feature. It helps to have some guidance so that every minute counts." **~San Diego Union-Tribune**

CiTY·SMaRT™ guides are written by local authors with hometown perspectives who have personally selected the best places to eat, shop, sightsee, and simply hang out. The honest, lively, and opinionated advice is perfect for business travelers looking to relax with the locals or for longtime residents looking for something new to do Saturday night.

ROME

Day 1 - Sat.

St. Peter's Basilica
Ate dinner at Antonio's
    Hostaria Dei Bastioni

Day 2 - Sun.

Villa Borghese
Borghese Gallery

Cappaccin Crypt
Spanish Steps
Trevi Fountain
Pal. Venezia dinner at L'Orso 80

Great Gelato at Giolitti's & coffee

Day 3 - Mon.

Vatican Museums -
Sistine Chapel

Colosseum
Roman Forum
Palatine Hill (Kind of)
Mamertime Prison - from the outside.
Ate Dinner at Al 34 Ristorante
              Da Giuseppi ☆

Day 4 - Tues.

early morning walk &
St. Peters - more photos a
    post office

Day 4 - Tues.   Florence

Train - arrived in Florence about 2:00

- Gallery Del Accedamia - David

- took walk around Santa Maria del Fiori Cathedral (Duomo) & down to River to Ponte Vecchio & piazza Vecchio.

- Trattoria Guelfa ~~&~~

- ~~Spent evening in Room resting~~

- ~~Room service~~.

Day 5 - Wed.

Tried to take bus to Siena — Bus drivers on strike

Santa Croce Church

Science Museum

Lunch at Gilli - overpriced

walked along Arno & Ponte Vecchio

Dinner at La Martinicca

Day 6 - Thurs.

Cooking Class - Judy Witts

- Central Market tour

- cooked - fried sage
  & zucchini flowers

  - Risotto & asaragus
  - Pork tenderloin in
    bread

  - figs & rasberries
  - almond cookies

→ ate quick dinner at pizzeria
→ looked at cooking stores

Day 7 - Fri

Pitti Palace
Central market for lunch
Medici Chapel
Uffizzi Galery
Casa Michaelangelo - great view of
                     sunset over florence

got lost.
Bought 2 pieces of art by Pitti
                              Palace

ate at Cafaggi

Day 8 – Sat

Train to Parma

ate at two great
restaurants

relaxed

Day 9 – Sun

Train to Venice

took Vaporretti down Grand Canal
to ~~the~~ San Marco

Walked around Venice

ate dinner at

Day 10 – Mon

Gallery Accadamia
Peggys Guggenheim Collection
walked around Venice
ate dinner at Al Covo
w/ John & Patty Houston